D0834185

MOROCCO

4th Edition

Where to Stay and Eat for All Budgets

Must-See Sights and Local Secrets

Ratings You Can Trust

Fodor's Travel Publications   New York, Toronto, London, Sydney, Auckland
www.fodors.com

FODOR'S MOROCCO

Editors: Mark Sullivan, Laura Kidder
Editorial Contributors: Rachel Blech, Maryam Montague, Simona Schneider, Victoria Tang, Sarah Wyatt, Jillian York

Production Editor: Tom Holton
Maps & Illustrations: David Lindroth, Ed Jacobus, *cartographers*; Bob Blake, Rebecca Baer, *map editors;* William Wu, *information graphics*
Design: Fabrizio La Rocca, *creative director*; Guido Caroti, Siobhan O'Hare, *art directors*; Tina Malaney, Chie Ushio, Ann McBride, Jessica Walsh, *designers*; Melanie Marin, *senior picture editor*
Cover Photo (Tuareg and camel, Erg Chebbi, Merzouga): SIME s.a.s/eStock Photo
Production Manager: Amanda Bullock

4th Edition

ISBN 978-1-4000-0804-9

ISSN 1527-4829

SPECIAL SALES

This book is available at special discounts for bulk purchases for sales promotions or premiums. Special editions, including personalized covers, excerpts of existing books, and corporate imprints, can be created in large quantities for special needs. For more information, write to Special Markets/Premium Sales, 1745 Broadway, MD 6-2, New York, New York 10019, or e-mail specialmarkets@randomhouse.com.

AN IMPORTANT TIP & AN INVITATION

Although all prices, opening times, and other details in this book are based on information supplied to us at press time, changes occur all the time in the travel world, and Fodor's cannot accept responsibility for facts that become outdated or for inadvertent errors or omissions. So **always confirm information when it matters,** especially if you're making a detour to visit a specific place. Your experiences—positive and negative— matter to us. If we have missed or misstated something, **please write to us.** We follow up on all suggestions. Contact the Morocco editor at editors@fodors.com or c/o Fodor's at 1745 Broadway, New York, NY 10019.

PRINTED IN THE UNITED STATES OF AMERICA

10 9 8 7 6 5 4 3 2 1

Be a Fodor's Correspondent

Your opinion matters. It matters to us. It matters to your fellow Fodor's travelers, too. And we'd like to hear it. In fact, we need to hear it.

When you share your experiences and opinions, you become an active member of the Fodor's community. That means we'll not only use your feedback to make our books better, but we'll publish your names and comments whenever possible. Throughout our guides, look for "Word of Mouth," excerpts of your unvarnished feedback.

Here's how you can help improve Fodor's for all of us.

Tell us when we're right. We rely on local writers to give you an insider's perspective. But our writers and staff editors—who are the best in the business—depend on you. Your positive feedback is a vote to renew our recommendations for the next edition.

Tell us when we're wrong. We're proud that we update most of our guides every year. But we're not perfect. Things change. Hotels cut services. Museums change hours. Charming cafés lose charm. If our writer didn't quite capture the essence of a place, tell us how you'd do it differently. If any of our descriptions are inaccurate or inadequate, we'll incorporate your changes in the next edition and will correct factual errors at fodors.com immediately.

Tell us what to include. You probably have had fantastic travel experiences that aren't yet in Fodor's. Why not share them with a community of like-minded travelers? Maybe you chanced upon a beach or bistro or B&B that you don't want to keep to yourself. Tell us why we should include it. And share your discoveries and experiences with everyone directly at fodors.com. Your input may lead us to add a new listing or highlight a place we cover with a "Highly Recommended" star or with our highest rating, "Fodor's Choice."

Give us your opinion instantly at our feedback center at www.fodors.com/feedback. You may also e-mail editors@fodors.com with the subject line "Morocco Editor." Or send your nominations, comments, and complaints by mail to Morocco Editor, Fodor's, 1745 Broadway, New York, NY 10019.

You and travelers like you are the heart of the Fodor's community. Make our community richer by sharing your experiences. Be a Fodor's correspondent.

Bon voyage!

Tim Jarrell, Publisher

CONTENTS

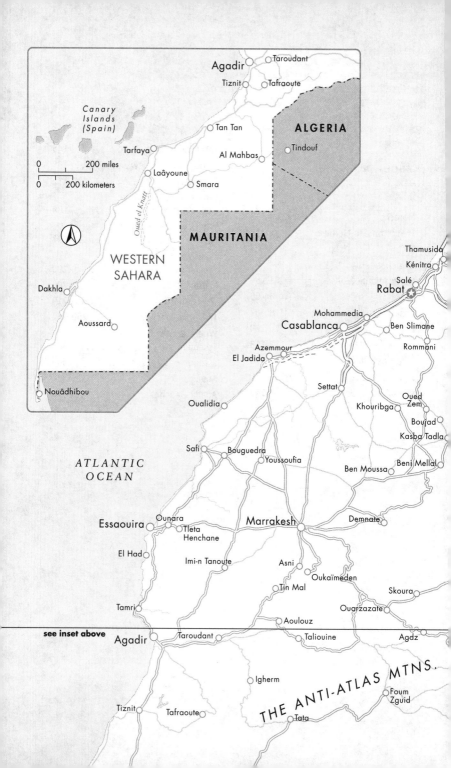

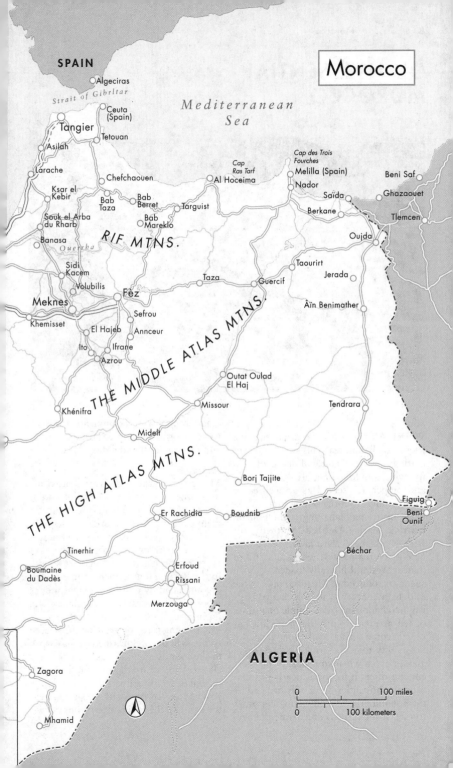

QUINTESSENTIAL MOROCCO

Mint Tea

When in Morocco, it's a good idea to make friends with mint tea. This sweet and aromatic brew is the national drink, offered for, with, and following breakfast, lunch, and dinner. It's served as an icebreaker for anything from rug selling in the Meknès souk to matchmaking at the Imilchil marriage market. Dubbed "Moroccan (or Berber) whiskey" *thé à la menthe* is Chinese green tea brewed with a handful of mint leaves and liberally loaded up with sugar. Introduced to Morocco only in the mid-19th century when blockaded British merchants unloaded ample quantities of tea at major ports, the tradition has now become such a symbol of Moroccan hospitality that not drinking three small glasses of tea when your host or business contact offers it to you is nearly a declaration of hostilities. Generally ordered by the pot and poured from on high in order to release the aromas and aerate the beverage, mint tea is recommended in cold weather or in sweltering heat as a tonic, a mild stimulant, and a digestive.

Music

Music is integral to daily and ritual life in Morocco, both for enjoyment and as a form of social commentary. It emanates from homes, stores, markets, and public squares everywhere you go. Joujouka music is perhaps the best-known, but every region has its own distinct sound. In the Rif you'll hear men singing poetry accompanied by guitar and high-pitched women's choruses; in Casablanca, *rai* (opinion) music, born of social protest, keeps young men company on the streets; cobblers in the Meknès medina may work to the sounds of violin-based Andalusian classical music or the more-folksy Arabic *melhoun*, sung poetry; and you know you've reached the south when you hear the banjo of the roving storytelling *rawais*

For a sense of Moroccan culture, a good start would be to embrace some of the ongoing rituals of daily life. These are a few highlights—customs and sites you can experience with relative ease.

in Marrakesh. Gnaoua music is best known for its use in trance rituals, but it has become popular street entertainment; the performer's brass *qaraqa* hand cymbals and cowrie shell–adorned hat betray the music's sub-Saharan origins. Seek out live music at public squares such as Marrakesh's Djemâa el Fna, or attend a festival, a regional *moussem* (pilgrimage festival), or even a rural market to see the performances locals enjoy.

Markets

Moroccan markets, souks, and bazaars buzz with life. Every town and city in Morocco revolves, in one way or another, around its market, and beginning your exploration at the hub of urban life is one of the best ways to start a crash course in wherever you find yourself. The chromatically riotous displays of fruit and vegetables are eye-bogglingly rich and as geometrically complex as the most intricate aspects of Islamic architecture and design. Fez el Bali is virtually all market, with the exception of the craftsmen and artisans preparing their wares for market. Fez's henna souk is famous for its intimate ambience and archaic elegance. Marrakesh's central market stretching out behind Djemâa el Fna square could take a lifetime to explore. The Meknès market next to Place el-Hedim is smaller but loaded with everything from sturdy earthenware tagines to a wide selection of Moroccan spices and fish fresh from the Atlantic. Casablanca's Marché Central in the heart of the city is one of the most picturesque and least Europeanized parts of an otherwise unremarkable urban sprawl. Essaouira's crafts and produce market shares this light and cheerful town's easygoing atmosphere, and shopping there becomes a true pleasure rather than a grim battle over haggling leverage.

IF YOU LIKE

Beaches

With coasts on both the Mediterranean Sea and the Atlantic Ocean, Morocco has hundreds of miles of sandy beaches, many of them little developed. Dangerous currents and national-park preservation explain why some beaches are unused, but gems abound. Surfing the Atlantic beaches has become popular, and surfing schools are increasingly easy to find along the beaches between Rabat and Essaouira. The port towns of Essaouira, Sidi Ifni, Asilah, and Al Hoceima make peaceful, low-key coastal getaways. Those familiar with Tunisia's topless beaches may be struck by the modesty that reigns on Moroccan public beaches, where picnicking local families spend their holidays.

■ **Sidi Ifni and Essaouira.** Well off the beaten beach paths, Ifni and Essaouira offer, respectively, burgundy rock formations and some of the strongest windsurfing breezes in all of Africa.

■ **Agadir.** Agadir is a major destination for the high-density European package-tour tanning crowd. For families looking for safe beaches and bathing with plenty of activities for the young, this is the spot.

■ **Oualidia.** With a first-class beach often compared to those of the French Riviera, and a surfing and windsurfing scene as hot as any in Europe, this is an important beach destination just 90 minutes southeast of Casablanca.

■ **Plage Robinson.** Just west of Tangier, this much-visited beach offers sun and sand, the Caves of Hercules where mythology has Hercules resting up after separating Africa from Europe, and a lively café and restaurant scene.

People-Watching

Morocco is a visual spectacle in every sense, and the human fauna are beyond a doubt the runaway stars of the show. French painters such as Delacroix and Matisse and the great Spanish colorist Marià Fortuny all found the souks, fondouks, and street scenes of Marrakesh, Fez, and Tangier irresistible. Today's visitors to this eye-popping North African brouhaha are well advised to simply pull up a chair and take in some of the most exotic natural street theater in the world.

■ **Djemâa el Fna, Marrakesh.** This cacophonous market square is unlike anything else on earth. Settle into a rooftop café for an unobstructed view of the acrobats, storytellers, musicians, dancers, fortune-tellers, juice carts, and general organized chaos.

■ **Fez el Bali.** The to-and-fro pulsing of Fez's medina makes it the perfect place to watch Moroccans doing what Moroccans do. Great spots include the cafés around Bab Boujeloud and Bab Fteuh, though the latter is much less amenable to travelers.

■ **Place Moulay Hassan, Essaouira.** Locals, temporary locals, and fishermen are all welcome to linger in this laid-back plaza, watching the world go by from an outdoor café. Try a cup of *louiza*—warm milk with fresh verbena leaves.

■ **Grand Socco, Tangier.** Every conceivable manifestation of Old Testament–looking humanity seems to have found its way to Tangier's Grand Socco from the Rif Mountains and the interior. A stroll down Rue de la Liberté into the food souk will put you in the middle of it all.

The Outdoors

A range of spectacular landscapes has made Morocco a major destination for rugged outdoor sporting challenges and adventure travel. Much of Morocco's natural beauty lies in its mountains, where the famous Berber hospitality can make hiking an unforgettable experience. You can arrange most outdoor excursions yourself or with the help of tourist offices and hotels in the larger cities. Rock climbing is possible in the Todra and Dadès gorges and the mountains outside Chefchaouen. Oukaïmeden has facilities for skiing, and a few other long, liftless runs await the more athletic. Golf is available in Rabat, Casablanca, Marrakesh, and Agadir. Several High Atlas rivers are suitable for fishing.

- **High Atlas.** People come from around the world to trek in these mountains, drawn by the rugged scenery, bracing air, and rural Berber (Imazighen) culture. Hiking is easily combined with mule riding, trout fishing, and vertiginous alpine drives.

- **Merzouga dunes.** Southeast of Erfoud, beyond Morocco's great oasis valleys, these waves of sand mark the beginning of the Sahara. Brilliantly orange in the late-afternoon sun, they can be gloriously desolate at sunrise.

- **Palm groves and villages, Tafraoute.** A striking tropical contrast to the barren Anti-Atlas Mountains and the agricultural plains farther north, the oases are scattered with massive, pink cement houses built by wealthy urban merchants native to this area.

Architecture

Refined Islamic architecture graces the imperial cities of Fez, Meknès, Marrakesh, and Rabat. Mosques and *medersas* (schools of Koranic studies) dating from the Middle Ages, as well as 19th-century palaces, are decorated with colorful geometric tiles, bands of Koranic verses in marble or plaster, stalactite crevices, and carved wooden ceilings. The *Mellahs* built by Morocco's Jews with glassed-in balconies contrast with the Islamic emphasis on turning inward. French colonial architecture prevails in the Art Deco and neo-Mauresque streets of Casablanca's Quartier des Habous. Outside these strongholds of Arab influence are the *pisé* (rammed earth) Kasbahs in the Ouarzazate–Er-Rachidia region, where structures built with local mud and clay range from deep pink to burgundy to shades of brown.

- **Aït-Benhaddou, near Ouarzazate.** Strewn across a hillside, the red-pisé towers of this village fortress resemble a melting sand castle. Crenellated and topped with blocky towers, it's one of the most sumptuous sights in the Atlas Mountains.

- **Bou Inania medersa, Fez.** The most celebrated of the Kairaouine University's 14th-century residential colleges, Bou Inania has a roof of green tile, a ceiling of carved cedar, stalactites of white marble, and ribbons of Arabic inscription.

- **La Bahia Palace, Marrakesh.** Built as a harem's residence, and interspersed with cypress-filled courtyards, La Bahia has the key Moroccan architectural elements—light, symmetry, decoration, and water.

WHAT'S WHERE

TANGIER & THE MEDITERRANEAN	Many of Morocco's most dramatic social and economic contrasts are immediately and painfully evident in Tangier and the Rif Mountains paralleling the northern Mediterranean coast. While the Spain–Tangier ferry crossing through the Strait of Gibraltar is geographically striking, arrival in Tangier can be pandemonium. Although the mountain stronghold at Chefchaouen is one of Morocco's most memorable towns, the harvest and sale of *kif* (a preparation of hemp leaves whose name comes from the Arabic word for "pleasure") in the nearby Rif region can cause problems with dealers and police. The Rif and the Mediterranean beaches comprise one of Morocco's most scenic and underexplored regions, low-key destinations for those weary of cities and tourist marketing. A drive through the rolling hills takes you past women working in the harvest with Spanish-style hats tied on with scarves, while Rifi tribesmen, known for their regional allegiance and fierceness, patrol the roads. Spanish influence is most palpable in the coastal cities of Tangier and Tétouan.
RABAT, CASABLANCA & THE NORTHERN ATLANTIC COAST	Morocco's economic capital, Casablanca, and political capital, Rabat, are the country's most Europeanized cities. Boulevards designed by French architects to highlight buildings inspired by Islamic architecture run alongside mazelike medinas. But whereas Rabat's streets are empty at night, Casablanca seems consistently rushed. Both cities attract travelers for their combination of colonial architecture and their colorful medinas. The magnificent Hassan II Mosque, reflecting polished French engineering and detailed Moroccan craftsmanship, is matched only by the pilgrimage center in Mecca. Meanwhile, the Atlantic beaches offer miles and miles of wild surf, sand, and sea.
FEZ & MEKNÈS	The alternating Arab-Islamic and Berber chapters in Morocco's history are most evident in these Imperial Cities, with their centuries-old arched gates built to be locked against invaders during uncertain times. The Fez medina contains the world's oldest university and the most exciting maze of shops, covered spice markets, tanneries, textile-weaving crannies, and food stalls in all of Morocco. This is an eminently lived-in medina, a first stop for rural migrant families crowded into single rooms inside mansions once owned by wealthy Fassis (residents of Fez). Meknès is a smaller and more-relaxed version of Fez, easier to feel at home in and offering less-pressured and largely hassle-free sightseeing. For the multiwalled

	"Versailles of Morocco," North Africa's most beautiful gate, and side trips to the Roman ruins at Volubilis and the holy town of Moulay Idriss, Meknès ranks right after Fez and Marrakesh as a must-see Moroccan city.
THE MIDDLE ATLAS	The Middle Atlas is an underrated mountain range of great natural beauty often passed through on the way to more dramatic destinations. Vast expanses of rolling hills, valleys, high peaks, and Kasbahs reward the trekker intrepid enough to abandon the beaten path. Taza, the Cirque du Djebel Tazzeka, and Friouato Cave complex provide natural adventure, while the Middle Atlas Berbers make and offer some of the country's most popular and sturdy deep-red carpets and delicate wool-embroidered straw mats in weekly markets for half what they command in Marrakesh.
MARRAKESH	Marrakesh is the turning point between Morocco's north and south, Arab and Berber, big city and small town. If you can see only one city in Morocco, make it Marrakesh. The legendary Djemâa el Fna Square is a sensorial feast, a highlight of any trip to this country: in late afternoon Moroccans as well as foreigners crowd the square to hear storytellers and musicians perform, be wooed by herbalists and acrobats, and sip some of the country's best orange juice, sold by rows of vendors. As the sun sets, smoke rises from the outdoor food stalls as they whip up traditional Moroccan fare. Djemâa el Fna can be overwhelming, but the medina beyond is a pleasure. The snowcapped High Atlas Mountains, rising beyond the lush gardens sprinkled throughout town, tempt you to forge on and out, and, indeed, the city is an ideal base for High Atlas day trips.
THE HIGH ATLAS	Although parts of the High Atlas can be mobbed with hikers at certain times of year, you can still get away from the package tours on foot or by mule and taste rural Morocco at its most colorful and hospitable here. These are some of Morocco's most densely populated areas. Free-flowing rivers and abundant underground springs keep the High Atlas verdant for much of the year. Ribbons of mountain peaks layer into the distance as you hike; Djebel Toubkal is North Africa's highest peak, sometimes retaining a snow cover well into the month of August. Decent roads offer pleasant rides to destinations popular with Marrakshis as well as foreign visitors, such as Setti Fatma and the ski resort Oukaïmeden.

WHAT'S WHERE

THE GREAT OASIS VALLEYS 	No trip to Morocco is complete without a taste of the desert. On the way out to Merzouga or M'Hamid, some of Morocco's most exotic scenery is in the southeast, where bone-dry hills and winding oases cling to the few rivers that sustain this region. Oases of date palms and apricot trees line the banks of the Ziz River, running north from Er-Rachidia to Rich and farther up. The single road down from Meknès makes the Tafilalt (source of the ruling Alaouite dynasty) accessible in a day's drive through the Middle Atlas. The narrow road between Er-Rachidia and Ouarzazate runs through some sleepy, picturesque villages, with homes decorated in a distinctive lace pattern painted on the exterior walls. The Dadès and Todra gorges and the sweeping landscapes on the way to and from them seem impossibly sculpted in the late-afternoon light. The Zagora Valley along the river Drâa south of Ouarzazate is known for its unique green-glazed pottery; and the silver jewelry of Rissani is renowned for its original designs and high quality.
ESSAOUIRA & AGADIR	Overdeveloped mass tourism at Agadir is contrasted by Essaouira's breezy grace. Essaouira oozes the kind of "cool" that independent travelers love, and offers artists, craftsmen, and a working port all within easy reach. For some travelers even Essaouira is now too popular to maintain its undiscovered, low-slung vibe. Agadir offers a more touristy beach vacation, with year-round crowds and a range of water sports
THE SOUSS VALLEY & ANTI-ATLAS	The triangle of Agadir, Tafraoute, and Tiznit is formed by curvy but manageable mountain roads studded with deserted hilltop Kasbahs, villages, and centuries-old rural Koranic schools. The southwest brings together Arab and Berber, ocean and mountain, luxury accommodations and guest facilities in rural homes. Coastal towns such as Sidi Ifni are temperate year-round, whereas the Souss plains and Anti-Atlas Mountains have intensely hot summers and cool winters. People-watching is interesting here, as women's wraps vary widely within the region, from austere black or navy full-body coverings in Taroudant to brightly flowered sheet-like garments along the southern coast.

WHEN TO GO

The best times to go to Morocco are spring and fall, specifically March, April, and October. Spring may be ideal—the sky is a beautiful deep blue, washed clear by the winter rain, and wildflowers blanket the landscape. Winter is the best time to see the desert and most of the south; summer is the best time to explore the High Atlas. If you like a hot sun, come in July, August, or early September. The months between late September and December are pleasant, with cool evenings. January, February, and March are changeable and can sometimes be chilly or rainy.

The Atlantic and Mediterranean coastal resorts are crowded during summer school vacation. It's best to see the coast another time; June is still warm, and the beaches are much less crowded.

Non-Muslim travelers will probably want to **avoid coming to Morocco during Ramadan.** During this monthlong fast all cafés and nearly all restaurants are closed during the day, and the pace of work is reduced. Ramadan starts in late August in 2009, mid-August in 2010, and early August in 2011. Ramadan lasts for 29 or 30 days.

Climate
Morocco enjoys a Mediterranean climate. Inland temperatures are high in summer—sometimes in excess of 40°C (104°F)—and cool in winter. The coastal regions have a more temperate climate, warmer in winter and less brutally hot in summer. Rain falls mainly in winter, from October through March, often with more in November and March. Northern Morocco, especially the Rif Mountains, gets more rain than the south.

At right are average daily maximum and minimum temperatures for Marrakesh and Rabat, a comparison of which reveals the tempering effects of the ocean on coastal destinations. Climate varies widely throughout Morocco, so consult the appropriate chapters for details on each region you'll be visiting.

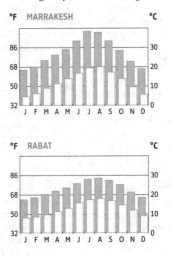

ABOUT THIS BOOK

Our Ratings

Sometimes you find terrific travel experiences and sometimes they just find you. But usually the burden is on you to select the right combination of experiences. That's where our ratings come in.

As travelers we've all discovered a place so wonderful that its worthiness is obvious. And sometimes that place is so unique that superlatives don't do it justice: you just have to be there to know. These sights, properties, and experiences get our highest rating, **Fodor's Choice**, indicated by orange stars throughout this book.

Black stars highlight sights and properties we deem **Highly Recommended**, places that our writers, editors, and readers praise again and again for consistency and excellence.

By default, there's another category: any place we include in this book is by definition worth your time, unless we say otherwise. And we will.

Disagree with any of our choices? Care to nominate a place or suggest that we rate one more highly? Visit our feedback center at www.fodors.com/feedback.

Budget Well

Hotel and restaurant price categories from ¢ to $$$$ are defined in the opening pages of each chapter. For attractions, we always give standard adult admission fees; reductions are usually available for children, students, and senior citizens. Want to pay with plastic? **AE, D, DC, MC, V** following restaurant and hotel listings indicate whether American Express, Discover, Diner's Club, MasterCard, and Visa are accepted.

Restaurants

Unless we state otherwise, restaurants are open for lunch and dinner daily. We mention dress only when there's a specific requirement and reservations only when they're essential—that said, it's always best to book ahead.

Hotels

Hotels operate on the European Plan (aka EP, meaning without meals), the Continental Plan (CP, with a Continental breakfast), Breakfast Plan (BP, with a full breakfast), or Modified American Plan (MAP, with breakfast and dinner), or are all-inclusive (AI, including all meals and most activities). We always list facilities but not whether you'll

be charged an extra fee to use them, so when pricing accommodations, find out what's included.

Many Listings

★	Fodor's Choice
★	Highly recommended
✉	Physical address
✛	Directions
✐	Mailing address
☎	Telephone
🖷	Fax
⊕	On the Web
✉	E-mail
🎟	Admission fee
☉	Open/closed times
Ⓜ	Metro stations
▭	Credit cards

Hotels & Restaurants

🏨	Hotel
⮨	Number of rooms
⚘	Facilities
🍽	Meal plans
✕	Restaurant
⚑	Reservations
⬃	Smoking
🍷	BYOB
✕🏨	Hotel with restaurant that warrants a visit

Outdoors

⛳	Golf
⛺	Camping

Other

☕	Family-friendly
⇨	See also
✉	Branch address
☞	Take note

Tangier & the Mediterranean

Updated
by Simona
Schneider

NESTLED BETWEEN THE EDGES OF THE MEDITERRANEAN SEA and the backbone of the Rif Mountains are the figurative golden gates through which many travelers enter Morocco. Though not associated with the *maroc typique* of deserts and oases, this northern region holds all the *Arabian Nights* allure that many people associate with the country—as well as an energy unparalleled in the rest of Morocco. The ancient cities of Tangier and Tétouan offer a glimpse of evolving urban Morocco with their Arab-inspired sophistication, European dress and languages, palm-lined boulevards, and extensive infrastructure for travelers. Here the vast majority of the population is under 25, and the streets are full of laughing children until late in the evening. In sharp contrast are the villages and small towns along the Rif Mountains routes, where regional dress and a traditional, agricultural way of life persist. As you travel farther east, the language shifts from Arabic to Rifi Berber, mingling with Spanish and French around the cities.

ORIENTATION & PLANNING

ORIENTATION

Tangier's location on the Strait of Gibraltar has made it a cosmopolitan city. This contrasts with the Atlantic and Mediterranean coastlines, which support a rich commercial and private fishery—with rocky coastal outcroppings where local anglers cast lines from long poles. In contrast, the Rif valleys and plateaus, extremely fertile thanks to the region's reliable annual rainfall—typically two weeks straight in late November and mid-April—yield some of the country's finest agricultural products, including olives, wheat, barley, and honey.

Tangier. Tangier seems a millennium removed from southern Spain, but the sights, sounds, and aromas of Morocco are never better highlighted than in this tumultuous collision of Rifi, Berber, Arabic, and European cultures.

The Ceuta Peninsula. with its lighthouse marking the meeting place of Atlantic and Mediterranean waters, the Ceuta Peninsula leads on to glorious beaches and modern resort towns. Tétouan's curiously Spanish medina is just one of the highlights.

Chefchaouen & the Rif. A mountain stronghold and sanctuary only opened to Christian visitors in the 20th century, Chefchaouen has always been a favorite of Moroccophiles. The cool, crisp mountain air; the bite-size medina; and the unique blue houses make this an indispensable destination.

The Northeastern Circuit. For windswept, lonely strands of beach and some of Morocco's least tourist-influenced villages and natural resources, this remote pocket isolated by the Rif Mountains combines highland and Mediterranean sights and landscapes with Berber culture and a Spanish enclave.

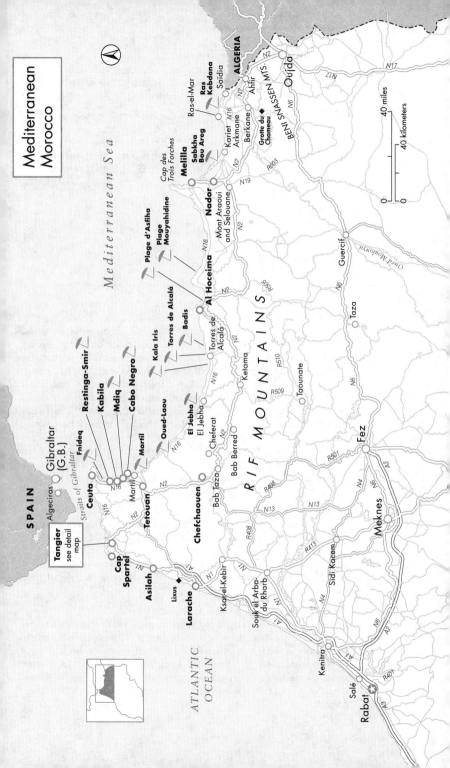

Mediterranean Morocco

SPAIN

Algeciras

Gibraltar (G.B.)

Straits of Gibraltar

Tangier
see detail map

Cap Spartel

Asilah

Lixus

Larache

Ksar-el-Kebir

ATLANTIC OCEAN

Mediterranean Sea

Ceuta

Fnideq

Restinga-Smir

Kabila

Mdiq

Cabo Negro

Martil

Martil

Tetouan

Chefchaouen

Bab Taza

Oued-Laou

El Jebha

El Jebha

Cheferat

Bab Berred

R408

N13

N13

Souk el Arba-du Rharb

Sidi Kacem

R413

R408

Meknes

Kenitra

Salé

Rabat

A3

R401

N6

A2

N4

N9

Fez

A2

R501

R509

Taounate

R510

Taza

N6

Guercif

Oued Moulouya

N6

N17

Oujda

ALGERIA

N2

Saïdia

Ahfir

Berkane

N6

BENI SNASSEN MTS.

Grotte du Chameau

N2

Kariet Arkmane

N16

Ras-el-Mar

Ras Kebdana

Sabkha Bou Areg

Melilla

Nador

N19

Mont Araoui and Selouane

N2

Cap des Trois Forches

Plage d'Asfiha

Plage Mouyahidine

Al Hoceima

N16

Torres de Alcalá

Torres de Alcalá

Badis

Kala Iris

Ketama

N2

RIF MOUNTAINS

R505

R603

40 miles

40 kilometers

TOP REASONS TO GO

Tangier: This city charms many new-comers with its eye-popping views, calm breezes, and friendly inhabit-ants who are always curious to know more about the outside world.

The Rif Mountains: Running parallel to the Mediterranean coast for 200 km (180 mi), this is the highest range in the north and offers some of the best scenery and trekking in Morocco.

Tétouan: Overlooking the verdant Martil Valley, Tétouan is famous for its Hispano-Moorish architecture and medina.

Chefchaouen: This charming blue-and-white mountain stronghold is one of Morocco's through-the-look-ing-glass fantasy spots, and is espe-cially popular with nature lovers.

PLANNING

WHEN TO GO

The region has a temperate, coastal climate throughout the year, though the bone-chilling winter weather can catch unprepared tour-ists off guard. Inland, the Rif Mountains areas see rain in winter and spring, and the high peaks are often snowcapped through April. Spring-time, particularly the month of May, is the region's finest season, with hundreds of varieties of hillside wildflowers in full bloom. The tradi-tional high season is from late July to the end of August; beaches teem with Moroccan families as well as substantial numbers of Europeans. Extensive beach campgrounds—full-fledged tent towns, really—stretch for miles in summer. During this time prices are higher, rooms are hard to find, beaches are packed, and roads are crowded. By contrast, spring and fall are quiet and peaceful periods in northern Morocco and are by far your best bet for ideal travel times.

GETTING AROUND

Trains connect Tangier with destinations farther south, although most of the region's destinations are not served. The C.T.M. bus line and *grands taxis* (taxis that travel long distances and leave only when full) are good ways to get from point to point. Renting a car is manageable, as is hiring local drivers (and their cars) for varying lengths of time through local travel agencies.

WHAT TO WEAR

In Tangier and other larger cities, locals often don't wear traditional clothing and are used to seeing tourists' bare legs. But outside the more-cosmopolitan areas it is wise to dress more modestly, opting for skirts or pants that come at least to the knee. Men in Tangier never wear shorts on the street; doing so is not offensive, but might provoke stares. If you're invited to someone's home, dress conservatively to show your respect.

A BIT OF HISTORY

Northern Morocco has a tumultuous history of invasion and revolt. Phoenician settlements dotted the coastline as early as 1200 BC, and were later taken over by Carthaginians; eventually they became an important part of the Roman province of Mauretania Tingitana, one of the Roman Empire's foremost agricultural production centers. Germanic Vandals and, later, Byzantine troops made claims to the area until Arab Muslim invaders entered the region in AD 682. The dawn of Islam in Morocco began more than 1,000 years of conflict, which reached through the north into Spain, involving the native Berbers, Arab dynasties, Moors, and Saharan tribes.

Recent Moroccan history is, of course, marked by European imperialism. Until Moroccan independence in 1956, northern Morocco was under Spanish and French control, except Tangier, which was ultimately under the rule of 14 different nations during its International Zone period. This colonial legacy is now evident in everything from architecture to gastronomy, from divergent languages to blue-eyed Rifi Berbers.

Light clothes are best in summer, but pack something warmer for the evenings when the temperature drops considerably. In winter bring plenty of layers.

GUIDES
In the port area there are still plenty of fake guides wanting to show you around. Simply walk quickly past these unsolicited assistants, pretend you know exactly where you're going, and show no sign that you're bewildered (not to mention astonished) by this sudden onslaught of new friends passionately interested in your welfare. Most licensed guides work for tour companies and can be seen leading large groups of tourists.

BARTERING
Negotiating for that handwoven rug or carefully crafted pair of silver earrings can be fun—if you start with the right attitude. You will undoubtedly be asked to pay more than the object is worth, but you shouldn't be offended. It's just the way bargaining begins. In inexpensive shops, the merchant will try to establish whether you really want to purchase an item. If you are serious about an item, chances are you will reach a compromise. At more high-end shops, the merchant usually starts off by giving you the "real" price, then offers to cut a deal right away. This makes bargaining more difficult, and sometimes impossible.

When deciding how much to offer, half of the original price is a good starting point. The real value of an object, however, is always how much you are willing to pay for it. Consider its originality, its quality, and how much you might find it for at home, if you could find it at all.

RESTAURANTS & CUISINE

As much of a mosaic as the region itself, northern Moroccan cuisine combines influences from several other cultures with native ingredients. Tagines are made with particular flair in the north, where olives, spices, and produce are all grown locally. *Barrogog b'basela* (lamb tagine with prunes), *djej m'qualli* (chicken tagine with lemons and olives), and *tagine b'lhout* (fish tagine) are all regional specialties. The abundance of fresh seafood makes it a natural choice in coastal areas. Fresh grilled sardines, shrimp, and calamari are standard fare here, and any one of them makes a wonderful lunch in a seaside eatery.

The finer Moroccan restaurants serve delicacies usually reserved within Moroccan culture for special occasions. *Pastilla* (pigeon pie), *mechoui* (roast lamb), and *tangia* (a meat dish roasted in clay pots over fire for more than 10 hours) are well worth a try here. More common but also enjoyable are Morocco's famous couscous, traditionally available only on Friday. Fresh local produce is found in dishes like *za'alook* (a cold, spicy, eggplant-based side dish) and *harira* (a tomato-based meat soup with vermicelli noodles).

WHAT IT COSTS IN DIRHAMS					
	¢	$	$$	$$$	$$$$
AT DINNER	under 50DH	50DH–100DH	100DH–150DH	150DH–200DH	over 200DH

Prices are per person for a main course at dinner or for a prix-fixe meal.

HOTELS

Accommodations in the north range from opulent to downright spare, with everything in between. You'll have a range of options in most areas. Hotels in Tangier can be on a par with those of Europe, but the farther you venture off the beaten path, the farther you might feel from Tangier's five-star welcome. Particularly in some of the smaller cities east of Chefchaouen and Tétouan, hotels lack the amenities to call themselves top-tier. Look a bit closer, though—what they lack in luxury these hotels often make up in charm, character, and, most of all, location.

In Tangier and Tétouan, advance reservations are a must if you want decent accommodations. Note that prices rise in July and August, and that if you'll be staying anywhere other than a five-star hotel you may want to inquire in advance (quite seriously) about the state of the hotel's credit-card machine.

WHAT IT COSTS IN DIRHAMS					
	¢	$	$$	$$$	$$$$
FOR TWO PEOPLE	under 250DH	250DH–500DH	500DH–1,000DH	1,000DH–1,500DH	over 1,500DH

All prices are for a high-season standard double room, excluding tax.

TANGIER

15 km (9 mi) across Strait of Gibraltar from Algeciras, Spain; 350 km (220 mi) north of Casablanca; 278 km (172 mi) north of Rabat.

Giddy from the rush provided by crossing the Strait of Gibraltar from the European continent to Africa, first-time visitors may find the Tangier port such a rude awakening that they fail to see the beauty of the place. Mobs of faux guides and bona fide hustlers greet the arriving ferries hungry for fresh greenhorns to fleece in any way they can. Once you hit your stride and start going places with confidence, Tangier has a charm that this raucous undercurrent only enhances: crumbling Kasbah walls, intimate corners in the serpentine medina, piles of bougainvillea, French balconies, Spanish cafés, and other remnants of times gone by.

Grab a seat at a sidewalk café and you'll begin to see how dramatically the urban brouhaha is set against the backdrop of the turquoise Mediterranean. Tangier is a melting pot—a place where it's not uncommon to see sophisticated Moroccans sharing sidewalks with rural Rifi Berbers wrapped in traditional striped *mehndis* (brightly colored blankets women wear tied around their waists). Saudi princes, American and European expats, and boats and busloads of day-trippers from Spain have all converged on the African continent's nearest point eager for a look into a cultural potpourri that has taken thousands of years to blend.

GETTING HERE & AROUND

Tangier's Boukhalef Airport, 15 km (9 mi) from the city center, is linked by taxis and buses to the Grand Socco (Nos. 17 and 70). Royal Air Maroc, Atlas Blue, and British Airways offer daily flights from many cities including Amsterdam, Brussels, Barcelona, London, Madrid, and Paris. EasyJet offers daily flights from Madrid. RyanAir flies from Brussels and Marseille.

The well-established Spanish company Trasmediterránia handles most ferry routes between Morocco and Spain. The Moroccan firm Comarit Ferry also connects the two countries in the warmer months and has added a one-hour hydrofoil trip to its ferry options. Southern Ferries Ltd. offers a car ferry with cabin accommodation from Sète (southern France) every four days, a 36-hour trip. Daily ferries connect Tangier with the Spanish port of Algeciras (two hours; 357 DH passenger, 1,189 DH car), Tarifa (30 minutes; 360 DH passenger, 920 DH car) and Gibraltar (two hours; 357 DH passenger, 892 DH car). Passenger-only hydrofoil service connects Tangier with the Spanish port of Algeciras once or twice daily (one hour; 357 DH).

Compagnie de Transports Marocains, or C.T.M., is the region's main and only recommended bus company. It runs several buses daily between Tangier, Tétouan, Chefchaouen, Al Hoceima, Nador, and many other cities. The company even has an overnight 10-hour bus to Marrakesh. The only northern city served by O.N.C.F., the Moroccan rail service, is Tangier. Tanger Ville station is 3 km (2 mi) west of town. Two daily trains connect Tangier with Casablanca, a journey of six hours. One daily train gets you to Fez in 5 hours, and an overnight train gets you to Marrakesh in 10 hours. First-class sleeping accommodations are highly recommended.

In the new part of the cities, abundant petits taxis are the safest and most efficient way to get around. They use meters, but make sure to insist that the driver turns it on. You can wave one down by indicating the general direction you wish to travel. If the driver is going your way, he'll stop. For longer distances you'll need a larger grand taxi. A 10-minute petit taxi ride should cost about 8 to 10 DH; in a grand taxi, the same journey would be about 30 DH. At night the fare increases by half.

TIMING & PRECAUTIONS

Tangier's reputation as a dangerous city has largely been propagated by wide-eyed tourists on day trips from Spain. The truth is that Tangier has become a much safer place because of increased police presence. Using common sense when exploring by day and staying out of dark alleys at night will help keep you out of harm's way. When in doubt about walking through dimly lighted areas, take a taxi. The medina in Tangier is still governed by its own security detail, and can be dangerous at night.

ESSENTIALS

Bus Contacts Compagnie de Transports Marocains (✉ *Ave. d'Espagne at Gare Routière* ☎ *039/96–16–23* ⊕ *www.ctm.co.ma*).

Ferry Contacts Comarit Ferry (✉ *7, rue de Méxique* ☎ *09/93–12–20* ⊕ *www. comarit.com*). **Southern Ferries Ltd** (✉ *179 Piccadilly, London, England* ☎ *207/491– 4968*). **Trasmediterránia** (✉ *31, ave. de la Résistance* ☎ *09/94–11–01*).

Internet Cyber Café Adam (✉ *19b, ave. Imar Ben Khattab* ☎ *039/94–83–97*). **Espace Net** (✉ *16, ave. Méxique* ☎ *039/93–25–26*).

Medical Assistance Hospital Al Kortobi (✉ Av. Asad Ibn Friate ☎ *039/93–10– 73*). **Pharmacie Jamilla "Depôt de Nuit"** (✉ *10, rue de Fès* ☎ *039/94–96–76*).

Post Office Tangier Main Post Office (✉ *33, ave. Mohammed V*).

Rental Cars Avis (✉ *54, bd. Pasteur* ☎ *039/93–30–31*). **Europcar/InterRent** (✉ *87, bd. Mohammed V* ☎ *039/94–19–38*). **Hertz** (✉ *36, bd. Mohammed V* ☎ *039/32–22–10*).

Train Contacts Office National des Chemins de Fer (✉ *8 bis, rue Abderrahmane el Ghafiki* ☎ *039/95–25–55* ⊕ *www.oncf.org.ma*).

Visitor & Tour Information Magic Carpet Adventures (✉ *Bd. Mohammed V* ☎ *039/32–12–72*). **Tangier Tourism Information** (✉ *29, bd. Pasteur* ☎ *039/94–80–50*).

A BIT OF HISTORY

Tangier's strategic position at the juncture of sea and ocean has long been hotly contested. Following ancient Phoenician, Roman, and then Arab conquerors, Portugal seized Tangier in the 15th century, only to hand it over to Britain in the 17th century as part of Catherine of Braganza's dowry on her marriage to King Charles II (a dowry that also included Bombay). England's control of Tangier was short-lived; in 1685 it fell into the hands of the Arab sultan Moulay Ismail. The French came to Tangier in 1912, but not without disputes from England and continued scurries over control, so that by 1923 Tangier was governed by international authority. The city's international status, complete with special tax laws and loose governance, attracted international crowds. In the first half of the 20th century Tangier was a sumptuous, rather anarchic, sensory feast that drew artists, writers, diplomats, heiresses, and free spirits from all over the world.

With Moroccan independence from French rule in 1956, Tangier was incorporated into the Moroccan state. The international population—and investors—dwindled, and the city's magnificence retreated to the realm of myth. Modern-day Tangier is much more subdued than the sybaritic haven of the glory days, yet it still has a distinct chiaroscuro appeal. Like Morocco's distinctive zellij tiles, the city is an amalgam—in this case of various periods and nationalities—that appears to change shape depending on the angle from which it's viewed.

EXPLORING

MEDINA

TOP ATTRACTIONS

⑧ American Legation. The Legation is housed in a typical Tangerine medina home with carved wooden doors, ornate plaster details, and high walls surrounding an outdoor courtyard. Preserved today as an American Historic Landmark, this property was given to the United States by the Moroccan sultan in 1821. Displays showcase Tangier's history, including handwritten correspondence between the sultan and George Washington. The museum hosts a regular lending **library**, which has a small but interesting collection of English-language books. To get here, follow Rue de Portugal as it climbs upward and look for a set of double stairs called "The American Steps" on the right, leading to an archway. When you find yourself under a balcony with a tile underside, walk up the stairs, go through the archway, and follow the winding street until you see the United States seal. ⊠8, *Zankat d'Amérique* ☎039/93–53–17 ⊕*www.legation.org* ⊗ *Weekdays 10–1 and 3–5; and by appointment.*

⑤ Kasbah. Sprawling across the ancient medina's highest point, Tangier's Kasbah can be blinding at mid-day as the infamous Mediterranean sun bounces off the pristine white walls. It has been tinkered with since the Roman era. During early Arab rule it was the traditional residence of the sultan and his harem. Since then the Kasbah has become a fashion-

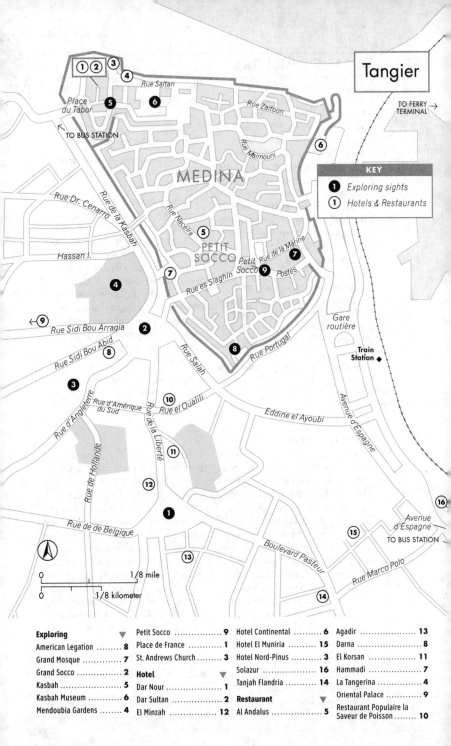

Tangier

TO FERRY TERMINAL →

← TO BUS STATION

KEY

❶ Exploring sights

① Hotels & Restaurants

Rue Saltan

Rue Zaitoun

Place du Tábor

Rue Maimouni

Rue Dr. Cenarro

Rue de la Kasbah

MEDINA

Rue Naceira

Hassan I.

PETIT SOCCO

Rue de la Marine

Petit Socco

Postes

Rue es Siaghin

Rue Sidi Bou Arragia

Rue Sidi Bou Abid

Gare routière

Train Station ◆

Rue Salah

Rue d'Angleterre

Rue d'Amérique du Sud

Rue el Oualili

Eddine el Ayoubi

Avenue d'Espagne

Rue de la Liberté

Rue de Hollande

Rue de de Belgique

Avenue d'Espagne

TO BUS STATION

Boulevard Pasteur

Rue Marco Polo

0   1/8 mile

0   1/8 kilometer

able residential area—particularly in the international era, but today as well. You can reach the Kasbah by climbing Rue d'Italie to its top and entering the huge Kasbah gate, Bab el Kasbah, at the top or by winding up the medina's Rue des Chrétiens to the Kasbah area.

> **DID YOU KNOW?**
>
> Morocco was the world's first nation to recognize the independent United States, and the document hangs at the American Legation. Established in 1777, the building was the first American ambassadorial residence and overseas property.

9 **Petit Socco.** Tennessee Williams based his play Camino Real on the square—and it is indeed dramatic, with the cast of characters that are passing through at any time of day. It has a theatrical range of seating, which is split among the three main cafés—parterre (Tingis), orchestra (Centrale), or balcony (Fuentes). The Fuentes used to be the German post office in the International Zone period—supposedly the most reliable one before the Germans got kicked out during WWII. It's a great place to take a break before plunging back into the souks that surround it.

WORTH NOTING

7 **Grand Mosque.** You can't miss the striking green-and-white-tile minaret of Tangier's Grand Mosque. Built in 1685 (on the site of a destroyed European-built church) by Moulay Ismail, the mosque was a tribute to and celebration of Morocco's return to Arab control. Although its entrances are blocked from view by wooden screens and entrance is strictly forbidden to non-Muslims, its bold colors make it one of the most recognizable of the medina's attractions. It's worth a look as you wander through the medina. ⊠ *Between Rue de la Marine and Rue des Postes in lower part of medina.*

6 **Kasbah Museum.** Constructed by the 17th-century sultan Moulay Ismail, this was the Kasbah's palace. The sultan's former apartments now house an interesting Moroccan-art museum, with mosaic floors, carpets, traditional Fez furniture, jewelry, ceramics, leather, daggers, illuminated manuscripts, textiles, and historic, finely crafted examples of carved and painted cedar ceilings. The marble columns in the courtyard were taken from the ancient Roman city of Volubilis. Don't miss the mosaic *Voyage of Venus* or the life-size Carthaginian tomb. Exit the palace via the former treasury of Moulay Ismail, the Bit el Mal; look for the giant wooden boxes that once held gold and precious gems. ⊠ *Pl. de la Kasbah* ☏ *039/93–20–97* 🎟 *10 DH* ☾ *Wed.–Mon. 9–4.*

NEED A BREAK?

Occupying the upper floors of a medina home with floor-to-ceiling windows is the fine tearoom **Salon de Thé/Restaurant le Détroit** (⊠ *Rue Riad Sultan at Pl. de la Kasbah* ☏ *09/93–80–80*), known as Café Détroit. Established in the early 1960s by beat writer Brion Gysin, it's the perfect place for the weary wanderer to sit and take in panoramic views of the Mediterranean Sea and palace gardens while enjoying fabulous Moroccan cookies and mint tea.

Look for the sign in a rather unassuming entrance across from the Kasbah's viewing belvedere. However, it can be quite packed with package tourists.

VILLE NOUVELLE

TOP ATTRACTIONS

❷ Grand Socco. Tangier's chief market area in times past, the Grand Socco (a combination of French and Spanish meaning "great souk") now serves as a local transportation hub. The main door to the medina, a white arch, stands at the bottom. As late as the 1940s, when the new city was just beginning, the door was locked at night to seal off outsiders. The main attraction of the Grand Socco is the recently restored movie theater, which displays photographs and old movie posters highlighting Tangier's glamorous past. It's on Place du 9 Avril. ⊠ *At bottom of Rue de la Liberté, just south of Mendoubia Gardens.*

❹ Mendoubia Gardens. Adjacent to the Grand Socco, this former residence of the Mendoub—the sultan's representative on the governing commission during the international years—is now a park with palm tree–lined paths that is popular with families on weekends. To the right of the entrance is a large banyan tree that locals claim is more than 800 years old. ⊠ *Rue Bouarrakia at Rue d'Italie.*

❶ Place de France. Famous for its café scene in the first half of the 20th century, Place de France is one of Tangier's main squares. It fills up after about 6 PM for a nightly promenade.

WORTH NOTING

Mohamed Drissi Gallery of Contemporary Art. Located in the stately former British Consulate building and surrounded by a lovely garden, this recently established gallery, run by the country's ministry of culture, highlights the works of Moroccan artists. ⊠ *52, rue d'Angleterre* ☎ *039/94–99–72* ⊙ *Wed.–Mon. 9–1 and 2–6.*

❸ St. Andrew's Church. This 19th-century Anglican church is one of the purest vestiges of Tangier's international days. The architecture and interior are both Moorish in flavor (the Lord's Prayer is inscribed in Arabic above the altar), while the cemetery hosts expats from the International Zone period. The priest comes from Gibraltar on Sunday for services. ⊠ *50, rue d'Angleterre* ☎ *039/93–46–33* ⊙ *Mon.–Sat. 9–6, Sun. noon–6.*

WHERE TO EAT

Tangier's cuisine has notable Moroccan, Spanish, and French influences, and a new crop of restaurants are successfully blending all three. Often the most delicious dishes are the simplest, such as freshly caught grilled fish with a touch of garlic. There's also the traditional dishes like tagines, couscous, or *baissara*, a bean soup. In the Ville Nouvelle there are a plethora of opulent choices in old palaces. In the medina, the restaurants are intimate and often associated with lodgings.

1

MEDINA

¢–$ **✗Al Andalus.** This no-frills restaurant specializes in a variety of fresh
SEAFOOD fish—including sole, swordfish, and dorado—expertly grilled or fried. The kitchen also prepares delicious and cheap Spanish-style tortillas (hearty omelets with deep-fried potatoes). ⊠ *7, rue de Commerce* ☎ *No phone* ⊟ *No credit cards* ⊘ *No lunch.*

$$–$$$ **✗El Korsan.** One of Tangier's most reliable restaurants, El Korsan is
MOROCCAN located in the peerless Minzah hotel. The kitchen serves traditional Moroccan cuisine in the most sumptuous manner possible. Specialties include succulent *mechoui* (roasted lamb or mutton), slow-cooked tagines, and couscous. The food is excellent, the staff is attentive, and the decor is classically Moroccan, with soaring arches and handicrafts. Andalusian music is performed nightly ⊠ *Hotel el Minzah, 85, rue de la Liberté* ☎ *039/93–58–85* ⊟ *AE, DC, MC, V.*

$ **✗Hammadi.** Decorated in an over-the-top Moroccan style, with ban-
MOROCCAN quettes covered with sumptuous pillows and rich brocades, Hammadi
★ is not to be missed. With a live band playing traditional Andalusian music and several nightly shows, it is anything but dull. The place is definitely touristy, but it also has a charm. Try the house pastilla, chicken tagine, or *kefta* (beef patties). ⊠ *2, rue de la Kasbah* ☎ *039/93–45–14* ⊟ *MC, V.*

$$$ **✗Hotel Nord-Pinus.** Boasting an unforgettably romantic ambience, this
SEAFOOD world-class restaurant serves traditional Moroccan dishes with a cre-
★ ative twist. Along with dishes like chicken and raisin tagine, there's a splendid array of vegetarian dishes such as eggplant caviar. Almost as delicious as the food is the windowed balcony overlooking the sea. Call around 11 AM for the menu of the day. ⊠ *11, rue Riad Sultan* ☎ *061/22–81–40* ⊕ *www.nord-pinus-tangier.com* ⊲ *Reservations essential* ⊟ *AE, DC, MC, V.*

TANGIER MOMENT **Disembarking from and embarking onto the Algeciras ferry in the port of Tangier add up to one of Morocco's most unforgettable experiences. Headed into Tangier, New Testament Western Europe has been suddenly replaced by Old Testament North Africa, complete with peak-hooded *djellabas* (long, hooded robes) and a press of phony guides, drivers, and hustlers. The chaos is breathtaking. On the way out of the country, having threaded your way through several tiers of ersatz customs agents offering to help you with your departure, the sudden peace and quiet aboard ship seem just as suddenly, and a little sadly, flat and unchallenging.**

VILLE NOUVELLE

$ **✗Agadir.** This cozy restaurant has an expansive menu of traditional
MOROCCAN Moroccan cuisine, including a number of delicious tagines (try the
★ lamb and prune, or chicken with vegetables). There's also plenty of continental fare. Romantic and relaxed, it's a great place to go after a long day of sightseeing, but not if you're starving. Expect a bit of wait, as the waiter is also the chef. ⊠ *Rue Prince Heritier* ☎ *068/82–76–96* ⊟ *No credit cards* ⊘ *No lunch. No dinner Fri.*

¢ **✗Darna.** Located in the old British prison, this restaurant is a favorite
MOROCCAN of Tangier's expat community. The students at this nonprofit women's
★

vocational training center prepare scrumptious home-style lunches. Tradition couscous is served on Friday, and should not be missed. ⊠*Rue Jules Cot off Pl. du 9 Avril* ☎*039/94–70–65* ▤*AE, DC* ☉*No dinner. No lunch Sun.*

$$$–$$$$
MOROCCAN

✕**Oriental Palace.** Lively belly dancers move between the tables at this chic lounge set in an opulent banquet hall with carved ceilings and authentic tile work. Superb dishes such as lamb with prunes are sure to satiate a gourmet palate, while a typical Mediterranean St. Pierre gets a fresh spin with Moroccan spices. ⊠ *3, rue de Cordoue Park Brooks* ☎*039/93–60–54* ▤*MC, V.*

$$$
SEAFOOD
★

✕**Saveurs de Poisson.** The owner of this restaurant doesn't hesitate to say the food here is extraordinary—in fact, he claims it has magical healing powers. Mohammed Belhadj likes to explain the effect of each recipe. The menu and the price are fixed, so there's no ordering at all. Be prepared for four courses, two of which come directly from the sea—St. Pierre, dorado, sole, or whatever is fresh. You'll also be served special fruit juice based on plum juice and infused with flowers, cloves, and other secrets. The flavors are exquisite, the vibe is relaxed, and Mohammed is a colorful character. ⊠*2, Escalier Waller* ☎*039/33–63–26* ▤*No credit cards* ☉*Closed Fri. No lunch.*

WHERE TO STAY

Whether the style is sparse modernism or over-the-top opulence, Tangier is all about leisure and luxury. Add Morocco's famous hospitality and Tangier's plethora of gorgeous views and you have an unforgettable experience. The service won't be especially efficient, but the sincere smiles of the staff are usually enough to remind you you're on vacation. Don't expect amenities such as full business centers or luxuries like casinos.

MEDINA

$$–$$$
★

▦**Dar Nour.** Located in the Kasbah, this pristine town house has an unbeatable location. The rooms are tastefully decorated with local artifacts and artwork. A short walk from the renowned Café Hafa, Dar Nour serves memorable breakfasts on the patio and an excellent prix-fixe dinner if arranged ahead of time. **Pros:** Personal attention, cozy atmosphere. **Con:** Limited facilities. ⊠*20, rue Gourna* ☎*062/11–27–24* ⊕*www.darnour.com* ➳*9 rooms* ⌂*In-hotel: restaurant* ▤*AE, DC, MC, V* ⋈*BP.*

$$–$$$

▦**Dar Sultan.** The chaotic harmony of every style of carpet known make this the exotic abode you'd expect in the Kasbah. The baronial palace, complete with crenellated battlements, gives you a well-stocked library, public rooms with fireplaces, and elegant bedrooms with an authentic feel. Three floors surround an interior courtyard in this chic Tangier hotel. **Pros:** In the heart of the medina, romantic atmosphere. **Con:** A bit hard to find. ⊠*49, rue Touila, La Kasbah* ☎*039/33–60–61* ⊕*www.darsultan.com* ➳*6 rooms* ⌂ *In-room: No a/c (some), Ethernet. In-hotel: room service.* ▤*AE, DC, MC, V* ⋈*BP.*

$

▦**Hotel Continental.** Morocco's very first hotel was built in 1865 in the Victorian style—appropriate, as Victoria's son Alfred was the first official guest. The yellowed pages of the 19th-century guest book also contain the simple quilled entry "Degas: Paris." Kept strictly to Victorian style until 1990, the Continental has made some changes since then, adding Moroccan arches and other decorative flourishes. Imbued with a slightly threadbare charm, it's nostalgic, romantic, and stately. You can relax in a variety of small parlors, reading rooms, and sunrooms, or on the open patio overlooking the port. Rooms 108 and 208 have the best views of the bobbing boats. With breakfast included, it's Tangier's all-around best value. **Pros:** Great views, excellent location, good value. **Cons:** Hot water is not always assured, some modernized rooms are a bit tacky. ⊠*36, Dar Baroud* ☎*039/93–10–24* ⊘*66 rooms* ⌂*In-hotel: restaurant, parking (no fee)* ▤*No credit cards* ⏧*BP.*

$$ ⏢**La Tangerina.** Across from the outer wall of the Kasbah, this four-
★ story hotel has a patio on which to enjoy a delicious full breakfast or tea and pastries whenever you desire. Some of the rooms gaze out over the ocean. **Pros:** Beautiful setting, stunning views from balcony. **Cons:** Far from the new city, a lot of stairs, many rooms have no view. ⊠*19, Riad Sultan* ☎*039/94–77–33* ⊕*www.latangerina.com* ⊘*10 rooms* ⌂*In-hotel: gym, public Wi-Fi* ▤*AE, DC, MC, V* ⏧*BP.*

VILLE NOUVELLE

$$$$ ⏢**El Minzah.** Tangier's top hotel was built in 1930 by the English Lord Bute. Decorated in Moorish style, it is located in the new city but is a short walk from the medina. A helpful staff in Ottoman costume, beautiful gardens, an elegant patio, the constant sound of falling water (much cherished by Moroccans), and fine views over the Strait of Gibraltar to Spain make it a classic experience. The spacious rooms are richly carpeted and lavishly decorated in an Andalusian style, with fabrics, brass, and traditional Moroccan tables, pottery, and artwork. **Pros:** Great service, excellent facilities. **Cons:** A bit impersonal, on the expensive side. ⊠*85, rue de la Liberté* ☎*039/93–58–85* ⊕*www. elminzah.com* ⊘*125 rooms, 15 suites* ⌂*In-room: safe. In-hotel: 2 restaurants, bars, pool, gym, laundry service, parking (no fee), no-smoking rooms* ▤*AE, DC, MC, V* ⏧*BP.*

¢ ⏢**El Muniria.** Made famous as the favorite hotel of the Beat Generation writers, El Muniria still offers clean and comfortable accommodations, a lovely garden, and Madame Rabia, the charming proprietress. Famous guests include Allen Ginsberg, Jack Kerouac, and William Burroughs, who wrote *Naked Lunch* in what was formerly Room 9. The hotel's legendary late-night bar, the Tanger Inn, still draws both locals and would-be beatniks. **Pros:** Nice views, away from the crowd. **Cons:** On poorly lighted alley, area gets sketchy at night. ⊠*1, rue Magellan* ☎*039/93–53–37* ⊘*8 rooms* ⌂*In-hotel: restaurant, bar* ▤*No credit cards* ⏧*BP.*

$$ ⏢**Solazur.** The best of Tangier's beachfront hotels, the Solazur gained a degree of notoriety when billionaire Malcolm Forbes held his 70th-birthday party here. The pastel rooms are spacious and comfortably posh. Treat yourself to one with a seaside view. Both restaurants are good choices for simple, international lunches, but most guests choose to venture into town for broader dinner options. **Pros:** Beachfront location, near nightlife. **Cons:** Impersonal feel, caters to tour groups, uphill

Tangier's Herculean Origins

The name Tangier is derived from the mythical Labors of Hercules. One of the hero's labors was to capture a golden apple from the Garden of the Hesperides (believed to be near the ancient site of Lixus, outside modern-day Larache, on Morocco's northwest Atlantic coast). In so doing, Hercules killed the giant Anteus, married his widow Tingis, and had a son with her. As a gift to their offspring, who would later become King Sophix,

Hercules grasped the rock of Gibraltar with one hand and Djebel (Mt.) Musa, near Tangier, with the other, and pulled Africa and Spain apart to give his son a city protected by the sea. Sophix named this city Tingis, in honor of his mother. Thousands of years later Tingis became Tangier, and the mythical land—although it does retain much of its magic—has evolved into a modern city.

walk to medina. ⊠*Ave. des FAR* ☎*039/32–07–60* ⊅*360 rooms* ⚭ *In-hotel: 2 restaurants, bar, pool, tennis court, public Wi-Fi* ▤*DC, MC, V* ⵔ*BP.*

$$
⚭
★
🏨 **Tanjah Flandria.** On Ville Nouvelle's main thoroughfare, this modern hotel has a rooftop pool, an atmospheric lounge, and an adjoining art gallery. The carpeted rooms have sunlight streaming through large windows. Moroccan touches such as handmade pottery, brass mirrors, and paintings add a touch of class. It's a good value and your best bet in the Ville Nouvelle. **Pros:** Close to beach, near markets, friendly staff. **Cons:** Impersonal feel, some rooms need renovation. ⊠*6, bd. Mohammed V off Bd. Pasteur* ☎*039/93-32-79* ⊅*150 rooms* ⚭ *In-hotel: 2 restaurants, bar, pool, public Wi-Fi, parking (no fee)* ▤*AE, DC, MC, V.*

NIGHTLIFE

Tangier's nightlife begins with the early-evening promenade and café hour, from about 6 to 9, when the streets teem with locals and expats alike. In summer many beachfront cafés are full well into the night. Late dining is another mainstay of Tangerine nightlife, with many restaurants open past 10 PM—rare in Morocco and another example of Spanish influence in the region.

BARS

Although there's a burly security guard at the front door, **Atlas Bar** (⊠*30, rue Prince Heritier*) is surprisingly mild-mannered on the inside. At the center is an island bar surrounded by high bar stools. The best part, however, is the generous selections of tapas served with every drink. **Cabaña** (⊠*Camping Miramonte, Marshan*) feels like you've stepped onto Gilligan's Island. You'll be greeted by monkeys and tropical fragrances at this cliff-side bar and restaurant. There are two restaurants, a pool, and a patio for dancing. Established in 1937, **Dean's Bar** (⊠*2, rue Amérique du Sud*) is a former expat favorite that is now full of local men watching soccer. The tapas are delicious. A late-night libation at the **Tanger Inn** (⊠*1, rue Magellan*) is an opportunity for literary nostalgia.

Knowing that your bar stool may have supported the likes of William Burroughs, Allen Ginsberg, Jack Kerouac, Paul Bowles, Jean Genet, Tennessee Williams, or Federico García Lorca always adds a dash of erudition to your cocktail. Approaching from Place de France is advisable, as the area can be sketchy by night. Weekends the place is packed with young locals.

CAFÉS

Cafés and writers seem inextricably linked, whether the substance sought is caffeine, hops, absinthe, or worse. Tangier café life is especially vibrant. Most patrons are men, as women tend to go to the salons de thé. Some men do all their business out of cafés, whether it be real estate, hustling, or philosophizing.

Ringside seating at the greatest show on Earth can be had at **Café Centrale** (⊠ *Petit Socco*), which sits on the Petit Socco. A good place to catch your breath with a *panaché orange* (orange-flavor fruit shake) and a *croque-monsieur* (grilled cheese sandwich) as you watch the strange cast of characters wander past. **Café Hafa** (⊠ *Ave. Mohammed Tazi*) west of the Kasbah overlooking the Strait of Gibraltar and set up on seven steps plunging toward the sea, this laid-back cliff café has been the favorite sunset-watching haunt of all Tangier glitterati from Paul Bowles to the Rolling Stones. People will test if you've been to Tangier by whether or not you have been here. With its tufted leather seats and impeccable service, **Gran Café de Paris** (⊠ *Pl. de France*) will make you feel like you're back in the '50s with Burroughs (he wrote here), or in The Bourne Ultimatum (it was filmed here). This is a perfect place to watch the *paseo* (evening promenade) on the boulevard. Andalusian musicians hold jam sessions every night in tiny **Les Fils du Detroit** (⊠ *Pl. du Méchouar off Pl. de la Kasbah*).

DANCE CLUBS

Discos, of which there is no shortage in Tangier, begin to fill around 11 and thump well into the morning.

Borsalino (⊠ *30, ave. du Prince de Moulay Abdellah*) is a retro disco complete with an enormous disco ball. This party may get started late, but pumps into the wee hours of the morning. Especially lively on summer nights, **Chellah Beach Club** (⊠ *Ave. Mohamed VI*) is tucked among the strip of clubs at Tangier Bay. A live jazz band and an outdoor dance floor keep this place swinging from 9 until the crowd disperses.

Morocco Palace (⊠ *11, ave. du Prince de Moulay Abdellah* ☎ *039/93–86–14*) is an energetic dance hall with a live band. The singers' vocals can be jarring—the flat tones come out of *sheikhates* (female Arabic vocalists from Morocco) traditions. The star lotar player, who accompanies belly-dancing shows, is a truly amazing musician. **Regine Club** (⊠ *8, rue el Mansour Dahbi* ☎ *039/34–02–38*) is a favorite of week-ending Spaniards, local professionals, and hip twentysomethings. The dance floor gets steamier and steamier as the night goes on.

SHOPPING

Tangier can be an intense place to shop; proprietors are accustomed to inflicting their hard sell on overwhelmed day-trippers from Spain. Ville Nouvelle boutiques offer standard Moroccan items, such as carpets, brass, leather, ceramics, and clothing at higher—but fixed—prices. The more unusual and creative high-quality items, however, are mostly in the specialty shops throughout the medina. Don't be afraid to stop at small, unnamed stores, as these often stock real off-the-beaten-path treasures.

ANTIQUES

One of the finest antiques shops in Morocco, **Boutique Majid** (⊠ *66, rue des Chrétiens* ☎ *039/93–88–92*) has an amazing collection of antique textiles, silks, rich embroideries, rugs, and Berber jewelry (often silver with coral and amber), as well as wooden boxes, household items, copper, and brass collected from all over Africa on his yearly scouting trips. Prices are high, but the quality is indisputable. As proprietor Abdelmajid says, "It's an investment!" **Galerie Tindouf** (⊠ *72, rue de la Liberté* ☎ *039/93–86–00*) is a pricey antiques shop specializing in clothing, home furnishings, and period pieces from old Tangier. The owners also run the Bazaar Tindouf, right down the street, which sells modern Moroccan crafts in ceramics, wood, iron, brass, and silver, plus embroidery and rugs. The staff here is relatively laid-back and has a large inventory of older rugs.

CRAFTS

The simple **Boutique Marouaini** (⊠ *65, rue des Chrétiens* ☎ *09/33–60–67*) sells ceramics, wood, rugs, clothing, and metalware, as well as paintings by local artists at very reasonable prices. The extensive collection of rugs at **Coin de l'Arts Berbères** (⊠ *66, rue des Chrétiens* ☎ *039/93–80–94*) includes samples from the Middle and High Atlas regions, made by Saharan and southern Berber tribes. Check out the collection of doors, locks, windows, and boxes from southern Morocco and the Sahara. You'll need to bargain here. The fixed-price, government-regulated **Ensemble Artisanal** (⊠ *Rue de Belgique at Rue Ensallah, 3 blocks west of Pl. de la France* ☎ *039/93–15–89*) offers handicrafts from all over Morocco. The store is a little pricey, but it's a good place to develop an eye for quality items and their market prices before you hit the medina shops. Attached to the Tanjah Flandria hotel, the **Tanjah Flandria art gallery** (⊠ *Rue Ibn Rochd* ☎ *039/93–31–64*) sells sculpture, paintings, and other works inspired by Tangier, featuring both Moroccan and expatriate artists. It's open later than most other shops: Monday through Saturday from 10 to 1 and 5 to 8.

OUTDOOR ACTIVITIES

New activities are popping up all the time—everything from quad riding to jet skiing to golf. There are also nature walks that take in the diverse fauna of the region. Though the majority of these are in French, more and more are offered in English.

GOLF

Golf, the favorite sport of the late King Hassan II, has spread through-out Morocco. The 18-hole **Royal Golf de Tánger** (⊠ *Rte. Boubana Tánger* ☎ *039/93–89–25*) is one of two premier courses in the north.

SAILING

Tangier Fishing Odyssey (⊠ *Port* ☎ *061/15–03–82* ⊕ *www.tangierfishing odyssey.ma*) offers full- and half-day fishing trips, as well as dolphin-watching excursions.

The **Tangier Yacht Club** (⊠ *Port* ☎ *039/93–85–75*) charters small day-sailing craft and windsurfing equipment in the port below the city. Sailing west out to Cap Spartel or east to Cap Malabata within sight of Tarifa across the strait would constitute a memorable event. The tourist office also has up-to-date lists of rental outfits.

THE CEUTA PENINSULA

The Ceuta Peninsula is such a peculiar phenomenon that it is difficult not to recommend it if you have the time and curiosity to spend a day there. The N16 coast road east from Tangier hugs the edge of the Strait of Gibraltar all the way to the Djebel Musa promontory.

CAP SPARTEL

16 km (10 mi) west of Tangier.

Minutes from Tangier is the jutting Cap Spartel, the African continent's extreme northwest corner. Known to Romans as Ampelusium ("cape of the vines"), this fertile area sits high above the rocky coast. A shady, tree-lined road leads up to the summit, where a large lighthouse has wonderful sweeping views out over the Mediterranean at the very point where it meets the Atlantic; ask the kindly gatekeeper to show you around. **Halfway to Cap Spartel, Rmilet** is a park popular with local families on weekends. It has shady pine, mimosa, and eucalyptus groves.

Cap Spartel's beaches vary widely from wide inlets to long stretches of sand. **Achakar** is a public beach protected by craggy cliffs. It becomes **Robinson Beach,** where Europeans tend to congregate.

EXPLORING

Five kilometers (3 mi) south of the cape are the **Caves of Hercules.** Inhabited since prehistoric times, the caves were used more recently to cut millstones, hence the hundreds of round indentations on their walls and ceiling. The caves are known for their windowlike opening in the shape of Africa, through which the surf comes crashing into the lagoon and lower cave. Stairs lead down to a viewing platform with a great vantage point and just a touch of sea spray. 🎫 *10 DH* ☉ *Daily 9–1 and 3–6.*

NEED A BREAK?

Above and to the right of the cave entrance, follow the tiled wall down to a path leading to a small platform café. Run by Abdelkader, this tiny café is the prime spot from which to view the caves from the outside. Its small wicker seats are ideal places to take in the stunning views down nearby Robinson Beach and to look down at local fishermen trying their luck on the rocks below. Besides these features, the tiny café offers a hidden secret. The small gray door near the kitchen opens into a two-story dining room inside Abdelkader's own personal cave; he will serve up one of his wonderful tagines while the surf's sound echoes off the cool cave walls. It's a one-of-a-kind place.

Leaving the caves and following the road straight for about 2 km (1 mi), look down toward the beach and you'll see the ruins of the 3rd-century AD Roman town of **Cotta** in the middle of the fields. Cotta was known for its production of garum, an anchovy paste that was exported throughout the Roman Empire. All that remains of the town now are the foundations of buildings, baths, and villas. You can walk to the site from the road or, more easily, from Robinson Beach.

WHERE TO EAT & STAY

$ ✕ **Chez Abdou.** Open for lunch and dinner, this laid-back restaurant
MOROCCAN   with indoor and outdoor seating serves up some of the most delicious
★   food in the area. The salt in the air as you eat only adds to the flavor. Abdou himself is known as one of a handful of great Tangier characters. ⊠ *Rte. de Rabat* ☎ *073/64–60–55* ▤ *No credit cards.*

$$$$ 🏨 **Hotel Mirage.** Located above the Caves of Hercules, this modern resort has appropriately stunning sea views. Favorites of the Moroccan elite and vacationing foreign nationals, the bungalows are very private, with lovely living areas and light, breezy bedrooms. Bougainvillea vines climb up whitewashed walls, and the sound of the surf is omnipresent. Enjoy the small yet verdant garden or walk down a staircase in the cliffs to the nearly endless stretch of sand. The restaurant, open to nonguests if there are tables available, serves excellent seafood and international cuisine. Be sure to have a glass of fresh-squeezed orange juice in the morning, or even better, a martini at sunset. **Pros:** Great service, excellent facilities, peaceful setting. **Con:** Long drive from the city. ⊠ *Grotte de Hercules, Rte. de Cap Spartel* ☎ *039/33–33–31* ⊕ *www.lemirage-tanger. com* ⇄ *30 bungalows* ⌂ *In-room: safe, Wi-Fi. In-hotel: restaurant, bar, pool, laundry service, parking (no fee)* ▤ *MC, V* ⊘ *Closed mid-Nov.–Feb.*

ASILAH

40 km (25 mi) southwest of Tangier.

Known as one of the country's most artistic communities, the sleepy fishing village of Asilah hosts a two-week festival every year in August in which artists from all over the world are invited to paint murals on the city's walls. Conquered by the Portuguese in 1471, the Old Town retains a Portuguese feel.

WHERE TO EAT & STAY

$
SPANISH
✕ **Casa Garcia.** People flock to this unassuming seafood restaurant for no-nonsense fresh fish. Its mouthwatering menu consists of nothing but the catch of the day served however you like it. Unlike its neighbors, this place serves alcohol. ⊠ *51, rue Moulay Hassan Ben el Mehdi* ☎ *039/41–74–65* ▭ *No credit cards.*

$–$$
MOROCCAN
✕ **Oceano Casa Pépé.** Reliable and friendly, this small restaurant is located outside Bab el Kasaba, the Old Town's main gate. The anchovy appetizer is not to be missed, and neither is the paella. The selection of tapas makes this place popular with groups. ⊠ *Rte. de Rabat* ☎ *039/41–73–95* ▭ *No credit cards.*

$
▦ **Zelis.** Located a stone's throw from the sea, this clean hotel has a great location in the center of town. Its decor is mostly modern, with some exotic touches. The sparkling pool is another selling point. **Pros:** Great location, friendly staff. **Con:** Decor is a bit cheesy. ⊠ *10, av. Mansour Eddahbi* ☎ *039/41–70–69* ⌕ *55 rooms* ⚲ *In-room: safe, TV. In-hotel: 2 restaurants, pool, parking (no fee)* ▭ *MC, V.*

LARACHE

80 km (50 mi) southwest of Tangier.

Known primarily for its proximity to the ruins of the ancient town of Lixus, Larache it is worth a stop for a stroll along the Balcon Atlantico, a seaside promenade that runs along the rocky shore. There are numerous cafés on the promenade where you can enjoy a fruit drink. Another enjoyable walk is to French writer Jean Genet's grave in the Catholic Cemetery just south of the medina. It's near the Muslim graveyard, which boasts decorative tile graves and dramatic views.

Larache's sleepy plaza feels like Spain all over again. Many of the people in this town grew up speaking Spanish as their first language, so strong was the Spanish colonial presence here up until Moroccan independence in 1956. Visible from afar, the 16th-century Geubibat Fort sits atop the highest cliff in Larache.

EXPLORING

You may have heard of Volubilis, Morocco's most famous Roman ruins in Meknès. On the Loukkos River, **Lixus** is a lesser-known but no-less-impressive site just 45 minutes away from Tangier. The main attractions are an amphitheater, a column-lined road, a mosaic of the sea-god—half man, half crab—and the religious center of the town, high on the hill, which retains the foundations for the places of worship of each civilization to have settled there. The hill held great importance to a series of seafaring civilizations, starting with the Phoenicians in the 7th century BC until the time of the Arabs. The guides at the entrance are official and informative. They are paid by the government to do their job, but appreciate a tip. ⊠ *Free* ⊙ *Daily 9–6.*

WHERE TO STAY

$ ⚹**La Maison Haute.** Located in the Kasbah, with great rooftop views
★ of the city and ocean, is this little gem. It's a traditional Moroccan
house, so it's organized around a central living room. The knowledgeable staff makes you feel like one of the family. The rooms are palatial
and visually exciting, with deep colors and rich patterns. Dinner can be
arranged ahead of time. **Pros:** Friendly staff, great location. **Con:** Steep
steps. ✉6, *Derb Ben Thami* ☎065/34–48–88 ⊕*http://lamaisonhaute.*
free.fr ⇄*7 rooms* ⚘*In-hotel: no elevator* ⊟*MC, V.*

CEUTA

94 km (58 mi) northeast of Tangier.

When it was incorporated into Spanish rule in 1580, Ceuta was one
of the finest cities in northern Morocco. Thriving under its Arab conquerors, the city was extolled in 14th-century documents for its busy
harbors, fine educational institutions, ornate mosques, and sprawling
villas. Smelling prosperity, the Portuguese seized Ceuta in 1415; the city
passed to Spain when Portugal itself became part of Spain in 1580, and
it remains under Spanish rule today.

Ceuta's strategic position on the Strait of Gibraltar explains its ongoing
use as a Spanish military town (many of the large buildings around the
city are military properties). Walls built by the Portuguese surround
the city, and together with the ramparts are impressive testimony to the
town's historic importance on European–Near Eastern trade routes.

Now serving mainly as a port of entry or departure between Spain and
Morocco, Ceuta has scant attractions for travelers, though the mere
existence of this Hispano-African hybrid that has successively belonged
to Phoenicians, Carthaginians, Romans, Vandals, Byzantines, Arabs,
Portuguese, and Spaniards is staggering. If you're short on time, you
might give it a miss. The most interesting sights are in the upper city,
away from the port's bustle.

GETTING HERE & AROUND

Ceuta has ferry service to and from the Spanish port of Algeciras (1½
hours; 238 DH passenger, 833 DH car). If you're driving, the N2 and
N16 connect Tangier, Ceuta, Tétouan, and the beaches.

ESSENTIALS

Internet Sal@Net (✉ *Calle General Aizpuru* ☎ *956/68–27–63*).

Visitor Information Ceuta (✉ *Edrissis [Baluarte de los Mallorquines]* ☎ *856/20–*
05–60). **Viajes Dato** (✉ *Muelle Canonero Dato* ☎ *956/50–74–57*).

EXPLORING

Castillo del Desnarigado. Located just under Ceuta's lighthouse, and
named for a pirate who ended up "noseless," this former fort now
houses a military museum. You can look out across Ceuta's port and,
on clear days, drink in a stunning view of Gibraltar. ✉*Carretera Del*
Hacho ☎*956/51–90–40.*

Foso de San Felipe. St. Philip's Moat was built in 1530 by Portuguese crusaders to strengthen the town's fortifications. Crossing the moat gives you grand views of the ramparts, including their inner walls and structures. ⊠ *Calle del la Independencia.*

Plaza de África. A lovely Andalusian-style space, the plaza is the heart of the old city. Check out the Plaza de África's noteworthy **war memorial,** honoring those who took part in the Spanish invasion of Morocco in 1859. Flanking the main plaza is a pair of impressive churches, both built on the sites of former mosques. To the north is the church of **Nuestra Señora de África** (Our Lady of Africa), an ornate baroque structure much frequented by Ceutíes (residents of Ceuta) looking for peace and quiet. On the southern end of Plaza de África, look for the city's **cathedral.** Constructed in an 18th-century baroque style—much like Nuestra Señora de África—it is larger and lushly ornate. ⊠ *Plaza de África.*

> **PRACTICALITIES**
>
> Crossing into Ceuta from Morocco involves a roughly 30-minute process of having your passport stamped and being shuffled through several checkpoints. A taxi from the border to downtown Ceuta costs about 7 euros. Note that euros are the standard currency here, with dirhams accepted only in some establishments. Cash machines are available downtown; try the Banco de España (Place de España). Large hotels will also change money for their guests, but you'll get a better rate if you just use an ATM. When calling Ceuta from Morocco or from overseas, use the country code for Spain, 34.

WHERE TO EAT

Much like Ceuta itself, the city's cuisine is a hybrid of Spanish and Moroccan influences. With the Mediterranean at its doorstep, Ceuta's culinary expertise lies in seafood. From shrimp sautéed in a spicy pepper sauce to creamy baked whitefish dishes and enormous grilled sardines to Spanish-style cold anchovy, garlic, and olive-oil tapas, Ceutan seafood is a pleasure not to be missed. Moroccan influences show up in the form of couscous, as well as sweet-salt combinations such as prunes with roast lamb. A favorite pastime here is eating Serrano ham and drinking wine (both totally impossible just a few minutes away).

$–$$
SEAFOOD
✕**La Tasca del Pedro.** A favorite with locals, this simple restaurant next to the Tryp Melia is prized for its carefully prepared, straightforward Andalusian fare. Fresh fish cooked *a la plancha* (grilled) is the signature house specialty every day but Monday. (The fishing fleet rests on Sunday). For the less adventurous, there are also Italian dishes. ⊠ *Ave. Alcalde Sánchez Prados 3* ☎ *956/51–04–73* ▤ *MC, V.*

$$–$$$
SPANISH
✕**La Torre.** Generally considered Ceuta's best restaurant, this charming dining room with exposed beams and tropical plants serves classic Andalusian dishes such as seafood paella, stuffed shrimp, shellfish in sauce, and creative daily specials. Reservations are advised. ⊠ *Gran Hotel Parador–La Muralla, Pl. de África 15* ☎ *956/51–49–40* ▤ *MC, V.*

WHERE TO STAY

$$$–$$$$ 🏨 **Gran Hotel Parador–La Muralla.** The top lodging in Ceuta, La Muralla
CONTEMPORARY is conveniently located on the main square, with views of the garden,
sea, or the plaza itself. Rooms are large and mostly modern, though a
few are in the neighboring Foso de San Felipe. All have good-size bath-
rooms and comfortable beds—but be aware that the decor is certainly
not as striking as that in the common areas. Furniture is a rather non-
descript blend of Mediterranean, Andalusian, and contemporary styles.
Nonetheless, it's ideally situated and offers beautiful grounds, lush pool-
side areas, and great ocean views. **Pros:** Central location, nice garden
views. **Con:** Rooms can be stuffy. ⊠ *Pl. de África 15* ☎ *956/51–49–40*
⊕ *www.parador.es* ↩ *77 rooms, 29 suites* ♿ *In-room: refrigerator. In-
hotel: restaurant, bar, pool, parking (no fee)* ▤ *AE, DC, MC, V.*

$$–$$$ 🏨 **Tryp Ceuta.** On a busy street in Ceuta's commercial center, the Tryp
offers comfort and amenities within walking distance of the main
sights. The rooms are simply but sleekly decorated in calming earth
tones, and the airy, sunny lobby is adjoined by some small boutiques.
The restaurant serves unremarkable international cuisine but does offer
a big breakfast. **Pros:** Good location, modern building. **Cons:** Stuffy
rooms, service not always attentive. ⊠ *Ave. Alcalde Sánchez Prados
3* ☎ *956/51–12–00* ⊕ *www.solmelia.com* ↩ *121 rooms* ♿ *In-room:
safe, refrigerator, Wi-Fi. In-hotel: restaurant, bar, pool, gym, parking
(no fee)* ▤ *AE, MC, V.*

OUTDOOR ACTIVITIES

HORSEBACK RIDING
Escuela Ecuestre Arantxa Márquez (⊠ *Complejo Rural Miquel Luque*
☎ *649/31–44–37*) organizes riding classes and horseback tours of
Ceuta and environs.

SAILING
El Puerto Deportivo (⊠ *Puerto de Ceuta s/n* ☎ *956/51–37–53*) can advise
on sailboat charters or windsurfing equipment rental.

SCUBA DIVING
Ceuta-Sub (⊠ *Carretera De San Amaro s/n* ☎ *669/28–80–00*) gives
classes and runs dives in select locations around the peninsula.

**EN
ROUTE**   Winding south out of Ceuta, back into Morocco, the N13 follows the
coast toward Martil. The road gives you easy access to a string of well-
developed beach resorts that combine modern amenities with gorgeous
Mediterranean beaches and northern Moroccan charm.

RESTINGA-SMIR

18 km (11 mi) south of Ceuta, 42 km (26 mi) east of Tangier.

Until recently Restinga-Smir was a small fishing village. Development
has come quickly: it's now one of the region's priciest summering spots,
rimmed by a long, uninterrupted beach. Diversions include windsurf-
ing, horseback riding, miniature golf, tennis, and camping, all of which
your hotel can arrange. The port, Marina Smir, is lined with shops,

Mediterranean Beaches

1

The one constant across northern Morocco is outstanding beaches. From crowded city beaches to miles of empty space, from fine sand to high cliffs, you'll find whatever combination of leisure, civilization, and scenery you have in mind on these shores.

On the far-northern Atlantic coast west of Tangier, Robinson Beach offers several uninterrupted miles of fine sand and good waves ideal for families and surfers alike. Like its counterpart at Tarifa across the Strait of Gibraltar, there is generally a lot of wind buffeting the strand at Robinson, making it also ideal for windsurfing. This is the last beach on the Atlantic Ocean before its waters merge with those of the Mediterranean Sea at Cap Spartel, so the winds and current can be tricky. Staying close to shore is recommended.

The northern Mediterranean beaches, centered on Cap Malabata, between Tangier and Ceuta, are some of the region's finest. Their water is classic Mediterranean turquoise, and secluded spots are easy to come by.

The road from Ceuta south to Martil passes more than 32 km (20 mi) of modern beach resorts that offer a wide array of sports and activities. These good, if somewhat touristy,

family beaches are heavily populated in summer, the North African answer to Spain's Costa del Sol.

Farther east, the road from Tétouan to Al Hoceima offers sweeping views along the Mediterranean coast. The water is calm here, and the beaches, usually empty, range from slightly pebbly to golden and sandy. The tiny fishing villages of Oued Laou, Torres de Alcalá, and Kalah Iris make good afternoon stops for lunch and a swim on the way east.

The area around Al Hoceima has some of the north's finest Mediterranean beaches. Quemado Beach, a busy urban strip in Al Hoceima proper, is a cove tucked between large hills, with fine sand and crystalline water—during a simple swim you can see coral and schools of fish below. A kilometer (0.5 mi) west of the city, the beach at Asfiha is a long stretch of pure sand wrapped around the bay; it's a popular family resort, and usually very crowded in summer.

Farther east, the beaches beyond Nador such as Kariet Arkmane, Ras Kebdana, and Saïdia are lonelier and less well equipped for family activities but excellent for communing with nature, your traveling companions, and the sun, sea, and sand.

cafés, and small restaurants geared toward tourists and affluent locals. Most upscale restaurants are in the hotels, but the seafood places on the marina are all good bets, grilling up the catch of the day in a pleasant outdoor atmosphere.

WHERE TO STAY

$–$$ 🏨**Karabou.** The Karabou is small and quaint, with a distinctly maritime feel. The rooms are simple rather than plush, but the staff is friendly, and you're a quick walk from the beach. The price is a steal, so reserve ahead in the summer months. **Pro:** Family-friendly atmosphere. **Con:** Basic rooms. ✉*Rte. de Ceuta, Km 27* ☎*039/97–70–70* 🛏*24* *rooms* ♿ *In-hotel: restaurant, bar, tennis courts, pool, parking (no fee)* ▭ *MC, V* ⊚|*BP.*

$$$　▦ **Sofitel Thalassa/Marina Smir.** Right on the beach, this luxurious hotel provides every comfort. Every one of the spacious rooms and suites has a balcony facing the pool and the private beach. The restaurant features Moroccan- and Spanish-inspired cuisine, the snack bar serves light grilled lunches poolside, and the bar has a patio with sea views. Outdoor activities are easily arranged. The staff is attentive, and the atmosphere breathes relaxation. Prices rise substantially in summer. **Pros:** On a beautiful coast, close to Ceuta and Tétouan, great views of the Rif Mountains. **Cons:** Impersonal vibe, no shuttle to the towns. ✉ *Rte. de Sebta* ☎ *039/97–12–34* ⊕ *www.accorhotels.com* ⇗ *110 rooms, 9 suites* ♿ *In-room: safe, refrigerator. In-hotel: restaurant, bar, pool, gym, spa, beachfront, water sports, parking (no fee)* ▭ *MC, V* ⊚|*BP.*

KABILA

20 km (12 mi) south of Ceuta, 114 km (71 mi) east of Tangier.

Kabila is quite literally a tourist village—a sprawling complex complete with hotel, villas, a helpful staff, a shopping center, and a marina with restaurants. The beaches—the majority of which are reserved for resort guests—are spotless (if a bit grainier than those farther north and south). Well-kept grounds and plenty of flowers keep the area green. Think California, with Moroccan food and decor. To arrange sailing and other outdoor activities, call Hotel Kabila.

WHERE TO EAT & STAY

$-$$　✕ **El Pueblo.** Dine indoors or out at this charming marina restaurant dec-
SEAFOOD　orated with Moroccan lanterns, pottery, and Tangerine paintings. The extensive menu features exotic salads and creative seafood and meat dishes, and is augmented by a good wine list. Portions are large, and the ambience is by far the best in the evening. ✉ *Marina* ☎ *039/97–71–94* ▭ *MC, V.*

$$　▦ **Hotel Kabila.** No expense was spared in creating this full-blown tourist outfit. The rooms are furnished with a distinctively Rifi Berber flair, featuring regional handicrafts, and each has a patio (or, on upper floors, a balcony) with clean footpaths leading to the hotel's private beach. The grounds are well maintained with blooming flowers. The restaurant serves regional Moroccan and Spanish dishes, and has live music most evenings. **Pros:** Exotic experience, plenty of activities. **Cons:** Outdated main building, garden a bit overgrown, service spotty. ✉ *Rte. de Ceuta, Km 20* ☎ *039/66–60–13, 039/66–60–71, or 039/66–60–90* ⇗ *82 rooms, 14 suites* ♿ *In-hotel: restaurant, bar, tennis courts, pool, gym, beachfront* ▭ *MC, V BP.*

MDIQ

22 km (13 mi) south of Ceuta, 74 km (45 mi) east of Tangier

Mdiq is a friendly seaside town with an appealingly lived-in feel. Unlike those in the more-touristy towns just north, Mdiq's hotels are more or less confined to the beachfronts, with the result that Mdiq is a functioning town in its own right. The main streets are lined with small stores and cafés, and there are plenty of side streets to explore. The hillside behind town is dotted with whitewashed and colorfully painted homes. At the port, fresh seafood is served both in a restaurant and at food stalls within view of fishing boats and the ongoing activity of local fishermen.

WHERE TO STAY

$$ ⊞ **Hotel Golden Beach.** This well-run waterfront hotel offers comfortable lodging in simple, modern rooms. The decor is an eclectic blend of cool pastel and airy Mediterranean colors with local rugs, lamps, textiles, and artwork. By no means the most charming or intimate of hotels, it is, nonetheless, a popular spot for group tours thanks to its easy town, road, and beach access and comfortable Western-style amenities. **Pros:** A good bargain, great place to snag last-minute rooms. **Con:** Decor needs refreshing. ⊠ *Rte. de Sebta* ☎ *039/97–50–77* ☞ *86 rooms* ⋄ *In-hotel: restaurant, bar, pool, parking (no fee)* ☰ *MC, V* ⑩ *BP.*

OUTDOOR ACTIVITIES

At the **port** (☎ *039/97–76–94*) you can rent sailboats and windsurfing and diving equipment, as well as arrange diving classes.

CABO NEGRO & MARTIL

40 km (25 mi) south of Ceuta, 72 km (45 mi) east of Tangier.

The beach here is more rugged and hillier than those around it, leaving Cabo Negro less developed than its neighboring towns. This is one of the quainter of the small towns along this coast, with numerous fish shacks lining the beach. From your seat you can watch fisherman bring in their catch.

Known as "Tétouan's beach," **Martil** comes alive mainly in summer, when it fills with Moroccans and feels more crowded than Cabo Negro. The rest of the year it's a good place to take a walk on the sand or enjoy lunch at a beachfront café—although the more-remote beaches farther north are often cleaner, less populated, and more scenic.

OUTDOOR ACTIVITIES

GOLF

★ The **Cabo Negro Royal Golf Club** (☎ *039/97–83–03*) is an 18-hole, par-72 course designed by the prestigious American golf architect (and Robert Trent Jones disciple) Cabell B. Robinson. The course undulates slightly with the natural terrain. Greens fees are 500 DH.

HORSEBACK RIDING

La Ferma (☎ *039/97–80–75* ✐ *la.ferma@hotmail.com*) arranges a series of equestrian experiences ranging from one-hour rides to a four-day trek along the coast and up into the hills. There are also a good restaurant specializing in French cuisine and seven inexpensive rooms to rent.

TÉTOUAN

40 km (24 mi) south of Ceuta, 57 km (35 mi) southeast of Tangier on the N2.

Andalusian flavor mingles with the strong Rifi Berber and traditional Arab identities of the majority of the populace to make Tétouan a uniquely Moroccan fusion of sights, sounds, and social mores. Nestled in a valley between the Mediterranean Sea and the Rif Mountains' backbone, the city of Tétouan was founded in the 3rd century BC by Berbers, who called it Tamuda. Romans destroyed the city in the 1st century AD and built their own in its place, the ruins of which you can still see on the town's edge. The Merenids built a city in the 13th century, which flourished for a century and was then destroyed by Spanish forces, who ruled intermittently from the 14th to the 17th century. The medina and Kasbah that you see today were built in the 15th and 16th centuries and improved upon in the centuries thereafter: Moulay Ismail took Tétouan back in the 17th century and the city traded with the Spanish throughout the 18th. Tétouan's proximity to Spain, and especially to the enclave of Ceuta, kept its Moroccan population in close contact with the Spanish throughout the 20th century. As the capital of the Spanish protectorate from 1913 to 1956, Tétouan harbored Spanish religious orders who set up schools here and established trading links between Tétouan, Ceuta, and mainland Spain. Their presence infused the city with Spanish architecture and culture.

GETTING HERE & AROUND

Tétouan's small Aéroport de Sania R'Mel, 5 km (3 mi) outside town, has domestic flights to Rabat, Casablanca, and Al Hoceima.

Compagnie de Transports Marocains is the region's main and only recommended bus company. It runs several buses daily between Tangier, Tétouan, Chefchaouen, Al Hoceima, and Nador. the N2 and N16 connect Tangier, Ceuta, Tétouan, and the beaches.

ESSENTIALS

Bus Contacts Compagnie de Transports Marocains (✉ *Ave. Hassan II* ☎ *039/96-16-88* ⊕ *www.ctm.co.ma*).

Medical Assistance Dépot de Médicaments d'Urgence (✉ *7, ave. al Wamda* ☎ *039/96-59-02*).

Visitor & Tour Information Akersan Voyages (✉ *Ave. des FAR* ☎ *09/96-30-34*). **Tétouan Tourism Office** (✉ *30, ave. Mohammed V* ☎ *039/96-19-15*).

EXPLORING

TOP ATTRACTIONS

A leisurely stroll through Tétouan begins most naturally in the **Place Moulay el Mehdi**, a large plaza ringed with cafés and aglow with strings of lights in the evening. ⊠*Bd. Mohammed V at Blvd. de Mouquauama.*

> NAVIGATING
>
> Tétouan's medina is fairly straightforward, so don't hesitate to deviate from the main path and explore; it's hard to get lost.

Follow Boulevard Mohammed V—past Spanish-style houses with wrought-iron balconies—to **Place Hassan II**, the open square near the Royal Palace. ⊠*East end of Bd. Mohammed V.*

The **medina** is one of Morocco's most active and interesting, and includes a rectilinear Jewish quarter, a Jewish cemetery with tombstones marked with pre-Columbian motifs brought back from South America, and 19th-century Spanish architecture from the period of the protectorate. Note the constantly flowing fountains, such as the one in the corner of Souk el Fouki; they are supplied by underground sources that have never failed and never been explained. Crafts, food, clothing, and housewares markets are scattered through the medina in charming little squares such as Souk el Houts and L'Ousaa. ⊠*Rue Terrafin at Bab er-Rouah.*

WORTH NOTING

West of Place Hassan II, the **Archaeological Museum** holds a large collection of Roman mosaics, coins, bronzes, and pottery found at various sites in northern Morocco. ⊠*2, rue Ben H'sain* ☎*039/96–73–03* ⊑*10DH* ☉ *Weekdays 9–4:30.*

The **Museum of Moroccan Arts** is housed in a former sultan's fortress surrounded by an Andalusian garden. The museum has a wonderful collection of traditional Moroccan costumes, embroidery, weapons, and musical instruments. (⊠*Ave. Hassan II, along medina wall* ☎*09/97–05–05* ⊑*10 DH* ☉ *Weekdays 9–noon and 2:30–5:30.*

WHERE TO EAT

Considering its substantial size, Tétouan has very few good restaurants and hotels. The ones listed below are clean and comfortable.

¢–$

MOROCCAN

✕**Restaurant Palace Bouhlal.** This palatial house in the upper medina was built in the 19th century by wealthy Spanish colonists. The elegant decor and furnishings are dazzling, and the prix-fixe menu includes Spanish and Moroccan dishes such as couscous and tapas. Head for Bab el Sebta from the Grande Mosque and be prepared to ask for directions. ⊠*48, Jamaa Kebir* ☎*039/99–87–97* ⊟ *No credit cards.*

¢–$

MOROCCAN

✕**Restaurant Restinga.** Here you'll find excellent value and well-made Moroccan dishes in a simple and quaint atmosphere. Try the house tagine or the mixed platter of fried fish. Dining is available inside or in the breezy courtyard. Service is friendly, and beer is occasionally available. ⊠*21, bd. Mohammed V* ☎*No phone* ⊟ *No credit cards.*

¢–$ ✕ **Restaurant Saigon.** This oddly named restaurant is very popular. Stan-
SPANISH dard Moroccan and Spanish fare are served in a charming environment,
with pottery and taped music for ambience. Try the chicken tagine or
the house paella. ✉ *2, rue Mohammed Ben Larbi Torres* ☎ *No phone*
═ *No credit cards.*

WHERE TO STAY

$$ ▦ **Hôtel Chams.** On the northern outskirts of town, this hotel offers
large, airy rooms with lovely views of the hillsides and valley around
Tétouan. If you have a vehicle at your disposal, it's a great choice,
but getting to and from town easily could prove tricky when relying
on local transportation. **Pros:** Peaceful setting, personal service. **Cons:**
Needs renovations, far from the action. ✉ *Ave. Abdelkhalek Tores,*
Rte. de Martil, Km 2.3 ☎ *039/99–09–01 or 039/99–09–02* ⊕ *http://*
membres.lycos.fr/hchams ➴ *72 rooms, 4 suites* ⌂ *In-hotel: restaurant,*
pool, parking (no fee) ═ *MC, V* ⦿ *BP.*

$ ▦ **Hotel Oumaima.** Moments from Place Moulay el Mehdi, this is one of
the few clean and respectable budget hotels in Tétouan's center. Private
bathrooms with showers are the only luxury, but what the hotel lacks
in amenities it makes up for in convenience. **Pros:** Great price, central
location. **Cons:** Can be noisy at night, rooms need renovations. ✉ *10,*
rue 10 Mai ☎ *039/96–34–73* ═ *No credit cards* ⦿ *BP.*

$ ▦ **Paris Hôtel.** The Paris is the best hotel downtown. True, that's not
saying much, but you should still call here first. Rooms are basic to the
point of drabness, but they're very clean and perfectly comfortable, and
each has a private shower. **Pros:** Central location, good value. **Con:** Just
a place to rest your head. ✉ *31, rue Chakib ArsaLa* ☎ *039/96–67–50*
➴ *40 rooms* ⌂ *In-hotel: restaurant* ═ *No credit cards.*

SHOPPING

The most interesting shopping is found in the medina where *mendils,*
the bright, multicolored cloth used by farmers from the Rif for all-pur-
pose protection from the elements, are made and sold in a little square
northeast of Bab er-Rouah. Wood and leather are other artisanal prod-
ucts to look for in the medina.

Ensemble Artisanal (✉ *Ave. Hassan II* ☎ *039/96–67–75* ⊙ *Daily 9–6*)
is a government-sponsored crafts center where rug weavers, leather
workers, woodworkers, and jewelry designers manufacture and sell
their wares. Prices are not negotiable here and the value is excellent,
especially if you factor in saved haggling time.

CHEFCHAOUEN & THE RIF

The trip south from Tétouan to Chefchaouen takes you through fertile
valleys where locals sell produce along the road, sheep graze in golden
sunshine, and the pace of life slows remarkably from that of the regions
just to the north. The route from Chefchaouen to Al Hoceima winds
through the Rif, northern Morocco's highest mountains.

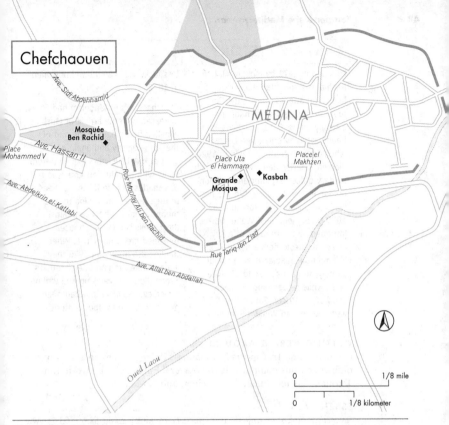

CHEFCHAOUEN

★ *64 km (38 mi) south of Tétouan, 98 km (61 mi) southeast of Tangier.*

Nestled high in the gray Rif Mountains, Chefchaouen, known as the "Blue City," is built on a hillside, and is a world apart from its larger, Spanish-style neighbors. The pace of life here seems somehow in tune with the abundant natural springs, wildflowers, and low-lying clouds in the surrounding mountainsides. From Rifi Berbers dressed in earth-tone wool djellabas (long, hooded robes) and sweaters (ideal for cold, wet Rif winters) to the signature blue-washed houses lining its narrow streets, Chefchaouen has managed to maintain its singular identity. Closed to Christians until the 1920s, the medina has been walled since its earliest days, and is still off-limits to cars. Somehow, even the burgeoning souvenir shops don't make much of a dent in the town's mystique. Chaouen, as it's sometimes called, is an ideal place to wander through a tiny medina, walk up into the looming mountains above the valley, and sip mint tea in an open square. No other place in Morocco (unless a maritime version, Essaouira, could be said to rival it) has Chefchaouen's otherworldly, bohemian appeal—a place that ranks as a consistent favorite among travelers to the region. The Alegria festival in mid-July brings together talented artists and musicians from Spain and Morocco.

A BIT OF HISTORY

Founded in 1471 by Moulay Ali ben Rachid as a mountain base camp for launching attacks against the Portuguese at Ceuta, Chefchaouen, historically off-limits to Christians, had been visited by only three Europeans when Spanish troops arrived in 1920. Vicomte Charles de Foucauld—French military officer, explorer and missionary—managed to make it inside the walls disguised as a rabbi in 1883. In 1889 British journalist Walter Harris, intrigued by the thought of a city closed to Westerners a mere 97 km (60 mi) from Tangier, used a similar strategy to gain access to Chefchaouen while researching his book *Land of an African Sultan*. The third visitor, American William Summers, less lucky, was caught and poisoned in 1892.

Chefchaouen's isolationism had increased with the arrival of Muslims expelled from Spain at the end of the 15th century and again at the start of the 17th. Jews expelled from Spain with the Muslims chose various shades of blue for the facades of their houses (according to one theory, as more effective against flies), while the Muslim houses remained green or mauve. When the Spanish arrived in 1920 they were stunned to find Chefchaouen's Sephardic Jews speaking and writing a medieval Spanish that had been extinct in Spain for four centuries.

GETTING HERE & AROUND

Compagnie de Transports Marocains is the region's main and only recommended bus company. It runs several buses daily between Tangier, Tétouan, Chefchaouen, Al Hoceima, and Nador.

ESSENTIALS

Bus Contacts **Compagnie de Transports Marocains** (☎ *063/57–27–63* ⊕ *www. ctm.co.ma*).

Internet **Echo Web** (⊠ *Ave. Ibn Rochd* ☎ *039/88–31–10* ⊕ *www.ctm.co.ma*).

Visitor & Tour Information **Chefchaouen** (⊠ *Pl. de Mohammed V* ☎ *No phone*).

EXPLORING

Established in 1989, Talassemtane National Park is just outside Chefchaouen's city walls. The 145,000-acre expanse boasts a Mediterranean ecosystem that hosts a unique variety of Moroccan pine as well as more than 239 plant species, many of which are endangered, such as the black pine and the Atlas cedar. There are short day hikes, and more ambitious hikes along a large loop trail. ⊠ *3, rue Machichi* ☎ *039/98–72–67*.

WHERE TO EAT

¢–$ ╳**Cafe Abdeslam.** This unassuming restaurant, away from the chaos
MOROCCAN of the main plaza, has intimate booths in which to enjoy Moroccan delicacies. The decor on its outdoor patio will take you into the world of Alice in Wonderland. ⊠ *17, Pl. Uta el Hammam* ☎ *039/98–69–88* ▭ *No credit cards.*

$$ ✕**El Baraka.** Set in a 150-year-old medina home and named for the Mus-
MOROCCAN   lim concept of auspicious divine protection, this restaurant serves tradi-
tional Moroccan dishes. The staff is charming, and the price makes the
experience a bargain. ⊠ *Just off Pl. Kharrazine (near Pension Andaluz)*
☎ *039/98–69–88* ▭ *No credit cards.*

WHERE TO STAY

$ ⌂**Casa Hassan.** Renowned throughout Morocco, this 350-year-old
★   family home combines an excellent restaurant with a handful of guest
rooms. The gorgeous suites are decorated with the best of local crafts,
including colorful tiles, wrought-iron balconies, and hand-painted
wood furniture. The rooftop terrace is a tranquil oasis, with hand-
woven carpets, richly covered banquettes, and lantern light in the eve-
nings. Tissemial serves homemade tagines, slow-roasted meats, and
succulent chicken dishes, not to mention lemon tarts and sweet cakes
for dessert. **Pros:** Friendly atmosphere, a real bargain. **Con:** Need to
reserve far ahead in high season. ⊠ *22, rue Targui* ☎ *039/98–61–53*
⟐ *6 rooms, 2 suites* ⌂ *In-hotel: restaurant* ▭ *MC* ⌑ *BP.*

¢   ⌂**Hostal Gernika.** This charming Spanish-run pension in the medina's
heart is wrapped around an interior courtyard. Built with Andalusian
archways and moldings and decorated with regional crafts, it feels
more like a house than a hotel. Guest rooms—only some of which
have showers—are cheery, simple, and clean; ask for one with a valley
view. The plant-lined roof, with both covered and open-air patios, is
perched above the medina's snaking streets and myriad rooftops, pro-
viding sweeping views across the valley and Old Town. Spanish lunches
and dinners are available if you place an order in the morning. **Pros:**
Interesting architecture, pleasant staff. **Cons:** Hard to find, reached via
narrow street. ⊠ *49, Ibn Askar* ☎ *039/98–74–34* ⟐ *10 rooms* ⌂ *In-
hotel: restaurant* ▭ *No credit cards* ⌑ *BP.*

$ ⌂**Hotel Madrid.** A short stroll from the medina walls, this airy, spa-
cious hotel has traditional Moroccan decor accented by the works of
local photographers. In the lobby, greenery and canary song fill an area
commanded by a tiled fountain. There's no restaurant, but there's an
inexpensive continental breakfast. The owners are cheerful locals. **Pros:**
Roomy and modern, easily accessible. **Cons:** In the new city, unsatisfy-
ing breakfast. ⊠ *Ave. Hassan II* ☎ *039/98–74–96* ⟐ *26 rooms* ⌂ *In-
room: safe. In-hotel: public Internet* ▭ *MC, V* ⌑ *CP.*

$–$$ ⌂**Hotel Parador.** Ideally situated on the medina's edge, within sight of
Place Uta el Hammam, the Hotel Parador is frequented by tour groups.
Guest rooms are comfortable yet plain, and some, along with the hotel's
outdoor terrace, have wonderful valley views. Relax by the pool in season. **Pros:** Comfortable rooms, friendly atmosphere. **Con:** Little of the
charm of the old city. ⊠ *Pl. el Mahkzen* ☎ *039/98–63–24* ⟐ *34 rooms,
4 suites* ⌂ *In-hotel: restaurant, bar, pool* ▭ *No credit cards* ⌑ *BP.*

SHOPPING

Chefchaouen is one of the north's best places to shop for quality traditional crafts. Wool items and leather goods are the main local export:
look in small medina stores for thick blankets, rugs, bags, and shoes.

Abdellah Alami (✉257, *Onsar Rasselma* ☎039/98–73–03) sells nothing but bronze products, made by a family of bronze workers who produce some of this region's finest handmade plates, bowls, and trays. Prices are reasonable, and the selection is vast. The small workshop **Artisanal Chefchaouen** (✉*Pl. el Makhzen, in parking lot of Hotel Parador*) produces beautiful, inexpensive hand-painted wood boxes, shelves, birdcages, chests, and mirrors of extremely high quality. Accredited by the Moroccan Ministry of Industry and Artisanal Commerce, **Casa Marbella/Coin de l'Artisanat** (✉*40, rue Grandade Hay Andalouss* ☎039/98–71–20) creates some of the country's finest zellij work, as well as metalwork, pottery, silver filigree, and bronze.

> **CAUTION**
>
> Driving at night can be dangerous in the Rif, where a false roadblock of stones can lead to robberies or forcible purchase of *kif* (hashish). Especially around Ketama, never accept invitations to private village ceremonies or even a mint tea, as this is usually a setup of some kind: someone slips a package of kif into your car and then the police are suddenly interested in searching your vehicle. Although kif is prevalent in both urban and rural areas of the north, it is still illegal. Foreigners caught in possession of the drug can be (and often are) arrested and subject to local laws.

Traditional henna application is also available for women. Prices are reasonable, and orders can be shipped via airmail around the world. (Retain all receipts and the store's contact information if you choose to ship directly.)

AL HOCEIMA

215 km (133 mi) east of Chefchaouen.

Surrounded on three sides by the Rif Mountains' foothills and rimmed on the fourth by turquoise Mediterranean waters, Al Hoceima is striking. From its perch in rolling hills, the town looks directly down on a stunning bay. It isn't nearly as developed as Tangier and Tétouan, and its natural sights and exquisite coastline make it the perfect place to relax for a day or two.

Established by the Spanish in 1925 as Villa Sanjuro, Al Hoceima was built as a stronghold against Rifi Berber rebellions. Al Hoceima is now a proudly Berber place, but its Spanish architecture and atmosphere remain. The finest Spanish edifice is the beautifully tiled **Collège Espagnol** (Spanish College) at the end of Boulevard Mohammed V. The Old Town is centered on the rather dingy **Place du Rif.** There are few sights here, but you can wander the town's markets, kick back at a café, and just enjoy the relative quietude. In the Ville Nouvelle, the cliff-top **Place Massira**, just above the main beach, is the focal point of the evening promenade. Festivals and citywide events are held here in the summer months, when many expatriate Al Hoceimans residing in Europe return home on vacation.

GETTING HERE & AROUND

Al Hoceima's Aéroport Côte du Rif, 17 km (11 mi) southeast of town, offers daily flights on Royal Air Maroc to Tangier, Tétouan, Casablanca, and Rabat, as well as weekly flights to Europe. Compagnie de Transports Marocains is the region's main and only recommended bus company. It runs several buses daily between Tangier, Tétouan, Chefchaouen, Al Hoceima, and Nador. If you're driving yourself, the N2 cuts east toward Al Hoceima, Nador, and Melilla.

ESSENTIALS

Bus Contacts **Compagnie de Transports Marocains** (⊠46, pl. Rif ☎039/98–22–73 ⊕ www.ctm.co.ma).

Internet **Cyber Club On-Line** (⊠103, bd. Mohammed V ☎039/98–86–23).

Visitor Information **Al Hoceima Tourism Office** (⊠Ave. Tariq Ibn Ziad ☎039/98–11–85)

EXPLORING

The real reasons to come to Al Hoceima are the beaches. The main city beach, **Plage Quemado,** sits in a natural bay formed by mountains on each side. The water is crystal-clear, perfect for snorkeling and scuba diving, and you can rent equipment from a very obvious stall on the beach. (However, be warned that the quality of the equipment is hit or miss. Be sure to check the equipment carefully before use, and if you're an inexperienced diver, you should take a pass.) Near Quemado Beach is Al Hoceima's **port,** where several restaurants cook up wonderful seafood. The coastline outside town is equally scenic; the beach at **Asfiha** stretches around the bay with miles of uninterrupted fine sand.

WHERE TO EAT

$ ✕**Club Nautique.** Fresh seafood reigns supreme here, and beer or wine
SEAFOOD are available to go with it. There are more grilled fish options that you can easily handle, and the house salads are well prepared and refreshing. The bay views from the outdoor tables are stunning. ⊠Port d'Al Hoceima ☎039/98–14–61 ⊟No credit cards.

$–$$ ✕**Hotel Karim.** This downtown hotel is better known for its restaurant
ECLECTIC than its rooms. The creative menu combines Moroccan, French, and Spanish dishes. Locals are fond of the seafood dishes, which include surprisingly large grilled sardines dressed up with lemon and cilantro—quite a treat. The roast chicken with preserved lemons and fresh vegetables is also good. Top it all off with a pot of mint tea. ⊠25, ave. Hassan II ☎039/98–21–84 ⊟MC, V.

$ ✕**Restaurant Karim.** The best of several restaurants in Al Hoceima's port,
SEAFOOD Karim serves excellent and varied seafood. The grilled calamari and shrimp are the specialty of the house—served up with rice and salad, they're not to be missed. Come early for tapas or a drink at the bar; then dine indoors or out. ⊠Port ☎039/98–23–10 ⊟No credit cards.

WHERE TO STAY

$$$–$$$$ ⊡**Chafarina's Beach.** This tourist complex 4 km (2 mi) north of Al Hoceima offers rooms with sweeping views over the Mediterranean as well as aquatic and sports activities and a splendid and spacious

dining hall. The Calypso nightclub keeps the action going until early morning at this thoroughly Europeanized spa. **Pros:** Lively in summer, plenty of activities. **Con:** Can be deserted in the off-season. ⊠*Plage Tala Youssef* ☎*039/84–16–01* ⌁*30 rooms* ⌂*In-hotel: restaurant, bar, tennis courts, beachfront* ⊟*MC, V.*

$ ⊞ **Hotel Maghred el Jadid.** Downtown, within walking distance of the beaches, this clean, comfortable, tasteful hotel has simple guest rooms with light and neutral color schemes, local artwork on the walls, and simple, functional furnishings. You won't find the kinds of rooms you lounge about in all day—rather, it's a comfortable base from which to explore the city and is the best bet, by far, in the downtown area for dining and lodging. Hotel staff can help you arrange jet skiing or scuba diving at the nearby beach. Try the top-floor restaurant and bar, which serves tasty Moroccan and Spanish dishes. Sample a beef or chicken tagine for lunch. **Pros:** Central location, near the beach. **Cons:** Nothing fancy, traffic is noisy. ⊠*56, ave. Mohammed V* ☎*039/98–25–04* ⌁*36 rooms* ⌂*In-hotel: restaurant, bar* ⊟*MC, V* ⦿*BP.*

$–$$ ⊞ **Hotel Mohammed V.** Al Hoceima's grand old hotel has remodeled rooms and classy bungalows. All are sparsely decorated, with simple beds, earth-tone tables, and quiet artwork. At the north end of town, you're just steps from the stairs down to the beach and port. The terrace, where breakfast is served in fine weather, and many of the rooms have lovely sea views. **Pros:** Away from the hubbub, near the beach. **Con:** Rooms feel utilitarian. ⊠*Pl. de la Marche Verte* ☎*039/98–22–33* ⌁*30 rooms* ⌂*In-hotel: restaurant, bar, beachfron, public Wi-Fi* ⊟*D, MC, V.*

$–$$ ⊞ **Hotel Quemado.** This modern seafront complex offers rooms, bungalows, and villas. Rooms are simple here, with whitewashed walls, Mediterranean decor, and plenty of windows with views over the peaceful bay at Quemado Beach. Bungalows and villas are situated on the hill above the beach, just a simple walk up from the hotel's beachfront terrace. The hotel is a short walk away from the town center. Prices soar—and reservations are scarce—in summer. **Pros:** Attentive service, up-to-date facilities. **Con:** Need to book months ahead. ⊠*Plage de Quemado* ☎*039/98–22–33* ⌁*22 rooms, 10 bungalows, 2 villas* ⌂*In-hotel: restaurant, bar, tennis courts, beachfront* ⊟*MC, V* ⦿*Closed Nov.–Mar.* ⦿*BP.*

THE NORTHEASTERN CIRCUIT

The Spanish enclave of Melilla, together with its border town of Nador, provides a mellow, distinctly Spanish environment. East of Nador the coastal road passes lagoons rich in plant and bird life near the mouth of the Moulouya River.

NADOR

1

20 km (12 mi) west of Mont Araoui, 145 km (90 mi) east of Al Hoceima, 225 km (140 mi) from Tétouan.

Controlled by the Spanish until 1957, Nador serves as a border town for the Spanish enclave of Melilla. In many ways it's a typical Moroccan border town, complete with contraband products for sale on the street and multilingual young boys running amok. Today it's very much an industrial center as well, with iron from nearby mines forged into steel here, and a bustling local port.

GETTING HERE & AROUND

Compagnie de Transports Marocains is the region's main and only recommended bus company. It runs several buses daily between Tangier, Tétouan, Chefchaouen, Al Hoceima, and Nador. If you're driving yourself, the N2 cuts east toward Al Hoceima, Nador, and Melilla.

ESSENTIALS

Bus Contacts **Compagnie de Transports Marocain** (⌗*612, rue Général Amezeane at Gare Routière* ☎*069/60–39–75* ⊕*www.ctm.co.ma*).

Visitor & Tour Information **Kemata Voyages** (⌗*146, bd. Mohammed V* ☎*039/98–23–76*). **Nador Tourism Office** (⌗*80, bd. Ibn Rochd* ☎*06/33–03–48*).

EXPLORING

Nador has a certain Spanish air, and a few hours' walk around this grid-patterned town is pleasant enough. The most attractive area surrounds **Boulevard Mohammed V,** which includes open plazas that lead off to Spanish-style churches, climbing bougainvillea, and windows trimmed with iron grilles and flower boxes.■**TIP➜** Because hotels are expensive in Melilla, Nador is a logical base for a day trip across the border. The border-crossing post is at Beni Enzar, a few miles out of town by bus, taxi, or car.

WHERE TO STAY

$ 🏨**Hôtel Méditerranée.** An economical choice, this airy seaside hotel has clean, simple rooms; the most coveted have balconies. The restaurant's charming cook makes tasty Moroccan cuisine. ⌗*2–4, bd. Youssef Ben Tachfine* ☎*036/60–64–95* ➥*24 rooms* ⚙*In-hotel: restaurant* ▤*MC, V.*

$$ 🏨**Hôtel Rif.** This upscale hotel has some amazing modernist architectural flourishes. What was once a masterpiece is now quickly deteriorating, although the lack of alternatives means it is still the best option in town. The rooms are clean and comfortable, with lovely floral motifs. Ask for a sea view. Pros: Unique architecture, central location. Cons: Needs refurbishing, can be cold in winter. ⌗*1, bd. Youssef Ibn Tachfine* ☎*036/60–65–35* ⊕*www.sogatour.ma* ➥*54 rooms, 3 suites* ⚙*In-room: Wi-Fi. In-hotel: restaurant, tennis courts, pool, parking (no fee)* ▤*MC, V* ⓞ*BP.*

$ 🏨**Hôtel Ryad.** This modern hotel in the center of the city offers plush accommodations, including well-furnished suites with Moroccan decorative touches. (Some border on cheesy, however.) The large reception area and salon is rich in Moroccan art and pottery, while rooms are comfortable and the upper floors have views out into the lagoon to the east. **Pros:** Unique decor, good location. **Con:** Can be cold in winter. ⊠*Ave. Mohammed V* ☎*036/60–77–15* ➚*22 rooms, 18 suites* ⌂*In-hotel: restaurant, bars, parking (no fee)* ▤*MC, V* ▯⃝|*BP.*

EN ROUTE

The village of **Mont Araoui,** 20 km (12 mi) south of Nador and on the way from Al Hoceima, is worth a stop for its Sunday souk. It's a sort of miniature version of Marrakesh's Djemâa el Fna, with lively story-tellers, tooth pullers, snake charmers, and displays of mountain crafts from the Rif.

If time permits, pass by **Selouane,** 11 km (7 mi) east of Mont Araoui, for a look at the impressive fortress, the **Kasbah of Moulay Ismail,** built in the late 17th century and later used by the early-20th-century pretender to the Moroccan throne, Rif tribal chieftain Bou Hamra.

EN ROUTE

Kariet Arkmane, 30 km (19 mi) east of Nador, is a salt-marsh area rich in migratory birds and insect life—spring is prime time to see the greatest variety. Follow the path opposite the town mosque that leads out into the salt marsh. A small shell beach here makes a lovely spot for an afternoon picnic, insect life permitting.

MELILLA

Border is 12 km (7 mi) north of Nador, 293 km (182 mi) southeast of Tangier.

For a day's vacation back in colonial Spain or just an evening layover in familiar peninsular comfort, this Spanish enclave beckons with coastal beauty, mainland Spanish charm, good shopping, a couple of good restaurants, and a handful of interesting sights. Settled by Phoenicians as the port of Rusadir, the strategic site was also inhabited by Greeks and Romans. The Spanish conquered the region from Rifi Berbers in the late 15th century.

GETTING HERE & AROUND

Tétouan's small Aéroport de Sania R'Mel, 5 km (3 mi) outside town, has domestic flights to Rabat, Casablanca, and Al Hoceima. Daily ferries connect Melilla with the Spanish ports of Málaga (eight hours; 357 DH passenger, 952 DH car) and Almería (seven hours; 297 DH passenger, 892 DH car).

Compagnie de Transports Marocains is the region's main and only recommended bus company. It runs several buses daily between Tangier, Tétouan, Chefchaouen, Al Hoceima, and Nador. If you're driving yourself, the N2 cuts east toward Al Hoceima, Nador, and Melilla.

ESSENTIALS

Bus Contacts Compagnie de Transports Marocain (☎*069/60–39–75* ⊕*www. ctm.co.ma*).

Visitor & Tour Information Anda-lucía Travel (⊠*Ave. de la Democracia* ☎*952/67–07–30*). **Melilla Tourism Office** (⊠*Fortuny 21 [Palacio de Congresos]* ☎*952/67–54–44*).

EXPLORING

TOP ATTRACTIONS

Restaurants and tapas bars line the main artery, **Avenida Juan Carlos I Rey**, between the Plaza de España and the lively municipal market. When you decide it's time for dinner, simply join the paseo and follow the crowds.

The ancient city center, the **Medina Sidonia** (⊠*Ave. General Macias*), is on the eastern promontory. Its imposing walled structure surrounds a series of three forts separated by drawbridges and gates.

> ## CAP DES TROIS FORCHES
>
> Twelve kilometers (7 mi) north of the Spanish enclave, this long peninsula juts into the sea, rocky, windswept, and wild. The name means "Cape of Three Forks," referring to the peninsula's three-pronged tip. Civilization here consists of a lighthouse and a few often-empty dwellings. The scenery en route to the tip is gorgeous, and small pockets of calm beach appear between the rocks. If you want to linger and swim, try the beaches at Cala Tramontana, 4 km (2 mi) past the cape village of Taourirt.

The Capilla de Santiago (Chapel of St. James) is by the Puerta de la Marina and the entrance to the medina. The medina is based on a Castilian fort and is more formal than some of the medinas in Morocco.

The area's main square, the **Plaza de la Maestranza** (⊠*Callede la Concepción*), is one of the oldest bullfighting rings in Spain. It is still a prestigious arena, hosting tournaments April to October.

Outside the Medina Sidonia all roads lead to the **Plaza de España** (⊠ *Ave. de la Democracia at Calle del General*), center of the new city and site of the paseo.

WORTH NOTING

Iglesia de la Concepción *(Church of the Immaculate Conception)* (⊠ *Calle de la Concepción*), built in the 17th century, holds some interesting baroque artwork and decoration and looks onto a cave cut into the rock below.

Across from the Puerta de Santiago, the **Museo Municipal** (⊠*Plaza de la Parada* ☎*952/68–01–44*) has a fine collection of local archaeological and historical treasures, most notably artifacts from the Carthaginian and Roman eras. The museum is open Sunday through Friday from 10 to 1 and 5 to 7; admission is free.

Parque Hernandez (⊠*Ave. de la Democracia*) is a typical mix of palm-lined walkways and tropical flowers. It's a lovely place for an afternoon stroll.

The Gothic **Puerta de Santiago** (⊠*Calle de los Jardines*), near the ramparts and beside the Chapel of St. James the Apostle, bears the coat of arms of Spain's King Charles V.

WHERE TO EAT & STAY

¢–$ ✕**Restaurant Brabo.** Named for
SPANISH the statue of the brave boy ("El
Brabo") in Amberes who cut off
the hand of a giant in defense of
the city, this Belgian-run restaurant
a short walk from Melilla is a well-
respected local dining landmark.
The live tank on display allows
you to choose your prey on the
spot, whether grouper, sea bass,
or lobster. Steak tartare is another
house favorite, and the economi-
cal set menu for lunch is a bargain. ⊠*5, Carretera Farkhana Calle C*
☎*952/69–16–95* ⊟*MC, V* ⊙*Closed Mon. No dinner Sun.*

> ### CALLING SPAIN
>
> When calling Melilla from Morocco
> or from overseas, use the country
> code for Spain, 34. Euros are the
> standard currency here, but dirhams
> are widely accepted. There are
> plenty of banks with ATMs around.
> As in Ceuta, crossing in and out can
> be slow in summer, but is usually
> only a 15-minute process.

¢ ✕**Los Salazones.** Fresh seafood and fish specialties are top choices at
SPANISH this spacious bar and restaurant well loved by Melilla residents and
regulars. The inside bar and four different dining spaces as well as a
wine cellar all make this dining and wine-tasting complex a welcome
change from surrounding northern Morocco's relatively scarce bacchic
opportunities. ⊠*15, Conde Alcaudete* ☎*952/67–36–52* ⊟*AE, DC,
MC, V* ⊙*Closed Mon. and Sept. 10–30.*

$$$$ 🏨**Melilla Puerto.** This modern resort towering over the waterfront may
CONTEMPORARY lack the charm of the Medina Sidonia, but the views are unsurpassed.
The halls and reception areas are grand, the rooms classically and comfortably furnished, and the restaurant, La Almoraima, has rocketed to
the top of Melilla's dining opportunities. **Pros:** Modern vibe, good service. **Con:** Not much bang for your buck. ⊠*Explanada de San Lorenzo*
☎*952/69–55–25* ⊕*www.hotelmelillapuerto.com* 🛏*134 rooms* ⌂*In-
hotel: restaurant, bar, parking (fee)* ⊟*AE, DC, MC, V.*

$$$–$$$$ 🏨**Parador de Melilla.** It's a bit of a walk from the town center, but this is
the best of Melilla's best-known hotels. The hotel lobby and grounds are
simply lovely: woodwork and tapestries are used throughout the open,
airy, indoor common areas, and lush palms and flowers line the patio
and pool. Rooms are done in a combination of rich and neutral colors
with Spanish influences—artwork, patterns, and textures—throughout.
Opt for a room with a private terrace and enjoy views out over the
walled city and nearby beach. You can exchange currency at the front
desk. **Pros:** All the trimmings of a big hotel, intimate feel. **Con:** A long
walk to the city center. ⊠*Ave. de Candido Lobera* ☎*952/68–49–40*
⊕*www.parador.es* 🛏*40 rooms* ⌂*In-room: safe, refrigerator. In-hotel:
restaurant, bar, pool, parking (no fee)* ⊟*AE, DC, MC, V.*

OUTDOOR ACTIVITIES

Extending out into the Melilla port, the **Club Marítimo** (⊠*Muelle*
☎*952/68–36–59*) offers advice on sailing and diving options as well
as a small restaurant serving some of Melilla's best cuisine at top-
value prices.

The Northern Atlantic Coast

WORD OF MOUTH

"The first place we stopped was really nice—the Chellah. These are Roman ruins dating back over a thousand years. We got there before the tourists in the early morning. The lighting was perfect for photography and the quiet peaceful nature of the place had just the right calming effect on us after the stressful previous day of traveling."

—danielsonkin

"You will be soooo disappointed in Casablanca. It is truly not worth a visit. It is a dingy city without charm or interesting architecture . . . O.K., except for the big mosque."

—NJriverchick

By Sarah
Wyatt

THE ATLANTIC BREAKERS ROLL IN FROM ASILAH TO SAFI, contrasting markedly with the placid waters of Morocco's Mediterranean coast. From here the ocean stretches due west to the United States. Much of this coast is lined with sandy beaches, and dotted with simple white *koubbas,* the buildings that house a Muslim saint's tomb.

This region contains Rabat, the political capital of the kingdom, and, less than 100 km (62 mi) to the southwest, Casablanca, the undisputed commercial capital. Morocco's main industrial and commercial axis stretches from Casablanca to Kenitra. Rich strata of history are piled here. A simple unmarked cave on the coast near Rabat is thought to be one of the first sites ever inhabited by humans. Rabat and its twin city Salé have some of the most important historical sights in the country. Rabat has monuments from successive Arab dynasties. The modern city of Casablanca was developed by the French from 1912 to independence.

Yet despite the historical riches, Rabat, Casablanca, and indeed the rest of this region are removed from the pressures of the larger tourist centers—Marrakesh, Fez, and Agadir. ■TIP➔ **If possible, come here at the beginning of your trip to relax and grow acclimatized to the ways of the kingdom.** Quite apart from the gentle climate, you'll generally find yourself—unlike in, say, Fez—free to wander around unmolested. This part of Morocco treats travelers gently.

ORIENTATION & PLANNING

ORIENTATION

This chapter divides the northern portion of Morocco's Atlantic coast in half. Driving from Asilah to Rabat works well if you're coming from Tangier or Tétouan; the other (Casablanca to Safi) leads nicely into a trip farther south, to Essaouira, Marrakesh, or the Atlas Mountains. Either way you'll absorb plenty of coastal scenery. If you're flying into Casablanca but can't spend much time in this region, you may want to go straight to Rabat, as it's only an hour and a half from the airport by car or train and is richer in traditional sights.

Rabat. Visitors are enticed by the beautiful tranquillity of Rabat, with its Moorish gardens bordered by charming cafés. They marvel at the Hassan Tower, which for more than eight centuries has overlooked the city. History buffs are attracted to the Hassan Tower and the Mohammed V Mausoleum. The Musée Archéologique houses the country's most extensive collection of archaeological artifacts. Golf fanatics may play at the Royal Golf Dar Es-Salam, while beach lovers will enjoy the shore south of Rabat.

Casablanca. With its spacious avenues of contemporary and Hispano-Moorish structures, public fountains, lush commons, and spacious shoreline, Casablanca appeals to Western visitors. International business executives are attracted to this center of Moroccan commerce,

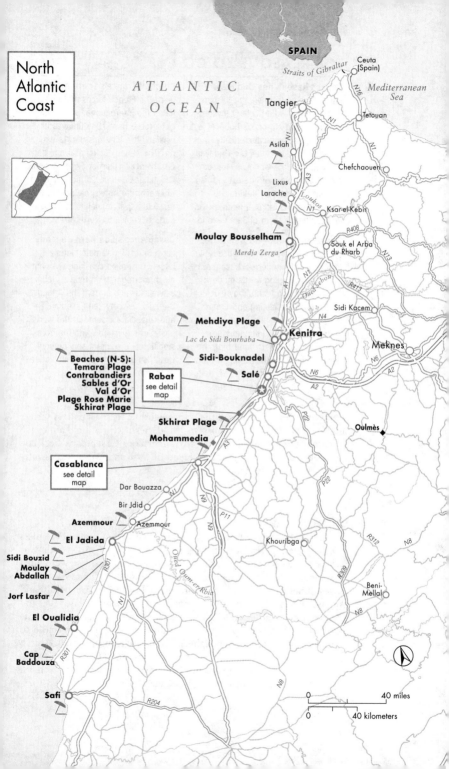

North
Atlantic
Coast

ATLANTIC
OCEAN

SPAIN

Straits of Gibraltar

Ceuta
(Spain)

Mediterranean
Sea

Tangier

Tetouan

Asilah

Chefchaouen

Lixus

Larache

Loukos

Ksar-el-Kebir

Moulay Bousselham

Souk el Arba
du Rharb

R408

Merdja Zerga

Oued Sebou

N13

Sidi Kacem

Mehdiya Plage

N4

Meknes

Lac de Sidi Bourhaba

Kenitra

N6

Sidi-Bouknadel

N6

Beaches (N-S):
Temara Plage
Contrabandiers
Sables d'Or
Val d'Or
Plage Rose Marie
Skhirat Plage

Salé

Rabat
see detail
map

A2

Oulmès

Skhirat Plage

Mohammedia

A3

Casablanca
see detail
map

Dar Bouazza

N1

P22

Bir Jdid

N9

Azemmour

Azemmour

P11

Khouribga

R312

N8

El Jadida

Oued Oum-er-Rbia

R301

Sidi Bouzid

Moulay
Abdallah

Beni-
Mellal

Jorf Lasfar

N8

El Oualidia

R301

N1

Cap
Baddouza

R204

Safi

N8

0   40 miles

0   40 kilometers

TOP REASONS TO GO

Rabat's Kasbah des Oudayas.
Rabat's medieval town, the Kasbah des Oudayas, is particularly mysterious given that Morocco's political capital sprawls bureaucratically around it. The mosque, the Oudayas Gardens, and the Oudayas Museum are all key points of interest in this ancient fortress overlooking the mouth of the Oued Bou Regreg river and the beach town of Salé beyond.

Casablanca's Tour Hassan II. Second only in scope to the mosque at Mecca, this modern extravaganza is less eye-popping for its modern engineering and technology (such as a retractable ceiling and a glass floor over the Atlantic) than for its elaborate use of traditional Moroccan craftsmanship. Beyond that, the sheer audacity of the project is staggering, especially since Hassan II, in the end, was interred in Rabat.

Colonial France's Southern Riviera. The French forces that dominated the international protectorate of Morocco from 1945 until 1956 wasted little time missing "la patrie." The alpine colony at Ifrane and Casablanca's Quartier des Habous in Casablanca and La Corniche (a strip of beachfront hotels, nightclubs, and restaurants) all managed to bring parts of France to North Africa.

Casablanca's Southern Beaches. For a refreshing ramble along a largely unspoiled coastline with not much more going on than surfable waves crashing in from the Atlantic, the beaches between Casablanca and Oualidia are some of the world's best. Surfing schools and the occasional port restaurant serving very fresh fish are the only manifestations of the real world.

while younger travelers seek the active nightlife. Its coast entices surfers and other water-sports enthusiasts. Modern structures amid a mosque shooting its laser beams to Mecca underscore Casablanca's eclectic spirit. This city is an appealing blend of East and West, successfully balancing history and innovation.

PLANNING

WHEN TO GO

Avoid this region in July, August, and the first half of September unless you only plan to visit Rabat, Salé, and Casablanca. Corresponding to Morocco's school vacation, the coastal resorts are extremely crowded in summer, hotels are packed, and prices are much higher. Moreover, huge numbers of Moroccans working in Europe return in July and August, driving down the coast from Tangier. In April, May, June, and October, the weather is delightful—easily warm enough to enjoy the beaches—and most resorts are pleasantly empty. If you don't need to swim or sunbathe, you can sightsee from November through March (and even then the weather can be quite warm). The relatively cold period (the *liali*) lasts from around Christmas through the end of January; temperatures on the coast can plunge to 4°C–6°C (39°F–43°F).

GETTING HERE & AROUND

For international visitors, Casablanca is best reached by air via the Mohammed V International Airport, which is located about 25 km (16 mi) south of the city. Many airlines fly directly from Middle Eastern and European cities, as well as those in the United States and Canada. Once at the airport, Casablanca can be easily reached via the numerous train, shuttle, or taxi services located outside the arrivals terminal.

The full length of the road from Rabat to Fez is now all autoroute. If your stay in this region is limited to Casablanca and Rabat, you won't need a car at all. There is excellent nonstop train service almost hourly between Casablanca Port, Rabat, and Kenitra, and even more frequently at the beginning and end of the day. If, however, your aim is to relax in small coastal towns like Moulay Bousselham and El Oualidia, a car is far more useful than the slow and complicated public transportation to those places.

SAFETY

Official guides in Casablanca are identified by large, brass badges. Be wary of the numerous unofficial guides, generally young men, who will offer to find you a hotel, take you on a tour of the city, or, in some cases, find hashish or "kif" for you. Some will falsely claim to be students who merely wish to practice their English. To avoid these hustlers, you should appear confident and aware of where you are going. If you feel bullied or harassed, do not hesitate to summon police.

ABOUT THE RESTAURANTS

Morocco's northern Atlantic coast is its center of seafood par excellence. From Asilah to Safi the menus are remarkably similar: *salades, crevettes* (prawns), *friture de poisson* (fried fish and octopus), *calamar* (squid), and various kinds of fish. *Fruits de mer* are shellfish and prawns, not fish. In addition to seafood, Casablanca and Rabat offer more international cuisine—lots of pizzerias and Chinese and Vietnamese eateries—and, of course, traditional Moroccan fare and French cuisine. Although it's tempting to think you can find good Moroccan restaurants anywhere, the best ones on this stretch of the coast are really limited to Casablanca and Rabat. (Moroccans eat Moroccan cuisine in the home, so when they dine out, they tend to want something more unusual.)

WHAT IT COSTS IN DIRHAMS					
	¢	$	$$	$$$	$$$$
AT DINNER	Under 40DH	40DH–80DH	80DH–120DH	120DH–160DH	over 160DH

Prices are per person for a main course at dinner.

ABOUT THE HOTELS

It's always a good idea to book ahead in this part of the country, as Rabat and Casablanca fill up with business travelers, and the beach resorts are packed in summer months. Most hotels require you to fax a request even after you're told that rooms are available. Ask for a faxed confirmation from them in return. Casablanca has branches of the familiar international business hotels, and most business hotels in both Casablanca and Rabat will discount their published rates by applying corporate rates at the drop of a company's name. In the smaller coastal resorts you'll typically find mid-range sea-view hotels with a pool.

WHAT IT COSTS IN DIRHAMS				
¢	$	$$	$$$	$$$$
FOR TWO PEOPLE	Under 400DH	400DH–900DH	900DH–1,500DH	1,500DH–2,000DH	over 2,000DH

Prices are for two people in a standard double room in high season, excluding tax.

FESTIVALS

Le Festival de Casablanca, a citywide arts event, attracts international visitors every July. The popular Amateur Theatre Festival, held in March, showcases Casablanca's growing thespian talent. Fatih Mouharam, the Islamic New Year, is also a popular March event.

RABAT

Southwest of Salé across river, 40 km (25 mi) southwest of Kenitra, 91 km (57 mi) northeast of Casablanca.

Rabat is an excellent place to get acquainted with Morocco, as it has a medina and an array of historical sites and museums, yet exerts none of the pressure that most foreign travelers experience in a place like Fez. You'll generally find yourself free to wander and browse without being hassled to buy local wares or engage a guide. As a diplomatic center, Rabat has a large community of foreign residents. Attractive and well kept, with several gardens, it's arguably Morocco's most pleasant and easygoing city.

The city has grown considerably over the last 20 years and today it has many important districts outside the Kasbah, the medina, and the original French New Town. These include L'Océan, the seaside area that was once Spanish and Portuguese (during the French protectorate); Hassan, the environs of the Hassan tower; Agdal, a fashionable residential and business district; Ryad, an upscale residential district; and Souissi, an affluent enclave of wealthy folks and diplomats. Take a ride in a taxi or your own car around the various neighborhoods to get a real understanding of the city as a whole.

GETTING HERE & AROUND

For international visitors, Rabat is best reached via Casablanca's Mohammed V International Airport. Rabat-Salé Airport, a domestic airport, is 10 km (6 mi) northeast of the capital. It has daily flights from Oujda and Agadir and weekly flights from Tétouan.

The bus station in Rabat is on the outskirts of the city in a neighborhood known as Kamara; from there you can take a taxi or a city bus (No.

17 or 30) into town. Rabat has two train stations: Rabat-Agdal, on the outskirts of town toward Casablanca, and Rabat-Ville, closer to most hotels and attractions. Rabat is three hours by train from Meknès, four hours from Fez, and four hours from Marrakesh. All these trains also call at Casablanca. In addition, there are overnight trains from Rabat to Oujda, and three direct trains daily to Tangier, which also have bus connections from an intermediate stop (just before Asilah) to Tétouan.

Guided tours of several cities in this region are best reserved in your home country. Generally speaking, you can't buy a place on a local guided tour upon arrival the way you can in many other countries. For customized tours, try Titanic Voyages in Rabat.

TIMING & PRECAUTIONS

Rabat is considered one of the safest, least harried cities in Morocco. Travelers can generally expect minimal harassment from vendors and fake tour guides. Nonetheless, streets can be somewhat desolate after sundown, so visitors should use taxis then.

ESSENTIALS

Bus Information Compagnie de Transports au Maroc (⊠ *Ave. Hassan II, Kamara* ☎ *037/79-51-24* ⊕ *www.ctm.co.ma*).

Emergencies Clinique Agdal (⊠ *6, pl. Talha* ☎ *037/77-77-77* 🖷 *www. clinique-agdal.com*). **Pharmacie de Nuit** (⊠ *Rue Moulay Rachid* ☎ *037/80-39-49*). **Polyclinique de Rabat** (⊠ *8, rue de Tunis, Agdal* ☎ *037/20-49-14*). **S.O.S. Médecins** (☎ *037/20-20-20*).

Internet Cafés Comête Info (⊠ *10, rue Damas*). **Gins Cyber** (⊠ *10, rue Annaba*). **Phobos** (⊠ *Ave. Hassan II*).

Rental Cars Avis (⊠ *7, rue Abou Faris el Marini* ☎ *037/72-18-18* ⊠ *www. avis.com*). **Budget** (⊠ *Rabat-Salé Airport* ☎ *037/70-57-89* ⊠ *www.budget.com*). **Hertz** (⊠ *Rabat-Salé Airport* ☎ *037/70-73-66* ⊠ *www.hertz.com*).

Train Information Office National des Chemins de Fer (⊠ *8 bis, rue Abderrahmane el Ghafiki* ☎ *037/77-47-47* ⊕ *www.oncf.org.ma*).

Visitor & Tour Information Office National Marocain du Tourisme (⊠ *Rue Oued el Makhazine* ☎ *037/67-37-56* ⊠ *www.visitmorocco.org*). **Titanic Voyages** (⊠ *16, Ave. Michlifen, Agdal* ☎ *037/67-54-09*).

EXPLORING

TOP ATTRACTIONS

❺ **Archaeological Museum.** Opened in 1931, the Musée Archéologique holds prehistoric, Roman, and Islamic-period artifacts discovered throughout the country. The emphasis is on Roman pieces, including many inscribed tablets; the Chellah and Volubilis sites are particularly well represented, and there's an ample collection of Roman bronze items. Also on display is a plaster cast of the early human remains found at Harhoura, on the coast south of town (⇨ *Temara Plage in Rabat's Southern Beaches, below*). ⊠ *23, rue Al Brihi* ☎ *037/70-19-19* 🖷 *www.minculture.gov. ma* 💴 *10 DH* ⏱ *Wed.–Mon. 9–11:30 and 2:30–5:30.*

KEY

1 *Exploring sights*

1 *Hotels & Restaurants*

2

A BIT OF HISTORY

Rabat gets its name from the Arabic word *ribat,* meaning "fortress." It was founded in the 12th century as a fortified town—now the Kasbah des Oudayas—on a rocky outcrop overlooking the River Bou Regreg by Abd al Mu'min of the Almohad dynasty. Abd al Mu'min's grandson, Yaqoub al Mansour, extended the city to encompass the present-day medina, surrounded it with ramparts (some of which still stand), and erected a mosque, from which the unfinished Hassan Tower protrudes as Rabat's principal landmark. Yaqoub al Mansour's ambitious city declined for a while, and after the Merenids took over from the Almohads in the 13th century, Chellah, a neighboring town now within Rabat, was developed as a necropolis. Chellah predated the original Ribat; it was probably

founded by the Phoenicians and was also a Roman town.

In the early 17th century Rabat itself was revived with the arrival of the Muslims, who populated the present-day medina upon their expulsion from Spain and whose descendents live here to this day. Over the course of the 17th century the Kasbah des Oudayas grew notorious for its pirates, and an independent republic of the Bou Regreg was established, based in the Kasbah; the piracy continued when the republic was integrated into the Alaouite kingdom and lasted until the 19th century.

Rabat was named the administrative capital of the country at the beginning of the French protectorate in 1912, and it remained the capital of the Alaouite kingdom when independence was restored in 1956.

❾ **Chellah.** Chellah was an independent city before Rabat ever existed. It
Fodor's Choice dates from the 7th or 8th century BC, when it was probably Phoeni-
★ cian. You'll see the remains of the subsequent Roman city, Sala Colo-
nia, on your left as you walk down the path. Though these remnants
are limited to broken stone foundations and column bases, descriptive
markers point to the likely location of the forum, baths, and market.
Sultan Abu Saïd and his son Abu al Hassan, of the Merenid dynasty,
were responsible for the ramparts, the entrance gate, and the majestic
portals. The Merenids used Chellah as a spiritual retreat, and at quiet
times the *baraka* (blessing) of the place is still tangible.

The entrance to the Merenid sanctuary is at the bottom of the path,
just past some tombs. To the right is a pool with eels in it, which is
said to produce miracles—women are known to toss eggs to the eels for
fertility. The ruins of the mosque are just inside the sanctuary: beautiful arches and the *mihrab* (prayer niche). Storks nest on the impressive
minaret. On the far side of the mosque is a beautiful wall decorated
with Kufi script, a type of Arabic calligraphy characterized by right
angles. To the left of the mosque is the *zaouia* (sanctuary), where you
can see the ruins of individual cells surrounding a basin and some
ancient mosaic work. Beyond the mosque and zaouia are some beautiful, well-maintained walled gardens. Spring water runs through the
gardens at one point, and they give the Chellah a serenity that's quite
extraordinary considering that it's less than a mile from the center of

a nation's capital. There is no place comparable in Morocco. From the walled gardens you can look out over the River Bou Regreg: you'll see cultivated fields below, and cliffs across the river. On the right is a hill with a small white koubba. ■TIP➜ **Tour groups are elsewhere at lunchtime, so try to come then to experience the Chellah at its most serene.** 🖼10 DH 🕙*Daily 8:30–6:30 (or until sunset if earlier).*

❸ **Hassan Tower.** At the end of the 12th century, Yaqoub al Mansour—fourth monarch of the Almohad dynasty and grandson of Abd al Mu'min, who founded Rabat—planned a great mosque. Intended to be the largest mosque in the Muslim world, the project

> **THEN & NOW**
>
> Rabat's medina was first populated by the Muslims who fled from Spain after the Christian Reconquest. True to tradition, the houses face inward, with rooms opening onto central courtyards and only a door exposed to the narrow alleys of the medina. The more sumptuous houses were at the top end, toward Avenue Al Alou, but Rabat's wealthy have long since left for the Souissi and Agdal districts to the west, and the medina is now inhabited by poor families, often several to a house.

was abandoned with the death of al Mansour in 1199. A further blow to the site occurred with the strong tremors of the 1755 Lisbon earthquake, and this tower is the only significant remnant of al Mansour's dream. A few columns remain in the mosque's great rectangular courtyard, but the great tower was never even completed (which is why it looks too short for its base). Note the quality of the craftsmanship in the carved-stone and mosaic decorations at the top of the tower. From the base there is a fine view over the river. Locals come here at dawn to have their wedding photos taken. 🖼*Free.*

❶ **Kasbah des Oudayas.** The history of the Kasbah is the early history of
★ Rabat. Built on high ground over the mouth of the Bou Regreg river and the Atlantic, the Kasbah was originally built here for defensive purposes. Still inhabited, it originally comprised the whole of the city, including the castle of Yaqoub al Mansour. ■TIP➜ **You may be approached by a potential guide at the entrance, but you won't really need one.**

Walk up the steps to the huge, imposing ornamental gate, built, like Bab Rouah, by the Almohads. The gate's interior is now used for art exhibits. Enter the Kasbah and turn right into Rue Jama (Mosque Street). The **mosque,** which dates from Almohad times (it was built in the mid-12th century), is on the left; it was supposedly reconstructed in the late 18th century by an English Muslim—Ahmed el Inglizi. Continue to the end of the road past a house called Dar Baraka, and you'll emerge onto a large platform overlooking the Bou Regreg estuary. Here you have a magnificent view across the river to the old quarter of Salé, and you can walk down to the water's edge. Go back along Rue Jama until you come to Rue Bazo on the left; this winds down the Kasbah past picturesque houses. Turn left, walk to the bottom of the street, and proceed down to the banks of the Bou Regreg river to see the beautiful **Jardin des Oudayas** (Oudayas Garden), a walled retreat that you can explore at your leisure. The garden was laid out in the early 20th century (and is now wheelchair accessible), but its enclosure dates from the beginning of the present Alaouite dynasty in the 17th century.

At the top of the garden, accessible by a bridge across a pool, is the **Musée des Oudayas** (Oudayas Museum), which holds various objects of traditional Moroccan art. The museum is set in a house built by Moulay Ismail in the traditional style, with rooms arranged around a courtyard. Thanks to fortuitous design, the rooms get sun in winter but not in summer. The two most valuable items are the 12th- or 13th-century Almohad Koran and the medieval astrolabe; other exhibits include Andalusian musical instruments, clothing, jewelry, and pottery from Fez. Leave the garden by the wrought-iron gate at the top and turn left as you come out to exit the Kasbah by the lower gate. ⊠*Oudayas Museum, 1, bd. Al Marsa* ☎*037/73–15–12* ⊠*Kasbah free, museum 10 DH* ⊙*Kasbah freely accessible, museum daily 8:30–noon and 3–5:30.*

NEED A
BREAK?

The Oudayas Café (*Oudayas Museum, 1, bd. Al Marsa* ☎*037/73–15–12)*is an excellent place to pause for a drink or snack; the shady terrace is decorated with mosaic-tile work and looks across the river to Salé.

❹ Mohammed V Mausoleum. Resting place of King Mohammed V, who died in 1961, the mausoleum is adjacent to the Hassan Tower and, thanks to a commanding position above the river, is similarly visible to anyone approaching Rabat from Salé. The tomb itself is subterranean; the terrace that overlooks it is approached by steps on each side. Looking down, you're likely to see someone ritually reading the Koran. Beyond the central sarcophagus of King Mohammed V are those of his sons Prince Moulay Abdallah and King Hassan II, who was interred here in July 1999 as world leaders stood by for his state funeral. Designed by a Vietnamese architect and built between 1962 and 1966, the tomb is cubical, with a pyramidal green-tile roof, a richly decorated ceiling, and onyx interior walls. A mosque, built at the same time, adjoins the tomb.

WORTH NOTING

❼ Bab Rouah *(Gate of the Winds).* This city gate was built by Yaqoub al Mansour in 1197. To see it, go outside the city walls and look to the right of the modern arches. Originally a fortification, the gate has an elaborately decorated arch topped by two carved shells. The entrance leads into a room with no gate behind it; you have to turn left into another room and then right into a third room to see the door that once led into Rabat. Bab Rouah is now used as an art gallery, but you don't need to go inside to appreciate the architecture. ⊠*Free* ⊙*Daily 8:30–noon and 2:30–7:30.*

❷ Ensemble Artisanal. Overlooking the River Bou Regreg is a series of small workshops where you can see artisans create Morocco's various handicrafts: everything from traditional mosaic-tile work, embroidery, leatherwork, traditional shoes, and painted wood to brass, pottery, and carpets. You can buy the items at fixed prices, which are a little higher than well-negotiated prices in nearby Rue des Consuls but which save you the trouble of bargaining. The small café has a river view. ⊠ 6, *Tarik el Marsa, Espace les Oudayas* ☎ 037/73–05–07 ⊘ *Free* ⊘ *Daily approximately 9–12:30 and 2:30–6.*

⑩ Lalla Soukaina Mosque. Just built in the 1980s by King Hassan II in honor of his granddaughter, this mosque is proof that the tradition of Moorish architecture that produced the Court of Lions in Granada's Alhambra is alive and well. Notice the exquisite sandstone work on the walkways surrounding the mosque, and look up at the colorfully painted geometrical designs on the ceilings. The mosque is surrounded by immaculately kept gardens. Non-Muslims may not enter, but there's plenty to admire from outside. ⊠ *Edge of Souissi, beyond Ibn Sina Hospital.*

❽ Royal Palace. Built in the early 20th century, Morocco's Royal Palace is a large, cream-color building set back behind lawns. Its large ornamental gate is accented by ceremonial guards dressed in white and red. Don't stray from the road down the middle of the complex; the palace is occupied by the royal family and closed to the public.

❻ Sunna Mosque. Rabat's most important mosque was built in the 1960s, but because it was designed in a traditional Maghrebi style, it was sheltered from the architectural anarchy of the time and remains beautiful and dignified today. In their day the French wanted to extend Avenue Mohammed V through this site, but the Moroccans resisted, and thanks to the martyrs of that confrontation, the mosque stands here on the site of an earlier one. Non-Muslims may not enter.

WHERE TO EAT

¢

MIDDLE EASTERN

✕ **Chawarma el Bacha.** These restaurants offer regionally authentic fast food and this is a great one for its cleanliness, quality, and service. Pita bread stuffed with zesty roast chicken or beef, and other Lebanese specialties such as falafel and hummus, will cost you next to nothing. ⊠ *Ave. Ibn Al Widanel, Agdal* ☎ *No phone* ⊟ *No credit cards.*

$$$$

MOROCCAN

★

✕ **Dinarjat.** Rabat's only truly palatial restaurant produces traditional Moroccan meals, but the real draw is the beautiful ambience of its setting in a medina house. Live Andalusian music creates a charming background. Start your à la carte meal with a spread of Moroccan salads, and then savor classic dishes like tagines or couscous. The restaurant is newly licensed to serve alcohol but still offers Oulmès or Sidi Ali mineral water. You can get here from Boulevard Laalou, not far from the Kasbah des Oudayas; in the evening a man stands at the nearest entrance to the medina with a lantern, ready to guide you to the restaurant. ⊠ *6, rue Belgnaoui, Medina* ☎ *037/70–42–39* ⊟ *www. dinarjat.com* ⊟ *MC, V.*

$$$–$$$$

JAPANESE

✕ **Fuji.** The Japanese diplomatic community eats here—a voucher for authenticity. The dining room has a pleasing ambience, with Japanese-style windows and a small rock pool with a fountain (not always operative). Adornments include little dolls and fans, and a tree made up of glass strips that change color. Entrées are mainly classics like sushi, teriyaki, and tempura (fried vegetables). Even the Berber waiters are dressed in passable imitations of Japanese style. ⊠*2, ave. Michlifen, Agdal* ☏*037/67–35–83* ⊟*V* ⊙*Closed Tues.*

\$\$–\$\$\$ ✕**Le Goeland.** Located near the flower market on Place Petri, Le Goeland
FRENCH   is an elegant restaurant with a warm yet dignified atmosphere. The French cuisine and the service are excellent. The catch of the day is showcased on ice near the entrance and the meats are well prepared. Try the huge and elegantly presented turbot encrusted in salt, and for dessert a delicious café *liégeois* (iced coffee with ice cream and whipped cream). ⊠*9, rue Moulay Ali Cherif* ☏*037/76–88–85* ⊟*AE, MC, V* ⊙*Closed Sun.*

\$\$ ✕**La Mamma.** This is the most popular of Rabat's many pizzerias, and
ITALIAN   with good reason. Pastas, pizzas, and grilled meats are excellent here, as are the pitchers of sangria. From the central brick oven to the garlands of garlic hanging from the rafters, the atmosphere is homey Italian kitchen. Though the place is always bustling, service is fast. ⊠*6, Zankat Tanta* ☏*037/70–73–29* ⊟*MC, V.*

\$ ✕**La Pagode.** Take a sharp right coming out of the Rabat-Ville train
VIETNAMESE   station and you'll hit this Vietnamese restaurant on the left, just before the city walls. The restaurant is upstairs, where an Asian look has been re-created. The menu offers spring rolls, shredded vegetable salad with mint, ginger beef curry, and various other temptations. ⊠*11, rue Baghdad* ☏*037/70–93–81* ⊟*MC, V* ⊙*Closed Mon.*

\$\$–\$\$\$ ✕**Paul.** Café, bakery, and distinguished French restaurant all rolled into
FRENCH   one, Paul is one of Rabat's most popular spots. In the evening there is a variety of fish, game, and meat dishes, such as *rôti du canard* (roast duck) and *rouget grillé* (grilled red snapper). You can lunch on delicious quiches, sandwiches, and crepes. The kitchen stays open late, the menu changes seasonally, and the dining room is occasionally animated by jazz performers. Sadly, the service doesn't match the food quality. The bakery is a standout in its own right, and makes what may be the best fresh-baked bread in town. ⊠*82, ave. Nations Unies, Agdal* ☏*037/67–20–00* ⊟*www.paul.fr* ⊟*MC, V.*

\$ ✕**Le Petit Beurre.** This attractive à la carte restaurant serves standard
MOROCCAN   Moroccan fare such as couscous, brochettes, tagines, and hearty *harira* (bean-based soup with vegetables and meat). Everything is well prepared and flavorful. The lovely tiled walls and painted ceilings give you the impression of dining in richer surroundings than the moderate prices and casual mood suggest. ⊠*8, rue Dumas* ☏*037/73–13–22* ⊟*MC, V.*

\$\$–\$\$\$ ✕**Restaurant de la Plage.** Fish takes many forms here, like *sole meunière*
SEAFOOD   (fillet of sole cooked in butter and almonds) or *filet St. Pierre* (fish cooked in fennel and green onions) served with little boiled potatoes and rice. Wines include the likes of Les Trois Domaines (a Guerrouane red from Meknès) and claret. You dine right next to the Kasbah des Oudayas, overlooking the Atlantic Ocean. ⊠*Plage Oudaya* ☏*037/20–29–28* ⊟*AE, MC, V.*

WHERE TO STAY

$$$ ⊞**Golden Tulip Farah Rabat.** Situated between the Hassan Tower and the medina walls, the Golden Tulip has an attractively decorated lobby and a rooftop pool graced with panoramic views of Rabat and Salé. Comfortable guest rooms are traditionally furnished and comfortable, and most offer nice views of the river. Fourth-floor rooms are more attractive, and have rich wood furnishings and wine-tone linens. The buffet breakfast, included in the room rate, offers a large, rotating selection. **Pros:** Great views, bus stop nearby. **Cons:** Small rooms, air-conditioning requires room key to operate. ⊠*Pl. Sidi Makhlouf* ☎*037/73–47–47* ⮑*www.goldentulipfarah.com* ⮑*188 rooms, 8 suites* ⌂*In-room: refrigerator, Ethernet. In-hotel: 2 restaurants, bar, pool* ⊟*AE, DC, MC, V* ⦿|*BP.*

¢   ⊞**Hotel Central.** If it's a reasonable rate that you want, come straight to this hotel. As the name suggests, it's centrally located, just off Avenue Mohammed V. What you get—a big room with high ceiling and sink—is very good for the price. Some rooms (14) offer showers just a step away from your bed for a slightly higher rate, and two have private toilets. **Pros:** Easy on the wallet, Internet connections in lobby. **Con:** No air-conditioning. ⊠*2, rue Al-Basra* ☎*037/70–73–56* ⮑*35 rooms, 2 with bath* ⊟*In-room: safe. In-hotel: no elevator, public Internet* ⌂*No credit cards.*

$ ⊞**Ibis Moussafir.** The Ibis Moussafir is adjacent to the Rabat-Agdal train station—that is, the first station you come to from Casablanca. The cheerful peach-and-turquoise rooms are small, but provide the basic comforts. There's a private lawn out back, and the buffet breakfasts, included in the room rate, are much better than those usually served at hotels in this price range. **Pros:** Good breakfast, near business district. **Con:** Views are not impressive. ⊠*32, rue Abderrahmane el Ghafiki, Agdal* ☎*037/77–49–19* ⮑*95 rooms* ⮑*In-room: Wi-Fi. In-hotel: restaurant, bar* ⊟*AE, MC, V* ⦿|*BP.*

$–$$ ⊞**Mercure Relais Sheherazade.** On a quiet street near the Hassan Tower, this hotel has what must be the city's most unusual dining: an Australian restaurant specializing in grilled meat. The small guest rooms are arranged so that the corners with windows jut out diagonally. Inside, furnishings are standard for the region: twin beds, curtains, and a rug on the floor. **Pros:** Unbeatable breakfast buffet, interesting restaurant. **Con:** Exposed plumbing in bathrooms. ⊠*21, rue Tunis* ☎*037/72–22–26* ⮑*78 rooms* ⌂*In-room: safe. In-hotel: restaurant, bar* ⊟*AE, MC, V* ⦿|*BP.*

$–$$ ⊞**Rabat Chellah.** The Chellah has been in business for some years and remains one of Rabat's best hotels. It's in the center of town, near the Sunna Mosque, but the area is relatively quiet. The building is fairly functional, but there's a pleasant courtyard near the breakfast area, with plants and cobblestones. The hotel's Kanoun Grill restaurant is a local favorite for grilled meats. **Pros:** Near the Royal Palace, reliable choice. **Con:** Rooms are small. ⊠*2, rue d'Ifni* ☎*037/70–10–51* ⮑*120 rooms, 3 suites* ⌂*In-room: safe. In-hotel: 2 restaurants, bar* ⊟*AE, DC, MC, V.*

$$$–$$$$ 🛏️**Rabat Hilton.** Visiting foreign dignitaries stay at this upscale hotel when breezing through Rabat. Near the Royal Palace, the hotel is surrounded by parks, including the one most favored by local joggers, Ibn Sina. The sumptuous lobby is neo-Roman, and there's a lush garden in back. The rooms have modern furnishings and tremendous views over the city. The luxury suites are very spacious and individually furnished, some with particularly fine carpets. **Pros:** Beautiful lobby, spacious grounds. **Con:** Common areas reek of cigar smoke. ⊠ *Quartier Aviation, Souissi* ☎ *037/67–56–56* ⊕ *www.hilton.com* ⇆ *222 rooms, 27 suites, 20 chalets* ♻ *In-room: safe, refrigerator. In-hotel: 3 restaurants, bar, tennis courts, pool, gym* ▭ *AE, DC, MC, V.*

> **FOR THE KIDS**
>
> With its spacious gardens, large pool, neighboring park, and baby-sitting service, the Rabat Hilton is one of the best all-around bets for children.

$ 🛏️**Rabat Yasmine.** This good-value hotel is not far from the Hassan Tower and offers a spacious lobby and a warm welcome. Rooms are small and simple, but brightly decorated, clean, and comfortable. The restaurant serves Moroccan and international delicacies. A generous breakfast is included in room rate. **Pros:** Well-maintained facility, soothing decor. **Con:** No gym. ⊠ *Rues Marinyne and Makka* ☎ *037/72–20–18* ⇆ *56 rooms* ♻ *In-hotel: restaurant, bar* ▭ *DC, MC, V* ⦿ *BP.*

$$$ 🛏️**Riad Oudaya.** With an intimate feel, this French-run hideaway in the
★ depths of the medina is one of the finest in Rabat. Rooms are sumptuously furnished and include fireplaces and balconies with views over the medina. The cuisine is traditional Moroccan with French accents, combining seafood and upland products such as lamb and pork. Rooms are attractive but simple. **Pros:** Authentic decor, central location. **Cons:** Unfriendly staff, basic rooms. ⊠ *46, rue Sidi Fateh* ☎ *037/70–23–92* ⊕ *www.riadoudaya.com* ⇆ *2 rooms, 2 suites* ♻ *In-room: no a/c, no phone, no TV, safe. In-hotel: restaurant, bar* ▭ *AE, DC, MC, V.*

$$$–$$$$ 🛏️**Sofitel Diwan.** Built on a busy intersection, this luxury hotel is remarkably quiet inside. Its architecture and interior design are an elegant, modern study in curves and waves: circular automated glass doors open onto the slick granite floors and wood columns of the lobby. Rates are expensive for the area, but rooms are plush, with subtle, sponge-painted yellow walls, mahogany details, and an array of deluxe amenities. **Pros:** Beautiful facility, free guarded parking lot. **Con:** Rates are high for the area. ⊠ *Pl. de l'Unité Africaine* ☎ *037/26–27–27* ⊕ *www.sofitel.com* ⇆ *88 rooms, 6 suites* ♻ *In-room: telephone, safe, refrigerator, dial-up. In-hotel: 2 restaurants, bar, parking (free)* ▭ *AE, DC, MC, V.*

¢ 🛏️**Terminus.** True to its name, this hotel is convenient for travelers arriving by train: as you come out of the Rabat-Ville station, turn right, cross the road, and you're there. The Moroccan salon–style lobby with tiled walls, carved ceilings, and plush couches is cozy but dim. Rooms come with a bed, desk, chair, and area rugs tossed about the bare floors. They're standard but satisfactory; those on the courtyard are quieter. **Pros:** Budget rates, stylish lobby. **Cons:** Unappealing entrance, basic rooms. ✉*384, ave. Mohammed V* ☎*037/70–52–67* 📞*130 rooms* ⟡ *In-hotel: restaurant, bar, parking (fee)* ▤*MC, V.*

$$$–$$$$ ⬚**La Tour Hassan Meridien.** If you want a luxury hotel that reflects classic Moroccan architecture, stay at the Tour Hassan. Its traditional arches are beautifully decorated with carved plasterwork. Although it's in the center of town, it has a large interior garden featuring walkways between flower gardens. Part of an international chain, the hotel's rooms are tastefully decorated in muted hues of red and gold. The hotel has three restaurants: La Maison Arabe serves Moroccan dishes, Le Valentino serves Italian food, and Restaurant Imperial offers French cuisine. **Pro:** Located in city center. **Cons:** Rooms in north wing are near a nightclub, some furnishings need updating. ✉*26, rue Chellah* ☎*037/23–90–00* ⊕*www.thassan.mtds.com* 📞*118 rooms, 21 suites* ⟡*In-room: refrigerator. In-hotel: 3 restaurants, bar, pool, gym* ▤*AE, DC, MC, V.*

$$$–$$$$ ⬚**Villa Mandarine.** This gorgeous villa in the residential neighbor-
★ hood between Agdal and the Royal Palace offers all the comforts of home along with smart hosts, savvy fellow guests, and fine French and Moroccan cuisine with contemporary touches. Cozy rooms with tasteful decorations and paintings overlook a lush garden centered on a bubbling fountain. The common rooms include a salon with a fireplace and a bar and a billiards room. The pool overlooks a lush orange grove. The property is best reached by taxi or rental car, as public transportation is limited. **Pros:** Romantic setting, relaxing hammam. **Con:** No public transportation. ✉*19, rue Ouled Bousbaa* ☎*037/75–20–77* ⊕*www.villamandarine.com* 📞*27 rooms, 9 suites* ⟡*In-room: safe. In-hotel: restaurant, bar, tennis court, pool, gym, spa, parking (free)* ▤*AE, DC, MC, V.*

SHOPPING

ANTIQUES

The Agdal neighborhood has a high concentration of furniture and antiques stores. **Arabesque** (✉*61, rue Fal Ould Oumeir, Agdal*) carries gorgeous old and new carved-wood furnishings, leather-covered chests, iron-framed mirrors, painted screens, and countless other decorative items. You may have to dig deeper into your pocketbook for the high-quality pieces here than you would in the souks.

CLOTHING

In addition to Rue des Consuls, the lower part of **Avenue Mohammed V** is a good place to buy traditional Moroccan clothing. Rabat is also a good place to get casual—if not necessarily high-fashion—Western clothes for men, women, and children at low prices, as this part of Morocco manufactures a good deal of clothing for export to Europe. **Casa Gallerie,** on Avenue Hassan II opposite Bab el Had, is a shop that has a good selection at fixed prices. For top-of-the-line leather jackets, try **Sedki** (✉*24, ave. Mohammed V*), on the right just after you leave the medina.

CRAFTS

The medina's **Rue des Consuls** is a great place to shop for handicrafts and souvenirs: it's pedestrian-only, has a pleasant atmosphere, and imposes no real pressure to buy. Here you can find carpets, Berber jewelry, leather goods, wooden items, brass work, traditional clothing, slippers, and more. For leather bags, wallets, and cases, go to the shop at No. 37; the affable owner, Abdelkader, speaks excellent English and can be trusted to bargain fairly. For carpets, try the shop with a birdcage outside, No. 200—it has a robust selection and will negotiate reasonable prices. You can peruse Zemour carpets (striped in white and burgundy) from Khémisset, near Meknès; deep-pile Rabati carpets, in predominantly blue-and-white designs; and orange, black, and white Glaoui carpets. Many of the larger shops take credit cards. ■TIP→ **Try to visit Rue des Consuls on a Monday or Thursday morning when the entire street turns into a carpet market.**

Embroidered tablecloths and napkins are traditional Rabati crafts and make nice gifts; **Arts de Marrakech** (⊠387, ave. Mohammed V), just beyond Sedki on the other side of the road, has a good selection.

NIGHTLIFE

BARS & CLUBS

Élysée Bar & Brasserie (⊠Pl. Ibn Yassine, Agdal ☎037/68–33–40) is a slice of Paris in Rabat, with a pulsating open terrace and a European feel. **5th Avenue** (⊠4, rue Bin Alaouidan, Agdal ☎037/77–52–54) is Rabat's Manhattan disco scene, complete with Claudia Schiffers waiting to be discovered and DJs spinning torrid tunes. **Le Puzzle** (⊠79, ave. Ibn Sina, Agdal ☎037/67–00–30) provides music, karaoke, dinner, rivers of beer, and a mixed and sophisticated mob. **Pachanga** (⊠10, pl. des Alaouites ☎037/26–29–31) is the Rabat pub of choice, offering drinks, music, food, and people-watching.

OUTDOOR ACTIVITIES

GOLF

FodorśChoice **Royal Golf Dar es Salam.** The best and most famous golf course in
★ Morocco is on the road toward Romani, at the far edge of Souissi on the right. Designed by Robert Trent Jones, it's considered one of the 50 best courses in the world. There are two 18-hole courses and one 9-hole course in 162 verdant acres. ⊠Rte. de Zaers, Km 10 ☎037/75–58–64.

RABAT'S SOUTHERN BEACHES

20 km (12 mi) southwest of Rabat.

Just southwest of Rabat, toward Casablanca, are a series of attractive beaches and the national zoo at Temara. If you're driving and happen to be here off-season (from October through May, excepting Easter week), any one of these beaches would be a convenient and lovely place to spend the night if you feel like staying outside of a city.

GETTING HERE & AROUND

This is a very compact area, and easy to get around—almost walkable, in fact. Temara is 13 km (8 mi) south of Rabat, and Plage Rose Marie is 9 km (6 mi) south of Temara, so the intermediate beaches are all about 3–4 km (2–2.5 mi) apart. All beaches as far as Val d'Or are accessible by Bus 33 from Rabat, which departs from Bab el Had (except in summer, when—essentially to keep crowds away—it only goes as far as Sables d'Or). Rabat's petits taxis (local taxis) can't come out here, as the beaches are beyond the city limits, but a grand taxi (long-distance taxis) can take you.

EXPLORING

TOP ATTRACTIONS

The coastal road south from Rabat starts at the Kasbah des Oudayas. The first beach it passes is **Temara Plage,** a small bay beach. (A slightly faster and safer, but less scenic, way to get here is to take the autoroute toward Casablanca and exit at Temara.)

Temara Plage is connected to the next beach, **Contrabandiers,** which is longer and has finer sand, by a walkway across the rocks.

On the other side of the coastal road, roughly level with Contrabandiers but under some white, Spanish-style apartments, is a **cave** with iron railings in front of it. There's no sign to identify the cave, and you can't go inside, but this site, known as Harhoura, is one of the earliest known sites of human habitation. Casts of the human skeletons found here are on display in Rabat's archaeological museum.

After Contrabandiers comes **Sables d'Or** *(Sands of Gold)*, a bay with a picturesque harbor for fishing boats.

Beyond Sables d'Or, and after a private beach belonging to Morocco's royal family, is **Val d'Or** *(Vale of Gold)*, the finest beach in this region. An island, which you can explore on foot at low tide, forms a lagoon. Near the northern end of the beach the lagoon's deep and protected water is perfect for swimming (except when the tide is lowest); at the other end is a sheltered bay with shallow water, ideal for small children. Beyond the hills—which present a profusion of wildflowers in spring— is an open beach intersected by the Ykem River whose dramatic breakers and dangerous undertow make swimming unsafe.

After Val d'Or comes the **Plage Rose Marie,** which looks out on a rocky area in the sea, though there are sandy sections, good waves for surfing, and protected areas for swimming.

Finally, beyond the summer Royal Palace of Skhirat, is the long, sandy, surfer-friendly **Skhirat Plage,** home of the luxury Amphitrite Palace hotel.

WORTH NOTING

☾ **Temara Zoo** is just north of the town of Temara, slightly inland from Temara Plage. Originally formed around the royal collection of Atlas lions, the zoo has a commendable array of creatures, including panthers, giraffes, elephants, hippopotamuses, snakes, and gazelles. The bird collection, near the entrance, is particularly attractive, with golden pheasants, various parrots, and eagles, among other feathered specimens. Everything is laid out in pleasant gardens and costs almost nothing. Children will enjoy the boating lake and the bumper cars. If you're not driving, take Bus 17 from Rabat's Bab el Had. ⊠*R.P. 1, Km 8, Temara* ☎*037/74–12–59* ☝*7 DH* ☉*Mon.–Sat. 9:30–6:30, Sun. 9–6:30 (closes earlier Oct.–Mar.).*

WHERE TO EAT

$–$$$ ✕**Le Miramar.** Sit outside on the terrace and let your eyes rest on the blue
SEAFOOD waters of the Atlantic; or in winter, sit inside by a crackling fire. Either way you'll have fine seafood here; the friture de poisson is particularly good. ⊠*Harhoura Plage, Temara* ☎*037/74–76–56* ▭*MC, V.*

$$–$$$$ ✕**Le Provençal.** Before present-day Temara ever existed, this restaurant
FRENCH was a country inn; it's now surrounded by what is essentially a rather poor suburb. Still, Le Provençal succeeds in creating a rural French atmosphere, and although it's somewhat pricey compared to others of its kind, it serves excellent French cuisine, with an emphasis on fish dishes like *loup au fenouille* (bass with fennel) and *brochettes de lotte* (monkfish kebabs). There's also a wide range of salads. If you like your prawns spicy, try *crevettes pil pil* (shrimp cooked slowly in oil so that a juice is created). ⊠*Ave. Hassan II, Temara* ☎*037/74–11–11* ▭*AE, MC, V.*

WHERE TO STAY

$$ ▦**L'Amphitrite Palace.** This luxury hotel is a good place to get away from it all. Miles of beach invite you to wander, watch the surfers, chat with fishermen, and soak in the Atlantic. Rabat is 20 minutes away but seems farther, while Casablanca is almost an hour distant and might as well be on another continent. This sleek and spotless beach refuge falls short of stellar in its construction, dining, service, and general savvy, but, for straight relaxation far from the madding crowd, it's a good option. The restaurant offers a continental breakfast (not included in room rate). **Pros:** Modern building, fresh decor. **Con:** Somewhat remote location. ⊠*Skhirat Plage, Skhirat* ☎*037/74–27–27* ⌨*www.lamphitrite palace.net* ☝*178 rooms* ⌂*In-room: safe, refrigerator. In-hotel: restaurant, bar, pools, spa* ▭*AE, DC, MC, V.*

$–$$ ▦**Kasbah Club.** As the name implies, the dark-rose-color clay exterior is modeled after an old fortress. There's plenty of space here, both around the pool and on the seaside terrace, and plenty of scope in the surrounding area for horseback rides. Rooms, decorated with traditional handicrafts, are a bit worn, and the air in those that don't open to the sea breeze can be stale. Guest rooms overlooking the sea are more expensive. The restaurant offers a continental breakfast (not included in room rate). **Pros:** Beachfront location, pretty pool. **Con:** Rooms are dark. ⊠*Plage Rose Marie, Skhirat* ☎*037/74–91–16* ☝*53 rooms, 2* *suites* ⚬ *In-room: refrigerator. In-hotel: restaurant, bar, tennis courts, pool, parking (fee)* ▤ *AE, DC, MC, V.*

$ ⊞ **Yasmine Club.** This family-friendly hotel is under the same ownership as the excellent Yasmine Hotel in Rabat. The rooms, arranged around a long, rectangular garden, are far more spacious than any in Rabat, and each even has a settee. The bungalows, arranged around a pool, all have two bedrooms, a living room, and a kitchenette. The restaurant has a tremendous view over the rock pools and the ocean. The restaurant offers a continental breakfast (not included in room rate). **Pros:** Good for families, plenty of space. **Con:** Public transportation is limited. ⊠ *Rte. Côtière de Rabat, Harhoura, Temara* ☎ *037/64–13–52* ⇗ *65 rooms, 40 bungalows, 4 suites* ⚬ *In-room: kitchen (some). In-hotel: restaurant, bar, tennis court, pool* ▤ *MC, V.*

SALÉ

37 km (23 mi) southwest of Kenitra, just 13 km (8 mi) northeast of Rabat across river.

Salé was probably founded around the 11th century. In medieval times it was the most important trading harbor on the Atlantic coast, and at the beginning of the 17th century it joined Rabat in welcoming Muslims expelled from Spain. Rabat and Salé were rival towns for more than 100 years after that, but Rabat eventually gained the upper hand, and today Salé is very much in its shadow. The medina, however, is well worth a trip even apart from its monuments, as it's particularly authentic; you're more likely to see people in traditional dress or practicing traditional crafts than you are in most other Moroccan medinas.

GETTING HERE & AROUND

Trains from Kenitra arrive every 30 minutes. Trains run between Rabat and Salé, but buses and taxis are easier options. If traveling by bus from Rabat, board Bus 16 and get off after passing under the railway bridge, then walk to the medina or Bab Fez. You can take the same bus back to Rabat.

TIMING & PRECAUTIONS

Most travelers stay in Salé for just one night, or even visit just for the day. Salé is a relatively safe city, with most hassles coming from vendors near the medina. If you feel harassed by them, do not hesitate to summon police.

EXPLORING

TOP ATTRACTIONS

A good place to start a tour of Salé is at the entrance to the **medina,** near the Great Mosque, which you can access from the road along the southwest city wall.

Enter the medina on Zanqat Sidi Abdellah ben Hassoun—a street named after the patron saint of Salé, whose **tomb** you pass on the left. Every year on the eve of Mouloud (the Prophet Mohammed's birthday), in June, a colorful procession with elaborate candles makes its way to this tomb.

On the right, before the tomb, is the **zaouia** *(spiritual meeting place, or sanctuary)* of the Tijani order, a mystical Sufi Islamic sect founded by Shaykh Ahmad al-Tijani (1739–1815).

Just after the tomb you come to the **Djemâa Kabir** *(Great Mosque)* which dates from the 12th-century Almohad dynasty and is the third-largest mosque in Morocco after the Hassan II in Casablanca and the Kairaouine in Fez.

★ Turn left around the corner of the mosque, and you'll see on your right the **Abou el Hassan Medersa,** built by the Merenid sultan of that name in the 14th century and a fine example of the traditional Koranic school. Like the Bou Inania in Fez or the Ben Youssef in Marrakesh, this medersa has beautiful intricate plasterwork around its central courtyard, and a fine *mihrab* (prayer niche) with a ceiling carved in an interlocking geometrical pattern representing the cosmos. Upstairs, on the second and third floors, you can visit the little cells where the students used to sleep, and from the roof you can see the entire city. The medersa is open daily from 8:45 to noon and 2:30 to 6, and admission is 20 DH.

When you come out of the medersa, turn right and take the first street on the right farther into the medina. Turn left at the end of the street and you'll come to a big triangular area on your right, the **Souk Alkabir,** or Great Market. Turn right (southwest) to emerge at the city walls, which you can then follow back to your starting point. The low gate on this wall once served as an entrance to the city from the sea. Just as the road around the medina turns to the northeast, you have a spectacular view over the wall across the cemetery to the Kasbah des Oudayas, on the other side of the River Bou Regreg—particularly lovely in the late afternoon, when the tombstones cast clear shadows across the cemetery and seem to be fringed by a halo of light.

Northwest of the medina, by the sea, is the tomb of **Sidi Ahmed ben Achir,** a much-venerated saint. Look through the windows in the wall by the sea for a fine view of the rocks and the ocean.

Beyond the northern corner of the city is a big round fortress called **Borj Ar Roukni.** If you follow the road around the other two sides of Salé, you'll also pass the gates Bab Sebta, Bab Fez, and Bab el Mrisa.

WORTHY NOTING

Salé's **pottery** complex, just off the road toward Fez (to the right after you cross the river from Rabat) is a whole series of pottery stores that sell their own wares. Each store has its own style, and you can walk around and see them all without any pressure to buy. Other crafts have been added to this complex, notably bamboo and straw work and mosaic-tile furnishings. The shops inside the large central building carry a variety of handicrafts at rather high prices.

WHERE TO EAT & STAY

$$ ✕**La Péniche du Bouregreg.** La
FRENCH Péniche is delightfully set on a
boat, a vessel brought from France
and moored in the river. There are
two decks outside—with wonder-
ful views of Rabat's Hassan Tower
and the Mohammed V Mauso-
leum—and two inside. Down a

NAVIGATING TIP

Don't worry if you lose track of
where you are in the medina;
many a shop will distract you, but
you're never far from an entrance
gate. Follow the car noise.

carpeted stairway you can hunker down at cozy little tables next to
brass portholes; upstairs, the tables are lined up along the railings. The
menu changes regularly, but it usually includes maritime specialties like
oysters, snails, mussels, and, of course, fish, as well as some Moroccan
food. Evenings bring live music, usually a keyboard-guitar duo singing
French and American songs. The place lives up to its location by serv-
ing excellent food. ✉*Rive Droite du Bou Regreg* ☎*037/78–56–59*
▭*DC, MC, V.*

$$ ▦ **Dawliz Rabat-Salé.** Set on a scenic bank of the River Bou Regreg, this
hotel enjoys brilliant views of the monuments of Rabat. The rooms,
decorated with wooden furniture and blue rugs, are unusually spacious, as are the bathrooms. There are some popular cinemas in this
complex, so if you want quiet evenings, ask for a room in the back,
overlooking the river—particularly on weekends. **Pros:** On the river,
nice views. **Con:** Rooms in front can be noisy. ✉*Ave. Prince Heri-
tier Sidi Mohammed, Rive Droite du Bou Regreg* ☎*037/88–32–77*
⊕*www.ledawliz.com* ⇆*43 rooms, 2 suites* ⚲*In-room: safe. In-hotel:
4 restaurants, bar, pool* ▭*MC, V.*

SIDI-BOUKNADEL

18 km (11 mi) northeast of Rabat.

Sidi-Bouknadel (also known as Bouknadel) isn't accessible from the
autoroute, but its attractions lie to the north, halfway between Kenitra and Rabat, and are accessible via the coastal road from either of
the two.

GETTING HERE & AROUND

Taxis run regularly from Salé to Sidi-Bouknadel in summer. If traveling from Rabat by bus, board Bus 28 at Avenue Moulay Hassan in
Rabat. You can take the same bus back to Rabat from Sidi-Bouknadel.
Taxis can be chartered to and from Rabat, Salé and Kenitra throughout the year.

TIMING & PRECAUTIONS

Most travelers visit Sidi-Bouknadel for the day en route to Rabat or
Kenitra. Sidi-Bouknadel is generally safe, with minimal hassling of visitors. The beach, however, is rather secluded after sundown, so caution
is advised for those desiring an evening walk on the shore.

EXPLORING

The **Plage des Nations** is a spectacular, long sandy beach with large Atlantic breakers. A heavy undertow makes it hazardous to swim here, which is why you'll see lifeguards patrolling the beach. Caution is advised, lifeguards or not.

In 1991 an entrepreneurial craftsman named Abdelila Belghazi was contracted to carve cedar decorations for the huge sliding domes on the Prophet's Mosque in Medina, Saudi Arabia. Thanks to this windfall, he established a workshop in this building in Bouknadel and founded the **Belghazi Museum** to exhibit his collection of traditional Moroccan art. Patronized (that is, publicly supported) by Princess Lalla Meriam, it is the first and only private museum in the country and houses a far larger collection than any state museum. On display are pottery, wood carvings, embroidery, manuscripts, musical instruments, agricultural tools, and weapons. One interesting room is full of Moroccan Jewish art, such as wedding clothes and temple furnishings. ⊠*Rte. de Kenitra, Km 17* ☎*037/82–21–78* ⊕*www2.maghrebnet.net.ma/~belghazi* ⊠*40 DH* ⊙*Sat.–Thurs. 8:30–6, Fri. 2:30–6.*

☾ South of Bouknadel are the **Jardins Exotiques** *(Exotic Gardens)*, created in the mid-20th century by a Frenchman named François, who used to play classical music to his plants. Since François's death the gardens have been maintained by the government, and although the landscaper's house has fallen into ruin, the leaves are still swept up daily. The gardens were originally planned to represent different regions, such as Polynesia, China, and Japan. They're a haven for birds and frogs, and the profusion of walkways and bridges makes them a wonderful playground for children. A touching poem by François about his life forms an epitaph at the entrance. ⊠*5 DH* ⊙*Daily 9–5.*

WHERE TO STAY

$ ⊡**Hotel Firdaous.** This hotel has a spectacular location on the Plage des Nations. The small guest rooms face the crashing ocean and have a standard beach-hotel design with light-wood furnishings, pastel linens, and small balconies. The restaurants serve good seafood. **Pros:** Peaceful setting, eye-popping location. **Con:** Rooms are small. ⊠*B.P. 4008, Plage des Nations* ☎*037/82–21–31* ⟳*17 rooms* ⚐*In-room: safe. In-hotel: 2 restaurants, bars, pool, beachfront* ⊟*DC, MC, V.*

KENITRA & MEHDIYA PLAGE

40 km (25 mi) northeast of Rabat.

Kenitra was only founded in 1913, so it has no monuments of great historical interest. If you find yourself longing, however, for a nice, juicy hamburger after your umpteenth plate of friture de poisson, stop in El Dorado restaurant. There was once an American air base nearby, so you can feel a slight American influence in the town; cafés have American names, and English is more widely spoken here than elsewhere in Morocco.

A slight detour—11 km (7 mi) west of Kenitra—will take you to the little seaside resort of Mehdiya Plage. Its long sandy beach is known for good surfing as well as swimming, although the strong undertow along Morocco's Atlantic coast is widely feared and respected. There's a great daily fish market where prawns are among the fresh (and inexpensive) treats on offer, and a handful of beachside cafés.

GETTING HERE & AROUND

A shuttle train connects Kenitra to Rabat and Casablanca every 30 minutes. The city has two train stations: Kenitra-Ville and Kenitra-Medina. The long main street, Avenue Mohammed Diouri, runs from Kenitra-Ville to the bus station by way of the central Place Administrative. It's a 15-minute walk from the square to the bus station or the Kenitra-Ville train station. For those traveling by car, the narrow S2301 is the best route.

TIMING & PRECAUTIONS

Most travelers stay in Kenitra for just one night. Kenitra is a relatively safe city, but some of its nightclubs have a reputation for attracting prostitutes. Unaccompanied females may be hassled by local men at the clubs. If you feel harassed, do not hesitate to summon police.

ESSENTIALS

Bus Contacts Compagnie de Transports Marocains (⊠ *Pl. Administrative* ☏ *037/37–62–38*).

Currency Exchange Agence Kenitra Salah Eddine (⊠ *Ave. Mohammed V at rue Salah Eddine*).

Emergencies Highway assistance (☏ *177*). Fire (☏ *15*). Police (☏ *19*).

Internet Access Pro (⊠ *12, rue Amira Aicha*).

Post Office Kenitra Main Post Office (⊠ *Ave. Hassan II*).

Taxis Kenitra Main Taxi Depot (⊠ *Ave. Mohammed V*) .

Visitor & Tour Information Lake Sidi Bourhaba Information Center (☏ *037/74–72–09* ⊕ *www.spana.org.ma*).

EXPLORING

You'll pass **Lake Sidi Bourhaba** on the way back to the main road. This freshwater lake is internationally famous for the number and variety of birds that pass through on their way to the south side of the Sahara desert. Ornithologists flock here nearly as eagerly as the itinerant birds themselves, looking especially for the rare marbled teal along with another 200 species. ☏ *037/74–72–09* ⊕ *www.spana.org.ma*

WHERE TO EAT & STAY

¢

AMERICAN

✕**El Dorado.** Think of this as a gold mine of such American delicacies as hamburgers and cheeseburgers. The food is appropriately tasty, and there's a menu in English. The small dining area attempts an American Southwest mood with high-back, vinyl cushioned booths and Western movie posters. ⊠ *64, Ave. Mohammed Diouri* ☏ *037/37–16–46* ▭ *No credit cards.*

¢ 🖼 **Hotel Mamora.** Despite its modest rates, this family-run establishment is the best hotel in Kenitra. It offers friendly service, attractive rooms decorated in pastels and blond wood, and continually changing local cuisine in the restaurant, El Kahima. Nightclub L'Araignee features live bands. Views take in the verdant poolside terrace or the trees of the town square. To get here, follow signs for the Hôtel de Ville. Hotel Mamora is across the town square from the Town Hall. **Pros:** Good prices, pleasant rooms. **Con:** Nightclub is noisy. ⊠*Ave. Hassan II* ☎*037/37–17–75* 🖅*hem.bredband.net/hana/mamora english* 🖅*69 rooms, 3 suites* ⚑*In-room: refrigerator. In-hotel: restaurant, bar, pool* ⊟*AE, DC, MC, V.*

MOULAY BOUSSELHAM

46 km (29 mi) southwest of Larache, 82 km (51 mi) northeast of Kenitra, 150 km (93 mi) northeast of Rabat.

The coastal resort town of Moulay Bousselham is popular with Moroccans. It's made up of little more than a single street crowded by cafés and souvenir shops. The saint Moulay Bousselham, a 10th-century Egyptian for whom the city is named, is buried above the Merja Zerga lagoon. Every July, Moulay Bousselham is the site of one of the region's largest moussems (pilgrimages).

This is one of northern Morocco's prime bird-watching locations, with boat trips organized to see thousands of birds—herons, pink flamingos, sheldrakes, and gannets. The best time for watching birds is just after dawn. The Moulay Bousselham sandbar is somewhat dangerous for swimmers due to a rapid drop-off that causes a continual crash of breaking waves.

GETTING HERE & AROUND
Moulay Bousselham has a train station with daily service from Larache and Rabat. There are frequent buses and taxis to Moulay Bousselham from Souk el-Arba du Rharb, which is accessible from Kenitra, Rabat, and Larache by grand taxi.

TIMING & PRECAUTIONS
Most travelers stay in Moulay Bousselham for one night. Moulay Bousselham is generally considered safe, with most annoyances stemming from vendors hawking their wares. The village becomes desolate after sundown, so it's wise to take the usual precautions.

ESSENTIALS
Currency Exchange **Banque du Populaire** (⊠ *Main village off S216* ☎*bponline. chaabinet.co.ma*). **Credit Agricole** (⊠*Main village off S216*).

Medical Assistance **Moulay Bousselham Pharmacy** (⊠ *Main village off S216*).

Post Office **Moulay Bousselham Main Post Office** (⊠*Souk el-Arba Rd., East of village*).

Visitor & Tour Information **Mansoury el Boukhary Tourism Office** (☎*063/09–37–94*).

EXPLORING

Moulay Bousselham is at the head of **Merdja Zerga** *(Blue Lagoon)*, which gives its name to the 17,000-acre national park that contains it. This is a major stopover for countless birds migrating from Norway, Sweden, and the United Kingdom to Africa: the birds fly south at the end of summer and stop at Merdja Zerga in September, October, and November before continuing on to West Africa and even as far as South Africa. They stop off again on their way back to Europe in spring, so spring and fall are the times for bird-watching. The pink flamingos on their way to and from Mauritania are particularly spectacular.

The legend of the lagoon and Moulay Bousselham dates from the 10th century, when the saint Saïd ben Saïd immigrated to the Maghreb from Egypt, following a revelation instructing him to pray where the sun sets over the ocean. He had a disciple called Sidi Abdel Jalil who (according to legend) saw Saïd ben Saïd fishing one day with a hook and asked him why a man with such great powers needed a hook. To show that he needed no such aids himself, Sidi Abdel Jalil put his hands into the water and pulled out fish as numerous as the hairs on his hand. Provoked by this act, Saïd ben Saïd took off his *selham* (cloak), swept it along the ground, called out, "Sea, follow me," and proceeded to walk inland. He did not stop until he had walked 10 km (6 mi). The sea followed him, and so the lagoon was formed. After this, Saïd ben Saïd was called Moulay Bousselham—"Lord, Owner of the Cloak."

Sidi Abdel Jalil begged his master to forgive him for his presumption, and Moulay Bousselham did so on the condition that he remain on the other side of the lagoon—and there **Sidi Abdel Jalil's tomb** remains to this day, on the large sand dune.

Moulay Bousselham's tomb is at the foot of the village, near the sea. Both tombs are cubic white buildings capped with a dome; Sidi Abdel Jalil's is somewhat smaller.

WHERE TO STAY

¢ ⓣ **Hôtel Le Lagon.** With panoramic views over the inland lagoon and the Atlantic as well, this comfortable hotel on the outskirts of Moulay Bousselham has breezy rooms and a spacious terrace for breakfast or evening cocktails. **Pros:** Good views, comfortable rooms. **Con:** Not much public transportation. ⊠ *Le Lagon, Front de Mer* ☎ *037/43–26–50* ⇦ *30 rooms* ⌂ *In-room: safe, Wi-Fi. In-hotel: restaurant, no elevator* ⊟ *MC, V.*

CASABLANCA

91 km (57 mi) southwest of Rabat.

Casablanca is Morocco's most modern city, and various groups of people call it home: hardworking Berbers who came north from the Souss Valley to make their fortune; older folks raised on French customs during the protectorate; pious Muslims; wealthy business executives in the prestigious neighborhood called California; new and poor arrivals from the countryside, living in shantytowns; and thousands of others from all over the kingdom who have found jobs here. The city has its own stock exchange, and working hours tend to transcend the relaxed pace kept by the rest of Morocco.

True to its Spanish name—*casa blanca,* "white house," which, in turn, is Dar el Beida in Arabic—Casablanca is a conglomeration of white buildings. The present city, known colloquially as Casa or El Beida, was only founded in 1912. It lacks the ancient monuments that resonate in Morocco's other major cities; however, there are still some landmarks, including the famous Hassan II Mosque.

GETTING HERE & AROUND

From overseas, Casablanca's Mohammed V Airport is the best gateway to Morocco itself: you're find a well-maintained arrivals hall, efficient and courteous staffers, and a trouble-free continuation of your journey by train or car. Trains connect the airport to the national network from 7:35 AM to 10:30 PM, and taxis are available to the city of Casablanca at relatively expensive but fixed rates (200 DH–250 DH).

Buses are fine for short trips, such as from Casablanca to El Jadida or Safi, but trips longer than a couple of hours can be interminable, hot, and dusty. Inquire at the station for schedule and fare information. In Casablanca the Compagnie de Transports au Maroc bus station is by far the most convenient, since the other stations are on the outskirts of town.

Casablanca has two stations: Casablanca Port, downtown, and Casablanca Voyageurs, for through trains between Marrakesh, Fez, and Rabat. The two are reasonably close together, and all trains from the airport call at both. Trains to Rabat depart hourly. (This is by far the best way to move between Casablanca and Rabat.) Casablanca is 3 hours by train from Marrakesh (nine trains daily), 3½ hours from Meknès (eight trains daily), and 4½ hours from Fez (nine trains daily). In addition, there are overnight trains from Casablanca to Oujda (three daily, 10 hours) and direct trains daily to Tangier (three daily, 6 hours).

There are numerous travel agencies in downtown Casablanca. Menara Tours is particularly good; it's on the left on the street next to Wafabank, opposite the Hyatt Regency on Place des Nations Unies.

TIMING & PRECAUTIONS

Most visitors stay in Casablanca for two nights. Travelers should be cautious at night when walking in the Casablanca city center and around the old medina. It is best to use a taxi late at night when returning from a restaurant or the nightclubs.

ESSENTIALS

Bus Information Compagnie de Transports au Maroc (✉ *23, rue Léon l'Africain* ☎ *022/54–10–10* ⊕ *www.ctm.co.ma*).

Emergencies Clinique Badr (✉ *35, rue el Allousi, opposite Badr Mosque, Bourgoune* ☎ *022/49–28–00*).

A BIT OF HISTORY

The earliest known settlement on this site was the port of Anfa, from which Berbers traded with Phoenicians and Carthaginians. Anfa started to grow in the 13th century, when the Berbers began trading with the Portuguese and Spanish, but in the 15th century the Portuguese destroyed the city in retaliation for Berber piracy, and in the 16th they named it Casa Branca. (Over the next century it became Dar el Beida, and finally Casablanca.)

At the end of the 18th century the important town was rebuilt under the Alaouite sultan Mohammed Ibn Abdullah and began trading with European ports once more. French general Hubert Lyautey's decision at the beginning of the French protectorate to build the present-day harbor paved the way for a rapid urban expansion that continues to this day. In 1943 Casablanca hosted the famous Anfa conference of Franklin D. Roosevelt, Winston Churchill, and Charles de Gaulle, at which Morocco's Prince Moulay el Hassan was also present.

Rental Cars Avis (⊠ *19, ave. des Forces Armées Royales* ☎ *022/31–24–24* ⊠ *www.avis.com).* **Budget** (*Rabat-Salé Airport* ☎ *022/53–91–57* ⊠ *www.budget. com).*

Internet Cafés Mondial Net (⊠ *Centre Allal Ben Abdellah, 47, rue Allal Ben Abdellah* ☎ *022/48–04–80).* **G@.Net** (⊠ *29, rue Abdel Kader Al Moftaker* ☎ *022/22–95–23).*

Train Information Office National des Chemins de Fer, Casa-Port (*O.N.C.F.* ⊠ *Bd. Houphouet Boigny* ☎ *022/22–30–11* ⊕ *www.oncf.org.ma).* **Office National des Chemins de Fer, Casa-Voyageurs** (*O.N.C.F.* ⊠ *Bd. Mohammed V* ☎ *022/24–38–18* ⊕ *www.oncf.org.ma).*

Visitor & Tour Information Menara Tours (⊠ *119, rue Chenier* ☎ *022/22–52–32).* Office National Marocain du Tourisme (*O.N.M.T.* ⊠ *55, rue Omar Slaoui* ☎ *022/27– 11–77 or 022/27–95–33* ⊠ *www.visitmorocco.org).* **Syndicat d'Initiative et de Tourisme** (⊠ *98, bd. Mohammed V* ☎ *022/22–15–24 or 022/27–05–38).*

EXPLORING

TOP ATTRACTIONS

❼ ★ Habous. At the edge of the new medina, the Quartier des Habous is a curiously attractive mixture of French colonial architecture with Moroccan details built by the French at the beginning of the 20th century. Capped by arches, its shops surround a pretty square with trees and flowers. As you enter the Habous, you'll pass a building resembling a castle; this is the Pasha's Mahkama, or court, completed in 1952. The Mahkama formerly housed the reception halls of the Pasha of Casablanca, as well as a Muslim courthouse; it's currently used for district government administration. On the opposite side of the square is the Mohammed V Mosque—although not ancient, this and the 1938 Moulay Youssef Mosque, in the adjacent square, are among the finest examples of traditional Maghrebi (western North African) architecture in Casablanca.

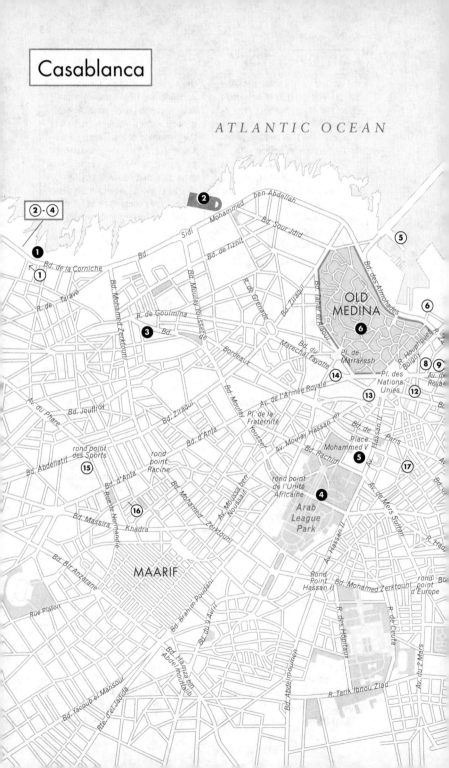

Casablanca

ATLANTIC OCEAN

②·④

① *Bd. de la Corniche*
②
③
④ Arab League Park
⑤
⑥ OLD MEDINA
⑧ ⑨
⑫
⑬
⑭
⑮ rond point des Sports
⑯
⑰

MAARIF

R. de Tarave
Bd. Mohamed Zerktouni
R. de Goulmina
Bd.
Bd. Moulay Youssef
R. de Grenade
Bordeaux
Bd. Ziraqui
Sidi Mohammed ben Abdellah
Bd. de Tiznit
Bd. Sour Jdid
Bd. des Almohades
Bd. Tahar el Alaoui
Bd. du Marechal Fayette
Pl. de Marrakesh
R. Houphouet-Boigny
Pl. des Nations Unies
Av. de l'Armée Royale
Av. de Roya
Bd.
Av. du Phare
Bd. Jouffroy
Bd. Ziraqui
Pl. de la Fraternité
Av. Moulay Youssef
Av. Moulay Hassan 1er
Bd. de
Place Mohammed V
Bd. Rachidi
Av. Hassan II
R. Paris
Bd. Abdellatif
rond point Racine
Bd. d'Anfa
Av. Moussa ben Noussair
rond point de l'Unité Africaine
Av. de Mers Sultan
Bd. d'Anfa
Rue de Normandie
Bd. Mohamed Zerktouni
Khadra
R. Haa.
Bd. Massira
Rond Point Hassan II
Bd. Mohamed Zerktouni
rond point d'Europe
Rue Platon
Bd. Bir Anzarane
Bd. Brahim Roudani
Bd. du 9 Avril
Bd. Hamza ben Abdel-moutalib
Av. Abdelmoumen
R. des Hôpitaux
R. de Ceuta
Av. du 2 Mars
Bd. Yacoub el Mansour
Rte. d'El Jadida
R. Tarik Ibnou Ziad

Look up at the minarets and you might recognize a style used in Marrakesh's Koutoubia Mosque and Seville's Giralda. Note also the fine wood carving over the door of the Mohammed V. The Habous is well known as a center for Arabic books; most of the other shops here are devoted to rich displays of traditional handicrafts aimed at locals. You can also buy traditional Moroccan clothes such as kaftans and *djellabas* (long, hooded outer garments). Immediately north of the Habous is Casablanca's Royal Palace. You can't go inside, but the outer walls are pleasing; their sandstone blocks fit neatly together and blend well with the little streets at the edge of the Habous.

> ## MAJOR MOSQUE
>
> Funded through public subscription, designed by a French architect, and built by a team of 35,000, the mosque went up between 1987 and 1993 and is now the third-largest mosque in the world, after the Haramain Mosque in Mecca and the Prophet's Mosque in Medina. It was set in Casablanca primarily so that the largest city in the kingdom would have a monument worthy of its size. Except for Tin Maland, this is the only mosque in Morocco that non-Muslims are allowed to enter.

❷ **Fodor'sChoice** **★** **Hassan II Mosque.** Casablanca's skyline is dominated by this massive edifice. No matter where you are, you're bound to see it thanks to its attention-grabbing green-tile roof. The building's foundations lie partly on land and partly in the sea, and at one point you can see the water through a glass floor. The main hall holds an astonishing 25,000 people and has a retractable roof so that it can be turned into a courtyard. The minaret is more than 650 feet high, and the mezzanine floor (which holds the women's section, about 6 feet above the main floor) seems dwarfed by the nearly 200-foot-high ceiling. Still, the ceiling's enormous painted decorations appear small and delicate from below. A eulogy to King Hassan II (written before he died, in July 1999) is inscribed inside. ■TIP➜ If you fly out of Casablanca, try to get a window seat on the left for a good view of the mosque in relation to the city as a whole. ⊠ *Bd. de la Corniche* ☏ *022/44–04–48* ✉ *120 DH* ⊘ *Guided tours Sat.–Thurs. at 9, 10, 11, and 2 (all visits by guided tour).*

❺ **Place Mohammed V.** This is Casablanca's version of London's Trafalgar Square: it has an illuminated fountain, lots of pigeons, and a series of impressive buildings facing it. Coming from the port, you'll pass the main post office on your right, and on your left as you enter the square is its most impressive building, the courthouse, built in the 1920s. On the other side of Avenue Hassan II from the post office is the ornate Bank Al Maghrib; the structure opposite, with the clock tower, is the Wilaya, the governor's office. The more modest buildings on the right side of the square house the notorious customs directorate (where importers' appeals against punitive taxes stand little chance). To avoid confusion, note that Place Mohammed V was formerly called Place des Nations Unies and vice versa, and the old names still appear on some maps.

WORTH NOTING

❹ **Arab League Park.** This is the most substantial patch of green in the center of Casablanca. There is a children's amusement park on the far side of Boulevard Moulay Youssef (2 DH) and, to the right of the amusement park an avenue of tall palm trees. Casablanca's modern cathedral, built in 1930, is at the park's northwest corner.

❶ **Corniche.** Get a feel for Casa's Atlantic setting by stopping at a Corniche café and basking in the sun and breeze. This is where the people of Casablanca go to relax—a seafront line of cafés, restaurants, and nightclubs, and a number of hotels. The Corniche goes on past a palace (home to resident Saudi Arabians) and a mosque to Aïn Diab, and finally to the tomb of Sidi Abderrahman, which is on a rock in the sea and accessible only at low tide.

NEED A BREAK?

La Petite Roche (⊠ 48, bd. de la Corniche ☎ 022/39–57–48), a bar with a restaurant downstairs, offers spectacular views of the Hassan II Mosque and candlelight in the evenings. Furnished with brass-topped tables and low-slung chairs, this is a good spot to cap off a day of sightseeing. Constructed in 1933 by French architect Georges Renaudin, **La Réserve** (⊠ 3, bd. de la Corniche ☎ 022/79–71–10), a flying-saucer-like architectural fantasy, is the most picturesque place for dinner or drinks on La Corniche. Live piano is played until midnight, when modern music and dancing begin.

❸ **Ensemble d'Artisanat.** This handicrafts center is much like the Ensemble Artisanal in Rabat. Here you can buy pottery, crafted wood, straw work, carpets, slippers, leatherwork, and handcrafted musical instruments in specialty shops, some of whose artisans create their wares in full view. ⊠ 195, bd. de Bordeaux ☎ 022/22–83–34 ☐ Free ☉ Daily approximately 9–12:30 and 2:30–6.

❻ **Old Medina.** The simple whitewashed houses of the medina, particularly those closest to the harbor, form an extraordinary contrast to Morocco's economic and commercial nerve center just a few hundred yards away. European consuls lived here in the 19th century, the early trading days, and there are still a youth hostel and a few very cheap hotels within. Near Place des Nations Unies a large conglomeration of shops sells watches, leather bags and jackets, shoes, crafted wood, and clothes, but the proximity of the Hyatt Regency makes negotiating a deal somewhat harder than usual.

WHERE TO EAT

$$–$$$$ ✕ **Aéropostale.** In line with its name, the walls of this popular French
FRENCH   bistro are covered with antique prints of air-post carriers. The menu is presented on large chalkboards and includes tasty seafood, duck

and meat dishes, generous salads, and a perfect fish soup poured into your bowl from a small clay pitcher. A daily three-course menu is available, and there's an impressive Belgian beer list. ✉ *6, rue Molière* ☎ *022/36–02–52* ▭ *MC, V* ⊘ *Closed Sun.*

$$$
MOROCCAN
✕ **Al-Mounia.** Come to this large Moroccan restaurant if you want to try the national dishes, such as couscous or tagines, in cosmopolitan Casablanca. The excellent cooking sometimes presents surprising flavors—a carrot salad is perfumed with oranges, and the chicken and almond tagine has a buttery, brown sugar sauce. You can dine in rooms with typically Moroccan decor or on the outdoor terrace under a hundred-year-old tree. ✉ *95, rue Prince Moulay Abdallah* ☎ *022/22–26–69* ▭ *AE, DC, MC, V* ⊘ *Closed Sun.*

$$–$$$$
FRENCH
✕ **A Ma Bretagne.** This restaurant is quite far out of town on the coast past Sidi Abderrahman and serves dinner only, but it's widely considered to serve the finest French provincial cuisine in Morocco. The setting is modern and elegant, with hardwood floors, sleek columns, and wall-to-wall ocean-view windows. The menu centers on fish and shellfish—the prawns make an excellent starter, and the grilled fish is particularly good. For sweets lovers, the warm chocolate tart is spectacular. ✉ *Bd. de la Corniche, Sidi Abderrahman* ☎ *022/36–21–12* ▭ *DC, MC, V* ⊘ *Closed Sun. No lunch.*

$$–$$$$
FRENCH
★
✕ **Le Cabestan.** Look down from a window seat onto blue rock pools as you savor delicious fish dishes. To wind down, you might have *tarte fine caramélisée aux pommes d'oulmès* (caramelized apple tart). This is French cuisine at its best, with fabulous sauces, and it's served in a great location near the lighthouse on the Corniche. ✉ *Phare d'El Hank, La Corniche* ☎ *022/39–11–90* ▭ *DC, MC, V* ⊘ *Closed Sun.*

$–$$
SEAFOOD
✕ **Cafétéria Chez François.** Dine on some of the freshest fish in the neighborhood at this out-of-the-way spot on a jetty overlooking part of the marina in Casablanca's port. This sunny, breezy spot with simple wooden tables and benches serves stuffed clams, calamari, and tiny fried sole, together with a huge mixed salad. ✉ *Jetée Moulay Youssef, S.N.C. Port de Plaisance* ☎ *022/31–58–22* ▭ *No credit cards.*

$–$$
CHINESE
✕ **Golden China.** For the best Chinese cooking in town, if not the entire region, try this centrally located restaurant. The lengthy menu offers a wide variety of poultry, seafood, meat, vegetarian, and noodle dishes. Start off with delicious spring rolls, dumplings, or hot-and-sour soup. The decor is elegant and authentic, with red, onyx, gold, and mahogany detail. ✉ *12, rue el Oraibi Jilali* ☎ *022/27–35–26* ▭ *MC, V* ⊘ *No lunch weekends.*

> **FOR THE KIDS**
>
> Casablanca's best opportunities for children are the beaches of the Aïn Diab section of town along the Boulevard de la Corniche.
>
> Le Miami, Le Lido, and KonTiki are a series of semiprivate clubs open to the public (60 DH for adults, 25 DH for children). They offer, along with sun and sand, swimming pools, waterslides, basketball courts, and other sports and amusements.

$–$$ ✕**Restaurant du Port.** Tucked inside
SEAFOOD the port, this is perhaps Casablanca's best-known fish restaurant, and as such gets rather crowded at lunchtime. The fried fish is particularly good at any time of day. To find the place, enter the port by the gate near the train station and turn left toward the fishing port. If you're arriving on foot, don't let the strong outdoor port odors deter you—the restaurant's interior is clean and fresh. ⊠*Port de Pêche* ☎*022/31–85–61* ▤*MC, V.*

$–$$ ✕**Taverne du Dauphin.** Decorated in
SEAFOOD a marine style, the popular Dolphin is a good alternative to its pricier counterparts for all fish and seafood dishes. You'll find it on the left side of the boulevard leading to the port station; the entrance is around the back. ⊠*115, bd. Félix Houphouet Boigny* ☎*022/22–12–00* ▤*DC, MC, V* ⊘*Closed Sun.*

$ ✕**Toscana.** For fashionable dining with hip crowds at reasonable prices,
ITALIAN come to this popular Italian eatery. Specialties include wonderful fresh pasta tossed with simple (garlic and olive oil) or rich (smoked salmon and crème fraîche) sauces. The wood-burning oven turns out excellent pizzas and breads. Don't expect a lot of elbow room in the stylish and intimate interior; still, coziness does help create a lively buzz. Service is pleasingly fast in spite of the constantly full house. ⊠*7, rue Yaalal Ifrani* ☎*022/36–95–92* ▤*No credit cards.*

CASABLANCA REDUX

Casablanca is probably most famous for the 1942 Humphrey Bogart–Ingrid Bergman film of the same name, which was shot entirely in Hollywood. Along with the apocryphal "Play it again, Sam" that was never uttered and Bogart's curious "I was mishinfawmed" line when told there were no thermal baths in Marrakesh, Casablanca surely ranks among the planet's greatest self-sustaining spurious cult myths. A visit to Rick's Café, where the waiters wear fedoras and trench coats, is de rigueur to complete this exercise in faux-nostalgia. And what the heck? It was just a movie in the first place, anyway.

WHERE TO STAY

$$–$$$ ▦**Golden Tulip Farah Casablanca.** The Farah has a bright and geometrically tiled lobby, offers full five-star comforts and services, and serves generous buffet breakfasts (not included in the room rate.) The hotel offers four restaurants: La Brasserie, serving a variety of local and international entrées; Al Johara, an Asian restaurant; El Ambra, serving Moroccan cuisine; and Le Lorenzo, specializing in Italian delicacies. **Pros:** Plenty of creature comforts, public transportation nearby. **Con:** No meal plan. ⊠*160, ave. des FAR* ☎*022/31–12–12* ⤳ *www.golden tulipfarah.com* ⤶*310 rooms, 12 suites* ⚬ *In-room: safe. In-hotel: 4 restaurants, pool, parking (fee)* ▤*AE, DC, MC, V.*

$ ▦**Hotel Bellerive.** Most rooms have ocean views at this hotel recommended for cost-conscious travelers. The accommodations, while not luxurious, modern, or aesthetically distinguished, are breezy, clean, and adequate. The terrace over the beach is an excellent spot for breakfast, which is included in room rate. There is a play area for children with games and amusements. There is a large garden area and a pool with solarium. **Pros:** Easy on the wallet, good for families with young children. **Cons:** Bland decor, rooms facing street are noisy. ✉ *Bd. de la Corniche* ☎*022/79–75–04* ⊕*www.belleriv.com* ⟿*37 rooms* ⌂*In-room: refrigerator, Wi-Fi. In-hotel: restaurant, bar, parking (free)* ▤*AE, DC, MC, V* ❢❘*BP.*

¢   **Hôtel du Centre.** Opposite the entrance to the Royal Mansour is this budget option with clean rooms and a central location. The staff is helpful, and management is beginning to touch up the rooms with new televisions and linens. You won't get the perks of the luxe lodging across the street, but at a fraction of the price, who's complaining? **Pros:** Convenient location, good price. **Con:** Very basic rooms. ✉*1, rue Sidi Balyout at corner of Ave. des FAR* ☎*022/44–61–80* ⟿*34 rooms* *In-room: safe. In-hotel: parking (fee)* ▤*No credit cards.*

$$ **Hotel Rivoli.** This place is hard to miss because of the life-size Egyptian reliefs marking its street-side discotheque. The Rivoli has the convenient location and all the facilities expected of a business hotel. Rooms are large, with smooth pastel bed linens. The hotel has its own Internet café, two bars, and four restaurants. **Pros:** Central location, reliable hotel. **Con:** Area is a bit sketchy at night. ✉*44, bd. Anfa* ☎*022/26–29–37* ⊕*www.hotelrivolicasablanca.com* ⟿*213 rooms* ⌂*In-room: safe. In-hotel: 4 restaurants, bars,* parking (free) ✉*AE, DC, MC, V.*

$$$$ **Hyatt Regency.** Casablanca's most conspicuous hotel occupies a large site next to Place des Nations Unies. The luxurious rooms have thoughtful touches like large executive desks and comfortable armchairs. Those on the top floors have some of the city's most spectacular views of the Hassan II Mosque. The bathrooms are splendid, with beautiful separate tubs and glass-door showers. Bar Casablanca is a big draw for tour groups who don't hesitate to don fez caps and trench coats to pose for photos by the oversize Bogart posters. Don't be surprised if the evening jazz performer breaks into "As Time Goes By" while you sip your cocktails. There are plenty of dining options: Asian, Mediterranean, Moroccan, a Parisian-style bistro, and poolside. **Pros:** Plenty of shopping nearby, great views. **Cons:** Too kitschy for many travelers, Internet access is $30 a day. ✉*Pl. des Nations Unies* ☎*022/43–12–34* ⊕*www. casablanca.hyatt.com* ⟿*222 rooms, 33 suites* ⌂*In-room: safe, refrigerator, Ethernet. In-hotel: 5 restaurants, bar, gym, pool, parking (free)* ▤*AE, DC, MC, V.*

$ **Ibis Moussafir.** The Ibis is right next to the Casablanca Voyageurs train station, which makes it very convenient for those catching the train to or from the airport. Service is excellent, and you get a particularly good breakfast included in the rate. Furnished in a dated but pleasing style, the rooms are simple and the double-glazed windows block out the train whistles. The hotel is often full, so reserve in advance. **Pros:** Friendly staff, near public transportation. **Con:** Could use updating. ✉*Ave. Ba Hmad, Pl. de la Gare–Casa Voyageurs* ☎*022/40–19–84* ⊕*www.ibishotel.com* ⟿*97 rooms* ⌂*In-room: Wi-Fi. In-hotel: restaurant, bar, no elevator, parking (free)* ▤*AE, MC, V* ❢❘*BP.*

$$$–$$$$ 🏨**Riad Salam.** The best lodging option available on the Corniche beachfront, this excellent hotel manages to provide the latest European technology, facilities, and comfort without abandoning North African esthetics and ambience. Standard rooms, suites, and bungalows are available at this gleaming white giant overlooking the Atlantic from a small promontory on Casablanca's most famous strip. The hotel offers a complimentary buffet breakfast. Al Fassia serves classic Moroccan dishes in a traditional setting. **Pros:** On the beach, indoor and outdoor pools. **Con:** Patio furniture is old and worn. ✉*Bd. de la Corniche s/n, Aïn Diab* ☎*022/39–13–13* ⤵*197 rooms, 9 suites* ♿*In-room: refrigerator. In-hotel: 3 restaurants, bar, tennis court, pools, gym, spa, parking (fee)* ▤*AE, DC, MC, V* ⧖*BP.*

$$$$ 🏨**Royal Mansour Meridien.** The Royal Mansour is the best hotel in Casablanca, especially for those looking for traditional luxury. Its service and attention to guests have no equal here, and all rooms overlook either the port or Avenue des Forces Armées Royales. The Moroccan restaurant is decorated like a typical Moroccan house on one side, a Moroccan tent on the other; breakfast is served in an attractive indoor garden. The health and fitness center is one of the most comprehensive in the country. **Pros:** Plenty of amenities, doting staff, impressive gym. **Con:** Internet access is about $45 a day. ✉*27, ave. des FAR* ☎*022/31–30–11* ⊕*www.lemeridien-casablanca.com* ⤵*159 rooms, 23 suites* ♿*In-room: safe, Ethernet. In-hotel: 2 restaurants, bars, gym, airport shuttle, parking (fee)* ▤*AE, DC, MC, V.*

$$$–$$$$ 🏨**Sheraton.** Casablanca's Sheraton has an impressive lobby and a mezzanine bar area with a high ceiling dangling pendant lamps. It's entirely convenient to the business district, including most airline offices. Comfortable rooms are tastefully furnished in pink and gray, with satellite televisions offering several English-speaking channels. The hotel offers Japanese, Moroccan, and French restaurants, and banquet service is sumptuous. Nightclub Caesar's Discotheque is open nightly. **Pros:** Many dining options, good for business travelers. **Con:** Pool area could use renovation. ✉*100, ave. des FAR* ☎*022/43–94–94* ⊕*www.sheraton.com/casablanca* ⤵*275 rooms, 31 suites* ♿*In-room: safe, refrigerator, Wi-Fi. In-hotel: 3 restaurants, bars, pool, no-smoking rooms, parking (free)* ▤*AE, MC, V.*

SHOPPING

ANTIQUES

For Moroccan antiques of all kinds, check out **Amazonite** (✉*15, rue Prince Moulay Abdallah*) You might find anything from a Berber carpet to a Delacroix. Antique furniture is the prime offering at **Abdou Alaoui-Belhassa** (✉*20, rue el Mourtada*).

CLOTHING

Casablanca also prides itself on fashionable Western clothing. The name of a small boutique for women in the Gautier district says it all: **AT751** (✉*42, ave. Hassan Souktani*), the number of a daily flight from Paris to Casablanca. Stroll the pedestrian Rue Prince Moulay Abdullah for a wide variety of stores. The greatest concentration of clothing boutiques by far is found in the **Maarif** area, west of Boulevard Brahim Roudani. Here you'll find a pedestrian street, the Twin Center shopping mall, and all manner of specialty stores from Belgian chocolatiers to fashionable shoe stores to Portuguese porcelain warehouses.

CRAFTS

Casa has three good places to shop for souvenirs and handicrafts. In close proximity to Casa's luxury hotels, the shops lining the **Boulevard Houphouet Boigny** offer few bargains, and their business is

> ### HERE ON BUSINESS?
>
> Morocco's French connection is most palpable in its most contemporary and, in many ways, most cosmopolitan city. Casablanca is by far the country's dominant commercial city, so if you're in Morocco on business you'll almost certainly be based here. If you have only a little time for excursions, head for the beach or the golf course at Mohammedia.

mostly geared to tourists. They do present a broad sampling of all things Moroccan however, and are convenient for last minute, one-stop shopping. The **Ensemble d'Artisanat** offers hassle-free shopping and a chance to see craftsmen at work; the prices are fixed at slightly higher rates than those you find in the markets, but the quality standards are high. The **Quartier des Habous** offers the best variety and prices, but you should still try to get an idea of the market prices before starting to bargain.

The **Exposition Nationale d'Artisanat** (✉*26, ave. Hassan II*) offers three floors of high-quality crafts from all over Morocco at generally high prices. Moroccan themes in household paraphernalia are the rule at **Thema Maison** (✉*27, rue Houssine Ben Ali*), a good choice for drapes, pillows, or minor decorative trinkets.

NIGHTLIFE

Most Casablanca nightlife for the young and wired develops out along the Boulevard de la Corniche, a 30 DH–35 DH taxi fare from the center of town. Exceptions are the major hotel discos such as the Caesar in the Sheraton Hotel or Black House in the Hyatt Regency, though these are also commercial love marts where both sexes are on the block, or suspected thereof.

Candy Bar Lounge (✉*Bd. de la Corniche, Aïn Diab* ☎*022/79–84–40*) in the Hôtel Riad Salam draws party animals from all over Casablanca for a torrid disco scene. **Mystic Garden** (✉*33, bd. de la Corniche, Aïn Diab* ☎*022/79–88–77*) is an oddity—a laid-back saloon with Scandinavian design and mellow sounds. **La Petite Roche** (✉*Bd. de la Corniche, Phare El-Hank* ☎*022/39–57–48*) over the restaurant of the same name has stunning views of the Hassan II Mosque and a young and thoroughly Europeanized Moroccan clientele.

Rick's Café (✉*248, bd. Sour Jdid* ☎*022/27–42–07*) is the place to wax nostalgic about the romantic Casablanca evoked in the Bogey film. The most recent renovation faithfully reconstructed the 1942 movie set.

HAMMAMS & SPAS

The following hammams are open to all (even nonguests, if in a hotel). (*For more on the hammam experience, see Chapter 10.*)

PUBLIC HAMMAMS

Hammam Le Pacha. Popular with modern Moroccans, this is one of the best private baths in Casablanca; hammam with exfoliation costs 40 DH; massage, 100 DH; towels, 40 DH. ⊠ *484, bd. Gandhi, Casablanca* ☎ *022/77–42–42* 🎫 *40 DH* ⊙ *Daily 8 AM–8 PM* ⊟ *No credit cards.*

Hammam Ziani. Opened in 1995, this upscale hammam offers exfoliation for 80 DH, soaping for 80 DH, and a package including massage and algae wrap for 270 DH. ⊠ *5, rue Abou Rakrak, Casablanca* ☎ *022/31–96–95* 🎫 *www.hammamziani.ma* 🎫 *50 DH* ⊙ *Daily 8 AM–10 PM* ⊟ *No credit cards.*

Moving Club. On the menu of this popular health club used by modern Moroccans is the Royal and Ancestral hammam with massage. ⊠ *33, ave. Mehdi Benbarka, Souiss, Rabat* ☎ *037/65–29–60* 🎫 *130 DH with exfoliation* ⊙ *Daily 8 AM–9 PM* ⊟ *No credit cards.*

HOTEL HAMMAMS

Royal Mansour Meridien. This is a great place to get rid of jet lag, or relax before you return home. The hammam is in a typical Moroccan setting with expert attendants. ⊠ *27, ave. des Forces Armées Royales, Casablanca* ☎ *022/31–30–11* ⊕ *www.lemeridien.com* 🎫 *Hammam 150 DH, 310 DH with exfoliation* ⊙ *Daily, women: 6 AM–3 PM; men: 3 PM–10 PM* ⊟ *AE, DC, MC, V.*

La Tour Hassan. Built in 1914 next to the famous unfinished tower of the Moorish Hassan Mosque, this elegant yet affordable hotel spa offers a hammam, massage, sauna, Jacuzzi, and beauty treatments. ⊠ *26, rue Chellah, Rabat* ☎ *037/70–42–01* 🎫 *210 DH* ⊙ *By appointment* ⊟ *AE, MC, V.*

SPA

La Sultana. La Sultana overlooks the turquoise-blue lagoon of Oualidia, the tiny seaside village on the Atlantic Coast famous for its oysters and spider crabs. It offers a hammam, indoor and outdoor massage, beauty treatments, Jacuzzi, sauna, and an indoor heated pool. ⊠ *Parc à Huitre, No. 3 Bled Gaïla, Oualidia* ☎ *024/38–80–08* ⊕ *www.lasultanaoualidia.com* 🎫 *Treatments 330 DH–5,400 DH* ⊙ *Open on request* ⊟ *AE, MC, V.*

–Pamela Windo

OUTDOOR ACTIVITIES

GOLF

★ The satellite commuter town of Mohammedia (which also happens to be Morocco's oil port), 25 km (16 mi) northeast of Casablanca, is home to an excellent golf course. The **Royal Golf de Mohammedia** (☎ *023/32–46–56*) is laid out between sea pines, eucalyptus trees, acacias, and oleanders. Par is 72 for 18 holes totaling 6,469 yards. To find it, take the Mohammedia exit from the autoroute and inquire when you get to the traffic circle (it's close by).

EL JADIDA

99 km (62 mi) southwest of Casablanca.

El Jadida's new town has a large, sandy bay and a promenade lined with palm trees and cafés. The name El Jadida actually means "the New" and has alternated more than once with the town's original Portuguese name, Mazagan.

GETTING HERE & AROUND

Train service to El Jadida is limited, and the train station is inconveniently located 4 km (2.5 mi) south of town. Buses are fine for trips from Casablanca to El Jadida. Frequent buses also come from the south from Safi and Oulidia. In El Jadida, one bus station, Gare Routière, serves all the bus companies and the grands taxis.

El Jadida has inexpensive metered petits taxis. For local runs, however, it is always advisable to establish an agreed-upon fare before getting in. The going rate for local trips is around 8 DH. The taxi station is next to the bus station. The larger, more-roadworthy grands taxis are available for intercity journeys, such as El Jadida to Safi (48 DH) or for longer trips to Marrakesh (69 DH) or Essaouira (62 DH).

TIMING & PRECAUTIONS

Most travelers stay in El Jadida for one or two nights. El Jadida is generally considered safe, however, the Cité Portugaise area is poorly lighted at night. Visitors should exercise caution if visiting the area after sundown.

ESSENTIALS

Bus Information Compagnie de Transports au Maroc (⊠ *Ave. Mohammed V, southeast end of El Jadida* ☎ *022/54-10-10* ⊕ *www.ctm.co.ma*).

Train Information Office National des Chemins de Fer (⊠ *4 km [2 mi]south of El Jadida* ☎ *023/35-28-24* ⊕ *www.oncf.org.ma*).

Visitor & Tour Information El Jadida Délégation de Tourisme (⊠ *Ave. Jaich el-Malaki* ☎ *023/34-47-88*). **Ricordi Voyages** (⊠ *Bd. Jamiâ Arabia Résidence el Morabitine* ☎ *023/35-59-69*). **Syndicat d'Initiative et du Tourisme d'El Jadida** (⊠ *33, pl. Mohammed V* ☎ *023/34-47-88*). **Travel Citerne International** (⊠ *Pl. el Hansali* ☎ *023/35-35-18*).

EXPLORING

To see El Jadida's attractions—about half a day's diversion—drive south along the coastal road until you see a sign pointing to the **Cité Portugaise,** where you can park opposite the entrance; or take a small white taxi there. The Portuguese city was originally a rectangular island with a bastion on each corner, connected to the mainland by a single

---

AFTER THE GAME

People come to **Restaurant du Port** (⊠ *1, rue du Port, Mohammedia* ☎ *023/32-24-66* ⊟ *MC, V* ⊙ *Closed Mon.*) from outside Mohammedia to eat fish and other seafood. It's worth the trip for the freshest catches, tasty preparations, and attentive service. Located right near the port, the restaurant is appropriately decorated in a nautical theme. The *crevettes au gratin* (baked shrimp and cheese) is particularly good.

causeway. Take the entrance on the right. You'll see that the original Portuguese street names have been retained, the contemporary ones written underneath.

Walk down Rua da Carreira (Rue Mohammed Al Achemi) and you'll see on the left the old **Portuguese church,** Our Lady of the Assumption, built in 1628 with a roof from the French period.

HERE'S WHERE

El Jadida's cistern was not rediscovered until 1916, when a Moroccan Jew stumbled on it in the process of enlarging his shop—whereupon water started gushing in. Orson Welles filmed parts of his famously low-budget *Othello* here.

2

Beyond the church is a fine old **mosque** with a minaret dating from Portuguese times.

Farther along Rua da Carreira on the left is the old **Portuguese cistern,** where water was stored when El Jadida was the fortress of Mazagan (some say the cistern originally stored arms). A small amount of water remains to reflect the cistern's Gothic arches, a lovely effect. ⊠ *Rua da Carreira* ☎ *10 DH* ☉ *Daily 9–1 and 3–6:30.*

Continuing along the *rua* (road), you'll pass the simple, yellow-stone **Spanish church** *(so called locally, despite having no real connection with Spain)* on your left.

At the end of the Rua da Carreira you can walk up ramps to the walls of the **fortress.** Looking down from the fortress, you'll see a gate that leads directly onto the sea and, to the right, El Jadida's fishing harbor.

Walk around the walls to the other side of the fortress and you can look down on the **Jewish cemetery.**

WHERE TO EAT

$–$$ ✕ **Ali Baba.** On the left side of the coastal road into El Jadida, Ali
SEAFOOD   Baba overlooks the sea and has a bright, airy ambience. The chef is French, and the focus is seafood. ⊠ *R.P. 8* ☎ *023/34–16–22* ▤ *MC, V* ☉ *Closed Mon.*

$–$$$ ✕ **Restaurant du Port.** Generally considered El Jadida's best restaurant,
SEAFOOD   this handy and picturesque seafood and fish specialist located, as its name suggests, in the port has splendid views over the harbor as well as the city ramparts. Wine and beer are served here, always a reassuring factor in Morocco, and the atmosphere is relaxed and elegant. ⊠ *Port El Jadida* ☎ *023/34–25–79* ▤ *No credit cards.*

WHERE TO STAY

¢   ⊡ **Palais Andalous.** The Palais Andalous is in fact a converted palace, and is remarkable for its elaborate decorations of intricately carved plaster. While some guest rooms have been renovated, the original artistry of the common areas has not been touched. The rooms, which can seem rather somber (light only comes in through windows facing the courtyard), are reached by a long staircase ornamented with zellij and face the central courtyard, which centers on a fountain. One unique room, originally a marriage suite, has a large raised bed requiring a three-step climb. Continental breakfast is included in the room rates. **Pros:** Authentic decor, unique furnishings. **Con:** Rooms are dark. ✉*Bd. Docteur de Lanouy* ☎*023/34–37–45* ☎*27 rooms* ▤ *In-room: safe. In-hotel: parking (fee)* ▤ *MC, V* ▥*CP.*

¢ ⬚**Le Relais.** On the quiet coastal road that runs from El Jadida down to Essaouira, this inviting blue-and-white inn stands alone overlooking miles of silver sand beaches. Its sunny seafood restaurant is a popular lunch destination with folks from nearby El Jadida for good reason: the lobster served here is the best in the area. The inn's airy, simply decorated rooms all have showers; some have panoramic sea views. **Pros:** Convenient to the beach, excellent restaurant. **Con:** Not all rooms have full bathrooms. ✉*Rte. d'Oualidia, Km 26* ☎*023/34–54–98* ☎*12 rooms* ⚲*In-room: safe. In-hotel: restaurant, no elevator* ▤*No credit cards.*

$$ ⬚**Sofitel Royal Golf.** The large, well-appointed rooms of this luxury hotel are brightened by cheery turquoise and yellow linens and blue-striped arm chairs. Two-story duplex suites with private terraces are particularly beautiful. Views abound on the lush green of the 18-hole golf course fairways surrounded by trees and the jogging trail overlooking the Atlantic. One of the restaurants serves traditional Moroccan cuisine, while the other two are international. The hotel is in a quiet area north of El Jadida, on the right as you drive south. It's out of the range of El Jadida petits taxis, but you can charter a grand taxi. **Pros:** Very quiet area, good for golf. **Con:** No public transportation. ✉*B.P. 116, Rte. de Casablanca, Km 7* ☎*023/35–41–41* ⊕*www.accorhotels. com* ☎*117 rooms, 18 suites* ⚲*In-room: safe, refrigerator, Ethernet. In-hotel: 3 restaurants, bar, golf course, tennis court, pools, gym* ▤*AE, DC, MC, V.*

OUTDOOR ACTIVITIES

GOLF

Royal Golf El Jadida (✉*Rte. de Casablanca Km 7* ☎*023/35–22–51* ⊕*www.golf-maroc.com/morocco/eljadida* ☑*Greens fees 400 DH*) is one of Morocco's finest golf courses. This 18-hole, 6,954 yard, par 72 beauty next to the Atlantic is well worth the journey.

EL OUALIDIA

★ *175 km (109 mi) southwest of Casablanca. 89 km (55 mi) southwest of El Jadida. From El Jadida, follow sign to Jorf Laser.*

As you enter El Oualidia you'll see salt pans at the end of a lagoon. This town is famous for its oysters, and if you visit the oyster parks you can sit right down and eat them after learning how they're cultivated. (Oyster Park 7 is best.) Turn right in the center of town to reach the beach. El Oualidia's bay must be one of the most beautiful places on Morocco's entire Atlantic coast. The fine sand is gently lapped by the calm turquoise waters of the lagoon, and in the distance you can see the white breakers of the sea. The beach is surrounded by a promontory to the south, a gap where the sea enters the lagoon, an island, and another promontory to the north. Around the corner is a beach that seems wholly untouched: sandy bays and dunes bearing tufts of grass

alternate with little rocky hills. The
month of August sees a large influx
of travelers and beach campers
here, and thus far less tranquillity.

GETTING HERE & AROUND

Grands taxis and local buses offer
services to Safi and El Jadida. Both
depart from a stop near the post
office on the main road. **Compagnie
de Transports au Maroc** offers regular

> **SURF'S UP**
>
> Gentle waves make the lagoon
> a good place to learn how to
> surf; experienced surfers will
> find waves to their liking on the
> straightforward Atlantic beaches
> south of town.

service north and south. If you are traveling by car from Marrakesh,
follow the road to Safi and take the scenic coast road to Oualidia. If
you are driving from El Jadida, follow the coast road down to Oualidia
and allow extra time for possible congestion.

TIMING & PRECAUTIONS

Most travelers stay in El Oualidia for one night. Some El Oualidia men
are offended by the presence of unescorted females. **The best approach to
handle unwelcome comments is to ignore them, followed by a verbal rebuke
if necessary. If this is ineffective, summon police.**

ESSENTIALS

Bus Information Compagnie de Transports au Maroc (⊠ *El Jadida-Safi Rd.*
☎ *www.ctm.co.ma*).

WHERE TO STAY

$$ ★ **L'Hippocampe.** This family-run hotel overlooks the lagoon, offering
direct access to the beach. Its spotless and charming rooms are arranged
around a lovely garden, which is at its finest in April and May. The staff
can easily organize a boat trip on the lagoon, possibly combined with
a bracing walk on the northern promontory from the tomb of Sidi
Daoud. Two impressive suites overlook the sea and have particularly
appealing bathrooms and private terraces with tables and chairs, but
most rooms do not have televisions, air-conditioning, or safes. The
combined restaurant-lobby area takes on a warm glow after the sun
goes down—a roaring fire is lighted, and guests are free to take refuge
with a good book, good company, or both. **Pros:** Easy beach access,
friendly staff. **Cons:** Few amenities. ⊠ *Oualidia Plage* ☎ *023/36–61–
08* ☞ *23 rooms, 2 suites* ⚒ *In-room: no a/c (some), no TV (some). In-
hotel: restaurant, bar, pool, no elevator* ☞ *MC, V* ◎ *MAP.*

¢ **Motel Restaurant à l'Araignée Gourmande.** This motel has sea views
and is a good place to eat at reasonable prices even if you aren't stay-
ing overnight. The lobster is, of course, more expensive than anything
else on the menu, but it's superb. The small rooms are less exquisite,
but they're perfectly adequate. While the original building resembles a
Cape Cod beach house, its larger satellite is a more-standard two-story
motor lodge. Rooms are clean and light, however, and the top floor
accesses an ocean-view roof terrace. **Pros:** Tasty restaurant, good value.
Con: Steps to climb. ⊠ *Oualidia Plage* ☎ *023/36–61–44* ☞ *47 rooms*
⚒ *In-room: dial-up. In-hotel: restaurant, no elevator* ▭ *MC, V.*

OUTDOOR ACTIVITIES

Surfland (⊠*B.P. 40, Oualidia, El Jadida* ☏*023/36–61–10*), a surfing school in El Oualidia, runs surfing holidays, including English-speaking instructors and camping accommodations for both adults and children. Surfers staying elsewhere can join up without a reservation if there's enough space.

EN ROUTE The coastal road from El Oualidia to Safi has magnificent views, especially in spring, when the wildflowers are out.

Just off the wild beach about 28 km (17 mi) south of El Oualidia, a **koubba** (*saint's tomb*) is built on a rock in such a way that it's only accessible at low tide. Some of the cliffs here are truly magnificent, reminiscent of the Atlantic coast of Ireland.

Plage Lalla Fatma, 16 km (10 mi) before Safi, is a wonderful discovery, a pristine, empty patch of orange-gold sand beneath rocky cliffs that's good for swimming.

> ### PLAY IT SAFE
>
> A woman traveling alone, or indeed merely walking around on her own, is a cultural problem for many Moroccan men. Don't think you'll enlighten them by flaunting your cultural liberty.
>
> The faux parking guard you ignore will be alone in the street with your car for many hours. It's best to give him 10 DH and figure he really might keep your car from being trashed.

SAFI

69 km (43 mi) southwest of El Oualidia, 157 km (98 mi) southwest of El Jadida, 129 km (80 mi) north of Essaouira, 209 km (130 mi) southwest of Casablanca.

GETTING HERE & AROUND

Buses are fine for trips from Casablanca to Safi. In Safi, one station, Gare Routière, serves all the bus companies and the grands taxis. In Safi the taxi station is next to the bus station. The larger, more roadworthy grands taxis are available for intercity journeys, such as Safi to Oualidia (26 DH) or for longer trips to Marrakesh (67 DH) or Essaouira (62 DH).

Safi has inexpensive metered petits taxis. For local runs, however, it is always advisable to establish an agreed-upon fare before getting in. The going rate for local trips is usually 8 DH.

TIMING & PRECAUTIONS

Most travelers stay in Safi for one night. Safi is generally considered safe, although some travelers may encounter offers for hashish. **The best approach to handle unwelcome offers is to ignore them.**

ESSENTIALS

Bus Information Compagnie de Transports au Maroc (⊠*Ave. President Kennedy* ☏*024/62–21–40*) .

Train Information Office National des Chemins de Fer (*O.N.C.F.* ⊠*Rue de R'bat* ☏*024/46–21–76* ⊕*www.oncf.org.ma*).

Visitor & Tour Information **Délégation du Tourisme de Safi** (⊠ *Rue Imam Malek* ☎ *044/73–05–62*). **Syndicat d'Initiative et du Tourisme de Safi** (⊠ *Ave. de la Liberté* ☎ *044/46–45–53*).

EXPLORING

Safi (Asfi, in Arabic) used to be a fishing port for sardines, but the sardines have since been killed off by pollution from the chemical factory south of town. Despite the industrial presence, however, Safi's **Old Town** retains its charm.

> ## QUINTESSENTIAL SAFI
>
> The clay kilns of the potters' hill surround a **koubba**; wander around and you'll see the different stages of a pot's creation, from throwing to firing to painting to glazing. 🎫 *10 DH* ⊙ *Daily 8:30–6.*
>
> *(For more information on Safi's renowned pottery-making tradition, see Chapter 10.)*

Place de l'Indépendance is next to the medina, and the medina itself is bisected by a street lined with shops. On the ocean side of the square is the **Dar el Bahr** (*House of the Sea*), a 16th-century Portuguese castle.

A few kilometers inland, and best reached by car or taxi, is the **National Ceramic Museum,** housed in a large, old Portuguese fort. Displays present Morocco's various native pottery styles, such as refined blue pieces from Fez and Safi's own pottery (made of red clay and finished in white, black, and green or turquoise and black), including some fine pieces by the renowned master Ahmed Serghini. ☎ *044/62–45–53* 🎫 *10 DH* ⊙ *Wed.–Mon. 8:30–6.*

From the walls of the old fort you have an excellent view of the city, and to the north you can look down onto the **potters' hill,** its clay kilns an attractive pinkish color.

WHERE TO EAT

¢–$$$$ ✕ **Refuge Sidi Bouzid.** On the coast a little north of Safi, this is a reliable
SEAFOOD place for seafood and panoramic views of Safi. A three-course, prix-fixe menu is available. ⊠ *Sidi Bouzid* ☎ *044/46–43–54* 🚫 *No credit cards.*

$–$$ ✕ **La Trattoria.** North of Safi, just beyond the potters' hill, this Italian
ITALIAN restaurant serves pizzas, fish, and other seafood in a pleasant Mediterranean atmosphere. The menu is large and varied, and if you need a break from seafood, there's homemade pasta on offer. ⊠ *Rue Aouinate* ☎ *044/62–09–59* 🚫 *DC, MC, V.*

WHERE TO EAT & STAY

¢ 🏨 **Assif.** On a quiet street in the new part of town, the Assif gets its character from its colors—painted murals enliven the reception area, and the white halls are lined with pink and purple columns. Rooms are substantial, and the suite with a double bed and two twin beds is ideal for a family with children. To get here, follow a series of yellow signs from the traffic circle by the ceramics museum. **Pros:** Spacious rooms, peaceful location. **Con:** Public transportation in area is limited. ⊠ *B.P. 151, Ave. de la Liberté, Plateau Safi* ☎ *044/62–29–40* 🛏 *62 rooms, 1 suite* ♿ *In-room: safe. In-hotel: restaurant* 🚫 *MC, V.*

¢   ⊡**Atlantide.** Once a grande dame, the Atlantide has been restored to some of its original glory. The renovated guest rooms have high ceilings and are equipped with satellite TVs and modern showers. If you prefer the romance of the antique, you can opt for an untouched room with a 1920s armoire and old-fashioned bathtub. The dining room is palatial, recalling perhaps a lodging on a Swiss lake. A large swimming pool is open year-round. **Pros:** Pretty pool area, old-fashioned charm. **Con:** Food is not impressive. ⊠*Rue Chaouki, Safi* ☎*044/46–21–60* ⇥*40 rooms, 2 suites* ⚿*In-room: safe. In-hotel: restaurant, bar, pool* ⊟*AE, MC, V.*

$ ⊡**Hotel Safir.** This hotel has a pleasant terrace with a commanding view over the city of Safi. Though somewhat dated in style and in need of new carpeting, the rooms are spacious, pastel in hue, and furnished with a small settee in an alcove. Facilities are ample, including a playground for kids. The hotel offers free shuttle to three area golf courses. **Pro:** Good for families with children. **Con:** Decor is old and worn. ⊠*Ave. Zerktouni* ☎*044/46–42–99* ⇥*86 rooms, 4 suites* ⚿*In-room: safe, refrigerator. In-hotel: restaurant, bar, pool* ⊟*MC, V.*

SHOPPING

Walk down the hill to the north of the fortress until you come to the **shops** at the foot of the potters' hill. In shop No. 7 you can buy works from the school of Ahmed Serghini; ask to see the room with the most precious pieces. ■ **TIP →** The pottery sold in all these shops is an excellent buy compared to what it would cost elsewhere in the kingdom; attractive turquoise bowls, for example, can be had for around 30 DH.

Fez & Meknès

WITH VOLUBILIS AND MOULAY IDRISS

WORD OF MOUTH

"If you want to step back in time and enjoy watching things crafted and sold the way they were ages ago, then Fez is for you. It is not charming or quaint—it is real and sometimes a bit shocking."

—gruezi

"Visiting the Saturday morning market in Moulay Idriss was fascinating. It was loud and messy and everything about it took me back a hundred years ago. Donkeys everywhere carrying merchandise, fruits and vegetables displayed on the ground, and locals unaware of tourism and the 21st century made it a great experience."

—Castellanese

Updated by
Victoria Tang

FEZ AND MEKNÈS ARE, RESPECTIVELY, the Arab and Berber capitals of Morocco, ancient centers of learning, culture, and craftsmanship that both deserve their standing as UNESCO World Heritage Sites. Long recognized as Morocco's intellectual and spiritual nerve center, Fez has one of the world's oldest universities as well as one of the largest intact medieval quarters with an active population of 100,000 (one-tenth of the city's total). Meknès, with 450,000 inhabitants, offers a chance to experience all the sights, sounds, and smells of Fez on a somewhat smaller, more manageable scale. Witnessing dynamic economic growth and attracting international events, both Fez and Meknès remain two of Morocco's most authentic and fascinating cities, outstanding for their history and culture and likely to rival Marrakesh as top tourist destinations.

ORIENTATION & PLANNING

ORIENTATION

Situated between the mountainous Middle Atlas and plains of the Rif, Fez and Meknès are rewarding visits with medieval monuments, sumptuous palaces, imposing ramparts, and vibrant markets. Fez is by far the grander city, known best for its artisanal craftsmanship, its ancient university, and the Kairouine Mosque, the second largest in North Africa. For a calmer experience, head to Meknès, where there will be fewer tourists and less hassle from hustlers. Side trips to the ancient Roman ruins in Volubilis and sacred village of Moulay Idriss Zerhoun add to the exotic experience for those who have more time to explore.

Fez. Founded in the 9th century, Fez is Morocco's grandest and oldest imperial city. Within the medieval stone walls of the medina there are two distinct historic areas: Fez el-Bali (Old Fez) and Fez el-Djedid (New Fez). Farther south, the Ville Nouvelle (New Town) is a modern district built in 1912, attracting wealthier residents and strong commercial activity. Most Fassis live outside the dense maze of more than 9,500 narrow passageways of the medina. Yet it is this labyrinthine heart of the city enclosing historic minarets, souks, mosques, museums, fountains, and squares that gets the well-deserved attention of most visitors throughout the year.

Meknès. Founded in the 11th century by the Almoravids, Meknès became an imperial city under the rule of Sultan Moulay Ismail, who provided the town with impressive palaces, gardens, fortresses, gates, squares, and mosques. A pleasure to discover by foot, taxi, or caléche (horse-drawn carriage), there are three distinct areas in Meknès—the ancient medina with its central Place el-Hadime, the Imperial City that contains the most impressive monuments, and the Ville Nouvelle (New Town), where many good restaurants and hotels are located.

TOP REASONS TO GO

Step into a time warp: Fez el-Bali is the world's largest active medieval city, and a sensorial vacation from modern life and technology.

Watch artisans in action: from leather-workers to wood-carvers, coppersmiths, weavers, and potters there are hundreds of shops and studios in both cities where you can buy fine wares and see how they're made.

Indulge your senses at the Meknès food souk: In Place el-Hedime

you can sample the famous olives, spices, and fruit, available in a dizzying of colors and flavors.

Explore an archaeological wonder in Volubilis: A short trip from Meknès, these well-preserved Roman ruins date back to the 3rd century BC and are considered the most impressive in the country.

PLANNING

WHEN TO GO

Busloads of tourists and intense heat tend to suppress the romance of just about anything. Try to visit Fez and Meknès between October and early March, before the high season or extreme sun kicks in. Spring is considered the best season to travel throughout Morocco since the weather is warm and clear in all regions. Summer months can be oppressive with crowds and stifling temperatures. Winters are typically mild with cold nights, occasional frost, and rainfall. Before planning your trip, keep in mind major Islamic holidays such as Ramadan (when operating hours are shortened, activities may be closed, and restaurants will have limited service) and annual international events, such as the Festival of World Sacred Music held every summer in Fez. Note that, as with everything in Morocco, travel commodities like hotel rooms and local car rentals are negotiable, and you'll have more bargaining power in the low season.

RESTAURANTS & CUISINE

Every Moroccan city has its own way of preparing the national dishes. *Harira,* the spicy bean-based soup filled with vegetables and meat, may be designated as Fassi (from Fez) or Meknessi (from Meknès) and varies slightly in texture and ingredients. *Tagines,* stewed combinations of vegetables and meat or fish cooked in conical earthenware vessels, are nearly always delicious, as is couscous, served traditionally on Friday in Moroccan households. *Pastilla,* a phyllo-pastry pie with pigeon or chicken, is a Fez specialty, cloyingly sweet with powdered sugar and cinnamon. *Mechoui,* roast lamb, must usually be ordered at least several hours in advance. *Kebabs* are grilled brochettes of meat. Some of Morocco's best and cheapest food is sold in the souks, where you can grab an excellent harira.

Note that few medina restaurants in Fez and Meknès are licensed to serve alcohol. Proprietors generally allow oenophiles to bring their own wine, as long as they enjoy it discreetly. Larger hotels and luxury riads have well-stocked bars that serve wine, beer and liquor, as do more-upscale restaurants.

WHAT IT COSTS IN DIRHAMS				
¢	$	$$	$$$	$$$$
AT DINNER under 100DH	100DH–200DH	200DH–300DH	300DH–400DH	over 400DH

Prices are per person for a main course at dinner.

HOTELS

Hotels in Fez range from the luxurious and the comprehensively comfortable, such as the Sofitel Palais Jamaï, Le Méridien's Mérinides, and the Jnan Palace, to more-personal, atmospheric riads (renovated guesthouses and villas) that offer everything from kitschy decor to authentic traditional living. Hotels nearest Fez el-Bali are best, as the medina is probably what you came to see. In Meknès, there is a more limited choice, with a few gems competing at the top end. The Palais Didi and Ryad Bahia are lovingly restored houses. The Hôtel Transatlantique is the best combination of old-world digs overlooking the Imperial City's walls. For a modern alternative, the Hôtel Rif is in the Ville Nouvelle.

WHAT IT COSTS IN DIRHAMS				
¢	$	$$	$$$	$$$$
FOR TWO PEOPLE under 600DH	600DH–1,200DH	1,200DH–1,600DH	1,600DH–2,000DH	over 2,000DH

All prices are for a standard double room, excluding tax.

WHAT TO WEAR

Comfort is key. In Morocco, consider climate and culture when deciding what to wear. Islam is a state religion and very short skirts and shorts, and tops that expose shoulders, arms, and chest are likely to be offensive. Bathing suits are acceptable only at the beach; bathing topless or nude anywhere is strictly forbidden. On the street, Moroccan men typically wear long pants, long-sleeved shirts, or kaftans. For women, most wear loose-fitting pants and shirts or full-length robes. Locals are usually tolerant of tourists, but it's advised to dress conservatively. You aren't expected to be covered from head to toe; however, skimpy dress will attract unwanted attention and be culturally insensitive. Pack lightweight cotton fabrics for summer and waterproof attire for winter. Leave formal attire and expensive jewelry at home.

SAFETY

In general, Fez and Meknès are very safe cities. In Fez, less in Meknès, pickpocketing and unwanted hassling from hustlers will be the biggest concern. Harassment from those offering to be guides is best avoided by smiling and firmly saying "no thank you," preferably in Arabic or French; never become visibly agitated, as it could exacerbate the situation.

Keep backpacks and bags close to the body. Never expose a wallet brimming with cash or expensive electronics. Pay attention to your surroundings, especially in crowded souks and squares, where the majority of pickpockets congregate. You can safely explore the medina during the day. At night, the many barely lighted passageways can be intimidating.

Women traveling alone or in small groups should exercise care and common sense. A lone female (tourists and locals alike) will attract unwanted attention, especially if dressed in what may be considered provocative clothes. Be aware of your surroundings, dress modestly, and use a registered guide to avoid constant hassling. Single women shouldn't travel alone in remote regions.

For gay and lesbian travelers, discretion is recommended in conservative towns like Fez and Meknès. Disabled and elderly travelers will have particular challenges negotiating poorly paved walkways, steep inclines, and ill-equipped hotels and restaurants.

FEZ

Fez is a living work of art and the perfect medieval labyrinth—mysterious, bewildering, mesmerizing. Passing through one of the *babs* (gates) into Fez el-Bali is like entering a time warp, and the occasional satellite dish is your only reminder that you're at the beginning of the third, not the second, millennium AD. The din of hammering coppersmiths and the cries of *"Balek!"* ("Watch out!") from donkey drivers pushing through crowded alleys mingle with the smells of cooking, spices, mint, dung, leather, and cedar wood, all dramatically illuminated by shafts of sunlight bursting down through the thatched roof of the *kissaria* (covered markets).

GETTING HERE & AROUND
The main gateway to the region is Fès-Saïss Airport. Driving to downtown Fez takes about 30 minutes. A taxi will cost around 120 DH; a local bus 4 DH. Hourly Compagnie de Transports Marocains buses cover the Fez–Meknès route. The trip takes about one hour and costs 20 DH. The bus to Marrakesh takes about 10 hours and costs 150 to 170 DH. The bus to Casablanca takes five hours and costs 90 DH. Three buses daily connect Fez with Tangier in six hours for 90 DH.

Ten trains run between Fez and Meknès each day. They cost 25 DH and take 45 minutes. There are seven daily trains to Casablanca (five hours, 155 DH) via Rabat (four hours, 90 DH). There are five daily trains to Marrakesh (eight hours, 250 DH). The train to Tangier leaves once a day, takes five hours, and costs about 125 DH. The Fez train station is on the north side of the Ville Nouvelle, a 10-minute walk from the center of town.

Grands taxis are large, usually shared taxis (up to six passengers) that make long-distance runs between cities. This can be faster, more comfortable, and better value than bus travel. The local *petits taxis* are

TAKE A TOUR

There's much to be said in favor of employing a guide in Fez; you'll be left alone by faux guides and hustlers, and if your guide is good you'll learn much and be able to see more of your surroundings than when having to read and navigate as you move around. On the other hand, getting lost in Fez el-Bali is one of those great travel experiences. Maps of the medina really do work, and the explanations of the sites to visit included in this guidebook are as good as you can get from any private guide, and, moreover, perfectly intelligible.

The tourist office and your hotel are the best sources for qualified guides.

An official guide from the tourist office costs around 200 DH–250 DH for half a day and 300 DH–350 DH for a full day.

Local Agent Referral Carlson Wagonlit (⊠ 5, Immeuble du Grand Hotel, Bd. Mohammed V s/n ☎ 035/62–29–58 ⊕ www.carlson wagonlit.com.

Travel Agencies Objective Maroc (⊠ 9, rue de Turquie s/n ☎ 035/65–28–16 ⊕ www.obmaroc.com).

Tour-Operator Recommendation ONMT (⊠ Pl. de la Résistance–Immeuble Bennani ☎ 035/62–34–60).

metered, take up to three passengers, and may not leave the city limits. If the driver refuses to turn on the meter or agree to a reasonable price, don't hesitate to get out. There's a 50% surcharge after 8 PM.

TIMING & PRECAUTIONS

Fez is an enigmatic, exotic city best explored on foot. Walking beneath one of the imposing arched babs, or gateways, and into the maze of cobbled streets stimulates all the senses. Summer months can be unbearably hot with little air circulation, especially beneath canopied and crowded alleys. The best time to tour is the morning; crowds and temperatures won't be too great. Nights are cool throughout the year with a refreshing desert breeze. Remember that Friday is a traditional day of prayer, and many establishments are closed.

ESSENTIALS

Bus Contacts Compagnie de Transports Marocains (⊠ Ave. Mohammed V ☎ 035/73–29–92 ⊕ www.ctm.co.ma).

Currency Exchange Société Generale (⊠ Ave. Lalla Meriem ☎ 035/62–13–47).

Internet Cyber Club (⊠ Rue Abdelkarim el-Khattabi s/n ☎ 035/62–62–86). **Espace Cyber** (⊠ Ave. Hassan II Ville Nouvelle ☎ 035/6– 37–52) **London Cyber** (⊠ Ave. Allal Fassi ☎ 035/62–61–53).

Mail & Shipping Main Post Office (⊠ Ave. Hassan II s/n ☎ 035/63–02–36) **Medina Post Office** (⊠ Pl. de l'Istiqlal s/n ☎ 035/63–92–61).

Medical Assistance Clinique Ryad (⊠ Pl. Hussein de Jordainie ☎ 035/96–00–00). **Hôpital Ghassani** (⊠ Dhar Mehraz district ☎ 035/62–27–77).

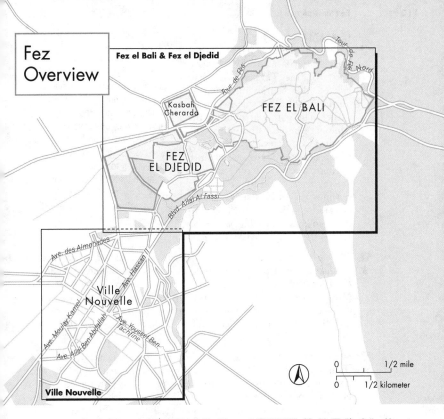

Fez Overview

Fez el Bali & Fez el Djedid

FEZ EL BALI

FEZ EL DJEDID

Kasbah Cherarda

Ville Nouvelle

Ave. des Almohads

Ave. Hassan II

Ave. Moulay Kamel

Ave. Allal Ben Abdallah

Ave. Youssef Ben Tachfine

Ville Nouvelle

Blvd. Allal Al Fassi

Tour de Fès

Tour de Fès Nord

0   1/2 mile
0   1/2 kilometer

Rental Cars Avis (✉ *50, bd. Chefchaouni* ☎ *035/62–69–69* ✉ *Fès-Saïss Airport* ☎ *035/62–67–46*). **Budget** (✉ *Bd. Lalla Asmaa* ☎ *035/94–00–92*). **Hertz** (✉ *Ave. Lalla Meryem* ☎ *035/62–28–12* ✉ *Fès-Saïss Airport* ☎ *035/65–18–23*).

Train Information Fez Station (✉ *Ave. des Almohads* ☎ *035/93–03–33*).

Visitor & Tour Info Fez Tourist Office (✉ *Pl. de la Résistance–Immeuble Bennani* ☎ *035/62–34–60*).

EXPLORING

FEZ EL-BALI

Fez el-Bali is a living crafts workshop and market that has changed little in the past millennium. With no cars and some 1,000 *derbs* (dead-end alleys), it beckons the walker on an endless and absorbing odyssey. Exploring this honeycomb of 9th-century alleys and passageways is a challenging adventure. Fez isn't really yours, however, until you've tackled it on your own, become hopelessly lost a few times, and survived to tell the tale. Once you have a sense of the place, about the worst that can happen is that a young boy will offer to take you wherever you want to go. Five or 10 dirhams will more than satisfy his commercial instincts; and for another five and a clear explanation that you would now prefer to continue alone, he'll vanish.

TOP ATTRACTIONS

13 Andalusian Mosque. This mosque was built in AD 859 by Myriam, sister of the Fatima who had erected the Kairaouine Mosque on the river's other side two years earlier. The gate was built by the Almohads in the 12th century. The detailed wood carvings in the eaves, which bear a striking resemblance to those in the Fondouk Nejjarine, are the main thing to see here, as the mosque itself is set back and elevated, making it hard to examine from outside. ⊠*Rue Nekhaline* ☞*Entrance restricted to Muslims.*

> **WHAT IS . . .?**
>
> The word *medersa* comes from *madrassa,* the classical Arabic word for "school"—which meant, of course, Koranic school, in which the only objective was the memorization of the Koran. Medersas housed students while they learned to recite the Koran and the Hadith, the words and deeds of the prophet; once they mastered these, they progressed to more analytical studies.

7 Attarine Medersa. ★ The Attarine Medersa (Koranic school) was named for local spice merchants known as *attar.* Founded by Sultan Abou Saïd in the 14th century as a students' dormitory attached to the Kairaouine Mosque next door, its graceful proportions, elegant, geometric carved-cedar ornamentation, and its excellent state of preservation make it arguably the loveliest medersa in Fez. ⊠*Boutouil Kairaouine* ☉*Daily 9–1 and 3–6:30.*

1 Bab Boujeloud. ★ Built in 1913 by General Hubert Lyautey, Moroccan commander under the French protectorate, this gate is 1,000 years younger than the rest of the medina, yet generally considered its most beautiful point of entry. The side facing out is covered with blue ceramic tiles painted with flowers and calligraphy; the inside is green, the official color of Islam—or of peace, depending on the interpretation. ⊠*Pl. Boujeloud.*

2 Bou Inania Medersa. ★ From outside Bab Boujeloud you will have seen this medersa's green-tile tower, generally considered the most beautiful of the Kairaouine University's 14th-century residential colleges. It was built by order of Abou Inan, the first ruler of the Merenid dynasty, which would become the most decisive ruling clan in Fez's development. The main components of the medersa's stunningly intricate decorative artwork are: the green-tile roofing; the cedar eaves and upper patio walls carved in floral and geometrical motifs; the carved-stucco mid-level walls; the ceramic-tile lower walls covered with calligraphy (Kufi script, essentially cursive Arabic) and geometric designs; and, finally, the marble floor. The most dazzling display is the carved cedar, each square inch a masterpiece of handcrafted sculpture involving long hours of the kind of concentration required to memorize the Koran. The black belt of ceramic tile around the courtyard bears Arabic script reading THIS IS A PLACE OF LEARNING and other such exhortatory academic messages. ⊠*Talâa Kebira* 💰*20 DH* ☉*Daily 9–7.*

4 Fontaine Nejjarine. This ceramic-tile, cedar-ceiling fountain is one of the most beautiful and historic of its kind in Fez el-Bali. The first fountain down from Bab Boujeloud, Fontaine Nejjarine seems a miniature version of the Nejjarine *fondouk* (medieval inn), with its geometrically decorated tiles and intricately carved cedar eaves overhead.

8 **Kairaouine Mosque.** This is considered one of the most important mosques in Morocco. One look through the main doorway will give you an idea of the immensity of this place. With about 10,760 square feet, the Kairaouine was Morocco's largest mosque until Casablanca's Hassan II Mosque came along in the early 1990s. Built by the Kairaouine Fatima in 857, the Kairaouine Mosque became the home of the West's first university and the world's foremost center of learning at the beginning of the second millennium. Stand at the entrance door's left side for a peek through the dozen horseshoe arches into the mihrab (marked by a hanging light). An east-facing alcove or niche used for leading prayer, the mihrab is rounded and covered with an arch designed to project sound back through the building. Lean in and look up to the brightly painted and intricately carved wood ceiling. If you're lucky enough to visit during the early morning cleaning, two huge wooden doors by the entrance swing open, providing a privileged view of the vast interior. For a good view of the courtyard, also head to the rooftop of the Attarine Medersa. ⊠ *Boutouil Kairaouine*

NEED A BREAK? Spend some time around the Fontaine Nejjarine, not only to view the intricately carved roof that covers this 14th-century cistern, but to appreciate the central role of water in the life of this medieval city. Carved cedar eaves and intensely decorated ceramic tile work are the setting for a meeting place where transport workers water their donkeys, young girls giggle in delight over some shared confidence, and young boys crouch next to the gushing faucet for a drink. Fundamental to prayer rituals as well as every other aspect of life, Fez's fountains bear inscriptions reminding the thirsty that the gift of water is Allah's first and most important blessing.

9 **Musée Nejjarine des Arts et Métiers du Bois** (*Nejjarine Museum of Wood Arts and Crafts*). This 14th-century fondouk is without a doubt the medina's most modern restored monument. The three-story patio displays Morocco's various native woods, 18th- and 19th-century woodworking tools, and a series of antique wooden doors and pieces of furniture. The rooftop tearoom has panoramic views over the medina. Don't miss the former jail cell on the ground floor, or the large scales—a reminder of the building's original functions, commerce on the patio floor and lodging on the three levels above. ■ TIP→ Check out the palatial, cedar-ceiling public bathrooms, certainly the finest of their kind in Fez. ⊠ *Pl. Nejjarine* ☎ 035/74–05–80 ☜ 20 DH ☼ *Daily 10–7.*

11 **Place Seffarine.** The wide, triangular souk of the *dinandiers*, or coppersmiths, is a welcome open space, a comfortable break from the medina's tight crags and corners. Donkeys and their masters wait for transport work here, and a couple of trees are reminders that this was once a fertile valley alongside the Fez River. Copper and brass bowls are wrought and hammered over fires around the market's edge, and the smells of donkey droppings and soldering irons blend in the sun. Looking into the Kairaouine Mosque at the top of the square is the

Fez el Bali & Fez el Djedid

KEY

❶ *Exploring sights*

① *Hotels & Restaurants*

↑ TO MEKNES

Army Museum

Kasbah Cherarda ◆

Cimetière de Bab Segma

Kasbah el Nouar ◆

Bab Mahrouk

⑨ Water Clock

Place Bagdadi

⑧ **①** **②**

Place Bou Jeloud **⑦**

Cimetière de Bab Mahrouk

⑮

Bab Boujat

Blvd. Moulay Hassan **⑩**

⑲ Jardin Jnan Sbil

BATHA

FEZ EL DJEDID

Bab Jebala

Ave. de l'Unesco

⑱

Grande Rue de Fès-Jdid

Ave. de Liberté

Bab Smarine

⑯

Palace Gardens

Blvd. Bou Ksissat

⑰

Place des Alaouites

Grande Rue du Mellah

Ave. du Batha

Blvd. des Saadiens

◆ taxi stand

Bab Lamar

Bd. des Alaouites

Blvd. Moulay Youssef

Blvd. Allal El Fassi

| 0 | | 1/4 mile |
| 0 | | 1/4 kilometer |

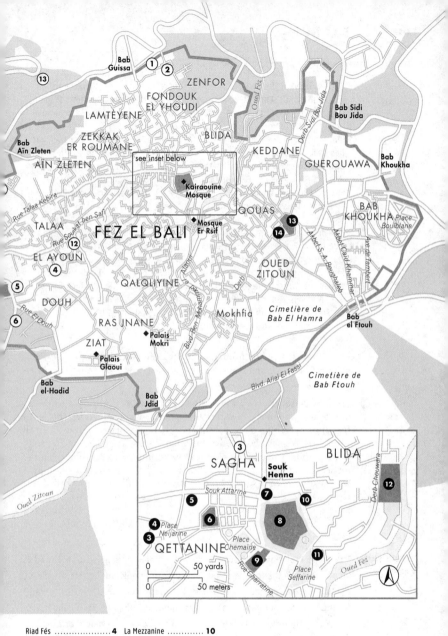

Bab Guissa ①②

ZENFOR

Bab Sidi Bou Jida

FONDOUK EL YHOUDI

⑬

LAMTÈYENE

ZEKKAK ER ROUMANE

Bab Aïn Zleten

AÏN ZLETEN

BLIDA

KEDDANE

GUEROUAWA

Bab Khoukha

see inset below

Kairaouine Mosque

QOUAS

BAB KHOUKHA Place Bouiblane

TALAA

Mosque Er Rsif

⑬
⑭

Rue Talaa Kebira

Rue Soukat ben Safi

FEZ EL BALI

EL AYOUN

⑫

④

OUED ZITOUN

⑤

QALQLIYINE

Rue El Douh

DOUH

⑥

RAS JNANE

Mokhfia

Cimetière de Bab El Hamra

Bab el Ftouh

Palais Mokri

ZIAT

Palais Glaoui

Cimetière de Bab Ftouh

Bab el-Hadid

Bab Jdid

Blvd. Allal El Fassi

Oued Zitoun

SAGHA

BLIDA

③

Souk Henna

Souk Attarine

⑫

⑤

⑦

⑩

④ Place Nejjarine

⑥

⑧

③

QETTANINE

Place Chemaïne

⑪

0   50 yards

⑨

Place Seffarine

Oued Fez

0   50 meters

Rue Chrarratine

Derb Chouwara

Riad Fés .... **4**   La Mezzanine **10**
Riyad Shéhérazade .... **12**   Le Kasbah **7**
Ryad Mabrouka .... **11**   Medina Café **8**
Sofitel Palais Jamaï .... **2**   Palais Tijani **9**

Restaurant   ▼

Al Firdaous **1**
Dar Saada **3**

A BIT OF HISTORY

Fez has been at the heart of Morocco's Arabic and Islamic development since shortly after the arrival of the first religious refugees from the Middle East in AD 788. Built in the Fez River's fertile basin—the Oued Fez, also known as Oued el-Yawahir, the River of Pearls—Fez el-Bali (literally, Fez the Old) was founded in AD 808 by Moulay Idriss II, son of Morocco's founder, Moulay Idriss I. The medina is divided into two quarters on either side of the Fez River. The Andalusian Quarter originally housed refugees from Moorish Spain, who had begun to flee the Christian Reconquest; the Kairaouine Quarter originally housed refugees from Kairaouine, Tunisia, who fled westward in search of a purer form of Islamic worship. Always the more important of the two demographically and commercially, the Kairaouine Quarter was especially expanded under the Merenid dynasty, during Fez's 14th-century golden age. Fez el-Djedid (New Fez) was founded in 1276 by the Merenid rulers, who needed extra space for their palaces as well as a sense of distance from the population itself. The original and the most imperial of Morocco's Imperial Cities, Fez was the nation's capital in the 9th, 12th–14th, and 16th centuries. The Ville Nouvelle was built by the French after they established their protectorate in 1912.

Kairaouine University library, which once housed the world's best collection of Islamic literature. Recently restored, it is open only to Muslim scholars.

⑭ Sahrij Medersa. Built by the Merenids in the 14th century and showing its age, one of the medina's finest medersas is named for the *sahrij (pool)* on which its patio is centered. Rich chocolate-color cedar wall carvings have visibly faded from intense sun exposure and the zellij mosaic tiling, some of the oldest in the country, are crumbling, but the medersa remains active, providing rooms and an open bathing area for mostly Senegalese students of Koranic studies. Head up the narrow steps leading to empty rooms over the central patio—you may hear the chanting of Koranic verses or see numerous birds roosting in the ancient eaves. ⊠ *Andalusian Quarter* ☜ *20 DH* ☉ *Daily 9–1 and 3–6:30.*

FEZ FACTS

The basic elements without which a traditional Islamic neighborhood is incomplete are the local mosque, medersa, fondouk (shelter for travelers), public fountain, and collective bakery, which simultaneously heats the water for the hammam, or public bath. Fez is composed of some 350 communities or neighborhoods, each of which contains all pillars of neighborhood life. Look for a small cluster of women carrying baking dishes under their arms and you'll know you have found two of the six essentials: the public bakery and the hammam.

❺ Souk el-Henna. This little henna market is one of the medina's most picturesque squares, with a massive, gnarled fig tree in the center and rows of spices, hennas, kohls, and aphrodisiacs for sale in the stalls and shops around the edges. The ceramic shops on the way into the henna souk sell a wide variety of typically blue Fassi pottery. At the square's end is a plaque dedicated to the Maristan Sidi Frej, a medical center and psychiatric and teaching hospital built by the Merenid ruler Youssef Ibn Yakoub in 1286. Used as a model for the world's first mental hospital—founded in Valencia, Spain, in 1410—the Maristan operated until 1944.

⑫ **Terrasse des Tanneurs.** The medieval tanneries are at once beautiful, for their ancient dyeing vats of reds, yellows, and blues, and unforgettable, for the nauseating smell of rotting animal flesh on sheep, goat, cow, and camel skins. The terrace overlooking the dyeing vats is high enough to escape the place's full fetid power and get a spectacular view over the multicolor vats. Absorb both the process and the finished product at No. 2 Chouara Lablida, just past Rue Mechatine (named for the combs made from animals' horns): the store is filled with loads of leather goods, including coats, bags, and babouches (traditional slippers). One of the shopkeepers will explain what's going on in the tanneries below—how the skins are placed successively in saline solution, lime, pigeon droppings, and then any of several natural dyes: poppies for red, tumeric for yellow, saffron for orange, indigo for blue, and mint for green. Barefoot workers in shorts pick up skins from the bottoms of the dyeing vats with their feet, then work them manually. Though this may look like the world's least desirable job, the work is relatively well paid and in demand for a strong export market. ✉2, *Chouara Lablida.*

⑥ **Zaouia of Moulay Idriss II.** Originally built by the Idriss dynasty in the 9th century in honor of the city's founder—just 33 at the time of his death—this *zaouia* (sanctuary) was restored by the Merenid dynasty in the 13th century and has became one of the medina's holiest shrines. Particularly known for his *baraka* (divine protection), Moulay Idriss II has an especially strong cult among women seeking fertility and pilgrims hoping for good luck. The wooden beam at the entrance, about 6 feet from the ground, was originally placed there to keep Jews, Christians, and donkeys out of the *horm,* the sacred area surrounding the shrine itself. Inside the horm, Moroccans have historically enjoyed official sanctuary—they cannot be arrested if sought by the law. Look through the doorway and you'll see the saint's tomb at the far right corner, with the fervently faithful burning candles and incense and touching the tomb's silk-brocade covering. Note the rough wooden doors themselves, worn smooth with hundreds of years of kissing and caressing the wood for baraka. ✉*Boutouil Kairaouine, on north side of mosque* ☉*Daily 24 hrs* ☞*Entrance restricted to Muslims.*

WORTH NOTING

⑨ **Cherratine Medersa.** Constructed in 1670 by Moulay er Rachid, this is one of Fez's two Alaouite medersas. Less ornate than the 14th-century medersas of the Merenids, this one is more functional, designed to hold more than 200 students. It's interesting primarily as a contrast to the intricate craftsmanship and decorative intent of the Merenid structures. ✉*Derb Zaouia* 🎫*20 DH* ☉*Daily 9–1 and 3–6:30.*

🔟 **Fondouk Tsetouanien.** Named for the traders from Tétouan who traded and lodged here, this fondouk is the medina's most original. With its jumble of balconies, ground-floor scales, and rug and leather dealers, it seems to come closest to the look of the fondouks in Delacroix and Fortuny paintings. Fondouks were great centers of ribaldry and intrigue in the Middle Ages, and some sense of this vitality seems to have survived the passage of time. ✉ *Boutouil Kairaouine* 🕙 *Daily 24 hrs.*

FEZ EL-DJEDID

TOP ATTRACTIONS

Fez el-Djedid (New Fez) lies southwest of Bab Boujeloud between Fez el-Bali and the Ville Nouvelle. Built after 1273 by the Merenid dynasty as a government seat and stronghold, it remained the administrative center of Morocco until 1912, when Rabat took over this role and diminished this area's visibility and activity. The three distinct segments of Fez el-Djedid consist of the Royal Palace in the west, the Jewish Quarter in the south, and Muslim District in the east.

> **DID YOU KNOW?**
>
> Founded in the 10th century, the Kairaouine University is, unbeknownst to many, the Western world's first center of higher education, predating Oxford, La Sorbonne, and Bologna. It has always enrolled some 2,000 students, and its library of 30,000 volumes, one of the world's greatest in the Middle Ages, is still one of the most significant in Arabic scholarship. Some of its most famous students are Averroës, Maimonides, and Pope Sylvester II. Sylvester II (died 1003), a master mathematician, introduced the zero into European mathematics.

🔟 **Bab es Seba.** Named for the seven (*seba*) brothers of Moulay Abdellah who reigned during the 18th century, the Gate of Seven connects two open spaces originally designed for military parades and royal ceremonies, the Petit Méchouar and Vieux Méchouar. It was from this gate that Prince Ferdinand, brother of Duarte, king of Portugal, was hanged head-down for four days in 1437. (He had been captured during a failed Portuguese invasion of Tangier, and Portugal had failed to raise the ransom for his release.) His remains were subsequently stuffed and displayed here for 29 years.

NEED A BREAK?   There are few restaurants in Fez el-Djedid. However, the quiet café **La Noria** (✉ *43, Batha* ☎ *035/62–54–22*), just down to the right of Bab Dekaken by the Fez River at the Bab Boujeloud gardens' southwest corner, is a welcome respite from the turbulent streets. Mint tea and tagines are available.

🔟 **Dar el-Makhzen.** Fez's Royal Palace and gardens are strictly closed to the public, but they're an impressive sight even from the outside. From Place des Alaouites take a close look at the door's giant brass knockers, made by artisans from Fez el-Bali, as well as the brass doors themselves. Inside are various palaces, gardens, and parade grounds, as well as a medersa founded in 1320. One of the palaces and wonders of Dar el-Makhzen, Dar el-Qimma, has intricately engraved and painted ceilings. The street running along the palace's southeast side is Rue

Bou Khessissat, one side of which is lined with typically ornate residential facades from the Mellah's edge. Note: Security in this area is high and should be respected. Guards watch visitors carefully and warn that photographs of the palace are forbidden.

⑰ Mellah. With its characteristically ornate balconies and forged-iron windows, the Mellah was created in the 15th century when the Jews, forced out of the medina in one of Morocco's recurrent pogroms, were removed from their previous ghetto near Bab Guissa and set up as royal financial consultants and buffers between the Merenid rulers and the people. Fez's Jewish community suffered repressive measures until the beginning of the French protectorate in 1912. Faced with an uncertain future after Morocco gained independence in 1956, nearly all of Fez's Jews migrated to Israel, the United States, or Casablanca.

> **WHAT IS . . .?**
>
> The word *mellah* essentially means "quarter," but it originally came from the Arabic word for salt (*melh*). Morocco's Jewish quarters allegedly got this name from the Arab rulers' onetime habit of draining and salting the heads of decapitated rebels before they were impaled on the city gates for public view (Jews were hired to assist in the salting). An alternate theory is that the name refers to the fact that when the Jews migrated from Spain in the 15th century they were allotted a salty swamp area in Fez by the ruling Merenids.

⑮ Museum of Moroccan Arts. Housed in **Dar Batha**, a late-19th-century Andalusian palace built by Moulay el Hassan, the museum of Moroccan Arts has one of Morocco's finest handicrafts collections. The display of pottery, for which Fez is particularly famous, includes rural earthenware crockery and elaborate plates painted with geometrical patterns. Other displays feature embroidery stitched with real gold, astrolabes from the 11th to the 18th century, illuminated Korans, and Berber carpets and kilims. ✉ *Pl. de l'Istiqlal* ☎ *035/63–41–16* 💰 *20 DH* ⊙ *Wed.–Mon. (except national holidays) 8:30–noon and 2:30–6.*

WORTH NOTING

⑱ Moulay Abdellah Quarter. Built by the Merenids as a government seat and a stronghold against their subjects, this area lost its purpose when Rabat became the Moroccan capital under the French protectorate in 1912. Subsequently a red-light district filled with brothels and dance halls, the quarter was closed to foreigners for years. Historic highlights include the vertically green-striped **Moulay Abdellah Mosque** and the **Great Mosque Abu Haq,** built by the Merenid sultan in 1276.

WHERE TO EAT

Culinary pleasures are everywhere in Fez. From simple food stalls and cafés (for grilled meat kebabs, honey-laden pastries, and fresh mint tea) to gourmet restaurants (for succulent tagines, couscous, and mechoui), there is no shortage of outstanding dining options for every budget.

FEZ EL-BALI

$$$–$$$$
MOROCCAN

✗ **Al Firdaous.** Moroccan tagines, pastillas, and couscous are just the beginning here: Al Firdaous (Arabic for "paradise") offers Moroccan art, belly dancing, and Berber Gnaoua music along with excellent cuisine and service. Occasional tour groups notwithstanding, it delivers a complete evening of Moroccan cuisine and culture. ✉ *10, rue Zenjfour* ☎ *035/63–43–43* 🖃 *AE, DC, MC, V.*

> ### WHAT ABOUT THE VILLE NOUVELLE?
>
> The Ville Nouvelle is a modern oasis with tree-lined avenues, contemporary hotels, fashionable boutiques, and upscale residences. Considerable commercial development is taking place to attract younger, affluent Fassis. There are no outstanding historical sites, but visit for newer cafés, restaurants, and lodging.

$$$–$$$$
MOROCCAN

✗ **Dar Saada.** This 16th-century mid-medina palace is one of Fez's well-established culinary retreats but is only open for lunch. The kitchen is known for the quality and quantity of everything from beef tagines to pigeon pastilla to mechoui, which must be ordered a day in advance. High ceilings and elaborate woodwork add to the sensorial rush of the place. ✉ *21, Souk el-Attarine* ☎ *035/63–73–71* ⚐ *Reservations essential* 🖃 *AE, DC, MC, V.*

$–$$
MOROCCAN

✗ **Le Kasbah.** The second-floor tables perched over the street at this handsome spot just below Bab Boujeloud offer an entertaining look down into the street life below. The harira, tagines, vegetarian couscous, and other Moroccan specialties are expertly interpreted here. ✉ *Rue Serrajine* ☎ *035/63–34–30* 🖃 *AE, DC, MC, V.*

$$$$
MOROCCAN

✗ **Medina Café.** Next to the most important gate into the medina, this reliable little winner offers excellent people-watching and simple Moroccan cuisine in a setting distinguished by well-crafted wood and ceramic elements and a lively buzz. Ask for the daily specials ✉ *6, Derb Mernissi Bab Boujeloud* ☎ *035/63–34–30* 🖃 *AE, DC, MC, V.*

$–$$
MOROCCAN

✗ **La Mezzanine.** A five-minute walk from Fez el-Djedid, sleek stainless-steel café tables stand outside a contemporary glass-and-gray-stone restaurant and lounge-bar that is fast becoming the "in" place for young and fashionable Moroccans. A haven of cool, enter the air-conditioned ground and upper floor, passing designer tables and well-stocked bar, and carefully maneuver the slick stairway to a rooftop terrasse lined with fuschia cushions and oversize lanterns that overlooks the lush garden flora. Enjoy a casual meal of salads, fusion tapas such as Roquefort-filled *briouates* (spicy dumplings) or tapenade of Moroccan olives with a refreshing cocktail or fresh fruit juice. A lemon tart or sorbet is a simple pleasure at this chic spot managed by an equally hip and friendly staff. ✉ *17, Kasbat Chams* ☎ *011/07–83–36* 🖃 *MC, V.*

$–$$
MOROCCAN

✗ **Palais Tijani.** Near the Tijani Mosque in Fez el-Bali, this commendable traditional restaurant serves homestyle Morocaan dishes with warm service and genuine Fassi ambience. Delectable *briouates au kefta* (ground-beef dumplings) and mechoui are staples. Wine is not served, but management will not object if you discreetly bring your own. ✉ *51–53, Derb ben Chekroune–La Blida* ☎ *035/63–33–35* 🖃 *MC, V.*

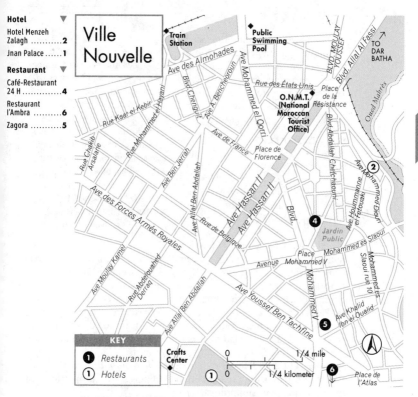

Hotel ▼

Hotel Menzeh
Zalagh **2**
Jnan Palace **1**

Restaurant ▼

Café-Restaurant
24 H **4**
Restaurant
l'Ambra **6**
Zagora **5**

Ville Nouvelle

◆ Train Station
◆ Public Swimming Pool
↗ TO DAR BATHA

Ave des Almohades
Rue des États Unis
O.N.M.T. (National Moroccan Tourist Office)
Place de la Résistance

Rue Mohammed el Qotri
Place de Florence
Ave de France

Rue Ksar el Kebir
Rue Mohammed el Hayani
Bivd Chenguit
Ave A. Bencheqroun

Rue Chakib Arsalane
Ave Ben Jerrah
Ave Allal Ben Abdallah

Ave des Forces Armées Royales
Rue de Belgique
Ave Hassan II
Ave Hassan II

Blvd

Bivd Abdallah Chefchaouni
Ave Hoummanne el Fetouaki
Ave Mohammed Diouri

Ave Moulay Kamel
Rue Abdelouahed Derraq

Jardin Public
④
Place Mohammed V
Avenue Mohammed V
Mohammed es Slaoui
Slaoui rue 10

Ave Allal Ben Abdallah
Ave Youssef Ben Tachfine
Mohammed V

⑤
Ave Khalid Ibn el Oualid

KEY

❶ *Restaurants*
① *Hotels*
◆ Crafts Center

0 ———— 1/4 mile
0 ———— 1/4 kilometer

① ⑥ Place de l'Atlas

VILLE NOUVELLE

¢ ✕**Café-Restaurant 24 H.** Market restaurants are always good, and this
MOROCCAN one is even better, as it remains open, as its title would suggest, around
the clock. Tagines, sandwiches, salads, scrambled eggs—"anything you
want" to quote the head chef. And any time you want, too. ✉*Marché
Centrale, Ave. Mohammed V* ☎*035/62–36–97* ▭*No credit cards.*

$ ✕**Restaurant L'Ambra.** A private home in the Ville Nouvelle on the
MOROCCAN road to Imouzzèr and Ifrane (N8), this cozy spot is like dropping by a
friend's place for dinner. Decorated with antiques, the house is small
but charming. The full range of Fassi gourmet specialties is available
here in an intimate and personable setting. ✉*47, rte. d'Imouzzèr*
☎*035/64–16–87* ▭*MC, V.*

$$$ ✕**Zagora.** This Ville Nouvelle standout is known for its classic Moroc-
MOROCCAN can and international cuisine. The beef and lamb tagines are especially
good, and the briouates (spicy dumplings) are nonpareil. The wine list
is an anthology of Moroccan vineyards, and the service is first-rate.
Decorated in a fusion of European and Moroccan motifs, Zagora has
a smart, sophisticated, and modern atmosphere. ✉*5, bd. Mohammed
V* ☎*035/94–06–86* ✍*Reservations essential* ▭*AE, DC, MC, V.*

WHERE TO STAY

Staying in Fez's medina offers such a unique experience that you're best off choosing a hotel either in or very near medieval Fez el-Bali. That said, there are also some good hotels in the Ville Nouvelle. There are no hotels in Fez el-Djedid.

RIAD RENTALS

Enjoying the privacy of an entire riad for a few days with your family or friends is an incredible experience. The following agencies can help you arrange a stay in your very own Moroccan palace. **Fez Medina** (☎800/714–3390 from U.S) ⊕www.fesmedina.com).   Founder Lon Wood and her international team have a passion for saving and maintaining historic medina homes. With a strong commitment to preserving historical integrity, a portion of the fees are donated to restore common treasures such as fountain tiling, mosaic floors, and cedar porticos.

Fez Riads (☎035/35–637–713 ⊕www.fez-riads.com). Helen Ranger, a Fez resident, will help you rent a room in a traditional guesthouse, or you can have a whole riad to yourself with cleaning service and breakfast included. Profits go to renovation projects.

Splendia (☎024/33–9–60 ⊕www.splendia.com/morocco.php). This Web site offers a unique selection of lodgings. The properties range from the simple to sumptuous.

FEZ EL-BALI

$$
MOROCCAN

Hôtel Batha. Near Bab Boujeloud, the Batha has a great location. The rooms are comfortable, but the decor is dated and the street noise can be bothersome. The staff is friendly and speaks English. **Pros:** Central location, good value, pretty pool. **Cons:** Uninspiring decor, unreliable service. ⊠Pl. de l'Istiqlal Batha ☎035/74–10–77 ⌨62 rooms ♿In-hotel: restaurant, pool, parking (fee) ☰AE, DC, MC, V ⦿BP.

$$$$
MOROCCAN
Fodor's Choice
★

La Maison Bleue. Originally the private residence of Sidi Mohammed el Abaddi, a famous judge and astrologer, this 19th-century family home has been handsomely renovated and expanded. High ceilings and intricately carved stucco and cedar walls surround central patios and fountains with Andalusian-style guest rooms. Age seems to be taking its toll, as some of the furnishings seem worn and the service is inconsistant. For the prices on the menu, you'd expect better than average food in the restaurant, although there is an authentic chwa'k dar, a beef tagine. Work off your dinner in a well-equipped gym that boasts a great view of the city and the surrounding countryside. **Pros:** Central location, historic building, private balconies. **Cons:** Unreliable service, dull decor. ⊠2, pl. de l'Istiqlal Batha ☎035/63–60–52 ⊕www.maisonbleue.com ⌨1 room, 18 suites ♿In-hotel: restaurant, pool gym, spa ☰AE, DC, MC, V ⦿BP.

> ### QUICK EATS
>
> For food on the run it's hard to beat a 50¢ bowl of cumin-laced pea or bean soup at one of the many little stands and stalls near the medina's main food markets just inside Bab Boujeloud. Lamb brochettes marinated in Moroccan spices and cooked over coals are another ubiquitous and delicious specialty. If pastries are on your mind in the heart of the medina, look for the Pâtisserie Kortouba next to the Attarine Medersa on Talâa Kebira, near the Kairaouine Mosque.

> **WORD OF MOUTH**
>
> "We recently stayed at the Riad Mabrouka in Fez. It was a beautiful place and we arranged a dinner there. It couldn't have been a more romantic spot and the meal was delicious." —I8Ds

$$$$ **Le Méridien Les Mérinides Hotel.** Strategically placed to overlook the city, Les Mérinides is deservedly popular, so reserve well in advance. The views of Fez el-Bali from the pool—nicely raised above the fray—are the best in town. The rooms are decorated in pale shades with glass and wood trim. The restaurant is subdued compared to some of the more exotic medina choices, but the cuisine, both international and Moroccan, is carefully prepared and elegantly served. The only drawback is coming and going by taxi, as it's a few minutes' drive above the medina. **Pros:** Stunning view, large pool, excellent for families. **Cons:** Out-of-the-way location, expensive rates. ✉*36, Chrablyne Borj Nord* ☎*035/64–52–26* 🌐*www.lesmerinides.com* *102 rooms, 4 suites* *In-hotel: 2 restaurants, bars, pool* *AE, DC, MC, V* *BP.*

$$$$ **Riad Fès.** For an architecturally refined interpretation of riad living, head to this well-equipped guesthouse. What you get is a perfect blend of character, modern convenience, creature comforts, and outstanding service. The place is magical in the evening, when weary guests are welcomed back with a warm smile into the glow of candlelight and mesmerizing rhythms of a lute player. The stunning Andalusia pavilion with an ornamental pool and intricately carved stone archways houses a sleek bar and lounge on one side and a plush crimson-color smoking room on the other. The excellent restaurant means you may have difficulty mustering the energy to leave the pleasurable confines of this memorable hotel. **Pros:** Quiet location, full of charm, luxurious appointments. **Cons:** Very expensive, no pool. ✉*5, Derb Ibn Slimane Zerbtana* ☎*035/94–76–10* 🌐*www.riadfes.com* *12 rooms, 14 suites* *In-hotel: restaurant, bar, parking (fee)* *AE, DC, MC, V* *BP.*

$$$$ ★ **Riyad Sheherazade.** Frequented by celebrities, this former home of a 19th-century minister makes you feel like Moroccan royalty. The converted palace is a perfect expression of traditional style, with spectacular woodwork and tranquil views onto the vast courtyard. Every detail is beautiful, from the hand-painted tiles in the courtyard to the wooden terrace overlooking the chemical-free pool. The proprietors, a doctor and architect who decorated with integrity and authenticity, strive to give each guest personalized service. There's an award-winning restaurant where you can sample an inventive assortment of flavorful dishes. **Pros:** Attentive service, spacious rooms, central location. **Con:** Steep stairs in some corridors. ✉*23, Arsat Bennis Douh* ☎*035/74–16–42* 🌐*www.sheheraz.com* *2 rooms, 11 suites* *In-hotel: restaurant, pool* *DC, MC, V* *BP.*

$$$$ **Ryad Mabrouka.** This carefully restored Andalusian town house in the heart of the medina is such a pleasure as to become instantaneously addictive. Every detail here is painstakingly polished, from the music of flowing water, to scents of cedar from the magnificent doors, ceilings, and closets. All suites are sumptuously furnished and decorated, and the proprietors are unfailingly helpful and smart about every detail

of your stay in Fez. **Pros:** Central location, elegant rooms, good service. **Con:** Not for families with young children. ✉*25, Derb el Mitar* ☎*035/63–63–45* ⊕*www. ryadmabrouka.com* ⇆*2 rooms, 6 suites* ⚷*In-hotel: restaurant, pool* ▤*AE, DC, MC, V* ☉*BP.*

FROM THE TOP

The Sofitel Palais Jamaï and the Batha are the only hotels that look right over the medieval city, but Le Meridien's Mérinides and the Zalagh, while farther away, have more-panoramic views.

$$$$
MOROCCAN
🏨**Sofitel Palais Jamaï.** With an unbeatable location near the medina, plenty of creature comforts, and a beautiful pool, the Palais Jamaï is a popular choice. Built more than 120 years ago, the hotel has rather tired rooms that overlook the city and the gardens. You can enjoy well-prepared international cuisine on the spacious outdoor terrace, lounge with drink in hand in the popular piano bar, or treat yourself to a massage and facial in the full-service spa. The prices for all this aren't cheap, however. **Pros:** Great location, historic building. **Cons:** Impersonal service, rooms need refreshing. ✉*Bab Guissa* ☎*035/63–43–31* ⊕*www.sofitel.com* ⇆*123 rooms, 19 suites* ⚷*In-hotel: 3 restaurants, bars, tennis court, pool, gym, spa* ▤*AE, DC, MC, V.*

VILLE NOUVELLE

$$$–$$$$
🏨**Hôtel Menzeh Zalagh.** Offering pretty gardens and a pool overlooking the medina, the Menzeh Zalagh is close to plenty of restaurants. Guest rooms vary from cedar-carved upper-floor suites with balconies to somewhat undistinguished chambers on the Ville Nouvelle side. The staff is friendly, but don't count on exceptional service. **Pros:** Panoramic views, pretty pool area. **Con:** Attracts large tour groups ✉*10, rue Mohammed Diouri* ☎*035/93–22–34* ⇆*143 rooms, 6 suites* ⚷*In-hotel: 3 restaurants, bars, pool, parking (no fee)* ▤*AE, DC, MC, V.*

$$$$
🏨**Jnan Palace.** For comfort and service, this glass-and-stucco structure is unsurpassed among the Ville Nouvelle's hotels. With ultramodern rooms worthy of any first-rate American hotel chain, the Jnan Palace seems to have little in common with the city around it. Take one look at the tranquil pool and the cosmopolitan bar and café and you'll be glad to escape from the hustle and bustle of the surrounding neighborhood. The restaurants—Italian, Moroccan, and international—are all among the Ville Nouvelle's best. **Pros:** Spacious rooms, tasty buffet breakfast, luxurious pool area. **Cons:** Overpriced food, far from the medina. ✉*Ave. Ahmed Chaouki* ☎*035/65–39–65* ⇆ *217 rooms, 17 suites* ⚷*In-hotel: 3 restaurants, bar, pool, parking (no fee)* ▤*AE, DC, MC, V* ☉*BP.*

NIGHTLIFE

Pretty much all of Fez's nightlife unfolds in the Ville Nouvelle, though many of the best hotel bars are in or near the edge of the medina.

BARS

The bar at the **Hôtel les Mérinides** (✉*Rte. Du Tour de Fès* ☎*035/64–52–26*) overlooking the city is a favorite watering hole. For a lively bar scene at an unpretentious address, the **Hotel Menzeh Zalagh** (✉*10, rue*

Mohammed Diouri (☎035/93–22–34) is near one of Fez's best discos. Also check out **Pub Cala Iris** (✉26, ave. Hassan II ☎035/74–10–77). The bar at the **Sofitel Palais Jamaï** (✉Bab Jamaï ☎035/63–43–31) is a prime spot for an evening libation at the piano bar.

DANCE CLUBS

The nightclub at the **Hôtel Menzeh Zalagh** (✉10, rue Mohammed Diouri ☎035/93–22–34) is wild (if a little sordid) every night. The disco in the **Hotel Sofía** (✉3, rue de Arabi Saoudite ☎035/62–42–65) gets active around 11 and, depending on the general level of frenzy, may stay open until 3 or 4. The bar at the **Jnan Palace** (✉Ave. Ahmed Chaouki ☎035/65–39–65) hotel

often has live performances (usually on the quiet side), while the hotel's disco, Le Phoebus, is among Fez's best. The small but trendy**La Mezzanine** (✉17, Kasbat Chams ☎011/07–83–36) attracts a young and hip crowd grooving to the beat of imported house music. The open-air terrace is a nice touch.

SHOPPING

Fez el-Bali is one big souk. Embroidery, pottery, leather goods, rugs and carpets, copper plates, brass pots, silver jewelry, textiles, and spices are all of exceptional quality and sold at comparatively low prices, considering the craftsmanship that has remained authentic for nearly 1,000 years.

CRAFTS

★ **Belmajdoub Mohammed** (✉270, Talâa ☎035/64–11–12) is a well-known master wood craftsman creating decorative items and furniture. **Bouchareb Mohammed** (✉8, Boutouil Kairaouine ☎035/63–57–69) crafts marquetry and other wood products. **Ensemble Artisanal** (✉Ave. Allah ben Abdullah ☎035/62–27–04) is across town on the southeastern edge of the city near the Hôtel Crown Palace, but the chance to see artisans working everything from leather to copper to pottery and wood is not only a rare treat but a chance to price goods for comparison with some of the opening bids you may hear elsewhere (the iron smith's lanterns are of a quality you won't easily find in the medina). **Fès Art Gallery** (✉2, Boutouil Kairaouine ☎035/63–46–63) has miscellaneous arts and crafts.

METAL

Akessbi Fouad (✉23, *rue Nejja-rine, Souk Sekatine* ☎*No phone*) is a master of the art of dama-scening (watered steel or silver inlay work) and the officially pro-claimed "Best Artisan of Fez." For copper, gold, and silver, stop into **Argenterie Fès** (✉6, *Aouadine Bab Sensla* ☎035/63–39–55). Loads of bronze, copper and silver objects, both antique and new, are sold at **La Maison de Bronze** (✉6, *Derb el Hara, Talâa Kebira* ☎061/28–03–11)For bronze, copper, and jew-els, visit **La Maison Bouanania** (✉6, *Derb ben Azahoum, Talâa Kebira* ☎035/63–65–66).

> ### READY, SET, GO
>
> Get used to the bargaining pro-cess: decide what the item is worth to you (which may come down to the question of whether or not you really want it) and stick with it as closely as you can. *(For more tips to help you brave this most intense of souks, see Chapter 10.)*

POTTERY

Au Bleu de Fès (✉*Boutouil i Safarine* ☎035/63–35–79) specializes in Fassi pottery. **Les Poteries de Fès** (✉*Aïn Nokbi [Rte. N6 to Taza, Km 2]* ☎035/63–15–26) is the place to buy the famous blue-and-white Fassi pottery and to see how it is made. From Bab el-Ftouh a 20-minute walk west (left coming out), a petit taxi ride, or the 79 bus will get you to the new potters' quarter. **Maison Sahara** (✉9, *pl. Nejjarine* ☎035/63–45–22) has pottery and assorted other goods.

RUGS

★ For the best rugs-and-carpets discussion in Fez and a good mint tea, make a trip to **Aux Merveilles du Tapis** (✉22, *Sebaâ Louyet [Seven Turns]* ☎035/63–87–35). The store takes credit cards and ships rugs overseas. The time you save buying from these weavers will more than make up for the slightly inflated fixed prices on the rugs and carpets at **Dar Ibn Khaldoun** (✉45, *Derb Bem Chakroune Lablida* ☎035/63–33–35).

MEKNÈS

60 km (37 mi) west of Fez, 138 km (85 mi) east of Rabat.

It's easy to understand why Meknès is considered the Versailles of Morocco. Meknès's three sets of imposing walls, architectural Royal Granaries, symmetrical Bab Mansour, and spectacular palaces are as beautiful as any French monarch's creations. Less inundated with tour-ists and more provincial than Fez, Meknès offers a low-key initiation into the Moroccan processes of shopping and bargaining. The souks and the Imperial City are just as impressive as their Fez counterparts, but the pace is slower and the pressure lighter. Whether it was post–Moulay Ismail exhaustion or the 1755 earthquake that quieted Meknès down, the result is a pleasant middle ground between the Fez brouhaha and the business-as-usual European ambience of Rabat.

Meknès occupies a plateau overlooking the Boufekrane River, which divides the medina from the Ville Nouvelle. Most travelers stay in the

Ville Nouvelle and approach the medina either on foot or by car.

GETTING HERE & AROUND

Fès-Saïss Airport serves both Fez and Meknès. The taxi or bus ride to Meknès takes about 30 minutes. Regular Compagnie de Transports Marocains buses cover the Fez–Meknès route hourly. There are buses to Casablanca buses (four hours, 80 DH). Tangier (five hours, 95 DH), and Marrakesh (eight hours, 200 DH). The most convenient train station in Meknès is the rue el Amir Abdelkader stop close to the administrative center of the city. If you're coming from Tangier, this will be the first stop; from Fez it will be the second. All trains stop at both stations.

> **GRAB A GUIDE**
>
> An official guide from the tourist office costs about 250 DH for a half day or 500 DH for a full day. Private guides are helpful for first-time visits to the medina and the Imperial City, though you'll almost certainly end up haggling over rugs for the last hour of your tour. However, the palaces that house these rug enterprises are usually architectural gems, and the historical background of the rug-weaving craft is fascinating. The problem comes when you attempt to depart without purchasing one.

Grands taxis taking up to six passengers make long-distance runs between Fez and Meknès. This can be faster, more comfortable, and a better value than bus travel. Metered petits taxis take up to three passengers, but may not leave the city limits. If the driver refuses to turn on the meter or agree to a reasonable price, do not hesitate to get out. There is a 50% surcharge after 8 PM.

TIMING & PRECAUTIONS

Meknès is a beautifully intact medieval city worth exploring as a short excursion from Fez. From the central Place el-Hedime you can discover the medina's network of small open and covered streets flanked by shops, artisan studios, and food stalls. To see the Imperial City quarter, take a petit taxi or a more atmospheric caléche (horse-drawn carriage).

ESSENTIALS

Bus Contacts **Compagnie de Transports Marocains** (✉Ave. des FAR s/n ☎035/52–25–85).

Currency Exchange **Banque Marocaine du Commerce Extérieur** (✉98, ave. des FAR ☎035/62–51–13).

Internet **Cyber de Paris** (✉6, Zankat Accra ☎035/62–53–33). **Quick Net** (✉28, rue el Amir Abdelkader ☎035/62–77–63).

Mail & Shipping **La Poste** (✉Pl. de l'Istiqlal s/n ☎035/62–39–41).

Medical Assistance **Hôpital Moulay Ismail** (✉Rte. 21 ☎035/52–28–05).

Rental Cars **Bab Mansour Car** (✉8, rue Idriss II ☎035/52–66–31). **Stop Car** (✉3, rue Essaouira ☎035/52–50–61). **Zeit Wagen** (✉4, rue Antsirabe ☎035/52–59–18).

A BIT OF HISTORY

Founded in the 10th century by the Zénète Meknassa tribe from the eastern Rif Mountains, Meknès has been called "the turntable of Morocco" for its pivotal position between the Rif and Middle Atlas mountains and between the Atlantic Ocean and the Sahara. The Romans chose nearby Volubilis as their Moroccan headquarters for its strategic central position, and this was probably Sultan Moulay Ismail's reasoning when he decided to govern from Meknès in 1673. As Sultan of Morocco between 1672 and 1727, this ambitious and tyrannical sultan built extensively, and as a result Meknès is often called the Versailles of North Africa.

Moulay Ismail encased the city within some 40 km (25 mi) of lime-and-earth walls. Surrounded and threatened by 45 regional Berber tribes, Moulay Ismail was obsessed with defense to a degree virtually unparalleled in world history. Meknès was developed to withstand a hypothetical 20-year siege, with protected granaries, a reservoir, and three concentric systems of ramparts surrounding the 9th-century medina, the 13th-century Imperial City, and the Royal Palace. In addition, Ismail was known to have maintained 500 concubines and a standing army, the Abid regiment, of 150,000 crack troops (the infamous Black Guard) originally purchased from the Sudan. Handed Arab and Berber women as wives, Ismail's army lived in a special camp where male offspring were impressed into service at an early age, officially at 15. Two hundred palace eunuchs, a 12,000-horse cavalry, and a labor force of 60,000 slaves (largely prisoners of war, condemned criminals, and random captives) completed Moulay Ismail's extraordinary personal staff. Somewhat surprisingly, Ismail is remembered and revered for his unique achievements rather than reviled for his equally unique excesses: under his leadership Morocco was united under government control for the first time in five centuries and experienced its last golden age to date. After Ismail's death, Meknès crumbled during the late 18th and early 19th centuries—as if sapped of strength after Ismail's reign of terror—and even Ismail's son tore down a palace or two before moving Morocco's capital to Marrakesh.

Visitor & Tour Info Carlson Wagonlit (✉ *1, rue Ghana* ☎ *035/52–19–95*). **Meknès Tourist Office** (✉ *Pl. de l'Istiqlal* ☎ *035/52–44–26*). **RAM** (✉ *7, ave. Mohammed V* ☎ *035/52–09–63*). **Wasteels** (✉ *45, ave. Mohammed V* ☎ *035/52–30–62*).

EXPLORING

THE IMPERIAL CITY

TOP ATTRACTIONS

A sweeping tour of Moulay Ismail's 40 km (25 mi) of walls (in three concentric rings), the granaries, the reservoir, a modern-day farm for training Arabian horses, and the walled corridor between the Royal Palace and the Imperial City is best accomplished by car. Driving will give you the most effective sense of the scale of Ismail's vision. You can easily hire a taxi and a good guide (useful, as there are no explanations at the monuments) through the tourist office. If you have more time, walk the medina to explore the souks, Grand Mosque, and Bou Inania Medersa.

Fodor'sChoice ★

❶ Heri el Souani *(Royal Granaries).* Also known as Dar eMa (Water Palace) for the reservoir beneath, the granaries were one of Moulay Ismail's greatest achievements and are the first place any Meknessi will take you to give you an idea of the second Alaouite sultan's exaggeratedly grandiose vision. The Royal Granaries were designed to store grain as feed for the 12,000 horses

DID YOU KNOW?

The granaries have such elegance and grace that they were once called the Cathedral of Grain by a group of Franciscan priests, who were so moved that they requested permission to sing plainsong here. Acoustically perfect, the granaries are now often used for summer concerts and receptions.

in the royal stables—not just for a few days or weeks but over a 20-year siege if necessary. Ismail and his engineers counted on three things to keep the granaries cool enough that the grain would never rot: thick walls (12 feet), suspended gardens (a cedar forest was planted on the roof), and an underground reservoir with water ducts under the floors. The room on the far right as you enter has a 30-foot well in its center and a towpath around it—donkeys circulated constantly, activating the waterwheel in the well, which forced water through the ducts and maintained a stable temperature in the granaries. Out behind the granaries are the remains of the royal stables (the roofs were lost in the 1755 Lisbon earthquake). Some 1,200 purebreds, just one-tenth of Moulay Ismail's cavalry, were kept here. At a point just to the left of the door out to the stables, you can see the stunning symmetry of the stable's pillars from three different perspectives. ✉ *Heri el Souani* 🎫 *20 DH* 🕑 *Daily 9–1 and 3–6:30.*

WORTH NOTING

❷ Haras Régional. Purebred Arabian and Berber horses and fine hybrids are the star performers at this equestrian breeding and training farm. Under the supervision of Berber horseman Ben Salm, these beautiful stallions receive hundreds of visitors daily during Morocco's high season. The horses, all of which used to be registered with Lloyds of London, are identified by plaques on their stable walls: red for Arabians; green for Berber stallions and mares; and red and green for hybrids. The ratio of the two colors indicates their exact percentages in the horse's bloodline. ■TIP➜ **Guided horseback outings can be arranged for about 400 DH** .

BAB MANSOUR & THE MEDINA

A walk around Bab Mansour and Place el-Hedime takes in nearly all of Meknès's major sites, including Moulay Ismail's mausoleum and the Prison of the Christian Slaves.

TOP ATTRACTIONS

❹ Bab Mansour. Widely considered North Africa's most beautiful gate, this ★ mammoth, horseshoe-shape triumphal arch was completed in 1732 by a Christian convert to Islam named Mansour Laalej (whose name means "victorious renegade"). The famous and much-repeated story of the gate's construction—sultan Moulay Ismail asked, "Can you do better?" to which Mansour replied in the affirmative and was immediately executed—is surely a legend, as the gate was finished five years after Ismail's death. The smaller marble columns supporting the two bastions on either side of the main entry were taken from the Roman ruins at Volubilis, while the taller Corinthian columns came from Marrakesh's El Badi Palace, part of Moulay Ismail's campaign to erase any vestige of the Saadian dynasty that preceded the Alaouites. Ismail's last important construction project, the gate was conceived as an elaborate homage to himself rather than (for once) a defensive stronghold, thus its intensely decorative character. ⊠ *Rue Dar Smen s/n.*

> **GREAT QUOTE**
>
> French novelist Pierre Loti (1850–1923) penned the definitive description of Bab Mansour: " . . . rose-hued, star-shaped, endless sets of broken lines, unimaginable geometric combinations that confuse the eye like a labyrinthine puzzle, always in the most original and masterly taste, have been gathered here in thousands of bits of varnished earth, in relief or recessed, so that from a distance it creates the illusion of a buffed and textured fabric, glimmering, glinting, a priceless tapestry placed over these ancient stones to relieve the monotony of these towering walls."

❼ **Bou Inania Medersa.** Begun by the Merenid sultan Abou el-Hassan and finished by his son Abou Inan between 1350 and 1358, the Meknès version of Fez's residential college of the same name is arguably more beautiful and better preserved than its better-known twin. Starting with the cupola and the enormous doors on the street, virtually every inch of this building is covered with decorative carving or calligraphy. The central fountain is for ablutions before prayer. Go upstairs to visit the small rooms that overlook the courtyard. These housed the 60 theology students who lodged here. ■ TIP→ **The rooftop terrace has the city's single best view of Meknès's medina.** ⊠ *Souk es Sebaat* 🖵 *10 DH* ☉ *Daily 9–1 and 3–6.*

■ **NEED A BREAK?** Near Bou Inania Medersa is a tiny, old-fashioned **café** dominated by a large brass tank, a good place for a mint tea prepared and served in the traditional manner.

❻ **Dar Jamai.** This 19th-century palace was built by the same family of viziers (high government officials) responsible for the Palais Jamaï hotel in Fez. The building itself is exquisite, especially the second-floor carved-cedar ceilings; and it now houses the **Museum of Moroccan Art,** which has superb collections of carpets, jewelry, and needlework and wondrous domed reception room on the upper floor. Facing away from Bab Mansour, the ceramics stalls on Place el-Hedime's left side sell oversize tagine pots for as little as 15 DH to 20 DH. ⊠ *Pl. el-Hedim* 🖵 *20 DH* ☉ *Daily 9–1 and 3–6:30.*

5 **Food souk.** A tour through this shady oasis stuffed with food products heaped in elaborately arranged piles and pyramids—prunes, plums, olives, spices, nuts, dates, meats, fish, in every conceivable shape, color, aroma, and taste—is synesthetic ecstasy, as well as a break from the sun and general sales pressure outside. ■ TIP→ **The kissaria (covered market) is a good place to stock up on Moroccan spices.** Look for the fish market (through to the right) for a surprising look at denizens of all descriptions straight from the Atlantic ocean an hour's drive away.

MEKNÈS MOMENT

The produce market just off Place el-Hedime is a sensorial feast and a good place to sample olives, purchase spices, or buy simple ceramic cooking wares such as the red-clay tagines typically used for slowly stewing meats and vegetables. The variety of olives on display and the painstaking care with which each pyramid of produce has been set out daily is nearly as geometrically enthralling as the decorative designs on the Bab Mansour gate, with the important difference that these patterns are more ephemeral and, in fact, edible.

3 **Moulay Ismail Mausoleum.** One of four sacred sites in Morocco open to ★ non-Muslims (the others are Casablanca's Hassan II, Rabat's Mohammed V Mausoleum, and Rissani's zaouia of Moulay Ali Sherif), this mausoleum was opened to non-Muslims by King Mohammed V (grandfather of Mohammed VI) in honor of Ismail's manifestly ecumenical instincts. Always an admirer of France's King Louis XIV—who, in turn, considered the sultan an important ally—Moulay Ismail maintained close ties with Europe and signed commercial treaties even as he battled to eject the Portuguese from their coastal strongholds at Asilah, Essaouira, and Larache. The mausoleum's site once held Meknès's Palais de Justice (Courthouse), and Moulay Ismail deliberately chose it as his resting place in the stated hope that he would be judged in his own court by his own people. The lovely ocher-hue walls inside (pale yellow on their sun-bleached upper parts) lead to the sultan's private sanctuary, on the left, heavily decorated with zellij tiles bearing colorful geometric patterns. To the right is Moulay Ismail's tomb, surrounded with hand-carved cedar-and-stucco walls and more zellij. ⊠ *Rue Palais next to Bab er-Rih* ⊠ *Free* ☉ *Sat.–Thurs. 9–noon and 3–6.*

WHERE TO EAT

There are only a few culinary gems in Meknès, but chances are you'll want to sample local delicacies, snack on exotic fruits, and savor the ritual sweet pastries and mint tea, purported to be the best in the country. Good cafés and restaurants are scattered in the medina (many near the Place el-Hedime). Avenues Mohammed V and Hassan II in the Ville Nouvelle provide a wide choice of Moroccan and French or Mediterranean dishes.

$ ╳**Annexe Restaurant Metropole II.** This family-friendly place on the TangMOROCCAN ier road is just a five-minute walk from the Hôtel Transatlantique. Don't be put off by the less-than-grand aesthetics; this is real Moroc-

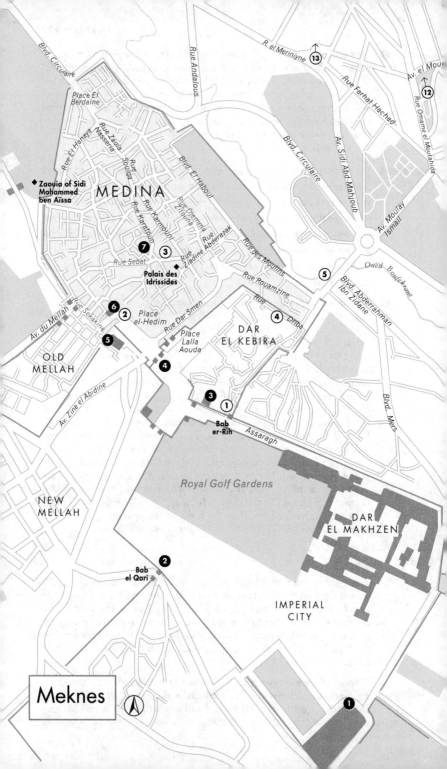

Meknes

3

KEY

❶ *Exploring sights*

① *Hotels & Restaurants*

can cooking. Mechoui is available without a day's advance notice and at a very reasonable price; order in advance anyway, just to be certain. ✉*4, bd. Yougoslavie (Rte. de Tanger)* ☎*035/51–35–11* 🔲*AE, DC, MC, V.*

$$$$
MOROCCAN

✕**Collier de la Colombe.** A five-minute walk to the left inside Bab Mansour, this graceful medina space with intricate carvings, giant picture windows, and terraces overlooking the Boufekrane River and Ville Nouvelle is an excellent place to enjoy authentic Moroccan specialties. The menu is a classic range with delectable pastilla, tender grilled lamb, spicy beef brochettes, and mouthwatering tagines. Local Moroccans regularly line up and wait for choice seating on the panoramic rooftop terrace. Prices are a steal for the experience and quality of cooking. ✉*67, rue Driba (access via Bab Mansour and P. Lalla Aouda)* ☎*035/55–50–41* 🔲 *MC, V.*

$$$–$$$$
FRENCH

✕**Le Dauphin.** Meknès's enclave par excellence for French and international cuisine, Le Dauphin is well respected for it extensive menu, lively ambience, and attentive service. Fresh fish, duck, and foie gras are reliable standards, as are wines from beyond North Africa. Desserts are decadent in a traditional French manner with crepes, tarts, and sorbets. ✉*5, ave. Mohammed V* ☎*035/52–34–23* 🔲 *MC, V.*

$$$–$$$$
MOROCCAN

✕**Palais Terrab.** This family-run restaurant in a residential part of the Ville Nouvelle is well known in Meknès for its serious cuisine, folkloric spectacles, and ability to serve 600 people at once. The downside is that you may find yourself either dining in a vast empty space or surrounded by 599 other tourists. The upside is that the food is excellent and the staff is warm and generous. Try the *brique Tetuan,* a kind of briouate (spicy dumpling). The *tagine de kabab maghdour* (hunks of meat stewed in onions and spices) is a Meknès specialty. ✉*18, ave. Zerktouni* ☎*035/52–61–00* 🔲*AE, DC, MC, V.*

$
MOROCCAN

✕**Restaurant Marhaba.** Fueling up has never been tastier than at this low-key eatery. Start with freshly made Berber bread and thick harira soup. Share a plate of grilled brochettes and sweet potato fries. Portions are generous, and will cost less than a cup of coffee back home. ✉*23, ave. Mohammed V* ☎*035/52–16–32* 🔲*DC, MC, V.*

$$–$$$
MOROCCAN

🏨 **Riad d'Or.** Hidden inside the ramparts of the Royal Palace, this stately yet intimate garden restaurant is so jarringly lovely that you almost rub your eyes upon arrival. The owner, Raouf Alaoui Ismail— a direct descendant of Moulay Ismail—speaks excellent English and serves fine Moroccan cuisine. Tables are arranged in and around the

Sidi Ben Aïssa: Morocco's All-Purpose Insurance Policy

Built in 1776 by Sultan Sidi Mohammed ben Abdellah, the **Zaouia of Sidi Mohammed ben Aïssa** is the focal point of the legendary Aïssaoua cult, known for such voluntary rituals as: swallowing scorpions, broken glass, and poison; eating live sheep; and cutting themselves with knives in prayer-induced trances.

Ben Aïssa was one of Morocco's most famous saints. He was said to have made a pact with the animal world and possessed magical powers, such as the ability to transform the leaves of trees into gold and silver coins. Thought to have been a 17th-century contemporary of Moulay Ismail (1646–1727), Ben Aïssa was known as the protector of Moulay Ismail's 50,000-man workforce, and persuaded hungry laborers that they were able to eat anything at all, even poisonous plants, glass, or scorpions. Ben Aïssa went on to become the general protector of all his followers. It was said that women, for example, could travel safely under his protection.

AÏSSA CELEBRATIONS

The cult is still around, and has in fact proliferated throughout North Africa to Algeria and beyond. Every year, during Ben Aïssa's *moussem* (pilgrimage) on the eve of the birth of the prophet Mohammed, members of the Aïssaoua fraternity from all over North Africa gather at the shrine. Processions form and parade through Meknès, snakes are charmed, and the saint's followers perform ecstatic dances, often imitating the behavior of certain animals. Although some of the Aïssaoua's more brutal practices have been outlawed, this moussem remains one of Morocco's most astonishing and mysterious events.

VISITING THE SHRINE

Koubba Sidi ben Aïssa (⊠ *Bd. Circulaire s/n* ⊡ *20 DH* ⊙ *Daily 9–noon and 3–6*).

–George Semler

central patio on the second floor. ⊠*4, rue Ain el Anboub* ☎*04/107–8625* ▤ *AE, DC, MC, V.*

$–$$
ECLECTIC

✕ **Le Tangerois.** An intimate hideaway near the Hotel Akouass and El Amir Abdelkader train station, this combination Moroccan, Vietnamese, and international restaurant in the Ville Nouvelle is good at everything it does. The candlelit dining room, with no more than a dozen tables, is decorated in European style. The menu is an eclectic hodgepodge ranging from Vietnamese *nuoc mam* (a salty fish sauce) to tagines of lamb, beef, or chicken. The wine list is first-rate, and you're guaranteed never to find a busload of tourists in this local favorite. ⊠*2, rue de Beyrout* ☎*035/51–50–91* ▤ *MC, V.*

WHERE TO STAY

Unlike Fez, Meknès has yet to attract strong commercial development and active restoration of riads. Staying within the medina in the limited choices available is especially exotic here. For more updated accommodations, there are several decent hotels in the Ville Nouvelle that are reasonably priced and a short walk or taxi ride from the train station.

$ **Hotel Akouass.** The rooms here are merely adequate, but the helpful staff, the tasty breakfast (including all the fresh-squeezed orange juice you can drink), and the glass-walled breakfast room perched over a busy street corner manage to compensate. Across the street from one of North Africa's better-stocked newspaper kiosks, the Akouass hosts an unbelievable downstairs disco scene (get a room as high up as you can to escape the noise), where men and women in *djellabas* (long robes) boogie alongside women in thongs and men in leather pants. **Pros:** Central location, ample breakfast. **Con:** Some rooms are noisy. ⊠*27, rue Zenkat el Emir Abdelkader* ☎*035/52–59–67* ⌨*52 rooms* ⌂*In-hotel: restaurant, bar* ▭*AE, DC, MC, V.*

$$ **Hôtel Rif.** This Ville Nouvelle lodging has a pool, making it a nice base for those exploring the surrounding area. The Moroccan restaurant usually has a belly dancer and live music, especially when tour groups are in residence. The air-conditioned rooms are spacious and comfortable, and some have views across the river to the medina. **Pros:** Wheelchair access, good value. **Con:** Noise from train station. ⊠*Rue d'Accra* ☎*035/52–25–91* ⌨*153 rooms* ⌂*In-hotel: 2 restaurants, bar, pool, laundry service, parking (no fee)* ▭*AE, DC, MC, V* ꙮ*BP.*

$$$ **Hôtel Transatlantique.** Across the river from Meknès, the Transatlantique has beautiful views. The rooms themselves are not luxurious, but the ones with balconies over the pool and orange trees have a solid colonial feel about them. Look for old-fashioned sinks and traditional furniture. **Pros:** Great views, spacious grounds. **Con:** Rooms need renovations. ⊠*Rue el-Meriniyne* ☎*035/52–50–50* ⌨*120 rooms* ⌂*In-hotel: 2 restaurants, bar, tennis court, pool* ▭*AE, DC, MC, V* ꙮ*BP.*

$ **Hotel Zaki.** Depending on which room you get at this traditional hotel, your experience will be either incredibly positive or justifiably negative. Ask to see a few before you decide. A salmon-hue low-rise block conceals a spacious garden with an outdoor pool. The restaurant food is nothing to write home about. **Pros:** Good value for money, fairly close to the medina. **Cons:** Inconsistent service, needs some refurbishing. ⊠*Bd. Al Massira* ☎*035/52–09–90* ⌨*169 rooms* ⌂*In-hotel: restaurant, pool* ▭*AE, DC, MC, V* ꙮ*BP.*

$$$$ **Palais Didi.** Next to Bab Mansour, North Africa's widely acclaimed most beautiful gate, this stately 18th-century palace was restored by owner Ismaili Raouf as an homage to his grandfather, who was affectionately known as Didi. Arranged around a classical patio and fountain, the ground-floor suites are elegantly distributed and composed of bedroom, drawing room, and handsome tiled bathrooms. Upstairs are the six rooms, some of them duplex, each decorated with different elements and styles including circular copper bathtubs or darkwood beams supporting the corners of the canopy beds. Breakfast is served around the fountain in the patio. There's a golf course next door, and the hotel arranges excursions to ski at Mischliffen or to visit the Roman ruins at Volubilis. **Pros:** Luxurious accommodations, medina location. **Cons:** Some rooms need updating, very expensive. ⊠*7, Dar*

el Kbira ☎035/55–85–90 ⊕www. palaisdidi.com ➭6 rooms, 5 suites ♿In-hotel: restaurant ⊟AE, DC, MC, V ⏩BP.

$$–$$$ ✦ ⊡**Ryad Bahia.** A 14th-century family house lovingly restored by a couple with years of experience working as Meknès guides, this impressive anthology of ceramic, rug weaving, and woodworking crafts is tucked away on the medina just a few steps from the Dar Jamai museum on the Place el-Hadime. Rooms are comfortable and sump-

> **SUMMER FESTIVITIES**
>
> Summer concerts in the Heri el Souani are great favorites for Meknès music lovers. Check with the tourist office for dates and dress warmly—those 12-foot walls built to cool oats and barley cool people as well. Meknès's inter-national animated **film festival** (*FICAM* ☎035/51–58–51) takes place in mid-May.

tuously appointed, and the rooftop garden is beautiful. The restaurant in the patio serves fine Moroccan dishes, and the owners are fascinating sources for the history and culture of Meknès and the rest of Morocco. **Pros:** Medina location, outstanding service, family-friendly atmosphere. **Con:** Long walk from parking lot. ✉*Tiberbarine* ☎*035/55–45–41* ⊕*www.ryad-bahia.com* ➭*2 rooms, 2 suites* ♿*In-hotel: restaurant* ⊟*AE, DC, MC, V* ⏩*BP.*

NIGHTLIFE

A thriving, if somewhat tawdry, disco scene thrives in the hotels around train station in the Ville Nouvelle.

Discothèque el Andalouse (✉*38, rue el-Emir Abdelkader* ☎*035/52–52–39*) has an underground club that pounds away until four in the morning. More interesting are the bar and live-music scenes in the better hotels, especially the Transatlantique and the Rif; sometimes you'll hear traditional Gnaoua, sometimes Western folk music.

SHOPPING

CRAFTS

The **Centre Artisanale** (✉*Ave. Zine el-Abidine Riad* ☎*035/53–09–29*), is, as always in Moroccan cities, a good place to check for quality and prices before beginning to haggle in the souks. At **Carreaux Traditionnels** (✉*27, Rahbat Zrâa el Kadima* ☎*035/53–04–96*) you can watch a zellij (ceramic-tile) artisan in action. **El Ouadghiri el Edrissi** (✉*77, Kou-rat Souk el-Attarin* ☎*035/53–34–41*) makes doors and other wooden items. **L'Art Traditionnel** (✉*7, Rahbat Zrâa Lakdimia Zaouia Tijania* ☎*035/53–10–05*) creates wooden sculpture and decorative objects of all kinds, including leather, ceramics, and copper. **Palais de l'Artisan** (✉*11, Koubt Souk Kissariat Lahrir* ☎*035/53–35–02*) is a specialist in damascening (watered steel or silver inlay work). **Produits Artisanaux Bennani Saâd** (✉*21, rue el Kissaria* ☎*035/55–78–90*) is the shop of a top damascening artisan.

A WALKING TOUR OF THE MEKNES SOUK

The Meknès souk, as with Meknès generally, seems somehow easier to embrace than vast Fez. Getting lost here is difficult; it just isn't that big. Beginning from the Place el-Hedime, just past the pottery stands, a narrow corridor leads into the **food souk,** a riotous display of everything from spices to dried fruit to multicolor olives. Work through the souk and emerge from the far-right corner; through the bird market outside and back to your right, in a corner, you'll find the fish market.

Continue right around the building, pass to the left of Dar Jamai, and you'll enter the Meknès souk. Continue straight in until you come to a T—on the left is a usually boisterous public auction area. The street crossing the T is the main artery through the souk. A left turn will take you through the **Souk Nejjarine,** the woodworkers' souk, and then into the rug and carpet souk. Farther on in this direction is the **Souk Bezzarine,** a general flea market along the medina walls. Farther up to the right are basket makers, iron smiths, leather workers, and saddle makers, and, near **Bab el-Djedid,** makers of odd items like tents and musical instruments.

A right turn at the T will take you through **Souk es Sebat** and the souk's more formal section, beginning with the babouche (leather-slipper) market. At the first right, take a quick look at an ancient fondouk, now in ruins.

Back on the main street you'll pass **Fondouk Oueda** on the left, and, shortly thereafter, the **Bou Inania Medersa.**

Once again back on the main thoroughfare through the souk, you'll pass one of the mosque's 12 doors before reaching the **camel-meat vendor** on a left-hand corner at stall No. 15, identifiable by the toy camel hanging in front of his stand. The butcher is more than willing to open his refrigerator and haul out a camel head in case you have any doubts.

Turn left here, leaving the main street, and take an immediate right. On the left you'll see a brass door surrounded by colorful ornamentation; this is an old fondouk. Farther down on the left, at No. 91, is a **beignet,** a maker of fritters, or doughnuts, one of the few of these traditional artisans remaining.

You will now be hit by a powerfully milky aroma from the *laiterie* (dairy shop) on the right-hand corner; this is a signal to turn right and proceed down into **Place du Murier** (named for its mulberry tree), where a 1,000-year-old mulberry, gnarled and about 3 feet in diameter, stands in the middle of what was once the salt vendors' souk.

On the right, where he's seated in a bucket car seat at stall No. 27, meet celebrated zellij-tile artisan **Ben Adada,** whose father was also a well-known zellij maker and whose grandfather was one of the master craftsmen of Moulay Ismail's Royal Palace.

Turn right just past Ben Adada's place (taking a look left into the ancient wood-burning public bakery as you leave the square) and follow signs to the **Palais des Idrissides,** a wonderful 14th-century palace and carpet emporium.

FOOD

Ben Moussa (⊠ *Food market, Pl. el-Hedime* ☎ *035/55–73–21*) is the place to stock up on Morocco's fragrant spices. Just inside the Place el-Hedime entrance across from Bab Mansour, it's in the first aisle to the right, last stall on the left; follow your nose.

RUGS

Fodor's Choice ★ The **Palais des Idrissides** (⊠ *11, rue Kermouni* ☎ *035/55–78–92*), in the souk near Dar Jamai, is the best place to look for Berber kilims, rugs, and carpets. Much more than a carpet emporium, this magnificent 14th-century palace built by the cult of the Idrissid dynasty is a treasury of art, artisanship, and architecture not to be missed. The proprietors speak excellent English.

> **A SIGH OF RELIEF**
>
> Meknès's merchants and craftsmen are as exceptional as those in Fez, and what's more, they're easier to negotiate with. Just be prepared, if you try to tell a rug salesman that you're pressed for time, to hear, "Ah, but a person without time is a dead person."

SIDE TRIPS

Volubilis and Moulay Idriss are highly recommended side trips from Fez and Meknès. Volubilis was the Roman Empire's farthest-flung capital, and Moulay Idriss has Morocco's most sacred shrine, the tomb of founding father Moulay Idriss I. Both sites are key to an understanding of Moroccan history. It's possible to see both places in one day, but if you're not independently mobile and need to sign up for a tour from Meknès or Fez, you might not get the chance to do both. If you must choose between trips to Volubilis and Moulay Idriss, go with the former. The Roman ruins at Volubilis are some of the best archaeological treasures in the country.

Another option is to head over to Oulmès (81 km [50 mi] from Meknès) for an excursion into the hinterlands.

MOULAY IDRISS

23 km (14 mi) north of Meknès, 3 km (2 mi) southeast of Volubilis, 83 km (50 mi) west of Fez.

Moulay Idriss is Morocco's most sacred town, the final resting place of the nation's religious and secular founder, Moulay Idriss I. It is said that five pilgrimages to Moulay Idriss are the spiritual equivalent of one to Mecca; thus the town's nickname: the poor man's Mecca. A view over the town is a panoramic and informative look at a provincial Moroccan village, but it must be said that Moulay Idriss, for all its importance to Moroccans, is of only marginal interest to visitors compared to other Moroccan sights and scenes. Non-Muslims are not allowed inside the tomb at all, and until recently were not allowed to spend the night in town.

GETTING HERE & AROUND

Buses (10 DH) leave Meknès for Moulay Idriss hourly from 8 AM until 6 PM. Getting afternoon buses back to Meknès from Moulay Idriss can be difficult.

TIMING & PRECAUTIONS

Moulay Idriss is a holy town and requires utmost respect for sacred rituals and customs. Dress conservatively and avoid taking pictures of people. Try to arrive on a Saturday, since this is the most active time of the week. Friday is a day of prayer, so expect to see many establishments shut down.

> ### FESTIVAL FOR ALL
>
> A splash of white against Djebel (Mt.) Zerhoun, Moulay Idriss attracts thousands of pilgrims from all over Morocco to its moussem in late August or early September. *Fantasias* (Berber cavalry charges with blazing muskets), acrobats, dancers, and storytellers fill the town, while hundreds of tents cover the hillsides. Non-Muslims are welcome to attend the secular events and can stay overnight at the nearby Hôtel Volubilis Inn.

EXPLORING

The one-hour climb to the vantage point overlooking the **zaouia of Moulay Idriss I** is an invigorating hike through the town's tiny alleys and whitewashed houses and a symbolic bow to Morocco's secular and spiritual history.

Your objective is the **Sidi Abdellah el Hajjam Terrace,** above the Khiber quarter on the left. The adjoining quarter across the gorge is called Tasga.

The **Moulay Idriss Medersa,** hidden in the town's steep and twisting streets, has Morocco's only cylindrical minaret, significant as an indication of the country's resistance to and independence from Turkish influence in the 15th and 16th centuries. Originally built with materials from Volubilis, the minaret is decorated with green ceramic tiles bearing some of the 114 *suras* (chapters) of the Koran.

WHERE TO EAT

The main street through Moulay Idriss (up to the parking area just in front of the zaouia) is lined with a series of small, indistinguishable stands and restaurants serving everything from brochettes of spicy meat to harira to mint tea. Look for **Baraka** (⊠22, *Aïn Smen Khiber* ☎*035/54–41–84*), the town's best, if somewhat overpriced, restaurant.

VOLUBILIS

28 km (17 mi) northwest of Meknès, 88 km (53 mi) northwest of Fez, 3 km (2 mi) west of Moulay Idriss.

Volubilis was the capital of the Roman province of Mauritania (Land of the Moors), Rome's southwesternmost incursion into North Africa. Favored by the confluence of the Rivers Khoumane and Fertasse and surrounded by some of Morocco's most fertile plains, this site has probably been inhabited since the Neolithic era.

CLOSE UP

Roman Morocco

The Roman epoch in Morocco began in about 40 BC. Juba I, king of Numidia (present-day Algeria), sided with Pompey in his rivalry with Caesar and lost, committing suicide after Caesar's victory at Thapsus. His son Juba II, educated in Rome, was nevertheless favored by Caesar and reinstated as king, first of Numidia and later, in 25 BC, of Mauritania. Highly learned, the young prince lived in Volubilis with his wife, Cleopatra Selene (daughter of Antony and Cleopatra), writing lengthy historical and geographical works.

A bronze bust of Juba II found in Volubilis is now displayed in Rabat's Archaeological Museum. It was probably the influence of Juba II that made Volubilis such an opulent outpost. Juba and his son Ptolemy did a great deal for the region, fostering trade, commerce with Rome, the arts, and diplomacy with the Berbers, until the emperor Caligula had Ptolemy murdered in 40 BC and the province rose up against Rome.

After quelling the revolt, Emperor Claudius divided the province into the eastern Mauritania Caesarea and western Mauritania Tingitana, with Tingis (Tangier) as capital. Volubilis prospered, exporting to Rome olive oil, wheat, and wild animals for slaughter in the Colosseum. The last resulted in the swift decimation of Volubilis's lion, bear, and elephant population over a period of 200 years.

Rome's ambitions to extend its empire beyond the Atlas Mountains were never realized, and the Roman garrison withdrew in AD 285 after three centuries in North Africa. Inhabited by a mixture of Berbers, Jews, and peoples from the eastern Mediterranean, Volubilis survived largely intact and still functioned in Latin when Moulay Idriss arrived in 786. With the construction of nearby Meknès, Volubilis's decline accelerated, and by the late 17th century Moulay Ismail was using parts of the Roman ruins to build his lavish imperial capital.

–George Semler

Volubilis's municipal street plan and distribution of public buildings are remarkably coherent examples of Roman urban planning. The floor plans of the individual houses, and especially their well-preserved mosaic floors depicting mythological scenes, provide a rare connection to the sensibilities of the Roman colonists who lived here 2,000 years ago.

If you prefer to see Volubilis on your own (less informative, more contemplative), proceed through the entrance and make a clockwise sweep. After crossing the little bridge over the Fertasse River, climb up to the plateau's left edge, and you'll soon come across a Berber skeleton lying beside a sculpture with his head pointed east, a deliberate placement suggesting early Islamization of the Berber populace here.

GETTING HERE & AROUND

Volubilis is just a 30-minute drive north from Meknès, and an hour's drive from Fez. Sometimes marked on road signs as OUALILI, Volubilis is beyond Moulay Idriss on Route N13, which leaves R413 to head northeast 15 km (9 mi) northwest of Meknès. Grands taxis to Volubilis are available from Meknès and Fez, for 350 DH and 400 DH respectively. From Moulay

Volubilis

Tangier Gate

North Gate

Gordian Palace

House of the Bathing Nymphs

Dionysus & the Four Seasons

House of the Labours of Hercules

Via Decumanus Maximus

House of the Cistern

Knight's House

House of the Columns

House of Ephebus

Arc de Triomphe

North Baths

fountain

fountain

Aqueduct

House of the Nereids

House of Venus

House of the Dog

House of the Athlete

Forum

Basilica

Capitol

Baths of Gallienus

House of Orpheus

Oil Presses

Oued Fertassa

Temple of Saturn

bridge

♦ Café

Entrance

Southeast Gate

Open-air Museum ♦

0   100 yards

0   100 meters

Idriss there are shuttles to Volubilis (6 DH). From Fez, the only regularly scheduled bus connection to Volubilis is via Meknès.

TIMING & PRECAUTIONS

Volubilis is an expansive site that requires intense walking and sun exposure. Tour earlier in the day, wear a hat, and carry a water bottle.

ESSENTIALS

Visitor & Tour Info **Volubilis Tourist Office** (⊠ *City entrance* ☎ *035/54–41–03*).

EXPLORING

Remains of **Roman olive presses** are visible to the left, 2 of some 55 such presses identifiable at Volubilis, proof of the importance of the olive-oil industry that supported the 20,000 inhabitants of this 28-acre metropolis. The first important mosaics are to the right in the imposing **House of Orpheus**: a dolphin mosaic and a mosaic depicting the Orpheus myth in the *tablinum,* a back room used as a library and receiving room. Past the public **Baths of Gallienus,** in a room to the right, are a dozen sets of footprints raised slightly above floor level. If you find this strangely reminiscent of European water-closet engineering, well, that's what this was: a communal bathroom. The wide paved street leading up to the **capitol,** the **basilica,** and the **forum** is the **Cardus Maximus,** the main east–west thoroughfare of any Roman town. Across the forum from the basilica were the market stalls. The **triumphal arch**—built in AD 217, knocked down by the 1755 Lisbon earthquake, and restored in 1932—is down to the left at the end of **Decumanus Maximus,** the main north–south street. The eroded medallions on the arch represent the emperor Caracalla and his mother, Julia Donna. As you look south through the triumphal arch, the first building to the left is known as the **House of the Dog,** since a bronze dog sculpture, now on display in Rabat, was discovered here. The **House of the Athlete,** with a mosaic depicting an acrobat performing an equestrian trick, is right after the House of the Dog. Just south is the entrance to the town brothel, or **Lupanar,** identifiable by an impressive phallus carved out of stone.

The town's greatest mansions and mosaics line the Decumanus Maximus from the town brothel north to the Tangier Gate, which leads out of the enclosure on the uphill end. Some of the most famous include the **House of Ephebus,** just west of the triumphal arch, named for the nude ivy-crowned bronze sculpture discovered here (now on display in Rabat). The *cenacula,* or banquet hall, has colorful mosaics with Bacchic themes.

Continuing up the Decumanus Maximus, the small spaces near the street's edge held shop stalls, while mansions—10 on the left and 8 on

---

PLAY IT SAFE

Volubilis can be hot and dry, as the ruins offer no shade. Wearing a hat and bringing plenty of water are essential.

Since walking is the cheapest and most convenient way to tour, the best pair of walking shoes you can find and break in are the only way to go.

3

the right—lined either side. The house of **Dionysus and the Four Seasons** is about halfway down the Decumanus Maximus; its scene depicting Dionysus discovering Ariadne asleep is one of the town's most spectacular mosaics.

The **House of the Bathing Nymphs** is named for its superb floor mosaics portraying a bevy of frolicking nymphs in a surprisingly contemporary, all but animated, artistic fashion. On the main street's right side, the penultimate house has a marble bas-relief medallion of Bacchus. As you move back south along the next street below and parallel to the Decumanus Maximus, there is a smaller, shorter row of six houses.

The fourth one down contains Volubilis's best set of mosaics and should not be missed. This is the **House of Venus,** with mosaics portraying a chariot race, a bathing Diana surprised by the hunter Actaeon, and the abduction of Hylas by nymphs. The path back down to the entrance passes the site of the Temple of Saturn, across the riverbed on the left.

WHERE TO STAY

$$$

MOROCCAN

🏨 **Hôtel Volubilis Inn.** Surrounded by olive trees high on a hillside, this comfortable hotel has exceptional views from its pool and terrace over the valley to the southwest. The hotel's two restaurants, one Moroccan and the other international, have outdoor dining areas overlooking the ruins. All guest rooms have balconies or terraces, are contemporary in design, and well equipped with modern appliances. The inn is a good bet if you either accidentally run out of daylight or deliberately decide to watch the sunset from Volubilis. If you're coming from Meknès, the hotel is 500 yards beyond the entrance to the Roman ruins, across the street. **Pros:** Modern rooms, outstanding views. **Con:** Popular with tour groups. ✉ *Rte. de Volubilis (N13,) Moulay Idriss Zarhoun* ☎ *035/54–44–05* ⊕ *www.hotelvolubinisinn.com* 🛏 *53 rooms* ⚑ *In-room: refrigerator. In-hotel: 2 restaurants, bar, room service, pool* ☰ *AE, DC, MC, V.*

The Middle Atlas

WORD OF MOUTH

"We were on our way to Fez via Midelt. As we passed through Azrou we got to see our first animal (besides the many stray dogs) . . . monkeys. Our guide was making us laugh trying to act like the monkey. He kept us well entertained. We stopped in Ifrane aka the Snow City and had a very good lunch at an outdoor eatery."

—lourdesmadrid

By Sarah
Wyatt

ALMOST CONNECTING FEZ AND MARRAKESH, the Middle Atlas is a North African Arcadia, where rivers, forests, and grasslands abound. Snowy cedar forests, ski slopes, and trout streams are not images normally associated with Morocco, yet the Middle Atlas unfolds like an ersatz alpine fantasy less than an hour from medieval Fez. To remind you that this is still North Africa, Barbary apes scurry around the roadsides, and the occasional *djellaba* (hooded gown) and veil appear in ski areas.

Most travelers to Morocco are content to glance at the Middle Atlas as they whiz between Fez and Marrakesh, or between Meknès and points south. Depending on how much time they have, this is only logical, considering that the High Atlas, the desert, the great oasis valleys, the Imperial Cities, and the Atlantic coast are all more emblematically Moroccan and more exotic to the Westerner than this mountain redoubt in between. Perhaps for this reason, some of this central highland's secret valleys and villages are doubly rewarding discoveries for their integrity and authenticity.

ORIENTATION & PLANNING

ORIENTATION

You didn't come to Morocco for evergreens and skiing, presumably, so the Middle Atlas is most recommendable as a brief surprise on your way to or from the Sahara. The Atlas mountain ranges separate the Mediterranean and Atlantic coasts from the desert. Azrou and Ifrane are the central mountain resorts and winter-sports stations. Farther afield, the Cirque du Djebel Tazzeka, the difficult mountain tracks through the Djebel Bou Iblane Massif, and, farther south, the Massif de Tichchoukt are great for adventurers with four-wheel-drive vehicles and loose schedules. Midelt is on the range's southern edge, with splendid views of the often snowcapped High Atlas, while Khénifra, Kasba Tadla, and Beni-Mellal are primarily base camps for exploring upland objectives like the source of the River Oum-er-Rbia, El-Ksiba, and (for the intrepid and well equipped) Imilchil. The loop south from Beni-Mellal on the S508 road makes a good final leg on a north–south (Fez to Marrakesh) tour of one of Morocco's least explored regions.

The main points of interest are well connected with surfaced routes, either main roads marked in red or secondary routes marked in yellow on the Michelin 959 road map. Routes marked in white may vary wildly from well-paved and passable thoroughfares to tracks only fit for four-wheel-drive vehicles with plenty of clearance. Generally speaking, the farther away from the red roads you get in Morocco, the more interesting and rewarding the terrain—and this is particularly true of the Middle Atlas. Avoid the main Fez-to-Marrakesh route, the N8, whenever possible (though you'll need it to reach Kasba Tadla and Beni-Mellal). ⚠ **You should usually believe the most pessimistic advice**

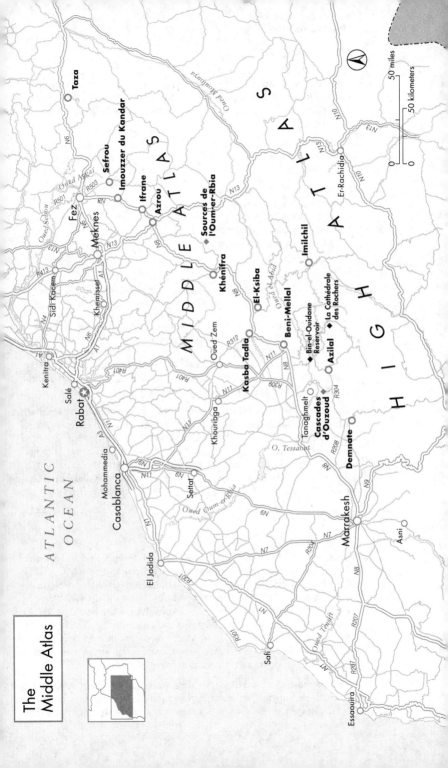

The Middle Atlas

ATLANTIC OCEAN

Taza
Sefrou
Imouzzer du Kandar
Ifrane
Azrou
Fez
Meknes
Sources de l'Oum-er-Rbia
Khénifra
El-Ksiba
Imilchil
Beni-Mellal
La Cathédrale des Rochers
Bin-el-Ouidane Reservoir
Azilal
Kasba Tadla
Tanaghmelt
Cascades d'Ouzoud
Kenitra
Salé
Rabat
Sidi-Kacem
Khemisset
Oued Zem
Khouribga
Demnate
Mohammedia
Casablanca
Settat
Marrakesh
Asni
El Jadida
Safi
Essaouira

MIDDLE ATLAS
HIGH ATLAS
SAHARA

Oued Moulouya
Oued Sebou
Oued Agaï
Oued el Abid
O. Tessaout
Oued Oum-er-Rbia
Oued Tensift

Er-Rachidia

50 miles
50 kilometers

N6
N13
R503
R501
N8
N13
N13
N10
N13
N11
R312
R401
N11
R309
N8
R304
R308
N9
N7
R204
N7
N8
N1
N9
R301
R207
R207
A1
A3
A4
N4
N6
R13

TOP REASONS TO GO

See stunning waterfalls: the cascading falls of Ouzoud are among the most stunning sights in the Middle Atlas.

Ski before a Sahara sunset: the Merzouga dunes in Mischliffen rise up to 492 feet.

Trekking to thrilling elevations: the Djebel Ayachi Massif, south of Midelt, and the Tessaout gorges, southwest of Demnate, offer physical challenge and breathtaking views.

Explore unusual flora and fauna: the Azrou Cedar Forest is Morocco's equivalent to Arcadia.

Take an overland safari: the September marriage moussem at Imilchil is best reached in a four-wheel-drive vehicle.

you hear on road conditions; optimists tend to be either misinformed or overeager to give you good news.

The Mediterranean Middle Atlas. Spreading south and east of Fez, the northern Middle Atlas is drained by the River Moulouya en route to the Mediterranean Sea near the Algerian border. The Azrou Cedar Forest and the Djebel Tazzeka Massif above Taza are the main attractions in this heavily forested northern zone, along with Midelt and the Cirque de Jaffar at the more-barren southern edge.

The Atlantic Middle Atlas. As you head toward Marrakesh, the southern Middle Atlas is drained by the River Oum-er-Rbia, which flows across the Tadla Plain to the Atlantic Ocean south of Casablanca. Forested with olive groves and live oaks on their lower slopes, the rugged mountains to the south of El-Ksiba and Beni-Mellal offer memorable trek and jeep excursions and form a striking contrast to Azilal's lush Cascades d'Ouzoud and Demnate's natural bridge at Imi-n-Ifri.

PLANNING

WHEN TO GO

This part of Morocco is relatively cool year-round, and often snow-bound in midwinter with temperatures dropping below 0°C (32°F). For skiing or driving through the snow-filled Azrou Cedar Forest (occasionally snowed in from January to March, but normally well plowed), come between December and April. April–June is the best time to hike and explore the headwaters of the region's many rivers. The high tourist season in the mountains (mid-March through summer) can draw the occasional crowd to sites you'd probably prefer to see in their natural state. Summer daytime temperatures average around 25°C (77°F).

The increasingly famous September marriage *moussem* (pilgrimage festival) in Imilchil, to which Berber families bring brides, including reluctant teenage girls, to meet and marry their husbands in mass ceremonies, is the Atlas's best-known moussem. Beni-Mellal's mid-March cotton festival, Sefrou's June cherry festival, and Imouzzer du Kandar's August apple festival are some other local revels.

GETTING HERE & AROUND

The only reasonable way to explore the Middle Atlas is by car, prefer-

<table>
<tr><td colspan="2">SOUK DAYS</td></tr>
<tr><td>Sunday: Demnate, Khénifra, Midelt
Monday: Imouzzer du Kandar
Tuesday: Azrou, Beni-Mellal
Wednesday: Khénifra
Thursday: Sefrou</td></tr>
</table>

ably by four-wheel-drive jeep. Most contracts for rented standard cars stipulate in fine print that traveling on unpaved roads violates the terms of the rental agreement—meaning that if you run into trouble on some mountain track, you're on your own. This can be expensive. Buses can get you to the main towns in the Middle Atlas if you're planning a hiking excursion, but you'll need a taxi from towns such as Beni-Mellal or Midelt to get you to trailheads like the Cirque de Jaffar. Hitching (or paying for) rides on trucks serving remote markets can be useful for exploring the backcountry between the Middle and High Atlas, but these are often several days apart, and fares can approach extortion.

Most travelers begin a Middle Atlas itinerary in Fez, terminating in Marrakesh. Visitors may fly directly into the Fès–Saïss Airport, or fly into Casablanca and take ground transportation to Fez. Touring the Middle Atlas with a dedicated guide is generally unnecessary and expensive; consider utilizing local guides in each city.

RESTAURANTS & CUISINE

Most of the Middle Atlas hotels we recommend have fair to excellent restaurants, but don't hesitate to stop at a small-town crossroads or souk for the odd bowl of *harira* (chickpea, lentil, and meat soup) for 5 DH or less. Brochettes (beef or lamb kebabs) cost about a U.S. dollar. You can also order a few lamb chops and some fresh countryside Moroccan bread at truck stops like the one at Itzer. ■TIP→ **You may want to carry a few bottles of wine with you, as wine is not often served in the mountains. Note that some Islamic villagers frown upon alcohol of any kind.**

WHAT IT COSTS IN DIRHAMS					
	¢	$	$$	$$$	$$$$
AT DINNER	under 40DH	40DH–70DH	70DH–90DH	90DH–110DH	over 110DH

Prices are per person for a main course at dinner.

ABOUT THE HOTELS

With the notable exceptions of Beni-Mellal's Hôtel Ouzoud, there are no luxury hotels in the Middle Atlas. Though perfectly survivable, lodging tends to be undistinguished. Some of the inns and auberges off the beaten path should be thought of as shelter rather than full-service hotels.

WHAT IT COSTS IN DIRHAMS				
¢	$	$$	$$$	$$$$
FOR TWO PEOPLE	under 175DH	175DH–250DH	250DH–350DH	350DH–500DH	over 500DH

All prices are for a high-season standard double room, including service and tax.

SAFETY

Even in the dead of winter, from December through February, the snow-removal system in the Azrou Cedar Forest is excellent. Ten-foot banks of snow may flank the road, but the driving surface will be clear unless you're in the middle of the snowstorm. The more remote roads (marked in white on the Michelin 742 National Morocco map) will be completely closed in snowy conditions and are often difficult even at the best of times. Beware particularly of the C1811 to the Cascades d'Ouzoud. The 63 km (37 mi) from the S508 to the P24 is also very rough going and should not be attempted in a car with low clearance. ■TIP➡ **A general rule of thumb is to consider all roads marked in white on the Michelin 959 map to be suitable mainly for vehicles with four-wheel drive.**

Accidents and medical emergencies in the Middle and High Atlas should be reported to the nearest Gendarmerie Royale or Protection Civile, both of which are Moroccan public safety groups. As helicopter assistance may be long in coming, it's best to pack as complete a first-aid kit as possible.

The minimum driving age in Morocco is 18, but some car-rental companies require drivers to be 21 or over. An international driving license is not required in Morocco if you carry your domestic license that bears a photograph. Driving in Morocco is on the right side, and speed limits are generally 120 km per hour (75 mph) on the extended highways and 100 km per hour (62 mph) on urban highways.

WHAT TO WEAR

Morocco can be a progressive country and most Moroccan women do not wear head scarves. Moroccans have been widely exposed to, and have an awareness of, Western culture and style. In rural areas of the Middle Atlas, women should dress conservatively and avoid wearing low-cut tops, midriffs, or shorts. In more urban areas including Taza and Sefrou, women can dress less conservatively but in general they should follow the lead from local women. Men and women should avoid baring their entire arms or anything above the knees. Swimsuits should be worn only at the pool or on the beach.

THE MEDITERRANEAN MIDDLE ATLAS

Spreading south and east of Fez, the northern Middle Atlas is drained by the River Moulouya en route to the Mediterranean Sea near the Algerian border. The Azrou Cedar Forest and the Djebel Tazzeka Massif above Taza are the main attractions in this heavily forested northern

OUTDOORS IN THE MIDDLE ATLAS

The contacts here organize tours beyond their immediate towns, so feel free to check out any of these when planning your trip.

HIKING & TREKKING

Major treks beckon from the Djebel Ayachi Massif, south of Midelt, as well as above Beni-Mellal, Azilal, and Demnate. The Tessaout gorges above Lac des Aït-Aadel, west of Demnate, have some of Morocco's best and most spectacular long-distance trekking. The Délégation Provincial du Tourisme recommends guides for hikes, treks, mule trips, ski outings, and fishing trips. Imilchil Voyages organizes treks as well as trout-fishing trips.

Contacts: **Délégation de Tourisme** (⊠ *Ave. Hassan II, Azilal* ☎ *023/45–87–22*). **Imilchil Voyages** (⊠ *333, bd. Mohammed V, Beni-Mellal* ☎ *023/48–90–60*).

HORSEBACK RIDING

A few outfits organize mountain outings on horseback. Try the Centre Equestre et de Randonnée, Club Omnisport, or the Royal Club Equestre de Randonnée.

Contacts: **Centre Equestre et de Randonnée** (⊠ *Aïn Amyer, Rte. d'Immouzzer, Km 2, Fez* ☎ *055/60–64–21*). **Club Omnisport** (⊠ *Rte. de Marrakesh, Km 4, Beni-Mellal* ☎ *023/48–22–02*). **Fédération Royale Marocaine des Sports Equestres** (⊠ *B.P. 742, Dar Es-salam, Rabat* ☎ *037/75–44–24*). **Royal Club Equestre de Randonnée** (⊠ *Dayet Aoua, Ifrane* ☎ *035/64–28–86*).

FISHING

Morocco, surprisingly, offers trout fishing in the foothills of the High Atlas and in the Azrou Cedar Forest. European brown trout and rainbows, nearly all stocked fish or descendants of repopulated fisheries, thrive in select highland environments. March through May are the prime angling months. Permits and further orientation are available through the Administration des Eaux et Forêts offices in Rabat.

Permits: **Administration des Eaux et Forêts** (⊠ *11, rue du Devoir, Rabat* ☎ *037/70–33–25*).

RAFTING

There are even white-water rafting opportunities in the area. Moroccan White Water Experience, in Marrakesh, runs three-day white-water rafting expeditions along the Ahansal River in the Middle Atlas. Trips leave every Monday, Wednesday, and Friday, February–May, and cost $250.

Contact: **Moroccan White Water Experience** (⊠ *41, ave. Yougoslavie, Guéliz* ☎ *077/84–37–06*)

SKIING

Mischliffen and Djebel Hebri are the two ski resorts nearest Ifrane and within day-trip range of Fez. Don't expect too much of these snow bowls—the trails are few and relatively simple—but if your ambitions are modest, a day on the slopes is a pleasant option here. For rental equipment and lodging, the Hôtel Aghlias is the place.

Contact: **Hôtel Aghlias** (⊠ *Station de Ski de Mischliffen* ☎ *035/56–04–92*).

A BIT OF HISTORY

The Berber tribes'that inhabited the Middle Atlas when the Phoenicians arrived in 1100 BC were aboriginal Caucasoid peoples who occupied the lands between the Sahara and the Mediterranean throughout North Africa, from Egypt to the Atlantic. The so-called Barbary Coast was named for the Berbers, who are thought to have originated in Central Asia, though various theories have also connected them to the Celts, Basques, and Canaanites.

Prior to Roman annexation and imperial rule in AD 24, the Berber kingdom of Mauritania was a loose federation of Berber tribes centered on Volubilis. Juba II (25 BC–AD 23), one of the first romanized Berber rulers, was educated in Rome and married the daughter of Antony and Cleopatra. The 7th-century Arab invasion initiated the Islamization of the Berbers, who up to that point had been a mixture of pagans, Christians, and Jews.

Morocco's modern history has included a series of only partly successful attempts to subjugate the staunchly independent Berber majority tribes, who even today remain largely aloof from Morocco's government.

zone, along with Midelt and the Cirque de Jaffar at the more barren southern edge.

GETTING HERE & AROUND

The Fès–Saïss Airport serves the Middle Atlas as well as Fez and Meknès. Azrou, Ifrane, Sefrou, Imouzzer du Kandar, Beni-Mellal, Azilal, Midelt, Kasba Tadla, and Khénifra are all served by Compagnie de Transports au Maroc buses, if somewhat sporadically. The bus from Casablanca to Ifrane to Azrou takes six hours from beginning to end; the one from Meknès to Azrou to Midelt takes four to five hours total. If you have any intention of wandering into the hinterland (and you will), be sure you're driving a four-wheel-drive vehicle, and consider carrying more than one spare as well as emergency fuel. Depending on where you're coming from, it's best to rent a car in Fez or Meknès.

ESSENTIALS

Bus Terminals Azrou (⊠ Bd. Moulay Abdelkader s/n ☎ 055/56–20–20). **Ifrane** (⊠ Ave. de la Marché Verte s/n ☎ 055/56–68–21). **Midelt** (⊠ Ave. Mohammed V s/n ☎ 055/58–14–20). **Taza** (⊠ Pl. de l'Indépendance s/n ☎ 055/67–30–37).

Currency Exchange BMCI (⊠ Er Rachidia Rd., Midelt). **Credit du Maroc** (⊠ Bd. Mohammed V at Ave. des Tilluels, Ifrane).

Internet Mahlabat Annas (⊠ 3, rue Esmara, Bit Ghoulam, Taza ☎ 035/67–43–44).

Post Office Midelt Main Post Office (⊠ Er Rachidia Rd, Midelt ☎ 055/58–14–20).

Rental Cars Avis (Fez-Saiss Airport, Fez ☎ 055/62–69–69 ⊠ www.avis.com) **Budget** (Fez-Saiss Airport, Fez ☎ 35/94–00–92 ⊕ www.budget.com). **Europcar** (45. ave. Hassan II , Fez ☎ 055/62–65–45 ⊕ car-rental.europcar.com).

Taxis **Ifrane** (⊠ *Ifrane-Meknès Rd., Ifrane*). **Midelt** (⊠ *Er Rachidia Rd., Midelt*).

Visitor & Tour Info **Délégation du Tourisme d'Ifrane** (⊠ *Ave. Prince Moulay Abdallah, Ifrane* ☎ *035/56-68-21*). **Délégation du Tourisme de Taza** (⊠ *30, ave. Mohammed V , Taza* ☎ *055/67-35-83*).

TAZA

120 km (72 mi) east of Fez.

Taza's medina is one of Morocco's most pristine, largely untouched by modern life or Western customs. An important capital during the Almohad, Merenid, and early Alaouite dynasties (11th to 16th century), Taza was used as a passage into Morocco by the first Moroccan Arabs—the Idrissids—and nearly all successive invaders en route to Fez. The Taza Gap separates the Rif from the Middle Atlas Mountains. Fortified and refortified, Taza was never easy to defend, and Berber tribes as well as succeeding dynasties managed to move through it like hot knives through butter.

PLAY IT SAFE

The sight of Berber children sprinting toward your car can be unnerving. Not running over them may require skillful maneuvering, but don't stop or you may find yourself in a roadblock with only one way out: buying something. Likewise, resist the temptation to pick up children offering to "guide" you through remote villages.

EXPLORING

The lovely and haunting city walls, first constructed in the 12th century, are in various stages of disrepair. **Bab er-Rih** (Gate of the Wind), the main entry, is panoramic and moving, with views up into the forested hillsides of the Djebel Tazzeka. The main street through the middle of town connects the medina's four mosques, the Grande Mosquée, the Sidi Azouz Mosque, the Mosquée du Marché, and the Andalous Mosque. With its perforated cupola, the **Grande Mosquée,** or Great Mosque, is the most striking and widely visible of the four. The mosque, founded by Sultan Abd el-Moumen, is possibly the oldest Almohad structure in existence and is believed to predate the mosque at Tin Mal. The **Mosquée du Marché,** or Market Mosque, is an unusual, upside-down-seeming structure, its base oddly more slender than the tower above. The covered stalls of the kissaria (commercial center) and the granary outside the mosque are worth a visit.

WHERE TO EAT & STAY

$ ✕**Les Deux Rives.** This small, bright Mediterranean restaurant offers light entrées including salads, soups, and pizzas. ⊠*20, ave. Oujda* ☎*035/67-12-27* ▤*No credit cards.*
MEDITERRANEAN

$ ▦**Grand Hôtel du Dauphiné.** This Art Nouveau building was once, like the town itself, an elegant and grandiose affair. It has seen better days, but retains some charm for this very reason. The rooms, some of which have balconies overlooking Place de l'Indépendance, have aging furniture and fixtures (no superfluous extras like televisions or refrigerators). The service is at best desultory, but the place's old-world feel gives it a novelistic allure. The restaurant, while no gourmet tour de force, pre-
MOROCCAN

pares hearty tagines of several varieties and a stick-to-your-ribs *harira* (a soup including lentils, chickpeas, lamb stock, onions, garlic, tomatoes, herbs, and spices). **Pros:** Old-fashioned vibe, near public transportation. **Cons:** Dowdy decor, no heat in winter. ⊠*Pl. de l'Indépendance* ☎*035/67–35–67* ⇌*26 rooms, 9 with bath* &*In-room: safe. In-hotel: restaurant, parking (fee)* ▤*No credit cards.*

SEFROU

33 km (20 mi) southeast of Fez, 136 km (82 mi) southwest of Taza.

A miniature Fez at an altitude of 2,900 feet, the white town of Sefrou lies in the fertile valley of the notoriously flood-prone River Agdal, at the foot of the Middle Atlas's first heights. A first stop on the caravan routes between the Sahara and the Mediterranean coast, it was originally populated by Berber converts to Judaism, who came north from the Tafilalt date palmery and from Algeria in the 13th century. The town remained a nucleus of Jewish life until 1956, when, upon the country's declaration of independence from France, virtually the entire Jewish community left Morocco.

EXPLORING

Sefrou's **medina** would be considered one of Morocco's great treasures were it not overshadowed by that of Fez, probably the world's largest and densest such quarters. The walls, *babs* (gates into the medina), and Jewish **Mellah** are all worth poking around. Separated from the medina by the River Aggai, the Mellah is now inhabited almost entirely by Muslims, with only a few Jewish families remaining. The **Thursday souk** is a nice opportunity for some relatively sedate shopping.

The *zaouia* (sanctuary) of **Sidi Lahcen Ben Ahmed** contains the remains of this 17th-century saint.

From the Mellah's dark and narrow streets, stone bridges cross the Aggai into the souks north of the mosque. During the town's Cherry Festival, in May or June, a procession ventures across the Aggai to the **Kef el-Mumen** cave, said to contain the prophet Daniel's tomb, a pilgrimage venerated by Jews and Muslims alike. According to legend, seven followers of Daniel (and, somewhat oddly, their dog) slept here for centuries before miraculously resuscitating.

West of Sefrou is the miraculous fountain of **Lalla Rekia,** believed to cure mental illness. Some visitors bring jugs and other containers to the site in order to carry away the alleged benefits. The area is best accessed by rental car or taxi, as public transportation in the area is limited.

WHERE TO STAY

$ 🏨**Hôtel Sidi Lahcen el Youssi.** Named for the local saint, this mountain chalet is blessed with a fine restaurant and a distinctly alpine ambience that is startling and welcome in North Africa. Menu choices include Moroccan specialties such as *mechoui* (roast lamb) and *pastilla* (sweet pigeon pie in puff pastry). The fresh wood decor and the pastoral surroundings combine to make this a favorite country getaway for Fas-

GREAT DRIVE: CIRQUE DU DJEBEL TAZZEKA

The 123-km (74-mi) loop around the Cirque du Djebel Tazzeka southwest of Taza is one of the most varied and spectacular day trips in the Middle Atlas. Packing a range of diversions from a picnic at the waterfalls of Ras el Oued to serious spelunking in the Gouffre du Friouato (Friouato Cave), cresting the 6,494-foot Djebel Tazzeka, or navigating the gorges of the Oued Zireg, this tour is a topographer's fantasy. The entire multisurface drive takes some five hours without stops.

The S311 road south from Taza is narrow and serpentine, though soundly guard-railed, with oncoming vehicles the primary hazard. The Cascades of Ras El, 10 km (6 mi) south of Taza, are a first stop, best in spring when hydraulic abundance makes them spectacular. The Parc National de Tazzeka entrance offers a handy picnic area. The right fork on the S311 takes you to the Friouato caves (part of the park) while the left leads out to the often dry lake bed of Daïa Chiker, most impressive in early spring when subterranean waters keep it filled.

The **Friouato Cave** complex, 26 km (16 mi) from Taza, is well marked; a guard will show you through North Africa's deepest caverns—they extend steeply down 520 stairs to a depth of 590 feet. Explored by the eminent French speleologist Norbert Casteret in 1930, the caves consist of various large chambers filled with enormous stalagmites in strange and fantastic shapes and colors. Chambers such as the Salle de Lixus, the Salle de Draperies, and the Salle Casteret lead through what has been referred to as an underground palace. This experience is not for claustrophobes or the faint of mind or limb. The caves are muddy and wet, the climb down and back is strenuous, and opportunities for minor injuries are many. As with many caves, the Friouato Caves are home to a large family of bats. Proper hiking footwear and warm clothes that you don't mind getting wet are recommended, as are powerful flashlights. Admission to the top gallery costs 10 DH, and a three-hour guided tour (including flashlight rental) costs 120 DH.

Beyond the caves, the road climbs through a pine forest to the village of Bab Bou Idir, abandoned except in summer when the campground and chalets fill with vacationers. After another 8 km (5 mi), the right-hand fork leads 9 km (5.5 mi) to the crest of Djebel Tazzeka, 6,494 feet, a tough climb by car or on foot. Your reward is the unique view over the Rif and south to the Middle Atlas.

From Djebel Tazzeka there are another 38 km (23 mi) north along the spectacular Zireg river gorges to Sidi Abdallah de Rhiata, where you can get on the N6 back to Taza or Fez.

⚠ **Note that the 7-km (4.5-mi) track to the crest of Djebel Tazzeka is a dangerous drive in bad weather.**

sis (residents of Fez). **Pros:** Clean rooms, nice ambience. **Con:** Not traditional Moroccan. ⊠ *Rue Sidi Ali Bou Serghine* ☎ *035/68–34–28* ↪ *20 rooms, 3 bungalows* ♿ *In-room: safe. In-hotel: restaurant, pool* ▭ *No credit cards.*

> **WHEN TO GO**
>
> Imouzzer du Kandar's Apple Festival, held in June, is the event of the year, and is well worth a stop for its music, dancing, and general atmosphere.

IMOUZZER DU KANDAR

38 km (23 mi) south of Fez, 23 km (14 mi) southwest of Sefrou.

A mountain retreat for stressed-out Fassis, Imouzzer du Kandar is a small town with little more than a central square and a Kasbah in ruins. It's virtually a suburb of Fez, but it's considered the first real stop in the Middle Atlas. Imouzzer holds a Monday souk, where Berber artisans bring natural and homemade products and are even more eager to close sales than the hardened negotiators in the big cities.

EXPLORING

Just 9 km (5 mi) south of Imouzzer du Kandar, **Dayet Aoua,** a lovely freshwater lake, is a pretty place to camp or rent a boat. Hiking, bird-watching, and horseback riding are also popular activities. Local guides are available for about 350 DH daily.

WHERE TO STAY

$ 🏨 **Hôtel des Truites.** This little mountain enclave—the Trout Hotel—is a welcome break after the intensity of Fez or Marrakesh, a pastoral sanctuary with excellent vistas over the Massif de Kandar and the Plaine du Saïss. The rooms are small and spartan but cozy and clean. The restaurant serves a standard range of Moroccan specialties as well as French and dishes such as fresh trout at dinner, and breakfast for an additional fee. About half the rooms have private baths. **Pros:** Quiet location, hearty breakfasts. **Con:** Rooms have just the basics. ⊠ *Rte. P24 from Fez entering Imouzzer* ☎ *035/66–30–02* ↪ *18 rooms* ♿ *In-room: safe. In-hotel: restaurant, parking (no fee)* ▭ *No credit cards.*

IFRANE

25 km (15 mi) southwest of Imouzzer du Kandar, 63 km (37 mi) southwest of Fez.

Built in 1929 during the French protectorate to form a deliberate "*poche de France*" (pocket of France) for expatriate French diplomats, functionaries, and business personnel, Ifrane's alpine chalets and broad, well-lighted boulevards seem almost like an officially organized sight gag or Potemkin village if you've just come from Fez or Marrakesh, and particularly if you've come from the desert. But if you could use a short break from the Moroccan-ness of Morocco, this is the place to find it.

EXPLORING

At an altitude of 5,412 feet, Ifrane is known for its cold-water trout fishery and its excellent hiking trails up to the **Cascades des Vierges** (Waterfall of the Virgins). Zaouia de Ifrane, the village to the north, is known for its artisans. The ruling Alaouite dynasty has a royal palace in Ifrane, identifiable by its green-tile roof (an exclusive royal privilege), so you may encounter extraordinary security measures.

WHERE TO EAT & STAY

$$$$
MOROCCAN
✕**La Paix.** This airy restaurant offers tagines and other Moroccan specialties. There's a range of international dishes as well, ranging from salads to pizzas. The menu is somewhat limited but the food is tasty, the staff is friendly, and the terrace is spacious. ⊠ *Ave. de la Marche Vert* ☎ *055/93–17–97* ⊟ *No credit cards.*

$$$$
MOROCCAN
▥**Hôtel Mischliffen.** It may be just an hour south of the world's largest medieval city at Fez, but this major European-style vacation hotel has as many comforts and as much action as you will find near the Mischliffen ski area. If courting culture shock is your cup of tea, don't miss this giant overlooking the Azrou Cedar Forest and the Djebel Hebri, another ski opportunity. Rooms are large and lushly carpeted and curtained; the restaurant and nightlife are excellent. **Pros:** Beautiful views, near dining and nightlife. **Con:** Limited public transportation. ⊠ *B. P. 18, Ifrane* ☎ *035/56–66–07* ⊕ *www.concorde-hotels.com* ⇱ *107 rooms* ☖ *In-room: safe, refrigerator. In-hotel: restaurant, bar, pool, parking (fee)* ⊟ *MC, V.*

AZROU

17 km (10 mi) southwest of Ifrane, 67 km (40 mi) southeast of Meknès, 78 km (47 mi) southwest of Fez.

Occupying an important junction of routes between the desert and Meknès and between Fez and Marrakesh, Azrou—from the Berber word for "rock"—is a significant ancient Berber capital. It was one of Sultan Moulay Ismail's strongholds after he built an imposing fortress here (now largely in ruins) in 1684; but Azrou was for centuries unknown, a secret mountain town that invading forces never fully located, thanks in part to a cave system designed for concealment and protection.

EXPLORING

Seeing a Berber nucleus, the French established the **Collège Berbère** here in an attempt to train an elite Berber opposition to the urban Arab ruling class; both Arabic and Islam were prohibited. After independence, Berber College became an Arabic school, and the movement faded.

Azrou's artisan center, the **Maison de l'Artisanat,** just off the P24 to Khénifra (and a mere five-minute walk from Place Mohammed V), is one of the town's main attractions—it's a trading post for the Beni M'Guild tribes, who are known for their fine carpets, kilims, and cedar carvings. Place Mohammed V, a square lined with numerous cafés, holds an important Tuesday souk where prices start significantly lower than in the major cities.

★ The **Azrou Cedar Forest** is a unique habitat in Morocco, as much a state of mind as a woodland. Moroccans are proud of their cedar forest, always one of the national geography's crown jewels. Even in the Fez medina you can sense a breath of fresh air when the forest is mentioned, usually as the source of some intricate cedar carving. Moroccan cedars grow to heights of close to 200 feet, and cover some 320,000 acres on the slopes of the Middle Atlas, the High Atlas, and the Rif at altitudes between 3,940 and 9,200 feet; the forest's senior members are more than 400 years old. Cedar is much coveted by woodworkers, particularly makers of stringed musical instruments. Living among the enormous cedars to the south of Azrou are troops of Barbary apes, and birdlife ranging from the redheaded Moroccan woodpecker to owls and eagles. Flora include the large-leaf peony, the scarlet dianthus, and the blue germander, all of which attract butterflies, including the cardinal and the colorful sulphur Cleopatra. If you'd like to visit, you should pick up information, guides, and maps of the forest showing trails and hikes at the **Ifrane Tourist Office** (⊠*Ave. Prince Moulay Abdallah, Ifrane* ☎*035/56–68–21*); it's open weekdays 8:30–12:30 and 2:30–6:30.

WHERE TO EAT & STAY

$$–$$$ ✕ **Patisserie Azrou.** This café, located near the mosque in the city center,
CAFÉ is smoky and dark on the ground floor but more pleasant and spacious upstairs or on the terrace. The coffee is flavorful and the service friendly. ⊠*Pl. Hassan II* ☎*No phone* ▭*No credit cards.*

$$$–$$$$ ▦ **Auberge Amros.** Outside town on the road to Meknès, this little inn is popular among Azrou natives for its restaurant, which serves excellent French and Moroccan cuisine. Try the *truite meunière* with almonds followed by a spicy Moroccan tagine for tastes from two worlds. Surrounded by oak and cedar forest, the auberge is a good base camp for hiking or fly-fishing in the Middle Atlas. Rooms are on the small side but are cozy and decorated in light tones with wood trim. Management is attentive. **Pros:** Great food, friendly staff. **Con:** Public transportation is limited. ⊠*Rte. P21, Km 3* ☎*035/56–36–63* ⤶*74 rooms* ⟳*In-room: safe. In-hotel: restaurant, bar, pool* ▭*MC, V.*

$$–$$$ ▦ **Hôtel Panorama.** This handy place near Azrou's center has good views over the forest and town as well as an excellent restaurant and reliable heating—more than welcome during Azrou's long, snowy winters. This hotel offers rustic charm with open fireplaces and pointed gables. The restaurant serves Moroccan fare with a hearty mountain emphasis strong in tagines, Atlas trout, and soups such as harira. A limited breakfast selection is available for an additional charge. Rooms are clean and equipped with TVs. The owners are conscientious and pleasant. **Pros:** Helpful staff, quiet location. **Con:** A bit old-fashioned. ⊠*Rue el Hansali, Azrou Center* ☎*035/56–20–10* ⤶*36 rooms* ⟳*In-room: safe. In-hotel: restaurant, bar, parking (no fee)* ▭*MC, V.*

SOURCES DE L'OUM-ER-RBIA

57 km (35 mi) southwest of Azrou.

Water always seems a rare treasure in Morocco, and a trip to the 40 or more springs that form the sources of the River Oum-er-Rbia is an interesting way to start a day that could end in the Sahara. The springs are best approached from Azrou and Aïn Leuh through the cedar forest. Flowing across nearly the entire Moroccan heartland from the Middle Atlas to the Atlantic Ocean (at Azemmour, south of Casablanca), the great Oum-er-Rbia, Morocco's longest river, has been diverted, dammed, and largely destroyed over the years in favor of irrigation and hydroelectric projects. Spawning shad used to swim upriver from the Atlantic until the proliferation of dams interrupted their life cycle. The sources are now impressive for the great volume of crystal-clear water exploding from the adjoining mountain's side, part of the Djebel Hebri Massif and the Mischliffen ski area (thus the snow runoff). The Aguelmane Azigza (Lake Azigza), another 20 km (12 mi) south of the sources on the 3211 road, is another impressive Middle Atlas site, with red cliffs surrounding the blue waters.

Several cafés and restaurants are built into the rock terraces around the flow, and as long as they're open (they're deserted when not overflowing with busloads of tourists), they'll fix you anything from mint tea to tagines. You'll be greeted here by a mob of youths racing across the parking lot to divvy you up: you'll want at least one boy to guard your car, as well as a guide or two for the 10-minute walk uphill. Although it can be tempting to flee, it's more rewarding to play along; hand out a few 5 DH pieces to avoid battling with these kids the whole time you're here.

KAYAKING ADVENTURES

Khénifra is a mere 10 hours by kayak, so if you happen to have brought a kayak to Morocco (many do: you can actually kayak in the Sahara, at the seasonal salt lake Dyet Sjri, near Merzouga), this is the place to start. There are no dams until after the River Oued Tessaout junction, 100 km (60 mi) north of Marrakesh.

4

KHÉNIFRA

82 km (49 mi) southwest of Azrou, 45 km (27 mi) southwest of Sources de l'Oum-er-Rbia, 327 km (197 mi) northeast of Marrakesh.

This dusty, red-clay city on the Oum-er-Rbia's banks is no paradise, but it does offer a good look at life in a Moroccan market town. Khénifra is known locally as Red City for its *pisé* (rammed earth) houses and relentless red dust. The town holds a carpet auction on Saturday and souks on Wednesday and Sunday; look for the *taraza,* the typical equestrian headgear made of straw and decorated with colorful wool tassels and pendants. Berber Zaiane tribesmen have long been known for their horsemanship and still compete on the local racetrack for moussems and other special events.

WHERE TO EAT & STAY

$$$
MOROCCAN

✕ **Restaurant de France.** A pleasant stop on the long road between Fez and Marrakesh, this small restaurant offers delicious Moroccan entrées. There are some international dishes as well. ⊠ *Quartier des Forces Armées Royales* ☎ *055/58–61–14* ⊟ *V.*

$$–$$$

⌐ **Atlas Zayane.** Previously named for the 19th-century *caid* (chief) Hamou Azzayani, leader of Khénifra's legendary resistance to centralized power, this modern building in the New Town is surprisingly comfortable considering its rudimentary surroundings. The restaurant serves passable Moroccan cuisine ranging from *kefta* (brochettes of marinated minced lamb) to couscous. Rooms are plain and unmemorable but perfectly serviceable. **Pros:** Clean rooms, good rates. **Cons:** Unexciting decor, few amenities. ⊠ *B.P. 94, Cité Al Amal* ☎ *035/58–60–20* ⌐ *58 rooms, 2 suites* ♿ *In-room: safe, refrigerator. In-hotel: restaurant, bar, pool, parking (fee)* ⊟ *AE, DC, MC, V.*

MIDELT & THE CIRQUE DE JAFFAR

206 km (124 mi) southeast of Khénifra, 232 km (139 mi) south of Fez, 126 km (76 mi) north of Er-Rachidia.

Midelt itself is nothing to go out of your way for, but the Cirque de Jaffar and Djebel Ayachi definitely are, and Midelt is the logical base camp for these excursions. The town has an interesting carpet souk—particularly active on Sunday—with rugs in original geometric designs and kilims made by Middle Atlas Berber tribes.

EXPLORING

The **Atelier de Tissage–Kasbah Miryem** is a workshop run by the Notre Dame d'Atlas convent and monastery. Off the road to the Cirque de Jaffar and surrounded by trees, it is a good place to buy carpets, blankets, and textiles of all kinds as well as to chat with the French Franciscan nuns, all of whom are experts on matters Moroccan. On-site is a small church with an icon of the Seven Sleepers of Ephesus, a legend referenced in both Christianity and Islam. A small community of Trappist monks from Algeria resides on the property.

A digression from Midelt takes you to the silver and lead mines at the **Gorges d'Aouli,** a 24-km (14-mi) round-trip negotiable by a standard car. Formed by the Oued Moulouya—Morocco's longest river, flowing all the way to the Mediterranean—the gorges are sheer rock walls cut through the steppe.

★ You'll need four-wheel drive to tackle the notoriously rough but spectacular 80-km (48-mi) loop through the **Cirque de Jaffar,** a verdant cedar forest running around the Ayachi peak's lower slopes. The 12,257-foot **Djebel Ayachi,** the dominant terrain feature in the Atlas Mountains south of Midelt, was long thought to be Morocco's highest peak before Djebel Toubkal, south of Marrakesh, was found to be 13,668 feet. The view of this snowcapped (from December to March) behemoth from the eponymous hotel's roof is inspiring; Djebel Ayachi is very much *there*. It calls you. If you have time for serious exploration, the 130-km (78-mi) loop around through Boumia and Tounfite will take you across the immense Plateau de l'Arid, through the gorges of the upper Moulouya river valley, and into the Cirque de Jaffar on your way back into Midelt. Overland adventurers with four-wheel drive might be tempted to bivouac in the Cirque de Jaffar and climb Djebel Ayachi. After that, the route over to Tounfite on the right fork of Route 3424 is another adventure, and even more rugged still is the left fork, Route 3425, over the 10,749-foot Djebel Masker to Imilchil.

4

WHERE TO EAT & STAY

$$$$
MOROCCAN
✕**Restaurant de Fes.** This small restaurant offers delicious Moroccan and international entrées, including tasty couscous and tagines. ✉*2, ave. Mohammed V, Midelt* ☎*No phone* ▱*V.*

$–$$
MOROCCAN
▭**Hôtel el Ayachi.** Both the dining room and the service are pleasant surprises this far from a major city. Waiters in dinner jackets, a pleasant terrace, an accessible wine list, and a piping-hot lamb tagine go a long way toward making up for the somewhat bizarre but amusing rooms. Overstuffed beds with cedar headboards, coarse (though clean) sheets, and rough, heavy blankets remind you that you're out in the wilderness. The hotel is surrounded by the High Atlas to the south and the Middle Atlas to the north and west, so the rooms do have nice views; scale the roof first thing to admire the 12,257-foot Djebel Ayachi and the snow-covered High Atlas in the morning sun. **Pros:** Beautiful views of Ayachi, excellent dining room. **Con:** Rooms reek of cigar smoke. ✉*Rue d'Agadir* ☎*035/58–21–61* ⊕*www.hotelelayachi.com* ⟳*28 rooms* ♿*In-room: safe. In-hotel: restaurant, bar, parking (fee)* ▱*AE, DC, MC, V.*

THE ATLANTIC MIDDLE ATLAS

As you head toward Marrakesh, the southern Middle Atlas is drained by the River Oum-er-Rbia, which flows across the Tadla Plain to the Atlantic Ocean south of Casablanca. Forested with olive groves and live oaks on their lower slopes, the rugged mountains to the south of El-Ksiba and Beni-Mellal offer memorable trek and jeep excursions and form a striking contrast to Azilal's lush Cascades d'Ouzoud and Demnate's natural bridge at Imi-n-Ifri.

GETTING HERE & AROUND

The Marrakesh Menara airport is 6 km (4 mi) southwest of Marrakesh. Try to avoid the marathon bus from Marrakesh to Fez (via Beni-Mellal, Kasba Tadla, Khénifra, Azrou, Ifrane, and Imouzzer du Kandar), a trip totaling 10 hours, unless you really have no other way to get around. Buses run from Beni-Mellal up to Azilal, a common departure point for excursions into the Middle and High Atlas; they depart approximately every three hours between 7 AM and 4 PM. If you have any intention of wandering into the hinterland (and you will), be sure you're driving a four-wheel-drive vehicle, and consider carrying more than one spare as well as emergency fuel. Depending on where you're coming from, it's best to rent a car in Fez or Meknès.

ESSENTIALS

Bus Contacts Azilal (⊠ *Ave. Hassan II* ☎ *023/45–87–22*). **Beni-Mellal** (⊠ *Ave. Hassan II s/n* ☎ *023/48–39–81*). **Demnate** (⊠ *Ave. Mohammed V s/n* ☎ *023/45–60–87*).

Currency Exchange Bank Al-Maghrib (⊠ *Bd. Hassan II, Beni-Mellal* ☎ *023/48–96–88* ⊕ *www.bkam.ma*).

Internet Cafés Cyber Itri Internet (⊠ *Ave. Hassan II, Azilal*). **Hansali 2000 Internet** (⊠ *Rue Tarik ibn Ziad, Beni-Mellal*).

Visitor & Tour Info Délégation du Tourisme d'Azilal (⊠ *Ave. Mohammed V, Azilal* ☎ *023/45–87–22*). **Délégation du Tourisme de Beni-Mellal** (⊠ *Ave. Hassan II, Immeuble Chichaoua, Beni-Mellal* ☎ *023/48–39–81*).

EL-KSIBA

74 km (44 mi) southwest of Khénifra, 209 km (125 mi) west of Midelt.

Just south of the P24 is the village of El-Ksiba, a busy Berber enclave surrounded by apricot, olive, and orange groves. It's most notable as a gateway for the backcountry to the south. The road into town is steep and can be dangerous in bad weather, but if you can get up into the highlands behind it, some of Morocco's least spoiled wilderness will unfold before you. Wide expanses of sparsely vegetated Middle Atlas countryside and mountains spread out in impossibly grandiose and sweeping panoramas that prove surprisingly difficult to capture on film. With the occasional pocket of cedars, live oaks, or olive trees, the Middle Atlas gives way to the High Atlas and the peak of 10,604-foot Djebel Mourik to the south.

IMILCHIL

113 km (70 mi) southwest of Midelt, 150 km (93 mi) northeast of Marrakesh.

The 113-km (70-mi) trip on the P24 from Midelt to Imilchil is an unforgettable adventure best enjoyed in a four-wheel-drive vehicle. You'll pass tents belonging to Berber nomads, marvel at harsh yet beautiful ter-

Romance Among the Rocks

Every year hundreds of people get married at the three-day marriage moussem, the engagement festival that takes place at Imilchil every August/September, at the northern end of the Todra Gorges. The reason? Long ago Isli and Tislit, a young man and woman from opposing tribes, fell in love. Sound familiar? It's Shake-speare with a twist. The warring tribes were so angered by their love that they separated the pair, whereupon they wept and wept until their tears formed the lake that rests there today. They threw themselves into it and drowned. The villagers were so shocked that they vowed to honor their love henceforward, and started the ceremony in their honor.

–Katrina Manson & James Knight

4

rain, and feel refreshingly removed from civilization. Here the joy is in the journey; however, if you find yourself in the area during September, you'll have an extra reason to visit. The September marriage moussem, which brings the Aït Haddidou tribe together to marry off eligible—but not always fully consenting—young people, is an event that over time has become more of a tourist attraction than a marriage mart. The surrounding **Plateau des Lacs** (Plateau of the Lakes) includes the lakes of Iseli and Tislit (His and Hers, or Fiancé and Fiancée). Lac Tislit is 5 km (3 mi) from Imilchil, while Iseli is another 10 km (6 mi) east.

KASBA TADLA

22 km (13 mi) northwest of El-Ksiba, 99 km (59 mi) southwest of Khénifra, 206 km (124 mi) west of Midelt.

Occupying a strategic position at the junction of the P24 to Marrakesh and the P13 to Casablanca, this town takes its name from the Kasbah built here by Moulay Ismail in the late 17th century as an advance post against the local Berbers. The Kasbah and the two mosques inside it are the only buildings of note, forming a little walk of an hour or so. The massive walls are in full decay as the palace crumbles around the smaller farms and the reddish-clay pisé structures that have gone up in and around the fortress and mosques over the centuries. The best place to look down on the building is from the River Oum-er-Rbia's left bank, just off the P24 toward Beni-Mellal. West of town, the Tadla Plain stretches out along the river.

BENI-MELLAL

198 km (148 mi) northeast of Marrakesh, 30 km (18 mi) south of Kasba Tadla, 211 km (127 mi) southwest of Azrou.

Ringed with fortifications built by Moulay Ismail in 1688, this rapidly growing country town nestles in the shadow of 7,373-foot Djebel Tas-semit, surrounded by verdant orchards that are well irrigated by the

Bin-el-Ouidane reservoir, 59 km (35 mi) to the southwest. Beni-Mellal is largely modern and of little architectural interest, but its Tuesday souk, known especially for its Berber blankets with colorful geometric designs, is an event to catch. ■TIP→The 10-km (6-mi) walk up to the Aïn Asserdoun spring and the Kasbah de Ras el Aïn is well worth the haul for the gardens and waterfalls along the way and the views over the olive groves and the Tadla Plain.

WHERE TO EAT & STAY

$$$ ✕**SAT Agadir.** This small restaurant offers light entrées like hearty soups
MOROCCAN and tagines. The upper dining-room area offers a lovely view of the square. ⊠ *155, bd. el-Hansali* ☎*023/48–14–48* ▤ V.

$ ▥**Hôtel Ouzoud.** Generally acclaimed as Beni-Mellal's best hotel for
★ its quality service and the general equipment and infrastructure, this modern building nonetheless lacks character on the outside. The large rooms are well equipped with good beds and hot showers—the kinds of minor amenities for which you may find yourself thirsting if you've just come from the wild country to the south. Rooms have balconies that face a lush garden. The restaurant serves fine Moroccan specialties ranging from couscous and kebabs to soups and tagines. **Pros:** Best restaurant in the area, excellent service. **Con:** Worn decor. ⊠*Rte. de Marrakesh* ☎*023/48–37–52* ☚*60 rooms* &*In-hotel: restaurant, bar, tennis courts, pool* ▤*AE, DC, MC, V.*

AZILAL

171 km (103 mi) northeast of Marrakesh, 86 km (52 mi) southwest of Beni-Mellal on the S508, off the P24.

Azilal is a small garrison town used as a jumping-off point for routes into the southern highlands, especially toward the M'Goun Massif in the High Atlas, north of Ouarzazate. The pistes south of here become a maze of loops and tracks, great for exploring, but the main route forks 28 km (17 mi) after Aït Mohammed. To the right (southwest), the 1809 road descends into the Aït Bou Guemés valley, passing *ksour* (villages or tribal enclaves) at El Had and Agouti and looping eventually back to Aït Mohammed after a tough, tremendous 120-km (72-mi) trek that's much more effectively absorbed on foot than from a car.

EXPLORING

The left (northeast) fork takes the 1807 road through the Tizi-n-Ilissi Pass to the Zaouia Ahanesal shrine and eventually reaches the 260-foot rock formations known and marked on the Michelin 742 National as **La Cathédrale des Rochers** *(Cathedral of Rocks)* for its resemblance to the spiky spires of a Gothic cathedral. The road eventually becomes 1803 and passes through a live-oak forest to reach the Bin-el-Ouidane reservoir after 113 km (68 mi) of slow and tedious, though wildly scenic, driving.

CLOSE UP

Moroccan Wines

South and west of Meknès, from Sidi-Slimane to Boufakrane, are Morocco's best vineyards, known since Roman times for producing fine wines. At a mean altitude of 1,970 feet, the vines grow in clay soils and benefit from the dry and sunny climate excellent for producing powerful, full-bodied, highly expressive wines. The cooling breezes from both the Atlantic and the Mediterranean keep the nights fresh and the grapes' acidity viable. The traditional varieties, originally imported from France, are Carignane and Cinsault for reds and Clairette and Muscat for whites. Cabernet Sauvignon and Merlot are also present in smaller quantities, as are Grenache and Syrah. Guerrouane, Medaillon, Cuvée du Président, Ksar, and Coquillage are some of the best wines to look for. French actor Gérard Depardieu's Meknès vineyard in the foothills of the Atlas Mountains produces a Syrah blend called Gérard Depardieu Lumière, made with 25-year old vines and described in tasting notes as a "jammy, ultra-concentrated Rhone-style" brew.

–George Semler

WHERE TO STAY

¢ ⌑ **Hôtel Tanoute.** This little hotel on the Beni-Mellal road into Azilal is the only viable lodging in Azilal. Don't expect too much from this country inn; rooms are small, plain, and generally clean, and they are adequately equipped with serviceable beds and clean sheets, but this is no luxury resort. The restaurant serves a passable lamb-and-fig tagine *sur commande* (upon advance request). **Pro:** The only hotel in the area. **Con:** Few amenities. ⌂*Rte. Beni-Mellal (S508)* ☎*023/45–87–78* ⬲*8 rooms* ⌂*In-room: no phone, no TV, safe. In-hotel: restaurant* ⊟No *credit cards*.

CASCADES D'OUZOUD

153 km (95 mi) northeast of Marrakesh, 22 km (14 mi) northwest of Azilal.

Cascades **d'Ouzoud** are among the most stunning sights in the Middle Atlas. Approachable from the S508 via the 1811, you'll rarely see this spectacular waterfall without a rainbow hovering over the twin falls. These crash into a basin from which the water again falls, this time in a single white torrent to the riverbed below. A path through a grove of olive trees leads to the pools carved out of the rock at the base of the falls; here you can swim. At dusk families of Barbary apes come out to drink and feed on the pomegranates along the banks. If you have a rental car, the falls are an easy day trip.

Downstream, past the Ouzoud falls on the 1811 road, is the Berber hillside village of **Tanaghmelt.** Nicknamed "the Mexican village," the small community is connected by a web of narrow alleyways and semi-underground passages.

Continue up the 1811 (toward the P24) to see the **river gorges** of the Oued-el-Abid.

WHERE TO EAT & STAY

$$$

MOROCCAN

✕**Dar Es-Salam.** Located near the parking area for the falls, this small restaurant offers delicious crudités and tagines, best enjoyed with the signature mint tea. ⊠ *Cascades d'Ouzoud* ☎*023/45–96–58* ▭ *V.*

$$$$

▥**Riad Cascades d'Ouzoud.** This restored *riad* (mansion) over the waterfalls is about as luxurious and aesthetically satisfying a place as you will find in the Middle Atlas. The rooms are comfortable and stylish, decorated in bright tones with fresh wood trim. Tastefully and intelligently run, the hotel requires *demi-pension* (breakfast and dinner) as part of the room price. With mesmerizing views over the falls, the terrace is ideal for morning and evening dining. **Pros:** Stylish rooms, good views of falls. **Con:** A lot of tourist buses. ⊠*Cascades d'Ouzoud* ☎*023/45–96–58* ⊕*www.ouzoud.com* ⇆*6 rooms* ♨*In-hotel: restaurant* ▭*AE, DC, MC, V* ▯*MAP.*

DEMNATE

72 km (43 mi) southwest of Azilal, 158 km (95 mi) southwest of Beni-Mellal, 99 km (59 mi) east of Marrakesh.

This walled town is a market center to which Berbers from the neighboring hills and plains bring multifarious produce, especially for the Sunday souk held outside the walls. Once famed for its ceramics artisans, Demnate still has some traditional kilns. The rectangular ramparts are made of an unusual ocher-color pisé and pierced by two monumental portals; within is a Kasbah built by T'hami el-Glaoui.

Up a 6-km (4-mi) piste above Demnate is the natural stone bridge **Imi-n-Ifri,** where the diminutive River Mahseur has carved out a tunnel inhabited by hundreds of crows. A path twists down through the boulders and under the "bridge," where stalactites and sculpted hollows dramatize the natural rock formations. Women come to bathe in the stream because it is said to bring them good luck, but the crows are considered harbingers of doom. The legend associated with these birds—a St. George and the Dragon–type saga in which a lovely maiden is saved from an evil genie who, when destroyed by the brave hero, dematerializes into crows—is told in several variations by imaginative guides.

Marrakesh

WORD OF MOUTH

"The food stalls, the noise, the fortune tellers, the chaos and the loud African and Moroccan music being played charms you like a cobra. However, during the day, Djemâa el Fna is just an ordinary and noisy square. I think it's better to first see it at night than during the day."

—castellanese

"The souk is an experience you will probably never find again anywhere in the world. It can be a bit of an intimidating place. It's all part of good-natured attempt to get business. No one will be offended when you walk on. Just smile, put your right hand on your heart and shake your head."

—dysfunctional

Updated
by Maryam
Montague

MARRAKESH IS MOROCCO'S MOST INTOXICATING city. Ever since Morocco's Jewel of the South became a trading and resting place on the ancient caravan routes from Timbuktu, the city has barely paused for breath. Lying low and dominating the Haouz Plain at the foot of the snowcapped High Atlas Mountains (a marvelous sight on a sunny day), the city was stubbornly defended against marauding tribes by successive sultans. They maintained their powerful dynasties and surveyed their fertile lands from the Menara Garden's tranquil olive groves and lagoon, and the Agdal Gardens' vast orchards. Today, exploring the city has never been easier. A crackdown on hustlers who hassle means that you're freer to wander and wonder than ever before.

> **TOP REASONS TO GO**
>
> Wander amid the sizzle and smoke of the Djemâa el Fna—the world's most exuberant marketplace.
>
> Lose yourself (literally) in the alluring lanes of the bizarre bazaars of the souk and the city.
>
> Stay in a riad and sip mint tea in the airy confines of your bougainvillea-filled courtyard haven.
>
> Step back in time to the elaborate tombs and palaces of the Saadian sultans, and the calm and beauty of the intricate medersa.

The medina is Marrakesh's miracle—a happy clash of old and new, both beguiling and confusing in turn. Virtually unchanged since the Middle Ages, Marrakesh's solid salmon-pink ramparts encircle and protect its mysterious labyrinthine medina, hiding palaces, mansions, and bazaars. Pedestrians struggle to find their balance on the tiny cobbled lanes among an endless run of mopeds, donkey carts, and wheelbarrows selling a mixture of sticky sweets and saucepans. But pick up your jaw, take your time, and take it all in, stewing in the Rose City like a mint leaf in a pewter teapot.

ORIENTATION & PLANNING

ORIENTATION

Medina. The medina, the old walled city, contains the bulk of the attractions, the *souks* (markets) and *riads* (mansion houses). It's a warren of narrow *derbs* (alleyways), in which you can lose yourself if you don't pay attention. Thankfully, there is a method to the madness with some of the souks organized by type, including the carpet souk, the spice souk, and the slipper souk.

Ville Nouvelle. The wide, tree-lined boulevards of the New Town lie directly to the west of the medina, and were largely planned and laid out by the French colonial authorities. The Ville Nouvelle is principally split into two main neighborhoods: Guéliz is the modern administrative center, home to the tourist information office, numerous tour agencies, fashionable boutiques, and many of the city's hottest restaurants; Hivernage, to the south, has chain hotels and chic bars and clubs.

A BIT OF HISTORY

From its beginnings as a stronghold in 1062, Marrakesh became, together with Fez, a center for trade, culture, and religion, and the capital from which Youssef ben Tachfine, the Almoravid sultan, controlled the whole of North Africa and Andalusia. Under Tachfine's pious son, Ali ben Youssef, whose mother was a Christian slave, an influx of craftsmen from Spain created the New City's buildings, including the ramparts, and an underground irrigation system.

Although conquered and sacked in 1147 by the Almohads, Marrakesh remained the dynastic capital and became even more significant under Yacoub el Mansour, the third Almohad sultan. Perhaps the greatest of Marrakesh's sultans, El Mansour built extensively—palaces, mosques, and gardens—with materials imported from Italy and the Far East. The completion of the extraordinary Koutoubia Mosque, begun by the Almohad sultan Abdel Moumen, is one of El Mansour's accomplishments. Peace did not last, however. By the early 13th century, after two centuries of control by the Almohads and Almoravids, Marrakesh relapsed into a long period of skirmishing between dissenting tribes that constantly attacked and ransacked each other's strongholds.

By the mid-13th century the conquering Merenids had arrived and taken Marrakesh as their capital; but they soon moved it to Fez, which then became the center of Moroccan culture. In the 14th and 15th centuries Marrakesh fell into decline, and was finally conquered in 1554 by the Saadians from the south, who restored it as their capital. The rich and powerful Saadian sultan Ahmed el Mansour ("the Golden One") was responsible for a prosperous period in Marrakesh during the late 16th century, thanks to his raids of caravan routes from Timbuktu. El Mansour was the creator of El Badi Palace and the Saadian Tombs, his own final resting place.

The 17th century saw the beginning of the Alaouite dynasty, during which Marrakesh suffered another decline. The power-hungry sultan Moulay Ismail turned north to Meknès for his capital, plundering every monument and palace in Marrakesh—especially El Badi—to build his version of Versailles there. The Alaouites have ruled Morocco ever since; today they reside in Rabat, administrative capital since the French protectorate (1912–56). In the 18th century, however, Moulay Ismail's successor Sidi Mohammed ben Abdellah restored many of Marrakesh's ruined palaces, as well as the ramparts and mosques, and added to gardens such as the Menara, but although Marrakesh remained one of Morocco's Imperial Cities because of its strategic location, it declined again.

In the 19th century Moulay el Hassan I, great-great-grandfather of the current king Mohammed VI, gave Marrakesh renewed importance by choosing to be crowned and building his palace here in 1873. When the French established a Moroccan protectorate they built the Ville Nouvelle, which facilitated new trade.

5

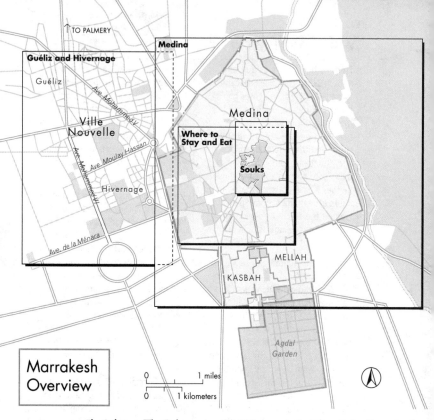

Marrakesh Overview

0 — 1 miles
0 — 1 kilometers

The Palmery. The Palmery is a 30,000-acre oasis, 7 km (4.5 mi) north of the medina between the roads to Casablanca and Fez. Once a source of wealth for the sultans because of its acres of date plantations, it's now a hideaway for the rich and famous (Jacques Chirac and Yves St. Laurent have owned properties here), with a crop of luxury hotels and secluded villas springing up among the palms.

PLANNING

WHEN TO GO

Morocco has been called "a cold country with a hot sun." With a chilly breeze off the High Atlas Mountains, Marrakesh can indeed get surprisingly cold in the winter and after the sun goes down. Although the sun shines almost year-round, the best time to visit is in spring, when the surrounding hills and valleys are an explosion of colorful flowers, and fall, when the temperature is comfortable enough to warrant sunbathing. The only exception in that period is during Easter week, which brings crowds.

Marrakesh's annual folklore festival of Moroccan music, theater, and dance—the **Festival National des Arts Populaires de Marrakech**—draws performers from all over Morocco and may even include an equestrian event. Held in July on the grounds of El Badi Palace, the festival lasts about 10 days and usually offers an evening program at 8:30. Don't miss it if you're here; just check with the Moroccan Tourist Office, as the date is never confirmed until a month or so beforehand.

GETTING HERE & AROUND

Menara Airport is Marrakesh's airport. It receives domestic flights as well as international connections from the United States, Europe, and the Middle East. There are no buses from the airport. The standard charge for a run into the medina in *petits taxis* (small taxis that serve the city and its suburbs) starts at about 100 DH during the daytime and 150 DH after dark.

> ### SORRY, I DON'T SPEAK ENGLISH
>
> You may occasionally encounter overly insistent wannabe guides in the streets, known by Marrakshis as *faux guides*. Local advice is to pretend not to speak French (not a problem in many cases) or even English. Try "I'm sorry, I speak little English; I'm Russian"—or another nationality with a tricky language—and then decidedly refuse to understand anything further.

Marrakesh is well served by train from Tangier, Rabat, Casablanca, and Fez. The train station on Avenue Hassan II is Morocco's main southern terminus. Advance reservations can be made for first-class only. Trains leave for Tangier five times a day; trains to Casablanca leave nine times a day.

Buses arrive here from Casablanca, Rabat, Fez, Agadir, and other cities at the Gare Routière at Bab Doukkala. Compagnie de Transports Marocains buses are considered the best; you can reserve a seat at the terminal or at an office on Boulevard Zerktouni. Supratours, which has its office next door to the train station on Avenue Hassan II, links up with Morocco's train network, and has bus routes to destinations south and west of Marrakesh.

Marrakesh is in Morocco's center, so it connects well by road with all other major destinations. Most of these roads are good, two-lane highways with hard, sandy shoulders for passing.

WITHIN MARRAKESH

Petits taxis in Marrakesh are small, beige, metered cabs permitted to transport three passengers. A petit taxi ride from one end of Marrakesh to the other costs around 20 DH. *Grands taxis* are the ubiquitous old Mercedes and other large four-doors and have two uses. Most often they simply take a load of up to six passengers on short hauls to suburbs and nearby towns, forming a reliable, inexpensive network throughout each region of Morocco.

Calèches are green, canopied, horse-drawn carriages that hold four to five people. Even if they do scream "tourist," they're a great way to reach your evening meal, and children love riding up front beside the driver. They're also picture-perfect for trips out to enjoy the Majorelle, Menara, and Agdal gardens. You should always agree on a price beforehand, but keep in mind that rides generally cost a minimum of

60 DH; trips to the Palmery might cost 300 DH, and round-trip excursions (circling the ramparts, say) might cost 200 DH. There are two main pick-up stops: one is in the medina, along the left side of the street stretching from the Djemâa el Fna to the Koutoubia Mosque; the other is in Guéliz, just south of the Place de la Liberté and west of Bab Nkob. You can also always try flagging one down.

Driving isn't the best way to get around. Cars can pass through many of the medina's narrow alleys, but not all, and unless you know the lay of the land you risk getting suddenly stuck and being hard-pressed to perform a U-turn. Instead, take the frequent public buses that run all over Marrakesh; fares are approximately 3 DH.

If you want a top-notch private guide for Marrakesh, you can't beat Mohammed Lahcen. Having grown up in the valley, his knowledge of the region is unsurpassed. His English is excellent, and he makes for great company if you're looking to experience Morocco with some help. Legendes Evasions is a highly respected local agency that runs chauffeured vehicle tours to some of the Berber villages around Marrakesh. Sahara Expedition is a well-recommended budget agency that runs excursions throughout the region, from jaunts down the Ourika Valley to trips to the beach at Essaouira; from trekking in the High Atlas to three-day sprints to the desert at Zagora and Merzouga.

ESSENTIALS

Bus Contacts Compagnie de Transports Marocains (⊠ *Gare Routière* ☎ *024/43–44–02* ⊠ *Bd. Zerktouni, Guéliz* ☎ *024/44–83–28*). **Supratours** (⊠ *Ave. Hassan II* ☎ *024/47–53–17*).

Internet C@fé Askmy (⊠ *Bd. Zerktouni, next to C.T.M. booking office, Guéliz* ☎ *024/44–74–76*). **Cyber Sihame Saida Ahouad** (⊠ *Riad Zitoune Elkadime Derb Skaya, 4, signposted right off Rue Riad Zitoun el Kedim running south from main square, Medina* ☎ *024/39–17–58*). **Tele Boutique Internet** (⊠ *Bd. Zerktouni, Guéliz* ☎ *No phone*).

Medical Assistance Pharmacie de Garde (⊠ *Djemâa el Fna, near C.T.M. hotel, Guéliz*. **Pharmacie du Nuit** (⊠ *Rue Khalid ben Oualid, just off Pl. de la Liberté, next door to fire station, Guéliz*).

Post Office Djemâa el Fna branch (⊠ *1 block from Banque du Maghreb*). **Place du 16 Novembre branch** (⊠ *Ave. Mohammed V*).

Rental Cars Avis (⊠ *137, ave. Mohammed V, Guéliz* ☎ *024/43–37–27*). **Europcar** (⊠ *63, bd. Zerktouni, Guéliz* ☎ *024/43–12–28*). **Hertz** (⊠ *154, ave. Mohammed V, Guéliz* ☎ *024/43–19–94*). **National** (⊠ *1, rue de la Liberté, Guéliz* ☎ *024/43–06–83*). **Rent Med** (⊠ *Résidence Al Morad, Ave. Mohammed V, Guéliz* ☎ *024/43–00–61 or 061/09–84–30*).

Train Contacts ONCF (⊠ *At station on Ave. Hassan II* ☎ *024/44–79–47* ⊕ *www.oncf.ma*).

Visitor & Tour Info Brigade Touristique (⊠ *Rue Sidi Mimoune, south of Koutoubia Mosque* ☎ *024/38–46–01*). **Legendes Evasions** (⊠ *212, ave. Mohammed V, Guéliz* ☎ *024/33–24–83* ⊕ *www.legendesevasions.com*). **Mohammed Lahcen** (☎ *061/33–81–02* ✎ *bab_adrar@hotmail.com*). **Moroccan National**

Tourist Office (✉ *Pl. Abdel Moumen at Ave. Mohammed V* ☎ *024/43–61–31 or 024/43–62–39*). **Sahara Expedition** (✉ *Angle el Mouahidine and Bani Marine* ☎ *024/42–79–77* ⊕ *www.saharaexpe.ma*).

SAFETY

Like other Moroccan cities, Marrakesh is quite safe. While women— particularly those traveling alone or in pairs—are likely to suffer from catcalls and whistles, there is generally little physical risk. The city does have its fair share of pickpockets, especially in markets and other crowded areas; handbags should be zippered and held beneath an arm, and wallets placed in front pockets. The old city shuts down relatively early, so don't wander its dark alleys late at night. The Moroccan Tourist Police take their jobs very seriously, so don't hesitate to call on them.

FESTIVALS

Marrakesh's annual folklore festival of Moroccan music, theater, and dance—the **Festival National des Arts Populaires de Marrakech**—draws performers from all over Morocco and may even include an equestrian event. Held in July on the grounds of El Badi Palace, the festival lasts about a week and usually offers an evening program at 8:30. Don't miss it if you're here; just check with the Moroccan Tourist Office, as the date is never confirmed until a month or so beforehand.

Aïd el Arch, or Throne Day, the commemoration of the king's coronation, is always on July 30. Parades and fireworks create a festive ruckus, and throngs of people fill the streets to listen and dance to live music. **Aïd el Seghrir** celebrates the end of Ramadan and is felt largely as a citywide sigh of relief. **Aïd el Kebir,** the Day of Sacrifice, has a somber tone; approximately 3½ months after Ramadan Muslims everywhere observe the last ritual of the pilgrimage to Mecca by slaughtering a sheep. The Youth Festival, **La Fête de Jeunesse,** held on July 9, celebrates children, who generally just run around the streets singing, dancing, and horsing around.

WHAT TO WEAR

While in Marrakesh, you're likely see everything from short skirts to billowing robes. But although Marrakesh is more modern than most Moroccan cities, it remains deeply traditional. Modest attire, particularly in the old city, is a good idea. For women, skirts to the knee or longer are appropriate, as are trousers. Both men and women should skip sleeveless tops and stick to those with sleeves. A shawl is a handy cover-up for women.

GUIDES

Guides can be helpful when navigating the medina's serpentine streets. They can point out little-known landmark, and help you understand the city's complicated history. You are best off booking a licensed guide through a tour company, and your hotel's staff will be able to suggest one to suit your interests. Although guides can be very knowledgeable about the city, don't rely on them for shopping. Store owners will inflate prices in order to give the guides kickbacks.

BARGAINING

Bargaining is part of the fun of shopping in the medina's souks. Go back and forth with the vendor until you agree on an acceptable price. If you are not sure if the vendor's "lowest price" is really the lowest, slowly leave the store—if the vendor follows you, then you can negotiate further. If bargaining is just not your thing and you don't mind paying a little extra, consider the shops of Guéliz. Although these shops are not as colorful as the souks, a reasonable variety of high-quality goods are on offer.

RESTAURANTS & CUISINE

Marrakesh has arguably the best selection of restaurants in Morocco; as a group they serve equal parts Moroccan and international cuisine. Restaurant dining, however, is a relatively new phenomenon for Moroccans, who see eating out as somewhat of a shame on the household. Even the wealthiest Marrakshis would prefer to invite friends over to sample home cooking than to go out for the evening. A treat is to spend an evening at one of Marrakesh's popular riad restaurants in the medina. These will give you an idea (albeit a rather expensive one) of traditional yet sumptuous Moroccan entertaining.

You can also eat well at inexpensive sidewalk cafés in both the medina and Guéliz. Here, don't miss out on a famous local dish called *tangia,* made popular by workers who slow-cook lamb or beef in an earthenware pot left in hot ashes for the whole day.

ABOUT THE HOTELS

Marrakesh has exceptional hotels. Five stars are dropped at every turn, the spas are superb, and the loving attention to detail is overwhelming. If, however, you'd prefer not to spend a fortune sleeping in the bed where a movie star once slumbered, solid budget and mid-range options abound. They're small, clean, and suitably Moroccan in style to satisfy adventurous penny-pinchers.

To take on the historic heart of Marrakesh and live like a pasha of old, head to one of the medina's riads. Riad restorations, many by ultra-fashionable European expats, have taken over the city; you'd trip over them, if only you know where they were. Anonymous doors in the narrow, twisting derbs of the medina, and especially the souks, transport you to hidden worlds of pleasure. There are cheap ones, expensive ones, chic ones, funky ones, plain ones . . . The list goes on.

EXPLORING

Negotiating the twisting and turning alleys deep in the medina is a voyage in itself. If you don't hire a guide, keep a guidebook with you at all times. The medina, although not quite as enclosed and intense as the one in Fez, takes some patience—street names are often signposted only in Arabic. A small street is called a *rue* in French or a *zencat* in Arabic; an even smaller alley is called a *derb*. If you get lost, keep walking and you'll eventually end up at one of the 14 original *babs* (arched gates) that lead in and out of this ancient quarter. Most of the medina's monuments charge an entry fee of 10 DH–40 DH and have permanent but unsalaried on-site guides; if you use one, tip him about 30 DH–50 DH.

Guéliz, in comparison, is easy to navigate. The wide streets are signposted in French and lined with orange and jacaranda trees, office buildings, modern stores, and a plethora of sidewalk cafés.

MEDINA

If you can see the ramparts, you're either just inside or just outside the medina. In some respects not much has changed here since the Middle Ages. The medina is still a maze of narrow cobblestone streets lined with thick-walled, interlocked houses; designed to confuse invaders, the layout now serves much the same purpose for visitors. Donkeys and mules still deliver produce, wood, and wool to their destinations, and age-old crafts workshops still flourish as retail endeavors.

> **YOUR NEW BEST FRIEND**
>
> A highly detailed map is key. The best one is "Marrakech Evasions," subtitled "La Carte." It's particularly helpful because it marks key riads, hotels, restaurants, and bars, as well as monuments, landmarks, and transportation hubs. It should cost no more than 20 DH, and is widely available at newsstands, bookstores, and tobacco shops.

TOP ATTRACTIONS

6 **Ali ben Youssef Medersa.** If you want a little breath taken out of you, don't pass up the chance to see this extraordinarily well-preserved 16th-century Koranic school, North Africa's largest such institution. The delicate intricacy of the *gibs* (stucco plasterwork), carved cedar, and *zellij* (mosaic) on display in the central courtyard makes the building seem to loom taller than it really does. As many as 900 students from Muslim countries all over the world once studied here, and arranged around the courtyard are their former sleeping quarters—a network of tiny upper-level rooms that resemble monks' cells. The building was erected in the 14th century by the Merenids in a somewhat different style from that of other medersas; later, in the 16th century, Sultan Abdullah el Ghallib rebuilt it almost completely, adding the Andalusian details. The large main courtyard, framed by two columned arcades, opens into a prayer hall elaborately decorated with rare palm motifs as well as the more-customary Islamic calligraphy. The medersa also contains a small mosque. ⊠ *Just off Rue Souk el Khemis* ☎ *024/44–18–93* ⌨ *50 DH for medersa, 60 DH combination ticket includes museum and Qoubba Almoravid* ☉ *Daily 9–6:30.*

9 **Dar Si Saïd.** This 19th-century palace is now a museum with an excellent collection of antique Moroccan crafts including pottery from Safi and Tamegroute, jewelry, daggers, kaftans, carpets, and leatherwork. The palace's courtyard is filled with flowers and cypress trees, and furnished with a gazebo and fountain. The most extraordinary salon is upstairs; it's a somber room decorated with gibs cornices, zellij walls, and an amazing carved-cedar ceiling painted in the *zouak* style (bright colors in intricate patterns). Look for the prize exhibit, a marble basin with

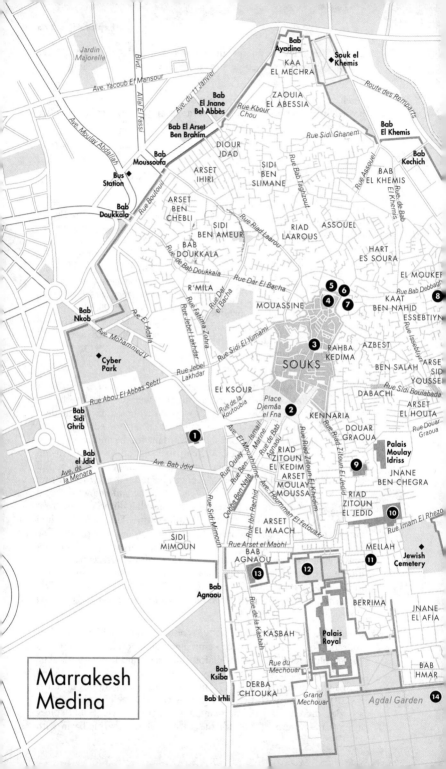

Marrakesh Medina

5

Route de Fès

TO →
FÈZ & MEKNES

Bab
Debbagh

Bab Lalla
Aouda Saadia

Rachidia

Bab
Aylen

Route des Remparts

Oued Issil

Rue Bab Ahmad

Rue El Qadi Ayad

Bab
Ghemat

Zaouia
Youssef
Ben Ali

Route de Ouarzazate

Rue Belaid

Ave. Houis

0   1/2 mile

0   1/2 kilometer

MARRAKESH THREE WAYS

It's best to visit the north of the medina in the morning, when you're likely to have plenty of energy for the rigors of the souk and the tanneries. Start by enjoying breakfast from a terrace café overlooking the **Djemâa el Fna** and watching the human bazaar on display. Then plunge into one of the roads running north into the **souk,** where you can window-shop on your way to the **Qoubba Almoravid,** the **Musée de Marrakesh,** and the **Ali ben Youssef Medersa.** You'll also pass some *fondouks,* medieval warehouses and inns that are still in use. From here you can continue on Rue Bab Debbagh toward the **tanneries.**

Take a tour of the southern medina, home to many of Marrakesh's historic monuments, for something slightly gentler. Start with a walk around the **Koutoubia Mosque,** then head down to Bab Agnaou and the **Saadian Tombs.** Afterward, retrace your steps and turn right into the narrow walled street just before the Bab Agnaou. Walk almost to the end of the wall; then turn right again and continue on this street to Place des Ferblantiers. When you go through the Bab Berrima arch you'll be in a large, rectangular enclosure. Look for the entrance to **El Badi Palace** to pay a visit. Return through the arch and walk a few minutes northeast through the **Mellah** to **La Bahia Palace** and **Dar Si Saïd,** two derbs north on Riad Zitoun Jdid. From here it's a short walk north on Riad Zitoun Jdid to **Djemâa el Fna,** where you can stop for lunch.

Scenic spots on the city's perimeter make for a lovely sunset jaunt, whether on foot or during a calèche ride. Relax in the **Menara Garden** or (on Friday and Sunday only) the **Agdal Garden,** via the **Méchouar;** or tour the **Ramparts** or, just outside town, the **Palmery.**

an inscription indicating its 10th-century Córdoban origin. The basin, which is sometimes on loan to other museums, was once given pride of place in the Ali ben Youssef Mosque in the north of the souk. It was brought to Morocco by the Almoravid sultan in spite of its decorative eagles and griffins, which defy the Koran's prohibition of artistic representations of living things. Guides are available on-site. ⊠ *1st derb on right just up from La Bahia Palace* 🎫 *20 DH* 🕙 *Wed.–Mon. 9–noon and 3:15–6:15.*

❷ **Djemâa el Fna.** The carnivalesque open square right at the center of the
Fodor's Choice   medina is Marrakesh's heartbeat. This centuries-old square was once
★   a meeting point for regional farmers and tradesmen; today it's surrounded by bazaars, mosques, and terraced cafés with perfect balcony views over the action. Transvestite dancers bat their eyelashes; cobras sway to the tones of snake charmers; henna women make their swirling marks on your hands; fortune-tellers reveal mottled futures; apothecaries offer bright powder potions and spices; bush dentists with Berber molars piled high on tables extract teeth; and, best of all, men tell stories to each other the old way, on a magic carpet around a gas lamp.

All day (and night) long you can get fresh orange or grapefruit juice from the green gypsy carts that line up round the square, for about 3 DH a glass. You can also buy a shot of cool water from one of the roving water sellers, whose eye-popping costumes carry leather water pouches and polished-brass drinking bowls. Or snack on sweet dates, apricots, bananas, almonds, sugar-coated peanuts, and walnuts from the dried fruit–and–nut stalls in the northwest corner. Meat and vegetable grills cook into the night, when Marrakshis come out to eat,

> **EXPLORING THE MEDERSA**
>
> To imagine how the medersa's young scholars lived and worked, look for an interesting display of how rooms differed between students from the countryside and the city. One has brass candle-sticks, an ornate cooking stove, and an elaborate writing desk; the other has some clay pots and simple floor mats. It isn't hard to guess which one's which.

meet, and be entertained. It might be a fun bazaar today, but once upon a time the Djemâa's purpose was more gruesome; it accommodated public viewings of the severed heads of sinners, criminals, and Christians. *Djemâa* actually means "meeting place" and *el Fna* means "the end" or "death," so as a whole it means something along the lines of "assembly of death" or "meeting place at the end of the world."

🕑 **El Badi Palace.** This 16th-century palace was once a playground for Saadian princes and visiting diplomats—a mammoth showpiece for opulent entertaining. Today it's a romantic set of sandstone ruins, policed by nesting storks. Sultan Ahmed el Mansour's lavish creation was ransacked by Moulay Ismail in the 17th century to help him complete his own palace at Meknès. But it's not hard to see why the palace, whose name translates as "The Marvel," was once among the world's most impressive monuments. A huge swimming pool in the center (still there today) is flanked by four others, along with four sunken orange orchards. The main hall was named the Koubba el Khamsiniyya, referring to its 50 grand marble columns. Along the southern wall is a series of below-ground corridors and underground dungeons. It's a vast, calm, and mystical place. Also on display is a collection of goods from the Minbar (pulpit from which the Imam gives services) of the Koutoubia Mosque. If you use an on-site guide (otherwise unpaid), who can bring the place to life, you should also tip 30 DH–50 DH. ⊠ *Enter ramparts and enormous gateway near Pl. des Ferblantiers* 🎫 *10 DH for palace, 20 DH for palace and display of the Koutoubia Mosque Minbar* ⊙ *Daily 8:30–11:45 and 2:45–5:45.*

🕙 **La Bahia Palace.** This 19th-century palace, once home to a harem, is a marvelous display of painted wood, ceramics, and symmetrical gardens. Built by Sultan Moulay el Hassan I's notorious Grand Vizier Bou Ahmed, the palace was ransacked on Bou Ahmed's death, but you can still experience its layout and get a sense of its former beauty. Don't forget to look up at smooth arches, carved-cedar ceilings, *tadlak* (shiny marble) finishes, *gibs* (stucco plasterwork) cornices, and zouak painted ceilings. Fancy a room? Each one varies in size accord-

Fodor's Choice
★

5

ing to the importance of each wife or concubine. The entire palace is sometimes closed when the royal family is in town, since their entourage often stays here. If you use an on-site guide, you should also tip 30 DH–50 DH. ⊠ *End of Ave. Houmman el Fetouki- near Pl. des ferblantiers* ☎ *024/38–54–65* 🖭 *10 DH* ⊙ *Daily 8:45–11:45 and 2:45–5:45.*

⓭ ★ **Saadian Tombs.** This small, beautiful 16th-century burial ground is the permanent resting place of 166 Saadians, including its creator, Sultan Ahmed el Mansour, the Golden One. True to his name, he did it in style—even those not in the lavish mausoleum have their own colorful zellij graves, laid out for all to see, among the palm trees and flowers. Because the infamous Moulay Ismail chose not to destroy them

> ## ROCKING THE KASBAH
>
> Today's partially walled Kasbah, in the southwest of the medina, houses the (inaccessible) modern royal palace and the Saadian relics—the tombs and El Badi Palace. Marrakesh's first Kasbah was built around 1062, on the site of what is now the Koutoubia Mosque, by Abu Bakr, leader of the Almoravid tribe of warriors from Mauritania. Abu Bakr was quickly overthrown by his cousin Youssef ben Tachfine, who became the Berber dynasty's first great sultan. The Almoravids, who also conquered Spain, essentially founded Marrakesh by adding a mosque to the Kasbah (of which no trace remains) in 1070.

(he was apparently superstitious about plundering the dead), these tombs are one of the few Saadian relics left. He simply sealed them up, leaving only a small section open for use. The complex was rediscovered only in 1917 by General Hubert Lyautey during the French protectorate. Passionate about every aspect of Morocco's history, the general undertook the restoration of the tombs.

The central mausoleum, the **Hall of Twelve Columns,** contains the tombs of Ahmed el Mansour and his family. It's dark, lavish, and ornate, with a huge vaulted roof, carved cedar doors and *moucharabia* (carved wooden screens traditionally used to separate the sexes), and gray Italian marble columns. In a smaller inner mausoleum, on the site of an earlier structure containing the decapitated body of the Saadian dynasty's founder, Mohammed esh Sheikh, is the tomb of El Mansour's mother. ■ **TIP➔** **Get here either early or late to avoid the crowds and to see the monuments swathed in soft golden light of a restful sun.** If you use one of the on-site guides (who are unpaid), you should tip 30 DH to 50 DH. ⊠ *Rue de la Kasbah, across small square from mosque* 🖭 *10 DH* ⊙ *Daily 8:30–11:45 and 2:30–17:45; closed May 1.*

➌ Fodor'sChoice ★ **Souks.** The vast, labyrinth of narrow streets and derbs at the center of the medina is the souk—Marrakesh's marketplace and a wonder of arts, crafts, and workshops. Every step brings you face-to-face with the colorful handicrafts and bazaars for which Marrakesh is so famous. In the past, every craft had a special zone within the market—a souk within the souk. Today savvy vendors have pushed south to tap trading opportunities as early as possible, and few of the original sections remain. Look for incongruities born of the modern era. Beside handcrafted wooden pots for kohl eye makeup are modern perfume stores; where there is a world of hand-sewn djellabas at one turn, you'll find soccer jerseys after the next; fake Gucci caps sit beside handmade Berber carpets, their age-old tassels fluttering in the breeze.

TIP→ As you wander through the souk, take note of landmarks so you can return to a particular bazaar without too much trouble. Once the bazaars' shutters are closed, they're often unrecognizable. The farther north you go the more the lanes twist, turn, and entwine. Should you have to retrace your steps, a compass comes in handy, as does a mental count of how many left or right turns you've taken since you left the main drag. But mostly you'll rely on people in the souk to point the way.

**MEDINA
MOMENT**

It's not every day you walk past a whole lamb being cooked. Follow a tiny street that leads off the Djemâa el Fna (to the left of Les Terrasses de l'Alhambra) and you'll see exactly that. Although the row of upstanding severed lambs' heads set upon tagines may not be everyone's idea of culinary heaven, Marrakshis love **Chez Lamias Hadj** (⊠ *Souk Ablouh, 18–26* ☎ *061/39–84–28*), and you'd be missing out not to try it. Ask to see the oven—a hole in the ground where the entire animal is cooked over hot wood ash. The meat is then hauled up and cut in front of you, served with bread for a cheap 20 DH sandwich, or for larger amounts at 140 DH per kilogram. If you're nervous, ask for a small taste first. However much you have, sprinkle the meat with a delicious cumin-and-salt spice mix and wash it all down with mint tea. For a more-adventurous experience, try the head (cheaper at 60 DH per kilogram) or the trotters. Get there between 11 AM and 12:30 PM.

WORTH NOTING

⑭ **Agdal Garden.** Some say dull scrub; others, pinnacle of romance. Stretching a full 3 km (2 mi) south of the Royal Palace, the Jardin de l'Aguedal comprises vast orchards, a large lagoon, and other small pools, all fed by an impressive, ancient system of underground irrigation channels from the Ourika Valley in the High Atlas. The entire garden is surrounded by high *pisé* (a mixture of mud and clay) walls, and the olive, fig, citrus, pomegranate, and apricot orchards are still in their original raised-plot form. The largest lagoon, the grandiose Tank of Health, is said to be the 12th-century creation of an Almohad prince, but, as with most Moroccan historic sites, the Agdal was consecutively abandoned and rebuilt—the latest resurrection dates from the 19th century. Until the French protectorate's advent, it was the sultans' retreat of choice for lavish picnics and boating parties. **TIP→ If you're here on a clear day, don't miss the magic and majesty of a 180-degree turn, from facing the Koutoubia Mosque (northwest) to facing the Atlas Mountains (southeast).** ⊠ *Approach via Méchouar; or, from outside the ramparts, walk left on Rue Bab Irhil and the garden will be on your right* ☉ *Fri. and Sun., usually 9–6.*

❺ **Ali ben Youssef Mosque.** After the Koutoubia, this is the medina's largest mosque and Marrakesh's oldest. The building was first constructed in the second half of the 12th century by the Almoravid sultan Ali ben

CLOSE UP

Drink in the Views

Nowhere is café culture busier than on Djemâa el Fna, where several terraces compete for the award for best view of the square.

Our favorite is the first-floor terrace (the middle level, not the upper) of **Café Argana** (⊠ *1, 2, pl. Djemâa el Fna* ☎ *024/44–53–50*), where the only drawback is that you have to eat (rather than drink) for the privilege of the best square-side table. On your way out you can also pick up a scoop of ice cream for 6 DH, choosing from among more than 20 ice-cream flavors (including such exotics as fig, avocado, and cinnamon).

Les Terrasses de l'Alhambra (⊠ *Pl. Djemâa el Fna, opposite Café de France* ☎ *065/04–74–11*) in the square's northeastern corner is the classiest option, with decent pizza and pasta and warm wood panels.

It's tucked away at the edge of the square, but still has lovely views. Bag a seat on the top terrace.

Just opposite Les Terrasses, **Café de France** (⊠ *Pl. Djemâa el Fna, in northeastern corner* ☎ *024/44–23–19*) is much past its prime, but as long as you're only interested in a late-night hot chocolate with a good view (it stays open until midnight—later than most), it does the trick; go right up to the top terrace corner.

To catch the sunset and the beginnings of the alluring smoke and sizzle of the grills, the rightly named **Grand Balcon du Café Glacier,** to the south of the square, is a top choice. It shuts relatively early, though, and you'll have to compete for elbow room with all the amateur photographers who throng the best spot.

–Katrina Mansono–James Knight

Youssef, around the time of the Qoubba Almoravid. In succeeding centuries it was destroyed and rebuilt several times by the Almohads and the Saadians, who changed its size and architecture accordingly; it was last overhauled in the 19th century, in the then-popular Merenid style. Non-Muslims may not enter.

NEED A BREAK?

One rule of thumb is that every old Marrakshi monument has a café nearby to rest your feet in after all those historical exertions. The **Café Palais El Badi** (⊠ *4, rue Touareg, Bab Berrima, Mellah* ☎ *024/38–99–75*) is a cheap and popular lunch spot (the 80 DH menu includes *kefta (beef patties)* and tagine). It's a pretty, wrought-iron terrace overlooking both the palace and the Place des Ferblantiers. Look, too, for the gracious storks nesting opposite.

❶ Koutoubia Mosque. Yacoub el Mansour built Marrakesh's towering Moorish mosque on the site of the original 11th-century Almoravid mosque. Dating from the early 12th century, it became a model for the Hassan Tower in Rabat and the Giralda in Seville. The mosque takes its name from the Arabic word for book, *koutoub*, because there was once a large booksellers' market nearby. The minaret is topped by three golden orbs, which, according to local legend, were offered by the mother of the Saadian sultan Ahmed el Mansour Edhabi in penance for fasting days she missed during Ramadan. The mosque has a large plaza, walkways, and gardens, as well as floodlights to illuminate its curved windows, a band of ceramic inlay, pointed *merlons* (ornamental edgings), and various decorative arches. Although non-Muslims may not enter, anyone within earshot will be moved by the power of the evening muezzin call. ⊠*South end of Ave. Mohammed V.*

⑪ **Mellah.** As in other Moroccan cities, the Mellah is the old Jewish quarter, once a small, walled-off city within the city. Although it was once home to a thriving community of native and Spanish Jews, along with rabbinical schools and scholars, today, it's home to only a few hundred Jewish inhabitants. You can visit the remains of a couple of synagogues with the help of a guide.

> **NAVIGATING TIP**
>
> No matter how lost you might think you are, the Koutoubia Mosque is the ultimate "where-am-I-now?" landmark. With a square minaret that rises 230 feet, the mosque is visible for 29 km (18 mi) in every direction, so just head toward it to get back to the nearby Djemâa el Fna square.

❼ **Musée de Marrakesh.** The main reason to come to this small but perfectly formed museum next door to the Ali ben Youssef Medersa is not the exhibitions, but rather the stunning central atrium, a tiled courtyard containing a huge lampshade that resembles a UFO descending. This is a perfect place to relax while enjoying Moroccan architecture and gentle strains of guitar music piped through speakers. The temporary exhibitions in the courtyard are often of beautiful artifacts and paintings (some for sale), but they're poorly displayed and lack English translations. The museum also has a good bookstore and a café. ■**TIP**➔ The toilets are spotless and worth the admission price if you find yourself far from your hotel. ⊠*Pl. ben Youssef* ☎*024/44–18–93* 💶*40 DH for museum, 60 DH combination ticket includes Ali ben Youssef Medersa and Qoubba Almoravid* ☉*Daily 9–6:30.*

❹ **Qoubba Almoravid.** This is the city's oldest monument and the only intact example of Almoravid architecture in all of Morocco (the few other ruins include some walls here in Marrakesh and a minaret in El Jadida). Dating from the 12th century, this masterpiece of mechanical waterworks somehow escaped destruction by the Almohads. It was once used not only for ablutions before prayer in the next-door Ali ben Youssef Mosque (relying on the revolutionary hydraulics of *khatteras,* drainage systems dug down into the water table), and also had a system of toilets, showers, and faucets for drinking water. It was only excavated from the rubble of the original Ali ben Youssef Mosque and Medersa in 1948. You can scramble around at your leisure. 💶*60 DH combination ticket includes Musée de Marrakesh and Ali ben Youssef Medersa* ☉*Daily 9–6:30.*

Ramparts. The medina's amazingly well-preserved walls measure about 33 feet high and 7 feet thick, and are 15 km (9 mi) in circumference. Until the early 20th century, before the French protectorate, the gates were closed at night to prevent anyone who didn't live in Marrakesh from entering. Eight of the 14 original babs (arched entry gates) leading in and out of the medina are still in use. Bab Agnaou, in the Kasbah, is the loveliest and best preserved of the arches. ■TIP➜ **The best time to visit the walls is just before 7 PM, when the swallows that nest in the ramparts' holes come out to take their evening meal. A leisurely calèche drive around the perimeter takes about an hour.**

MEDINA MOMENT

Just when you start wondering where the quiet, traditional areas are, the quintessential derb comes along. The second left going south from the Saadian tombs is a tiny covered lane lined with fresh beetroot, zucchini, beans, and peppers. Look for the stall (on the left) with vats of couscous piled high, meat and olive stands, and (again on the left) an amazing zellij-and-stucco arched door; currently masked by a street stand, it's just waiting to be turned into a grand entrance to tomorrow's trendy riad. See it and smell it, before it goes.

⑧ Tanneries. For a whiff of Marrakesh life the old way, the tanneries are a real eye-waterer, not least because of the smell of acrid pigeon excrement, which provides the ammonia that is vital to the dyeing process. The method relies on natural dyes such as wild mint, saffron, cinnamon, and henna. Six hundred skins sit in a vat at any one time, resting there for up to two months amid constant soaping, scrubbing, and polishing. Goat and sheep skins are popular among Berbers, while Arab dye-masters rely on camels and cows and tend to use more machine processes and chemical dyes.

Thirteen tanneries, mixing both Berber and Arab elements, are still in operation in the Bab Debbagh area in the northeast of the medina. Simply turn up at Rue de Bab Debbagh and look for the tannery signs above several open doorways to both the right and left of the street. To visit one of them, just pop in and the local manager will offer you mint leaves to cover the smell, explain the process, and guide you around the vats of dyes. In return he'll hope for a healthy tip to share with his workers; this is a dying art in a poor dyeing area, so the more you can tip, the better.

■TIP➜ **Finding the rue de Bab Debbagh can be frustrating.** You'll be inundated with offers from young would-be guides to take you to their favorite (or more likely, the one that will pay them). These guides may demand money and pass you on to unscrupulous managers who aren't the real thing, barely understand the process themselves, and demand yet more money.

MEDINA MOMENT

Berbers regularly come down from the mountains to barter for tanned leather in exchange for their own carpets. If you happen to stumble across one of these impromptu auctions, you're in for a treat.

GUÉLIZ & HIVERNAGE

In addition to office buildings and contemporary shops—none of which may exceed the nearest mosque's height—Guéliz has plenty of sidewalk cafés, international restaurants, upscale boutiques, and antiques stores.

TOP ATTRACTIONS

Fodor'sChoice **Majorelle Garden.** The Jardin
★ Majorelle was created by the French
painter Louis Majorelle, who lived
in Marrakesh between 1922 and
1962. It then passed into the hands
of another Marrakesh lover, the late
fashion designer Yves Saint Laurent.
If you've just come from the desert,
it's a sight for sore eyes, with green-
bamboo thickets, little streams, and
an electric blue gazebo. There's also
a villa housing a small Islamic art
museum, a nice museum shop, and
a delightful café. ⊠ *Ave. Yacoub el
Mansour (main entrance on side
street)* ☎024/30–18–52 ✉ *Garden
30 DH, museum 15 DH additional*
⊙ *Daily 8–6:30.*

WORTH NOTING

Marché Central. The vivid Central
Market is the Western expatriate
crowd's favorite place to shop for meat, fish, fruits, flowers, and vegetables. It also includes a handicrafts bazaar. The market is in Guéliz's
center, on Avenue Mohammed V near Rue de la Liberté, which in turn
has a few sunny cafés ideal for breakfast.

Menara Garden. The Menara's lagoon and villa-style pavilion are
ensconced in an immense royal olive grove, where pruners and pick-
ers putter and local women fetch water from the nearby stream, said
to give *baraka* (good luck). A popular rendezvous for Marrakshis, the
garden is a peaceful retreat. The elegant pavilion—or *minzah,* meaning "beautiful view"—was created in the early 19th century by Sultan
Abd er Rahman, but it's believed to occupy the site of a 16th-century
Saadian structure. In winter and spring snowcapped Atlas peaks in
the background appear closer than they are; and, if you are lucky, you
might see green or black olives gathered from the trees from October
through January. ⊠ *From Bab el Djedid, garden is about 4 km (2.5 mi)
down Ave. de la Menara* ☎024/43–95–78 ⊙ *Daily 8–7.*

IN THE KNOW

For the Real McCoy, visit Berber
tannery El Guezmiri, a door on
the right and the fourth tannery
you come across when arriving
from the southwest. Soulimane,
the kind manager, can guide you
around with expertise. There's also
a boutique at the end where you
can buy the wares more cheaply
than in the souk. Look for No.
84, Chez Abdel Jalil. Or, to see
ironmongers hard at work on the
lanterns that bring atmosphere
to the halls of Marrakesh's plush-
est hotels and riads, head to the
medina's Place des Ferblantiers,
where you may even be able to
get a better deal than in the souk,

5

WHERE TO EAT

Restaurants in Marrakesh tend to fall into two categories. They're
either fashionable, flashy affairs, mostly in Guéliz and the outlying
areas of Marrakesh, which serve à la carte European and Moroccan
cuisine, or they're more-traditional places, often tucked inconspicu-
ously into already-out-of-the-way places in the medina. Both types
can be fairly pricey, and, to avoid disappointment, are best booked in
advance. They also tend to open quite late, usually not before 7:30 in

Guéliz and 8 in the medina, although most people don't sit down to eat until 9 or 9:30.

There's no set system for tipping. Your check will indicate that service has been included in the charge; if not, tip 10% or 15% for excellent service.

> **DID YOU KNOW?**
>
> For fruit and vegetables, forget the souk. The place Marrakesh's top restaurateurs swear by for fresh produce is the market in the Bab Doukkala neighborhood.

WHAT IT COSTS IN DIRHAMS					
	¢	$	$$	$$$	$$$$
AT DINNER	under 125DH	125DH–200DH	200DH–350DH	350DH–450DH	over 450DH

Prices are per person for a main course at dinner.

MEDINA

$$$
MOROCCAN

✕**Al Baraka.** It's easy to fancy yourself one of Morocco's 19th-century elite in this grand, white-tile riad, once home to the pasha. Set menus for different budgets feature traditional *briouates* (spicy dumplings) as well as tagines and couscous. You have the choice of dining on brocade divans in the salon or in the enormous courtyard filled with orange trees, musicians, and the odd belly dancer. ⊠*1, Djemâa el Fna, next to Commissariat de Police* ☎*024/44–23–41* ▤*MC, V.*

$
MOROCCAN

✕**Café Arabe.** This three-story restaurant in the heart of the medina is a happening place by day and by night. Homemade pastas are on offer at this Italian-owned place, making it a great spot for lunch and dinner. The lantern-lighted terrace, complete with a trickling fountain, is a good place to stop for drinks. ⊠*184, rue el Mouassine* ☎*024/42–97–28* ▤ *AE, MC, V.*

¢
CAFÉ

✕**Café des Epices.** In the medina's spice market, this little café is a surprisingly glamorous and modern affair. It teeters over three levels, and has a great rooftop view over the spice square below. Suitably enough, it offers spiced tea and cinnamon coffee along with a good complement of drinks and light meals. ⊠*75, Rahba Lakdima* ☎*024/30–17–70* ▤ *No credit cards.*

¢
MOROCCAN

✕**Chez el Bahia.** It won't win prizes for design, but this cheap joint is perfect for a lunchtime pit stop. Locals and visitors alike frequent this friendly and atmospheric canteen tucked into a small derb leading to Djemâa el Fna. Tagine pots stand two rows deep on the street stall outside, and a barbecue sizzles away. ⊠*Riad Zitoune el Kdim, 206* ☎*061/31–78–20* ▤*No credit cards.*

$$$$
MOROCCAN
Fodor'sChoice
★

✕**Dar Marjana.** If you can only visit one of Marrakesh's traditional riad restaurants, make it this one. Cocktails featuring *mahia*—fig liqueur— are served on low-slung tables around a delightful courtyard. Then you move to salons (ask for the larger minzah) to recline on brocade divans and enjoy wave after wave of classic Moroccan cuisine. The couscous is impossibly fluffy, and if the lamb tagine came off the bone any easier it would be floating. To round this off, a troupe of lively Gnaoua musicians brings you to your senses before a belly dancer brings you to your feet. The fixed price includes unlimited drinks, and the staff is charming. ⊠*15, Derb Sidi Tair, Bab Doukkala, opposite Dar el Basha* ☎*024/38–51–10* ⚒*Reservations essential* ⊟*AE, MC, V* ⊗*Closed Tues. No lunch.*

$$$$
MOROCCAN

✗**Dar Moha.** This isn't the most stylish riad, but it has an established reputation for its fixed menu of *nouvelle cuisine marocaine*. Delicious adaptations of traditional dishes include a tiny melt-in-the-mouth *pastilla* (sweet pigeon pie) filled with a vegetable purée, and strawberries wrapped in wafer-thin pastry and rolled in ground almonds. Steer clear of the poky salons; head instead for the outside tables arranged around a small pool and shaded by lush banana palms. With the accompaniment of Andalusian lutes, these are where it's at. ⊠*81, rue Dar el Bacha* ☎*024/38–62–64* ⊟*MC, V* ⊗*Closed Mon.*

¢–$
FRENCH

✗**Le Foundouk.** This French-run place hidden at the souk's northern tip is regularly booked with upscale tourists and expats, and is good for an intimate evening for two. The sunny rooftop garden is a good lunch or afternoon tea spot. A lighter terrace adorned with statues and masks from West Africa rounds out the dining-room options. Chic à la carte dishes include foie gras and fig tagine; for a lighter snack at lunchtime try a *croque monsieur* (hot ham-and-cheese sandwich). The drawback is that it desperately wants you to know how seriously stylish it is. ⊠*55, Souk Hal Fassi, Kat Bennahid, near le Mokef square and the Musée de Marrakesh* ☎*024/37–81–90* ⊟*MC, V* ⊗*Closed Mon.*

$$
MOROCCAN

✗**Le Marrakchi.** With zellij walls, wood ceilings, and white-tile floors, this old palace serves up good Moroccan cuisine with modern flair at reasonable prices. You can choose from à la carte dishes, or choose one of the set menus. Book a table on the top floor for the panoramic view of the square. ⊠*52, rue des Banques, just off Djemâa el Fna* ☎*024/44–33–77* ⊟*MC, V* ⊗*No lunch.*

$$
FRENCH
★

✗**Le Pavillon.** If you arrive early in the evening, have an aperitif on the riad terrace of this chicest of chic French restaurants. Dine in the small courtyard under bountiful fig trees or behind glass in the (warmer) red salon alcoves, and watch the magic in the courtyard unfold. Highlights include pink duck with apples and impeccable service. ⊠*47, Derb Zaouia, opposite Bab Doukkala Mosque* ☎*024/38–70–40* ⊟*AE, MC, V* ⊗*Closed Tues. and 1 month in summer. No lunch.*

$
CONTEMPORARY

✗**Ryad Tamsna.** Hidden among the alleys of the medina's southern part, this handsome, neutral-tone riad offers a subtle African twist on Marrakesh dining. Delicious African, modern Moroccan, and international plates are served in a beautiful courtyard. The menu changes daily. Check out the first-floor boutique selling lovely—if pricey—items, and pretty rooftop terrace if you're here for lunch or a predinner aperitif. ⊠*Riad Zitoun Jdid 23, Derb Zanka Daika, 4th derb on left in Riad Zitoun Jdid* ☎*024/38–52–72* ⊟*MC, V.*

$–$$
MOROCCAN

✗**Le Tanjia.** This swanky restaurant has rose-filled fountains on each of its three floors. By day, dine on elegant arugula salads and other items on the lunch menu on the covered terrace overlooking a busy souk. By night, enjoy dinner and a glass of wine while marveling at the shimmying of belly dancers. The Sunday bunch is not to be missed. ⊠*14, Derb J'did Hay Essalam* ☎*076/04–67–67* ⊟ *V.*

Sidewalk Grills

Marrakshis have perfected the art of cooked street food, traditionally the province of the working class. There are hundreds of sidewalk grills scattered throughout both the medina and Guéliz. Step up for a tasty, satisfying meal at one of these institutions; it's a priceless experience that costs next to nothing. From midday to midnight, choose from grilled minced beef, sausage, lamb chops, brochettes, Moroccan salads, and french fries, supplemented by bread, olives, and hot sauce. No credit cards, clearly.

DJEMÂA EL FNA

✕ For the ultimate grilling experience, there's only one place (although some cautious travelers save their sensitive stomachs until their last night). By dusk, more than a hundred stalls sizzle and smoke their way through mountains of fresh meat and vegetables. Step up to the stall of your choice and order from the wild array of perfectly done veggies, salads, *kefta* (beef patties), *merguez* sausages, beef brochettes, couscous,

and even french fries. In cooler months or during Ramadan, try a bowl of hearty *harira* (chickpea, lentil, and meat soup) or country eggs in homemade bread. The meal starts with free bread (to weigh down your paper place setting) and a hot dipping sauce called *harissa*. The mint tea at the end should be free, too.

There's little continuity of quality, even at the same stall, so it's potluck and instinct all the way for each sitting. Vendors will do anything to attract your attention, from dragging you to a seat, chasing you down the lanes, and best of all, performing the occasional comic rundown of classic English phrases ("it's bloody marvelous") with matching cockney accent. If you're feeling superadventurous, try one of the outer stalls selling local standards: steamed snails served in porcelain bowls, and delicacies such as sheep's head and brains.

Tips:

Everything is fresh, as vendors give leftovers to the poor every night. Watch the Moroccans: they know what to order, and they really get into their food.

If there's a strong wind, avoid sitting in the path of billowing smoke. Don't be afraid of using other diners as windbreakers if there's a chill in the air.

OTHER MEDINA GRILLS

✕ **Haj Brik.** In a row of grill cafés on a narrow side street running south off Djemâa el Fna, Haj Brik is one of the best. Everything is prepared so well that it has been in business longer than most. The menu focuses on grilled lamb chops, merguez sausages, kefta, and kidneys, each served with

5

bread, olives, tomato salad, and hot sauce. Everything cooks on an indoor grill at the front of the shop, sending billowing smoke and smells over the diners. ⊠ *39, rue Bani Marine, through arch just left of post office in Djemâa el Fna* ☎No phone.

✕**Kasbah.** If you're feeling bold, step up to this down-and-dirty smoky den, a couple of doors south of the more-upscale Nid Cigogne café (you'll recognize it as the smokiest in the area). It's usually buzzing with Marrakshis, who may fall over flat at the prospect of a tourist turning up without so much as a flicker of the eye. You'll pay 10 DH for a mince sandwich. So long as it's cooked through, it's good to go. ⊠*Rue de la Kasbah* ☎No phone.

✕**Restaurant Bab Fteuh.** The much-loved and best grill in town is a total meat feast, serving up heart, liver, kidney, merguez, and mincemeat, for 24 DH a portion. It's tiny, but good. ⊠*On small derb linking Djemâa el Fna with Bab Fteuh, north of Café Argana on the right* ☎No phone.

✕**Restaurant el Bahja.** This small, tiled medina café next door to Marrakesh institution Haj Brik is just as popular and has almost the same food at the same prices. You can also get beef and chicken tagines and *loubia* (bean stew) in addition to standard grill fare. ⊠*41, rue Bani Marine* ☎024/44–03–43.

—Katrina Manson & James Knight

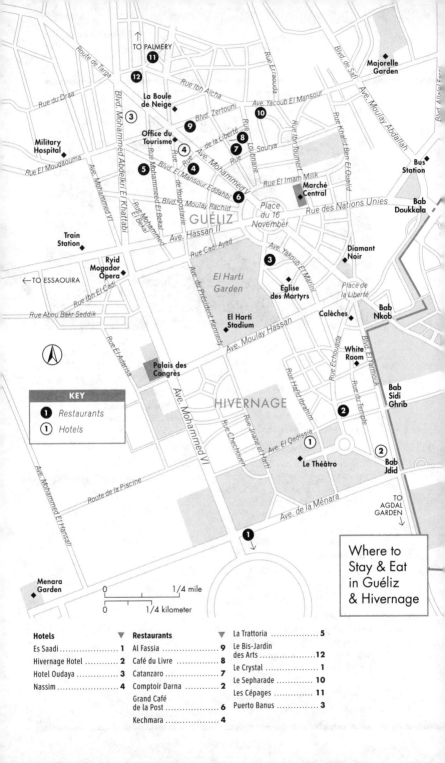

Where to Stay & Eat in Guéliz & Hivernage

KEY
- ● Restaurants
- ① Hotels

Hotels	▼
Es Saadi	1
Hivernage Hotel	2
Hotel Oudaya	3
Nassim	4

Restaurants	▼
Al Fassia	9
Café du Livre	8
Catanzaro	7
Comptoir Darna	2
Grand Café de la Post	6
Kechmara	4

La Trattoria	5
Le Bis-Jardin des Arts	12
Le Crystal	1
Le Sepharade	10
Les Cépages	11
Puerto Banus	3

$$$ **✕Tatchibana.** Take a break from
JAPANESE nonstop tagine and couscous at this
elegant Japanese eatery. Dine on the
wide array of sushi specialties, or
simply ask the chef to prepare you
the freshest catch of the day. ✉*38
Bab Ksiba, Kasbah,* ☎*024/38–71–
71* ▤ *AE, MC, V.*

$$$$ **✕Le Tobsil.** The name may be Ara-
MOROCCAN bic for "dish," but get ready for
several. The traditional Moroc-
can fixed menu, featuring not one
but two tagines (first poultry, then
lamb) followed by couscous, not
to mention starter and dessert, is
wheeled out in serious style. Dine
among lanterns and petals in the
intimate yellow-ocher courtyard of
the small riad just inside Bab Lakh-
sour. It's stylish and friendly, and the cuisine is very good. ✉*22, Derb
Abdellah ben Hessaien, R'mila Bab Ksour* ☎*024/44–15–23* ▤*MC, V*
🕙*Closed Tues. and July and Aug. No lunch.*

$$$$ **✕Le Yacout.** The palatial Yacout is in a house designed as a *Thousand
MOROCCAN and One Nights* restaurant. Its location deep in the medina only adds
★ to its mystery. Aperitifs are taken on the rooftop to the haunting chants
of a Gnaoua musician. A traditional Moroccan feast is served in sev-
eral different settings: beside the pool in a vaulted upstairs room; in
an intimate glassed-in salon; or in the lush, cushion-filled main salon.
Courteous, discreet waiters in white djellabas and red fezzes scurry
about to fulfill your every need. ✉*79, Sidi Ahmed Soussi, near Bab
Doukkala* ☎*024/38–29–29* ⚼*Reservations essential* ▤*AE, MC, V*
🕙*Closed Mon. No lunch.*

NEIGHBORHOOD
WATCH

Marrakesh's restaurant scene
changes faster than a belly dancer
at quitting time, and today's
hot tagine can quickly become
tomorrow's soggy couscous.
This is especially true in trendy,
finicky Guéliz. Some of the most
celebrated restaurants have built
their reputations around stunning
decor rather than stunning food,
but they're still worth going to as
long as you know this. Sound out
local opinion, and don't be afraid
to take a chance.

5

GUÉLIZ AND HIVERNAGE

$ **✕Al Fassia.** Serving some of the best à la carte Moroccan food in the
MOROCCAN city, Al Fassia breaks the mold in several ways. It's run by women,
★ avoids the dictates and giant portions of normal set menus, and brings
classic cooking to the modern district. ✉*55, bd. Zerktouni* ☎*024/43–
40–60* ▤*AE, MC, V.*

$$–$$$ **✕Le Bis-Jardin des Arts.** This restaurant's gorgeous decor, with lacy
FRENCH plasterwork around the fireplace and sparkling crystal in the pendant
lights, catches your attention right away. The delicious and complex
French dishes, such as lamb with a confit of prunes and raisins, help
make up for the somewhat diffident management. ✉*6–7, rue Sakia el
Hamra, Semlalia* ☎*024/44–66–34* ▤ *AE, V.*

$ **✕Café du Livre.** Peruse a small and quirky collection of English-language
FRENCH books while ordering lunch or an early dinner. It closes at 9, rather
early by Moroccan standards. Enjoy continental fare like a delicious
entrecôte or American-style dishes like a tasty cheeseburger. For des-

sert, enjoy the chocolate cake while relaxing on the comfortable velvet seating. ⊠*44, rue Tarik ben Ziyad* ☎*024/43–21–49* ▤*No credit cards* ☉*Closed Sun.*

¢   ✕**Cantanzaro.** One of Marrakesh's
ITALIAN   most popular restaurants, this homey Italian spot has dining on two floors, brightened by red-chintz tablecloths. The menu has a

good selection of basic Italian dishes and pizzas at prices that make them fabulous values. Pizza Royal—that is, with everything on it—is a favorite. ⊠*Rue Tariq Ibn Ziad, behind Marché Central* ☎*044/43–37–31* ⌕*Reservations essential* ▤*MC, V* ☉*Closed Sun.*

$ ✕**Les Cépages.** Chef Patrick and his wife, Véronique, opened this res-
FRENCH   taurant in a salmon-pink villa on a quiet residential street in Guéliz. You can sip cocktails and nibble on homemade pâté while browsing the haute-cuisine French menu in the cool shaded garden. Options include lobster with homemade mayonnaise, poached sea bass with sorrel sauce, and even a T-bone steak with three separate sauces. All are served by a polite and smiling staff. Sampler menus are available on request. ⊠*9, rue Ibn Zaidoun (in a street on the left, diagonally opposite Hôpital Civil entrance)* ☎*024/43–94–26* ▤*MC, V* ☉*Closed Mon.*

$–$$ ✕**Comptoir Darna.** Like the dark mahogany beams and panels that give
MOROCCAN   the interior its clubby feel, the place has aged well. À la carte dining blends traditional Moroccan and European cuisines. It remains a nighttime draw for hip Marrakshis and visitors alike; musicians, belly dancers (starting at 9:45), and an upstairs DJ and small dance floor provide added bite. ⊠*Ave. Echouhada, Hivernage* ☎*024/43–77–02* ▤*MC, V* ☉*No lunch.*

$$–$$$ ✕**Le Crystal.** Located in the trendy Pacha complex, this restaurant's huge
CONTINENETAL   glass doors open onto a magical pool setting. The Art Deco restaurant has artfully arranged food in fashionably small quantities. Look for such Italian-influenced dishes as ravioli with foie gras. Not only is the food chic, but you should be, too—be prepared to dress the part. Make reservations for weekend evenings to listen to live jazz. ⊠*Bd. Mohammed VI, Zone Hoteliere de l'Aguedal* ☎*024/38–84–00* ▤*V.*

$–$$ ✕**Grand Café de la Poste.** The colonial atmosphere provides a fabulous
MOROCCAN   backdrop for excellent salads and pastas. In spring and summer, enjoy a cold Casablanca beer on the covered veranda. The management is very attentive and friendly. ⊠*Bd. el Mansour Eddahbi at Ave. Imam Malik* ☎*024/43–30–38* ▤*AE, MC, V.*

$–$$ ✕**Kechmara.** Marrakesh doesn't get hipper than this. Ice-cool mid-cen-
CONTINENTAL   tury design and exhibitions by Moroccan and European artists put this on a par with something that might sprout in New York's East Village. Local cognoscenti believe the food could be better—this makes it better as a lunch drop-in than an all-out dinner option. You can always go back in the evening for relaxed drinks if you like. ⊠*3, rue de la Liberté* ☎*024/42–25–32* ▤*MC, V.*

Start the Day Right

Early birds should make the most of morning life in Marrakesh by having breakfast at a café, where locals sit languorously with their newspapers and chat with friends. Although you can find good café au lait and croissants almost anywhere, a typical Moroccan breakfast is harder to find (outside the hotels that serve it). The meal consists of: doughnuts called *sfinge*; and various hot pancakes called *bghrir* and *msaman*, that are served with butter, honey, and argan oil or *amalo* (a mixture of ground almonds and argan oil).

La Boule de Neige, on Rue de Yougoslavie in Guéliz, serves most of the above, in addition to continental breakfasts. You can get piping-hot sfinge with a glass of mint tea at a minuscule, unnamed café on Rue Mauritania, a side street that leaves Avenue Mohammed V at the Derby shoe store.

5

¢–$ **✕Puerto Banus.** This cozy eatery in the town center might remind you
SPANISH of Seville or Granada. In addition to paella full of seafood, the kitchen serves a wide variety of fish. A favorite is the sea bream, which come daily from El Oualidia. A table in the quiet courtyard takes you far from the madding crowd; in winter or on cool evenings meals are taken indoors, near a log fire. ⊠*Rue Ibn Hanbal (opposite police station)* ☎*024/44–65–34* ⊟*MC, V.*

$$$ **✕Le Sepharade.** This comfortable kosher restaurant is set in a large,
KOSHER salmon-pink villa just around the corner from the Beth-El Synagogue. The fixed menu includes kosher specialties and versions of various Moroccan tagines and cooked salads. ⊠*Between Rue Ibn Toumert and Rue Loubnane, off Bd. Zerktouni* ☎*024/43–98–09* ⊟*MC, V* ⊘*No lunch.*

¢–$ **✕La Trattoria.** Due partly to the pizzazz of its late owner, Juan Carlo, La
ITALIAN Trattoria has long held a place among Marrakesh's top restaurants. His chef Mohammed has taken over, and with neo-Moorish renovations overseen by Bill Willis, this ornate restaurant is flourishing. You can sit beside the pool and enjoy a good entrecôte or one of the many seafood pastas. ⊠*179, rue Mohammed el Béqal* ☎*024/43–26–41* ⚐*Reservations essential* ⊟*DC, MC, V* ⊘*No lunch.*

THE PALMERY

$–$$ **✕Le Blokk.** A fabulous addition to the dining scene in the Palmery, Le
MOROCCAN Blokk is well worth the taxi ride. The decor is chic, and dishes like duck
Fodor's Choice with balsamic vinegar and lamb with thyme are reasonably priced. The
★ live music, however, takes center stage. Tap your feet while talented singers perform songs from the last 50 years. ⊠ *Ennakhil, Propriete Farah, Prefecture Syba, 40000 (next to Mehdi Palace)* ☎*074/33–43– 34* ⊟*AE, V.*

$ **✕Dar Ennassim.** Indulge with top-notch French cuisine prepared by chef
FRENCH Fabrice Vulin. By day enjoy an artfully arranged salad and other light menu options on the terrace. By night, partake in the stunning restaurant interiors and feel like one of "the beautiful people." It's not cheap,

so consider this a special splurge. ⊠*Pavillon du golf, Circuit de la Palmeraie,* ☎*024/33–43–08* ☰ *AE, MC, V.*

WHERE TO STAY

Marrakesh is something of a Shangri-la for designers who, intoxicated by the colors, shapes, and patterns of the city, are free to indulge themselves in wildly opulent and ambitious designs. Although it isn't all tasteful, much of the decor and style in Marrakesh hotels and riads is fascinating and easy on the eye.

Most of the larger hotels (classified as three, four, or five stars by the Moroccan government) are in Guéliz, Hivernage, and the surrounding areas of Marrakesh. If you prefer something authentic and inexpensive near the action, choose one of the numerous small and clean hotels in the medina near Djemâa el Fna.

Hotels and riads vary their prices wildly between high and low season. This means that if you time your trip right you can find some great deals. High season runs from October to May, with spikes at Christmas, New Year's, and Easter. Most hotels provide their own free parking or oversee parking in the street nearby with a permanent guardian, who wears a badge. The fee for street parking is 5 DH for the day, and 10 DH–20 DH overnight.

WHAT IT COSTS IN DIRHAMS					
	¢	$	$$	$$$	$$$$
FOR TWO PEOPLE	under 400DH	400DH–1,000DH	1,000DH–2,500DH	2,500DH–4,000DH	over 4,000DH

Prices are for two people in a standard double room in high season, including service and tax.

MEDINA

$ **Dar Alfarah.** You enter this riad through a quiet garden near La Bahia Palace. All the house's original doors, ceilings, and tiles remain, and the guest rooms have painted wrought-iron window grilles and private bathrooms finished in *tadelakt* (a traditional, shiny, smooth-wall effect). Jasmine, bougainvillea, and banana palms surround a small courtyard pool. You can request meals on the secluded terrace, which has great views of Marrakesh and the High Atlas. **Pros:** Good location, plenty of atmosphere. **Con:** Small pool. ⊠*Riad Zitoun Jdid* ☎*024/43–15–60* ⊕*www.daralfarah.com* ⇆*5 rooms* ⌂*In-room: safe, Wi-Fi. In-hotel: pool* ☰*No credit cards.*

$ **Equity Point.** Hidden in the souk down twisting, turning derbs, this handsome, brooding affair doesn't make for a great daytime hangout, but it's a perfect home to come back to after a long day of souk exploration. Rooms are cheaper and more fun than suites; each room has two levels linked by its very own spiral staircase, and the calm bedrooms on the mezzanine level are devoid of anything but a bed. The candlelit, Berber-tented dining room comes alive at night and serves traditional cuisine. **Pros:** Lovely restaurant, gorgeous bathrooms. **Con:** Hard to find. ✉*80, Derb el Hammam, Mouassine, take Mouassine street in the souk going north, past Fnac Berbère and after 110 yards double back through arch to the right and follow signs* ☎*024/44–07–93* ⊕*www.equity-point.com* ⟿*2 rooms, 4 suites* ♿*In-hotel: restaurant* ▤*MC, V* ⫿⃝*BP.*

¢ 🏨**Hotel Ali.** Backpackers pile into sparsely furnished rooms or stay on the crowded roof terrace. All rooms are en suite and guests have free use of the adjoining cybercafé, as well as access to a 24-hour currency exchange bureau and a hammam. There are great views over Djemâa el Fna, and Rooms 204–207 have private balconies overlooking the street and the Koutoubia gardens. Buffet dinners are included in the rate during high season. **Pros:** Great place to meet fellow travelers, free Internet access. **Con:** A little noisy. ✉*Rue Moulay Ismail, 55 yards from Dejmâa el Fna.* ☎*024/44–49–79* ⊕*www.hotel-ali.hotel-marrakech.com.uk* ⟿*45 rooms, 2 dorms* ♿*In-hotel: restaurant, hammam, public Internet* ▤*AE, MC, V* ⫿⃝*MAP.*

> ### TADELAKT & ZELLIJ
>
> Morocco's nicest hotels often have *tadelakt* and *zellij* touches, but what exactly are they? Tadelakt is a traditional, shiny, smooth-wall effect, much more lustrous than simple matte paint. It's achieved by smoothing plaster, painting over it with egg white, and then rubbing it until it shines, as you would with a brass lamp. It's especially popular on bathroom walls, but can be used for entire guesthouses. Zellij is a kind of elaborate tiling for floors, walls, and skirting that uses small hand-made tiles that can be fashioned into complex mosaics.

¢ 🏨**Hotel Essaouira.** This is without doubt the best value in town. So
★ long as you're happy sharing bath facilities (one shower and toilet per floor—the better shower is on the first floor), the hotel will be nothing but a delight. Pretty ceramics, painted wooden ceilings, cascading green plants, helpful staff, and small but perfectly formed rooms don't come cheaper. The rooftop terrace has meals and snacks all day long, and you're just a twist and a turn away from Djemâa el Fna. **Pros:** Great value, central location. **Con:** Shared bathrooms. ✉*3, Sidi Bouloukate* ☎*024/44–38–05* ⊕*www.jnanemogador.com* ⟿*28 rooms without bath* ♿*In-hotel: restaurant* ▤*No credit cards.*

¢–$ 🏨**Hotel Sherazade.** A series of gorgeous rooftop terraces, stylish tents,
★ and plant-filled courtyards of two conjoined riads beguile you into thinking this is a much more expensive hotel. The family-run place is superfriendly and helpful, and a backpacking gold standard minutes from Djemâa el Fna. **Pros:** Good location, restful setting. **Con:** Few amenities. ✉*3, Derb Djemâa, Riad Sitoun Elkedim* ☎*024/42–93–05* ⊕*www.hotelsherazade.com* ⟿*19 rooms, 15 with bath* ♿*In-hotel: restaurant* ▤*MC, V.*

$ 🏨**Hotel du Tresor.** A haven for artists and design lovers, this beautifully converted hotel has been featured in design magazines. The Italian owner balanced a respect for the old and a love of the new, so you might find a modern sculpture against lovingly restored tiles. There's a small heated pool where you can relax after a day of exploring. This place is located near the Djemaa el Fna. **Pros:** Fantastic location, top-notch design, helpful management. **Con:** Pool area not private. ✉*77, Sidi Boulokat, Riad Zitoun Kdim* ☎*024/37–51–61* ⊕*www.hotel-du-tresor. com* ⏎*11 rooms, 3 suites* ⚘*In-hotel: public Wi-Fi* ⊟*AE, MC, V* ⦿*EP.*

$$–$$$ ⛺**Les Jardins de la Koutoubia.**After La Mamounia, this might be the sultan of the medina. Despite its location on an unprepossessing street, the interior's grand scale and opulence impress. The carved pillars of the garden give the air of an ancient temple, with four salons around an enormous pool and a giant fireplace at one end. The ambassador suite has great views of the medina and nearby Koutoubia Mosque. **Pros:** Plenty of atmosphere, great pool area. **Con:** Terrible exterior. ✉*26, rue de la Koutoubia* ☎*024/38–88–00* ⊕*www.lesjardinsdelakoutoubia. com* ⏎*102 rooms, 51 suites* ⚘*In-hotel: 2 restaurants, bar, gym, hammam* ⊟*DC, MC, V* ⦿*EP*

$ ⛺**Jnane Mogador.** Run by the same proprietor as the long-standing and nearby backpackers' Hotel Essaouira, this budget option is a cut above the rest. Fountains, tadelakt columns, wood-clad rooms, a rooftop terrace, and cascading plants contribute to an air of elegance. **Pros:** Near the main square, very good value. **Cons:** Some rooms can be dark, unoriginal decor. ✉*116, Riad Zitoun Kedim, Derb Sidi Bouloukate* ☎*024/42–63–23* ⊕*www.jnanemogador.com* ⏎*17 rooms, 1 suite* ⚘*In-room: Ethernet. In-hotel: restaurant, spa, hammam* ⊟*MC, V.*

$$ ⛺**La Maison Arabe.** Owner Fabrizio Ruspoli created this small hotel for
★ those craving old-fashioned charm. The hotel artfully blends Moorish and European design (note the Italianate reading room), and each of the four courtyards offers grandeur on an intimate scale. Rooms are small and staunchly Arabian, but are well appointed and air-conditioned. Many suites cover two or three levels. In the medina near Bab Doukkala, the house was once a famous restaurant, the first to serve Moroccan cuisine to such European notables as Winston Churchill. Breakfast and afternoon tea are complimentary, and the service is excellent. **Pros:** Lots of little nooks, renowned cooking school. **Cons:** Small rooms, a bit pricey. ✉*1, Derb Assehbe, Bab Doukkala* ☎*024/38–70–10* ⊕*www.lamaisonarabe.com* ⏎*9 rooms, 8 suites* ⚘*In-room: Wi-Fi. In-hotel: restaurant, hammam* ⊟*MC, V.*

$$$ ⛺**Riad Fawakay.** Lovingly restored by two charming British expats, this riad is long on charm. The public areas are filled with lovely vintage textiles and some wonderful artworks. It's only rented out in its entirety, making it perfect for a big family or couples traveling together. The food is so tasty that you'll hesitate to dine out. Skinny-dip in the plunge pool . . . no one will tell. **Pros:** Beautiful terrace, great private chef. **Cons:** Must rent entire house, no parking. ✉*74, derb El Cadi* ☎*075/13–01–42* ⊕*www.daralfarah.com* ⏎*3 rooms* ⚘*In-room: Wi-Fi. In-hotel: pool* ⊟*No credit cards.*

$$$–$$$$ ⛺**Riad el Fenn.** For high-octane creative types who want real style, Vanessa Branson's (sister of the British entrepreneur) riad "adventure" is where it's at. Behind an anonymous door hidden down a derb in the western reaches of the medina is a palace of individually conceived rooms designed with a stylish modern aesthetic. Most guests stay four to five days—some even two weeks—and together with the staff they create an atmosphere worthy of a private club. **Pros:** Dripping with good taste, an exclusive vibe. **Con:** Very expensive. ⊠*2, Derb Abdellah ben Hessaien, R'mila Bab Ksour* ☎*024/44–12–10* ⊕*www.riadel fenn.com* ➴*17 rooms* ⌂*In-hotel: restaurant, pool, hammam* ▤*AE, MC, V.*

$$ ▦**Riad Lotus Privilège.** With exquisite decor, this lovely riad will leave you breathless. One of the carefully designed rooms even offers a hand-carved bathtub. A small pool is located in the beautifully designed courtyard. **Pros:** Romantic enough for a honeymoon, decadent decor. **Cons:** Smaller rooms are considerably less stylish, tricky to find. ⊠*9 Derb Sidi Ali Ben Hamouch, Medina* ☎*024/43–59–29* ⊕*www.riads lotus.com* ➴*5 rooms* ⌂*In–room: safe, refrigerator, Wi-Fi. In-hotel: pool, hammam, laundry service* ▤*AE, MC, V* ⦿*EP.*

$$ ▦**Riad Malika.** The rambling, relaxing Malika was one of the first riads to reinvent itself in the 1990s, and owner Jean-Luc Lemée and his English-speaking wife are full of anecdotes about Morocco. They've created an exuberantly styled collection of travel mementoes and Art Deco relics. The winter lounge—with a book of Chopin mazurkas on the piano for anyone brave enough to play—is one of the coziest in Marrakesh. **Pros:** Plenty of charm, congenial hosts. **Con:** A bit small for some. ⊠*29 to 36, Arsat Aouzal, Bab Doukkala* ☎*024/38–54–51* ⊕*www.riadmalika.com* ➴*8 rooms, 5 suites* ⌂*In-hotel: pool, hammam, airport shuttle, public Internet* ▤*MC, V* ⦿*MAP.*

$ ▦**Riad Al Mamoune.** This French-owned riad is a peaceful retreat amid the chaos of the souk. Rooms are decorated with extreme care, artfully blending Moroccan colonial flair with Indochine chic. Ask for the first-floor room with the four-poster bed. The manager goes out of her way to make sure that guests are pampered, and will help plan special meals and interesting outings. **Pros:** Local cell phones loaned to guests, piping-hot water at all times. **Con:** A bit hard to find. ⊠*140, Derb Aarjane, Rahba Kédima, east of Rue Semarine through Souk aux Epices, then follow signs from Rahba Lakdima* ☎*024/39–19–58* ⊕*www.riadalmamoune.com* ➴*5 rooms, 1 suite* ⌂*In-hotel: hammam* ▤*MC, V.*

$$$ ▦**La Sultana.** There's a certain over-the-top charm to this series of four riads. The rooftop walkway has good views to the zellij of the Saadian tombs below. A nighttime aperitif beside the pool on the terrace amid rows of man-size lanterns is hard to beat. The decent and well-priced restaurant is open to nonguests and has both French and Moroccan menus, with an emphasis on fish. **Pro:** Fireplaces in every room. **Con:** Decor is a bit gaudy. ⊠*403, rue de la Kasbah, on a tiny alley heading left just south of Saadian tombs, Kasbah* ☎*024/38–80–08* ⊕*www. lasultanamarrakech.com* ➴*21 rooms* ⌂*In-room: Wi-Fi. In-hotel: restaurant, bar, spa, hammam* ▤*AE, MC, V* ⦿*Closed Aug. 6–26 (check ahead)* ⦿*BP.*

$$ ▦**Talaa 12.** This achingly trendy temple to modernist riad chic is in the
★ middle of the medina. Rooms are an exercise in minimalism. They're drenched in natural creams and browns, but have just enough color to make them inviting. The overall cool quotient would verge on icy if not

5

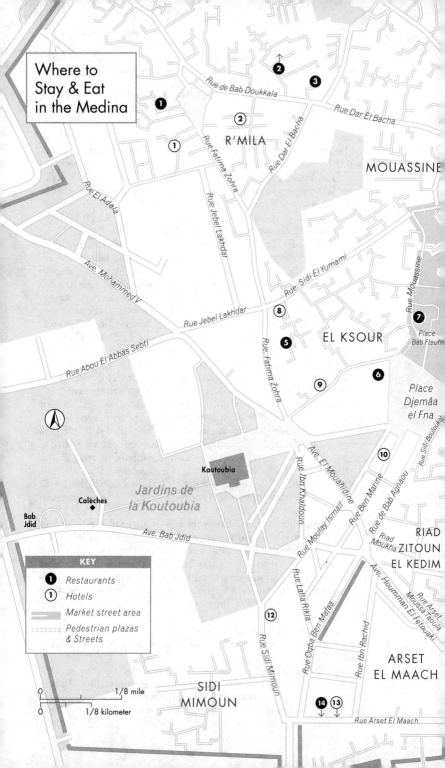

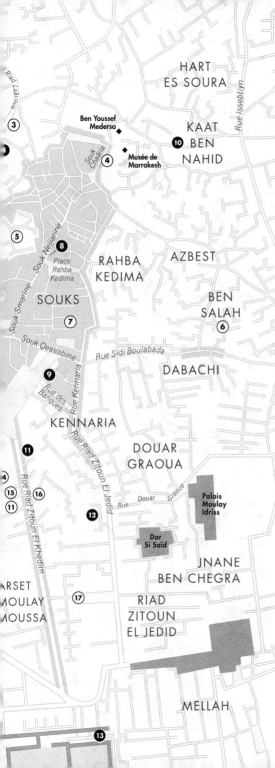

RIAD RENTALS

Nothing beats taking over a riad for a few days. We mean booking the whole darn thing—not just a room. Staying in a beautifully restored 16th-century palace isn't cheap, but riads in the medina and small villas in the Palmery are geared up for this. Their staffs can help organize meal plans, special itineraries, weddings, birthday parties, and literary salons. There are more than 800 riads in Marrakesh, and at least half of these claim to be the trendiest. The choices may seem overwhelming, but as long as you find one that appeals to you (not hard!), you're set for a special night. In addition to the individual riads listed below, try the following agencies:

Boutique Souk (☎ +44 (0)7900/195261 [U.K.] ⊕ www.boutiquesouk.com).

Marrakech Medina (✉ 72, Derb Arssat Aouzal, Bab Doukala ☎ 044/24–24–48 ⊕ www.marrakech-medina.com)

Marrakech Riads (✉ 8, Derb Cherfa Lakbir ☎ 024/42–64–63 or 24/39–1– 39 ⊕ www.marrakech-riads.net).

Secret Morocco (✉ 120, Dar el Bacha Souika, Sidi Abdelaziz ☎ 024/24–24–48 ⊕ www.marrakech-medina.com).

for the warmth of English-speaking host Laurent and the orange trees in the central courtyard. You can swim at the Nikki Beach complex at the Palmeraie Golf Palace. **Pros:** Very stylish, friendly staff. **Con:** Some find it overdesigned. ✉ 12, Talaa ben Youssef, on the way to Ali ben Youssef Medersa ☎ 024/42–90–45 ⊕ www.talaa12.com ⟲ 4 rooms, 4 suites ☒ In-hotel: hammam, airport shuttle ☰ AE, MC, V ☉ CP.

$$$–$$$$ ☷ **Villa des Orangers.** This property has all the understated glamour and class you'd expect from a Relais & Chateaux hotel, with unobtrusive service, libraries to hide away in, and bedrooms with enormous bathrooms. The best (and more-expensive) option is a room on the first floor, which gives you access to a private terrace with a rooftop shower and lounge chairs. Dine on the excellent contemporary French and Moroccan food in the restaurant (nonguests welcome), or take your meals by the pool or fireside on a private, orange tree–filled patio. **Pros:** Unsurpassed luxury, plenty of privacy. **Con:** Very expensive. ✉ 6, rue Sidi Mimoune ☎ 024/38–46–38 ⊕ www.villadesorangers.com ⟲ 19 rooms ☒ In-hotel: restaurant, pools ☰ AE, MC, V ☉ BP

VILLE NOUVELLE

Unless you're with a family in need of a big hotel to drown out the noise you make, the towns of Guéliz and Hivernage in Ville Nouvelle mostly cater to expensive package holidays. They overflow with facilities but lack the character or service you find elsewhere. Still, we've found a few that buck the trend.

$$ ☷ **Es Saadi.** This large family hotel started as Marrakesh's first casino, ↺ and then grew and grew. The 1950s design does little to inspire, but this family-run hotel with every amenity does the job. The gardens, blooming with orange trees and roses, are lovely, and children are constantly splashing their way into the large pool. **Pros:** On-site casino, family-friendly atmosphere. **Con:** Dated design. ✉*Rue Quadissia* ☎*024/44–88–11* ⊕*www.essaadi. com* ⇆*150 rooms* ⚐*In-hotel: 3 restaurants, bar, tennis courts, hammam* ☰*AE, DC, MC, V.*

$$ 🏨**Hivernage Hotel & Spa.** Hip cou-
★ ples with serious pampering needs will enjoy this exclusive pleasure dome nestled among the Hivernage megachain hotels. The pool area is small, but rooms are more boutique than brash, incorporating Moroccan design with African and Art Deco flourishes. If that's not enough, the restaurant is under the aegis of Christophe Leroy, chef to the French jet set on the Côte d'Azur, and a patisserie turns out delicious treats all day. If your wallet is up to it, request a junior suite for the pool view through the wonderful bay window that comes with it. **Pros:** Impressive design, great food. **Con:** Chain-hotel feel. ✉*Ave. Echouhada at Rue des Temples, Hivernage* ☎*024/42–41–00* ⊕*www.hivernage-hotel.com* ⇆*85 rooms, 10 suites* ⚐*In-room: safe. In-hotel: 2 restaurants, bar, pool, gym, hammam* ☰*AE, MC, V* ⦿*EP.*

$ 🏨**Hotel Oudaya.** The unpretentious Oudaya, on a busy tree-lined side street in Guéliz, is popular with young travelers, particularly those from France. The aesthetic is modern Moroccan, and the entrance hall is impressive. Rooms are small and clean, with well-appointed bathrooms. For a quieter stay, ask for one of the newer rooms at the back of the hotel in the annex. **Pro:** Spic-and-span rooms. **Con:** Some accommodations are noisy. ✉*147, rue Mohammed el Bequal* ☎*024/24–85–12* ⊕*www.oudaya.ma* ⇆*144 rooms, 15 suites* ⚐*In-room: safe. In-hotel: 2 restaurants, pool, hammam* ☰*MC, V.*

$ 🏨**Nassim.** If you want to stay in the city center, this modern hotel is ideal—it's near Place Abdel Moumen and all the surrounding cafés. The good-size, air-conditioned rooms are nicely decorated, if a bit businesslike, and facilities include a small pool, a quiet bar, an exercise room, and a rooftop terrace. **Pro:** Pool is great on a hot day. **Con:** Not a lot of charm. ✉*115, ave. Mohammed V* ☎*024/44–64–01* ⊕*www. hotelnassim.ma* ⇆*52 rooms, 4 suites, 1 apartment* ⚐*In-room: safe. In-hotel: restaurant, bar, pool, gym, hammam* ☰*MC, V* ⦿*EP.*

ROOMS WITH A VIEW

No matter how good your riad or hotel, most rooms tend to face inward to the gentle sound of a bubbling fountain in a central courtyard rather than out over the medina. Here are a few places to stay that have great views across the city.

Hotel Ali: Rooms 204–207, 212, 213, and 215–217

Hivernage Hotel & Spa: medina-view rooms

Les Jardins de la Koutoubia: medina-view rooms

5

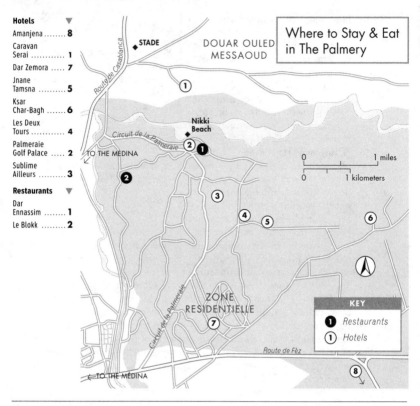

THE PALMERY

Staying in the Palmery is a good choice if you're looking for a relaxing vacation and won't feel guilty about exchanging the medina's action for an idyll in your own private country palace. It's also close to Marrakesh's famous golf courses. The drawback is the 7-km (4.5-mi) distance from Marrakesh, which necessitates a car, a taxi, or use of infrequent hotel shuttles.

$$–$$$ **Caravan Serai.** The name means "resting place" originally for the
★   merchants crossing the Sahara, and nowadays guests lounge happily in the garden, pool, and beautifully restrained bedrooms. This is the ultimate in rustic charm, perfect for lovebirds and uptight city slickers looking to unwind. Design is a feast of exposed brick, lightly hued walls, and simple wooden pillars. For real privacy ask for the Majorelle Suite; it's entirely blue and has its own swimming pool. **Pros:** Lovely design, laid-back service. **Con:** Garden can feel cramped. ⊠264, Ouled Ben Rahmoune, Palmery, take route to Casablanca then turn right after sign to Chez Ali, then take dirt track on right side at sign ☎024/30–03–02 ⊕www.caravanserai.com ➷4 rooms, 13 suites ⌂In-room: Wi-Fi. In-hotel: pool, hammam, airport shuttle ☰MC, V ⫮CP.

$$$ ⛺**Dar Zemora.** The unpretentious charms of this country villa will ease
★   your guilt about staying in the Palmery and possibly seeing less of Marrakesh. The rambling, English-style garden is a delight, and in-season bouquets from the rose garden adorn the house. Service is attentive, and for once design isn't too over the top. Belgian manager Valerie is an authority on all aspects of the city, particularly its restaurants. **Pros:** Regal views, friendly staff. **Con:** Minimum stay required. ⊠*72, rue el Aandalib, Ennakhil, Palmery, just off road to Fez* ☎*024/32–82–00* ⊕*www.darzemora.com* ☞*3 rooms, 2 suites, 1 apartment* ⌂*In-hotel: pool, airport shuttle, public Internet* ⊟*MC, V* ⦿*CP.*

$$–$$$ ⛺**Les Deux Tours.** The Two Towers has the advantages of a luxurious garden setting and classic Charles Boccara architecture. The communal areas, particularly the poolside terrace and cathedral-like restaurant, are a delight, and the site is crammed with romantic nooks and crannies. Rooms contain wonderful Moroccan writing desks and unconventional painted oleander-branch ceilings. **Pros:** Lovely common areas, pretty pool. **Con:** Some unattractive appliances. ⊠*B.P. 513, Douar Abiad, Circuit de la Palmeraie* ☎*024/32–95–25* ⊕*www.les-deux-tours.com* ☞*31 suites* ⌂*In-room: safe, Wi-Fi. In-hotel: restaurant, pool, hammam, airport shuttle* ⊟*MC, V.*

$$$$ ⛺**Hotel Amanjena.** Just south of the Palmery, Hotel Amanjena is a blend of Moorish and ancient Egyptian architecture. The terra-cotta-color villas and pavilions all surround a turquoise lagoon from which a series of smaller lagoons spread out through the manicured gardens. Each pavilion and villa is secluded and enveloped by lush plants, and the stylish, generously sized bedrooms have high domed ceilings. Some units have private dipping pools, fountains, and garden courtyards with drapes and white divans; each unit has a bath with a view of the blue sky and the tops of palm trees. **Pros:** Stunning architecture, incredible attention to detail, great Thai restaurant. **Con:** Marrakesh's priciest hotel—you will need deep pockets to stay here for any length of time. ⊠*Rte. de Ouarzazate, Km 12* ☎*024/40–33–53* ⊕*www.amanresorts.com* ☞*32 pavilions, 7 villas* ⌂*In-room: refrigerator. In–hotel: 2 restaurants, bar, tennis courts, pool, gym, bicycles* ⊟*AE, DC, MC, V.*

$$$–$$$$ ⛺**Jnane Tamsna.** The word *jnane* means "garden," and this, the third
Fodor'sChoice of Meryanne Loum-Martin's jet-set luxury properties, lives up to its
★   name. Modeled in a hacienda style that blends Moroccan with Mexican, the five cottages and main house that make up this oasis complex are surrounded by palms and olive trees. Each cottage is tastefully decorated with shiny tadelakt finishes and colorful rugs and drapes, and there are fireplaces in bedrooms and bathrooms. Meals use fresh produce from Loum-Martin's husband's garden in the Atlas Mountains. **Pros:** Plenty of pampering, attentive staff. **Con:** Expensive rates. ⊠*Douar Abiad, Circuit de la Palmeraie* ☎*024/32–84–84* ⊕*www.jnanetamsna.com* ☞*9 rooms, 5 cottages* ⌂*In-hotel: airport shuttle* ⊟*AE, MC, V* ⦿*BP.*

$$$$ ⛺**Ksar Char-Bagh.** Rising like a Byzantine, 14th-century Kasbah from
★   the Palmery and surrounded by its own moat and acres of grounds, this hotel is the last word in sumptuous, escape-it-all luxury. From the moment its giant wooden doors swing open to reveal the central

courtyard, restaurant, and swimming pool beyond, everything is calculated to impress. Ruins to explore at the bottom of the garden also contain a boutique from which visitors can purchase replica furniture. **Pros:** Beautiful decor, heated pool. **Con:** Service sometimes falls short. ⊠*Djnan Abiad, Circuit de la Palmeraie* ☎*024/32–92–44* ⊕*www.ksarcharbagh.com* ➪*12 suites, 1 apartment* ⚒*In-hotel: restaurant, tennis courts, pool, hammam, airport shuttle, public Internet* ▤*AE, MC, V* ☉*Closed July 20–Aug. 10* ⊚*BP.*

$$$–$$$$ 🏨**Palmeraie Golf Palace.** Tasteful
☺ it isn't, but this giant, gaudy self-contained bubble in the middle of the Palmery offers every kind of distraction, and plenty to keep children amused. The biggest draw is the demanding championship golf course (par 72). Guest rooms have plenty of gilt and marble. A sense of space, a lively pool scene, and all the various amenities and restaurants are the biggest advantages. **Pros:** Great for golfers, plenty of pampering. **Con:** Not much charm. ⊠*Les Jardins de la Palmeraie, Circuit de la Palmeraie* ☎*024/36–87–04* ⊕*www.pgpmarrakeh.com* ➪*286 rooms, 28 suites* ⚒*In-room: safe. In-hotel: 8 restaurants, bars, golf course, tennis court, pools, spa* ▤*AE, MC, V* ⊚*EP.*

$$$$ 🏨**Sublime Ailleurs.** Two villas and a riad stand in 5 acres of gardens, each with its own pool and terrace. The design and decor are a thoughtful blend of Asian and Art Deco styles and furnishings in warm terracotta tones. Rooms in the riad can be rented individually; the villas have two suites each and are rented as a whole unit. The live-in staff takes care of everything and prepares meals on request. **Pro:** Lots of privacy. **Con:** Villa rooms must be rented as pairs. ⊠*Circuit de la Palmeraie* ☎*024/32–96–44* ⊕*www.sublimeailleurs.com* ➪*4 rooms, 2 villas* ⚒*In-room: safe. In-hotel: pool, airport shuttle* ▤*AE, MC, V* ⊚*FAP, MAP.*

DON'T MISS

Late-night drinking is one of the few ways to sample the interiors of Marrakesh's most prestigious hotels.

The attractive Art Deco stylings and extensive cigar rack of **Les Jardins de la Koutoubia** (⊠*26, rue de la Koutoubia* ☎*024/38–88–00*) are decadent enough, although the more-intimate surroundings of the African bar at **La Maison Arabe** (⊠*1, Derb Assehbe, Bab Doukkala* ☎*024/38–70–10*) provide a less-starchy environment and tapas for late-night munchies.

NIGHTLIFE

Without doubt, Marrakesh is Morocco's nightlife capital. Options include everything from the free but fascinating goings on at the Djemâa el Fna square to the nightly over-the-top show at Chez Ali.

BARS

Alcohol was once frowned upon in the medina, and while it's still unthinkable to swig liquor on the streets, there is now a reasonably good group of places to go for a drink within the city walls.

However, despite this development, things tend to wind down early in the medina. Night owls in search of something more lively will have to take a taxi over to the trendy hangouts in Guéliz and Hivernage.

MEDINA

One of the most beautiful settings is **Café Arabe** (⊠*184, rue el Mouassine, Medina* ☎*024/42–97–28*), a galleried, bougainvillea-strewn riad with a sleek roof-top bar and two dance floors. Pastas are homemade, so come for dinner and make an evening of it.

> ### GREATEST SHOW ON EARTH
>
> Don't leave the city without visiting **Chez Ali** (⊠*La Palmeraie,* ☎*024/30–77–30*), a Vegas-meets-Marrakesh experience. After your multicourse dinner in breezy tents, the show begins. Featuring hundreds of performers and dozens of horses, this singing-and-dancing extravaganza is a celebration of traditional culture. It's somewhat cheesy but very enjoyable.

The cuddly sounding **Kosy Bar** (⊠*47, pl. des Ferblantiers, Kzadria, Medina* ☎*024/38–03–24*) and restaurant has been criticized for poor service in the past, but the sushi and a jazz pianist make it worth a look. Inventive cocktails can be enjoyed on the large roof terrace and the interiors are camera worthy, as well.

HIVERNAGE

La Casa Tapas Bar (⊠*Hotel Andalous, Hivernage* ☎*024/44–82–26*) attracts young Marrakshis and tourists alike and plays a selection of Latin and Top 40 hits.

A lively crowd gathers regularly at the popular darkened corners of **Comptoir Darna** (⊠*Ave. Echouhada, Hivernage* ☎*024/43–77–02*) to dance to the tunes of the top-floor DJ.

CASINOS

The casino at **La Mamounia** has a large room for roulette and blackjack, a slot-machine hall, and is open until 4 AM.

The only other casino of note is the one in the gardens of the **Es Saadi** hotel, set apart from the main building. The first in Marrakesh, it has undergone a revamp and contains a mixture of one-armed bandits and tables for roulette and blackjack.

NIGHTCLUBS

GUÉLIZ

In the town center, **Le Diamant Noir** (⊠*Pl. de la Liberté, Guéliz* ☎*024/43–43–51*), a Marrakesh institution, piles on the R&B, remains popular, and is gay-friendly.

The **Havana Club** (⊠*Triangle d'O, Guéliz* ☎*024/43–13–77*), in the Hotel Kenzi Semiramis, draws a good crowd.

The Cuban-theme surrounds and sounds of **Montecristo** (⊠*20, rue Ibn Aicha, Guéliz* ☎*024/43–90–31*), complete with Che Guevara portraits, has also caught the imagination of the city's groovers and shakers.

Another popular nightclub is **Paradise** (✉ *Ave. Mohammed VI, Guéliz* ☎024/44–82–22), at the Hotel Mansour Eddahbi.

HIVERNAGE

One of the hippest nightspots is the Indian-tinged **Jad Mahal** (✉ *10, rue Fontaine de la Mamounia, Bab Jdid, Hivernage* ☎024/43–69–84), with its exorbitantly priced drinks and lavish belly-dancing display that manages to soothe your empty wallet.

For a rococo treat that sends you back to 1970s Miami, try **Le Théâtro** (✉*Hotel Es Saadi, Rue Quadissia, Hivernage* ☎024/44–88–11 ⊕*www.essaadi.com*).

Part of the Hotel Royal Mirage Deluxe, **White Room** (✉*Rue de Paris, Hivernage* ☎024/44–89–98) puts the disco back into discotheque, and has free entry for women every Wednesday night. Monday is disco night, and there's a Sunday special.

PALMERY

Le Palace Lux Clubbing (✉ *Palmeraie Golf Palace & Resort, B.P. 1488, Jardins de la Palmeraie* ☎024/36–87–35), at the Palmeraie Golf Palace, is worth the short trek from Marrakesh. It's been totally revamped and now has a resident DJ.

PACHA COMES HOME

The supertrendy super-club has finally launched in Marrakesh. About time, too, given that the city was actually once ruled by pashas. Out on the Ourika road, **Pacha** (✉*Ave. Mohammed VI* ☎024/38–84–00 ⊕*www. pachamarrakech.com* ✉*From 150 DH*) sits like a desert palace among the scrub, with two restaurants, a swimming pool, bar, boutique, chill-out room with live music, and, of course, a dance floor. Restaurants Crystal and Jana offer Mediterranean and Moroccan menus, respectively. The nightclub plays 50,000 watts worth of music, and hosts international DJs.

SHOPPING

Marrakesh is a shopper's bonanza, full of the very rugs, handicrafts, and clothes you see in the pages of magazines back home. Most bazaars are in the souk, just north of Djemâa el Fna and spread through a seemingly never-ending maze of alleys. Together, they sell almost everything imaginable and are highly competitive. Bargaining here is hard, and you can get up to 80% discounts. So on your first exploration, it's often a better idea to simply wander and take in the atmosphere than to buy. You can check guideline prices in some of the more well-to-do parts of town, which display fixed price tags for every object.

There are a number of crafts and souvenir shops on Avenue Mohammed V in Guéliz, as well as some very good Moroccan antiques stores and designer shops that offer a distinctly modern take on Moroccan clothing, footwear, and interior decoration. These have sprung up as part of a movement toward allowing buyers to browse at their leisure, free of the souk's intense pressures. Many show fixed prices, with only 10% discounts after haggling. Most of these stores are happy to ship your purchases overseas. The Central Market also has a bazaar section.

Bazaars open between 8 AM and 9 AM and close between 8 PM and 9 PM; stores in Guéliz open a bit later and close a bit earlier, some breaking for lunch. Some bazaars close on Friday, the Muslim holy day.

THE SOUKS

SOUK SEMARINE

Your first mission is to find Rue Semarine, one of the two main souk arteries stretching north. From Djemâa el Fna take the street just to the left of the **Café Argana,** which leads into the small **Bab Fteuh** square. To the left there is a **kissaria,** (covered market), with dried fruits, herbs and spices, essential oils, and traditional colored eye kohls (expect to pay about 10 DH for a kohl holder and 5 DH for the kohl itself). Veer right into the covered market, past a couple of stands selling teapots and mint tea glasses, and take a left onto Rue **Souk Semarine.** It's signposted and lined with fabrics and inexpensive souvenirs.

LA CRIÉE BERBÈRE & SOUK LGHZAL (OLD SLAVE SOUK)

Bypass a fairly prominent derb turning on the left (Rue R'mila Bab Ksour, also called **Rue el Ksour**), and take the next right turn. Wander down and turn right again toward the square for **La Criée Berbère,** once the old slave market. Look for the overhead sign to Souk Lghzal (the same place as Criée Berbère), which translates as the Wool Souk. Today women sell secondhand clothes in the square, and the odd djellaba. A real treat can be found in the apothecary stalls leading up to the entrance to the square, and immediately to the right on entering it. There are spices and potions galore, as well as animal skins (zebra, snake, leopard), used by women for magic: mostly in their desire for marriage and pregnancy.

SOUK RAHBA QDIMA (SPICE SOUK)

Retrace your steps, rejoin Souk Semarine, and take the next right, which leads into an even larger square, **Souk Rahba Qdima.** Pushier and more mass-market than the spice street, this is the souk's main spice center. There are also lots of woven baskets and hats for sale here. Pause for a pleasant pit stop at the **Café des Epices.**

SOUK EL ATTARINE (OIL & PERFUME SOUK)

Souk el Attarine is traditionally the market street for perfumes, essential oils, and spices. This street is one of the main left turns, leaving the road at a "10 o'clock" angle. If you'd like to curtail your souk exploration, take this turn now and do a counterclockwise loop up to the central medina mosque (perhaps an easier route into the souks for both leather slippers and wool dyers, which are just to the right of the mosque), turning left to go back south eventually, down Rue Mouassine to rejoin Bab Fteuh square.

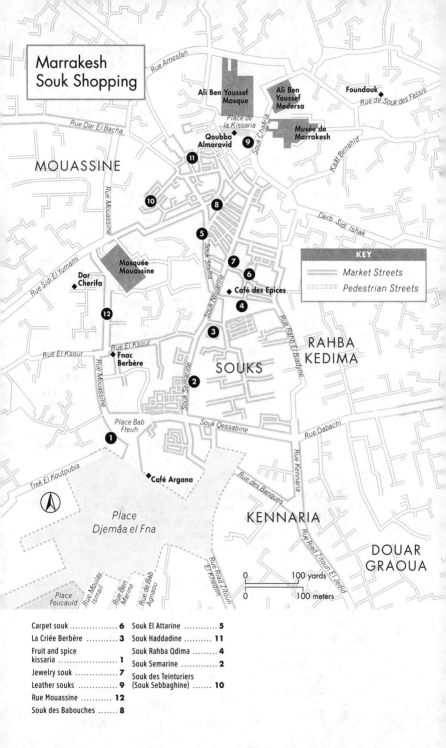

Marrakesh Souk Shopping

MOUASSINE

Rue Amesfah

Rue Dar El Bacha

Ali Ben Youssef Mosque

Ali Ben Youssef Medersa

Foundouk

Rue de Souk des Fassis

Place de la Kissaria

Qoubba Almoravid **9**

Musée de Marrakesh

Kâat Benahid

11

10

Rue Mouassine

Souk Chaaria

Derb Sidi Ishak

8

5

Mosquée Mouassine

Rue Sidi El Yumami

Dar Cherifa

7

6

Souk Stalla

Souk Nejjarine

Café des Epices

4

Rue Rahb El Bladyne

RAHBA KEDIMA

12

3

Rue El Ksour

SOUKS

Rue El Ksour

Fnac Berbère

Rue Mouassine

2

Souk Semarine

Rue Dabachi

Place Bab Fteuh

Souk Qessabine

Rue Kennaria

1

Trek El Koutoubia

Café Argana

Rue des Banques

KENNARIA

DOUAR GRAOUA

Place Djemâa el Fna

Rue Riad Zitoun El Jedid

Place Foucauld

Rue Moulay Ismail

Rue Ben Marine

Rue de Bab Agnaou

Rue Riad Zitoun El Khedim

0 — 100 yards
0 — 100 meters

KEY

Market Streets

Pedestrian Streets

NEED A BREAK?

Tired of lamb and almonds? Try the only camel tagine in Marrakesh at **Ma Cousine** (⊠*Rue Mouassine, just north of Pl. Bab Fteuh*), in the middle of the souk. Not only does it provide much-needed respite, but the food is great, and cheap at 30 DH to 40 DH. There's a wide-ranging menu for the less adventurous and a rooftop terrace that puts a completely different angle on the market.

RAHBA QDIMA (CARPET SOUK)

> **TO GUIDE OR NOT TO GUIDE?**
>
> Many guides have (undeclared) affiliations with certain shops, and taking on a guide may mean you'll be delivered to the boutique of their choice, rather than your own discovery. You should be fine on your own, as long as you keep your eyes peeled for mini-adventures and touts. Small boutique shopkeepers who can't afford to tip guides will thank you for it.

Head back down to where you left Rue Semarine and continue north on that street. The next right turn from Rue Souk Semarine (now more properly named Rue Souk el-Kebir—the Big Souk Street) brings you into the main **carpet souk.** The flat shiny floor in the middle of the surrounding boutiques makes a change from the cobbles, and is used to roll out the rugs to display to potential buyers. ■TIP➡ **There are auctions at 5 PM daily (except Friday), when Berbers come down from the mountains to sell their wares to the vendors. This is strictly "trade" only, but a marvelous sight.** You can also ask a vendor in advance to buy for you, at reduced rates.

SOUK DES BIJOUTIERS (JEWELRY SOUK)

Head back to Rue Souk Semarine. Farther north along the street is an overhead sign for the **Souk des Bijoutiers** (also labeled Souk Tagmouty-ime). Follow that into a thin mall, full of jewelry stores displaying their wares behind glass. It is by no means the only place to buy jewelry, however, especially the bulky kind.

SOUK DES BABOUCHES (SLIPPER SOUK)

Now for some left turns. A small but perfectly formed left, just before a small leather boutique also on the left-hand side, will take you toward the central medina mosque, into the **Souk Principal des Babouches** (on the right), filled with the pointed leather slippers so beloved of Moroccans. The small doorway opens up to an enormous emporium with examples in every color imaginable.

EN ROUTE

Look for the tiny wool boutique on the left as you come to the arch before the right turn for the babouches market. It's on the way to the **Souk des Teinturiers** (Dyers' Souk). You can see men rolling out wool to make into fetching striped handbags, and, best of all, into small balls and looping them up into the most unusual necklaces going.

SOUK DES TEINTURIERS (DYERS' SOUK)

Retrace your steps to the entrance to the babouches souk, turn right in front of the central medina mosque, and take an immediate turn on your left. Follow that and look for the helpfully daubed word "teinturies" in spray paint on the left (clearly a modern addition), and then head right. **Souk des Teinturiers** is also called Souk Sebbaghine. The main square for fabric dyeing is hidden down a little shimmy to the right and then immediately left, but anyone can direct you. Here you'll see men dipping fabrics into vats full of hot dye. Don't forget to look up—there are scarves and trains of wool hanging all over, in individual sets of the same bright colors.

> **SLIPPERS GALORE**
>
> It can be hard to judge the proper value of these fairy-tale leather slippers, since price depends on so many things, such as the thickness of the sole, the number of layers, the presence or absence of a stepped heel, and of course the decoration. Use your nose, but be warned that a fair price can vary from 30 DH to 400 DH, depending on quality. *(For more on buying slippers, see Chapter 10.)*

SOUK MOMENT

For the best view, head into the dyers' square and ask to be led into the boutique. A dyer can show you the powders that the colors come from. A lovely bit of magic involves the fact that green powder dyes fabric red; red powder dyes things blue; and yellow powder dyes things purple. Head up the steep spiral stairs and onto the roof. A spectacular view of industry unfolds, with head scarves and threads of every color hanging up to dry in separate color blocks all over the rooftops.

SOUK HADDADINE (METAL SOUK)
From there, head back to Rue Souk el-Attarine. Following that main souk street as faithfully as possible will take you north, looping clockwise to the east, through the ironmonger's souk, where you'll see blacksmiths at work, hammering out lanterns and wrought-iron chairs.

LEATHER SOUKS
At the northeastern edges of the souk are the leatherworkers—busy cutting out templates for babouches, hammering and polishing, and making up bags and satchels from several types of animal skins. Look for signs to the Souk des Sachochiers (bag makers), Souk Chairia, and Souk Cherratine, all leather-working areas. Also in the northeast are a range of instruments, especially drums (Souk Moulay aii), and woven baskets (Souk Serrajine).

NEED A BREAK?

You'll most likely be souked out by the time you reach this point. Once you're anywhere near the northern edges of the souk, you're not far from a well-earned cultural break. Visit the medersa, museum, and Qoubba, relatively well signposted once you reach the top of Rue Azbest (if in doubt, just ask, as everyone knows where they are).

RUE MOUASSINE
The easiest way to head back to Djemâa el Fna is to find Rue Mouassine, the souk's other main north–south artery, running along its westernmost edge. Rue Mouassine is quite easy to find, and it's almost impossible to veer away from the correct path once you're on it; the simplest route is to take a counterclockwise loop from behind the

Fondouks

If you tire of the haggling in the souk but still want to pick up a bargain, try visiting a *fondouk*. These were originally storehouses, workshops, and inns frequented by merchants and artisans on their journeys across the Sahara (known as *caravanserai* in the Middle East), and are still in use today. Some of them are used as overnight dormitories, particularly by Berber merchants bringing carpets and other goods from surrounding villages; others are staffed by artisans at work on goods destined for the market. They're easily recognized by courtyards full of junk, usually with galleries on upper levels. Fondouks always keep their doors open, so feel free to look around. Because you deal with the artisans directly, there's less of a markup on prices. There are a couple of fondouks on the Dar el Bacha as you head towards the souk, and on Rue Bab Taghzout by the fountain known as Shrob ou Shouf ("Drink and Look").

Ben Medersa Mosque—when you hit the big mosque, you've hit Rue Mouassine. This is heavy souvenir territory, with the whole gamut of goods on display—lanterns, teapots, scarves, babouches, djellabas. It's an easy trip south. ■TIP➜Look for Fnac Berbère, the Berber bookshop, on Rue Mouassine. It's a good landmark. The street spits you out into the northeast corner of Bab Fteuh square, and from there it's a short hop down to Djemâa el Fna.

SOUK MOMENT

Wind down at **Dar Cherifa** (⊠ *8, Derb Cherfa Lakbir, Mouassine* ☎ *024/42–64–63*) an airy riad turned café turned library turned art gallery. It puts on the occasional cultural evening, including poetry readings and storytelling. It also styles itself as a literary café, so you can take a book on Morocco down from the shelves, sit on the low-slung cushions at the foot of the four pillars, and sip mint tea. Alternatively, you can gaze for hours at the outsize modern art (all for sale) hanging on the 16th-century white walls below the stucco and cedar carvings. Magical.

MEDINA

ANTIQUES

ETs. Bouchaib Complexe d'Artisanat (⊠ *7, Derb Baissi Kasbah Boutouil, Kasbah* ☎ *024/38–18–53*) is usually either full or empty, depending on whether the latest tour bus has dropped off a load of shoppers. Still, don't let that put you off. Originally a carpet store, it has expanded to three floors of ornate goods ranging from Jewish-Berber handwritten scrolls to man-size Oriental teapots, and each one has an individual price tag. The best thing about it is that the reliable shipping department will wrap fragile items in more rolls of bubble wrap than you thought possible. On large orders, haggle up to 25%.

Fodor's Choice ★ Popular with the international jet set, the reputable **Khalid Art Gallery** (⊠ *Rue Dar el Basha, Mouassine* ☎ *024/44–24–10* ⊕ *www.ilove-mar rakesh.com/khalid.html*) is a gorgeous riad stuffed full of the most sought-after Moroccan antiques. Owner Khalid speaks excellent English, and is an authority on most of the art coming out of Marrakesh.

Le Trésor des Nomades (⊠*128, rue Mouassine* ☎*024/44–59–06*) sells antique doors and all kinds of lamps. **Twizra** (⊠*361, Bab Agnaou* ☎*024/37–65–65*) is a general antiques and bijous store in the Kasbah.

Zimroda (⊠*128, rue Dar el Bacha, Mouassine* ☎*024/44–31–12*) has a small collection of curios, jewelry, and pottery.

ART

Atelier de Marrakech Art et Culture (⊠*Fontaine Lalla Aouda, Bab Doukkala, behind the Bab Doukkala mosque* ☎*068/32–84–74* ⊙*Mon.–Sat. 10:30–12:30 and 4–7:30*) puts on exhibitions by local artists and showcases artists at work. Visitors can then buy work they like.

Light Gallery (⊠*2, Derb Chtouka* ☎*024/38–45–09*) has a reliable hip collection of art shown off in an all-white setting. **Miloud Art Gallery** (⊠*Souk Cheratine* ☎*024/42–67–16*) has a very nicely curated collection of upscale Moroccan items for the home. Clothing and bags for women are in the back.For something a bit more cutting edge, **Ministero del Gusto** (⊠*22, Derb Azzouz el Mouassine* ☎*024/42–64–55* ⊕*www. ministerodelgusto.com*) combines boutique and gallery and shows off gorgeous items in both.

La Quobba Galerie (⊠*91, Souk Talaa, Souks* ☎*024/38–05–15* ⊕*www. art-gallery-marrakech.com*) has a range of modern but "safe" art from all over the country.

BOOKS

Fnac Berbère (⊠*Rue Mouassine* ☎*No phone*) has a city-renowned range of books on Berber life and culture.

Librarie el Ghazali Ahmed Ben Omar (⊠*51, Bab Aganou, Mouassine* ☎*024/44–23–43*) has a range of guidebooks, cookery books, volumes on Moroccan history in English, and maps.

CARPETS

Bazaar Jouti (⊠*19, Souk des Tapis, Rahba Lakdima* ☎*024/44–13–55*) has a wide selection of rugs and carpets in its spacious two-story shop. They can also arrange for shipping on the spot.

Ask Mr. Sarmi, of **Mohamed Taieb Sarmi at Bazaar ben Rahal** (⊠*10, Souk des Tapis* ☎*024/42–74–54*), to take you to his warehouse near Rahba Qdima, the carpet souk, to see his stock of Berber tribal rugs and carpets, where he will painstakingly explain their origins and value. Sarmi sends rugs and carpets anywhere in the world; for packages to the United States, the import tax is paid in Morocco.

Palais Saâdiens (⊠*16, rue My Taib Kssour* ☎*024/44–51–76* ⊕*www. tapis-marrakech.com*) has an enormous selection of Berber, Bedouin, and Arab carpets.

CLOTHING

Bouriad Karim (✉ *Rue Fatima Zahra R'mila, Dar el Bacha* ☎ 024/38–65–17) turns out some of the most fashionable handmade clothes in Marrakesh, and many end up on the hangers of boutique stores in the United States and Europe. His colorful selection of Moroccan-style shirts is perfect for beach or evening wear, while a made-to-measure djellaba will keep out the cold back home. **Kasbek** (✉ *216, rue Riad Zitoun J'did, Medina* ☎ 063/77–56–90) sells fabulous vintage caftans. Newer caftans are also on offer, and the stretchy jersey ones are particularly comfy. **Warda La Mouche** (✉ *Rue Kennaria, Medina* ☎ 024/38–90–63) stocks reasonably priced clothing for women in great fabrics. The tunics are especially wearable and figure flattering.

CRAFTS

Antique Jewelery Saharian (✉ *176, Rahba Lakdima* ☎ 024/44–23–73) specializes in handcrafted jewelry from southern Morocco.

Ensemble Artisanat (✉ *Ave. Mohammed V* ☎ 024/38–66–74) is a great way to see all the wares of the souk under one hassle-free umbrella. Several boutiques in modern confines display fixed prices for handicrafts including babouches, embroidery, lanterns, bags, jewelry, carpets, and paintings. There's even a snack bar.

La Joie (✉ *44, pl. des Ferblantiers* ☎ 041/19–09–50) sells tiny lanterns that are so inexpensive that you'll be tempted to buy a dozen. **La Maison Berbère** (✉ *23, rue el Mouassine Fhal Chidmi* ☎ 024/39–08–48) has a variety of handicrafts.

GUÉLIZ

ANTIQUES

Marco Polo (✉ *55, bd. Zerktouni, Immeuble Taieb* ☎ 024/43–53–55) has been in Guéliz for years, selling all kinds of antique Moroccan and Asian furniture as well as other artifacts. **L'Orientaliste** (✉ *11 and 15, rue de la Liberté* ☎ 024/43–40–74) is a charming mixed bag of a place, with old bottles, copper bowls, candlesticks, early-20th-century engravings, Fez pottery, furniture, perfume, and all sorts of antiques. There are two locations on the same street.

La Porte d'Orient (✉ *9, bd. Mansour Eddahbi, next to Glacier Oliveri* ☎ 024/43–89–67), a sibling of the medina's Porte d'Or, sells Moroccan and Asian antiques. It's geared toward those who prefer to browse before buying.

BOOKS

The **American Language Center** (✉ *3, Impasse du Moulin, Guéliz* ☎ 024/44–72–59) has a small English-language bookstore.

CLOTHING

Atika Boutique (✉ *34, rue de la Liberté* ☎ 024/43–64–09) is best known for its shoes, especially its soft leather moccasins in every shade of the rainbow. **Intensite Nomade** (✉ *139, ave. Mohammed V* ☎ 024/43–13–33) carries chic and rather expensive Moroccan-inspired clothing for

HAMMAMS & SPAS

The following hammams and spas are open to all (even nonguests, if in a hotel).

PUBLIC HAMMAMS

Hammam el Basha (The Pasha's Bath). As far as public hammams go, this is one of the largest and most accessible (it's 10 minutes north of Djemâa el Fna). Even in its current rundown condition you get a good sense of how impressive this hammam must have been in its heyday. Instead of the typical series of small low rooms, here you bathe in large, white-tiled chambers that give a pleasant sense of space. After your bath, dry and dress in a huge domed hall skirted with inset stone benches. ⊠ *20, rue Fatima Zohra* ☎ *No phone* 🖂 *10 DH* ⊗ *Daily: men 4 AM–noon and 7:30–11 PM; women noon–7:30 PM* ⊟ *No credit cards.*

Hammam Majorelle/Es Salama. This is a clean and modern hammam located 165 yards from the famous Majorelle Garden in Guéliz ⊠ *57, Quartier Rouidate, off Ave. Yacoub el Mansour* ☎ *No phone* 🖂 *10 DH* ⊗ *Daily 6 PM–10 PM* ⊟ *No credit cards.*

PRIVATE HAMMAMS

Hammam Hilton. A short petit-taxi ride (15 DH–20 DH) will bring you to an upscale private hammam in the Targa district of Marrakesh that few tourists know about. In addition to the hammam, it also offers massage (100 DH). ⊠ *Ave. de Targa* ☎ *024/49-31-29* 🖂 *40 DH* ⊗ *Daily 6 AM–10 PM* ⊟ *No credit cards.*

★ **Fodor's Choice** **Hammam Ziani.** Sister to Casablanca's Ziani, this hammam is highly recommended, and is located not far from Bahia Palace in the medina. Both men and women are welcome. It's

traditional without being in the slightest bit down-at-heel. The full hammam and *gommage* (exfoliation) works cost 60 DH, while a 270 DH package includes hammam, scrubbing, massage, and an algae wrap. ⊠ *14, Riad Zitoune Jdid, near Bahia Palace* ☎ *062/71-55-71* ⊕ *www. hammamziani.ma* 🖂 *50 DH* ⊗ *Daily 8 PM–10 PM* ⊟ *No credit cards.*

HOTEL HAMMAMS

Les Couleurs de l'Orient. This hammam is in a riad near the Djemâa el Fna, with affordable prices from 50 DH for massage and hammam. Relax with a mint tea on the terrace. ⊠ *22, Riad Zitoune Lakdim, Derb Lakhdar* ☎ *024/42-65-13* ⊟ *No credit cards.*

Hotel Nassim. Right in the city center, opposite Café des Negocants in Guéliz, the small but smart Nassim is a convenient place to take a hammam. ⊠ *115, ave. Mohammed V* ☎ *024/44-64-01* 🖂 *130 DH, including exfoliation* ⊗ *Daily, by appointment* ⊟ *MC, V.*

La Maison Arabe. Worth a try, especially in order to visit this charming hotel, a morning or afternoon spent in this hotel's hammam will make you feel like royalty. The staff may not scrub you quite as hard as you like, but the hammam room is beautiful and the small pool filled with roses is just for you. It's popular, so call at least two days in advance. ⊠ *1, Derb Assehbe, Bab Doukkala* ☎ *024/38-70-10* ⊕ *www.lamaisonarabe.com* 🖂 *650 DH for hammam and massage* ⊗ *By appointment* ⊟ *MC, V.*

La Mamounia. An afternoon at the Mamounia's hammam is a good way to spend some time at this celebrated establishment without denting your wallet. ⊠ *Ave. Bab el Djedid* ☎ *024/44-44-09* ⊕ *www. mamounia.com* ≥ *200 DH hammam, 350 DH with exfoliation* ⊘ *Daily by appointment* ☰ *AE, DC, MC.*

La Sultana Spa & Boutique Hotel. La Sultana is in the Kasbah district, close to the Royal Palace, and offers bath therapy, affusion showers (showers with lukewarm water combined with hand massage), hammam, Jacuzzi, and sauna. ⊠ *403, rue de la Kasbah* ☎ *024/38-80-08* ⊕ *www. lasultanamarrakech.com* ≥ *350 DH for hammam, 385 DH for massage* ⊘ *Upon request* ☰ *AE, MC, V.*

SPAS

★ **Caravan Serai.** Converted from an enclave of Berber houses with an encircling mud wall, this stylishly simple inn has a divine spa that offers desert-sand exfoliating treatments with orange-flower water, jasmine, rose, and amber oils; hammams with rhasoul wraps; aromatherapy massage; argan oil facials; and shiatsu. ⊠ *264, Ouled Ben Rahmoune* ☎ *024/30-03-02* ⊕ *www.caravanserai.com* ≥ *400 DH hammam plus treatments* ⊘ *By appointment* ☰ *MC, V.*

Jnane Tamsna. An oasis of calm and lush vegetation, this is the perfect place for total relaxation. The hammam is situated in an aromatic garden, and has two massage rooms. Treatments include scrubbing, aromatherapy, massage, mud facials, and meditation. ⊠ *Douar Abiad, Circuit de la Palmeraie* ☎ *024/32-94-23* ⊕ *www.jnanetamsna.com* ≥ *Complete hammam 450 DH* ⊘ *By appointment* ☰ *AE, MC, V.*

★ **Fodor's Choice** | **Kasbah Agafay.** Situated just outside Marrakesh on the road to Agadir, this spectacular spa is in the Kasbah's grounds, with fountains and aromatic herb gardens. You can book a hammam, massage, clay mask, henna, and yoga. ⊠ *20 km (12 mi) on Rte. de Guemassa* ☎ *024/36-86-00 or 024/42-09-60* ⊕ *www.kasbahagafay.com* ≥ *Treatments from 300 DH* ⊘ *By appointment* ☰ *AE, MC, V.*

Riad des Eaux. In the simple elegance of this renovated riad just a few steps south of Djemâa el Fna you can relax in an apricot-color tiled hammam and be treated to clay beauty masks and massaged with essential oils from plants gathered in the Ourika Valley. ⊠ *24, Derb Lakhdar, Riad Zitoune Lakdim, Medina* ☎ *067/66-18-55* ⊕ *www. ryaddeseaux.com* ≥ *hamman 150 DH, treatments from 250 DH* ⊘ *By appointment* ☰ *MC, V.*

Riad Mehdi/Les Bains de Marrakech. The spa annex of this opulent riad includes milk baths with orange water and rose petals, massages with argan oil, body treatments with essential oils, and rubdowns with mint-steamed towels. ⊠ *2, Derb Sedra, Bab Agnaou, Kasbah* ☎ *024/38-47-13 or 024/38-47-17* ⊕ *www.riadmehdi.net* ≥ *hamman 150 DH* ⊘ *By appointment, 2-3 days in advance* ☰ *MC, V.*

–Pamela Windo

5

MASTER CLASS

With so many chic riads serving up a culinary storm, it's no surprise that cooking schools in Marrakesh have taken off in recent years. Tagines, couscous, and briouates are all on the menu for the Maghrebian master chef in the making.

Dar les Cigognes. For a quick introduction to Moroccan cooking in the medina, this hotel offers a one-hour class every day at 6:30 for two people, for 150 DH each. Book ahead if you want to get in before the guests. ⌧ *108, rue de Benima* ☎ *024/38–27–40* ⊕ *www.lescigognes.com.*

Jnane Tamsna. Peggy Markel leads the "Feast for the Senses" culinary tours in the charming cottage compound with a thriving organic garden in the middle of the Palmery. A female Moroccan chef gives instruction in the preparation of exquisite Moroccan recipes that are easy to replicate back home. ⌧ *Douar Abiad, Circuit de la Palmeraie* ☎ *024/32–94–23* ⊕ *www.jnanetamsna.com* ✉ *700 DH per person for outside groups, minimum 6 persons* ☰ *AE, MC, V.*

Kasbah Agafay. Hidden away in a quiet corner of the Kasbah's grounds is the garden in which cooking classes are held. At the start of class

you'll pick the herbs and vegetables for the dishes to be prepared, which include various tagines and couscous. Lessons also include bread and pastry making, and you'll use the traditional ovens that give these foods their distinctive flavor. Advice is also given about the excellent variety of Moroccan wines. ⌧ *20 km (12 mi) on Rte. de Guemassa* ☎ *024/36–86–00 or 024/42–09–60* ⊕ *www.kasbahagafay.com* ✉ *1,600 DH 1-day lesson* ☰ *AE, MC, V.*

La Maison Arabe. This boutique hotel began its life as a famous restaurant and, aptly, and is now one of the best places for cooking workshops for amateurs and professionals alike. The workshops are conducted by a *dada* (Moroccan cook, traditionally female), and are organized in small groups around easy-to-use modern equipment. A translator (Arabic, English, French) provides detailed preparation and cooking instructions. At the end of each workshop participants dine on the meal they have prepared. ⌧ *1, Derb Assehbe, Bab Doukkala* ☎ *024/38–70–10* ⊕ *www.lamaisonarabe.com* ✉ *1,600 DH 1–2 persons; 600 DH per person in groups of 3–5 persons; 500 DH per person in groups of 5–8* ☰ *MC, V.*

–Pamela Windo

men and women. **Michele Baconnier** (⌧ *6, rue de Vieux* ☎ *024/44–91–78* ⊕ *www.ilove-marrakech.com/baconnier*) sells high-end clothing, jewelry, babouches, and bags that offer a hip twist on contemporary design.

Place Vendome (⌧ *141, ave. Mohammed V* ☎ *024/43–52–63*) stocks gorgeous leather goods of much better quality than what is offered in the souks.

CRAFTS

Al Badii (⌧ *54, bd. Moulay Rachid* ☎ *024/43–16–93*) sells artworks, crafts, and antiques in a quiet setting.

The **Matisse gallery** (⊠ *61, rue de Yougoslavie* ⊠ *43, Passage Ghandouri* ☎ *024/44–83–26*) has a nice collection of works by young Moroccan artists, Moroccan masters, and the Orientalists.

The gallery **TinMel** (⊠ *38, rue Ibn Aisha* ☎ *024/43–22–71*) sells artworks, antique carpets, and furniture.

JEWELRY

Bazar Atlas (⊠ *Rue de la Liberté* ☎ *024/43–27–16*) sells an enormous selection of jewelry, including the heavy silver *filbules* favored by Berber women to weigh down their dresses; the filbules have become a symbol of the Berber way of life. Owner Said speaks good English, and has another store in the medina.

> ### SWIRL YOUR NAME IN ARABIC
>
> Stucco plasterwork in riad courtyards and above ornate medina doors isn't there simply for effect. Deep in the carvings are Arabic phrases, curving their lines into the fabric of the building forever. "Aneqsh" for example, means "on behalf of God," while other elegant writings hope for good health or guidance. To meet local artists and Arabic writing experts, and even learn a little of the beautiful calligraphy yourself, take a course with **Marrakech Pulsations** (⊠ *6, Derb Sidi Abdelwsaa Ben Saleh* ☎ *066/30–43–46* ⊕ *www.marrakech-pulsations.com*).

OUTDOOR ACTIVITIES

With more than 300 days of sunshine a year, Marrakesh residents pretty much live outdoors. Beat the heat in one of the upscale swanky pool complexes or meander through the public gardens and stop to smell the roses. Whatever you do, don't forget the sunscreen.

GOLF

There are three championship golf courses in and around Marrakesh. With 9 new holes added in 2008, the 27-hole **Golf Amelkis club** (☎ *024/40–44–14*) offers plenty of challenges. The greens fee is 500 DH. Robert Trent Jones designed the 18-hole course at the **Palmeraie Golf Palace** (☎ *024/30–10–10*), 7 km (4½ mi) north of Marrakesh in the Palmery,and 9 new holes are set to open in March 2009. Facilities include a clubhouse and restaurant, pro shop, and equipment rental, and greens fees are 500 DH. The well-established **Royal Golf club** (☎ *024/40–47–05*), founded in 1923, is a tree-filled haven, with a 27-hole course 6 km (4 mi) south of Marrakesh on the Ouarzazate road. The greens fee is 500 DH but save a little extra cash for an open-air lunch at the casual restaurant.

QUAD BIKING

Marrakesh is in the grip of a quad frenzy, and outfits offering four-wheeled miniexcursions are springing up faster than you can say bandwagon. Most of these take advantage of the sandy tracks of the

Palmery for half a day or so of fun, but some can organize treks that range farther afield.

Dunes & Desert Exploration (☎061/24–69–48 ⊕www.marrakechquad. com) is for those who like more-adrenaline-pumping entertainment of quad bikes.

Rhino Quad Aventure (☎062/48–84–93 ⊕www.marrakechquad.com) head ups the Ourika Valley for 1,300 DH per day with lunch.

SWIMMING

☾ The jewel in Marrakesh's aquapark crown is **Oasiria** (⊠*Rte. d'Amezmiz, Cherifa, 4 km [2.5 mi] from town opposite Club Equestre* ☎024/36–87–00 ⊕*www.oasiria.com*), where children will enjoy a kids lagoon, a pirate ship, a wave pool, an inner-tube ride, and three twirly water-slides, while parents chill out at the Bellevue restaurant.

ARTIFICIAL BEACHES The Palmeraie Golf Palace complex is home to the more-grown-up **Nikki Beach** (⊠*Circuit de la Palmeraie* ☎024/33–24–94 ⊕*www.nikki beach.com*), part of a fashionable global chain that started in Miami. It comprises an artificial beach and restaurant area. There's even a DJ spinning some tunes in the evening. It has proven a bit too louche for some visitors, but it's worth a look if you want a livelier atmosphere than the average hotel pool.

Fodor'sChoice ★ Just outside the city, **La Plage Rouge** (⊠*Rte. de l'Ourika Km 10* ☎024/37–80–86) is the latest and most gorgeous addition to Marrakesh's collection of sexy beaches. A huge, sunken pool edged with sand is the centerpiece of this pool-restaurant-bar complex. During the day, it's great for kids, and at night DJs spin house music and a beautiful waitstaff brings you cocktails as you relax on terry-cloth beds under white canvas tents. Entrance fee is 250 DH. A shuttle bus leaves the Palais des Congrès every half hour.

The High Atlas

WORD OF MOUTH

"The drive through the High Atlas Mountains was intense, even for us who are used to driving the Sierra Nevada and Rockies."

—danielsonkin

"The real highlight of our holiday was being out of the cities. Our route was not uncommon—Telouet, Ouarzazate, Dades, Tamttatoucht, Merzouga; we stayed in clean and basic but mainly cold hotels, but our trade-off was the luxury of taking things more slowly than most."

—kahwahlib

Updated by
Jillian York

THE HIGH ATLAS REGION IS PERFECT for outdoors adventure and the perfect antidote to the concentration and animation of Marrakesh. You can hang-glide, ski, hot-air balloon, quad-bike, and ride mules. Best of all, you can walk. And if trekking in the snowy mountain ranges for days on end with only Berber women and their mules for friends isn't your thing, you can wimp out and drive.

In fact, there's nothing wimpy about it. The roads career around bends for miles on end, carving their way through the rock. You and your fellow passengers will ooh and aah at every vista and every new combination of snow and sun. Stretching from the ocean to the desert, the mountain scenery is utterly compelling.

The High Atlas Mountains rise as a natural fortress between the fertile Haouz Plain around Marrakesh and the deserts of the south. Trapping moisture that blows in from the Atlantic, the mountains pass this bounty along to the land and to the thin rivers that vanish into the southern desert. To reach the mountains, even today's travelers must pass through one of the routes guarded by age-old passes: Tizi-n-Test in the west and Tizi-n-Tichka in the east. They benefit from some glorious spots to stay, and the chance to take a quiet look at some intriguing relics of Moroccan history.

ORIENTATION & PLANNING

ORIENTATION

The two routes over the Tizi-n-Test (Test Pass) and Tizi-n-Tichka (Tichka Pass) are spectacular. For serious trekking, the area around Imlil is justifiably famous. There are also less strenuous walks along many of the dirt roads in the region, for instance along the Agoundis River. Alternatively, visitors can make the hotels around Ourigane their bases, exploring the area on muleback or simply lounging by the pool. The Tin Mal Mosque and the Goundafi Kasbah can easily be reached from Ourigane on a day trip.

Imlil. A village between Marrakesh and Mount Toubkal, Imlil is the center of adventure tourism in Morocco. Trekkers en route to the mountain stop here for rest, relaxation, and to breathe in the fresh mountain air so rarely found elsewhere. Cherries, walnuts, and apples are grown here, and a walk through the forests might garner many fruits.

Ourika Valley. The verdant Ourika Valley, just south of Marrakesh, is home to a string of charming villages. Visitors to the region marvel at the waterfalls of Setti Fatma and pause for pictures in front of Morocco's only brick mosque at Aghbalou.

Tizi-n-Tichka. Completed in 1936, the Tizi-n-Tichka can be a daunting prospect. Though the road is safer and wider than its counterpart, it can be a dangerous drive, particularly in winter weather conditions. Still, the views from the pass are nothing like else.

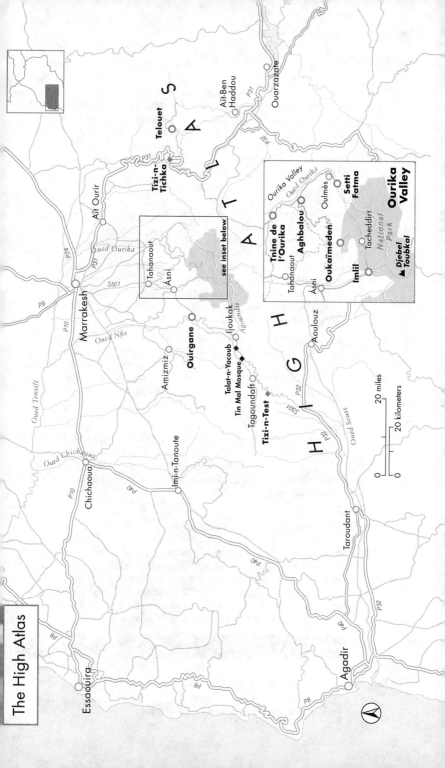

The High Atlas

PLANNING

WHEN TO GO

There's a season for everyone. For some the High Atlas is at its best in April, when the trees are flowering and the mountains are still cloaked in white. High-country hiking is safest and easiest in late summer. Winter can be cold but very peaceful, and on sunny days the lower passes just south and north of Imlil and the area around the Agoundis can make for pleasant day hikes. Summer is hot and humid, but the hotels with pools can take the edge off. The high passes should be attempted in winter only by serious alpinists with serious gear, and even in summer the higher peaks are worthy of respect.

GETTING HERE & AROUND

Getting to the High Atlas region isn't as difficult as it seems. The closest airport is Marrakesh Menara. From there, most travelers find it easiest to rent a car. But if driving is not your thing, you can hop on a bus. Perhaps the best, and most expensive, option for nondrivers is to hire a *grand taxi* to explore the area.

SAFETY

The High Atlas is no longer the wily region it used to be, but travelers should take precautions. Rural sentiments are quite different from urban ones, so women should dress more conservatively than in larger cities. The biggest safety concern is, of course, for trekkers; beginners should consult a local expert or join a group.

RESTAURANTS

There are a few excellent restaurants in the hotels around Ouirgane, and a couple near Imlil, but beyond these, fare is limited mostly to what's available in small hotel restaurants and cafés—mostly tagines. Avoid alcohol except in hotels. In general, drinking won't raise any eyebrows as long as you're among other tourists, but the practice of carrying wine and spirits into the backcountry is not appreciated by villagers. Alcohol is *haram* (forbidden by the Koran), but on a more earthly level it's simply not very socially acceptable.

TOP REASONS TO GO

The chance to hike North Africa's tallest peak: Djebel Toubkal, which soars to 13,671 feet, is only a two-day climb. Trekkers can find everything they need at the base of the mountain.

Experience rural Moroccan life: Many travelers say their favorite experience was staying with a traditional Berber family. Known for their hospitality, locals will open their hearts and homes to you.

Get the best of Morocco's nature: Quiet valleys and rushing streams offer a chance for gentle walking, horseback riding, and bird-watching.

WHAT IT COSTS IN DIRHAMS				
	¢	$	$$	$$$	$$$$
AT DINNER	under 60DH	60DH–90DH	90DH–120DH	120DH–150DH	over 150DH

Prices are per person for a main course at dinner.

A BIT OF HISTORY

Four periods stand out in High Atlas history. The first is the arrival of Islam in the 12th century—exemplified by the mosque at Tin Mal, the crowning glory of the religious reformer Ibn Tumart. The nominally Islamic tribesmen of the High Atlas converted to the austere version of Islam that Tumart articulated. Some families in the valley of the Upper Nfis, around Tin Mal, trace their arrival in the mountains to this time, pointing to their earlier origins in the Haouz Plain around Marrakesh, the southern desert regions, and the Anti-Atlas Mountains.

The second significant period was that preceding the 1912 arrival of the French, when most of the High Atlas was dominated by local tribal caids. These overlords were often ruthless—even today a few locals can mesmerize you with tales of their power, of their arbitrary violence and brutal repression of dissent. Each of the passes over the mountains was dominated by a different tribal confederation. The Tizi-n-Tichka (Tichka Pass) was ruled by the Glaoui from the Kasbah at Telouet. To the west, the Tizi-n-Test was controlled by the Goundafi caid based in Tagoundaft and later Talat-n-Yacoub. The most westerly route, heading south to Agadir, was ruled by the Mtougi.

In 1912 the Glaoui became allies of the French, and played a significant role in Moroccan politics during the French protectorate. Many High Atlas residents remember the French protectorate with great ambivalence, as a time when infrastructure improved (the French built roads into the mountains to extend the reach of central government) and constant tribal warfare was finally put to rest, but also as a time of forced labor, excessive taxation, and humiliating domination by Christian colonizers.

Independence from France in 1956 saw the ascendancy of King Mohammed V and the downfall of the French-Glaoua alliance. Today, as roads are paved, schools built, and electric poles march ever deeper into remote valleys, mountain Ishelhin are more integrated into the Moroccan nation.

6

HOTELS

Most of the better hotels in the High Atlas are located in or around Ouirgane, which is quickly becoming a sought-after refuge from the sometimes excessive stimulation of Morocco's cities. There are a couple of stunning Kasbahs around Imlil. Most other lodging in the region consists of inexpensive backpackers' refuges (*gîtes*). Heterosexual couples staying in private homes while trekking will be assumed to be married. It's best not to disabuse your hosts of their assumptions.

WHAT IT COSTS IN DIRHAMS				
¢	$	$$	$$$	$$$$
under 250DH	250DH–400DH	400DH–650DH	650DH–1,000DH	over 1,000DH

FOR TWO PEOPLE (row label)

All prices are for a standard double room, excluding tax.

FESTIVALS

The most famous of festivals in this region is the Imilchil Marriage Festival, held each year in September. Legend has it that a Romeo and Juliet story happened here ages ago; since then, an annual festival is held for young people to choose their own partner. Though lately the festival has been attracting more and more tourists, it's still a sight to behold. The Setti Fatma Moussem, held in August, still contains the religious elements of a *moussem* (pilgrimage festival). Foreigners are welcome and will be pulled into the games and entertainment.

WHAT TO WEAR

As weather in this region can be unpredictable, it's best to bring layers. Having a wool sweater or fleece pullover is a necessity, as it can get quite frigid at night. Solid footwear, such as boots or sneakers, is important. Although sandals are socially acceptable, they're mostly useless here.

Both women and men should dress conservatively: no shorts or sleeveless tops. Women will be better received by locals if they wear longish sleeves and long pants or skirts. And although locals are used to seeing uncovered heads, some travelers report that keeping a scarf handy is a good idea.

HIKING THE HIGH ATLAS

A trek up North Africa's highest mountain or through its valleys doesn't just exercise your legs and your lungs. It's a village experience extraordinaire. Goatherds and other locals are your companions, and even if you don't know a crampon from an ice pick you can make it to the top hands-free in summer. It's hard to beat the literally high level of achievement, spectacular views, and Moroccan life seen up-close.

KNOW-HOW

PREPARATION & EQUIPMENT

Even amateurs can turn up in Imlil and enjoy a good couple of days hiking. It's best to book your first night's stay in Imlil well in advance, but not much more preparation is needed; you can arrive independently and organize a guide, hire equipment, and choose your route once you arrive. It's best to buy a map of the region when in Marrakesh (they're difficult to find in Imlil). Hotel Ali, in Marrakesh, sells them for 140 DH.

You can get almost everything else you might need in Imlil, including boots, jackets, sleeping bags, crampons, axes, and, of course, the perfect mountain luggage holder—a donkey or mule. Serious walkers are better off bringing their own boots if they plan on days of trekking. Likewise, a compass is best brought from home. A mule is generally 100 DH a day, and can carry two people's luggage. It's much harder to get a tent, so it's best to bring one with you or rent from a tour operator or travel agency ahead of time.

ROUTES

At 13,671 feet, Djebel Toubkal might be the highest and best-known option around, but it is by no means your only choice in the High Atlas. Depending on your level of fitness, experience, the time of year, and whether you want to spend half a day wandering around or eight days exploring peak after peak, you can make the most of the stunning sights and traditional life of the area. There are numerous trails, and the best bet is to consult

SOUK DAYS
Monday: Tnine Ourika
Tuesday: Tahanout, Aït Ourir
Wednesday: Ijoukak
Thursday: Ouirgane
Friday: Jemaa Rhemat
Saturday: Asni
Sunday: Setti Fatma

your guide for a route that takes in what you're most interested in for the time and money you have available.

If getting to the top quickly offers the excitement you crave, then you can climb Djebel Toubkal (and back) in two days from Imlil. The first day of the route is fairly clear, heading south from town past Sidi Chamarouch. You can do it without a guide (make sure you have at least one walking partner though, and let someone else know where you're going), as long as you have a good understanding of a compass, a good map, and mountain-climbing experience. Spend the night on the mountain at the Nelter refuge (80 DH per person), farther south of Sidi Chamarouch. The ascent the next morning takes you on a steep, rewarding climb east, up to the highest peak.

Imlil is the biggest but only the first Berber village you're likely to reach. Nearby Ait Souka, northeast of Imlil, is a traditional Berber village where you can share mint tea or even arrange to stay the night with a family. You can also go farther east, via Tamatert, up to Ouanesekra or Tinerhourhine, and then back up west and on to Ikkiss. This is best done as a two- or three-day loop, passing back west and south through Aguersioual and Taddert to Imlil.

Farther south, Lac d'Ifni offers a sea change from the rocky views, far enough out of the way to offer a new twist on the idea of "remote." You can go on a five-day clockwise loop out of Imlil, staying first at Tacchedirt, to the east, heading south to Tizi Likemt (11,663 feet) and spending the night at Azib Likemt, then on to spend the third night at Amsouzerte. In the morning, loop westward to the lake and on to the refuge at Nelter for the night. If you really want to push it, you can climb Djebel Toubkal the next morning and come back down to Imlil by lunch.

For a hearty walk likely to last between three and six days, depending on your route, you can bridge the gulf between Imlil and the Ourika Valley, trekking northeast to Oukaïmeden or even as far as Setti Fatma. In the opposite direction, you can trek to Ouirgane and its superb hotel options, where you can relax after your exertions. Stay in family homes on the way.

WHEN TO GO

If you aren't up for mountain-eering proper—if you've had no experience, don't make this your first time—then late April to early October is the perfect time to climb Djebel Toubkal, as you won't need specialist knowledge. During the winter months (late October to early April) you'll be climbing with your fingers as well as your feet,

> **CAUTION**
>
> Any trip into the mountains means hairpin bends, improbably thin and twisting lanes, and for some, taking chances with passing. It's a gorgeous winding road through peak after peak, but watch out and honk as you round corners.

clinging to the rock face and banging in those crampons to haul you to the top. Don't go without a guide.

If you're staying only a short time in Morocco, combining a trip to the High Atlas with a stay in nearby Marrakesh makes perfect sense. Spend three days in the hectic whirl of the souk, and then disappear into the fog of the mountains for a few days before rounding off the week with a huge meal back in Marrakesh.

WHERE TO STAY

There are many friendly and cheap, if sometimes well-worn, backpacker options in Imlil for before and after your trip into the mountains, as well as the award-winning luxury ecolodge Kasbah du Toubkal.

When it comes to multiday treks, your overnight options once among the peaks are fairly limited. There are a few simple refuges run by the French mountaineering association CAF, which you can book in advance (at the head office in Oukaïmeden, not Imlil), or ask the guardian at the Café d'Aksoual (opposite the refuge in the center of Imlil), but there's no guarantee they'll be able to get the mountain refuges ready in time for you. Two other options are to camp or to arrange a home-stay with the Berbers who live up the mountains—a wonderful opportunity if living life simple and authentic is your kind of thing. Ask your hotel or the Imlil guide office to arrange either of these; despite famous Berber hospitality, turning up unannounced and expecting to bed down for the night is pushing your luck.

Kasbah du Toubkal has opened a luxury lodge on the mountainside, up to a day's trek away from Imlil, in the Id Issa village. You can stay overnight amid solar-powered under-floor heating, a wood-burning stove, hearty meals, and the luxury to end all luxuries: a flushing toilet. Such fripperies don't come cheap: it's 300 euros a night for two.

TOUR OPERATORS & LOCAL GUIDES

Unless you're an intrepid and experienced hiker, it's best to hire a guide for any treks you take in this region. It isn't hard to get lost, and expert advice on how to approach treacherous areas may be necessary, depending on what route you're taking. Having a local Berber speaker on hand also means you may be able to enjoy interactions with local people you may meet on the way.

The easiest way to find a guide is to ask at your hotel or at the official guides' booths in Imlil and Setti Fatma. Hotels are more used to putting together entire packages that include equipment hire, food, and mules and are slightly more expensive as a result. Guides often work for both the official booths and the hotels. Tour operators also tend to use local guides, as they know the routes and can speak the local Berber language. These guides tend to work solely for one hotel. The bonus with a tour operator is the no-hassle element—transfers from Marrakesh and all-inclusive (although also more expensive) prices, with the high standards to match.

LOCAL GUIDES

Imlil is filled with guides in every flavor of legitimacy, some bearing little plastic cards with their pictures, others just earnest looks. The best place to find an official guide is the **Bureau des Guides et des Accompagnateurs à Imlil** in Imlil's main square. It has several accredited guides who can arrange all-inclusive treks (350 DH each per day, including guide, mule, and overnight lodging), and equipment rental, including crampons, ice axes, and sleeping bags (50 DH each). They know the routes well and can tailor-make a tour depending on fitness, time and interests.

You can also ask about guides at hotels or any of the town's small cafés. Expect to pay close to 300 DH a day plus 100 DH a day per mule. Bargaining is acceptable. ⚠ **Not every guide includes food or overnight stay in the price, so be sure to establish who will pay for what before you leave.**

Guided trips arranged by the popular Café Soleil cost 350 DH per person per day, including guide, mule, overnight, and food. Equipment hire costs extra, and you can store your luggage for the duration of your trekking in a locked room for free. They can arrange anything from a few hours to eights days and more.

To arrange to stay in one of the refuges of the **Club Alpin Français (CAF)**, an association of French mountaineering buffs, or to pick up a guide or information, contact either the guardian Hassan, an excellent local guide with bags of local knowledge and tips on trekking ideas who also runs Imlil's nearby Café Aksoual (☎ *024/48–56–12*), or Michele at the Club Alpin Français in Oukaïmeden (☎ *024/31–90–36*).

TOUR OPERATORS

Adrar Aventure (✉ *No 111, Cite Saada-Menara, Marrakesh* ☎ *024/43–56–63* ✉ *Opposite main square, Imlil* ☎ *024/48–56–18* ⊕ *www.adrar-aventure.com*) has a local branch in Imlil, where you can hire equipment and organize a trek. The better option is to organize a trip in advance, by e-mail or by visiting their offices in Marrakesh.

British-based **Discover Ltd** (✉ *Timbers, Oxted Rd., Godstone, Surrey, England* ☎ *+44 (0)1883/744392* ⊕ *www.kasbahdutoubkal.com*) owns Kasbah du Toubkal and can arrange stays as well as a series of treks from one to six days' walking. Prices aren't cheap, but the standards and attention to detail are second to none.

The Moroccan division of Discover Ltd., **Mountain Voyage** (✉ *Mountain Voyage Sarl, Immeuble el Batoul, 2eme étage, 5, ave. Mohammed V, Guéliz, Marrakesh* ☎ *024/42–19–96* ⊕ *www.mountain-voyage.com*) can tailor-make any trip you like, including transfers from Marrakesh into the mountains.

IMLIL

64 km (40 mi) southeast of Marrakesh.

The village of Imlil is the preeminent jumping-off point for the high country, a quiet mountain retreat whose existence has been given over to preparing walkers for various climbs around the peaks. It's filled with guides, cheap rooms, and equipment-rental shops. Imlil is a long strip of a village, built up around the main road. The main square is a parking area on the left, often crammed with the camper vans and cars of trek-minded travelers. Simple terraced cafés teem with *accompagnateurs* (guides), people offering you lodging in their homes, and mule owners renting the services of these essential means of mountain transport. ⚠ **Storms may occasionally make the road into town impassable, something to consider if you're heading up in rough weather.**

GETTING HERE & AROUND

Rental cars are available from numerous international and local agencies in Marrakesh. You can get as far as Asni by bus (20 DH–30 DH from Marrakesh, heading to Taroudant), and then for 15 DH get a seat in a grand taxi to Imlil.

TIMING & PRECAUTIONS

Depending on how adept you are at trekking, you could enjoy hiking for a day or spend an entire week trekking about the region. The best time to visit is early or late summer, but winter is best avoided except for by the most avid of outdoors enthusiasts.

ESSENTIALS

Bus Contacts Compagnie de Transports Marocains (✉ *12 Blvd. Zerktouni, Bab Doukala* ☎ *024/44–83–28* ⊕ *www.ctm.co.ma*).

Internet Cyber Imlil (✉ *Next to Pharmacie Imlil*).

Medical Assistance Pharmacie Asni (✉ *Marrakesh-Taroudant Rd.* ☎ *024/46–20–06*).

Visitor & Tour Info Bureau des Guides (✉ *Village Center* ☎ *024/48–56–26*).

EXPLORING

The mountain everyone wants to climb, or at least get close to, **Djebel Toubkal** is a two-day ascent from the small village of Imlil. The road to Imlil is a left turn off the S501 (the Tizi-n-Test road that leads south from Marrakesh), just after Asni. The 17-km (11-mi) stretch between Asni and Imlil is always spectacular, taking you from what are essentially foothills of scrub and cactus to the very foot of the Ouanoukrim Massif. In spring the trip is particularly beautiful: the snowcapped mountains just above Imlil contrast with the green, irrigated fields of the valley; the fields along the way overflow with flowering apple and quince trees; and the red poppies scattered among their trunks are glorious.

WHERE TO EAT

The restaurants in Imlil are fairly basic, so don't expect much on the menu besides tagines and brochettes. **You can't purchase beer or wine in Imlil, so stock up in Marrakesh if you'd like a drink during your stay.**

¢–$ ╳**Café Aksoual.** Run by a local guide, Café Aksoual has a more rustic
MOROCCAN   look than some of the other options. Popular with locals and with hiking groups out to experience authentic Morocco, it serves reasonably good local fare. There's also a lively pool table where you can test your skills against the locals. ⊠ *Before the main square in Imlil, on right as you approach from Asni* ☎024/48–56–12 ▤*No credit cards.*

WHERE TO STAY

Most of Imlil's hotels are right on the main square as you enter the village. There are a couple of stunning and luxurious places to stay nearby, but in general accommodations are fairly basic; you'll find hot water and sometimes a towel, but don't count on niceties like soap. You can always stay in a private home for about 50 DH a night per person, if invited; this can be a nice way to see something of everyday Moroccan life. If you go this route, pay special attention to our etiquette suggestions and make sure you find out before nightfall what and where the bathroom facilities are. Bring your own toilet paper if you'd rather not go all that local.

¢ ▥**Auberge La Vallée.** This is a basic choice a little way beyond the center of town. You can camp in the bumpy garden (30 DH) or stay in simple rooms with shared bathroom facilities. It's under the same management as the popular Café Soleil. All rooms have twin beds rather than doubles. **Pros:** Clean and simple rooms, budget price. **Cons:** Shared bathrooms, stiff sheets. ⊠ *Follow main Imlil road from Asni and veer right up hill. It's on the left* ☎024/48–52–16 ⤶*5 rooms without bath* ⌂*In-hotel: no elevator* ▤*No credit cards.*

$ ▥**Café Soleil.** The best backpacker accommodation in Imlil, Café Soleil is a firm favorite because of helpful owner Mohamed Aziam. It's regularly booked up, not least because it's right on the main square and opposite the official guides' office. With a lovely smell of incense, rooms are bare but pleasant. They can arrange all-inclusive treks (350 DH each per day, including guide, mule, and overnight lodging), and equipment rental, including crampons, ice axes, and sleeping bags (50 DH each). You can also leave heavy backpacks in the secure lockup for free. **Pros:** Restaurant makes good tagines, staff can help book trips. **Cons:** Some shared bathrooms, rooms are bare. ⊠ *On town square.* ☎024/48–56–22 ⤶*10 rooms* ⌂*In-hotel: restaurant, no elevator* ▤*No credit cards* ⍑CP.

$$$$ ▥**Kasbah du Toubkal.** Perched on the rocks a little outside the town center, this ecolodge is a wonderful mountain retreat that never sacrifices
Fodor'sChoice   tradition for style. You can eat indoors or on the terraces (nonguests,
★   too). There's no booze on offer, but you can bring your own. Visitors

must trek the short uphill climb to get to this hillside oasis (or take a 60 DH transfer by mule). There's a reception center in the town center, opposite the main square, where you can arrange for a mule transfer. Treks can be arranged, including a two-day ascent of Djebel Toubkal that costs €450 for two, including guides, mules, accommodations, and food. **Pros:** Luxury in the midst of nowhere, everything is catered. **Cons:** Very expensive, often booked solid. ⊠ *Follow main road through Imlil and go right at fork, follow signs up hill, and keep going until you reach the top* ☎ 024/48–56–11 ⊕ *www.kasbahdutoubkal.com* ⇨ *5 rooms, 6 suites, 1 house, 3 dorms* ⚑ *In-hotel: restaurant, hammam* ☰ *MC, V* ⦿ *CP.*

$$$$ 🏠 **Kasbah Tamadot.** Richard Branson's country villa has quickly established itself as *the* luxury destination of choice in the High Atlas. The place is filled with decadent *objets* accumulated from his travels, particularly from India, and a wander around the castellated terraces is an exercise in fairy-tale splendor. Although the location, overlooking the river Issktan and the Berber village of Tanzgart, is stunning, and the staff highly capable, some small touches, such as the metallic reception doors and window frames and highly visible air-conditioning units in rooms, detract slightly from what should be a flawless experience. For nonguests, the restaurant is open for lunch daily and serves a lip-smacking good selection of light dishes, such as cumin-roasted chicken sandwiches. ■ **TIP ➡** Don't take your cell phone around with you. The only ring permitted in the Kasbah is that of a classic Berber song. **Pros:** Unbelievable luxury, amazing views. **Cons:** Luxury comes at a high price, less interaction with locals. ⊠ *B.P. 67, 042150 Asni, Rte. d'Imlil, just after Asni on road to Imlil, on left* ☎ 024/36–82–00 ⊕ *www.virgin. com/kasbah* ⇨ *18 rooms* ⚑ *In-hotel: tennis court, pools, gym, hammam, spa, public Internet* ☰ *MC, V* ⦿ *CP.*

¢   🏠 **Refuge de Club Alpin Français.** This is one of a series of refuges maintained by an association of French mountaineering buffs and is a good place to pick up a guide or information. You can stay here, too, in one of two desultory dormitories (tired bunk beds in bare rooms), or camp if you have your own gear. The low prices match the basic accommodation. There's also a kitchen if you want to prepare your own food. First-aid equipment is available at all refuges. **Pros:** Great place to start a trek, knowledgeable staff. **Con:** Very basic accommodations. ⊠ *Across main square from Café Soleil* ☎ 024/31–90–36 ☰ *No credit cards.*

OURIKA VALLEY

A great day trip from Marrakesh, the Ourika Valley is prime hiking territory in all seasons, especially if you aren't up to hitting the heights of Djebel Toubkal. It's also stunning. Less than 20 minutes out of Marrakesh you can see green gorges, sparkling yellow wheat fields at the foot of snowcapped mountains, and the ferocious flush of the Ourika River, where women wash clothes in the spray of waterfalls at the roadside. Look out, too, for flat Berber homes; they're assembled in stacked villages the same red as the earth they merge into. The only vertical line that breaks the slither of horizontal roofs is that of the village mosque, whose minaret towers above it all. As you leave Marrakesh, the approach to the valley is lined with flat, spiky cactus and eucalyptus trees, before reaching the foothills of the Atlas and hugging the left-hand bank of the fast-flowing River Ourika.

The best and most free-spirited way to enjoy the valley is probably from the window of a rental car, with plenty of pit stops and a couple of days trekking. There are also five daily buses from Marrakesh (6 DH to Ourika) and grands taxis (10 DH to Ourika, 20 DH to Setti Fatma).

OUKAÏMEDEN

20 km (13 mi) from Imlil.

So you probably didn't go to Morocco for the snow. But if Vail's novelty value has worn off, and you have a day or two to kill, then a bit of powder isn't out of the question. The ski station at Oukaïmeden is also a good place for novices to get in some practice without the stress of jam-packed slopes, and is becoming an increasingly popular retreat. A range of walks is available outside the ski season. Taxis from Tnine de l'Ourika are available for about 20 DH, although most visitors make the journey in hired vehicles.

Unless you're Moroccan, or a ridiculously enthusiastic ski bum, it's highly unlikely you'll arrive with any of the right gear. Numerous shops are ready to help out. As in the souk, nothing has a fixed price, so you may need to bargain. As a general rule, expect to pay around 150 DH per day for some warm clothing, boots, skis, and poles. The next step is the ski-lift pass, which is in fact a frustratingly long distance away (particularly in ski boots). To ride on the big lift to the very top of the mountain (known as the *télésiège* in French) a lift pass costs 100 DH per day; access to the six smaller chairlifts (*téléskis*) costs 50 DH per day.

Although Oukaïmeden is small, don't think its 20-odd runs (pistes) are basic. Apart from three green (easy) runs and four blue (medium), everything else is either red (advanced) or black (difficult). Only red and black runs go down the télésiège, so go ready for a challenge. The long red run starts to the right of the lift drop-off point—everything else to the left is black, and with names like *Combe du mort* (Vale of Death) they aren't for the faint-hearted. It's currently undergoing massive investment. The ski season lasts from December until late March.

GETTING HERE & AROUND

The easiest way to get to Oukaïmeden from Marrakesh is by grand taxi. There is no scheduled bus service, but you can request the taxi to return at a given time. During the busy ski season, you will have no difficulty in finding a taxi or even a minibus to Marrakesh.

Though a tour guide is not necessary for this small town, U.K.-based Do Something Different offers a wonderful walking tour of Oukaïmeden and environs.

TIMING & PRECAUTIONS

For skiers, Oukaïmeden is often a day trip from Marrakesh. There are a few hotels for those wishing to spend the night. Oukaïmeden, being a resort, is extremely safe. Just be sure to bring warm clothes.

ESSENTIALS

Visitor & Tour Info Do Something Different (☎ *020/8090–3790* ⊕ *www. dosomethingdifferent.com*).

WHERE TO STAY

¢ 🍽️ **Club Alpin Français.** The rooms here are basic dormitory-style standard, but the surroundings are nice for the price, and the welcome as warm as the fire. French managers Michele and Jean are a mine of helpful local information, particularly on walks in the region. They also coordinate stays at the four other CAF outposts in the High Atlas, making this place a worthwhile contact for any trips in the region that may involve CAF accommodation. Dinner at the refuge costs 80 DH per head. **Pro:** Budget-friendly price. **Con:** Extremely basic rooms. ⊠ *Oukaïmeden, on right as you first enter town* ☎ *024/31–90–36* 🛏️ *163 dormitory beds.* ⅙ In-hotel: Restaurant. ▭ *No credit cards.*

$$$$ 🍽️ **Kenzi Louka.** This hotel may look retro from the outside, but the luxurious rooms, public areas, and restaurant are purely modern. The hotel also runs a range of walks and activities for the well-heeled traveler, including rock climbing and mountain biking, and even ski instruction. **Pros:** Luxurious suites, centrally located. **Con:** A bit pricey if you're spending the whole day outside anyway. ⊠ *Oukaïmeden, on right after Club Alpine Français* ☎ *024/31–90–80* 🛏️ *100 rooms, 5 suites* ⅙ *In-hotel: 2 restaurants, bar, pool* ▭ *MC, V* 🍽️ *MAP.*

SHOPPING

Small stands line the road from before Ourika to Setti Fatma, at the end of the road, selling crafts, pottery, and the carpets for which the Berbers are so famous. Many of these small stands supply the great boutiques and bazaars of Marrakesh, so if you're in the mood for bargain-hunting, you're likely to find a better deal here. Two shops stand out, a couple of kilometers apart and both a few kilometers before the right turn to Oukaïmeden (heading south), as the road starts to climb.

La Source de Tapis (⊠ *Ourika Valley Amassin, 37 km [23 mi] from Marrakesh* ☎*024/48–24–58* ▭*AE, MC, V*) is a Berber women's cooperative with more than 7,000 carpets on sale. Five hundred women from villages all over the region bring their carpets down to the enormous three-level shop, and are paid when their own carpet sells. There's a plethora of choices, but it's particularly good for *embroidered rugs.* Expect to be offered a 8 foot by 5 foot rug for 2,200 DH–2,500 DH. The shop also ships.

Pottery at Le Kasbah de Tifirte (⊠ *On Ourika road, 39 km [24 mi] from Marrakesh* ☎*067/34–49–06*) is a marvelous emporium of tagine pots, plates, and vases. You can watch experts sitting at a clay wheel knock off a tiny tagine pot and lid within minutes, judging everything expertly by eye and experience. Pieces are then fired in a kiln, decorated, and fired again. It's an excellent place to learn the difference between *tadelakt*, a hand-polished finish that takes an entire day, and painted stucco imposters.

OUTDOOR ACTIVITIES

Auberge Le Maquis (⊠ *To right of the Ourika road heading south, just after Oukaïmeden turnoff* ☎*024/48–45–31*) is a springboard into the hills and a great place both to plan local walks. They employ Berber guides and have a large selection of hand-drawn maps to take you around the surrounding hills. The night watchman doubles as a daytime guide, and can organize walks to a nearby farm and his home village of Tamzerdit, explain the flora and fauna of the valley, and even enable guests to have a go at pottery or tadelakt (50 DH for a half day, 100 DH for a full day). For more-demanding treks, this is also a gateway into the mountains, and a bit of luxury compared to camping and other local lodging options. Working in conjunction with the guides at Setti Fatma, it's possible to organize a two-day hike to the snow station of Oukaïmeden (from 870 DH per person) and a three-day hike, including a night under the stars, to the Yagour Plateau to see ancient rock carvings (from 1,370 DH per person). The hotel also has a good range of drives for four-wheel-drive junkies hankering after some dirt-track action.

SETTI FATMA

65 km (40 mi) south of Marrakesh.

This small town at the end of the road for the Ourika Valley as far as cars go is crammed with cafés and cheap hostels. For those wanting to make the jump into the mountains ahead, it's a perfect alternative to Imlil. Good trekking options include visits to the seven local waterfalls, which can be accessed by up to five different routes. (There are actually nine waterfalls at Setti Fatma, but only seven are accessible without risking your neck.)

GETTING HERE & AROUND

Many travelers to Setti Fatma arrive on foot from Imlil. This two-to-three-day trek is quite popular, and guides from Imlil can help show

Who Are the Berbers?

Berbers live in every part of Morocco and move in every social class, from the poorest rural farms to the wealthiest neighborhoods in Rabat. The genes of invading Vandals, Greek settlers, Roman bureaucrats, Phoenician sailors, and Arab scholars flow through the High Atlas's present Berber population, along with those of sub-Saharan soldiers, slaves, gold miners, and salt traders.

The word "Berber" is thought by many to derive from "barbarian," used by the Romans to describe foreigners, especially those from the untamed hinterlands of their empire. These negative connotations have led some contemporary activists to argue that the word "Berber" should be replaced with the indigenous word "Imazighen" ("Amazigh" in the singular), an umbrella term that refers to all the people in North Africa who speak some variety of Berber.

Berbers themselves are manifold, dividing into three broad groups (Masmouda, Sahanja, and Zénètes). Although there were numerous Berber-speaking Jewish communities until the mid-20th century (when many moved to Israel at its foundation in 1948), the population is now almost entirely Muslim.

There are three main language divisions, too: Taririft in the Rif area; Tamazight in the Mid-Atlas, and Tashelhit in the Anti-Atlas and Souss; however, the divisions don't necessarily match the broad groups mentioned above. High Atlas Berbers call themselves Ishelhin, and also speak Tashelhit. The language seems to have arrived with migrants from somewhere in the Middle East at least 3,000 years ago, perhaps in several waves.

THE BERBER WAY

Many guides are urban Arabic speakers with a limited ability to talk to Berbers, and even Tashelhit-speaking guides may be urbanized and have little patience for "backward" mountain mores. But attention to local sensitivities is much appreciated and often rewarded with the celebrated Amazigh hospitality. Keep these suggestions in mind:

Say hello: "*Salaamu aleikum*" ("Peace unto you").

Say thank you. The Arabic "*Shokran*" works fine, or you might try "*Baraka Allahu fik*" ("God's blessings upon you").

Smile. This goes further than anything else in creating good will. If you find that you've made a faux pas, say, "*Smahaliyi*" ("Excuse me") and smile some more.

Wear trousers or a long skirt, not shorts or anything above the knee. Wear something on your head if you're female (even a baseball cap). It is always appreciated, and asking about the local way of tying scarves

6

can be a good way of striking up a friendship.

Smoke discreetly. Smoking is typically an urban, male phenomenon. In the mountains women never smoke, and the men who do are gently disparaged.

Many High Atlas villagers are outraged that their children behave as beggars by demanding money, pens, or sweets from foreigners. The polite way to refuse is to say, "*Allah esahel,*" which means "God make it easy on you." It's far better to accept a family invitation to tea and discreetly present your host with tokens of your appreciation when you leave.

Ask permission before you photograph Moroccans. Children tend to be especially keen to pose ("t*soura, tsoura*" means they are imploring you to snap them.) Many adults are fond of stiff, Victorian arrangements, and getting them to smile for a camera can take some doing. Get a name and address, and send prints to anyone you photograph.

HOME DINING ETIQUETTE

If you're lucky enough to be invited to a private home for a mountain meal, bear the following in mind:

Use only your right hand to eat with (the left is traditionally for the toilet).

Meat is eaten last and is usually dished out by your host, so don't serve yourself.

Ending a meal can be difficult, especially since the Ishelhin may continue to tell you to "*ish*" (eat) indefinitely. Say that you'll perish if you have one more bite. Hold your stomach, groan, and say: "*shabagh*" ("I'm full"), "*alhamdullilah*" ("thank God"), or "*safi, shokran*" ("that's enough, thank you").

you the way. You can also take a bus or grand taxi from Imlil or Marrakesh.

TIMING & PRECAUTIONS

Setti Fatma is best known for its seven wonderful waterfalls; take care, as the climbs can be slippery. The area is quite safe, with little risk of hassle or hustle.

WHERE TO STAY

¢ **Hotel Asgaour.** For budget travelers keen to save cents for treks and other adventures, this place is dirt cheap. All rooms are basic but serviceable, and greatly cheered up by views across to the other side of the valley—try not to get stuck with a room that faces the unappealing rocky hill behind the hotel. The roof terrace is an option for meals served in the trusty canteen below, serving tagines for 50 DH. **Pros:** Clean rooms, budget rates. **Con:** Not much character. ⊠*Setti Fatma* ☎*024/48–52–84* ↩*26 rooms* ⚘*In-hotel: restaurant* ▤*No credit cards.*

$ **La Perle d'Ourika.** Bold in orange and blue, this is the best place to
★ stay in town. A series of cozy terraces and salons have lovely views over the river, and somehow manage to avoid views to any of the nearby backpacker junkets. Rooms are very basic (one en suite), but all with excellent mattresses. Food is great, with homegrown quince tagine and delicious couscous. English-speaking owner Ammaria Mounassib is very friendly. **Pros:** Comfortable rooms, delicious food. **Con:** Often booked up. ⊠*On left at beginning of Setti Fatma* ☎*024/48–52–95* ↩*6 rooms* ⚘*In-hotel: restaurant* ▤*No credit cards* ⏏*CP.*

OUTDOOR ACTIVITIES

The seven local guides (including English-speakers) of the **Bureau des Guides et Accompagnateurs en montagne Vallée de l'Ourika** (⊠*Toward end of Setti Fatma, on right* ☎*070/72–10–56 cell number for English-speaking guide Noureddine Bachar* ✎*nourifun@yahoo.fr*) offer tours to the surrounding hills, including a three-day walk to see the rock carvings at Yagour and a five-day trek to the top of Djebel Toubkal, via Imlil. They also have several walk options, including visits to the waterfalls and the local area, that last from one to seven hours (80 DH–250 DH). They can arrange overnight bivouacs, homestays with Berbers in the mountains, food and mules (with muleteer), as well as expert guides. You'll need your own sleeping bag.

AGHBALOU

45 km (30 mi) from Marrakesh.

Aghbalou is only about a kilometer past the turnoff for Ouakaïmeden, and has a lovely setting close to the Ourika River. Although there's little to the village, it's a well-situated base from which to explore the valley. With a four-wheel-drive vehicle and a bit of derring-do (provided you know the route, of course), it's also possible to navigate, via Ouakaïmeden, to the mountain village of Imlil in the neighboring valley.

GETTING HERE & AROUND
Grands taxis from Marrakesh, going in the direction of Ouakaïmeden, can take you as far as Aghbalou. Once there, it's all on foot.

TIMING & PRECAUTIONS
Aghbalou is a lovely place to spend the afternoon. Although there's a little tourist hustle, the area is safe to wander.

EXPLORING
Before the creation of Israel in 1948, the mountains of Morocco were home to a large population of Jewish Berbers. Nearly all have now left, but you'll see one of the few vestiges a couple of kilometers before the town itself. Jews can enter the **Sanctuary of Grand Rabbi Saloman Bel-Hench** and pray with the rabbi for a small fee. ✉ *Just after pottery shed on left heading south, before turning to Oukaïmeden.*

WHERE TO STAY
$$$ 🏨 **Auberge Le Maquis.** Blocky and cheerful rather than stylish, this hotel comes into its own with its fun and friendly embrace of families. It offers basic en-suite rooms, a swimming pool, games galore, and trekking. **Pro:** Comfortable rooms. **Con:** Often booked up. ✉ *Aghbalou, on right shortly after the turn to Oukaïmeden* ☎ *024/48–45–31* ⊕ *www.le-maquis.com* ⇆ *6 rooms* ⚐ *In-hotel: restaurant, pool, hammam* ▭ *No credit cards.*

$$ 🏨 **Auberge Restaurant Ramuntcho.** It's all 1950s colorful concrete, but this best of a fairly soulless bunch centered around Aghbalou is a good bet for lunch or dinner, with a great terrace face-to-face with the cliffs at the back. The outdoor areas (including pool) are much prettier than the barren rooms. Three-course meals come with several good options. Nonguests are welcome to swim as long as they stay and eat. **Pros:** Tasty tagines, lovely pool. **Cons:** Some rooms lack views, not a lot of charm. ✉ *Iggir, just after Aghbalou, on right heading south* ☎ *024/43–82–63* ⇆ *14 rooms* ⚐ *In-hotel: restaurant, pool* ▭ *V.*

OUTDOOR ACTIVITIES
Just at the edge of Tnine Ourika, on the road to Aghbalou, is a **Centre d'informations Touristique** (✉ *Tnine Ourika* ☎ *068/96–55–45* ⊙ *Mon.– Sat. 8–6*). This easily missed shack is a grotto of helpful trekking information, including photocopies of detailed maps of the region for 10 DH. The guide, Hassan Saktine, is helpful and authoritative, and can organize treks, homestays, and cultural and folklore evenings with surrounding Berber communities.

TNINE DE L'OURIKA

35 km (22 mi) south of Marrakesh.

GETTING HERE & AROUND
The Tnine de l'Ourika, at the start of the Ourika Valley, is best reached by car or grand taxi, though a few buses stop here on their way to Oukaïmeden. Once here, you can explore the small village on foot.

TIMING & PRECAUTIONS

Tnine de l'Ourika's Monday souk ranks among the best in the region. Aside from that, the only thing to see is the local *zaouia* (sanctuary) and the ruins of an ancient Kasbah.

ESSENTIALS

Visitor & Tour Info Centre d'informations Touristique (✉ *Tnine Ourika* ☎ *068/96–55–45* ⏱ *Mon.–Sat. 8–6*).

HERE'S WHERE

On the way into Aghbalou, look out for a pink house to the right of the road perched high on the hillside. It belongs to Mick Jagger, and is a reminder of Morocco's popularity as a hippie hangout in the 1960s, when the young rock stars of the day were rolling more than just stones.

EXPLORING

★ The absolute pièce de résistance of any visit to the Ourika Valley is a trip to **Nectarome** (✉ *B.P. 142, Tnine d l'Ourika Haouz* ☎ *024/48–24–47* ⊕ *www.nectarome.com* ⏱ *Sept.–May, daily 9–5; June–Aug., daily 9–7*), the region's first aromatic garden. It produces essential oils for massages, spas, and hammams in the classiest of hotels and riads back in Marrakesh. Started by two Moroccan brothers (one a biochemist, the other a pharmacist), it grows 50 species of aromatic and medicinal plants, all in 2.5 acres of beautifully maintained and colorful gardens. They pick the plants on-site, then extract, process, and bottle the oil in the top-secret perfume workshop. You can take a guided tour (80 DH–120 DH depending on number in tour) through the grounds and learn about the healing properties of each plant (lavender for rest; rosemary for blood circulation; thyme for digestion; geraniums for menopause, etc.), or wander on your own (for 15 DH). You can also have an essential-oils open-air pedicure in specially constructed basins dug into the ground (70 DH for 15 minutes) or bake your own Berber bread in one of three types of clay oven to accompany your lunch (100 DH–150 DH per person). Whatever you do, don't miss the seven-plant tea infusion, taken in a garden gazebo or Berber tent, or the boutique, where you can buy the goods. ■ TIP➔ **Don't munch on the leaves of the oleander rose; they're pretty on the outside but poisonous on the inside. Two leaves are enough to kill a man.**

La Safranière de l'Ourika (✉ *Ferme Boutouil, Takateret* ☎ *024/48–44–76* ⊕ *www.safran-ourika.com*), just before the turn to Nectarome, also has guided tours around its gardens of the valuable saffron plant. For the ultimate saffron experience, go between October 30 and May 15, when the plants are in flower and you can even participate in the picking and drying process.

To get to either Nectarome or La Safranière, take the left turn at Ourika for the road that heads for Tnine de l'Ourika and Dr. Caid Ourika. The turn is signposted to both Nectarome and La Safranière, but easy to miss. La Safranière is down one of the first left turns down a small track (signposted); Nectarome is also a left, a little farther up (also signposted); then through a gate on the left after a few minutes' drive. Any local can give directions.

TO TIZI-N-TEST

To the west of Djebel Toubkal the southern road from Marrakesh through Asni and Ouirgane carves its way through the High Atlas Mountains and offers spectacular views all the way to the Tizi-n-Test pass and beyond. Ouirgane is a great base for trekking and playing in the hills, and has the best lodging options for miles around. South of Ouirgane is best done as a road trip, with stops for occasional sights and breathtaking views.

OUIRGANE

60 km (37 mi) south of Marrakesh.

Ouirgane is the most luxurious base for mountain adventure Morocco has to offer. It doesn't have the highest peaks, but it has a glorious choice of charming hotels and day trips that take in captivating scenery toward the mountainous Tizi-n-Test to the south. You can climb Djebel Toubkal in three days or stay up in the High Atlas for a little longer, safe in the knowledge that you have a snug hotel waiting for you back in Ouirgane. Even if you keep close to town, you can explore the surrounding hills on two "wheels" (foot or bicycle) or four (mule, horse, or quad bike) with ease. In town there's a lively morning souk on Thursday.

GETTING HERE & AROUND

If you have your own car, Ouirgane is a fairly short drive from Marrakesh. Failing that, a grand taxi costs 25 DH per person from Marrakesh. The cheapest way is by bus (15 DH), which leaves Marrakesh's Gare Routière five times daily.

TIMING & PRECAUTIONS

For many, Ouirgane is just a pleasant stop before tackling Tizi-n-Test. But the charming village has a few auberges that make it a good starting point for treks.

EXPLORING

Although counting sheep isn't everyone's idea of fun, seeking out Morocco's wild Berber sheep (*mouflon* in French; *aoudad* in Tashelhit) at the **Mouflon Rouge** will by no means put you to sleep. The wooly creatures are famed throughout the region, and can be seen at a lovely viewing area just before Ouirgane. It's worth it to see what all the fuss is about. ⊠ *On approach to Ouirgane from the north, look for a right turn signposted to "La Bergerie" near the village of Marigha. Keep going south on main road for about 0.5 km (0.25 mi), then take left turn for the viewing area, which parallels Ouirgane River.*

You'll need four-wheel drive to get to the **salt mines,** or stop at the turning for the Amizmiz road and walk. Here salt has been mined for centuries by traditional methods, and Berber merchants still ride from village to village selling salt from the backs of their donkeys. Tip the workers after a tour, but don't go on a Saturday, when all the miners go to the souk at Asni. ⊠ *From Ouirgane, take the Amizmiz Rd..*

6

Shrine of Haïm ben Diourne. Site of one of the few Jewish festivals still held in Morocco, this complex contains the tombs of Rabbi Mordekai ben Hamon, Rabbi Abraham ben Hamon, and others. The shrine, known locally both as the "tigimi n Yehudeen" and "marabout Juif" (House of the Jews), is a large white structure. The moussem generally happens in May. Tip the gatekeeper after a tour. About 4 km (2.5 mi) outside Ouirgane, the shrine is accessible on foot or by mule in less than an hour, or you can drive right up to gate on a dirt piste. Drive south from Au Sanglier and turn left after about 1 km (0.5 mi) at Ouirgane's souk; follow road as it winds through village until you reach a pink cubic water tank. Turn right and go to the end of road, about 3 km (2 mi).

> **GREAT DRIVES**
>
> To drive the stunning mountain road that winds south toward Tizi-n-Test, you'll need a car. You can pick up a bus (the scariest option) or grand taxi from Ouirgane, but it's best to rent a car through one of the agencies in Marrakesh.

WHERE TO EAT

$ ✕ **La Bergerie.** Surrounded by swaying wheat fields, La Bergerie combines
FRENCH Little-House-on-the-Prairie simplicity with Shaker-style elegance—
★ there are even red-and-white checkered tablecloths. The kitchen serves excellent French and local cuisine, including trout, boar, and frogs' legs. There's also a lovely auberge, with 16 rooms and a private gardens. ⊠ *Marigha, B.P. 64, Rte. de Taroudant, Km 59, Par Marrakesh, Asni* ☎ *024/48–57–16 or 024/48–57–17* ⊕ *www.labergerie-maroc. com* ⊟ *MC, V.*

$ ✕ **Chez Momo.** This cheery little place is a pleasure palace hidden in
MOROCCAN deepest Ouirgane. Cocktails around the small pool are all the rage, as
★ are chairs fashioned out of tree trunks. On outdoor grill nights dinner is served to guests who sit round a campfire on cushions in a luscious Berber tent. Chez Momo also has several rooms amid pretty rose gardens and orchards. The dirt road to Chez Momo is roughly 1 km (0.5 mi) south of the bridge over the Ouirgane River. Turn right at the sign and proceed about 164 feet downhill. Turn right again and park in a clump of olive trees. ⊠ *Rte. d'Asni, Km 61 from Marrakesh* ☎ *024/48–57–04 or 061/58–22–95* ⊟ *MC, V.*

WHERE TO STAY

$$ 🖼 **Auberge Au Sanglier Qui Fume.** "The Smoking Boar" has been a favor-
☾ ite with the French for generations. Plenty of families stay here, so kids will feel as much at home as the hotel's many cats and dogs. Guest rooms, spread around the grounds in several buildings, range from small, viewless doubles to suites with private decks and fireplaces. Proprietors Richard and Annick Pousset can arrange all kinds of guided and unguided tours to local sights, and you can rent mules just outside the main gates. Moroccan specialties are always available at the restaurant, but the menu can be a blessed relief from tagines, with Asian options and occasional delicacies such as duck *à l'orange,* frogs' legs, and trout. ■ **TIP→** Don't miss the chance to prepare your own lunchtime bread in clay Berber ovens. **Pros:** Activities for the whole family, excel-

lent cuisine. **Con:** Rooms are a bit overpriced. ⊠ *Vallée d'Ouirgane, Km 61 from Marrakesh* ☎024/48–57–07 ⊕*www.ausanglierquifume. com* ➪*15 rooms, 10 suites* ♿*In-hotel: restaurant, bar, pool, bicycles, hammam* ☰*MC, V* ⦿*MAP.*

$$
FodorsChoice
★

Kasbah de Ouirgane. This small Kasbah outdoes every other hotel in town when it comes to unbeatable views. Perched on a promontory above La Roseraie and Sanglier, it overlooks the Ouirgane and Nfis rivers. With only two beautifully appointed rooms, you'll need to book early, but it's worth the hassle. Owner Mohamed Ladib, previously chef at some of the best hotels around, has gone his own way in delightful style. Not only does he cook up memorable meals, but he has also created a simple, private idyll; along with *pisé* (rammed earth) walls and knotted woolen rugs there are modern bathrooms and a perfectly situated patio. **Pros:** Best food this side of Marrakesh, lovely accommodations. **Con:** Nice rooms if you can get them. ⊠ *On the way into Ouirgane, take right turn up toward reservoir* ☎024/48–48–37 *or 066/38–95–63* ➪*2 rooms* ♿*In-hotel: restaurant, bicycles* ☰*No credit cards.*

$$$$

La Résidence de la Roseraie. A hotel surrounded by gardens, La Roseraie is undoubtedly plush. Creature comforts are in evidence: every room has a television and refrigerator, and each of the "junior" and "senior" suites has a fireplace and deck. The grounds are beautiful, with great swaths of roses. Certain spa facilities cost extra, so ask before you sign up for that pedicure. The restaurant is open to the public. **Pros:** Plenty of pampering, excellent service. **Con:** For the price there ought to be more character. ⊠*B.P. 769, Rte. de Taroudant, Km 60, Marrakesh* ☎024/48–56–93 ⊕*www.laroseraiehotel.com* ➪*21 rooms, 21 suites* ♿*In-room: refrigerator. In-hotel: restaurant, tennis court, pool, spa* ☰*MC, V* ⦿*MAP.*

6

OUTDOOR ACTIVITIES

"Sights" aside, by far the best thing to look at here is the surrounding countryside with its poppies, yellow wheat, snowcapped mountains, rushing rivers, and glorious, looming hills. You can get out there in so many different ways, and your hotel (or a better-equipped one nearby) is the best way to rent equipment for outdoor activities.

BIKING

You can rent bikes from Kasbah d'Ouirgane, La Roseraie, Au Sanglier Qui Fume or, for the cheapest option, La Bergerie (from 20 DH an hour). Quad-biking adventurers can rent the beasts from Au Sanglier Qui Fume for 300 DH an hour (550 DH for half a day).

HORSEBACK RIDING

For horseback riding, La Roseraie is *the* place for the entire region. You can rent horses for local rides or for full-blown tours in the mountains, complete with food and lodging in Atlas villages. Prices start at 200 DH for an hour. As there might be an additional levy elsewhere, it's best to come straight here.

WALKING

Every hotel will be able to fix you up with a walking guide to wander the local hills and rivers, dropping in on the salt mines, the remains of the Jewish settlement, and a Berber house, as you like. It's also only three days on foot (with the help of a mule or two) to the summit of Djebel Toubkal. The route bypasses Imlil altogether, a significant benefit for anyone keen to avoid the trekker base camp.

TIZI-N-TEST

The road to Tizi-n-Test is the most glorious mountain drive in Morocco. The route south from Ouirgane to Tizi-n-Test takes you through the upper Nfis Valley, which was the spiritual heart of the Almohad Empire in the 12th century and later the administrative center of the Goundafi caids in the first half of the 20th century. It's best enjoyed as a day trip by car from Ouirgane, especially as lodging options are seriously basic and few. There are plenty of cafés on the way, however, and a great stop off at Tin Mal Mosque.

EXPLORING

Most of the massive **Goundafi Kasbahs**, strongholds of the Aït Lahcen family that governed the region until independence in 1956, have long since crumbled away. But just past the small village of Talat-n-Yacoub, look up. A great hulking red Kasbah sits at the top of the hill, amid a scene that is today eerily peaceful, with hawks nesting among the scraps of ornately carved plaster and woodwork still clinging to the massive walls. Built as a counterpart to the original Goundafi redoubt in Tagoundaft, the Kasbah is a compelling testament to the concentration of power in an era said to be governed "tribally." Locals say the hands of slack workers were sealed into the Kasbah's walls during construction. There's usually not a tourist in sight. Better yet, its future is secure, since it has been bought for conversion into a restaurant, what will surely become one of the best-placed spots to eat in the area. It's a rocky, although fairly easy, walk up to it. From the Kasbah you can see the Tin Mal Mosque to the south, across the juncture of the Nfis and Tasaft rivers. Just southeast are the mines of Tasaft. The Ouanoukrim Massif (the group of big mountains at the center of the High Atlas Mountains) dominates the view to the north. ⊠ *Above Talat-n-Yacoub, about 40 km (25 mi) south of Ouirgane.*

★ One of only two mosques in the country that non-Muslims may enter (the other is the enormous one in Casablanca), **Tin Mal Mosque** sits proudly on the hills and is well worth a visit. Built by Ibn Tumart, the first Almohad, its austere walls in the obscure valley of the Nfis are the cradle of a formidable superstate. This was the birthplace and spiritual capital of the 12th-century Almohad empire. Today the original walls stand firm, although covered in several extra layers of renovation work. It's filled with pale brick arch after pale brick arch, on a huge scale built to impress. It's free, but tip the guardian, who can also show you around and explain a little of the history. ⊠ *The signposted turnoff for mosque is about 4 km (2.5 mi) south of Talat-n-Yacoub. Turn right, cross bridge, and follow path up other side of valley.*

Ibn Tumart, the First Almohad

A Tashelhit speaker from the hills in the Souss Valley, Ibn Tumart (died 1128) traveled north to the great Kairaouine University in Fez and then east, to Baghdad. Studying with various scholars along the way, Ibn Tumart developed a particularly strict interpretation of the Koran, one that emphasized each believer's personal responsibility for the faith of his community. As he moved back west to Morocco, he collected followers and proclaimed himself "Mahdi"—the "rightly guided one," chosen to purify the community of the faithful before the end of the world. This millennial vision was tolerated uneasily by the Almoravid authorities, who had themselves ridden to power on a wave of religious fervor a couple of centuries earlier. In Marrakesh the tension finally came to a head when the Mahdi threw the sultan's own sister from her horse for appearing in public without a veil. Ibn Tumart was forced to flee to the mountains, where he sought protection from the sultan's cavalry. Eventually he landed among the tribes settled around Tin Mal, and here he set about converting the locals to his version of Islam.

History books and local lore agree that Ibn Tumart's conversion methods were ingenious, if sometimes brutal. One story has it that he would teach the Koran to the mountain Ishelhin (Berbers) word by word. Men were lined up, taught their word, and then made to recite in turn. Working together in this way these Tashelhit speakers could reproduce the resonant Arabic poetry of the Koran and embody the holy text. Another (less quaint) story has it that the Mahdi had thousands of men killed in a four-day purge, with family members directed to put one another to the sword. True or not, these stories suggest the ability of Ibn Tumart to reorganize the fractious mountain tribes into a new social, religious, and military order.

Although their first assault on Marrakesh was brutally thwarted, Abd al-Mumin, the Mahdi's successor, eventually conquered all of the Moroccan mountains, followed by Fez and Marrakesh. The leaders of the empire that resulted became known as the Almohads, or Unifiers, and they rose to replace the Almoravids as rulers of the western Mediterranean.

6

The **Tizi-n-Test**, at 6,889 feet, provides wonderful views to the north and south. It's the summit of any trip from Ouirgane, and a moment's rest from the hair-raising road trip. ⊠ *76 km (47 mi) southwest of Ouirgane.*

WHERE TO EAT & STAY

¢ ✕**Café/Restaurant du Col Tizi-n-Test Bellevue.** This small café right at the

CAFÉ summit of Tizi-n-Test is the perfect place to take in the astounding view with some Berber biscuits and mint tea on beautiful wrought-iron chairs made by the owner's son. It's a good spot to stop and wander up the hills. Although the restaurant has a hotel, it's best avoided. ⊠ *Tizi-n-Test summit, 6,889 feet* ☎ *066/93–47–65* ▭ *No credit cards.*

¢ 🛏**La Belle Vue.** A kilometer down the road from the pass, this concrete block of a hotel has a totally different *belle vue* (beautiful view) from the café at the top. Perched on the edge of the abyss that peers into the Souss Valley, the two terraces are superb places to watch the earth disappear from beneath you. The rooms are clean, simple, and, sadly, have no good views themselves. Bathroom facilities are shared. Meals include tagines, salads, and *mechoui* (roasted lamb; if ordered in advance). The hotel can organize paragliding from 6,000 DH each in groups of at least six. **Pros:** Breathtaking views, the spotless rooms. **Cons:** Shared bathrooms, disappointing views from the rooms. ⊠ *1 km (0.5 mi) south of Tizi-n-Test summit* ☎ *061/38–76–22 or 067/05–58–44* ⊳ *12 rooms without bath* ⚘ *In-hotel: restaurant* ⊟ *No credit cards.*

HIGH-ALTITUDE DRIVING

The route to Tizi-n-Test clings to the mountainside, sometimes triple-backing on itself to climb the heights in a series of precipitous hairpin bends. It's often only a narrow single lane, with sheer drops, blind corners, and tumbling scree. Expect every bend to reveal a wide and furiously fast Land Rover coming right at you, or worse, a group of children playing soccer. Honk as you round sharp corners, and give way to traffic climbing uphill. If you control your speed and stay alert, you'll enjoy a wonderful day.

THE TICHKA PASS

The scenery around the Tichka Pass is peaceful and more low key than that of the rest of the High Atlas. It's soothing and stunning in equal measure, a good bet for stimulating walks and a relaxing hotel stay. If you're just passing through en route to the southern oases, the vista from the Tichka road itself is amazing—especially in spring—and the Glaoui Kasbah at Telouet is worth a look.

TIZI-N-TICHKA

110 km (68 mi) southeast of Marrakesh.

Winding its way southeast toward the desert, the Tichka Pass is another exercise in road-trip drama. Although the road is generally well maintained and wide enough for traffic to pass—and lacks the vertiginous twists of the Tizi-n-Test—it still deserves respect. Especially in winter, take warm clothes with you, as the temperature at the pass itself can seem another latitude entirely from the balmy sun of Marrakesh. ■ TIP→ **Sometimes gas can be difficult to find, particularly unleaded, so fill up before you hit the mountains. There's a station at the town of Aït Ourir, on the main road to Ouarzazate.**

The road out of Marrakesh leads you abruptly into the countryside, to quiet olive groves and desultory villages consisting of little more than a *hanut* (convenience store) and a roadside mechanic. You'll pass the R'mat River, the Oued Zat, and the Hotel Hardi. From here the road begins to rise, winding through fields that are either green with barley and wheat or brown with their stalks. At Km 55 you'll encounter the Hotel Dar Oudar in Touama. In springtime magnificent red poppies dot the surrounding fields.

The road begins to climb noticeably, winding through forests and some of the region's lusher hillsides. A broad valley opens up to your left, revealing red earth and luminously green gardens. At Km 67 stands Mohammad Noukrati's Auberge Toufliht. From Toufliht there is little between you and the Tichka Pass but dusty villages, shepherds, and rock. You might find a decent orange juice, trinket, or weather-beaten carpet in villages like Taddert, but you'll probably feel pulled toward the pass. The scenery is rather barren, and as the naked rock of the mountains begins to emerge from beneath the flora, the walls of the canyon grow steeper, more enclosing.

> ## ALL THAT GLITTERS
>
> On the way up into the hills, look for men and boys, often standing in the middle of the road, waving shiny bits of rock. These are magnificent pieces of quartz taken from the mountains that they sell for as little as 5 DH. On your left at Km 124 from Marrakesh you'll see the **Palais-n-Tichka**, a sort of Wal-Mart for these shiny minerals, as well as other souvenirs. It's also a good restroom stop.

NEED A BREAK?

La Maison Berbère (⊠ *5 km [3 mi] before Taddert, Rte. de Ouarzazate* ☎ *024/37–14–67* ⊙ *Daily 6–5*) has made more of an effort than most of the rest stops on this route, with a high-ceiling, traditionally decorated salon permeated by the unmistakable smell of real coffee. Take a late breakfast or a tagine on the terrace at the back, overlooking a small garden and poppy-dotted fields.

Around Km 105 you'll see several waterfalls across the canyon. The trail down is precipitous but easy enough to follow; just park at the forlorn-looking refuge and the Café Tichka at Km 108. The trail winds to the left of the big hill, then cuts to the right and drops down to the falls after a short walk of half an hour or so. The Tichka Pass is farther along, at 7,413 feet above sea level. Depending on the season and the weather, the trip over the pass can take you from African heat to European gloom and back.

WHERE TO EAT & STAY

$

MOROCCAN

✕**Dar Oudar.** More a restaurant with rooms than an out-and-out hotel, this is a good stop-off point before the climb to the Tichka Pass. The kitchen is justifiably proud of its reputation, and does delicious french fries, as well as tagines and grills. The *kefta* (beef patties) brochettes are outstanding. ⊠*Rte. de Ouarzazate, Km 55, Province Al Haouz* ☎*024/48–47–72* ▭*No credit cards.*

¢

Auberge Toufliht. As the SPECIALE sign suggests, beer, wine, and cocktails are available here, and the place has a pleasantly rowdy feel, particularly on weekends. The main balcony has a wonderful view and is a delightful place to spend a warm afternoon. Basic rooms have en-suite baths, and the cute touch of his-and-hers sandals for the duration of the stay. For views and some privacy, ask for Room 1 or 2. Even less-expensive rooms without bath are available for 100 DH. **Pros:** Sweet little touches, charming rooms. **Cons:** Can get noisy, sometimes closed without warning. ⊠*P31, Km 67 from Marrakesh (Km 135 from Oua-*

6

rzazate) ☎*024/48–48–61* ⟳*9 rooms* ⌂*In-hotel: restaurant, bar, no elevator* ▭*No credit cards.*

$ ⊡ **Le Coq Hotel Hardi.** The riverside Hardi makes a reasonable base for exploring Marrakesh from the relative peace of the countryside. Although it is fairly run down, rooms are inexpensive and have private showers. Most of the year the large pool is open and makes the heat something to savor rather than bear. The bar is sometimes more popular than many family-oriented travelers might like. **Pros:** Cozy poolside seating, well-manicured gardens. **Cons:** Rooms are bare, restaurant is overpriced. ⊠*B.P. 18, Rte. d'Ouarzazate, Km 38 from Marrakesh, Pont du Zat, Aït Ouir* ☎*044/48–00–56 or 044/48–02–29* ⟳*18 rooms* ⌂*In-hotel: restaurant, bar, pool, no elevator* ▭*No credit cards.*

$$$ ⊡ **I Rocha.** Hidden on a promontory above Tizirine, a somewhat inhospitable Berber town, is one of the best lodges in the region. This rustic

Fodor'sChoice   farmhouse on the side of a hill is a quiet idyll, with a small pool and ter-
★   race dining overlooking the valley. Most rooms are arranged around a small courtyard, or set beyond the terrace. All have private bathrooms. Make sure you reserve a double bed if you want one (some are simply two singles pushed together). It's a great base for a day trip to Telouet or for walking—it's a 45-minute walk from a tumbledown red-earth Kasbah. **Pros:** Lovely terrace, sparkling rooms. **Con:** Wine prices are very inflated. ⊠*Take a signposted left at Tizirine (also called Douar Tisselday), halfway down the main road that runs from Tizi-n-Tichka to Ouarzazate. Follow a steep dirt track for 500 feet* ☎*067/73–70–02* ⊕*www.irocha.com* ⟳*7 rooms* ⌂*In-hotel: restaurant, pool* ▭*No credit cards* ⎮⊙|*MAP.*

TELOUET

116 km (72 mi) southeast of Marrakesh, 20 km (12 mi) east of P31.

The main reason for visiting this otherwise unremarkable village is to see the incredible Kasbah of the Glaouis (which is sometimes referred to simply as "Telouet"). Built in the 19th century, the Kasbah is now in near-ruin, but the interior still hints of the luxury that once was.

GETTING HERE & AROUND
Getting to Telouet isn't always easy. The best way, aside from with a tour group, is to take a grand taxi from Marrakesh or drive yourself.

TIMING & PRECAUTIONS
The Kasbah itself takes no more than three hours to explore. Take care, as parts of it are beginning to crumble.

EXPLORING
About five minutes south of Tizi-n-Tichka is the turnoff for the **Glaoui Kasbah** at Telouet. The road is paved but narrow, and winds from juniper-studded slopes down through a landscape of low eroding hills and the Assif-n-Tissent (Salt River). In spring, barley fields soften the effect, but for much of the year the scene is rather bleak. Just before the Kasbah itself is the sleepy little town of Telouet, where you might find a café open, especially if it's Thursday (souk day).

REGIONAL HISTORY

It was from Telouet that the powerful Glaoua family controlled the caravan route over the mountains into Marrakesh. Although the Goundafi and Mtougi caids (local or tribal leaders) also held important High Atlas passes, by 1901 the Glaoua were on the rise. Having secured artillery from a desperate Sultan Moulay el Hassan, the Glaoua seized much of the area below the Tichka Pass, and were positioned to bargain when the French arrived on the political scene. The French couldn't have been pleased with the prospect of subduing the vast, wild regions of southern Morocco tribe by tribe. Thus the French-Glaoua alliance benefited both parties, with Mandani el Glaoui ruling as Grand Vizier and his brother Tuhami serving as pasha of Marrakesh.

Parking for the Kasbah is down a short dirt road across from the nearby auberge Chez Ahmed. Entry is free, although tips for the parking attendant and the guardian of the gate are appreciated. Inside, walking through dusty courtyards that rise to towering mud walls, you'll pass through a series of gates and big doors, many threatening to fall from their hinges. Different parts are open at different times, perhaps according to the whims of the guard. Most of the Kasbah looks ravished, as though most of the useful or interesting bits had been carried off when the Glaoui reign came to its abrupt end in 1956. This sense of decay is interrupted, however, when you get upstairs: here, from painted wood shutters and delicately carved plaster arabesques, exquisitely set tile and broad marble floors, you get a taste of the sumptuousness the Glaoui once enjoyed. Because it was built in the 20th century, ancient motifs are combined with kitschy contemporary elements, such as traditionally carved plaster shades for the electric lights. The roof has expansive views.

NEED A BREAK? The café next door to the Kasbah parking lot, **Chez Ahmed** (also known as Auberge Telouet), has one decent bathroom. The café's nomad-camp atmosphere is pleasantly goofy.

The Great Oasis Valleys

WORD OF MOUTH

"In Merzouga, we woke up to two sounds—one of this animal snorting noise, the other a soft, gentle voice saying, "Wake up." We got up to find our three camels sitting in the sand outside our tents, ready to be mounted and walk up the dunes to watch the sunrise. It was an incredible experience that none of us will ever forget."

—danielsonkin

"It was amazing!! We loved the night in the desert, the Todra Gorge, Ouarzazate and all the scenery between them. . . ."

—africama

By Rachel
Blech

MOROCCO WITHOUT THE SAHARA IS LIKE SWITZERLAND without the Alps, and a trip to the desert is fundamental to an understanding of the country. After you've seen the Atlas Mountains, followed by gorges, oases, palmeries, and Kasbahs, a trip down to the desert may seem a long way to go to reach nothing, and some Moroccans and travelers will warn you against it. Don't listen to them. The void you encounter in the Sahara will remind you why prophets and sages sought the desert to purge and purify themselves.

Once caravan routes from the Sudan, Timbuktu, and Niger to Marrakesh and Fez, Morocco's Great Oasis Valleys have been of fundamental importance to its history. From the Drâa Valley came the Saadian royal dynasty that ruled from the mid-12th to mid-17th century, and from the Ziz Valley and the Tafilalt oasis rose the Alaouite dynasty, which relieved the Saadians in 1669 and which still rules (in the person of King Mohammed VI) in 21st-century Morocco.

A trip through the oasis valleys doesn't just get you sand for your trouble. The asphalt might end and the desert begin at Merzouga and M'Hamid, but in between are the oases flanked by the High Atlas Mountains and the Todra and Dadès gorges—sister grand canyons separating the High Atlas from the Djebel Sarhro Massif.

Doing the entire circuit in the Great Oasis Valleys is a serious undertaking, and you might easily miss the best parts for all the whirlwind traveling. Walking in the Dadès or Todra gorge could easily take three days, and you should stay in at least one for a few days. Whichever gateway you choose, you should allot two days and a night at the very minimum for a trip to the desert. Unless you have oodles of time you'll have to choose between the dunes at Merzouga and M'Hamid, which are separated by 450 km (279 mi) of long, hard driving.

ORIENTATION & PLANNING

ORIENTATION

The Great Oasis Valleys cover a huge area, in a sort of lopsided horseshoe from Ouarzazate, the largest town in the northwest corner, east past the magnificent Dadès and Todra gorges on the northern road, south to the dunes at Merzouga, and looping back west on the southern road, farther south, through the Drâa Valley to Zagora, M'Hamid, and the great expanse of desert that reaches all the way across Erg Chagaga to Foum Zguid. To miss any of these roads would be to miss some of Morocco's most characteristic immensity—wide-open spaces and tundralike desolation.

PLANNING

WHEN TO GO

For off-season rates, better temperatures, and fewer convoys of travelers, try to travel the oasis routes between October and April. The high season begins in early March but doesn't kick in until April. Summer is extremely hot in the desert and the oases and gorges are crowded.

■ TIP➜ **Keep yourself stocked up on bottles of water: it's very hot.**

GETTING HERE & AROUND

The most convenient arrival and departure points for touring this vast region is via the towns of Ouarzazate (if you're traveling from Marrakesh and the Atlantic coast) or Er-Rachidia (if you're traveling from Fez, Meknès, or the Mediterranean coast). Given a choice, opt for Ouarzazate, as it is an interesting town in its own right. Ouarzazate is a key transport hub for exploring the Dadès and Todra gorges, Drâa valley, and the desert regions beyond Zagora. Er-Rachidia, aside from being a stop for those en route to Erfoud, Rissani, and Merzouga, is itself of little interest to travelers.

Ouarzazate's Taourirt International Airport, 1 km (0.5 mi) north of town, receives direct flights from Paris and domestic connections. Er-Rachidia also has an airport for domestic flights. *Petits taxis* (local taxis) are available for the 10-minute ride into town. If you need to catch an early flight, it's best to arrange transportation through your hotel the night before.

There are no train connections south of Marrakesh. Compagnie de Transports Marocains buses run to Ouarzazate, through the Drâa Valley, and down to Zagora, but busing around southern Morocco is not recommended unless you don't mind assuming a full-time study of transport logistics. The only practical way to tour the Great Oasis Valleys is to drive. Being surrounded by gorgeous and largely unexplored hinterlands like the Todra or Dadès gorges without being able to explore safely and comfortably defeats the purpose of coming down here. Driving the oasis roads requires full attention and certain safety precautions: slow down when cresting hills, expect everything from camels to herds of sheep to appear in the road, expect oncoming traffic to come down the middle of the road, and be prepared to come to a full stop if forced to the right and faced with a pothole or other obstacle.

WHAT TO DO

Hikes, treks, and even camel safaris can be the highlight of any trip through the southern oases, dunes, or gorges. Unless you have a four-wheel-drive vehicle, hiking is the only reasonable way to see the Todra Gorge, for instance, as the rocky piste (track) is lethal to most cars' oil pans and underpinnings. The Dadès Gorge, while paved, is still more spectacular when seen on foot. North of Msemrir, a trekker with a fly rod in his backpack might even find a trout or two. Serious trekking adventures through the M'Goun Massif (above the Dadès Valley) or around Djebel Sarhro, south of Tinerhir, are by far the best way to see this largely untouched Moroccan backcountry.

7

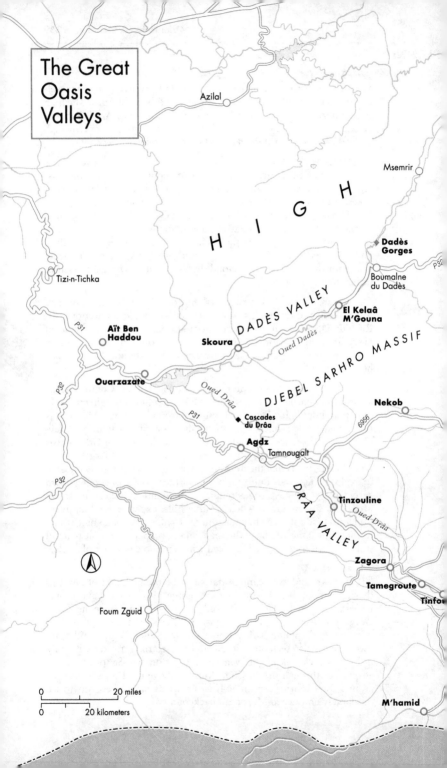

The Great Oasis Valleys

Azilal

Msemrir

H   I   G   H

Tizi-n-Tichka

◆ **Dadès Gorges**

P32

Boumalne du Dadès

DADÈS VALLEY

El Kelaâ M'Gouna

Aït Ben Haddou

P31

Skoura

Oued Dadès

DJEBEL SARHRO MASSIF

Ouarzazate

P32

Oued Drâa

P31

◆ **Cascades du Drâa**

Nekob

6956

Agdz

Tamnougalt

DRÂA VALLEY

Tinzouline

Oued Drâa

P32

Zagora

Tamegroute

Tinfou

Foum Zguid

0   20 miles
0   20 kilometers

M'hamid

SAFETY

You shouldn't have problems traveling this part of Morocco, but always exercise caution if going into remote areas. Don't stop for hitchhikers or for people whose car has broken down, as there are still some dishonest individuals wanting to take advantage of tourists.

Be prepared to be followed by local kids who may want to engage you in conversation. Rather than money, give them items such as pens or pencils. If they are selling homemade handicrafts, then of course give them a few dirhams for their efforts.

RESTAURANTS

Far from the set-menu Moroccan cuisine of the urban palaces, the

> ### TOP REASONS TO GO
>
> **Desert dreams:** live out those Lawrence of Arabia fantasies by sleeping on dunes under the stars.
>
> **Dadès Gorge:** follow mountain trails in some of Morocco's most beautiful scenery.
>
> **Kasbah trail:** marvel at and stay in ancient strongholds that dot the landscape.
>
> **Morocco's Hollywood:** spot celebs in Ouarzazate, home to visiting film crews.
>
> **Flower power:** spring is perfect for a visit to the Valley of Roses to see endless specimens in the wild.

fare along the southern oasis routes leans to hearty *tagines* (stewed combinations of vegetables and meat, usually lamb) and couscous. *Harira* (bean-based soup with vegetables and meat) is more than welcome as night sets in and temperatures plunge. *Mechoui* (roast lamb) is a standard feast, if you can order it far enough in advance. Some of the best lamb and vegetable tagines in Morocco are simmered over tiny camp stoves in random corners and campsites down here. You may want to keep a bottle of wine in the car or in a day pack, as many restaurants don't serve alcohol but have no problem with customers bringing their own. Always ask first, though, as some places object.

	¢	$	$$	$$$	$$$$
WHAT IT COSTS IN DIRHAMS					
AT DINNER	under 40DH	40DH–70DH	70DH–100DH	100DH–150DH	over 150DH

Prices are per person for a main course at dinner.

HOTELS

Hotels on the southern oasis routes generally range from mediocre to primitive, with several charming spots and a few luxury establishments thrown in. Come here with the idea that running water and a warm place to sleep are all you really need, and accept anything above that as icing on the cake. Sleeping outdoors on hotel terraces is common (and cheap) in summer, as are accommodations in *khaimas* (Berber nomad tents). The stars and the sky are so stunning here that failing to sleep at least one night *à la belle étoile* (under the stars) seems almost criminal.

	¢	$	$$	$$$	$$$$
WHAT IT COSTS IN DIRHAMS					
FOR TWO PEOPLE	under 200DH	200DH–350DH	350DH–500DH	500DH–700DH	over 700DH

All prices are for a high-season standard double room, excluding service and tax.

FESTIVALS

There are a number of *moussems,* or festivals, that take place in villages throughout the year that are linked to holy days and to the agricultural calendar. These often don't have specific dates, so encountering one is largely a matter of luck. There are few festivals which you can largely rely on: the **Rose Festival** of Kelaâ M'Gouna (Dadès Valley) in May, the **International Nomads Festival** in M'Hamid el Ghizlane (Drâa Valley) at end of March, the **Erfoud Date Festival** (Ziz Valley) in October, and the **Festival of Ahouach Music** in Ouarzazate (Drâa Valley) in early April. Check with a local tourist office or tour operator to check on the exact dates.

SEEING THE SAHARA

Life's truly picture-perfect moments come few and far between. A sea of sand dunes, shimmering gray, yellow, orange, and red throughout the day, is one of them. The Sahara is the most beautiful and awe-inspiring piece of geography you can come up against in Morocco, a piece of perfection. It isn't huge, though. From Merzouga, you can get to the other side within two days (no, it doesn't link up to the Algerian Sahara), and in peak season there are an awful lot of people trying to lose themselves in the same sandy spots. For the vast emptiness of the desert scrub and *hamada* (stony desert), you'll have to head to M'Hamid, miles from anywhere else, at the literal end of the road. From here a flat scrubby sandscape stretches out into undulating *ergs* (dunes) for days. The desert is partly a state of mind, a bowing to nature in the search for humility, so prepare for enlightenment here.

WHAT TO EXPECT

You might think there's not a lot to do in the desert. Of course, you're right. But when there are no shops, no stereos, and no kitchens, just getting by becomes wonderfully time-consuming. You can cook bread in hot ashes packed into the sand; you can count stars until the sky caves in; and you can listen to hypnotic Berber drumming deep into the night. Everyone has a favorite part of the day, be it waking to see the muted colors of the sand at first light, the fury of the midday sun, or cresting a dune on foot at dusk. No matter when you go, the image stays with you.

Most camel treks into Erg Chebbi, in Merzouga, rarely last more than three hours at a time, and palms, tents, and dinner are generally waiting for you at your oasis destination. Beyond M'Hamid, farther south,

Desert FAQ

When it comes to the Sahara, there's a first time for everyone, and no question is too silly. Here are some classics:

Will I fry?: Quite possibly. Temperatures can reach 55°C (131°F) in June, July, and August. The easy answer? If you must go in summer, don't go out in the day (even the camels won't); rather, take sunset camel rides into the dunes, spend the night, and head back at dawn. The best (and busiest) time is between March and the beginning of May. October to February is nice, too, although it can be chilly at night December through February.

What should I wear?: Cover up. People who've been living in the desert for years know that one light cotton or silk layer is better than a tank top and shorts.

What about my head?: Donning the *sheish* (head scarf), beloved of Saharaouia and Berbers, is really fun. Knot the end of a lightweight dyed fabric (most often blue, hence the desert moniker "the blue men") and put it on your head. Wrap the rest around your head and take the end across your nose and tuck it in. Didn't get it? No worries. Ask the experts and prepare to laugh.

What if I prefer skiing?: Believe it or not, you're in the right place. If camels, four-wheel drives, and long walks don't interest you, think of the sands as a miraculous cross between snow and sea. There are opportunities to ski, sand-board, and body-board. You can rent equipment from the auberges that surround Erg Chebbi near Merzouga. Make sure you ask an expert if the sand is suitable—as with snow, you need it heavy and compact to get a good chance of going like the wind.

And yes, it sounds weird, but that's why it's so cool.

What's all this talk of faux guides?: Guiding visitors around the desert has kept hard-up locals in cash for years. Now that the road to Merzouga is entirely paved, it's proving harder to capture customers early on, in Rissani, Erfoud, and even Er-Rachidia. Watch out for people on buses who claim not to be interested in selling you anything, but whose "uncle" has a place you can stay in for cheap. Most of these touts get a commission when they bring visitors to an auberge. Likewise, some may try to convince you that the auberge you think you're staying at has shut down, or is poorly run, and offer you a "better" alternative. Strangers may sometimes follow you by moped and urge you into the auberge of their choice. By far the best way to play this is to book an auberge in advance and arrange pickup if you don't have your own transport, or a roadside meeting even if you do.

Which dune should I visit?: The impressive Erg Chebbi near Merzouga are more amenable to a quick "in-out" overnight, but then again, they're far away from Ouarzazate. The small dunes near Zagora, at Amezrou and Tinfou, aren't worth writing home about, although some hurried tourists only ever make it that far. There might be some lovely places to stay nearby, but it just isn't the desert proper. Southwest of M'Hamid, however, you have eye-popping dunes that stretch for miles, including the Erg Chagaga. Allow for at least two days (by camel) to get there from M'Hamid.

Where should I stay?: In the desert is the short answer. Most operators and auberges have permanent tented

camps hidden among the oases and dunes, so there's no hassle once you arrive. They even have tents for two, so there's no need to start thinking this is Woodstock. If you want to keep the stars within eyeshot all night, you can also just sleep on a rug over the sands. There are also some traditionally styled guesthouses of varying quality around the dunes at Merzouga and M'Hamid; these generally offer private bathrooms, more luxury, and the chance to organize a trip through local guides.

TIPS

If you're driving and have a GPS, consider bringing it, especially if you're headed for Merzouga: not so much to find the dunes as to locate your auberge! They are scattered throughout the area, and can be hard to find on the scrubby pistes. Most auberges know their GPS fixing, so call ahead and ask.

Bring water-purifying tablets. The more hard-core excursions through the desert stretching from Foum Zguid to M'Hamid can go on for days, requiring too much water to carry yourself.

Pick a place to stay before you get to the town, call them up and confirm. You'll avoid so much hassle with persuasive local touts if you know where you're going and can say so confidently. Better yet, get your hosts to pick you up or meet you at an appointed place.

Bear in mind that riding a camel for a number of days can be painful. The second day, with soreness from the preceding day, is thought to be the worst. So either keep your camel trips short or do the intrepid thing and ride through the pain barrier and out the other side, at which point you might well never want to dismount from your trusty but bad-tempered steed.

–Katrina Manson & James Knight

there's a much greater range of dunes, salt lakes, and emptiness than at Merzouga, although you generally spend the night by an oasis.

While camel trekking (along with imbibing that particularly delectable camel scent and temper) is pretty much an obligatory part of the experience, you can mix things up a little. Quad bikes and buggies are becoming increasingly popular, and it's possible to arrange four- or five-day motorized dune safaris with companies based in Zagora. There are also skis, snowboards, and body boards for hire from many of the auberges that face the sands in Merzouga. Or you can take it easy, kicking back and watching the changing shades of the dunes all day long.

POINTS OF ENTRY

The two main desert areas in Morocco are very different. Merzouga and its dune, Erg Chebbi, has sand piled high like a fancy hairdo, and you can dip your toe in as you like. You can spend a night very happily in an oasis, sleeping under the stars, and another back at an auberge with front-row dune seats and a bit of luxury. M'Hamid is the entry point for the more adventurous. The sands go on for miles, and 10- to 15-day trips by camel are not uncommon. If you're pressed for time or money, or not a fan of camel travel (which is not entirely unsmelly), you can compromise. A two-day camel trek will get you to Erg Chagaga, the largest dune in the area. You can camp overnight and your tour operator can have a four-wheel drive waiting to take you back the next day.

OUARZAZATE

There's no desert in Ouarzazate, but the quickest and most comfortable way to get to your window on the desert is by car, and Ouarzazate is a great place to pick up a rental vehicle. You can also take a combination of buses and taxis, but it's more hassle and you're liable to bump into insistent and inventive touts along the way. If you'd like to travel in total security and style, you can also join an organized tour at one of the many tour agencies in town.

MERZOUGA

If you're coming from Fez and want to include a trip to the Sahara in your itinerary, Merzouga is the most convenient entry point. You can spend the night under the stars at Erg Chebbi and climb sand dunes at dusk and dawn. From there you can head back to Ouarzazate via the northern oasis road, passing the entry points for the Todra and Dadès gorges along the way. You can also take the southern oasis route back, from Rissani and then southwest through the glorious Kasbah-filled village of Nekob and south through the Drâa Valley, passing Zagora and on to M'Hamid, nearly 100 km (62 mi) farther south.

ZAGORA

Whatever you do, don't get all the way to Zagora and decide to venture no farther. There are numerous agencies offering camel treks and desert camps through the Drâa Valley, but M'Hamid is where the desert truly begins. The small excuses for sand dunes near Zagora give a taste of the desert but no more. You've barely started. That said, Zagora is a good place to arrange a desert tour by car or camel that starts from M'Hamid or Foum Zguid. The road between Ouarzazate and Zagora is faster than between Ouarzazate and Merzouga, and as a result this town, which has no real dunes of its own, is a popular desert stop off. When the adventure is over, hot-foot it back to a bit of luxury either in Zagora, or in the strip of hotels that line the road just 3 km (2 mi) before M'Hamid village itself.

> ### A NOTE ABOUT CAMELS
>
> For those of you who've never had a camel for a traveling companion before, know that they generally have wild, unpredictable dispositions. Treat them with care. To avoid discomfort when riding a camel, don't make the mistake of treating it like a horse. Relax and try and adjust to the rolling movement rather than tensing against it.

M'HAMID

If you're coming from Marrakesh, M'Hamid is your best bet for a Sahara side trip. Another boon is that it's also less touristy and overdeveloped than Merzouga. Although it's your true destination, M'Hamid can be pretty tough on tourists arriving in search of a desert tour. Why? Because it's the end of the road and the nomad families who live here are all struggling to survive on desert tourism. As a result there are touts everywhere, a little depressed and desperate. Many people drive in, are put off by the mayhem, and drive straight out again. The village now has several reputable tour agencies that can smooth out the process, and some have experienced English-speaking guides. They can organize treks for any length of time, traveling by camel or four-wheel drive, and staying in tents overnight.

TOUR OPERATORS

There are hundreds of tour operators offering trips throughout the oasis valleys and deserts of Morocco of which the larger companies will be fully licensed by the Office of Tourism. Though this is recommended if booking for large groups involving significant cash advances, it is not necessary for individual travelers and private groups. Many of the smaller operators offer a far more satisfactory personal service with in-depth local knowledge. In all cases ensure that your tour operator has a patent number and carries public insurance.

Tour Operators Atlas Voyages (✉ *131, ave. Mohammed V, Marrakesh* ☎ *024/43–03-33* ⊕ *www.atlasvoyages.com*), one of the larger Marrakesh-based tour operators, has a variety of excursions available.

Marmara (✉ *Hotel Marmara le Marrakesh, Pl. de la Liberté , Marrakesh* ☎ *024/43–43-51* ⊕ *www.marmara.com*) has a variety of short and long desert tours. Prices are reasonable, but expect to be part of a large group traveling by bus.

Destination Evasion (✉ *Villa el Borj, Rue Khalid Ben Oualid , Marrakesh* ☎ *024/44-73-75* ⊕ *www.destination-evasion.com*), a well-run Moroccan company, offers desert and valley excursions from their Marrakesh base.

Sahara Expedition (✉ *Angle el Mouahidine and Bani Marine, Marrakesh* ☎ 024/42–79–77 ⊕ *www.saharaexpe. ma*) is a small agency in Marrakesh that runs excursions throughout the region, with two- and three-day sprints to the desert at Zagora and Merzouga. Prices are significantly cheaper for groups of more than six.

OUARZAZATE

204 km (122 mi) southeast of Marrakesh, 300 km (180 mi) west of Erfoud.

Ouarzazate is Morocco's Hollywood, and the industry can regularly be found setting up shop in this sprawling desert crossroads with wide, palm-fringed boulevards. Brad Pitt, Angelina Jolie, Samuel L. Jackson, 50 Cent, and many more have graced the suites and streets. Despite the Tinseltown vibe and huge, publicly accessible film sets, Ouarzazate remains at its heart a dusty ghost town. Its main recommendation is the dramatic surrounding terrain that makes it a mainstay for filmmakers: the red-glowing Kasbah at Aït Ben Haddou; the snow-capped High Atlas, and the Sahara, with tremendous canyons, gorges, and lunarlike steppes in between.

GETTING HERE & AROUND

There are daily fights to Ourzazate's Taourirt Airport from Casablanca and flights twice weekly to Paris. The airport is 2 km (1 mi) from the town center and can be reached by petits taxis.

Oaurzazate is well served by buses from Marrakesh (4 hours), Agadir (8½ hours), Casablanca (8½ hours), Taliouine (3½ hours), Taroudant (5 hours), Tinerhir (5 hours), Er-Rachidia (6 hours), Erfoud (7 hours), Zagora (4½ hours), and M'Hamid (7 hours). Compagnie de Transports Marocains buses run from the eastern end of Avenue Mohammed V. Other public buses run from the Mahta bus station about 2 km (1 mi) from the town center just off the N9 route to Marrakesh (a petit taxi will get you here for about 15 DH). Shared grands taxis (long-distance taxis) also bring you here from Marrakesh, Er-Rachidia, Agadir, and Zagora.

There are many travel agencies in Ouarzazate, so shop around. If you book a tour in Ouarzazate, you'll avoid being hassled when you reach Merzouga or M'Hamid. Zbar Travel is a well-regarded company with English-speaking local guides who have an in-depth knowledge of the region. Cherg Expeditions, Iriqui Excursions, and Ksour Voyages are also good choices. If you want to drive yourself, there are many car rental agencies along Avenue Mohammed V.

TIMING & PRECAUTIONS

For those traveling to the desert, this is an important town for stocking up on cash. It's also a good place to purchase essentials like map, batteries, and other supplies. It is the last town where you will find a supermarket selling wine, beer, and liquor.

ESSENTIALS

Bus Contacts Compagnie de Transports Marocains (✉ *Ave. Mohammed V* ☎ *024/88-24-27*)

A DAY OUT

Interesting excursions from Ouarzazate into the High Atlas begin with the Glaoui Kasbah at Telouet, 70 km (42 mi) north of town on Route 6802–6803 *(⇨ Tizi-n-Tichka in Chapter 6)*. Another option, for the fit and courageous, would be to walk from the P31 to Aït-Benhaddou and back in a loop, a four- or five-day jaunt of 77 km (46 mi), to be attempted only with full camping and backpacking equipment *(⇨ Chapter 6 for more on trekking in the High Atlas)*.

Currency Exchange Banque Populaire (✉ *Ave. Mohammed V* ☎ *024/88-28-74*). **BMCE** (✉ *Ave. Mohammed V* ☎ *024/88-24-45*).

Medical Assistance Hôpital Bougafer (✉ *Ave. Mohammed V* ☎ *024/88-24-44*). **Pharmacie du Nuit** (✉ *Ave. Mohammed V opposite tourist office* ☎ *024/88-24-90*).

Post Office Poste Maroc (✉ *Ave. Mohammed V*).

Rental Cars Amzrou Transport (✉ *41, ave. Mohammed V* ☎ *024/88-23-23* ⊕ *www.amzroutrans.com*). **Hertz** (✉ *33, ave. Mohammed V* ☎ *024/88-20-84* ⊕ *www.hertz.com*). **Tafoukt Cars** (✉ *88, rue Er-Rachidia* ☎ *067/35-87-99* ⊕ *www.tafouktcars.com*).

Visitor & Tour Info Cherg Expeditions (✉ *2, pl. el Mouahidine* ☎ *024/88-79-08* or *061/24-31-47* ⊕ *www.cherg.com*). **Iriqui Excursions** (✉ *Pl. 3 Mars at Ave. Mohammed V* ☎ *024/88-57-99* ⊕ *www.iriqui.com*). **Ksour Voyages** (✉ *11, pl. du 3 Mars* ☎ *024/88-29-97* ⊕ *www.ksour-voyages*). **Ouarzazate Tourism Office** (✉ *B.P. 297, Ave. Mohammed V* ☎ *024/88-24-85*). **Zbar Travel** (✉ *Appt 4, Bab Sahara, Pl. Al Mouahidine* ☎ *024/88-56-10* or *068/51-72-80* ⊕ *www.zbartravel.com*).

EXPLORING

Known for its fine artisan traditions in ceramics and carpet making, the **Kasbah Taourirt**, once a Glaoui palace, is the oldest and finest building in Ouarzazate, a rambling *pisé* (a sun-dried mixture of mud and clay) castle built by those so-called Lords of the Atlas in the late 19th century. There are two lovely places to stay inside the Kasbah—both are worth it.

WHERE TO EAT

$$–$$$ ✕ **Chez Dimitri.** If Ouarzazate is the crossroads of the southern oasis
MOROCCAN routes, Chez Dimitri is at the heart of it. Founded in 1928 as the first
★ store, gas station, post office, telephone booth, dance hall, and restau-

CLOSE UP

Camel or Jeep?

Those cash-rich and time-poor are likely to plump for travel by jeep, especially to the desert south of M'Hamid that stretches west to Foum Zguid. Getting to Erg Chagaga, for example, takes two hours by four-wheel drive and two days by camel. There are also great off-road routes around Zagora, M'Hamid, and Foum Zguid for those who love four-wheel-drive adventure. Some even prefer to go by quad bikes, which are also readily available.

But spare a thought for the poor desert, which thrives on being alone and slowly buckles under the weight of car fumes, carelessly discarded rubbish, and intrusive revving and whooping in an otherwise noiseless environment. Camels may take longer, but they're quieter, more authentic, and fit with the nomadic way of life.

–Katrina Manson & James Knight

rant in Ouarzazate, Chez Dimitri may look unimpressive on an initial sweep down the town's banal main drag, but the food, whether international or Moroccan, is invariably excellent. The owners are friendly and helpful, and the signed photographs of legendary movie stars on the walls are sometimes enhanced by real stars at the next table. ✉22, ave. Mohammed V ☎024/88–73–46 ▤MC, V.

$$$–$$$$ ✕**Le Relais Saint-Exupéry.** In a town not renowned for its restaurant
MOROCCAN scene, this French-run restaurant is a glorious exception. Checkered tablecloths and floors give it the air of a French canteen, but the cuisine is high Moroccan, with some Bordelais touches. House specialties include *pastilla* (salty-sweet pigeon in puff pastry), and veal in Atlas honey. ✉13, Moulay Abdellah, Quartier el Qods ☎024/88–77–79 ⊕www.relaissaintexupery.com ▤No credit cards.

WHERE TO STAY

$$$$ 🏨**Le Berbère Palace.** Movie stars and magnates tend to stay at this ultraexpensive hotel when on location in Ouarzazate. The pool, the gardens, the public rooms—everything about it is impeccable. Even when the stars aren't in town you can luxuriate in the thought you might be sleeping in the same bed where Brad Pitt or Cate Blanchett rested a weary head. The elegantly furnished rooms and bungalows, the personal service, and the level of poolside chic are the best in Ouarzazate. First-floor rooms have terraces with views for the same price. The Moroccan cuisine is on a par with the hotel's high standards. The half-board option means nightly dining from the buffet. **Pros:** Plenty of creature comforts, top-notch service. **Cons:** Rooms feel a bit charmless, air-conditioners too close to the bed for comfort. ✉Ave. Elmansour Eddahbi ☎024/88–31–05 ⊕www.ouarzazate.com/leberberepalace 🛏235 rooms, 20 bungalows ♻In room: safe, refrigerator, Wi-Fi. In-hotel: 3 restaurants, bars, tennis courts, pool, gym, public Wi-Fi, public Internet, no elevator, parking (no fee) ▤AE, DC, MC, V.

$$$$ 🏨**Dar Kamar.** For anyone seduced by tales of Glaoui wealth and influ-
★ ence, this 17th-century pasha's courthouse has magisterial appeal. Filled with artifacts from all over Africa, the dark, lantern-lighted courtyard

CLOSE UP

A Different Take

If you're looking for things to do in Ouarzazate, visit **Atlas Studios**, opposite the Hotel Oscar. Flanked with beautiful impropriety by two giant Egyptian statues, these are Morocco's most famous studios. Guided tours start every 45 minutes and cost 50 DH, 30 DH if you're a guest of the hotel. It isn't Disney World, but you do get a sense of just how many productions have rolled through town, from Jean-Claude Van Damme kickathons to Hollywood blockbusters like *The Mummy Returns* and *Alexander*, and

classics such as *Cleopatra* and *Lawrence of Arabia*.

For another angle on the Ouarzazate film industry, check out the rather grand-looking Kasbah off to the right just out of town on the way to Skoura. One enterprising local producer, frustrated by the increasingly expensive charges being levied on film crews wanting to film around real Kasbahs, decided to build his own and undercut the competition.

–Katrina Manson & James Knight

envelops with its dusky grandeur. Rooms are effortlessly chic, with wrought-iron beds, Berber rugs, inventive lanterns, and bathrooms as smooth and polished as the service. The hotel can also arrange a variety of excursions, including four-wheel drives, quad biking, mountain biking, camel riding, trekking, and overnight bivouacs. **Pros:** Beautiful interiors, doting service. **Con:** No liquor license. ⊠*45, Kasbah Taourirt* ☎*024/88–87–33* ⊕*www.darkamar.com* ⇆*12 rooms* ⌂*In-hotel: restaurant, hammam* ⊟*MC, V* ⦿*MAP.*

$$ ☷**Hotel Oscar.** For its proximity to one of Ouarzazate's biggest silver-screen attractions, Atlas Studios, this is the movie buff's hotel of choice. Rooms are straightforward—more Jimmy Stewart than Errol Flynn—although the service can sometimes be sleepier than Bedford Falls. The lively restaurant makes good nighttime hangout. If you're not staying here, you can use the pool for 7 DH per person. **Pros:** Ideal for families with children, good restaurant. **Con:** Tired decor. ⊠*Tamassint, Rte. de Marrakesh, Km 5* ☎*024/88–22–12* ⇆*65 rooms* ⌂*In-hotel: restaurant, bar, pool, laundry service, no elevator* ⊟*MC, V* ⦿*CP.*

$ ☷**Hotel La Vallée.** Across the river from Ouarzazate on the road to Zagora, this hotel is popular with tour groups. The rooms are clean and simple, though they can be very cold in the winter months, There's an immaculate pool with a terrace café and a restaurant with a magnificent view of the palmery and the snowcapped peaks of the Atlas Mountains. The food is ample and delicious and the English-speaking staff very welcoming. **Pros:** Well-run hotel, friendly service. **Con:** Bathrooms need a face-lift. ⊠*Km 1, Rte. de Zagora, Tabount* ☎*024/85–40–34 or 066/17–76–10* ⊕*www.hotellavallee.com* ⇆*41 rooms* ⌂*In-room: no phone (some), Wi-Fi (some). In-hotel: 2 restaurants, pool, no elevator, public Wi-Fi, parking (no fee)* ⊟*AE, MC, V* ⦿*CP.*

¢–$ ☷**Hotel Zaghro.** You really can't beat this budget hotel. There's a great ★ zellij reception hall, decent traditional restaurant, a choice of rooms with or without bathroom, and even a swimming pool. Breakfast costs 30 DH and the set menu 85 DH, with three courses. **Pros:** Friendly staff, easy on the wallet. **Con:** Not all rooms have air-conditioning. ✉*B.P.193, Tabount* ✛*1.5 km (0.75 mi) on route to Zagora, in south of town over bridge* ☎*024/85–41–35* ⊕*www.hotel-restaurant-zaghro. com* ⤳*50 rooms, 30 with bath* ⚏*In-hotel: restaurant, pool, no elevator* ▤*AE, MC, V* ⎮⊙⎮*CP.*

$$ ▦ **La Kasbah Zitoune.** This hotel sits proud on the site of an ancient
☺ olive grove, hence the name, Arabic for "olive." It has fantastic views across the Ouarzazate palmery to the Kasbah Tiffoultoute. Rooms are enormous and use traditional materials, but there's not much furniture and very little storage for clothes. The surrounding gardens are a work-in-progress, and a swimming pool is planned for 2009. Moroccan-French couple Lahcen and Claudie have an encyclopedic knowledge of the region, and have run trips in it for years. **Pros:** Peaceful and spacious surroundings, cooking classes. **Cons:** Still under construction, need a car to get around. ✉ *B.P. 740, Zone Touristique de Tiffoultoute* ✛*from Marrakesh, take turn to Tiffoultoute/Agdz, pass the Kasbah on left, and it's 1st right turn after bridge* ☎*024/88–35–24* ⊕*www. kasbahzitoune.com* ⤳*10 rooms, 3 suites* ⚏ *In room: no TV. In-hotel: restaurant, bar, public Internet, no elevator* ▤*MC ,V* ⎮⊙⎮*CP.*

$ ▦ **Nadia Hotel.** What it might lack in architectural charm, the Nadia makes up for with dedicated service. Rooms with high stucco ceilings are a touch larger than at the nearby Zaghro, and the hotel has a calmer feel. Chef Raja, drawing on her years of experience, cooks some of the best hotel fare in town. **Pros:** Relaxed atmosphere, great food. **Con:** Architecture lacks charm. ✉*Rte. de Zagora, Km 2* ☎*024/85–49–40* ⊕*www.ouarzazate.com/hotelnadia* ⤳*30 rooms* ⚏*In-hotel: restaurant, pool, public Internet, no elevator, parking (no fee)* ▤*MC, V* ⎮⊙⎮*CP.*

$$–$$$ ▦ **Rose Noire.** Jmiaa and Bernard Rose lovingly restored a 300-year-old riad in the Kasbah, with rooms arranged around a courtyard open to the sky. Using traditional Berber construction and decorative techniques, they have made comfortable and tasteful accommodations. Look for nice touches like handwoven carpets and genuine artifacts. The hotel's reputation for home-cooked food has traveled far. All the food—which must be ordered in advance—is cooked by Jmiaa herself, who was taught Berber cooking by her grandmother. **Pros:** Beautiful building, welcoming hosts, tasty meals. **Cons:** Hard to find, not for those with mobility issues. ✉*Quartier de la Mosquée, Kasbah Taourirt* ☎*024/88–20–16 or 061/61–05–68* ⊕*www.maisondhote-rosenoire. com* ⤳*7 rooms, 1 suite* ⚏*In-room: safe, Wi-Fi. In-hotel: restaurant, parking (fee)* ▤*No credit cards* ⎮⊙⎮*CP.*

OUTDOOR ACTIVITIES

You can rent quad bikes from **Quad Aventure** (☎*024/88–40–24*), at the Marrakesh end of town, opposite Atlas Studios. They're good for day trips to the natural and historic wonders that have become backdrops to blockbuster films, including the Kasbah at Aït Ben Haddou and a plateau used in *Gladiator*. They also have canoes, great for the sparkling lake just southeast of town. Two hours cost 135 DH per person, half a day 180 DH, and a full day 330 DH.

AÏT BEN HADDOU

32 km (20 mi) northeast of Ouarzazate.

The *ksar* (fortified village) at Aït Ben Haddou is something of a celebrity itself. This group of earth-built Kasbahs and homes hidden behind defensive high walls has come to fame (and fortune) as a backdrop for many films, including David Lean's *Lawrence of Arabia*, Ridley Scott's *Gladiator,* and Oliver Stone's *Alexander.* Of course, it hasn't always been a film set. It got going in the 11th century as a stop-off on the old caravan routes, with salt heading one way and ivory and gold heading back the other. Strewn across the hillside and surrounded by flowering almond trees in early spring, the red-pisé towers of the village fortress resemble a sprawling, dark-red sand castle. Crenellated and topped with an ancient granary store, it's one of the most sumptuous sights in the Atlas.

When it's not seething with camera crews, it can get inundated with visitors desperate to capture the postcard-perfect snap. You can usually manage a moment or two alone with the ksar to take in its beauty, no matter how many people are there. You can get here in a standard car from Ouarzazate, or take a superb four-wheel-drive outing from Telouet to Ouarzazate, detouring to the village and ksar.

GETTING HERE & AROUND

The village of Aït Ben Haddou, 29 km (18 mi) northwest of Ouarzazate, is easily reached by road. There are very few buses to Aït Ben Haddou, so if you don't have a car the best and cheapest option is to charter a grand taxi in Ouarzazate. On arriving in the village, there are two main entrances to the Kasbah. The first entrance, by the Hotel-Restaurant Le Kasbah, has ample safe parking. Farther down the road is the second entry point opposite the Riad Maktoub. Here you can leave your car at the side of the road.

TIMING & PRECAUTIONS

The narrow road to Aït Ben Haddou is filled with vehicles traveling faster than they should. Proceed with caution and keep well over to the right.

To reach the Kasbah itself involves crossing a river. It's usually dry between April and October, but locals have installed stepping stones. Wear suitable footwear with a solid grip.

WHERE TO STAY

$ **Auberge Kasbah du Jardin.** To escape the hordes in the town center, flee to this outpost at the far edge of town. The service is friendly and enthusiastic, and the rooms are basic but cheerful. Not all have individual bathrooms, so look at a few before you decide. The pool, rather

HAMMAMS & SPAS

The following hammams and spas are open to all (even nonguests, if in a hotel).

PUBLIC HAMMAM

Hammam. There is a good public hammam five minutes from town center, two minutes from Kasbah Taourirt, in the Erac *quartier.* ✉ *Bd. Mohammed V, Ouarzazate* ☎ *No phone* 🖾 *5 DH* 🖃 *No credit cards.*

HOTEL HAMMAM

Le Berbere Palace. Home to movie stars filming in the nearby studios, this Kasbah-style hotel has a ham-

mam, sauna, and Jacuzzi. ✉ *Ave. Elmansour Eddahbias, Ouarzazate* ☎ *024/88–31–05* 🖾 *50 DH hammam, 135 DH with exfoliation* � *Daily 10 AM–8 PM* 🖃 *AE, DC, MC, V.*

SPA

Dar Ahlam. Set in the oasis of Skoura, 40 km (25 mi) east of Ouarzazate, Dar Ahlam (House of Dreams) is a renovated 19th-century Kasbah that offers a hammam, Jacuzzi, pool, and massages. ✉ *Douar Oulad Cheik Ali, Skoura* ☎ *024/85–22–39* 🕤 *Upon request..*

–Pamela Windo

starkly exposed in the garden, is a boon on dusty days. The staff can organize three-day mule trips to Telouet. Shorter, more-practical day trips are also available. **Pros:** Kitchen uses produce from its own garden, friendly staff. **Con:** Rooms on ground floor are depressing. ✉ *At far end of Aït Ben Haddou* ☎ *024/88–80–19* ⊕ *www.kasbahdujardin. com* 🛏 *15 rooms* 🔑 *In room: no a/c. In-hotel: pool, no elevator, parking (no fee)* 🖃 *No credit cards* ⦿| *MAP.*

$$$ 🏨 **La Kasbah.** Despite being a favorite of tour groups, this is a good choice because has stunning views of the Kasbah. It styles itself a "tourist complex," and has several restaurants, lovely terraces, and a pool that looks out over the city. The rooms in the new block (don't stay in the old block at any cost) are well appointed and decorated with nods to Berber style. You can also just stop for lunch (95 DH) or take a dip in the pool (50 DH for nonguests). **Pros:** Gorgeous pool, excellent restaurant, stunning views. **Con:** Lacks a personal touch. ✉ *Complexe Touristique, Aït Ben Haddou* ☎ *024/89–03–02* ⊕ *www.hotellakasbah. com* 🛏 *110 rooms* 🔑 *In-hotel: 3 restaurants, pool, laundry service, spa, no elevator* 🖃 *MC, V* ⦿| *MAP.*

$ 🏨 **Riad Maktoub.** Former photographer Abdellah Hassoun stumbled upon his Maktoub, or "destiny," when he found himself starting a small restaurant back in 2000. Since then he has added traditional Berber-style accommodations with comfortable beds, air-conditioning, and tiled bathrooms. Some of the larger suites have cozy fireplaces perfect for winter nights. There is a shaded terrace restaurant on the roadside and a large indoor restaurant with Berber motifs carved into earthen walls. The kitchen serves what is possibly the best chicken-and-lemon tagine in the village. Trekking with mules, bicycle rentals, and horseback-riding excursions can be organized for guests. **Pros:** Family-run business, attention to detail. **Con:** Remote location. ✉ *Ait Ben Haddou* ☎ *024/88–86–94* ⊕ *www.riadmaktoub.com* 🛏 *7 rooms, 12* *suites* ⚓*In-room: no TV (some). In-hotel: 3 restaurants, pool, bicycles, no elevator, parking (no fee)* ⊟*No credit cards* ⍟*MAP.*

SKOURA

★ *50 km (30 mi) southwest of El Kelaâ M'Gouna, 42 km (25 mi) northeast of Ouarzazate.*

Surprisingly lush and abrupt as it springs from the tawny landscape, Skoura deserves a lingering look for its Kasbahs and its rich concentration of date palms and olive, fig, and almond trees. Pathways tunnel through the vegetation from one Kasbah to another within this fertile island—a true oasis, perhaps the most intensely verdant in Morocco.

EXPLORING

With so many grand deep orange–hue and majestic Kasbahs in Skoura, a tour of the palmery is compulsory. The main Kasbah route through Skoura is approached from a point just over 2 km (1 mi) past the town center toward Ouarzazate. The 17th-century **Kasbah Ben Moro** is the first fortress on the right. The family next door is usually more than willing (for a small fee) to watch your car and guide you through the palmery, past the Sidi Aïssa *marabout* (shrine to a learned holy man). By the Amerhidil River is the tremendous **Kasbah Amerhidil,** the largest Kasbah in Skoura and one of the largest in Morocco.

Down the (usually bone-dry) river is another Kasbah, **Dar Aït Sidi el Mati,** while back near the Ouarzazate road is the **Kasbah el Kabbaba,** the last of the four fortresses on this loop. North of Skoura, on Route 6829 through Aït-Souss, are two other Kasbahs: **Dar Lahsoune,** a former Glaoui residence, and, a few minutes farther north, the **Kasbah Aït Ben Abou,** the second largest in Skoura after the Amerhidil.

WHERE TO STAY

$$$ ▦**Auberge Chez Talout.** Run by one of Morocco's friendliest hoteliers, this farmhouse is worth the trek for Talout's warm welcome, his wife's wonderful cooking, and the roof-terrace views across the palmery to Skoura's Kasbahs. The rooms are simple but homey, with traditional Berber clay sinks. Excursions to learn more about village crafts such as pottery and basket weaving are also available. **Pros:** Excellent cuisine, great for pottery lovers. **Con:** Hard to find. ✉*Oulad Aarbia, Skoura,* ✛*7 km (4.5 mi) before Skoura if coming from Ouarzazate, turn left off main road just after Idelssane* ☎*024/85–26–66 or 062/49–82–83* ⊕*www.talout.com* ➪*10 rooms* ⚓*In-hotel: restaurant, pool, public Internet* ⊟*No credit cards* ⍟*CP.*

$$$$ ▦**Dar Ahlam.** If money is no object, then consider a stay in this restored
Fodor'sChoice Kasbah, Morocco's most exclusive and sumptuous hideaway. Without
★ a signpost in sight, you have to know about this Relais & Chateaux property to find it. Each stunning suite takes up an entire side of the building, and an adjoining riad offers every last pampering treatment you could imagine, including an olfactory chamber with smells flown in from a Parisian parfumeur. Meals are served whenever you like, and never with other guests. The dining area changes nightly, so in the

company of glorious food, petals, and candles, you can discover different parts of the Kasbah with each passing day. For a stunning, secret overnight among the dunes there's also a permanent luxury camp in the desert at El Khiam Ahlam. Nonguests are welcome for lunch, but must phone in advance to reserve. **Pros:** Heavenly accommodations, pampering beyond your wildest dreams. **Con:** It's well beyond the reach of most mortals. ⊠*Kasbah Madihi, Skoura Palmery* ☎*024/85–22–39* ⊕*www.darahlam.com* ⊷*9 suites, 3 villas* ⚿*In room: no telephone, no TV. In-hotel: restaurant pool, spa, laundry service, public Internet, public Wi-Fi, no elevator, parking (no fee)* ⊟*AE, MC, V* ⦿*AI.*

$$$$ ▥ **Les Jardins de Skoura.** Styling itself as a *"maison de repos,"* this
☺ restored farmhouse throws such a charm over guests that many of them find it difficult to leave, staying on for days in its warm, lazy embrace. The laid-back feel disguises an incredible attention to detail; each room and suite was individually designed under French owner Carole's watchful eye. Extensive gardens, slung with the odd hammock and Berber tent, offer unlimited distraction for younger visitors, while for adults, doing nothing has rarely felt so worthy. **Pros:** Idyllic surroundings, excellent facilities. **Con:** May be too isolated for some. ⊠*Skoura Palmery, 45000* ⊕*2 km (1 mi) before Skoura (from direction of Ouarzazate), and after passing Kasbah Aït Ben Moro follow yellow arrow signs for left turn, additional 4 km (2.5 mi) of track to get to house* ☎*024/85–23–24* ⊕*www.lesjardinsdeskoura.com* ⊷*5 rooms, 3 suites* ⚿*In-hotel: pool, hammam, spa, no elevator* ⊟*No credit cards* ⦾*Closed end of June* ⦿*CP.*

$$$–$$$$ ▥ **Kasbah Aït Ben Moro.** This stunning pisé Kasbah is a 17th-century
★ desert castle that overlooks the palmery, the Kasbah Amerhidil, and the High Atlas Mountains. Amid lush gardens and handsome fortress walls, the hotel has simple, cozy rooms tucked into the Kasbah's turrets. The restaurant serves fine Moroccan and international cuisine based on local and imported products (including fresh fish from Agadir during winter months), and has a fully licensed bar. Although rooms do not have modern air-conditioning, the ancient pisé structures are naturally cool in summer and warm in winter. The staff can arrange for cycling tours of the local area, buggy rentals, and horse and camel treks. It's also a great lunch stop. Book ahead. **Pros:** Splendid terraces, rooms are in a Kasbah. **Con:** Restaurant lacks charm. ⊠*Douar Taskoukamte, Rte. P32, 38 km (23 mi) east of Ouarzazate, Skoura* ☎*024/85–21–16* ⊕*www.aitbenmoro.com* ⊷*16 rooms, 13 with bath* ⚿*In room: no a/c, no phone, no TV. In-hotel: restaurant, bar, pool, public Internet, no elevator* ⊟*MC, V* ⦾*Closed July* ⦿*MAP.*

OUTDOOR ACTIVITIES

On the way into Skoura, about 35 km (22 mi) from Ouarzazate and before Kasbah Aït Ben Moro, look out for signs on your left to **X.trem Explorer** (☎*066/43–53–77* ⊕ *www.darikram.net*). Here you can rent buggies from 300 DH an hour and drive them around the sands, palms, and Kasbahs.

EL KELÂA M'GOUNA

24 km (13 mi) southwest of Boumalne du Dadès, 92 km (57 mi) northeast of Ouarzazate.

Between Kelâa M'Gouna and Boumalne du Dadès stretches the region known as the Valley of the Roses. It is in fact a confluence of several valleys that meet at the village of Bou Thaghrar. The local Berber population cultivates the Rosa Damascena on the slopes of the High Atlas, and the richness of the soil boosts the pigment of the blooms. The town of Kelâa M'Gouna is known for its annual three-day Rose Festival held each May, when the roses are in full bloom.

Throughout the drive from Kelâa M'Gouna to Boumalne du Dadès (N10) you'll see thousands of small pink Persian blossoms dividing the fields and fringing the highway. To reach the terraced rose gardens of the Valley of the Roses, take the signposted route north from Kelâa M'Gouna as far as Bou Thaghrar. From there you have to proceed on foot. Guides are essential and can be found in Bou Thaghrar for about 250 DH per day.

GETTING HERE & AROUND

Kelâa M'Gouna is on the main route from Ouarzazate to Boumalne du Dadès and is served by buses and grands taxis from both directions. The route N10 is a principal road and is easily navigable. There are minibuses in Kelâa M'Gouna for tourists visiting the Valley of the Roses.

TIMING & PRECAUTIONS

A trip to explore the Valley of the Roses can take anything from a day to a week, depending on how much hiking you want to do. The best time to plan a visit is for the Rose Festival held at harvest time in May. On Wednesday there is a lively local souk.

ESSENTIALS

Currency Exchange Banque Populaire (✉ *Bd. Mohammed V, Kelâa M'Gouna* ☎ *024/83-61-51*).

Visitor & Tour Info Bureau des Guides et Accompagnateurs (✉ *B.P. 393, Zaouiat Aguerde, Kelâa M'Gouna* ☎ *024/83-73-71 or 024/83-73-72*).

WHERE TO EAT & STAY

$ ✕ **Les Arcades.** A simple restaurant frequented by the locals, Les Arcades MOROCCAN serves tasty salads, brochettes, and tagines. Set back from the main road in a small square, it sits next door to an intriguing spice shop. The canopy of plastic flowers might be a bit tacky, but for a relaxed light lunch or dinner you can't go wrong. ✉ *Bd. Mohammed V, Kelâa M'Gouna* ☎ *024/83-66-76* ▭ *No credit cards.*

$$$ ⌂ **Hotel Ksar Kaissar.** On an expansive piece of property near the town of Kelâa M'Gouna sits the Hotel Ksar Kaissar. This recently built Kas-

bah offers an excellent range of accommodation at reasonable prices. Rooms are sumptuous, and the reception areas and *salon de thé* are cool and elegant. For families, the most unusual and appealing accommodations are the troglodyte rooms, excavated out of the hillside to create spaces that will keep you cool in summer and toasty in winter. The hotel restaurant serves traditional Berber cuisine and alcoholic beverages. There's a massive garden to explore and a magnificent swimming pool. **Pro:** Ideal for families. **Con:** Can feel impersonal. ⊠*Km 1, Rte. de Kelâa M'Gouna* ☎*024/83–67–76* ⊕*www.ksarkaissar.com* ⇆*110 rooms, 4 suites* ⌂*In-room: no a/c (some), no phone, (some), no TV (some). In-hotel: restaurant, room service, bars, pool, no elevator, parking (no fee)* ▭ *MC, V* ⦿*CP.*

$$–$$$
Fodor'sChoice
★

▦**Kasbah Itran.** This small outfit could be the younger and less well-known brother of the High Atlas's Kasbah du Toubkal. Its location, perched on the edge of a cliff overlooking the Valley of the Roses, is equally stupendous, but more easily accessible. Inside its stone walls is an exceptionally cozy warren of colorful, tasteful rooms and terraces, all suffused with incense, smoke, and cinnamon from the kitchen. The Taghda brothers, whose knowledge of the rose valley is legendary, can organize all manner of tours, on foot, four legs, or four wheels. **Pros:** Stunning views of the valley, atmospheric rooms. **Con:** English-speaking staff not always on hand. ⊠*Box 124, Kelâa M'Gouna,* ⊹*4 km (2.5 mi) from Kelâa M'Gouna* ☎*024/83–71–03* ⊕*www.kasbahitran.com* ⇆*9 rooms, 5 with bath* ⌂ *In-room: no a/c, no phone, no TV. In-hotel: restaurant, no elevator, parking (no fee)* ▭ *No credit cards* ⦿*CP.*

OUTDOOR ACTIVITIES

Abdelaaziz (☎*062/13–21–92 or 024/83–73–71*) runs walking tours of the underexplored Valley of Roses. He also has a Kasbah up in the mountains and staffs the guide office in Kelâa M'Gouna.

THE DADÈS & TODRA GORGES

The drive through Morocco's smaller versions of the Grand Canyon is stunning, and the area merits several days' exploration. The Dadès Gorge is frequented more by independent travelers than tours, while the Todra is much more about mass-organized tourism. So many buses stop at the most beautiful point that you almost forget it's supposed to be beautiful. If you avoid lunchtime (when all the tour buses disgorge), however, and venture on, there are some great walks and lovely spots where you can feel much more alone.

THE DADÈS GORGE

Boumalne du Dadès is 53 km (31 mi) southwest of Tinerhir, 116 km (70 mi) northeast of Ouarzazate.

GETTING HERE & AROUND

The easiest access point for the Dadès Gorge is the town of Boumalne du Dadès. The N10 brings you here from Ouarzazate in the west or Er-Rachidia in the east. Buses frequent this route. The road through the gorge itself is paved as far as Msemrir. Beyond Msemrir requires a four-wheel-drive vehicle, and even then only if conditions are right. The piste routes can be treacherous, especially during the rainy season between December and February. If you do not have your own transport, grands taxis from Boulmane du Dadès will take you on the scenic drive.

TIMING & PRECAUTIONS

The Dadès Gorge is beautiful all year. In summer the steep canyon walls and rushing rivers are refreshing after the heat of the desert. In winter, however, the region gets considerable rainfall that makes the pistes impassable. Always ensure you have a full tank of gas, a spare tire, and plenty of water if embarking on cross-country routes.

ESSENTIALS

Bus Contacts **Compagnie de Transports Marocains** (⊠*Ave. Mohammed V*).

Currency Exchange **Banque Populaire** (⊠ *Ave. Mohammed V* ☎*024/80–86–23*).

Medical Assistance **Pharmacie du Dadès** (⊠*Ave. Mohammed V* ☎*024/80–76–83*).

Visitor & Tour Info **Bureau des Guides a Boumalne Dadès** (⊠*West end of Ave. Mohammed V* ☎*067/59-32-92*).

EXPLORING

The town of **Boumalne du Dadès** marks the southern entrance to the Dadès Gorge, which is even more beautiful—longer, wider, and more varied—than its sister, the Todra Gorge. The 63 km (38 mi) of the Dadès Gorge, from Boumalne through Aït Ali and on to Msemrir, are paved and approachable in any kind of vehicle. Beyond that are some great rocky mountain roads for four-wheel-drive vehicles with good clearance. Boumalne itself is only of moderate interest, though the central market square is a good vantage point for a perusal of local life. The shops Artisanale de Boumalne and Maison Aït Atta merit a browse for their local products at local prices, particularly rosewood carvings and rosewater.

The lower Dadès Gorge and the Dadès River, which flows through it, are lined with thick vegetation. While the Todra has its lush date palmery, the Dadès has figs, almonds, Atlas pistachio, and carob trees. A series of Kasbahs and ksour (plural of ksar, or fortified house) give way to Berber villages such as Aït Youl, Aït Arbi, Aït Ali, Aït Oudinar, and Aït Toukhsine—*Aït* meaning "of the family" in the Tamazight Berber language. Two kilometers (1 mi) up the road from Boumalne is the **Glaoui Kasbah,** once part of the empire of the infamous pasha of Marrakesh, T'hami el-Glaoui. The ksour at **Aït Arbi** are tucked neatly into the surrounding volcanic rock 3 km (2 mi) farther on from Glaoui Kasbah. Ten kilometers (6 mi) from Aït Arbi is the **Tamnalt Valley,** the "Valley of the Human Bodies," where the eroded rock formations seem curiously organic, like soles of feet or elephant hides. Just as you enter the Tamnalt Valley, the Café-Restaurant Meguirne appears, offering panoramic views, good meals, and several rooms; a few minutes' north is the Auberge Gorges du Dadès, another option for a temporary halt, an exploration of the river, or an overnight stay.

After Aït Oudinar, where most of the lodging options are clustered, the road crosses a bridge and gets substantially more exciting and empty, and the valley narrows dramatically, opening up around the corner into some of the most dramatic views in the Dadès. Six kilometers (4 mi) north of the bridge are three little inns, the best of which is the Kasbah de la Vallée, offering different levels of comfort ranging from tent to terrace to rooms with bath.

Aït Hammou is the next village, 5 km (3 mi) past the Kasbah de la Vallée. It makes a good base camp for walking and climbing north to vantage points over the Dadès River or, to the east, to a well-known cave with stalactites (ask the Hotel la Kasbah de la Vallée for directions). At the top of the gorges is **Msemrir,** a village of red-clay pisé ksour that has a café with guest rooms. To go farther from Msemrir, you'll need four-wheel drive to follow the road that leads north over the High Atlas through Tilmi, the Tizi-n-Ouano Pass, and Agoudal to Imilchil and eventually up to Route P24 (N8), the Marrakesh–Fez road. The road east climbs the difficult Route 3444, always bearing right, to another gorge-top town, Tamtattouchte. It makes for a great off-road drive.

WHERE TO EAT

$$$–$$$$ ✕**Chez Pierre.** This Belgian-run operation is chicest spot in the gorges.
MOROCCAN Many travelers stop at this French-Moroccan restaurant, which serves
★ some of the best food in the area (255 DH per person for three courses), including cheese grilled with honey and apples (45 DH) and *briouates* (spicy dumplings) with mint leaves (45 DH). ⊠ *Aït Oufi* ☎ *024/83–02–67* ⊕ *www.chezpierre.ifrance.com* ▤ *No credit cards* ⊙ *Closed June, July, and Nov. 15–Feb. 15.*

WHERE TO STAY

$ ▦ **Auberge des Gorges de Dadès.** The Berber designs that adorn the walls give this spacious hotel an Andean feel well suited to the surrounding scenery. Ideal for a clientele made up predominantly of small groups, it has the reassuring feel of a mountain lodge. The restaurant serves up large portions without setting taste buds on fire, but the hotel's real strength is as a base for organizing walking tours in and around the valley. **Pro:** Ideal for trekkers. **Con:** Lacks charm of smaller auberges. ⊠ *Aït Oudinar* ⊹ *27 km (16 mi) north of Boumalne* ☎ *024/83–01–53* ⊕ *www.aubergeaitoudinar.com* ⯆ *30 rooms* ⯅ *In-hotel: restaurant, no elevator* ▤ *MC, V* ⧖⊙ *MAP.*

$$ ▦ **Hôtel la Kasbah de la Vallée.** Halfway between Boumalne and Msemrir, the hotel overlooks one of the most dramatic parts of the canyon. Rooms are decked out in a modern style that is more functional than beautiful—ask for one that looks across the narrow valley—while the main areas are traditional Moroccan. It's also a hot spot in the evening, when nonguests return from a day's bushwhacking, thirsty for a beer. The outdoor terrace is difficult to beat. The hotel also does one of the best breakfasts in the valley, serving wonderfully eggy Moroccan bread, inspired by the owner's 10 years in New York. **Pros:** Owners have in-

depth knowledge of area, plenty of activities. **Con:** Feels a bit "municipal." ⊠*Aït Oufi* ✛*27 km (16 mi) north of Boumalne* ☎*024/83–17–17* ⊕*www.kasbah-vallee-dades.com* ⟲*42 rooms* ⚿*In room: no a/c (some), no telephone, no TV. In-hotel: restaurant, bar, public Wi-Fi, no elevator* ▤*MC, V* ⏁⃝*MAP.*

$$ \quad $$

\$\$ ⊡ **Hotel Source de Dadès.** Situated at exactly the point where the gorge narrows dramatically, this tiny place has one of the best locations in the valley. Rooms are cozy and management is friendly and welcoming. **Pros:** Great location, helpful staff. **Con:** Rooms are small. ⊠*Km 33 from Boumalne* ☎*024/83–12–58* ⟲*4 rooms* ⚿*In room: no a/c, no telephone, no TV. In-hotel: restaurant, no elevator, parking (no fee)* ▤*No credit cards* ⏁⃝*MAP.*

¢ ⊡ **Kasbah des Roches.** Set in well-tended gardens, this simple guesthouse run by Lahcen and Lucia is filled with laid-back ease. It's also away from the relative throng of Aït Oudinar, a little farther north on the right, near the rocks after which it is named. Meals are tasty and traditional—don't miss the *gallia*, a Berber specialty with a plate of stewed vegetables. Walking trips can be arranged (100 DH for two hours, 200 DH for five hours). A night in a camp with nomads is 250 DH with mules, and a walking picnic is 250 DH. **Pros:** Lovely terrace, great views. **Con:** Rooms a little sparse. ⊠*Rte. R704* ✛*32 km (20 mi) north of Boumalne du Dadès* ☎*024/83–12-57* ⟲*5 rooms, 3 with bath* ⚿*In-room: no a/c, no telephone, no TV. In-hotel: restaurant, no elevator, parking (no fee)* ▤*No credit cards* ⏁⃝*CP.*

OUTDOOR ACTIVITIES

Mohamed Amgom (☎*066/59–41–42*) is an experienced local Berber guide who can organize treks throughout the Dadès Valley for 400 DH. He can also organize four-wheel-drive vehicles for excursions throughout the Dadès and Todra gorges. He frequently works with the Chez Pierre guesthouse. You can also arrange three- to five-hour walks into the gorge (200 DH–250 DH for a guide) with Auberge Tissadrine (☎*024/83–17–45*).

THE TODRA GORGE

194 km (107 mi) northwest of Rissani, 184 km (101 mi) northeast of Ouarzazate.

GETTING HERE & AROUND

The town of Tinerhir (also spelled "Tinghir") is the most convenient access point for visiting the Todra Gorge. It sits on the main N10 route from Ouarzazate and Er-Rachidia. To reach the gorge, take route R703 (3445) north toward Tamtattouchte and follow the riverbed upwards for about 15 km (9 mi). The lush date palmery and rugged landscape change dramatically when steep walls of the gorge and glacial waters begin to tower above and block out the sunshine.

7

GREAT DRIVES: TODRA GORGES

If you have a four-wheel-drive vehicle with good clearance, you can take the adventurous route from the top of the Todra Gorge: pop over into the Dadès Gorge by the difficult but passable Route 3444 from Aït Hani (first village after Tamtattouchte) to **Msemrir.** (If you try this by jeep, take the second left after Tamtattouchte up a steep incline. Go right at the first fork, left at the second fork, and right at the third fork. Travel 6 km (4 mi) to the next fork, where you take the road on the left. From there it's a slow 45 km (28 mi) to Msemrir. (Disregard signs and markers, which will have been falsely rigged by the local hustlers.)

Hikers in top condition can do this as well, forming an ideal five- or six-day walk up the Todra and over to, down, and out the Dadès Gorge, including one night camping between Tamtattouchte and Msemrir.

Other four-wheel-drive options include continuing north to Agoudal and **Imilchil** (see Chapter 4), or heading east through Aït Hani, Tiidrine, and Assoul to Rich, a tortuous but stunningly beautiful route on which you ford several (shallow) rivers and see no one except Berber villagers and the occasional nomad.

■TIP→**Watch out for the children of Aït Hani, who have marked up their town with bogus road signs. They'll attempt to climb aboard your vehicle and, for a price, "direct" you on your way.**

Long-distance buses travel here from Agadir, Casablanca, Marrakesh, Fez, Meknès, and Rabat. Buses also arrive from Ouarzazate (5 hours), Er-Rachidia (3 hours), and Erfoud (4 hours). Most buses stop on Avenue Mohammed V, on the northern side of the main square. The **Compagnie de Transports Marocains office** is on the southwestern corner of the square on the corner of Avenue Hassan II. If you don't have your own vehicle, you can catch a grand taxi to take you up through the Todra palmery as far as the Todra Gorge. The drive takes about 30 minutes and should cost about 20 DH per person. There are also minibuses that transport locals to the villages above the Todra Gorge. You can ask to be dropped off at the gorge.

TIMING & PRECAUTIONS
The steep sides of the gorge can often mean that the route through the gorge itself is in shade, but the effect of angled sunlight shifting across the rock face during the day creates a spectacular sublime canvas of red and orange. Mid- to late afternoon is deemed the best time to visit.

ESSENTIALS
Currency Exchange Banque Populaire (⊠ Ave. Mohammed V ☎ 024/89–41–38). BMCE (⊠ Ave. Mohammed V ☎ 024/87–06–94).

Medical Assistance Pharmacie Todra (⊠ Ave. Mohammed V ☎ 024/83–41–66).

Post Office Poste Maroc (⊠ Ave. Hassan II).

EXPLORING

The 15-km (9-mi) drive up from Tinerhir to the beginning of the Todra Gorge will take you through lush but slender palmeries, sometimes no wider than 100 feet from cliff to cliff. An inn and a café await near the spring, but you're better off not stopping, as the site itself isn't remarkable, and the concentration of hustlers and overhelpful children is dense.

> ### FISHY FOLKLORE
>
> La Source des Poissons Sacrés (Springs of the Sacred Fish), about halfway to the beginning of the gorge, is so named for the miracle performed by a sage, said to have struck a rock once to produce a gushing spring, and twice to produce fish.

The 66-foot-wide entrance to the Todra Gorge, with its roaring clear stream and its 1,000-foot-high rock walls stretching 325 feet back on either side, is the most stunning feature of the whole canyon, though the upper reaches aren't far behind. The farther off the beaten path you get, the more rewarding the scenery; a walk or drive up through the gorge on paved roads to Tamtattouchte is particularly recommended.

From the thin palmery along the bottom, the walls of the Todra Gorge remain close and high for some 18 km (11 mi), dappled only with occasional families of nomads and their black khaimas (tents) tending sheep, goats, or camels (dromedaries) up on the rocks. Colorfully attired young Berber shepherdesses may appear from nowhere; sometimes you can hear them singing Berber melodies from high in the crags, their sounds echoed and amplified by the rock walls of the canyon. Eagles nest in the Todra, along with choughs (red-beaked rooks), rock doves, and blue rock thrushes.

WHERE TO STAY

$ **Auberge Baddou.** Once your eyes have recovered from the garish electric pink of this faux-Kasbah, the brightness and the spotless rooms are real selling points. The restaurant serves creditable tagines, mechoui, and other specialties if you order far enough ahead. Owner Ahmed Abaz organizes hiking and four-wheel-drive excursions and serves as a general outfitter and adviser to travelers in the upper Todra Gorge. After a grueling day of activities, unwind with a gin and tonic on the roof, after hauling it up on the ingenious dumbwaiter. On a tight budget? Sleep in a nomad tent for around 30 DH per person. *The hotel is 30 km (19 mi) north from Tinerhir.* **Pros:** One of few liquor licenses in area, spotless rooms. **Con:** Eye strain from hot-pink exterior. ⊠*Douar Tamtattouchte* ☎*072/52–13–89* ⊕*www.aubergebaddou.com* ⊅*13 rooms, 6 with bath* ⚭*In-room: no a/c. In-hotel: restaurant, bar, no elevator* ⊟*No credit cards.*

$$ **Dar Ayour.** Tucked down an alley just before the Todra Gorge is this guesthouse. Dar Ayour is perched on the edge of the Dadès River, with its own garden of fig, olive, and palm trees. The scent of incense creates an exotic feel as you enter the house or wander to the lantern-lighted roof terrace overlooking the towering canyon walls. There is a comfortable restaurant and salon where you can stretch out on handmade cushions and listen to the chatter of birds. The snug rooms are taste-

fully outfitted with rustic furniture and woven mats. Painting courses run by a local French artist and rock-climbing excursions can also be organized by owner Adnan Majdoubi. **Pros:** Peaceful setting, lovely garden. **Con:** Not much parking. ✉️*Rte. des Gorges de Todra, Tinerhir* ☎️*024/89–52–71 or 072/52–12–51* ⊕*www.darayour.com* ☞*7 rooms, 2 suites* ⚸*In-room: no a/c, no phone (some), no TV. In-hotel: restaurant, no elevator, laundry facilities, public Internet* ▭*MC, V* ☽⃝*BP.*

$$ ⊡ **Le Festival.** Made from the same mountain rock that surrounds it,
Fodor's Choice this hotel is a much beloved addition to the gorge. Owned and run by
★ the charming Addi Sror, who speaks excellent English, the rooms are simple but the stay magical. The best bit is that it's the only building in sight, just a few kilometers past the gorge, with great mountain views in every direction. The kitchen offers an à la carte menu for guests and nonguests alike, with mechoui, curry chicken, and a great range of salads. Bring your own liquor. You can also take wonderful local walks through the nomadic lands. Recently added are five atmospheric caves hewn from the mountainside and four turret rooms with balcony. Trekking, climbing, and bike rides are organized also. **Pros:** Made of gorgeous stone, great meals. **Con:** Not all rooms have bathrooms. ✉️*5 km (3 mi) north of the Todra Gorge, 12 km (7 mi) south of Tamtattouchte* ☎️*061/26–72–51* ⊕*www.aubergelefestival.com* ☞*15 rooms* ⚸*In-hotel: restaurant, bicycles, no elevator* ▭*No credit cards* ☽⃝*MAP.*

$ ⊡ **Hôtel Yasmina.** The closest hotel to the gorge is almost too close, and is choked with buses for most of the day. Most people come only for group lunches, however, so if you stay the night you'll have it much more to yourself. The hotel itself, designed in the 1950s, is more than adequate. Rooms 26 and 27 are among the best—they overlook the stream and the entrance to the gorge. The restaurant prepares creditable Moroccan fare; no wine is served, but you can bring your own. The hotel can also arrange a series of guided tours throughout the region, including to the top of the gorge. **Pros:** It's right on the gorge, good place to book tours. **Con:** Filled with tour groups. ✉️*B.P. 29, Gorges du Todra, Tinerhir* ☎️*024/89–51–18* ⊕*www.hotelyasmina.ma* ☞*48 rooms* ⚸*In room: no a/c. In-hotel: restaurant, laundry facilities* ▭*MC, V* ☽⃝*CP*

TO MERZOUGA & THE DUNES

This particular southeastern corner holds some of Morocco's greatest sights, principally the Sahara's picture-perfect undulating dunes near Merzouga, and the Tafilalt date palmery. It's best to avoid Er-Rachidia, a colonial town with little to offer, and even Erfoud, too, if possible, as it's full of touts. Now that the road to Merzouga is completely paved, you can drive straight there without stopping.

ERFOUD

81 km (49 mi) south of Er-Rachidia, 300 km (180 mi) northeast of Ouarzazate.

GETTING HERE & AROUND

Erfoud sits at the southern end of the Ziz Oasis. From the north, the only way here is the N13 via Er-Rachidia. From Ouarzazate, take the N10 and turn onto the R702 just after the village of Tinejdad, and onto the R702. This direct route avoids Er-Rachidia.

Buses to Erfoud depart from Er-Rachidia (1½ hours), Fez (11 hours), Rissani (1½ hours), and Tinerhir (3½ hours). From Er-Rachidia you can take buses to Ouarzazate, Marrakesh, Midelt, and Meknès. The **Compagnie de Transports Marocains** bus station in Erfoud is located on Avenue Mohammed V.

TIMING & PRECAUTIONS

The biggest event of the year is the annual Erfoud Date Festival, coinciding with the date harvest in October.

ESSENTIALS

Bus Contacts **Compagnie de Transports Marocains** (⊠ *Ave. Mohammed V*).

Currency Exchange **BMCE** (⊠ *Ave. Moulay Ismaile* ☎ *035/53–02–84*).

Medical Assistance **Hopital Erfoud** (⊠ *Ave. Moulay Ismail*).

Post Office **Poste Maroc** (⊠ *Aves. Moulay Ismail and Mahammed V*).

EXPLORING

A French administrative outpost and Foreign Legion stronghold, this frontier town on the Algerian border has a definite Wild West (in this case, Wild South) feel to it. The military fortress at Borj-Est, just across the Ziz to the east, provides the best possible view over the date palmery, the desert, and Erfoud from its altitude of 3,067 feet above sea level. Between Borj-Est and the Auberge Kasbah Derkaoua are quarries famous for their black marble, one of Erfoud's principal products; interestingly, this luxurious solid is rich in petrified marine fossils.

Erfoud itself is not without its peculiar charm, though this dusty, fly-bitten border post is best known as a traveler's jumping-off point for the Merzouga Dunes. Its finest architectural feature is the main gate into the medina, designed in the typical Almohad style with flanking crenellated bastions and an intricately carved stucco portal.

WHERE TO STAY

$$$$ 🏨 **Auberge Kasbah Derkaoua.** This lovely lodging sits at the edge of the desert, a half hour's drive from the Merzouga Dunes. Michel Auzat (who once served in the French army's camel corps) and his daughter, Bouchra, serve excellent Moroccan and French cuisine and offer well-designed accommodations of various kinds. To find the auberge, which is 24 km (14 mi) southeast of Erfoud, follow signs for DUNES SABLES D'OR. Don't be surprised when you find yourself driving across the Ziz River—this is not a mirage, but a dam *over* which, in early spring, the river flows at a depth of an inch or two. Once the pavement ends, follow the green-and-white markers. **Pros:** Splendid food, expert local knowledge. **Con:** Difficult to find. ⌂ *C/o Michel Auzat, Erfoud* ☎ *035/57–71–40* ⊕ *www.aubergederkaoua.com* ↝ *11 rooms, 2 bungalows, 2 tents, 1 apartment* ♿ *In-hotel: restaurant, tennis court, pool* ☰ *AE, DC, MC, V* ⊘ *Closed Jan., July, and Aug.* ℗ *MAP.*

$$$$ ⊞ **Kasbah Xaluca.** Constructed using authentic methods, this hotel is much beloved for its rustic charm. Rooms have twin beds that can be joined together, and the bathrooms have basins made of 350-million-year-old fossilized marble. The evening buffet has a tempting range of Moroccan and international dishes, so the half-board option is well worth considering. In addition to camel treks and four-wheel-drive journeys into the desert dunes, you can rent quad bikes and motorbikes. **Pros:** Pretty pool area, attentive service. **Con:** Distance from dunes. ⊕ *5 km (3 mi) out of Erfoud on way to Er-Rachidia* ☎ *035/57–84–50 or 061/25–13–94* ⊕ *www.xaluca.com* ↝ *110 rooms, 24 suites, 8 bungalows* ♿ *In room: refrigerator. In-hotel: 2 restaurants, bar, pools, tennis court , no elevator, public Wi-Fi* ☰ *No credit cards* ℗ *CP.*

RISSANI

17 km (11 mi) south of Erfoud, 40 km (24 mi) northwest of Merzouga.

Rissani stands on the site of the ancient city of Sijilmassa, Morocco's first independent southern kingdom, which thrived here from the 8th to the 14th century. Founded in 757 by dissident Berbers, who had committed the heresy of translating the Koran to the Berber language (Islamic orthodoxy forbids translation from the Arabic of the direct revelations of God), Sijilmassa and the Filalis, as they were known, prospered from the natural wealth of the Tafilalt oasis and the Tafilalt's key role on the Salt Road to West Africa. Sijilmassa was almost completely destroyed in civil strife in 1393; archaeological excavations are now attempting to determine the city's size and configuration. All that remains of Sijilmassa today is the excellent 13th-century gate Bab Errih, notable for the green ceramic-tile frieze over its three horseshoe arches.

GETTING HERE & AROUND

There are two main routes into Rissani, the N12 from Tazzarine (west) or the N13 from Erfoud (north). Buses arrive from Erfoud (1½ hours), Er-Rachidia (3 hours), Meknès (8 hours), Tinejdad (3½ hours), Tinerhir (4 hours), and Zagora (10 hours). Grands taxis run to Erfoud and Merzouga. Compagnie de Transports Marocains buses operate from the main square, while other companies use the new station just outside the arched entrance to the town.

TIMING & PRECAUTIONS

Rissani hosts a souk on Sunday, Tuesday, and Thursday.

EXPLORING

Modern Rissani is known as the cradle of the Alaouite dynasty, of which King Mohammed VI is the still-reigning sultan. The well-marked Circuit Touristique guides you through the main remnants of the Alaouite presence here. The **Zaouia of Moulay Ali Sherif**, the mausoleum of the dynasty's founder, is 2 km (1 mi) southeast of the center of Rissani. Next to the zaouia is the **Ksar Akbar**, to which rebellious Alaouite family members and the wives of deceased sultans were exiled. Moulay Ismail had two of his sons sent here to put some distance between his heirs and his power base at Meknès. The **Ksar Oualad Abdelhalim**, the largest and most impressive of these Alaouite structures, is 1 km (0.5 mi) beyond Ksar Akbar; it was built in 1900 for Sultan Moulay el Hassan's older brother, who had been named governor of Tafilalt. After Ksar Oualad Abdelhalim, loop around past the remaining ksour and climb the high ground at **Tinrheras**, correctly marked on the Michelin 959 map as an excellent lookout point over the Tafilalt.

The drive back north from Merzouga through Rissani brings you to the **Tafilalt date palmery.** The presence of a million-plus date palms here seems doubly miraculous after you have seen the desert. The palmery is a phenomenon created by the parallel Ziz and Rheris rivers, which flow within 3 km–5 km (2 mi–3 mi) of each other for 26 km (16 mi).

> ## LIKE A LOCAL
>
> Here's how to navigate Rissani without resorting to outside assistance. On the approach to Rissani from Erfoud is the first of two gates. Just afterward, follow the road as it curves left; don't take a right-hand fork for the "Circuit Touristique." You'll quickly reach town, at which point you'll go under a second arch. Ahead are the walls of the Kasbah. Turn right so that they are on your left, and follow them until the road ends in a T-junction. Turn left, and you should be on the road that winds through the palmery and leads, eventually, to the dunes.

7

WHERE TO STAY

$$$ 🏨 **Kasbah Ennasra.** Constructed using traditional materials and designs, the Kasbah Ennasra has a laid-back charm. It is one of few hotels in the area offering meals for passing travelers. The pool facilities are also available for nonresidents. Rooms in the hotel are charming and spacious, and some have huge four-poster beds. **Pro:** Plenty of activities. **Con:** Far from the dunes. ⊠*B.P. 167, Ksar Labtarni, Rte. de Rissani, 2 km (1 mi) north of Rissani , Er-Rachidia* ☎*035/77–44–03* ⊕*www.kasbahennasra.com* ⬥*13 rooms, 2 suites* ⚒*In-room: no phone, no TV (some), Wi-Fi (some). In-hotel: restaurant, bar, pool, no elevator, public Internet, public Wi-Fi* ▭*MC, V* ⧖*BP.*

MERZOUGA

53 km (32 mi) southeast of Erfoud, 134 km (83 mi) southeast of Er-Rachidia.

A sunrise trip to Erg Chebbi has become a classic Moroccan adventure. A series of café-restaurant-hotels overlooks the dunes, and most run camel excursions out to the top of the dunes, a 45-minute walk on foot, and to oases where you can camp for the night in permanent bivouacs.

GETTING HERE & AROUND

The N13 from Erfoud can now be driven in an ordinary car. Minibuses and grands taxis bring tourists from Rissani and Erfoud.

Adventures with Ali, run by Ali Mouni, has all-inclusive tours into the desert. Blue Men of Morocco runs tours from an ecotourist lodge near the Merzouga Dunes in Hassi Labied. Les Petales de Merzouga Maroc rents bikes and four-wheel-drive vehicles and arranges camel treks

TIMING & PRECAUTIONS

Temperature can soar in summer, so always have plenty of bottled water, sunglasses, and sunblock. In winter the nights can be viciously cold, so be prepared with extra layers if camping out. ■TIP➡The fine sand of the Sahara will find its way into everything. Carry sealable plastic bags for keeping items sand-free, especially electronic equipment and cosmetics.

ESSENTIALS

Visitor & Tour Info Adventures with Ali (✉ *Merzouga* ☎ *061/56–36–11* ⊕ *www. adventureswithali.com*). **Blue Men of Morocco Company** (✉ *B.P.17, 52202, Hassi LabiedMerzouga* ☎ *035/57–72–89* ⊕ *www.bluemenofmorocco.com*). **Les Petales de Merzouga Maroc** (✉ *On left as you approach Merzouga* ☎ *015/05–63–89* ⊕ *www.quadmaroc.net*).

EXPLORING

Fodor'sChoice
★

In most cases your hotel is your best bet for an organized tour of **Erg Chebbi**. Every auberge near the dunes is there because it's the best jumping-off point for a sunrise or sunset journey into the dunes, either on foot or by camel. Most auberges have their own permanent bivouac in the dunes, often not far from others but generally fairly well concealed, so you can pretend no one else is around even if they are. Most bivouac areas are organized into series of small tents for couples and larger groups, so you don't have to share with everyone. If you want to be utterly private, make sure your auberge doesn't share a tented site with any other, or ask to camp in the dunes on your own.

For anything more than camel-riding and staying in a desert oasis, such as quad-biking, you'll need to go to the right hotel (Tombuctou rents quads) or a local rental agent. Most auberges can get their hands on a four-wheel drive, even if they don't always have them on-site.

Near the dunes, the seasonal salt lake **Dayet Sjri** is a surprising sight and is filled in early spring with pink flamingos. The village of Merzouga itself has little to recommend it other than a few not-too-compelling but survivable hotels. Between Erg Chebbi and the town, have a look at the underground aqueduct, Merzouga's main water supply. It's flowing (oozing) proof that sand dunes form as a result of moisture, which causes the sand to stick and agglomerate. The dune at Merzouga towers at more than 815 feet over the surrounding desert.

WHERE TO STAY

There are few decent options in Merzouga. The best places are north of Merzouga in the desert village Hassi Labied; these also benefit from being closest to the towering sands.

$$ 🔲 **Auberge Atlas du Sable/Ali "El Cojo."** A peg-legged camel is the logo for his simple auberge, named for Spanish-speaking owner Ali Anaam. He himself is missing a leg, but that doesn't get in his way. He and his brothers arrange camel, quad, and four-wheel-drive outings. Besides the large and inexpensive auberge in Hassi Labied, there's also a nomad camp in the dunes. Guests can bring their own wine or beer. **Pros:** Reasonably priced, all the necessary comforts. **Con:** Not all rooms have air-conditioning. ✉*Hassi Labied* ☎*035/57–70–37* ⊕*www.alielcojo.com* ✍*40 rooms* &*In room: no a/c (some), no phone, no TV. In-hotel: restaurant, pool, no elevator* ☐*No credit cards* ⦿*MAP.*

$ 🔲 **Les Hommes Bleus.** This is a robust place, with rooms filled with colorful carpets. Ask for one of the larger rooms at no extra cost. There are plenty of dune activities, including skis and sandboards. Four-wheel-drive rental costs from 900 DH for four hours. **Pro:** Owner speaks very good English. **Con:** Twin rooms are cramped. ✉*North of Hassi Labied* ☎*035/77–01–75 or 061/21–61–52* ⊕*www.hommebleu.net* ✍*15 rooms, 6 with bath* &*In-hotel: restaurant, no elevator* ☐*No credit cards* ⦿*MAP.*

$ 🔲 **Kasbah Erg Chebbi.** Appropriately named after the sand dunes everyone
★ is here to see, this lodging is one of the closest auberges to Erg Chebbi, and it's pretty isolated, to boot. An attentive staff, a lovely courtyard, and en-suite rooms make this place simple, stylish, and a good value. It shares a bivouac in the dunes with two other hotels, and can arrange for camel rides (75 DH an hour), overnight stays (350 DH per person), and four-wheel drives (1,300 DH a day). The owner's son, Hassan, speaks excellent English and is a reliable guide. They'll pick you up from Erfoud. **Pros:** Great staff, close to dunes. **Con:** No air-conditioning in rooms. ✉*North of Hassi Labied* ☎*070/77–83–15* ⊕*www.hotel-ergchebbi-merzouga.com* ✍*17 rooms* &*In-room: no a/c. In-hotel: restaurant, no elevator* ☐*No credit cards* ⦿*MAP.*

$$ 🔲 **Kasbah Mohayut.** There are arches, fountains, and lanterns all over
★ this sweet and sultry auberge. Rooms are beautifully appointed with warm colors, wrought-iron beds, and comfortable chairs. It's right beside the dunes, and a private bivouac overnight in the desert costs 350 DH per person. They can also arrange four-wheel drives and camels. **Pros:** Proximity to dunes, pretty pool. **Con:** No air-conditioning in rooms. ✉*Hassi Labied* ☎*066/03–91–85* ⊕*www.mohayut.com* ✍*21 rooms, 1 suite* &*In-room: no a/c. In-hotel: restaurant, bar, pool, no elevator* ☐*AE, MC, V* ⦿*MAP.*

$$$$ ★ 🏨**Kasbah Tombuctou.** This magnificent camp gets a lot of complaints for being big and noisy, but the fact is that the facilities here are excellent. The rooms in the newer wing are all opulent. There are desert trips including camel rides (200 DH for two hours), quad bikes, and nights in private bivouacs, as well as free snowboarding, skiing, and body-boarding in the sand once you're out there. The pool and restaurant are also popular with nonguests. To find the hotel, look for the sign with two enormous kissing camels. **Pros:** Magnificent view of the dunes, luxurious lodging. **Con:** Lights in rooms are very dim. ✉ *B.P. 44, Hassi Labied* ☎ *035/57–70–91 or 061/25–56–84* ⊕ *www.xaluca.com* ➪ *56 rooms, 2 suites* ⚒ *In-hotel: 2 restaurants, bar, pool, spa, hammam, public Wi-Fi, public Internet, no elevator* ▤ *AE, DC, MC, V* ⦿ *MAP.*

> **NORTH TO SOUTH**
>
> Hotels are ordered by price, but here's the list of hotels in order from the northernmost point beyond the village of Hassi Labied, through the village to Merzouga itself and farther south: Les Hommes Bleus, Kasbah Erg Chebbi, Auberge Atlas du Sable, Kasbah Mohayut, Kasbah Tombuctou, Le Petit Prince, and Nomad Palace.

$ 🏨**Nomad Palace.** Owner Ali Mouni arranges all manner of desert and mountain outings from this budget-friendly auberge. It has an excellent location far from other lodgings. Rooms are set off a large rectangular courtyard. Overnight desert stays cost 250 DH–300 DH per person. **Pros:** Full range of desert activities, removed from the crowds. **Con:** Basic needs satisfied but no luxuries. ✉ *A little south of Merzouga on way to Taoz* ☎ *061/56–36–11* ⊕ *www.adventureswithali.com* ➪ *15 rooms* ⚒ *In-hotel: restaurant, no elevator* ▤ *AE, MC, V* ⦿ *MAP.*

$ 🏨**Le Petit Prince.** You're a little way from the dunes, as this reliable option is in Merzouga. Rooms are simple but a good value. You can also sleep on the terrace or in a Berber tent for 10 DH or take the camel caravan to the bivouac in the oasis with all meals included of 300 DH per person. Set meals go for 60 DH. **Pro:** Desert activities abound. **Cons:** Very simple accommodations, not much English spoken. ✉ *B.P.48* ☎ *062/18–99–22* ⊕ *www.lepetitprince-merzouga.com* ➪ *11 rooms, 3 with bath* ⚒ *In-hotel: restaurant, no elevator* ▤ *No credit cards* ⦿ *MAP.*

DJEBEL SARHRO & NEKOB

★ *95 km (57 mi) east of Agdz, 165 km (99 mi) southwest of Rissani.*

If you pick the southern oasis route, don't miss the chance to stay in Nekob, Morocco's most Kasbah-filled village. Locals have come up with all sorts of reasons for why there are 45 of them. The amusing and believable theory is that members of a rich extended family settled here in the 18th and 19th centuries and quickly set to work trying to outbuild and outimpress each other. There's little in the way of showing off in the village today. The children are wild and the place a little untouched for the moment.

Just when you thought there's nothing to do here but pass through, you find out that the trekking potential to the north of town stretches as far as Boumalne du Dadès, 150 km (93 mi) away and on the northern oasis route. It's a five-day trek to Tagdift or Iknioun to the north. You can pick up handmade carpets and head scarves made by local women at the weekly Sunday souk. Or you can do very little; simply sit back, stare over the palmery, and enjoy. ■TIP➡ At the moment, Nekob is a nature-lover's dream; it may not be like this in 10 years' time, so get here soon.

GETTING HERE & AROUND

Nekob lies on the southern oasis route between Agdz and Rissani, skirting the southern slopes of the Djebel Sarhro. Minibuses and grands taxis travel here from Rissani, Zagora, and Ouarzazate.

> ### AN EMPTY BOAST
>
> "The desert," wrote composer and novelist Paul Bowles, "will tweak your sense of time." Nowhere is this better exemplified than in an anecdote about French writer Antoine de Saint-Exupéry (1900–44), celebrated for his beloved children's book *The Little Prince* and his mail flights across the Sahara. Having landed his aircraft near a camel caravan somewhere in the desert one day, he boasted to a nomad, "Look, my airplane made it here in two hours, whereas it took your caravan two months . . ."—to which the camel driver, unimpressed, responded, "And what did you do with the rest of the time?"

Exploring the mountain ranges and peaks of Djebel Sarhro requires a four-wheel-drive vehicle.

TIMING & PRECAUTIONS

Nekob's Kasbahs make an overnight stop if your itinerary allows.

EXPLORING

The wonderfully panoramic oasis Route 6956/R108 (which becomes 3454/N12 after Tazzarine) still appears as a desert piste on Moroccan tourist-office maps, but it has since been paved. Indeed, it's one of the safest, fastest, and least crowded in Morocco, and it offers unparalleled views up into the **Djebel Sarhro Massif** and all the way over to the Tafilalt date palmery. Count on three hours for the 233-km (140-mi) trip from Route P31/N9 (the Ouarzazate–Zagora road) to Rissani, in the date palmery.

NEED A BREAK? Morocco is a magnet for fossil fans, and much of the activity centers around the town of Alnif, on Route 3454/N12 between Rissani and Tazzarine. About 13 km (9 mi) west of Alnif is **Auberge Kasbah Meteorites** ☎ *035/78-38-09* ⊕ *www.kasbahmeteorites.c.la*) where you can enjoy a simple lunch, a dip in the pool, and a two- to three-hour excursion with a guide who'll show you the best place to hunt for fossils.

7

WHERE TO STAY

$-$$ **⌂Auberge Ennakhile Saghro.** This charming auberge has an entrancing view of the palmery below. You could sit on the terrace and sip mint tea for hours. The place specializes in a variety of guided treks all over the area, staying in bivouacs overnight and traveling on foot or by mule (400 DH a day). Five "Kasbah" rooms have private baths where the shower base is made from a couscous pan and the water flows from a honey jar. If you're just passing through, the lunches are delicious, and the views sublime. **Pros:** Great views, plenty of activities. **Con:** Not all rooms have private bathrooms. ⌂*N'kob, at Erfoud end of town* ☎*024/83–97–19 or 072/64–15–11* ⥽*15 rooms, 5 with bath* ⌂*In room: no a/c. In-hotel: 3 restaurants, no elevator* ⊟No credit cards ⎟⊚⎟*MAP.*

$ **⌂Baha Baha.** This is the truest rendition of a traditional Kasbah
★ you're likely to find. The Moroccan owner has faithfully restored the building, so it has plenty of charm. The place sometimes hosts Berber marriages—traditional except for the fact that they tie the knot next to a shimmering swimming pool. There are plenty of trips on offer, on foot or by camel, mule, or four-wheel-drive vehicle. "Sand bath therapy" (1,400 DH for two people) involves surrounding yourself in hot sands as treatment for rheumatism. **Pros:** In a restored Kasbah, full of traditional style. **Con:** Spotty service. ⌂*N'kob* ⊹*Follow signs to right from main road if heading west* ☎*024/83–97–63* ⊕*www.kasbahaba. com* ⥽*11 rooms, 2 with bath* ⌂*In-hotel: restaurant, pool, no elevator* ⊟No credit cards.

$$$-$$$$ **⌂Kasbah Imdoukal.** This lovely Kasbah sits in the heart of the town. Simple but spacious rooms have beautifully finished wood furniture. Ask for one of the rooms with a terrace, connected by a beautiful spiral staircase made of rope. The Moroccan owner's local contacts mean that it's possible to organize folklore evenings with well-known local groups, as well as a good range of local trips from camelback tours to rock carvings. **Pros:** In center of Nekob, plenty of atmosphere. **Con:** Prices are a bit high. ⌂*N'kob* ☎*024/83–97–98* ⊕*www.kasbahimdoukal. com* ⥽*20 rooms* ⌂*In-hotel: restaurant, bar, pool, no elevator* ⊟No credit cards ⎟⊚⎟*CP.*

$$$-$$$$ **⌂Ksar Jenna.** This beautiful and calm riad-style lodging could have
Fodor'sChoice been plucked from Marrakesh. Youssef and Stella, the Italian/Moroc-
★ can couple that runs it, have built it all from scratch in impeccable style. Flowering gardens are full of isolated spots for quiet contemplation, rooms are chic and intimate, and the palace restaurant comes complete with a fountain and a magnificent hand-painted ceiling. **Pros:** Cool gardens, nice architecture. **Con:** Not staffed all year. ⌂*N'kob* ⊹*on right, 2 km (1 mi) after end of town, heading west* ☎*024/83–97–90* ⊕*www. ksarjenna.com* ⥽*5 rooms, 3 with bath; 1 suite* ⌂*In-hotel: restaurant, bar, no elevator, parking (no fee)* ⊟No credit cards ⎟⊚⎟*MAP.*

THE DRÂA VALLEY

Morocco's longest river, the Drâa once flowed all the way to the Atlantic Ocean just north of Tan-Tan, some 960 km (600 mi) from its source above Ouarzazate. With the sole exception of a fluke flood in 1989—the only time in recent memory that the Drâa completed its course—the river now disappears in the Sahara southwest of M'Hamid, some 240 km (150 mi) from its headwaters. The Drâa Valley and its palmery continue nearly unbroken from Agdz through Zagora to M'Hamid, forming one of Morocco's most memorable tours.

As wild as you may have found certain parts of Morocco thus far, the trip down to the Sahara will seem more so, something like steady progress into a biblical epic. The plains south of Ouarzazate give way to 120 km (75 mi) of date palmeries and oases along the Drâa River, and between Agdz and Zagora more than two dozen Kasbahs and ksour line both sides of the river. The occasional market town offers a chance to mingle with the diverse peoples you'll see walking along the road in black shawls. Though most of the inhabitants are in fact Berbers, the Drâa Valley also contains Arab villages, small communities of Jews or the Mellahs they once inhabited, and numerous Haratin, descendants of Sudanese slaves brought into Morocco along the caravan routes that facilitated salt, gold, and slave trading until late in the 19th century.

After Zagora and Tamegroute, the road narrows as the Tinfou Dunes rise to the east and, farther south, a maze of jeep tracks leads out to Erg L'Houdi (Dune of the Jew). Finally, in M'Hamid el Gouzlane (Plain of the Gazelles), with sand drifting across the road and the Drâa long since gone underground, there is a definite sense of closure, the end of the road.

7

AGDZ

69 km (41 mi) southeast of Ouarzazate.

Agdz, at the junction of the Drâa and Tamsift rivers, marks the beginning of the Drâa palmery. A sleepy market town and administrative center, Agdz (pronounced *ah*-ga-dez) has little to offer other than the 5,022-foot peak Djebel Kissane, and the Kasbah Dar el Glaoui. From Agdz south to M'Hamid, the P31/N9 road follows the river closely except for a 30-km (18-mi) section between the Tinfou Dunes and Tagounite, where the Drâa again draws close before temporarily looping east again.

GETTING HERE & AROUND
Agdz is served by buses and grands taxis traveling between Ouarzazate and Zagora. The trip is approximately two hours from either town.

TIMING & PRECAUTIONS
A great time to visit is in October when the date harvest is in full swing. The market is stacked with boxes of the most delicious and succulent varieties.

Schistosomiasis, a parasite, has been reported in the Drâa River, so don't be tempted to swim or even wade across.

EXPLORING

Lining virtually the entire Drâa Valley from Agdz to Zagora are some two dozen ksour and Kasbahs on both sides of the river. Perhaps the most amazing ksour in this region are at **Tamnougalt**, 6 km (4 mi) south of Agdz—the second group of red-pisé fortifications on the left. The resident Berber tribe, the Mezguita, governed its own independent republic from here until the late 18th century; the crenellated battlements and bastions were a necessary defense against nomadic desert tribes.

Kasbah Timiderte, 8 km (5 mi) south of Tamnougalt on the left side of the road, was built by Brahim, eldest son of the pasha of Marrakesh.

The truncated pyramidal towers and bastions of the **Ksar Igdâoun** are visible 15 km (9 mi) past the turnoff onto Route 6956/R108 to Tazzarine. There used to be three gates for the ksar: one for Jews; one for other people who lived nearby; and one for the local governor. Entry to the ksar costs 10 DH.

EN ROUTE Look for the turnoff to the **Cascades du Drâa** on the left, 30 km (19 mi) south of Ouarzazate and 10 km (6 mi) before Agdz. The 10-km (6-mi) track down to the waterfalls is steep, rough, and all but impassable in bad weather, but the falls are magnificent. Natural pools invite swimming, and a falls-side café serves good tagines.

WHERE TO STAY

$$–$$$ 🏨**Chez Yacob.** Wander through the heavy wooden door into this old house at midday, and its tiny central courtyard will be packed to the rafters with lunching tour groups—it may be noisy, but it's a big thumbs up for the kitchen. The rest of the time guests in the higgledy-piggledy corridors of this glorious old palace right next to the Tamnougalt ksour have the place to themselves. The English-speaking host can set up all manner of tours and visits, although some of the best-spent time is out on the roof terrace overlooking the palmery and Drâa Valley. **Pros:** Full of charm, great views over palmery. **Con:** Very little parking. ✉ *Tamnougalt* ✛ *4 km (2.5 mi) from Agdz on route to Zagora* ☎ *024/84–33–94* ⊕ *www.chezyacob.com* ✍ *8 rooms* ⚲ *In room: no a/c, no phone, no TV. In-hotel: restaurant, no elevator* ⊟ *No credit cards* 🍴 *MAP.*

$$ 🏨**Kasbah Itrane.** Much quieter and roomier than the boisterous Chez Yacob, this converted Kasbah on the edge of town has considerable charm. The extensive gardens and pool area afford good views of Tamnougalt. Rooms are simple but comfortable; the better-equipped ones are off a courtyard, although the more atmospheric ones (Room 6, in particular) are inside the Kasbah. Sleeping on mattresses in Berber tents is also possible. **Pros:** Large pool, ideal for children. **Con:** Rooms near entrance feel a bit like a holiday camp. ✉ *Tamnougalt* ✛ *4 km (2.5 mi) from Agdz on route to Zagora* ☎ *024/84–33–17* ✍ *24 rooms* ⚲ *In-hotel: restaurant, pool, no elevator* ⊟ *No credit cards* 🍴 *MAP.*

$$ \;\;\; \boxed{}$$ **Kissane Hotel Agdz.** This little inn near the ceremonial entryway to Agdz is bright, clean, and competently managed. The manager can arrange anything from an overnight bivouac under the stars to visits to local Kasbahs or the waterfalls. The rooms here, although adequate for an overnight, are modern, plain, and undistinguished. **Pros:** Friendly and efficient staff. **Con:** Dreary rooms. ⊠ *Ave. Mohammed V* ☎ *024/84–30–44* ⤳ *47 rooms, 2 suites* ⟨ *In-hotel: restaurant, pool, no elevator* ⊟ *MC, V* ⦿ *MAP.*

TINZOULINE

59 km (35 mi) southeast of Agdz, 130 km (81 mi) southeast of Ouarzazate.

About 59 km (35 mi) southeast of Agdz, Tinzouline holds an important weekly souk. If you're here on a Monday, take this opportunity to shop and make contact with the many peoples of this southern Moroccan region where communities of Berbers, Arabs, Jews, and Haratin (descendants of Sudanese slaves) have coexisted for centuries. The Tinzouline ksour are clustered around a majestic Kasbah in the middle of an oasis that includes several villages. Tinzouline is also one of the most important prehistoric sites in pre-Saharan North Africa: from the ksour a 7-km (4.5-mi) gravel path leads west of town to cave engravings depicting mounted hunters. These drawings are attributed to Iron Age Libyo-Berbers, lending further substance to the theory that Morocco's first inhabitants, the Berbers, may have originally come from Central Asia via central and eastern Africa.

ZAGORA

95 km (57 mi) southeast of Agdz, 170 km (102 mi) southeast of Ouarzazate.

Zagora is—and does feel like—the boundary between the Sahara and what some writers and travelers have referred to as "reality." After Zagora, time and distance are measured in camel days: a famous painted sign at the end of town features a camel and reads, TOMBOUCTU 52 DAYS—that is, "52 days by camel." The town of M'Hamid, 98 km (65 mi) farther south, marks the actual end of the paved road and the beginning of the open desert, but Zagora is where the sensation of being in the desert kicks in.

On your way into Zagora from Agdz, bear immediately left down to the Ksar Tinsouline hotel. You'll pass La Rose des Sables restaurant, complete with sidewalk tables, about halfway down on the left. See the town of Amazraou and, just across the river, **La Kasbah des Juifs** (Kasbah of the Jews).

GETTING HERE & AROUND

Zagora is easily reached by the main road from M'Hamid and Ouarzazate. Buses and grands taxis navigate this route. The Compagnie de Transports Marocains bus station in Zagora is on the main street, as is the main bus station.

Zagora is easy to explore on foot or by inexpensive petit taxi. There are numerous tour agencies in town offering everything from camel trips to desert camping. Caravane du Sud is a well-respected local organization based just outside the center of Zagora in the town of Amezrou, just off the main road to M'Hamid. Reima Voyages is a local tour operator with a conscience. It's a little more expensive than other options, but 8% of your fee supports the local community. Tombouctour has a great range of circuits through the desert. You stay in bivouacs and travel on foot and by camel and four-wheel drive as you please.

ESSENTIALS

Bus Contacts Compagnie de Transports Marocains (⊠ *Bd. Mohammed V* ☎ *024/84–73–27*).

Currency Exchange Banque Populaire (⊠ *Bd. Mohammed V* ☎ *024/85–93–72*). **BMCE** (⊠ *Bd. Mohammed V* ☎ *024/87–96–49*).

Medical Assistance Hopital Darrak (⊠ *Ave. Hassan II*). **Pharmacie Zagora** (⊠ *Bd. Mohammed V* ☎ *024/89–53–90*) .

Post Office Poste Maroc (⊠ *Bd. Mohammed V*).

Visitor & Tour Info Caravane du Sud (⊠ *B.P 13, Amezrou, Zagora 45900* ☎ *024/84–75–69 or 061/34–83–83* ⊕ *www.caravanesud.com*). **Reima Voyages** (⊠ *Ave. Mohammed V* ☎ *024/84–70–61 or 061/34–83–88* 🖷 *024/84–79–22* ✍ *fmazizi@hotmail.fr*). **Tombouctour** (⊠ *79 Ave. Mohammed V* ☎ *024/84–82–07* ⊕ *www.tombouctour.ch*).

EXPLORING

Djebel Zagora, reached via the first left turn south of the Asmaa hotel, is worth a stop. (There's also a twisting footpath up the 3,195-foot mountain from the hotel itself.) The town's promontory, with its 11th-century Almoravid fortress, is an excellent sunset vantage point, overlooking the Drâa palmery and the distant Djebel Sarhro Massif to the north and the Tinfou Dunes to the south.

WHERE TO EAT

$–$$
MOROCCAN
★

✕ **La Rose des Sables.** This unpretentious little restaurant is a local favorite—and with good reason. The salads and tagines are first-rate, the staff is quick and congenial, and the afternoon sun slants in nicely on the terrace overlooking the street. A mechoui can be rustled up with two hours' notice, and the tagine *de poulet* (chicken stewed in lemon, onions, olives, potatoes, and spices) is excellent. Sleep elsewhere, though. The old hotel rooms are very depressing. ⊠ *Ave. Allal ben Abdallah* ☎ *024/84–72–74* 🖃 *No credit cards.*

WHERE TO STAY

$$ ⬛**Dar Raha.** There's more than a touch of adventure to this converted
☪ Kasbah. The guesthouse is in a residential area just outside Zagora
★ so that guests can see a bit more of everyday Moroccan life. Rooms
are economically accessorized with bright colors, simple designs, and
thoughtful touches, such as a djellaba and slippers for guests to wear
on their way to the shared bathrooms. The labyrinth of passages and
doorways will have visitors enjoyably lost and children enchanted for
hours. Dar Raha runs a range of absorbing local tours, not only to
the local synagogue but also to nearby villages and homes. **Pro:** Feels
like living with the locals. **Con:** Shared bathrooms. ⬛*B.P. 142, Hay
Amazraou, Zagora ✛2 km (1 mi) from Zagora on road to M'Hamid
☎024/84–69–93 ⊕http://darraha.free.fr ⬥9 rooms without bath
⬙In room: no a/c, no phone, no TV. In-hotel: restaurant, no elevator
⬛No credit cards ⊘Closed July and Aug.* ⦿*CP.*

$$$ ⬛**Kasbah Sirocco.** A bit like a rambling French country hotel, this is
one of Zagora's favorite destinations. Rooms are simply decorated in
a resolutely old-fashioned style, the majority with views of the relaxed
pool area. **Pros:** Excellent reputation, full range of services. **Con:** Can
be noisy. ⬛*On road to M'Hamid, turn left just after bridge ☎024/84–
61–25 ⊕www.kasbah-sirocco.com ⬥20 rooms ⬙In-room: no phone.
In hotel: restaurant, bar, pool, laundry service, public Internet, airport
shuttle, no elevator ⬛MC, V* ⦿*MAP.*

$$ ⬛**Ksar Tinsouline.** With high ceilings and a general air of elegance, this
colonial-style hotel is a Saharan version of Fez's Palais Jamai, albeit
on a far more modest scale. Rooms overlook a garden of palms and
bougainvillea that shelters what must be the largest and most musical
community of desert sparrows in the Drâa Valley. The restaurant is
dark and restful, and the quality of the tagines is excellent. **Pro:** Ele-
gant chandeliers grace public spaces. **Con:** Bedrooms small and rather
plain. ⬛*Ave. Hassan II ☎024/84–72–52 ⊕www.zagora-desert.com/
ksar_tinsouline.htm ⬥96 rooms ⬙In-room: refrigerator. In-hotel:
restaurant, bar, pool, public Internet, public Wi-Fi, no elevator ⬛AE,
DC, MC, V.*

$$$ ⬛**Palais Asmaa.** Everything is on a grand scale at Zagora's most presti-
gious address: the impressively lofty lobby leads to a restaurant, bar, and
gardens all filled with Brobdingnagian-size copper kettles and zellij tiles.
By comparison, rooms are merely functional, but comfortable and well
appointed. **Pro:** Good range of facilities. **Cons:** Full of tour groups, dull
room decor. ⬛*B.P. 78 ☎024/84–75–55 ⊕www.palais.asmaa-zagora.
com/ ⬥68 rooms ⬙In-room: refrigerator. In-hotel: restaurant, bar,
pool, no elevator, parking (no fee) ⬛AE, MC, V* ⦿*MAP.*

¢–$ ⬛**La Palmeraie.** The best of budget options is at the end of the main drag.
It's large, with a good range of facilities and a friendly staff. Rooms on
the top floor have TVs at no extra charge. Ask for a room with a pool
view. **Pros:** Friendly service, good prices. **Con:** Public areas feel worn.
⬛*Ave. Mohammed V, ☎024/84–70–08 ⊕www.lapalmerie-zagora.
com ⬥56 rooms, 51 with bath ⬙In-room: no a/c (some). In-hotel:
restaurant, bar, pool, no elevator ⬛MC, V.*

7

$$$$ ⚏ **Riad Lamane.** You can't go wrong with this for a little bit of Mar-
★   rakesh living at the edge of the desert. The palm-filled gardens are
astounding, and rooms and tented restaurants are all beautifully decorated. If you can, stay in one of the newer villas, which have lots of
character, and private terraces on the roof that double as private dining
areas. They arrange quad and camel hire, overnights to Erg Chagaga
(2,000 DH a day with four-wheel drive), and a sunset trip to local
dunes through the palmery. For fun and to save money, try one of their
nomad tents for 300 DH per person half-board (but not in the heat
of summer). **Pros:** The shaded gardens and pool are a paradise. **Con:**
Service can be sluggish. ⊠ *Amazraou, at end of town headed towards
M'Hamid* ☎024/84–83–88 ⊕*www.riadlamane.com* ⇌*7 rooms, 8
villas, 5 deluxe tents* ⅋*In-room: refrigerator. In-hotel: 2 restaurants,
bar, pool, hammam, public Wi-Fi, no elevator* ▭MC, V ⅋◯MAP.

$ ⚏ **Zagour.** Friendly and unpretentious, this is an instantly likable bud-
get hotel. Bathrooms are modern, but elsewhere the design alternates
between Arab-style communal areas and more traditionally Berber
rooms. The rose-shaded terrace bar, looking out across the palmery,
is a picturesque spot for breakfast. **Pros:** Peaceful surroundings, pretty
terrace. **Con:** Rooms lack storage space. ⊠ *Amazraou, on road to
M'Hamid* ☎024/84–61–78 ⊕*www.zagour.com* ⇌*18 rooms* ⅋*In-
hotel: restaurant, pool, public Internet, no elevator* ▭MC, V ⅋◯CP.

TAMEGROUTE

18 km (11 mi) southeast of Zagora.

Tamegroute (literally "the last town before the border," an accurate
toponym when the Algerian border was closer than it is now) is the
home of the **Zaouia of Sidi Mohammed Ben Naceur,** a sanctuary devoted to
this extraordinary *marabout* (sage). Closed to non-Muslims, the sanctuary itself can be admired from the outside—the door bears an intricately decorated archway of carved cedar and stucco. The surrounding
courtyard is perennially filled with dozens of mental patients hoping
for miraculous cures or just for charity from the Naciri brotherhood.
Outside to the left are onetime slave quarters still inhabited by descendants of Sudanese slaves.

GETTING HERE & AROUND

Buses en route Zagora to M'Hamid stop at Tamegroute, but depart in
the evening, so for a daytrip to Tamegroute it is best to hire a grand
taxi or drive yourself.

TIMING & PRECAUTIONS

A visit to Tamegroute will take no more than two hours.

EXPLORING

Pass **Amazraou,** 3 km (2 mi) south of Zagora, where Jewish silver-
smiths made famous jewelry until the creation of the Israeli State in
1948, when all but 30,000 of Morocco's 300,000 Jews left for Israel.
Berber craftsmen continue the tradition in the Mellah here, an interest-

ing stop if you don't mind the clamor of children eager to be hired as your guide.

★ Just north of the Zaouia of Sidi Mohammed Ben Naceur is a 17th-century **medersa** (school) that still lodges 400 students preparing for university studies. The accompanying Koranic library was once the largest such collection in Morocco, with 40,000 volumes on everything

> **PLOW ON THROUGH**
>
> Only if you have no time at all should you be satisfied with getting this far and turning back. The Tinfou Dunes simply aren't the desert, and offer only the slightest taste of the real thing. Stay the course until you get to M'Hamid.

from mathematics, philosophy, medicine, and astronomy to linguistics and Berber poetry. The remaining volumes are plenty impressive: a genealogy of the prophet Mohammed, manuscripts adorned with gold leaf, a medical book with afflictions written in red and remedies in black, and hand-illuminated manuscripts written in mint (green), saffron (yellow), and henna (red) on gazelle hide. Ask for a look at the 13th-century algebra primer with Western Arabic numerals, which, though subsequently abandoned in the Arab world, provided the basis for Western numbers. Although there is no official admission charge, a small donation is expected.

Don't miss Tamegroute's **ceramics cooperative** at the south end of the library, medersa, and slave quarters. The characteristic green-glazed pottery sold here is all handmade.

TINFOU

10 km (6 mi) southeast of Tamegroute, 29 km (18 mi) southeast of Zagora.

The hamlet of Tinfou is famous for the freak (and very small) sand dunes that circling winds have deposited 2 km (1 mi) north of the Tamegroute–M'Hamid road. Beyond the dunes the sheer cliffs of the Djebel Tadrart Massif loom darkly on the horizon, while to the south and west is the high surrounding plateau of the Djebel Bani Massif. The dunes are a result of the Drâa River's narrow slot in high ground, a gap that sucks wind and sand from the desert and sticks them onto the moist edge of the Drâa palmery here.

GETTING HERE & AROUND

Tinfou is just a few minutes by car from nearby Tamegroute, so you can visit both from Zagora or M'Hamid.

WHERE TO STAY

$$–$$$ **Kasbah Hôtel Sahara Sky.** This is a place to see stars—literally. With
★ five latest-edition telescopes, from manageable to huge ("it costs the price of a car," says German owner Fritz Koring), the rooftop observatory puts 180,000 stars within reach. With not another building in sight, there's no light pollution, and both amateur and professional stargazers make the trek with glee. Nonresidents can also stargaze between 10 PM and midnight (50 DH each), or for free if you dine (120 DH

KSOUR & KASBAHS

Ksour (plural for *ksar*) and Kasbahs are fortified villages, houses, and granaries built of *pisé*, a sun-dried mixture of mud and clay. Ksour were originally tribal settlements or villages, while Kasbahs were single-family fortresses. The Erfoud–Ouarzazate road through the Dadès Valley is billed as the "Route of the Thousand Kasbahs," with village after village of fortified pisé structures, many decorated with intricate painted and carved geometrical patterns. The Drâa Valley is lined with Kasbahs and ksour the length of the Agdz–Zagora road. Highlights are the Kasbah Amerhidil, at the Skoura oasis; the Tifoultoute and Aït-Benhaddou Kasbahs, near Ouarzazate; the Tamnougalt and Timderte Kasbahs, just south of Agdz; and the 11th-century Almoravid fortress at Zagora.

each). Other than that, the rooms are merely adequate and the facilties rather graceless. There's a well-stocked bar on the premises. **Pros:** Stargazing equipment is top-notch, near the dunes. **Con:** Rooms lack the sparkle of the skies overhead. ⊠*B.P. 28, Tinfou Dunes, Tamegroute, Zagora* ☎*024/84–85–62 or 061/17–28–66* ⊕*www.hotel-sahara.com* ➹*16 rooms* ᗕ*In-hotel: restaurant, bar, public Internet, no elevator, parking (no fee)* ⊟ *MC, V* ❶*MAP.*

EN ROUTE Between Tinfou and M'Hamid lies more dramatic scenery. A Monday souk is held at the junction of the P31/N9 and the Drâa. The first pass through the Djebel Bani is the Anagam, after which the road leaves this dry steppe and enters a lush palmery. Note that as you approach the Algerian border at Tagounite you might be asked for your passport by police controls—a routine check of no consequence. After Tagounite, a second pass, Tizi-Beni-Selmane, descends to the turnoff for **Erg L'Houdi** *(Dune of the Jew),* a favorite dune for bivouacs. Dozens of sets of four-wheel-drive tracks mark the way to the dune, some 5 km (3 mi) from the P31/N9. The route is not suitable for standard cars.

M'HAMID

68 km (40 mi) south of Tinfou, 162 km (97 mi) south of Zagora, 260 km (157 mi) southeast of Ouarzazate, 395 km (237 mi) southwest of Rissani.

Properly known as M'Hamid el Gouzlane, or Plain of the Gazelles, M'Hamid neatly marks the end of Morocco's Great Oasis Valleys. Despite a distinct absence of attractions, it is definitely worth reaching. The sand drifting like snow across the road (despite the placement of palm-frond sand breaks or fences), the immensity of the horizon, and the patient gait of camels combine to produce a palpable change in the sense of time and space at this final Drâa oasis.

The town has a famous Monday souk notable for the occasional appearance of nomadic and trans-Saharan traders of the Saharan Reguibat tribe. Much chronicled by writer Paul Bowles, these ebony-skinned fellows habitually wear the indigo *sheish*, a linen cloth wrapped around the head and face for protection from the cold and from sandstorms. The dye from the

> **DID YOU KNOW?**
>
> M'Hamid was once an outpost for the camel corps of the French Foreign Legion. Looking at it now, it's difficult to imagine what's there worth defending, but the training would have been harsh enough to make a soldier out of any man.

fabric runs, tinging the men's faces blue and leading to their nickname, the Blue Men. Don't expect too much in the way of merchandise; the souk has lost much of its exotic appeal in recent years.

The ocean of dunes 7 km (4.5 mi) beyond M'Hamid will satisfy any craving for some real Saharan scenery.

GETTING HERE & AROUND
M'Hamid is the last village before the pavement ends. Buses arrive here twice daily from Marrakesh via Zagora and Ouarzazate. Grands taxis also make the journey to and from Zagora.

Arriving in M'Hamid without accommodations or excursions can be intimidating due to fiercely competing touts, so book ahead. That said, there are several agencies trying to use a community-based approach. **Nomadic Life** and **Bivouac L'Erg** are both committed to this approach. Other recommended companies are **Bivouac Mille & Une Nuits, M'hamid Travel, and Sahara Services.**

TIMING & PRECAUTIONS
The International Nomads Festival takes place at the end of March. The small event is run by local volunteers aiming to promote the traditions of the Moroccan Sahara.

ESSENTIALS
Visitor & Tour Info **Bivouac L'Erg** (⊠ *M'Hamid town center, opposite mosque* ☎ *061/87–16–30*). **Bivouac Mille & Une Nuit** (⊠ *Ouled Driss, 5 km before M'Hamid* ☎ *024/84–86–85*). **M'hamid Travel** (⊠ *M'Hamid town center* ☎ *024/88–59–49* ⊕ *www.mhamid-travel.com*). **Nomadic Life** (⊠ *M'Hamid town center, next to Hotel Elghizlane* (☎ *062/84–26–76* ⊕ *www.nomadiclife.info*). **Sahara Services** (⊠ *M'Hamid town center* ☎ *061/77–67–66* ⊕ *www.saharaservices.info*).

EXPLORING
The ruins of the ksar **Ksebt el-Allouj**, across the Drâa riverbed, are interesting to poke around in.

WHERE TO STAY
$ **Auberge Al Khaima.** For travelers on a tight budget who want some traditional accommodation, this option at the edge of town offers basic comfort in a quiet garden. Showers are spotless, and the hammam is an unexpected and welcome extra. The owner organizes desert tours. **Pro:** Clean accommodations. **Con:** Absolutely no frills. ⊠ *Turn left at*

town square and cross river, M'Hamid ☎062/13–21–70 ⌔3 *rooms* ⌂*In-hotel: hammam* ▤*No credit cards* ⍾*MAP.*

$$$–$$$$ ⌕**Chez Le Pacha.** A onetime camel trekker has realized his dream with this sumptuous site full of luxurious Berber tents, four sumptuous suites done up with enormous beds and 10 ravishing rooms using traditional finishes and decorative motifs. Youssef Dakhamat is committed to revealing the cultural complexity of the region. As a start, every room is named after a different prominent woman in the Drâa Valley's history, whether she be Berber, Arab, or Jewish. There is also a library to explain more about local culture and traditions. The pool is stunning, particularly at night. Tents for two are simple, with private terraces and sultry lanterns at night. As well as trips into the desert, you can also have sand therapy and children will be amused by the menagerie of birds, peacocks, donkeys, and camels. **Pros:** Stylish accommodations, helpful staff. **Con:** Tents unbearably hot in summer months. ⌧*Bounou, near Ouled Driss,* ☎024/84–86–96 *or* 016/34–84–36 ⊕*www.chezlepacha.com* ⌔*10 rooms, 4 suites, 16 tents* ⌂*In-hotel: restaurant, pool, public Internet, public Wi-Fi* ▤*MC, V* ⍾*MAP.*

$$ ⌕**Dar Azawad.** One of the finest addresses in southern Morocco awaits dusty arrivals who want a few better-than-home comforts with their desert adventures. Each room has been designed with the flair of the choicest Marrakshi retreat, and the bathrooms take inventiveness to new levels. The restaurant turns out fine French-Moroccan cuisine, and residents of the Berber tents have their own bathroom in a brilliantly designed shower block. **Pro:** Luxury at the edge of the desert. **Con:** Nomad tent rooms are expensive. ⌧*Douar Ouled Driss* ☎024/84–87–30 ⊕*www.darazawad.com* ⌔*10 rooms, 3 suites, 8 tents* ⌂*In-hotel: restaurant, bar, pool, spa, no elevator, parking (no fee)* ▤*MC, V* ⊘*Closed July* ⍾*MAP.*

$$$ ⌕**Kasbah Azalay.** The only luxurious lodging in the village of M'Hamid is this Spanish-owned Kasbah at the edge of the palmery. Named after the camel caravans that once passed through M'Hamid, Kasbah Azalay has boldly colored rooms with huge bathrooms finished in traditional tiles. There is a courtyard garden, roof terrace with expansive views, and a bar with what is possibly the last cold beer for miles. The restaurant has a Spanish colonial feel and serves both Moroccan and international cuisine. **Pros:** Plenty of creature comforts, good restaurant, at the edge of the desert. **Con:** Swimming pool still under construction. ⌧*M'Hamid el Ghezlane* ☎024/84–80–96 ⊕*www.azalay.com* ⌔*34 rooms, 8 suites* ⌂*In-room: no phone (some), refrigerator (some), Wi-Fi. In-hotel: restaurant, bar, spa, no elevator, public Wi-Fi* ▤*AE, DC, MC, V* ⍾*MAP.*

Essaouira & Agadir

WORD OF MOUTH

"I did greatly enjoy Essaouira, especially because it is such a visual contrast to Marrakesh, and really to the rest of the country—whites, blues, the sea. Also to me it had a nice relaxed feel that invited you to slow down and catch your breath for a minute and sit and watch people go by."

—tahl

"Personally I feel Essaouira is a great place to start a trip in Morocco. It's got a lot going for it: infrastructure, fantastic views and a good vibe. But it's low pressure and as such a good place to get your feet wet."

—Clifton

Updated by
Jillian York

THEY'RE BOTH ON THE COAST, and they both have beaches that people rave about, but Essaouira and Agadir couldn't be more dissimilar. A hippie hangout whose secret travelers refused to tell for years, Essaouira is only now coming into the limelight as a mainstream destination, but it nevertheless retains its slightly "other" feel. Windy beaches attract water-sports enthusiasts rather than sunseekers, and riad-hotels cater to independent travelers. Agadir, on the other hand, was made for mass tourism. It's a modern resort city with every kind of singing, dancing, and casino-betting distraction on hand and long stretches of hot, sandy beaches and calm seas perfect for sunbathing families. Both, however, have lively ports worth seeing in action and superb fresh fish and seafood. In between are less-frequented spots good for diving, surfing, windsurfing, kayaking, and body boarding, or, for the less active, sunbathing and hiding out from the world a little. Whatever your interest, whether holing up in luxury or diving into the surf, this coastal area has a great deal to offer.

ORIENTATION & PLANNING

ORIENTATION

Morocco's southern coastal towns might be just a few hours from bustling Marrakesh, but their laid-back vibe makes you feel you're a world away. Everyone flocks to this region in summer for the sandy beaches, the luxurious resort, or the numerous festivals that ensure that there's always music in the air.

Agadir. The resort town of Agadir has long been popular with European sun worshipers. It's also a good base for sampling regional beaches and the Souss Massa Bird Estuary, or for a day trip to Taroudant and Tafraoute. South of town is a strip of tarmac commonly referred to as "the tourist area," which runs alongside the beach, with hotels and restaurants galore. Northwest of the beach are the marina development and the port, as well as the old Kasbah walls. To the southeast are more secluded beach areas and classier hotels. Heading farther back from the beach, you're in a busy modern city with a smattering of cheaper hotels, souvenir shops, and a little bit of real life.

Essaouira. Essaouira is quieter and more emblematically Moroccan. It's becoming more popular with bus tours coming up for a day from Agadir, but still remains a quiet, pretty idyll that at least will never have Agadir's hordes. The beach stretches for miles in a curving bay, attracting water-sports enthusiasts. Most other visitors will spend their time in the car-free medina, which offers fresh fish from the port, wonderful sea views beyond the western medina walls, and hotels and restaurants tucked into narrow alleys.

TOP REASONS TO GO

Catch a wave: Known as "Windy City Africa," Essaouira draws hundreds of surfers every year to ride its huge breaks.

Satisfying seafood: Whether haggling down by the port for your own fish, or enjoying calamari on a rooftop terrace, Essaouira is a seafood-lover's paradise.

Mysterious music: Essaouira is known for its yearly Festival of Gna-

oua Music, and throughout the year retains its reputation as a music-lover's haven.

Family fun: Donkey rides, playgrounds, and ice-cream stalls make Agadir heaven for children.

Pampering yourself: Don't lift a finger, as stylish resort hotels serve up every luxury you could possibly want.

PLANNING

WHEN TO GO

Unlike inland destinations that get too hot in summer, high season for the coast is August, with peaks at Christmas, New Year's Day, and June. One of the nicest times to come is during October and November, out of season with prices and space to match, but still warm. Summer tends to be busy with vacationing Moroccan families from Casablanca, Rabat, and elsewhere. Vacationers and families from abroad tend to hit Agadir in spring, when the weather is pleasant but not too hot. Surfers and divers come year-round, although early spring is by far the best time for surf.

GETTING HERE & AROUND

International travelers coming to this region typically arrive via Marrakesh's Menara International Airport. Compagnie de Transports Marocains and Supratours both offer many buses to your final destination. Grands taxis, the large taxis that travel between cities, and minibuses are also popular options. Agadir is also accessible via Al Massira Airport, which has connections to other Moroccan airports.

SAFETY

Essaouira and Agadir are quite safe, with almost no violent crime. Lone female travelers will feel more comfortable in these towns than in the rest of Morocco. Travelers should keep an eye on their personal belongings, however, as pickpockets are common.

RESTAURANTS

All along the coast you can get great grilled and battered fish and seafood. It's inexpensive and good for both lunch and dinner. Cheaper places tend to batter all kinds of fish, which, depending on the fish, can make it lose its flavor. For a better fish experience, you'll have to go to nicer places, or try fish tagine, which is never battered. Both Agadir and Essaouira offer a couple of first-class restaurants that would hold their own in Marrakesh or Rabat.

Argan oil is a delicacy, drawn from the nuts of a tree that grows only in southern Morocco and South America. It's often served with good fish dishes all over the coast. Roadside stands lining the route between Agadir and Essaouira sell pure honey, which comes from bees feeding on regional herbs. It's expensive by local standards, but highly valued and worth tasting.

WHAT IT COSTS IN DIRHAMS					
	¢	$	$$	$$$	$$$$
AT DINNER	under 40DH	40DH–70DH	70DH–90DH	90DH–110DH	over 110DH

Prices are per person for a main course at dinner.

HOTELS

You'll find a full range of options, from small budget hotels to Agadir's five-star behemoths. There's a growing trend in Essaouira for converting grand family homes into beautiful *riads* (the Moroccan equivalent of a bed-and-breakfast). In summer it's best to reserve rooms in advance, but during the rest of the year you can usually find a clean bed with little effort. For the more upscale riad options you may have to book several months advance whatever the time of year.

An appealing alternative for travelers with time to spare is to set up house in a central location and take day trips. There's an increasing number of rental apartments in Essaouira and "apartment hotels" in Agadir; both offer self-catering options.

WHAT IT COSTS IN DIRHAMS					
	¢	$	$$	$$$	$$$$
FOR TWO PEOPLE	under 250DH	250DH–450DH	450DH–700DH	700DH–1,000DH	over 1,000DH

All prices are for a high-season standard double room, excluding service and tax.

FESTIVALS

Agadir and Essaouira are music hot spots, so it is no surprise that both cities host popular music festivals. Held in July, Agadir's Festival Timitar celebrates native Berber music, while Essaouira's world-famous Festival of Gnaoua, held each June, hosts international musicians as well as native ones.

ESSAOUIRA

171 km (102 mi) west of Marrakesh, 351 km (211 mi) southwest of Casablanca.

Make Essaouira the very last stop on your Moroccan vacation and you'll leave the country relaxed and wishing you never had to leave. Once famed as a hippie hangout for surfers and expat artists, Essaouira offers its cool breezes and relaxed atmosphere to a broader range of visitors.

Despite losing a little of its no-hassle niche and in-the-know cool, the Windy City remains a favorite destination, full of pink medina walls, blue shutters, twisting *derbs* (alleyways), and sea, sand, and surf.

Essaouira pretty much has a nine-month high season, from mid-March until the first week of November, with extra peaks around Christmas and New Year's. Increasing popularity means that more hotels are opening, and prices are rising. The town remains peaceful in its bustle, however—an enticing blend of fishing port and seaside haven.

GETTING HERE & AROUND

Most travelers arrive at Marrakesh's Menara International Airport. As parking is difficult and few rental agencies service the town, it

> ### GO INTO A TRANCE
>
> The end of June is always packed, as 400,000 people from all over the world come to enjoy the annual four-day **Gnaoua and World Music Festival**. It's one of the best times to listen to traditional Gnaoua musicians. These descendants of African slaves established brotherhoods across Morocco and are healers and mystics as well as musicians. Among their troupes of metal castanet players, lute players, and drummers, they have mediums and clairvoyants who perform wild, spellbinding acts. For more information, visit ⊕ *www.festival-gnaoua.co.ma*.

is sensible to arrive by public transport. The drive from Marrakesh to Essaouira takes about 2½ hours. Grands taxis and minibuses ply this route. Like most Moroccan cities, Essaouira is highly walkable. The local *petits taxis* (smaller, in-town taxis) are blue and metered. You can pick them up outside the medina, notably at Bab Sbâa.

A'V Voyages is the only local travel agent. It can arrange a number of trips and circuits from €50 per person (minimum three people), including transport, to towns such as Diabat and Sidi Kaouki.

TIMING & PRECAUTIONS

Weekend visitors to Essaouira often leave wishing they had more time. If you can, plan to spend several days in this relaxing seaside town. The best (and most popular) time to visit is summer. Although the temperature is tolerable year-round, this is a windy city, so don't expect to swim before May or after August.

ESSENTIALS

Bus Contacts Compagnie de Transports Marocains (☎ 024/78–47–64).

Currency Exchange Banque Populaire (✉ Pl. My Hassan ☎ 024/47–52–16).

Internet Espace Internet Mogador (✉ 8 bis, rue du Caire ☎ 024/78–35–84).

Medical Assistance De Nuit (✉ Siége de la Municipalité, Ave. Al Massira ☎ 024/78–31–52). **Mellah Elkdim** (✉ 122, ave. Sidi Mohammed Ben Abdellah ☎ 024/47–60–22). **Skala** (✉ 28-29, Lot Regraga, ave. Al Aqaba ☎ 024/78–36–84).

Post Office Poste Principale (✉ Ave. Lalla Aicha ☎ 024/47–30–13).

Rental Cars Araucariacar (☎ 024/47–22–25). **Avis Mogador** (✉ 28, rue Oued el Makhazine ☎ 024/47–49–26). **Jouhara Car** (✉ 2, bd. de Fes ☎ 024/47–45–58).

Visitor & Tour Info **A'V Voyages** (✉ Immeuble Habous, Quartier des Dunes
☎ 024/78-31-90). **Syndicat d'Initiative
et de Tourisme** (✉ 10, rue du Caire
☎ 024/78-35-32).

EXPLORING ESSAOUIRA

Medina. This isn't so much a sight as
the very essence of Essaouira, where
you are most likely to stay, eat,
shop, and wander. Brown volcanic
stone is the characteristic building
material of Portuguese architecture
in Morocco, and its best examples
(outside El Jadida) are Essaouira's
medina and main portal. Unlike the rust-color earth used for southern
Moroccan buildings farther inland, this stone is a light brown. Like Fez,
Essaouira is benefiting from preservationists' attention—its walls, ramparts, and Portuguese church are being carefully restored—so painted
walls such as those around the main square and near the port have been
restored from a light pink to their former natural beige.

> ### PEOPLE-WATCHING & ICE CREAM
>
> Place Moulay Hassan stretches
> far and wide, taking in fishermen,
> tourists, hecklers, and local coffee
> fiends glued to televised soccer
> games. Pick up an ice cream from
> **Gelateria Dolce Freddo** (✉ 25
> bis, pl. Moulay Hassan, right on the
> main Sq. ☎ 063/57-19-28), which
> has shiny scoops of flavors such
> as After 8, tiramisu, and hazelnut
> for 5 DH each, and off you go.

There are two other sections within the city walls: the Kasbah, used
to house urban aristocrats and governing authorities and thus double-
secured with additional walls; and the Mellah, the old Jewish quarter,
which once housed merchants who benefited from preferential tax and
commercial laws designed to establish Essaouira as a market center.

North Bastion. The distinctive outlines of the bastion's corner tubular
moldings frame the waves dramatically at sunset. It once held emergency supplies of fresh water. ■ TIP➔ If you stand in the middle of the
circle and stomp your foot or yell, you'll hear the echo ring far.

Fodor's Choice ★ **Port.** Built in 1769 in the reign of Sidi Mohammed Ben Abdellah by an
Englishman who had converted to Islam, the port is still going strong
in the southwest corner of town. Trawlers and other boats bob along
the quay, and middlemen and independent sailors sell the daily catch of
sardines, calamari, and skate from small dockside tables.

Sidi Mohammed Ben Abdellah Ethnological Museum. The stunning former
French-colonial town hall holds this smartly arranged collection of
items from everyday and ritual life in and around the Essaouira area.
Ground-floor displays of musical instruments distinguish between
Gnaoua and Sufi sects; upstairs, exhibits survey regional carpet styles,
wood-carving techniques and motifs, and Muslim, Jewish, and rural
Ishelhin Berber dress. ✉ 7, rue Laalouj ☎ 024/47-53-00 ☎ 10 DH
☉ Wed.–Mon. 8:30-6:30.

Sqala. Essaouira has three *sqala* (bastions), with fabulous cannons: the
Kasbah sqala (also known as the medina sqala), the port sqala, and
the sqala currently housing the Ensemble Artisanal, on Rue Modhem
el Qorry near Bab Marrakesh. Each was a strategic maritime defense

A BIT OF HISTORY

The Phoenicians established a commercial center called Migdal here in the 7th century BC; the Romans came six centuries later in search of the royal purple dye murex, extracted from sea snails stuck fast to the surrounding rocky islets (known as "les îles purpuraires"). The Portuguese took over the port briefly, from 1506 to 1510, and left behind distinctive ramparts when the populations of Chiadma Arabs and Ishelhin Berbers joined to oust the Christians from what *they* called Mogador.

The port became a city when in 1764 Moroccan sultan Sidi Mohammed Ben Abdellah decided to punish coastal Agadir, then in revolt, by building a rival naval base at Ess-

aouira. It became a coastal outlet for trans-Saharan trading of gold, slaves, and ivory from Timbuktu in Mali. He commissioned French fortification architect Theodore Cornut to design what is now the Essaouira medina, at the time a very modern, urban affair designed on a grid system. The sultan also wooed a large Jewish population to develop commerce, and they remained a significant presence until the mid-20th century—some locals say that there were more Jews in Essaouira in the 19th century than there were Muslims—when almost all of Morocco's Jews emigrated to France and Israel, leaving roughly 6,000 Jews in Morocco today.

point. Unlike the straight-edged Moorish constructions in other Moroccan cities, the ramparts in Essaouira are triangular, so the insider looking out has a broader field of vision than the enemy peering in. Check out the cannon engravings: the second and third to the right are signed CARLOS III, BARCELONA 1780, and a Dutch cannon dated 1743 is inscribed with a lion and the Latin phrase VIGILANTE DEO CONFIDENTES—"Those who trust in God are under his protection." Orson Welles filmed scenes of his film *Othello* from the tower of the port sqala, picking up a magnificent panorama of town, port, and bay all in one. 🎫 *10 DH.*

BEACHES

ESSAOUIRA BAY

Essaouira's beach is a sweeping bay that curves from the sheltered north through the east to the south. You nearly always feel warm when you're bathed in sunlight, but as the wind and treacherous riptides are consistently strong, sunbathers and swimmers won't have much fun. Deck-chair or sun-bed rental costs about 25 DH.

The wind comes from the north and creates three main areas. The most northerly part, tucked up into the armpit of the port, has wind that comes in gusts. Just south of this the wind strengthens, with fewer gusts. Farther south are the steady, strong winds the town is known for, and that make it a mecca for wind- and kite-surfers. This range of areas makes the bay perfect for every level of water-sportsman and -woman.

You can also visit the surrounding islets by boat; these islands (Iles de Mogador) are home to nine bird species, including the endangered

Eleanor falcon. If you want to visit outside of breeding season, you'll need a (free) visitor's permit from the port office. After that, haggle for a ride with local fishermen or rent a boat.

DIABAT

Essaouira's beach is fine for an early-morning jog or a late-afternoon game of soccer, but serious sunbathers typically head south to quiet Diabat. A few miles south of town, nestled in eucalyptus fields, are some ruins. Opinions differ on whether the ruins are of Portuguese or more-recent French vintage. On a windy day the only escape is a two-story rock that affords a nice resting spot at low tide.

> **CATCH OF THE DAY**
>
> Opt for lunch or dinner in one of the seafood grills along the port: feast on charcoal-grilled sardines, calamari, red snapper, sea bass, whiting, and shrimp (crab is usually too dry) from among the dozens of stalls, and experience the color and bustle of the port. You choose your fish, establish a price, find a table, and wait while your meal is cooked. Since it gets so windy, enjoying a nice big meal at an outdoor spot in the sun makes much more sense for lunch than for dinner, when it's better to head indoors than brave the cold.

GETTING HERE   The Number 5 bus leaves from Bab Marrakesh in Essaouira for Diabat about every two hours. If you're driving, the turnoff for Diabat is 7 km (4.5 mi) south of Essaouira, and 3 km (2 mi) west of the Agadir road.

SIDI KAOUKI

For the Essaouira ascetic who really wants to concentrate on sand and sea, the tranquil, wind-blasted beach village of Sidi Kaouki is the destination of choice. "Town" consists of an abnormally high number of guesthouses and auberges (most of them not functioning particularly well) and very little else, apart from pristine stretches of sand beach. Unlike Essaouira Bay, which is protected by the city, there's nothing to stop the fearsome winds in summer, making this a top spot for surfing and windsurfing. At press time a surf center and restaurant were under construction—it was already possible to borrow equipment. It's also easy to rent ponies and camels for rides at about €10 per hour. Sidi Kaouki's wide sand beach is also ideal for racing sail buggies; check with the surf center to see if they have any.

GETTING HERE   Sidi Kaouki is 27 km (17 mi) southwest of Diabat. The turnoff is 15 km (9 mi) south of Diabat on the Agadir road. The same Number 5 bus that gets you to Diabat continues on to Sidi Kaouki.

FARTHER AFIELD

Numerous paved roads jut off the road to Agadir heading toward the beaches along the coast, including the fishing and camping site at Plage Tafadna, 37 km (23 mi) south of the Sidi Kaouki turnoff. Accessibility to beaches and the locals' enthusiasm for foreign visitors lessen as you move south until you leave Haha territory (the land of the Ishelhin Berbers) behind and move into Cap Rhir.

WHERE TO EAT

There are some great restaurants in Essaouira. From port catches grilled in front of you to inventive and expensive fish dishes in the swankiest restaurants, seafood tends to headline menus when the surf permits. There are also lots of traditional Moroccan options and excellent examples of French, Italian, and Asian fusion. ■TIP➔ **Most of the local places fill up quickly, but if you can hang on for the second sitting, the crowds thin out again by 9.**

$$–$$$
FRENCH

✕ **Les Chandeliers.** Run by an attentive French family, Les Chandeliers styles itself a tapas bar and specializes in southwestern French–style dishes, with fish, pasta, and the occasional duck topping the menu. The spaghetti *de la mer* is a tasty combination of tomatoes, shrimp, calamari, and garlic with a splash of white wine. ⊠*14, rue Laalouj* ☎*024/47–58–27, 069/64–88–42, or 067/96–53–85* ✉*info@leschandeliers.net* ▭*No credit cards* ⊗*No lunch.*

$–$$
FRENCH

✕ **Chez Françoise.** There's a daily range of delights, including quiches, salads, tarts, and the occasional crepe, at this nice little lunch place. With only two rows of four small tables, it makes a perfect stop for afternoon tea. ⊠*1, rue Hommane el Fetouaki* ☎*068/16–40–87* ▭*No credit cards* ⊗*Closed Sun.*

$$$–$$$$
FRENCH
Fodor's Choice
★

✕ **Le Cinq.** Ask local riad owners where they dine out, and five times out of five they'll say Le Cinq. In a stylish setting of huge ceiling lamps and exposed brick, chef and restaurateur Anne Marie Teillou cooks up "Atlantic cuisine"—stunning and inventive French food, often with an Asian twist. From your first mint, rum, and ginger aperitif to your final mouthful of chestnut tart, it's a culinary marvel. The crab au gratin is a favorite not to be missed. A house menu and weekly specials keep fans coming back. ⊠*7, rue Youssef el Fassi* ☎*024/78–47–26* ▭*No credit cards* ⊗*Closed Tues. No lunch weekdays.*

$–$$
ITALIAN
★

✕ **Dar Baba.** A night with Orianna and Vincenti Gianfranco's cooking is not to be missed. This family-run Italian restaurant with only five tables on the first floor of their riad and home is affordable and charming. All the pastas and the cheeses are made in-house, and the menu is written in Italian. Tables are surrounded by fish and pasta charts, plants, a tarnished saxophone, a map of the world, and crooning Italian music. ⊠*2, rue de Marrakech* ☎*024/47–68–09* ▭*No credit cards* ⊗*Closed Sun.*

$$
SEAFOOD

✕ **Dar Loubane.** Here you can sit among cascading plants in the airy courtyard of an 18th-century riad and dine on fish to your heart's content. It's decorated with 1920s photos and Oriental-style bric-a-brac collected by Jean-Claude and Evelyne Dulac, the aging French couple that runs the restaurant. There's a daily lunch menu, but you can order à la carte anytime. The menu includes *pastilla* (sweet pigeon pie), *briouates* (spicy dumplings), ray with capers, grills, and tagines. There's a full wine

8

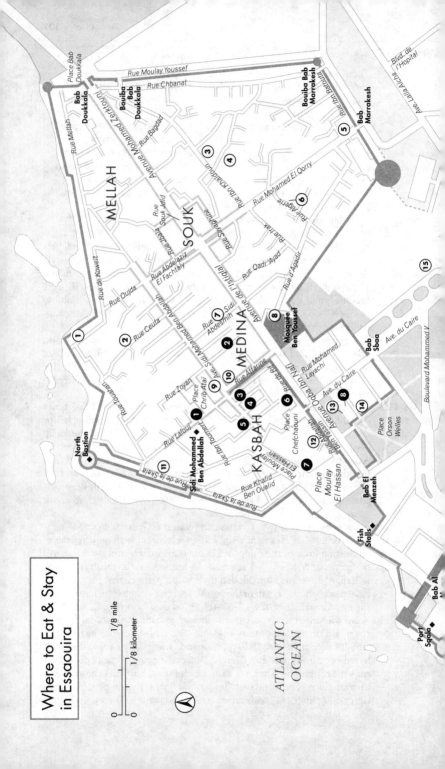

Where to Eat & Stay in Essaouira

ATLANTIC OCEAN

0   1/8 mile
0   1/8 kilometer

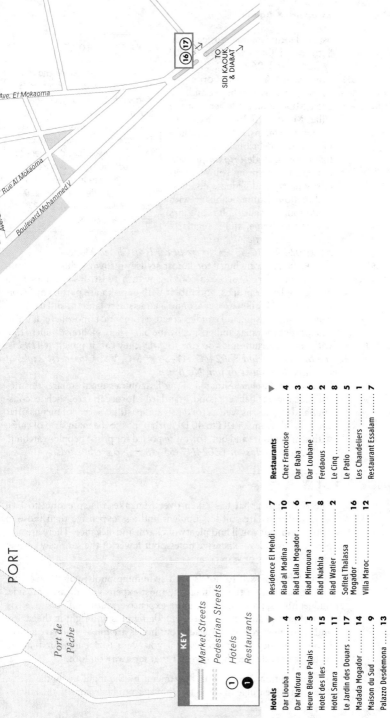

Ave. El Mokaoma

Rue Al Mokaoma

Ave. Lalla Aicha

Boulevard Mohammed V

TO
SIDI KAOUK,
& DJABAT →

PORT

Port de
Pêche

KEY

Market Streets

Pedestrian Streets

① Hotels

① Restaurants

8

list, and local Gnaoua musicians on Saturday night. ⊠*24, rue de Rif* ☎*024/47–62–96* ▭*MC, V.*

$$$
MOROCCAN
Fodor's Choice
★

×**Ferdaous.** At our favorite for Moroccan cuisine, the formidable chef, Mme Souad, formerly of the Villa Maroc, cooks up excellent starters and mains. Fish tagines bubble and boil deliciously, and inventive twists include *briq au poisson* (an enormous spring roll of ultra-crispy pastry and Chinese noodles) and *malfouf* (stuffed cabbage with thick tomato sauce). It's upstairs in a private home, and is regularly packed. ⊠*27, rue Abdesslam Lebadi* ☎*024/47–36–55* ▭*No credit cards* ☉*Closed Mon.*

> **SWEET SNACKS**
>
> You won't find the same choice of sweet shops in Essaouira as in Marrakesh, but for a quick, sticky bite on the move you can't beat **Patisserie Moderne Chez Driss**. This long-standing patisserie on the main square may date back to 1929, but the French and Moroccan pastries are fresh every day, and cost as little as 4 DH. ⊠*10, rue el Hajali* ☎*024/47–57–93* ▭*No credit cards.*

$$$–$$$$
MOROCCAN
★

×**Le Patio.** A sure winner for "most stylish in town," this French-run restaurant offers Moroccan cooking with a twist. Fish tagines with pears, apples, or prunes, and rabbit with paprika are particular favorites. The small tables are set around a large starry lantern, and deep-red walls, white muslin, and candles create a romantic atmosphere. It's also a great spot for tapas and posing by the bar. There's a house punch, too, with so much rum in it you can see why they call it punch. ⊠*28 bis, rue Moulay Rachid* ☎*024/47–41–66* ▭*MC, V* ☉*Closed 1st 3 wks of Dec. and last 3 wks of Jan. No lunch.*

¢
SEAFOOD

×**Restaurant Essalam.** Situated along Essaouira's main square, this no-frills local place delivers good, standard Moroccan fare, such as couscous and tagines, as well as fried fish and pastilla. Seven set menus offer cheap meals from 28 DH to 40 DH. It's opposite the main strip of cafés, with seats indoors and out, so you're poised for prime people-watching. ⊠*Pl. Moulay Hassan* ☎*024/47–55–48* ▭*No credit cards.*

WHERE TO STAY

The riad mania that has taken over Marrakesh is spreading to Essaouira. Rooms are still less opulent and less expensive than those in Marrakesh, but you'll find plenty of charm and elegance. There are also plenty of even less expensive hotels, but fewer of the seriously budget hippie hangouts of yesteryear.

Don't limit yourself to hotels with swimming pools; you'll have only one option within the medina (the most expensive) and two outside. Budget hotels, riads, and new, more-expensive, *maisons d'hôte* give you the ocean instead. Besides, medina lodging puts you right in the action and is far more romantic. Beachfront hotels are fine if you have a large family, but they aren't necessary if you want to spend your time on water sports; the beach really isn't that far away on foot.

Another option is to rent an apartment, by the night or by the week. There's a wide range of options, from spartan bedrooms with showers that don't work to an entire super-styled riad. Renting is often a better deal than staying in a hotel, especially if you're with a group. Simply let an agent know your budget and something will usually turn up.

Rooms book up quickly, especially in summer, so reserve (sometimes months) ahead.

APARTMENT RENTALS

Arriving in the city's New Town, you'll see men dangling keys by the side of the road, hoping to rent you an apartment. It's best to go through official agents, however.

> **DOWN THE DERBS**
>
> You can only take a car as far as a medina gate, so you'll have to heave your luggage to that dear little out-of-the-way spot down 10 twisting derbs yourself. The best option? Pick up a *charette* (a small cart on wheels) from the parking lot outside Bab Sbâa and pay the owner and cart wheeler 20 DH for his trouble.

Castles in the Sand (☎067/96–53–86 ⊕*www.castlesinthesand.com*) rents out two villas by London-based interior designer Emma Wilson. Dar Beida, the "White Room," is one of Essaouira's most sumptuous addresses. The villa is filled with a hip range of furniture and decor from the 1950s and 1960s. Cool 21st-century perks include iPod speakers and wireless Internet. Dar Emma has a more-traditional feel. **Jack's Apartments** (⊠*1, pl. Moulay Hassan* ☎024/47–44–38 ⊕*www. essaouira.com/apartments*) has 16 beautiful old medina apartments, riads, and houses. Each is serviced daily, and all are equipped with Moroccan-style kitchens, bedrooms, bathrooms, and salons. Many have great sea views, too. **Karimo Immobilier** (⊠*Pl. Moulay Hassan* ☎024/47–45–00 ⊕*www.karimo.net*) can locate apartments all over the medina for pretty much any price.

MEDINA

$$$–$$$$ ▦**Dar Liouba.** Designed in a much more open style than many other Essaouira riads, Dar Liouba contains a central atrium that lets in plenty of light. Each room is a delight, employing primary colors and rustic furniture—ask for one with its own fireplace. It's in one of the highest parts of town, so you can enjoy the views while breakfasting on the roof terrace. **Pros:** Amazing rooftop views, airy central atrium. **Con:** Far from the medina. ⊠*28, Impasse Moulay Ismail* ☎024/47–62–97 ⊕*www.darliouba.com* ➯*6 rooms, 1 suite* ⚐*In-room: no phone* ⊟*No credit cards* ¶⊙*CP.*

$$–$$$ ▦**Dar Nafoura Mogador.** A kitchen that seems constantly on the go, and a warm welcome from husband and wife Sylvie and Jackie make for a homier take on chic riad living. Each room is themed according to color; tones of yellow, red, and mauve warm up the uniform Essaouira whitewash, and there are *tadelakt* (hard, polished finish) and zellij tiles everywhere. **Pros:** A short walk to the beach, delicious made-to-order meals. **Cons:** Bathrooms are particularly small, some rooms lack windows. ⊠*30, rue Ibn Khaldoun* ☎024/47–28–55 ⊕*www.darnafoura. com/en-home.html* ➯*5 rooms, 4 suites* ⚐*In-room: no phone* ⊟*MC, V* ¶⊙*CP.*

8

$$$$ **Heure Bleue Palais.** On paper at least, this Relais & Chateaux property is Essaouira's most prestigious lodging. Fans of Marrakesh's Villa des Orangers will find a similar colonial charm in the cream, granite, and dark-wood decor, which, to Moroccans, represents the "English" style. The facilities are second to none—there are few other places in Essaouira where for evening

> **WINDING DOWN**
>
> End your tour of town by doing as the locals (and temporary locals) do: people-watch while sipping a coffee or *louiza* (warm milk with fresh verveine leaves) in one of the outdoor cafés on Place Moulay Hassan.

entertainment one can choose between an in-house cinema and a heated rooftop swimming pool with the some of the best views in town. To top it all, the kitchen is overseen by an expert French chef who brings together a blend of earth and sea in the sumptuous Moroccan-French menu. **Pros:** In-house cinema, relaxing hammam, pretty pool. **Cons:** More British than Moroccan, out of the reach of mere mortals. ⊠*2, rue Ibn Batouta* ☎*024/78–34–34* ⊕*www.heure-bleue.com* ➹*16 rooms, 19 suites* ⌂*In-hotel: restaurant, pool, spa* ▤*AE, MC, V* ⊙*CP.*

$$–$$$ **Hôtel des Iles.** It's a 1950s concrete jungle, but Hôtel des Iles does have a smallish pool (although you may end up sharing it with the seagulls who use it as a bathtub) and is conveniently near both the beach and the medina. The bungalows with private terraces overlooking the pool have a better view than rooms overlooking the sea, since you have to first look past the uninspiring parking lot full of tour buses. **Pros:** Clean and comfortable. **Cons:** Full of tour groups, lacking in character. ⊠*Bd. Mohammed V* ☎*024/78–36–36* ➹*40 bungalows, 31 rooms, 4 suites* ⌂*In-room: refrigerator. In-hotel: 3 restaurants, bars, pool* ▤*AE, DC, MC, V.*

¢   **Hotel Smara.** It's little more than a concrete block in the middle of a very touristy street, but this budget option's ocean view and proximity to the ancient medina walls make up for it. A room with a view costs almost twice as much as one without, but you can always look out from the windy rooftop terrace. It's regularly full, so book in advance. **Pros:** Easy on the wallet, great location. **Cons:** Sheets are a bit stiff, staff doesn't speak English. ⊠*26, rue de Skala* ☎*024/47–56–55* ➹*20 rooms* ⌂*In-room: no TV* ▤*No credit cards.*

$$$$ **Madada Mogador.** Stylized, elegant, and designed to perfection, this is
Fodor'sChoice   Essaouira's ultimate riad. It's perfectly poised within the medina walls
★   to get great ocean views. The rooms are exquisitely decorated with a chic modern take on Moroccan style. If you want traditional, rugged, and real, you won't find it here. If you want minimalist high fashion and smooth lines, make sure to call ahead. **Pros:** Marvelous massages, range of activities, plenty of pampering. **Cons:** Books up months in advance, very expensive. ⊠*4, rue Youssef el Fassi* ☎*024/47–55–12* ⊕*www.madada.com* ➹*6 rooms* ⌂ *In-hotel: restaurant, spa, public Wi-Fi* ▤*MC, V* ⊙*CP.*

$$–$$$ **Maison du Sud.** There's a twist to this great traditional option through
★   a heavy stone arch on a medina street: each room has a Moroccan salon with stairs leading up to a charming mezzanine level that fits a bed and

leather lamp shades. The courtyard, set around a fountain filled with roses, is so comfortable you may be reluctant to finish your breakfast and start your day. The manager is prepared to meet any request. The set dinner menu costs 90 DH. **Pros:** Delicious meals, cozy lounges. **Con:** Pricey for what you get. ☒29, *ave. Sidi Mohammed Ben Abdellah* ☎024/47–41–41 ⊕*www.riad-mai sondusud.com* ⌨7 rooms, 7 suites ⚄*In-hotel: restaurant, bar, bicycles* ▤*AE, MC, V* ��⊙⸠*CP.*

$$$ ▦ **Palazzo Desdemona.** This classy small hotel has rooms with sophisticated decor: white woolen blankets, low divans, and delicate accents of selectively placed Moroccan antiques. Some rooms have fireplaces, and others come with ornate wrought-iron four-poster beds. Rooms in the back have wide-board floors and are quieter than those facing the busy street. There's a roof terrace for breakfast or an evening aperitif. **Pros:** Large rooms, relaxed atmosphere. **Con:** Creaky floors make for noisy evenings. ☒12–14, *rue Youssef el Fassi* ☎024/47–22–27 ⌨15 *rooms, 7 suites* ⚄*In-hotel: bar* ▤*No credit cards.*

$-$$ ▦ **Résidence el Mehdi.** Inexpensive rooms with private bathrooms surrounding a pleasant courtyard trimmed with blue shutters make this is a pretty option. **Pros:** Spic-and-span rooms, good value. **Con:** Decor is a bit outdated. ☒15, *rue Sidi Abdessmih* ☎024/47–59–43 ⊕*www. residence-el-mehdi.com* ⌨13 *rooms, 3 suites, 2 apartments* ⚄*In-hotel: restaurant, bar* ▤*No credit cards* ⸠⊙⸠*CP.*

$$$ ▦ **Riad Al Madina.** Near the Maison du Sud, this beautiful riad is
★ wrapped around a stone courtyard where you'll find a trickling fountain. Greenery tumbles down from the balconies above, creating a magical space. The sumptuous rooms are some of the city's most expensive, but they offer unmatched sophistication. The restaurant is also lovely, with low arches and pressed-tin lamps providing atmosphere. The hotel has its own hammam, which can be used by nonguests, too (from 70 DH for a hammam to 350 DH for the works—hammam, exfoliation, and clay wrap). **Pros:** Sun-filled rooms, plenty of pampering, in-house hammam. **Con:** Often very crowded. ☒9, *rue Attarine* ☎024/47–59–07 or 024/47–57–27 ⊕*www.riadalmadina.com* ⌨54 *rooms* ⚄*In-hotel: restaurant, bar, spa, no elevator* ▤*MC, V* ⸠⊙⸠*CP.*

$$-$$$ ▦ **Riad Lalla Mogador.** There's a kind of dollhouse charm to this tiny riad. No two rooms are the same; some cover two floors, and one has a private terrace. Plenty of colorful touches and a castellated sun terrace for looking out across the city complete the exceedingly pretty picture. Five languages are spoken by the staff, who will also organize excursions for guests. **Pros:** Unique rooms, filled with tiny treasures. **Con:** Family rooms are small. ☒12, *rue de l'Iraq* ☎024/47–67–44 ⊕*www.riadlallamogador.com* ⌨6 *rooms, 2 suites* ⚄*In-room: no phone* ▤*No credit cards* ⸠⊙⸠*CP.*

8

$$$$ 🏨 **Riad Mimouna.** Tight against the northern side of the medina walls,
★ this riad sits over the water's edge, letting you have the raging sea all
to yourself. The riad was once an enormous family home, and boasts
traditional dark carved wood and stained glass. For a real treat, ask
for Suite 210, which has magnificent sea views on two sides. **Pros:**
Beautiful views, central heating in winter. **Con:** Expensive rates. ✉62,
rue d'Oujda, Sandillon ☎024/78–57–53 ⊕*www.riad-mimouna.com*
🛏*24 rooms, 9 suites* ♿*In-hotel: beachfront* ▭*MC, V* ❙○❙*CP.*

$ 🏨 **Riad Nakhla.** This favorite of budget travelers offers the pleasure of
riad living at budget-hotel prices. Rooms are well decorated and have
satellite television. The English-speaking staff goes out of its way to
please. It lacks the class of the better-appointed riads, but only just,
and a great location adds to its appeal. **Pro:** Great budget choice.
Cons: Windows face interior, rooms aren't always well kept. ✉*12
rte. d'Agadir, Quos Ben Attar* ☎024/47–52–30 ⊕*www.essaouiranet.
com/riad-nakhla* 🛏*16 rooms, 2 suites* ♿*In-room: no phone* ▭*No
credit cards.*

$$$–$$$$ 🏨 **Riad Watier.** Roomier than the average Essaouira riad, the Watier
↺ seems as though it's showing off with the size of its rooms. Each of the
★ 10 individually designed suites is on a palatial scale, with bedrooms,
living rooms, and beds you could fit most of the port into. It's an ideal
choice if you have children but don't want to miss out on riad life. The
tiny dining room actually looks like it can accommodate all the guests
at once. The cubbyhole of a library, stocked with books on the his-
torical trials and tribulations of Essaouira, is constantly growing. **Pros:**
Lovely communal spaces, wonderful dining. **Con:** In a noisy part of the
medina. ✉*16, rue Ceuta* ☎024/47–62–04 ⊕*www.ryad-watier-maroc.
com* 🛏*10 suites* ♿*In-hotel: no elevator* ▭*MC, V* ❙○❙*CP.*

$$$ 🏨 **Villa Maroc.** Embodying much of what international travelers seek in
★ a Moroccan hotel, the intimate Villa Maroc is delightfully decorated to
epitomize a "traditional" Moroccan style that never really was. It takes
up four connected 18th-century riads and has you climbing, turning,
and ducking as though you're navigating a medina. There's little in
the way of grand luxury about the rooms. White keeps the look fresh,
but the place is also cluttered with Moroccan textiles, metalwork,
and ceramic tiles. Try to reserve Room 2, 5, 6, or 7; these have great
views. Room 30, a suite, takes up an entire floor of a tiny riad, and is
a delight. The restaurant serves a different sophisticated three-course
dinner each day in nooks around the second floor, and a breakfast of
assorted pancakes on the sunny central terrace upstairs. Half-board is
required in April, July, and August. **Pros:** Delicious breakfasts, sizable
rooms. **Con:** Faux-Moroccan style. ✉*10, rue Abdellah Ben Yassine*
☎024/47–61–47 ⊕*www.villa-maroc.com* 🛏*7 rooms, 13 suites* ♿*In-
hotel: restaurant, spa, no elevator* ▭*MC, V* ❙○❙*CP.*

ON THE BEACH

$$$$ 🏨 **Le Jardin des Douars.** Beachfront life will seem raucous after a few
↺ hours at this tranquil, out-of-the-way country retreat. It's an architec-
★ tural tour de force; almost every surface is rendered in glorious dark
pink tadelakt, and each individually designed room is guarded by ogre-
size wooden doors. Most rooms occupy either two levels or multiple

rooms, and are intended specifically for families or two couples. The sunken fireplace area brings added coziness to cool winter nights, and the pool and gardens are a perfect antidote to sultry summer afternoons. **Pros:** Lovely pool, a restful retreat. **Con:** It's not near anything. ✉*Sidi Yassine on road to Marrakesh* ☎*024/79–24–92* ⊕*www.jardindesdouars.com* ⇆*10 rooms, 5 suites, 2 bungalows* ♿*In-hotel: pool, bar* ▤*AE, MC, V* ⎮⎰⎮*CP.*

$$$$ ⌶ **Sofitel Thalassa Mogador.** Looming over the beach, this five-star hotel has little of the magic that is Essaouira. Rooms fail to inspire, service is harried, and you miss all the fun of the medina. However, it offers everything else one would expect from a full-service major international chain, with the addition of thalassotherapy clinics for massage, aquatic gymnastics, two restaurants (including one on the beach), and a pool. **Pros:** Large pool, plenty of activities. **Cons:** Lacks character, quite expensive. ✉*Bd. Mohammed V* ☎*024/47–90–00* ⊕*www.sofitel.com* ⇆*117 rooms, 8 suites* ♿*In-hotel: 2 restaurants, bar, pool, water sports* ▤*AE, DC, MC, V.*

> **DID YOU KNOW?**
>
> Inspector Watier was the French engineer who masterminded the reclamation of Essaouira from the dunes that surrounded it, paving the way for the modern town that exists today. He managed to reclaim 37 acres of dunes by furiously planting trees, which kept the sand at bay. Check into Riad Watier to read up on the details.

SHOPPING

ANTIQUES

Galeria Aida (✉*Rue Sakala, next door to Taros restaurant* ☎*061/70–50–45*) has an interesting selection of glassware and bric-a-brac, but the real draw is the impressive collection of antique daggers, all surrounded by multilingual commands not to touch. There's also a bookshop selling classics such as Paul Bowles's *The Sheltering Sky.* **Galerie Jama** (✉*22, rue Ibn Rochd* ☎*024/78–58–97*) seems more museum than shop, and as such is a good bet for specialists. You can browse among wooden doors, mosaic vases, and all sorts of wonderful odds and ends. Prices aren't marked, so get ready to negotiate if you see something you like.

ARGAN OIL

Argan d'Or (✉*5, rue Ibn Rocha* ☎*024/78–40–69 or 061/60–14–71*) is a little boutique with a great selection of argan-oil products from women's cooperatives all over the country. There are also more-expensive cosmetic oils for the face, hands, and body.

If you want to try out the delights of argan oil before you buy, Sanda, who runs **Massage du Monde** (☎*077/54–28–88*), offers argan-oil massages galore, from 450 DH for 75 glorious minutes. Other massages start at 100 DH for 15 minutes.

ART

Many galleries clustered in one quarter of the medina display contemporary Moroccan and expatriate mixed-media productions.

Essaouira's Best Buys

Essaouira is Morocco's best shopping destination south of Marrakesh, and has a vast range of high-quality products and very few hustlers. If you've gotten used to haggling in Marrakesh or Fez, you can relax here, as starting prices are often reasonable.

Essaouira is famed as an artisanal center expert in marquetry and inlay. Boxes, platters, and picture frames made of local **thuya wood** make excellent gifts, and the wood-carvers' souk below the sqala is the best place to purchase them. A hard local wood that shines up to almost plastic perfection, thuya is sculpted for both artistic and practical use. Almost-life-size statues and sculptures sit alongside boxes, bowls, and chess sets. Scan a number of stores to see whether you prefer the even-toned thuya branch inlaid with mother-of-pearl or walnut or one with swirling root designs. To get a bulk price, buy a bunch of picture frames from a craftsman who specializes in them.

Carpets, goatskin lamps, and **metal candlesticks** are sold in the square next to the clock tower; compare their prices with those in the shops on side streets off Avenue de l'Istiqlal. The goatskin lamps are etched with

henna and are highly fashionable at the moment.

There's a veritable warehouse of carpets and **carpet-scrap pillow covers** down Route de Marrakesh, off Avenue de l'Istiqlal; tell the store owners that you're looking for a bigger selection than they offer, and they'll lead you to the warehouse.

Colorful, square **woven baskets** hang from herbalists' stores in the medina. New and old **silver jewelry** is sold in the extensive silver souk between the medina's inner gates and in the shops starting from the BMCE Bank, heading off Place Moulay Hassan down Avenue de l'Istiqlal.

For tasteful used **pewter platters and goblets** and **ceramic teapots,** as well as new and used English and French books, check the **Galérie Aida** (⊠ *2, rue de la Skala* ☎ *024/47-62-90*), underneath the ramparts. The gallery's owner, Joseph Sebag, a Jewish multimedia artist, and his staff are knowledgeable about remnants of the city's Jewish history.

If you packed too light to brave the chilly Atlantic wind, buy a **handwoven sweater** in Place Moulay Hassan or the square off Rue Laalouj.

★ The **Gallerie d'Art Fréderic Damgaard** (⊠ *Ave. Oqba Ibn Nafiaa* ☎ *024/78-44-46*), across from the clock tower, has well-curated displays, with artists' biographies, of work by Essaouira painters and sculptors; the gallery also sells books and pamphlets on regional art and culture. It's open daily 10–1 and 3–7. Another standout is the **Espace Othello Gallerie d'Art** (⊠ *9, rue Mohammed Layachi* ☎ *024/47-50-95*), where part of Orson Welles's *Othello* was shot. It's open daily 9–1 and 3–8. The lithe, lunar figures in the paintings of **Slimane Driss** (⊠ *Rue Ibn Rachid* ☎ *065/66-06-30* ⊕ *www.artmajeur.com/soulaiman*) are a departure from usual art, but with plenty of take-home potential. The gallery is open daily from 9 to 9.

Morocco's Art Town

Essaouira has developed into a hub for contemporary Moroccan art, and draws artists, poets, and craftsmen from all over the country. It's therefore thronged with art galleries, with both expatriates and numerous local and regional artists producing works year-round. Among the better-known artists are Nurredin Alioua, Mohammed Bouada, and Mohammed Tabal.

GNAOUA ART

Essaouira is considered the spiritual home of the Gnaoua, whose cultural roots lie in sub-Saharan Africa, and whose powerful, mysterious blend of Islam with animism and fetishism continues to fascinate today. As well as trancelike music for which Gnaoua are known, the beguiling fantastic designs and bold colors of Gnaoua art have become fashionable in recent years.

Some see this "tribal," "native," or "trancelike" art as having similarities with Caribbean-island-style painting in its colors and fluid designs. Danish collector Frederic Damgaard saw echoes of the Tahitian work of Gauguin in the nature and color of the paintings of Mohammed Tabal and others; he was one of the first to bring the work to international attention in 1988. At the time, Tabal was something akin to a troubadour, wandering the countryside happily performing Gnaouan rites in return for a night's lodging and a little food.

As with the music, Gnoauan painting is considered autodidactic, as the artist gives himself over to quasi-possession by another, higher force that guides the strokes of the brush and takes the artist into a trancelike state. Other practitioners include Ali Maimoune and Fatima Ettabi.

CALLIGRAPHY

There's also a great calligraphy tradition here. Artists are bringing the beauty and inspiration of Arabic and Berber script to the canvas, and many of their works hang in the more-affluent riads.

Three artists in particular are going strong in this area. The first is Essaouira-born Mohammed Zouzaf, a Berber artist who marks signs and symbols on lamb's skins. (To see his work, head for the Espace Othello Gallerie d'Art (⇨above) and look out for the walls in the long-established riad-hotel Villa Maroc.) Another is Casablanca native Mohamed Boustous, whose elegant works on skins and paper focus on calligraphy in the grand Arab tradition. Mohammed Tifardine, an Essaouira native, also paints with calligraphy, taking inspiration from the great philosophers. His work tends to be soothing and magnificent, and manages to communicate a clear beauty to viewers, even if they don't understand the script.

8

HOUSEWARES

You can't beat **Jamade** (✉*Pl. des Artistes, 21 Bab Doukala* ☎*068/76–41–76*) for just about anything you might like to put in your home. Tadelakt vases, lamp stands, and bowls in bright, bold colors sit alongside beaded goods, candleholders, and bags. **Kifkif** (✉*204, Marché aux Grains* ☎*061/08–20–41*) has textiles, accessories, and desirable objects for the home, all made using local artisanal techniques.

JEWELRY

La Fibule Berbère (⊠*51, 53, rue Attarine* ☎*024/47–62–55 or 66/64–19–89*) has stunning ethnic jewelry, such as huge silver pendants and bulky necklaces made in the Berber and Toureg styles. Delve into an astounding array of brightly colored fabric handbags at **Poupa Litza** (⊠*135 bis, rue Mohamed el Kory* ☎*024/78–35–65*). Goods from this atelier also sell in Europe, but prices are much cheaper here, plus you have the joy of seeing where it's all made. They also have a selection of jewelry.

> **DON'T MISS**
>
> Rue el Mahdi is delightful for browsing. Running away from the Cap Sim hotel, this small derb has endless little boutiques, but hasn't yet been overrun with tourists. Many shops are unnamed; for example, a very chic one opposite Beldy sells fabulously stylish bags and lighters. Other shops have henna-painted lanterns made of calfskin.

WOODWORK

Thuya wood furniture is as unavoidable on the streets of Essaouira as in-line skaters in Malibu Beach, and just as painful if you bump into it. If you want to find some untouristy workshops off the main streets, take a right onto Rue Khalid Ibn el Walid, just off Place Moulay Hassan.

Chez Hassan (⊠*15, rue Khalid Ibn el Walid* ☎*024/78–40–63*) turns out lovely boxes and trinkets ideal for taking home from as little as 20 DH.

Coopérative Artisanale des Marqueteurs (⊠*Rue Khalid Ibn el Walid* ☎*024/47–56–76*) turns out finely decorated tables and larger furniture. Everything has a price tag, and prices are highly reasonable.

OUTDOOR ACTIVITIES

CYCLING

You can rent bikes at many hotels. You can also hire from **Velo Location Chez Youssef** (⊠*10, rue el Mohajir* ☎*072/04–40–67 or 068/25–46–02*). Their bicycles go for 80 DH a day, or 120 DH with a guide who can point out good local trails depending on interest, distance, and time.

HORSEBACK & CAMEL RIDING

You can arrange horseback riding with **Les Cavaliers d'Essaouira** (⊠*Rte. de Marrakesh, Km 14* ☎*065/07–48–89*). **Equitation Randonées** (☎*062/74–34–97 or 068/09–80–11* ⊕*www.randocheval.com*) offers a wealth of horseback-riding itineraries of 2 to 15 days for 400 DH a day. They tailor tours to the season, so it's off to the desert in winter and to the mountains in summer. **Location de Chameaux** (☎*061/94–35–68 or 061/99–70–25*) offers camel riding from an hour (100 DH) to a full day (400 DH) with Rachid el Filali, and can organize longer treks and overnight camping in bivouacs.

HAMMAMS & SPAS

The following hammams and spas are open to all (even nonguests, if in a hotel).

PUBLIC HAMMAMS

Hammam Bagdad. This basic but user-friendly hammam for men is located in the medina—ask for directions at any kiosk on Rue Bagdad. ⊠*Rue Bagdad, Essaouira* ☏*No phone* 🖅*5 DH* ☉*Daily* ⊟*No credit cards.*

Hammam Pabst. Located in the Mellah, this is one of the oldest hammams in Essaouira. Now brightly painted, it has a plaque indicating that Orson Welles once used it as a location during the filming of *Hamlet.* ⊠*Rue Annasr, Essaouira* ☏*No phone* 🖅*10 DH* ☉*Daily* ⊟*No credit cards.*

PRIVATE HAMMAM

Hammam Mounia. In addition to hammam, this nicely renovated old spa offers four-hand massages with essential oils, and has a relaxation room–cum-café. Be prepared for crowds, as it's very popular. ⊠*17, rue Oum Errabia, Essaouira* ☏*024/78–42–47* 🖅*50 DH, 70 DH with exfoliation* ☉*Men: daily 7:30–9:30 AM, 12:30–4:30 PM, and 8–10:30 PM; women: daily 9:30 AM–12:30 PM and 4:30–8 PM* ⊟*No credit cards.*

HOTEL HAMMAMS

Hotel Riad Al Madina. This unreasonably expensive riad near the Maison du Sud has a rather good hammam that nonguests can use. It's 70 DH for a hammam and 350 DH for the works (hammam, gommage, and clay wrap). ⊠*9, rue Attarine, Essaouira* ☏*024/47–59–07 or 024/47–57–27* ⊕*www.riadalmadina.com* 🖅*15 DH hammam, treatments 60 DH–180 DH* ⊟*MC, V.*

Lalla Mira Hotel. This small "bio-hotel" in the medina has nicely renovated the oldest hammam in Essaouira, located next door. It's heated by thermo-solar power instead of wood. ⊠*14, rue d'Algerie, Essaouira* ☏*024/47–50–46* 🖅*15 DH hammam, treatments 60 DH–180 DH* ☉*Daily 8:30 AM–8:30 PM, by appointment* ⊟*No credit cards.*

Villa Maroc. The first riad in Essaouira has a small private hammam perfect for one person or a couple. ⊠*10, rue Abdellah Ben Yassine, Essaouira* ☏*024/47–31–47 or 024/47–61–47* 🖅*500 DH per person or couple* ☉*Upon request* ⊟*MC, V.*

SPAS

L'Heure Bleue. Located in a busy alley in the medina, this palatial riad hotel has a hammam, massage room, and swimming pool. ⊠*2, rue Ibn Batouta, Bab Marrakesh, Essaouira* ☏*024/78–34–34* 🖅*250 DH with exfoliation* ☉*Upon request 1–2 days in advance* ⊟*AE, MC, V.*

Hotel Sofitel. Situated on the seafront, this hotel specializes in thalassotherapy, water jet showers, hydrating baths, massages, and aqua gym workouts. There's also a heated outdoor pool and solarium. ⊠*Bd. Mohammed V, Essaouira* ☏*024/47–90–00* 🖅*360 DH with exfoliation* ☉*Upon request* ⊟*AE, DC, MC, V.*

–Pamela Windo

8

KITING
Kite Adventure (☎ *064/89–41–59* ⊕ *www.kiteadventuressaouira. com*) is run by Raynaud Christophe, a qualified instructor who can teach lessons from beginner to advanced. Under the direction of Jean-Louis Marchand, **Mogador Evasion** (☎ *078/95–50–17*) offers buggies with parachutes and windsurfing on wheels down the beach.

QUAD-BIKING & BUGGIES
Aladin Aventure (☎ *078/45–80–95*) can organize trips on quads and buggies from an hour to a full day, with guide. **Essaouira Quad** (☎ *072/15–32–95* ⊕ *www.essaou iraquad.com*) rents out both one- and two-seater quads. They suggest several local tours around Essaouira that last between three hours and a day.

SAILING
Base Nautique (✉ *Bd. Mohammed V* ☎ *024/47–90–00*), a sailing school owned by Sofitel, and just across the way from the hotel on the beach, gives lessons.

WATER SPORTS
★ **Club Mistral and Skyriders Centre** (✉ *Bd. Mohammed V* ☎ *024/78–39–34* ⊕ *www.club-mistral.com* ☉ *Daily 9–6*) is the biggest outfit in town. It prides itself on the quality of its equipment and its multidisciplinary and multilingual instruction. Factor this into the cost of courses, which are pricier, but also more comprehensive than elsewhere along the bay: three days of surfing instruction cost 660 DH, while a 10-hour windsurfing starter course costs 1,980 DH, and 10 hours of kite surfing costs 3,080 DH.

Fun System (✉ *Bd. de la Plage, across from the Sofitel* ☎ *024/47–65–28* ⊕ *www.fun-system.com*) is German-run, but there are plenty of English-speakers on staff. You can rent new boards and take windsurfing lessons and kiting lessons (€90 for three hours). You can even take a free one-hour taster surfing lesson before signing up for any courses. Experienced water-sports enthusiasts can also rent equipment (€15 for an hour of windsurfing).

★ **Magic Fun** (✉ *Bd. de la Plage, beyond Sofitel* ☎ *061/10–37–77* ⊕ *www. magicfunafrika.com*) can set you up for just about anything, including kayaking (from 100 DH an hour, 330 DH for a day), surfing (300 DH for a 2-hour lesson, 1,000 DH for 10 hours), and windsurfing (150 DH for an hour, 450 DH for a day). Lessons are kept to a maximum of four people, so the focus is really on learning. They will pick you up for no extra charge.

BEACHING IT

The stretch between Essaouira and Sidi Ifni presents the most spectacular coast anywhere in Morocco. The first half of the trip north from Agadir on the P8 road to Essaouira is particularly stunning. A drive is pleasant in itself, but you can stop and relax at several turnoffs from the main road both north and south of Agadir. Unspoiled beaches lie just 10 km (6 mi) north of Sidi Ifni; the only travelers who find the unmarked dirt road come in campers during the summer months.

AGADIR

172 km (103 mi) south of Essaouira.

Agadir is a holiday resort. Don't hope for a medina, a souk, or a Kasbah (although it does have all three, after a fashion). Think sun, sea, and sand. These are what it does best, as hundreds of thousands of visitors each year can testify.

There's no reason to begrudge the city its tourist aspirations. Razed by an earthquake in 1960 that killed 15,000 people in 13 seconds, Agadir had to be entirely rebuilt. Today it's a thoroughly modern city where travelers don't think twice about showing considerable skin, and Moroccans benefit from the growing number of jobs.

There's a reason why this popular European package vacation destination is overrun with enormous, characterless beachfront hotels. The beach, all 10 km (6 mi) of it, is dreamy. A 450-yard-wide strip, it bends in an elegant crescent along the bay, and is covered with fine-grain sand. The beach is sheltered and safe for swimming, making it perfect for families. Farther north, where small villages stand behind some of the best waves in the world, is a surfers' paradise.

Even if you have no interest in surfing, diving, jet skiing, golf, tennis, or horseback riding down the beach, you can treat Agadir as a modern bubble in which to kick back. It's equipped with familiar pleasurable pursuits—eating, drinking, and relaxing next to the ocean—and modern amenities such as car-rental agencies and ATMs. It isn't quite Europe, but neither is it quite Morocco.

GETTING HERE & AROUND

Most travelers fly directly into Agadir's Al Massira airport. Although there are no flights from North America, connections through European airports are easy. Inexpensive buses are easy ways to get here from Essaouira, Marrakesh, and beyond. If all else fails, grands taxis can take you just about anywhere for the right price.

Once in Agadir, you'll find that the city is easily navigable on foot. The city's orange petits taxis are easy to flag down. Agadir also has all the major car-rental agencies, including Hertz and Avis.

Complete Tours is an English-run operation based in Agadir that can put together your whole trip, including hotels, excursions, and meals—everything but the flight. Massina Travel has a great range of trips to Imouzzer, Tafraoute, Tiznit, and as far as Tata, Essaouira, and Marrakesh. You can pick up good local and regional maps at Info Touriste Agadir, as well as brochures and seasonal guides to dance, music, and theater around town. It's closed Sunday but open weekdays 9–noon and 3–6, Saturday 9–noon.

TIMING & PRECAUTIONS

Many first-time travelers to Morocco never leave Agadir, but that would be a mistake; a great idea for first-timers is to make Agadir home base and take day trips to other towns in the area. Agadir is on

8

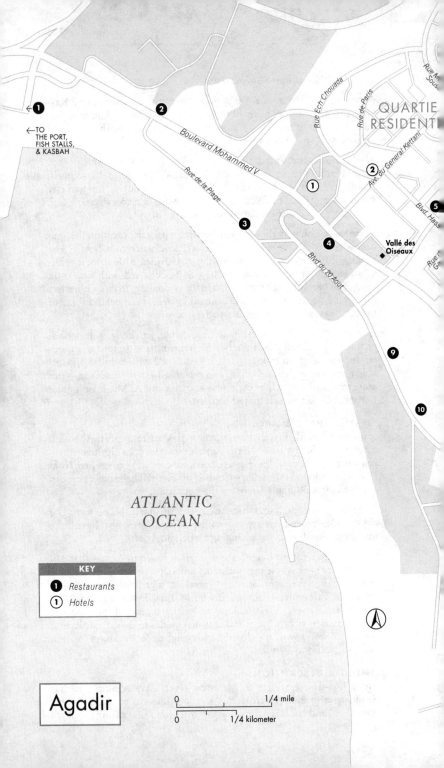

Agadir

ATLANTIC
OCEAN

KEY
❶ Restaurants
① Hotels

0   1/4 mile
0   1/4 kilometer

←TO
THE PORT,
FISH STALLS,
& KASBAH

Boulevard Mohammed V

Rue de la Plage

Blvd du 20 Aout

Rue Ech Chouada

Rue de Paris

Ave. du General Kettani

Rue M.
Sous...

Blvd. Hass...

Rue de
Ga...

QUARTIE
RESIDENT

Vallé des
Oiseaux

❷ ❸ ❹ ❺ ❾ ❿ ② ①

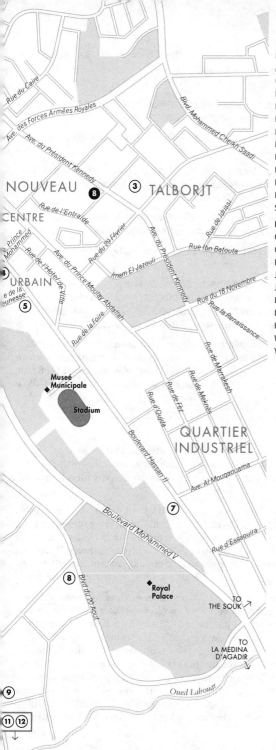

8

the whole fairly safe, though it's a good idea to keep an eye on your wallet, as pickpockets are a problem.

ESSENTIALS

Bus Contacts C.T.M (⊠*Bd. Zerktouni, Guéliz, Marrakesh* ☎*024/44–83–28*). **Supratours** (⊠*Ave. Hassan II* ☎*024/43–55–25*).

Currency Exchange Banque Populaire (⊠*Bd. Hassan II*) **Wafa Bank** (⊠*Bd. Hassan II*).

Internet Cyber Café Indrif (⊠*60, ave. Prince Moulay Abdellah*). **Internet Swiss** (⊠*Bd. Hassan II*). **Sannad@Sahelnet** (⊠*48/3, bd. Mohammed V*). **Streamnet** (⊠*Rue Allal ben Abdellah, Talborjt*).

Medical Assistance Clinic Al Massira (⊠*Ave. du 29 Février* ☎*028/84–32–38*) **Night Pharmacy** (⊠*Ave. Sidi Mohammed* ☎*028/82–03–49*).

Post Office Poste (⊠*Corner of Ave. du Prince Moulay Abdellah and Ave. PS Sidi Mohammed*)

Rental Cars Avis (☎*028/82–14–14, 028/83–92–44 airport*). **Budget** (☎*028/84–82–22, 028/83–91–01 airport*). **Diamant Cars** (⊠*Corner of Ave. du Prince Moulay Abdellah and Ave. PS Sidi Mohammed* ☎*028/82–22–12*). **Europcar** (☎*028/84–03–37, 028/83–90–66 airport*). **Hertz** (☎*028/84–09–39, 028/83–90–71 airport*).

Visitor & Tour Info Complete Tours (⊠*No. 26, Immeuble Oumlil, ave. Hassan II* ☎*028/82–34–01 or 028/82–34–02* ⊕*www.complete-tours.com*). **Info Touriste Agadir** (⊠*Bd. Mohammed V* ☎*028/82–53–04*). **Massina Travel** (⊠*Bd. du 20 Août, in Tagardirt complex by Blue Orange restaurant* ☎*028/82–67–05 or 061/16–55–52*).

EXPLORING

Kasbah. High up on the hill to the northwest that looks over Agadir is the old Kasbah. It's in need of restoration, but still worth the exertion to make it to the top and back down to the port for a hearty fish lunch.

Emblazoned on the side of the hill below the Kasbah are three Arabic words that keep guard over Agadir at all times. Their meaning? God, country, and the king. By day they're a patchwork of huge white stones against the green grass. By night they're lighted up powerfully against the dark. The huge hill is really a burial mound, covering the old medina and the impromptu graves of those who died in the earthquake.

La Medina d'Agadir. In Aghroud, a few miles south of Agadir on the Inezgane road, is a remarkable 13-acre project-in-progress orchestrated by Moroccan-born Italian decorator-architect Coco Polizzi. He dreamed of replacing the medina Agadir lost to the 1960 earthquake with a new medina on his own land. This combination of living ethnological museum and high-quality bazaar is being constructed by Moroccan craftsmen following centuries-old techniques. Each stone is laid by hand, and the buildings are made of earth, rock from the Souss, slate from the High Atlas, and local woods such as thuya and eucalyptus. Decorations follow both Berber and Saharan motifs. Mosaic craftsmen, painters, jewelers, a henna artist, metalworkers, and carpenters welcome spectators as they practice their crafts (and welcome customers for the results) in workshop nooks throughout the medina. The grand plan is to have a restaurant, hotel, and even an amphitheater. To get here, pick up one of the regular shuttles (60 DH round-trip, including entry) that pass by several of the big hotels. ⊠*B.P. 230, Bensergao* ☎*028/28–02–53* ⊕*www.medina polizzi.com* ⊠*40 DH* ⊙*Daily 8:30–6:30.*

> ## ALL ABOARD
>
> ☪ A ridiculous yet amusing way to see the town is with the Petit Train, a small white train with three carriages pulled by a motorcar at the front. It leaves every 35 minutes (9:15 AM until nightfall) from the kiosk south of the Vallée des Oiseaux. It's as touristy as a Hawaiian shirt, but kids love it and it's a great way to get off your feet. Tickets cost 18 DH and the ride lasts half an hour.

Musée Municipale. Agadir's municipal museum features photography and local handicrafts, but is open only when an exhibition is mounted. Check with the tourist office in the Hôtel de Ville (town hall) for details. ⊠*Ave. du Prince Héritier Sidi Mohammed* ☎*28/82–28–94.*

☪ **Souk Al Had.** In the northeastern corner of the city is a daily bazaar selling both souvenirs and household goods. You'll need to bargain hard. ⊙*Tues.–Sat.*

☪ **Vallée des Oiseaux** (*Valley of the Birds*). It's not so much a valley as a great route connecting Avenue Hassan II to the beach. It not only has birds, but also monkeys, fountains, and lovely green surroundings. ⊠*Ave. du Prince Héritier Sidi Mohammed* ☎*28/82–28–94* ⊠*5 DH* ⊙*Daily 9:30–12:30 and 2:30–6:30.*

BEACHES

AGADIR BEACH

Agadir beach swings around a crescent from southeast to northwest. You're more likely to find a quiet spot if you wander south. The most crowded areas, frequented year-round by families and locals, are to the north. Along the flanking thoroughfare, known as the Corniche (promenade), you'll find inexpensive cafés, bars, and restaurants. It can be a little sketchy at night, but it's still a good spot to stop and watch the world go by. The northern tip is also the place to rent a catamaran or surf equipment. Toward the northern end of the beach, next to Place Al Wahda, is a children's fun fair. There are small trains, individual toys to sit in (5 DH), and minicarts (10 DH for 15 minutes).

TAGHAZOUTE

In late summer the beaches north of Agadir on the Essaouira road—especially those in rapidly expanding Taghazoute—are crammed with camping Moroccan families, but it empties out in winter. The Number 12 bus runs from Agadir to Taghazoute.

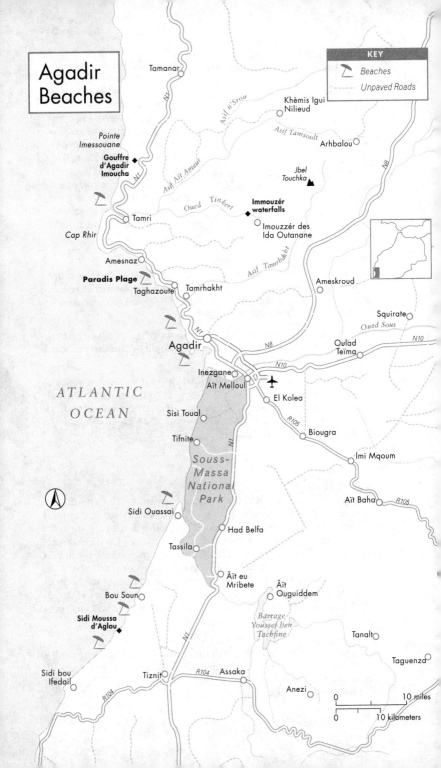

CAP RHIR

The rest of the year, a few stray Western surfers seek out waves around the bend from the lighthouse at Cap Rhir, but otherwise the neighboring village of Aghroud is, like Taghazoute, quiet—a pretty detour, with empty sands and calm waters. You may come across a bald ibis, as their preserve is nearby at the Souss Massa National Park & Estuary (⇨ *For the Birds box in Chapter 9*).

OFF THE BEATEN PATH

Imouzzer. From Aourir (12 km [7 mi] north of Agadir), take the paved road 50 km (31 mi) up into the Ida Outanane Mountains to the waterfalls here, near Isk. Check with locals – the waterfalls are often dry when the region is experiencing drought. Dry hills closer to the coast give way to the palm gorge of Paradise Valley, where the rocky riverbank welcomes picnicking Moroccan families and foreigners alike.

WHERE TO EAT

Neon signs throughout Agadir lure you in to sample not so much the delights of Moroccan cuisine as the woes of fast food and international menus. Nevertheless, many of these restaurants have good locations along the beachfront or in the town center. The main joy of eating in Agadir is the chance to dine in fish restaurants, which also tend to be the least brash and pretentious. All major hotels have both Moroccan and continental restaurants, and many now have Mexican, Asian, and Lebanese options. There's also a good selection of Italian food and pizza. ■TIP➔ For some of the town's best seafood and a refreshing change of scenery, head to the warehouses and wharves of the port.

8

¢ MOROCCAN

✕**Café les Arcades.** The farther north out of the tourist zone you go, the closer you get to what Moroccans really eat. This spit-and-sawdust roadside café is the perfect antidote to the high-rolling resorts by the beach. Locals hang out there all day long, and you can get a set meal of three tasty dishes (salad, soup, or omelet; meat or fish; dessert) for an incredible 35 DH, and watch the real world go by to boot. ✉*Bd. Allal ben Abdellah, Talborjt* ☎*No phone* 🚫*No credit cards.*

$–$$ SEAFOOD ★

✕**Chez Mimi la Brochette.** Run by Mimi and her husband for over 25 years, this place brings a little style to the chain of cheapos at the northern end of the beach. Everything is grilled over a wood fire, and you can get great fish, including lobster and prawns. Don't miss the fig-based digestif, Mahia, or the chance to have hot prawns or smoked eel saladThe house specialty is, of course, brochettes of any kind; there's plenty of meat on the menu, too. The only downside is that you can't eat here Friday night. ✉*Promenade du Bord de mer, Complexe Al Moggar* ☎*028/84–03–87* 🚫*No credit cards* ⊘*No dinner Fri., no lunch Sat.*

¢–$ ENGLISH

✕**English Pub.** Just when you thought you couldn't get Yorkshire pudding in Morocco, you come across this street-side bar and restaurant. It prides itself on comfort food—burgers and fries—and full English breakfasts. There's a special Sunday lunch of roast beef with the works, and all sorts of traditional meat pies. The food is a little on the bland side, but it's familiar and cozy for English-speaking guests, who can also be found glued to the televisions inside. ⊠ *Bd. du 20 Août* ☎ *028/84–53–53* ▤ *AE, DC, MC, V.*

$$$
MOROCCAN
✕ **Jean Cocteau.** You might think it strange to find a good restaurant on top of one of Agadir's most happening casinos, but Jean Cocteau is a cut above it all. Choose from a sumptuous international menu with French selections and Moroccan tagines. ⊠ *Bd. Mohammed V, 1st fl., above Shem's Casino* ☎ *028/82–79–23* ▤ *MC, V.*

$$$
MOROCCAN
✕ **Johara.** It's right in the middle of tourist central, and owned by a hotel to boot, but it's one of the best fine-dining options for Moroccan cuisine in the area. Lanterns, low seats, and painted tables are de rigueur, as are pigeon pastillas, tagines, and pastries. With 24 hours' notice you can order such specialties as *mechoui* (roasted lamb) and stuffed royal sea bream. ⊠ *Al Madina Center, Bd. du 20 Août* ☎ *028/84–53–53* ▤ *MC, V.*

> **FISH STALLS**
>
> Agadir's lively deep-sea fishing port is Morocco's busiest. And best of all, you can eat there, too. Frequented by locals and travelers alike, it's a great bet for cheap and fun eats. Each stall offers nearly identical food, including squid, prawns, sole, lobster, and whiting, and for nearly identical prices. So walk around and pick what you'd like; the better-organized stalls have chalkboards listing the catch of the day and the price. Eating at the stalls is a better choice for lunch (after visiting the hilltop Kasbah, say), since at night the area is unlighted and stall owners can be a little aggressive.

$$–$$$
✕ **Little Italy.** The best of Italian dining in the area, the restaurant is a little more dulcet in tone than others on the strip. You'll eat pasta and pizza surrounded by black-and-white photos and dark wooden banisters. ⊠ *Ave. Hassan II, Immeuble Goumri, opposite Pl. Al Amal* ☎ *028/82–00–39* ▤ *MC, V* ☉ *Closed Mon.*

$$$$
SEAFOOD
✕ **Le Miramar.** Sumptuous fish and pasta dishes are served at small tables in Agadir's smartest restaurant. It's particularly popular with Western expats. ■ **TIP➔** Chef's night off is Sunday, so it's best to sample the tasty delights on a different night of the week. ⊠ *Hotel Miramar, Bd. Mohammed V (toward port)* ☎ *048/86–26–73* ▤ *AE, DC, MC, V.*

$
PIZZA
✕ **La Siciliana.** This Moroccan-run Italian eatery has really good wood-fired pizza. Run by friendly husband-and-wife team Jalila and Rachid, it's a sweet little place among the busy restaurants that line Avenue Hassan II. It also delivers, should you crave a quiet night in. ⊠ *Ave. Hassan II, Immeuble K2 (2 blocks north of Ave. du Prince Héritier Sidi Mohammed)* ☎ *028/82–09–73* ▤ *No credit cards.*

$–$$$
ITALIAN
✕ **Via Veneto.** The decor is distinctly kitschy, but the food is robust, with a good selection of fish dishes (hot shrimp, bass with fennel, and sole) and great pizzas. Go for a window seat. ⊠ *Ave. Hassan II (down the street from La Siciliana restaurant)* ☎ *048/84–14–67* ▤ *MC, V.*

$$$–$$$$
SEAFOOD
★
✕ **Yacht Club.** You can't beat fresh-caught fish eaten beside the port. This lively family-run restaurant grills, batters, and fries the catch of the day to simple perfection. Watch the swing of the kitchen doors and enjoy the clatter. At the entry to the port, go through the police

checkpoint and take the second right. ✉*Agadir port* ☎*028/84–37–08* ▤*MC, V.*

WHERE TO STAY

You can forget riad-style intimacy in Agadir; your choices are executive-style functionality or giant beachfront complexes that cater primarily to European package tours. As a general rule the luxury (and price) increases as you move down from the northern tip of the beach. A room with beach views and access right off the property often costs a supplement of about 300 DH.

START THE DAY RIGHT

For breakfast have a buttery *pain au chocolat* (chocolate croissant) and strong coffee at the **Boulangerie Pâtisserie Yacout** (✉*Ave. 29 Février, Talborjt* ☎*028/84-65-88*). For a light meal or coffee at any time of day, go straight to the open-air **Pâtisserie La Fontaine** (✉*Pl. de L'Esperance off Ave. Hassan II*), which serves outstanding individual pastillas and spicy shrimp rolls as an alternative to plain old toast.

The hotels along Boulevard du 20 Août have so many amenities and restaurants that you'll feel no need to leave the beach complex. Indeed, more and more hotels are becoming all-inclusive properties. Be wary of these, however, as they don't guarantee fine dining and many local experts think they will lead to a slip in standards. If you just need a bed while passing through, there are less-expensive, basic hotels in the center of town, north of the beach. There's also a lively trade in "résidences," apartments with kitchens you can rent by the night. These even have communal hotel facilities such as swimming pools and restaurants and are an affordable bet for families.

$$$$ **Al Madina Palace.** Set back from the beach, this complex of rooms and restaurants lacks the wide-open vistas of other resorts, but is slightly quieter. The decor won't win any awards, but it's a highly regarded five-star bet with a pleasant feel, and much closer to the rest of Agadir than other similar hotels. Pros: Lovely pool, close to beach. Cons: Tacky decor, no real views. ✉*Bd. du 20 Août* ☎*028/84–53–53* ⊕*www.lti-almadinapalace.com* ⇨*180 rooms, 26 suites* ⌂*In-room: safe, refrigerator. In-hotel: 6 restaurants, bars, pool, gym, laundry service* ▤*DC, MC, V.*

$$$$ **ClubHotel Riu Tikida Dunas.** As all-inclusive options go, this one gives you serious value for your money. Although rooms are nothing special, the complex as a whole is exceedingly well designed. The lavish gardens and pool areas are great for kids. Thoughtful touches such as juice for day-trippers returning to the lobby, nightly entertainment for children, and efficient service create a warm atmosphere. Pros: Pretty pools, lovely gardens. Cons: Not everything is included in the "all-inclusive" price. ✉*B.P. 901, Chemin des Dunes* ☎*024/84–90–90* ⊕*www.riu.com* ⇨*406 rooms, 8 suites* ⌂*In-hotel: 2 restaurants, bars, pools, gym, spa* ▤*MC, V* ⦿*AI.*

$$$$ **Dorint Atlantic Palace.** Owned by a royal cousin, this ornate affair is the king's choice when he's in town. The rooms are a little inelegant for the price, but the gardens, including row after row of rosebushes, are very nice. You can't fault the facilities and outdoor options, which include all water sports, fishing, quad bikes, golf, and four-wheel-drive adventures on request. **Pros:** Relaxing spa, royal treatment. **Con:** The beach is a 15-minute walk from the hotel. ⊠*B.P. 194* ☎*028/82–41–46* ⊕*www.atlanticpalace-agadir.com* ⬎*280 rooms, 49 suites, 2 duplexes* ⬚*In-room: safe, refrigerator. In-hotel: 5 restaurants, bars, tennis court, golf, pool, gym, spa, water sports* ⊟*AE, DC, MC, V* �Ⓞ⫙*CP.*

$ ⓘ**Hotel el Bahia.** If you're not desperate for beach views and don't want to spend five minutes finding your room each evening, El Bahia is a central and good-value option. It's popular with families, European and Moroccan alike. It has comfortable rooms (although the bathrooms could do with shower curtains) with satellite TV that picks up English channels. Some rooms also have small terraces. There's a multilevel central patio for eating breakfast or resting in the sun or shade. **Pros:** Inexpensive rates, clean rooms. **Con:** Few amenities. ⊠*Rue el Mehdi ben Toumert* ☎*028/82–39—54 or 028/82–27–24* ⬎*27 rooms* ⬚*In-hotel: no elevator* ⊟*MC, V.*

$ ⓘ**Hôtel Les Palmiers.** This is a fine mid-range choice in town, and it has a good restaurant. The rooms (all with private bath) are basic with a minimum of decor, but street-side rooms overlook Agadir and the mountains to the north. Ask for one with a balcony for the same price. **Pros:** Beautiful views, clean rooms. **Cons:** Few amenities, restaurant is only so-so. ⊠*Ave. du Prince Héritier Sidi Mohammed at corner of Rue de la Jeunesse* ☎*028/84–37–19 or 028/82–25–04* ⬎*24 rooms* ⬚*In-hotel: restaurant* ⊟*MC, V.*

$ ⓘ**Hotel Marhaba.** Tucked behind a street a little way back from the beach, this is a resort hotel with the works, but without the prices to match. Rooms are simple but pleasant, all with en-suite bathrooms, and you can request a private balcony at no extra cost. **Pros:** Great value, very clean rooms. **Con:** Pool could use a scrubbing. ⊠*Ave. Hassan II* ☎*028/84–06–70* ⬎*69 rooms, 6 suites* ⬚*In-hotel: restaurant, pool* ⊟*AE, DC, MC, V.*

$ ⓘ**Hotel Solman.** Behind a charming, old-school entrance is a well-worn, good-value hotel with a street-side bar, zellij-tiled reception area, and restaurant and pool at the back. Noisy rooms with twin beds face out onto the street, but the better choice (for the same price) are the rooms with double beds looking out over the pool. Two rooms on each floor also have balconies, so try to book one of those. **Pros:** Clean rooms, nice swimming pool. **Cons:** Lots of street noise, bar is smoky. ⊠*Ave. Hassan II* ☎*028/84–45–65* ⬎*55 rooms* ⬚*In-hotel: restaurant, bar, pool* ⊟*MC, V.*

¢   ⓘ**La Petite Suède.** It's a decent choice for an inexpensive hotel in town, and the staff is friendly, but rooms here are simple and rather characterless. Only four have en-suite toilets, but all have their own private shower. **Pros:** Very affordable, spic-and-span rooms. **Con:** Most rooms have shared bathrooms. ⊠*Aves. Hassan II and General Kittani* ☎*028/84–07–79 or 048/84–00–57* ⬎*20 rooms,4 with bath* ⊟*MC, V* ⓄⓁ*CP.*

$$$–$$$$ ⓘ**Résidence Flathotel.** It doesn't have the most inspiring of names, but
ↂ   it's one of the best of the self-catering options. The spotless, mod-

ern apartments are near the beach and have balconies, huge kitchens with granite work surfaces, and every amenity. The massage and fitness center, the Berber Palace, is just downstairs, so you'll have a relaxing time all around. **Pros:** Beautiful fitness center, Olympic-size pool. **Con:** Generic decor. ⊠ *Cité Founty Sonaba, Baie des Palmiers* ☏ *028/84–26–60 or 028/84–30–84* ⊕ *www.flathotelagadir.com* ⇆ *47 apartments* ⌂ *In-room: safe, kitchen. In-hotel: restaurant, bar, pool, gym* ☰ *MC, V.*

$$ 🏨 **Résidence Yamina.** The common areas with their hand-painted tiles
♺ and trickling fountains are more impressive than the apartments themselves. These are outdated and a little shabby, although in perfect working order. Yamina is close to the royal tennis courts and a good bet for families, as there's a separate swimming pool for kids. Apartments have living rooms with televisions, kitchens, and balconies. **Pros:** Large pools, balconies with great views. **Cons:** Shabby decor, not much character. ⊠ *Rue de la Jeunesse, south of Ave. Hassan II* ☏ *028/84–26–60, 028/84–25–65, or 028/84–30–84* ⇆ *68 apartments, 8 suites* ⌂ *In-room: kitchen (some). In-hotel: pools* ☰ *MC, V.*

$$$$ 🏨 **Sofitel.** This is the beach strip's most glamorous and sophisticated
★ option, and it manages to provide privacy and intimacy on a grand scale. It's decked out in teak, and mixes elegant Kasbah style with Oriental warmth. It also has the best beach access, a daily fish market at lunchtime, and the most exclusive nightclub in town. Four-poster beds and large hammocks surround the divine private swimming pool. Children can enjoy the farm on the beach; it has goats, camels, and ponies for seaside trekking. You can take golf lessons or go out on quad bikes or Jet Skis. It's worth spending a little extra for a room with pool or ocean view and balcony, rather than a garden view. **Pros:** Luxury to the extreme, excellent amenities. **Cons:** Lacks Moroccan feel, very expensive. ⊠ *Cité Founty P4, Baie des Palmiers* ☏ *028/82–00–88* ⊕ *www. sofitel.com* ⇆ *273 rooms, 25 suites* ⌂ *In-room: refrigerator, Wi-Fi. In-hotel: 4 restaurants, bars, pool, spa, gym* ☰ *AE, DC, MC, V.*

$$$ 🏨 **Le Tivoli.** This is a less expensive option than many of the Agadir behemoths, and there's no direct access to the beach, but you can buy a ticket at reception for the Palm Beach enclosure. The rooms are lovely, in mint-green, pale blue, or ocher-yellow, and all have a private balcony. If you want a double bed (rather than sheets made over two singles pushed together), you'll need to upgrade to a suite (200 DH extra). **Pros:** Good value, pleasant decor. **Cons:** Twin beds in standard rooms, rooms aren't squeaky clean. ⊠ *Bd. du 20 Août, Secteur Touristique* ☏ *028/84–76–40* ⇆ *256 rooms, 24 suites* ⌂ *In-room: safe. In-hotel: 2 restaurants, bar, pool, gym, hammam* ☰ *DC, MC, V* ⏚ *CP.*

NIGHTLIFE

With its relaxed mores, Agadir is a clubbing hot spot, particularly for young people looking to cut loose. Many places don't get going until 3 or 4 AM, but the beachfront is always busy earlier on, with diners and drinkers making the most of the beach environment. Although Agadir lacks the class of Marrakesh, a number of places, mostly based in the resort hotels, are putting up some decent competition.

Note: Nighttime also attracts many prostitutes, some underage, who throng the cheap bars. The authorities aren't afraid to imprison foreigners who patronize them, and several Europeans were being held at the time of writing.

> **A BIT OF HISTORY**
>
> Agadir wasn't always a modern city of white block buildings, broad, straight streets, and resorts. The name "Agadir" means fortified granary, and refers to the abandoned one perched on the cliff north of town. The Portuguese first set up a trading post here in 1505. From then on to this day, Agadir has been the world's largest sardine-fishing port. The Saadians wrested it from the Portuguese in 1541, under Mohammed Echeikh el Mehdi. Sugarcane, silk, dates, wax, skins, oil, cotton, spices, and gold—and sardines—all graced the port, which eventually surrendered to Essaouira as a commercial center.

BARS & CLUBS

A long-standing favorite is **Papagayo** (✉*Hotel Riu Tikida Beach, Chemin des Dunes* ☎*028/84–54–00* *100 DH* ⏲*Daily midnight–dawn*), which has an easy, laid-back feel and pumps out fairly mainstream tunes.The chicest and best nightclub is without doubt **SO** (✉*Sofitel Hotel, Baie des Palmiers* ☎*028/82–00–88*), which charges a hefty admission price for nonguests of the hotel (300 DH each, including a small drink). There's live music every night, a chic although loud restaurant, two levels, and three bars. It's so trendy you could scream, or simply dance the night—and morning—away.

Those looking for post-dinner, pre-club drinks with a touch of East African colonial elegance should stop by **Zanzibar** (✉*Hotel Riu Tikida Beach, Chemin des Dunes* ☎*028/84–54–00* ⏲*Daily 7–1*).

CASINOS

Part of the Dorint Atlantic Palace, **Casino Atlantic** (✉*Hotel Atlantic* ☎*028/84–33–66* ⏲*Daily 2* PM*–8* AM) is the long player of the bunch, with blackjack, roulette, poker, and 70 slot machines going all afternoon, night, and early morning. **Casino Le Mirage** (✉*Village Valtur, Chemin des Dunes* ☎*028/84–87–77* ⏲*Daily 6* PM*–5* AM) has blackjack, poker, roulette, and slot machines. **Casino Shem's** (✉*Bd. Mohammed V, next to tourist information office* ☎*028/82–11–11* ⏲*Daily 4* PM*–6* AM*)* is a good option for people staying in town.

SHOPPING

You'll have to bargain hard for any of the leather goods for sale at **Drugstore Fabrique** (✉*91, ave. Hassan II, near the turning for Pl. Prince Heriter Sidi Mohammed* ☎*028/84–14–98*). **Madd** (✉*38–40, ave. Hassan II* ☎*028/84–05–92*) is a boutique jewelry store that entices you with 18-carat gold from behind a warm wooden exterior. For an emporium of carpets, ceramics, leather, lanterns, and ornate boxes, visit **Palais du Sud** (✉*Rue de la Foire, north of Ave. Hassan II* ☎*No phone*).

Ardent About Argan

The **Argane-Spa** (✉ *Caribbean Village Agador, Bd. du 20 Août* ☎ *028/84–13–19*) offers the gamut of baths and scrubbing. A fragrant hot bath followed by a massage costs 400 DH and lasts an hour. Or try "erg-therapy," an active sand wrap at the beach for 150 DH (30 minutes).

Diar Argan (✉ *Bd. du 20 Août, opposite Hotel Kasbah* ☎ *028/21–00–22 or 028/23–97–96* ⊕ *www.diarargan. com*) offers two hours of Berber massage with argan oil for 300 DH.

Les Massages d'Argan (✉ *Bloc 9, No. 20, Hay Sidi Mohammed, Ihchach* ☎ *028/21–08–84* ⊕ *www.lesmassagesdargan.com*) offers a range of massages, from relaxation to lymphatic drainage. Two-hour massages cost 350 DH. There's also a boutique where you can buy the massage products. It's located a little far out in the north of the city, but if you call, they can pick you up for free.

Palais Berbère (✉ *Cité Founty Sonaba, Baie des Palmiers, beneath Résidence Flathotel* ☎ *028/21–07–66*) has private massage areas with every kind of essential oil imaginable. They offer the works, from four-hand massages to massages to combat weight gain or back pain. An hour costs 200 DH, two hours 300 DH. Ask for a demonstration to explain how argan oil is extracted from the fruit. You can buy the resulting argan oils, soaps, and creams, too; a small bottle of cosmetic argan oil costs 150 DH. There's also a hammam, sauna, and fitness center.

–Katrina Manson & James Knight

Behind the golden doors, all goods have price tags, which makes buying hassle-free.

Scarlette Idées K-do (✉ *Eastern end of Ave. Hassan II* ☎ *028/82–32–93*) is a lovely boutique selling everything you could possibly want for the home, from candles and lanterns to mirrors, fabrics, and small chests of drawers.

Focusing on stylish crockery, **Tawarguit** (✉ *Lotissement Faiz No. 1, Rue 206, 1 block north of Rue d'Oujda* ☎ *028/84–82–25 or 061/13–29–47*) also sells lamps, stools, coffee tables, gifts, and artisanal work.

SPORTS & OUTDOOR ACTIVITIES

GOLF

There are two grand courses within 15 minutes of Agadir. Both **Golf du Soleil** (✉ *Chemin des Dunes, Rte. d'Inezgane* ☎ *028/33–73–30* ⊕ *www. golfdusoleil.com* 💳 *€130 for a 7-day pass, May 1–Sept.*) and **Golf les Dunes** (✉ *Rte. d'Inezgane* ☎ *028/83–46–90*) are American-style, with three courses of 9 holes each. Les Dunes has Bermuda and Pencross grass and the greens fees are 600 DH, including caddie; du Soleil, in Bensergao, has Tifway grass across 110 acres. The greens fees for 9 holes are 460 DH, including caddie. For both courses, there is a regular, free shuttle bus that picks up at the big hotels throughout the day.

The smaller **Royal Golf Club** (✉ *KM 12, Rte. d'Inezgane* ☎ *028/24–85–51*), is 12 km (7 mi) from Agadir on the road to Aït Melloul. It has

Surf's Up

Surf dudes the world over rate Morocco's southern Atlantic coast one of the world's best places to catch waves. There has recently been something of a surfer boom in the region. Today there are about 25 surf schools, many run by foreigners who came to surf and then simply couldn't tear themselves away. Board rentals tend to cost about 100 DH. An hour's training generally costs 200 DH, and a week's worth of lessons can go for between 2,500 DH and 4,000 DH. Here's a rundown of some of the top spots:

At the small village of Taghazoute, 22 km (14 mi) north of Agadir, is the famed Anchor Point (*Les pointes des ancres*). This pleasant bay among the rocky peaks attracts pro surfers from around the world for its point breaks of more than a kilometer. British surfers in the 1970s named it Anchor Point after the nearby row of anchors that used to secure an enormous fishing net to catch tuna. The best surf here is October through February.

Cap Rhir, jutting out into the ocean 40 km (25 mi) north of Agadir, is well known for its large waves. Farther north still, the divers' favorite, Imesouane, is also great for surfers. Beginners especially can benefit from the long portal wave.

South of Agadir, experienced surfers can try to catch the Cathedral and Rif waves, while farther south still, Sidi Ifni and Massa are quieter spots with lovely beach breaks. Mirleft has a beautiful beach, with great surf spots; it's a reminder of how hippie and empty Essaouira once was.

SURFING SCHOOLS

In Mirleft, south of Agadir, try **Aftas Trip** (☎ 066/02–65–37 ⊕ *www. aftastrip.com*), which can also arrange diving.

In Tamghart and Aourir, try **La Maison de la Glisse** (☎ 060/23–78–74).

Océan Aventure (☎ 066/77–01–67 ✉ *toimbert@aol.com*) is in Agadir proper.

Vagues et Vents (☎ 061/21–57–46 ✉ *info@kitesurfing-maroc.com*), in Agadir, specializes in kite surfing.

---

9 holes over 30 acres, with English-style Bermuda 419 and Cucuyo grass. Greens fees are 250 DH for 9 holes and 360 DH for 18, including caddie. Half an hour's training costs 150 DH, up to 2,400 DH for 10 hours.

SCUBA DIVING

Located within the Anezi Hotel, **Taffs Diving** (✉ *Bd. Mohammed V, Bloc D, Rez de Chaussé, Complexe Anezi* ☎ *028/82–10–27* ⊕ *www.taffs diving.com*) is run by Welshmen, and offers diving in 12 highly rated main dive areas, from just north of Agadir right up to the point at Imesouane. From first-timers (250 DH for a dive in a pool) to pros, there's something for everyone, including PADI certification. Many of the sites have never been dived before—you even have the chance to have a site named after you.

The Souss Valley & Anti-Atlas

WORD OF MOUTH

"We were excited about the bird-watching possibilities in Morocco, and the Souss Massa bird sanctuary exceeded our expectations. We saw bald ibises and flamingos. It was a wonderful extension of our trip to Agadir. We also took another daytrip out to Taroudant for the souk there. Everything under the sun was in the market, from slippers to rugs to pottery."

—Anne-Sophie

By Rachel
Blech

FEW TRAVELERS VENTURE THIS FAR SOUTH in Morocco, but those who do are rewarded with a slice of life in the great Sahara. The Moroccan southwest combines glorious beaches and arid mountains flanked by lush palm, olive, and orange groves. The region's character is strongly flavored by its Tashelhit-speaking Berbers, who inhabited these mountains and plains before Arabs ever set foot in Morocco: there are no imperial cities anywhere in the south, and the feel is distinctively rural.

Vast dunes follow the coast from Tan-Tan south to Laayoune, broken by stretches of *hamada*—flat expanses of rocky desert, sometimes accented by scrub and the sporadic sand dune. On the desert's western edge the Atlantic Ocean provides the fish that help support this region economically, meeting the land in surf that ranges from wild to calm. It's a sparse but striking landscape, and it forms Morocco's southernmost gateway to the rest of the African continent.

ORIENTATION & PLANNING

ORIENTATION

The Souss Valley & Anti-Atlas. The region around the Anti-Atlas Mountains, comprising Taroudant, Tafraoute, and Tiznit, is relatively compact, and most easily reached from family-friendly Agadir, providing a completely different kind of travel experience. This area also provides a great alternative jumping-off point for forays into the desert toward Zagora and M'Hamid (⇨ *Chapter 7*).

Southern Coast & Western Sahara. Western Sahara is Morocco's tail, a vast tract of mostly empty land. The few small cities breaking the journey seem to rise out of the sand as isolated clumps of civilization. Distances here are huge—the roughly 1,000 km (620 mi) between Tiznit and Dakhla is greater than between Tiznit and Tangier. Traveling the ribbon of coastal road toward the Mauritanian town of Nouadhibou marks the beginning of the transformation from North Africa to sub-Saharan Africa: it's a lonely trip, with the raging surf of the Atlantic on one side, and the raging heat of the desert on the other.

PLANNING

WHEN TO GO
In the Souss Valley, spring is the most spectacular time to visit, when almond trees and wildflowers are in bloom, the harvest is near, and the weather is sunny but not too hot. Fall temperatures are moderate, but landscapes are a bit more drab after the summer harvest. As long as rains don't wash out the roads, winter is pleasant as well—coastal areas are warm, although inland temperatures can be cold and heated rooms hard to find. If you must come in summer, stick to the coast: even an hour inland, in Taroudant, the July and August heat is unbearable in all but the nighttime hours.

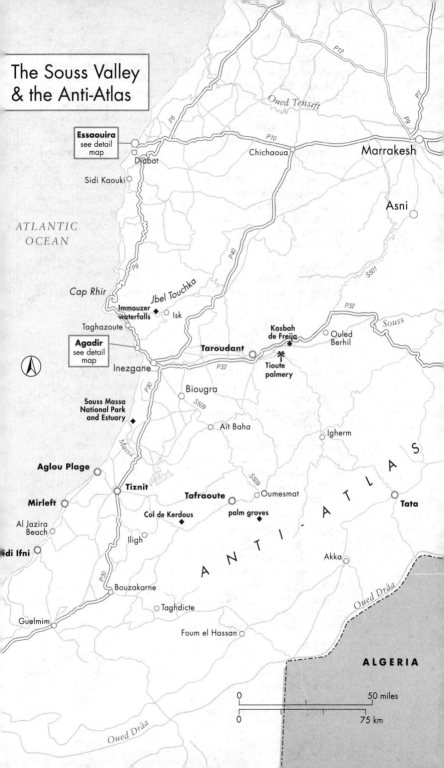

The Atlantic coast keeps local temperatures lower than the name "Sahara" might imply; except in July and August, the area near the Atlantic route remains temperate. Inland towns, such as Smara and Boukra, tend to be much hotter. Summer brings Moroccans from the northern regions down to western Saharan beaches, so spring and fall are the ideal times to come. The cities are devoid of travelers then, the lagoons teem with migratory birds and plant life, and the warm sun hovers beneath its summer peak.

GETTING HERE & AROUND

Agadir's Al Massira Airport is 35 km (21 mi) east of town. *Grands taxis* (large shared taxis) to downtown Agadir cost 150 DH during the day, 200 DH at night. There is also a modern shuttle bus nine times a day the airport and downtown Agadir (60 DH). Grands taxis also connect the airport to other major towns. Inezgane, 13 km (8 mi) southeast of Agadir, is a major transport hub with buses and grands taxis going to most southern destinations. For venturing into the very southern desert area of western Sahara there are regional airports in Dakhla, Tan-Tan, and Laayoune.

Explorations of the area around Taroudant and Tafraoute can be done as side trips from Agadir. One of the most enjoyable ways to cover this broad area is to organize a tour through one of several agencies based in Laayoune or in Tafraoute. These companies provide transport, arrange accommodations or camping, and offer guided tours to points of interest, often well off the beaten path.

WHAT TO DO

Whether it's hill walking, camel trekking, or surfing that floats your boat, this region offers the kind of isolated adventure that more established activity centers such as Imlil, Essaouira, and Merzouga can only dream of. Just don't expect much in the way of organizational infrastructure. Tourist offices work with local contractors and guides and provide services on an as-needed basis. Taroudant and Tafraoute have a clutch of companies with good specialist knowledge of this particular region.

SAFETY

If you plan to strike out for long distances along the coast, advance planning is crucial, particularly when organizing far-flung accommodation options and fuel requirements. Be prepared to take some supplies with you in case you get stuck, and stock up on local currency, as cash machines are few and far between south of Agadir. Consider taking a

TOP REASONS TO GO

Walking in the Anti-Atlas: spectacular scenery around Tafraoute, without another tourist in sight.

Taroudant: a beautiful walled city with strong crafts tradition and wonderful accommodations.

Unmissable stretches of wild, deserted beach: such as Tan-Tan Plage and the Mirleft surroundings.

Desert gateways: such as Guelmim and Tiznit, on the edge of the great Sahara.

Reaching the end of the road: getting to Dakhla, simply because it's there.

local flight to Laayoune or Dakhla if you want to cut down on driving time. Alternatively, if you only have time for a few days in the region, it may be a better bet to head straight for the Souss coast, with its sleepy pace and small towns, for a few days of peace and quiet.

Outside the major beach resorts like Agadir and Essaouira and in any town, women should cover their upper arms and legs. Immodest clothing will not invoke ire or glares, just laughing, staring, and pointing, especially from the ever-present adolescent boys who have nothing better to do but follow a woman around town.

RESTAURANTS

Basic Moroccan fare can be had in any medium-size town or rest stop catering to travelers. For breakfast try *harira* (or, in Tashelhit Berber, *azzakif*), the barley-flour-and-olive-oil soup that serves as a regional staple for hardworking farmers. Southern couscous is mild, usually containing lamb or chicken and vegetables. Self-caterers can pick up locally grown supplies for the road in any town center or weekly market. Dates range from the firmer, drier varieties to the sticky, melt-in-your-mouth kind to small yellow dates, considered a delicacy here. Fresh seafood, hauled into most cities daily from nearby ports, is a sure bet; the local grilled sardines are particularly delicious. Black olives are popularly served with lemon and garlic, spicy green olives with red pepper. Olive oil from the plains around Taroudant is known throughout Morocco, though it's not yet exported internationally.

WHAT IT COSTS IN DIRHAMS					
	¢	$	$$	$$$	$$$$
AT DINNER	under 60DH	60DH–90DH	90DH–120DH	120DH–150DH	over 150DH

Prices are per person for a main course at dinner.

HOTELS

The Souss has some choice small hotels: restored palaces, riad-like houses decorated with an antique Moorish aesthetic, small *auberges* (inns), and one luxury hotel that's among the best in Morocco. Apart from the preferable few, hotels here are mostly modest affairs.

WHAT IT COSTS IN DIRHAMS					
	¢	$	$$	$$$	$$$$
FOR TWO PEOPLE	under 200DH	200DH–500DH	500DH–800DH	800DH–1,200DH	over 1,200DH

All prices are for a high season standard double room, excluding tax.

THE SOUSS VALLEY & ANTI-ATLAS

East and south of Agadir you leave the world of beach vacations and enter Berber country. Scenic drives take you past hills covered with barley and almond trees, palm groves, Kasbahs, and the Anti-Atlas Moun-

GREAT BEACHES

The Atlantic coast of the western Sahara has some of Morocco's finest and most pristine beaches. The stretch between Tan-Tan and Tarfaya is lined with long stretches of golden sand and good surf, which Europeans and Australians like to ride in winter. Try the area around Akhfenir for seaside solitude. Laayoune Plage offers excellent surfing and windsurfing as well as calmer areas for swimming.	The almost-400-km (248-mi) route from Boujdour to Dakhla passes lovely swaths of often desolate beaches, the finest of which are centered on Dakhla itself. The region's coastal lagoons also attract many species of native and migratory birds as well as unique plants, all adapted to life in the consistently temperate coastal Saharan climate.

tains themselves. In town, poke around the monuments and souks of Taroudant or shop for Morocco's finest silver in Tiznit.

TAROUDANT

85 km (51 mi) east of Agadir, 223 km (134 mi) southwest of Marrakesh.

Imagine a mini-Marrakesh, with much of the hectic hustle removed, and you've pretty much got Taroudant. It's a historic market town where people, customs, and the Arabic and Tashelhit Berber languages mix. The town's relaxed feel, the easy interaction with locals, and inexpensive dining make Taroudant an ideal base for exploring the Souss Valley and the western High Atlas.

After a few glory days in the 16th century as a center of the Saadian empire, Taroudant retained allegiance to the sultan even when the Souss Valley plains and Anti-Atlas Mountains revolted. Its population held steady between 5,000 and 10,000 until the 1970s, when rural emigrants to Europe returned to the region, built houses, and opened businesses and the population boomed to 60,000. Nevertheless, the place retains a small-town feel, with narrow streets and active markets.

GETTING HERE & AROUND

The principal road routes to Taroudant are easily navigable and well signposted. The N10 runs east from Agadir and leads eventually to Taliouine, Tazenakht and Ouarzazate. There are also scheduled buses from Agadir (1½ hours), Ouarzazate (5 hours), Casablanca (10 hours), Rabat (13 hours), and Marrakesh (6½ hours). Efficient and comfortable Compagnie de Transports au Maroc buses leave from Bab Targhount on the western side of the medina.

Once you arrive in the city, everything is within walking distance. For a treat you could hop aboard a *calèche* (horse-drawn carriage) and tour the ramparts for about 30 DH.

Local guide Abdelaziz Tali organizes trekking in the High Atlas Mountains. Contact him at the Hotel Taroudant on Place al Alaouyine. Tafraout Aventure is a recommended local tour agency.

TIMING & PRECAUTIONS

Taroudant attracts visitors all year round thanks to it's favorable climate. Most visitors stay a day or two.

ESSENTIALS

Bus Contacts Compagnie de Transports au Maroc (⊠ *Pl. al Alaouyine*).

Currency Exchange Banque Populaire (⊠ *Ave. Hassan II* ☎ *028/85-25-88*). BMCE (⊠ *Pl. al Alaouyine at Rue du Souk* ☎ *028/85-20-15*.

Medical Assistance Hopital Mokhtar Soussi (⊠ *Ave. Moulay Rachid* ☎ *028/85-24-26*). **Pharmacie Taroudant** (⊠ *Pl. al Alaouyine* ☎ *028/85-13-92*).

Rental Cars Malja Cars (⊠ *Complexe Ouled Lourzal, Gas Station Afriquia, 2 km [1 mi] from Taroudant* ☎ *061/16-18-01*).

Visitor & Tour Info Abdelaziz Tali (⊠ *c/o Hotel Taroudant, Pl. al Alaouyine* ☎ *028/85-24-16*). **Tafraout Aventure** (⊠ *Opposite post office in the center of town, Tafraoute* ☎ *028/80-13-68 or 061/38-71-71* ⊕ *www.tafraout-aventure.com*).

EXPLORING

A good place to begin a walk is outside the double-arch **Bab el Kasbah** along Avenue Moulay Rachid, one of half a dozen major doors that locked residents in every night during the French protectorate.

Facing the Kasbah door, you'll see the hospital on your left, across from which is the **Dar Baroud,** the French ammunition-storage facility. This building is closed to the public—and is locally rumored to be haunted—but you can admire its delicate carved stone walls from the exterior.

Continue along Avenue Moulay Rachid and take the first right, following the signs toward the Hôtel Saadiens. The mosque on your right marks **Farq Lhbab,** the "loved ones' parting place." In the 16th century, it is said, five holy men reached this spot after years of religious study in Baghdad; each threw a stone, and each settled where his rock landed. The best loved of these saints are Sidi Beni Yaqoub, of the province of Tata; Sidi u Sidi, who stayed in Taroudant; and Sidi Hmed u Moussa, who went on to Tazeroualt (in the province of Tiznit).

Keep following signs to the Hôtel Saadiens, passing **Sidi bu Sbaa**'s tomb on your right and a French church with magnificent gardens on your left.

Just past the hotel, on your left, is the French lookout post **Talborjst.**

Head straight into the residential area here, emerging on a narrow street lined with fish vendors, produce carts, and men selling cilantro from their bike baskets. A short jog to the right lets you peek into the **tomb of Sidi u Sidi**, patron saint of Taroudant.

WHERE TO EAT

$
MOROCCAN

✕**Chez Nada.** If you want to stick within the city walls for some no-hassle Moroccan food, you can't go wrong at this father-and-son joint. While the decor is nothing special, the views over the medina are sublime, and dishes such as hearty couscous, harira, and pigeon *pastilla* (sweet pigeon pie; order in advance) are part of a top-value set menu. ⊠*Rue Moulay el Rachid* ☎*028/85–17–26* 🗀*No credit cards.*

> ### TAROUDANT MOMENT
>
> Whatever you do in the late afternoon, don't miss the sight of colorfully dressed Roudani (Taroudant native) women lined up against the ramparts near the hospital like birds on a ledge, socializing in the cool hours before sunset.

$
MOROCCAN
☻

✕**Restaurant Jnane Soussia.** Between olive groves and the ramparts just outside Bab Zorgan, this restaurant's location is only bettered by its food. Traditional Moroccan cuisine is served under a *caidal* (white canvas) tent around two small swimming pools, in a garden full of orange, fig, and papaya trees and flowers. Weekending Moroccan families are drawn to the excellent specialties of the house, such as the *briouates* (spicy dumplings) and *mechoui* (roasted shoulder of lamb, best ordered in advance), and a relaxed ambience that can easily turn a quick bite into a long lunch. ⊠*Just outside Bab Zorgan, on right side of road as you head west* ☎*028/85–49–80* 🗀*V.*

WHERE TO STAY

$$$$

🏨**Dar Zitoune.** Rooms at this countryside retreat are spaced out in a fragrant garden of roses and orange trees, with outdoor patios ideal for breakfast. Bathrooms are a feast of colorful tiles, with deep-welled showers. With a team and a cook poached from La Gazelle d'Or, standards among the English-speaking staff are high, making this a welcome upscale addition to the Taroudant accommodation and dining scene. **Pros:** Delightful gardens, English-speaking staff. **Con:** Bland rooms. ⊠*Boutarialt el Barrania, on road to Agadir, 2 km (1 mi) from town* ☎*028/55–11–41* ⊕*www.darzitoune.com* 🛏*14 bungalows, 8 suites* ⚒*In-room: refrigerator (some). In-hotel: restaurant, bar, pool, gym, spa, public Internet, public Wi-Fi* 🗀*AE, MC, V* 🍴*CP.*

$$$$
★

🏨**La Gazelle d'Or.** One of the most exclusive and expensive hotels in Morocco, the Gazelle d'Or has secluded bungalows with airy, exquisitely tasteful rooms and terraces. These are arranged around manicured lawns and an excellent pool—beside which is served possibly the finest luncheon buffet in the country, open to nonguests if they reserve ahead. All vegetables come from the hotel's own organic farm, and dairy comes from the hotel's melancholy cow—Ermintrude Organica. The staff is gracious and inconspicuous, the clientele is largely British, and the atmosphere tends to be respectful and private. Horseback riding can also be organized if required. **Pros:** Exclusive feel, first-rate service. **Con:** Prices put it out of reach for most. ⊠*Taroudant* ⊹*2 km (1 mi) outside Taroudant on Amskroud–Agadir road* ☎*028/85–20–39* ⊕*www.gazelledor.com* 🛏*28 rooms, 2 suites* ⚒*In-room: refrigerator, safe. In-hotel: 2 restaurants, bar, tennis courts, pool, spa, public Wi-Fi, no elevator* 🗀*AE, MC, V* 🍴*MAP* ☉*Closed mid-July–mid-Sept.*

$$$–$$$$ ⊞**Hôtel Palais Salaam.** Any hotel that manages to accommodate the presidents of France and the United States must have pretty wide-ranging appeal. This friendly hotel, built into the ramparts of the former pasha's court, likes to think of itself as the best place in town. While it may not actually hold that crown, the hotel's surroundings are stunning. Newer rooms are often duplexes located off little alleys. Older, less expensive rooms are still peaceful, set around a series of courtyards shaded with lush banana palms. Bike trips or treks can be arranged. **Pro:** Plenty of activities. **Cons:** Rooms are disappointing, unattractive pool. ⊠*Bd. Mouly Ismail, outside ramparts* ☎*028/85–11–04* ⊕*www. palaisalam.com* ⟿*92 rooms, 48 suites, 4 apartments* ⌂*In-room: safe, refrigerator, Wi-Fi. In-hotel: 2 restaurants, bar, room service, pools, gym, bicycles, no elevator* ▭*MC, V* ⦿*CP.*

$ ⊞**Hôtel Saadiens.** Simple rooms and friendly management make this hotel a good choice. There's an excellent pastry shop downstairs with improbable red-leather couches, and thank goodness for the big pool surrounded by hibiscus and sun umbrellas—a must if you're in Taroudant in summer. To avoid noise, ask for a room overlooking this area rather than the busy main street. The management can also put guests in touch with local guides. **Pro:** Good budget option. **Cons:** Rooms not always clean, poor service. ⊠*Ave. 20 Août, Bordj Oumansour* ☎*028/85–25–89* ⟿*45 rooms* ⌂*In-hotel: restaurant, pool, no elevator* ▭*No credit cards.*

$ ⊞**Hotel Tiout.** The accommodations here are playfully cheery: the rooms are busily stenciled with colorful paints, and the hallways have murals of sunsets, palm trees, camels, and anything else vaguely Moroccan. Ask for a room with a balcony that faces the morning sun. Managers are eager to please. The restaurant specializes in southern Moroccan dishes, and the popular café serves real coffee. **Pro:** Great location near the souks. **Con:** Jumbled decor. ⊠*B.P. 228, Ave. Prince Heritier Sidi Mohammed* ☎*028/85–03–41* ⊕*www.hoteltiout.com* ⟿*50 rooms, 5 suites* ⌂*In-hotel: restaurant, public Internet, no elevator* ▭*MC, V* ⦿*CP.*

$ ⊞**Riad El-Aissi.** Don't be deceived by the riad tag—there's no overdone
☾ decor here, rather elegance and a wonderful atmosphere amid the 72
★ acres of this Moroccan-run fruit farm just outside Taroudant. Host Latifa has turned her family home, staffed entirely by women, into a collection of spacious but spare rooms. The kitchen turns out top-quality food with fresh produce, much of it from surrounding fields. Ask for a room in the older wing, where interiors stay cooler in the hot months. Children are well catered for and adults will simply marvel at the tranquillity. **Pros:** Huge rooms, excellent food. **Con:** No air-conditioning. ⊠*Village Nouayl, off Amskroud–Agadir Rd.* ☎*028/55–02–25* ⊕*www.riadelaissi.com* ⟿*9 rooms* ⌂*In-room: no a/c. In-hotel: restaurant, pool, public Internet, no elevator* ▭*No credit cards* ⦿*CP.*

SHOPPING

Colorful round-toe Berber slippers, some with sequins and fanciful pom-poms, are a favorite with both locals and travelers. Other local products include saffron and lavender, sold by the ounce in Jnane Edjemâa herbal stores. The locally pressed olive oil is nationally renowned; ask the herbalists if they can get you a liter.

9

Sculpteur De Pierre (⊠*Fondouk el Hare, Rahra Kedima* ☎*068/80–78–35*) is the best place to go for sculpture, both for quality and range of workmanship. Small stone masks start at 80 DH. They also serve some of the best mint tea in town, brewed by the erstwhile team of draftsmen polishers. For serious collectors, **Antiquaire Haut Atlas** (⊠*Souk el Kabir, No. 61* ☎*028/85–21–45*) has one of the best collections of Berber jewelry in southern Morocco, some of it dating from the 17th and 18th centuries. Even if you're not in the market for a trinket, wandering around the dusty rooms of carpets, candlesticks, and charms makes for a diverting half hour. And if you *are* in the market, Mr. Houssaine accepts all major credit cards.

OUTDOOR ACTIVITIES

If you're hankering after some responsible tourism, you can't do better than **Naturally Morocco** (⊠*Glas, Penbryn, Sarnau, Ceredigion, U.K. SA44 6QG* ☎*+44(0)1239–654–466* ⊕*www.naturallymorocco.co.uk*). This U.K.-based operator has special links with Taroudant, and has its own accommodation in town (only bookable from the United Kingdom), and the best local guides. Jane Bayley, who set up the company, brings her experience as a researcher and lecturer in environmental geography to bear in setting up trips that sample the best in Moroccan rural life: the refreshingly original "Real Morocco" tour that comprises cultural outings in the Taroudant area.

EAST OF TAROUDANT: THE SOUSS PLAINS

A loop drive east of Taroudant will take you through the agriculturally rich Souss Valley plains and a tour of colonial-era *caids'* (local dignitaries') former homes. From the main circle outside Taroudant's Bab Kasbah, take the road toward Tata/Ouarzazate to Aït Iazza; then turn right toward Igherm/Tata, crossing the Souss River (provided it's not flooded, as it sometimes is in winter) into Freija. Back on pavement, look on your right for a decorated mud house, the **Kasbah de Freija.** It's now largely deserted, but you can usually find someone to show you around. Continue on until a sign marks the turnoff to Tioute. The **Tioute palmery,** about a 45-minute drive from Taroudant, was the base used by merciless colonial caid El Tiouti, whose French-armed forces broke some of the last pockets of mountain resistance to French rule. From the Kasbah or a short hike up the hillside, you have superb views over the palmery and verdant fields of mint.

From here you can continue the scenic loop northeast to Aouluz, then turn back west toward the Tizi-n-Test pass until argan trees give way to olive groves and you reach **Ouled Berhil,** which houses the unique and delightful hotel Riad Hida. As an alternative, if you're pressed for time, simply return to Aït Iazza and take the Ouarzazate road straight to Ouled Berhil.

WHERE TO STAY

$$ 🏨 **L'Arganier d'Or.** About 22 km (14 mi) east of Taroudant, these clean, albeit pricey, rooms are arranged around a lovely central courtyard. Meals are served in a tasteful tented restaurant, and folklore shows provide evening diversion. The real treats are the 10-acre orange farm directly behind the hotel and the range of local excursions on offer. **Pros:** Lots of local color, plenty of activities. **Con:** Overpriced accommodations. ⊠*Zaouiat Ifergane, Aït Igass* ☎*028/55–02–11* ⊕*www. larganierdor-hotel.com* ⇆*10 rooms, 1 suite* ♿*In-hotel: restaurant, pool, public Internet, bicycles, no elevator* ☐*MC, V* ⦿*CP.*

$$ 🏨 **Riad Hida.** Don't be dissuaded from staying at this gem because of
★ the approach through grimy streets. Surrounding a large courtyard crowded with wildly overgrown grapefruit trees, oleanders, bougainvillea, and olive and palm trees, the guest rooms are simply decorated, each in a different style. Colorful tiles make the bathrooms almost as lovely as the sleeping quarters. High ceilings and correspondingly tall windows lure the fresh breeze from outside. The pasha's bedroom is the best value, with woodwork dating from the 1850s and two private terraces granting superb views over the surrounding fields. **Pros:** Beautiful rooms, good reputation. **Con:** Not all rooms have air-conditioning. ⊠*Ouled Berhil, 45 km (30 mi) east of Taroudant* ☎*028/53–10–44* ⊕*www.riadhida.com* ⇆*13 rooms* ♿*In-room: no a/c (some). In-hotel: restaurant, bar, pool, no elevator* ☐*No credit cards* ⦿*MAP.*

TATA

200 km (124 mi) southeast of Taroudant

Tata is a four-hour drive from Taroudant on a frequently narrow road, but allow for more time for frequent photo stops. The contrast between Anti-Atlas hills of barley and almond trees and the pre-Saharan plain farther south makes this a rewarding drive. En route you'll pass through **Igherm,** with a Wednesday market and a Wild West feel; women travelers should cover their heads and dress modestly, as this is very conservative territory. Tata itself is an uninteresting military and administrative post, but nearby villages, abandoned Kasbahs, and saints' tombs make interesting exploring. Coppersmiths have been crafting mugs and buckets in the Tata region for at least a thousand years, and small shops dotted around commercial parts of town sell their wares at fair prices.

GETTING HERE & AROUND

There are five daily buses from Agadir (9 hours), as well as service from Ouarzazate (5 hours), Taroudant (5 hours), Marrakesh (10 hours), and Casablanca (16 hours). Buses arrive and depart from the Place Marche Verte. Grands taxis are a more-comfortable option. Tata is a small town and can easily be explored on foot.

TIMING & PRECAUTIONS

The weekly souk takes place on Sunday in the center of town. On Thursday there's a date market in El Khemis, 6 km (4 mi) toward Akka.

ESSENTIALS

Visitor & Tour Info **Délégation de Tourisme** (⊠ *La Montagne, Ave. Mohammed V* ☎ *028/80–20–75*).

WHERE TO STAY

¢–$ ▦**Hôtel de la Renaissance.** The rooms are merely functional, with not much more than a lumpy bed and a basin for washing your face and hands, but the suites are very affordable and the location is convenient. **Pro:** Ideal for budget travelers. **Con:** Uncomfortable beds, no air-conditioning. ⊠*96, ave. des FAR* ☎*028/80–22–25* ⇥*28 rooms, 4 suites* ⬩*In room: no a/c. In-hotel: restaurant, bar, pool, no elevator* ▬*No credit cards.*

$$ ▦**Le Relais des Sables.** This is Tata's most comfortable option. Rooms in muted hues are arranged around pools, and dinner is served poolside. The suites have air-conditioning and telephones. Bird-watching excursions are available. **Pros:** Comfortable rooms, liquor license. **Con:** Not all rooms have air-conditioning. ⊠*Ave. des FAR* ☎*028/80–23–01* ⇥*54 rooms, 10 suites* ⬩*In-room: no a/c (some). In-hotel: restaurant, bar, pool, no elevator* ▬*No credit cards* ⏐◎*MAP.*

TAFRAOUTE

152 km (94 mi) southeast of Agadir.

Tafraoute is a pretty and quiet regional market and administrative center, nestled at the bottom of a valley. Usually overlooked by groups, it's a great base for exploring an area rich in natural beauty and overflowing with walks, many of which can be undertaken without bumping into another tourist. Although the dizzying mountains around Tafraoute may prove forbidding to cyclists or light hikers, half-day excursions can take you to prehistoric rock carvings, the Ammeln Valley, or the villages off the main road to Tiznit. It's also worth planning a day's excursion to the Aït Mansour gorges to the south of town.

Tafraoute is a great place to visit some spectacular *agadirs*—hilltop granaries perched at the top of sheer cliffs. They include Amtoudi, Tasguint, and Ikouka.

GETTING HERE & AROUND

The R105 runs from Agadir to Tafroute via Aït Baha. There are buses from Aït Baha (2 hours), Agadir via Tiznit (5 hours), Marrakesh (10 hours), and Casablanca (14 hours). There are also grands taxis from Tiznit. Once in Tafraoute, your best bet is to travel on foot or by bicycle.

TIMING & PRECAUTIONS

Travelers report being harangued by persistent fake guides. Your best bet is to hire a guide from Tafraout Aventure or another local agency.

ESSENTIALS

Currency Exchange Banque Populaire (✉ *Pla. al Massira*). **BMCE** (✉ *Ave. Mokhtar Souissi* ☎ *028/80–15–82*).

Medical Assistance Pharmacie al Massira (✉ *Pl. al Massira* ☎ *028/80–01–60*).

Post Office Poste Maroc (✉ *Pl. al Massira*).

Visitor & Tour Info Tafraout Aventure (✉ *Opposite taxi rank in the center of town* ☎ *028/80–13–68* ⊕ *www.tafraout-aventure.com*).

EXPLORING

★ The **palm groves** southeast of Tafraoute deserve a full day's excursion, and the former piste circuit through them is increasingly paved.

From the rotary take the road in the opposite direction from the Agadir sign. Follow the signs toward Tiznit, and after 2 km (1 mi) you'll see the so-called "Napoleon's cap" of massive boulders on your right. Occasionally you'll see foreign climbers here, with their incongruously high-tech rock-climbing gear. Follow signs toward Agard Oudad. When the road forks, the right one going to the Painted Rocks, take the left branch. A winding paved road takes you higher into the Anti-Atlas Mountains, with views over the Ammeln Valley below; 20 km (12 mi) out of Tafraoute, turn right toward Aït Mansour, which you'll reach after another 14 km (9 mi) of winding down into the palm groves. Five kilometers (3 mi) farther on is the village of Zawia; another 5 km (3 mi) brings you to Afella-n-Ighir. Along the paved road you'll pass shrouded women, either transporting on their backs palm-frond baskets of dates supported by ropes around their foreheads or walking to Timguilcht to visit its important saint's shrine. Continue on the piste to Souk Lhad, whose busy market is held on Sunday. From there the piste loops back to Tafraoute.

A walk in the **Ammeln Valley** might start at the village of Oumesmat, where for once the ubiquitous **Maison Berbère** is worth a trip. Here the gentle, blind Si Abdessalem will take you through his traditional Anti-Atlas home, introducing you to domestic implements, and with agility will cloak women visitors in the local gold-laminated black wrap, the *tamelheft*. Express your appreciation for the tour by tipping generously. From Oumesmat you can follow paths to the neighboring villages. **Taghdicte** makes a good base for ambitious Anti-Atlas climbers; Mohammed, in Souq Al Had Afella (☎ *028/80–05–47*), can help with arrangements.

A trip to the **Painted Rocks** outside Tafraoute (follow signs) is most dramatically experienced in late afternoon, when the hillsides stacked with massive round boulders turn a rich mustard hue before sunset. Belgian artist Jean Veran painted a cluster of these natural curiosities in varying shades of blue in 1984; checking out amateur copies is as much fun as looking at the originals.

The prehistoric **gazelle rock carving** just 2 km (1 mi) south of Tafraoute is an easy walk or bike ride from town. The sparse etching has been retouched, but it's still interesting and gives you an idea about how long these desolate mountains have sustained human cultures. To get here,

9

follow signs to Tazka from behind Hôtel Les Amadiers; go through the village to the palm and argan fields beyond, taking along a local child to point out the way. (Be sure to thank kids for such services with a small gift, such as a pen or an elastic ponytail holder. Try to avoid giving them money.)

WHERE TO EAT & STAY

$ ✕ **Café Marrakech.** Fatima, the café's owner, cooks all the dishes here
MOROCCAN herself. The fare tends toward simple omelets and brochettes, but the tagines are fresh and tasty, too. Cool, fresh-squeezed juices make this a nice spot to catch your breath and get out of the sun. You might even try a game of billiards with one of the sharp-shooting local kids. ⊠ *Ave. Hassan II, just down hill toward center of town from Restaurant L'Etoile du Sud* ☎ *028/80–10–23* ⊟ *No credit cards.*

$$–$$$ ✕ **Restaurant L'Etoile du Sud.** Since 1968 the "Star of the South" has been
MOROCCAN serving delicious couscous and tagines in a red-velvet dining room or under a huge red-and-green velvet tent. The harira is hearty and satisfying after a long day's drive, and the salads are surprisingly fresh. The staff is friendly, but not overly so, and the atmosphere is cheery. No one would bat an eye if you kicked off your shoes and rested your weary feet on the couches. Azzizi Hassan, who can be found at the restaurant's entrance, is a knowledgeable polyglot guide to the region's sites. The restaurant also serves alcohol. ⊠ *Ave. Hassan II* ☎ *028/00–00–38* ⊟ *V.*

WHERE TO STAY

$$ ▦ **Hôtel Les Amandiers.** Designed in a mock-Kasbah style, this hotel
★ dominates the town, providing panoramic views of the mountains that surround it. Arranged around two courtyards, all of the immaculately maintained rooms have spacious bathrooms, phones, and TV, and many have mountain views, although the decor feels a little dated. **Pros:** Great views, pretty pool. **Con:** Mediocre restaurant. ⊠ *B.P. 10* ☎ *028/80–00–88* ⊕ *www.hotel-lesamandiers.com* ⇌ *60 rooms, 7 suites* ⟡ *In-hotel: restaurant, bar, pool, public Internet, no elevator* ⊟ *MC, V.*

¢ ▦ **Hotel Salama.** Staffed by a helpful team of English-speakers, the Salama offers cool rooms with excellent showers overlooking the busy area around the market, where old men sell dates and local women bring their homemade argan oil. The comfortable public lounge on the roof has panoramic views of the town and rocky mountains beyond. **Pros:** English-speaking staff, nice views. **Con:** Rooms overlooking market can be noisy. ⊠ *Tafraoute center* ☎ *028/80–00–26* ⊕ *www.hotel salama.com* ⇌ *37 rooms* ⟡ *In- room: no a/c (some), no TV (some). In-hotel: restaurant, no elevator* ⊟ *No credit cards.*

SHOPPING

Tafraoute's central market has a good selection of woven palm-frond baskets, argan oil, and *amalou* (almond and argan paste). The obligatory **Maison Touareg** (⊠ *Rte. de l'Hotel Les Amandiers* ☎ *028/80–02–10*) is difficult to miss, carries a good selection of regional Berber carpets, and accepts credit cards.

EN ROUTE

The newer road from Tafraoute to Tiznit (follow signs out the back of Tafraoute, beyond the post office) is flat and bike-accessible for about the first 15 km (9 mi), after which it begins an incline into the mountains.

As the road winds over the Anti-Atlas peaks and through the valleys, you'll see many sights, of which the former Kasbah site **Col du Kerdous**, almost exactly halfway between Tafraoute and Tiznit (54 km [34 mi] and 53 km [33 mi] respectively), and standing at 1,203 feet, is a highlight.

> **DID YOU KNOW?**
>
> Tafraoute is the place to come for mountain *babouches* (slippers). These are different from the slip-on varieties found in the souks of Marrakesh and Fez, as they are specially made with a heel to aid mountain walking. The local market is full of examples at reasonable prices. Take note of Berber babouche color coding: yellow for men, red for women, and spangled designs only for special occasions.

TIZNIT

100 km (62 mi) west of Tafraoute, 98 km (61 mi) south of Agadir.

Tiznit suffers from its uncomfortable location on a flat, hot plain, which makes it look ugly in comparison to the picturesque towns of the mountains or the laid-back beach hangouts of the coast. Yet markets in Tiznit's medina offer a great selection of silver jewelry, and the ambience, especially in the evening, is more relaxed than that of Marrakesh or Fez.

Park your car in the main square, the Méchouar, and walk or rent a bike from the bike shop just inside the square's southern entrance.

GETTING HERE & AROUND

Tiznit is well signposted if traveling by road, with the N1 bringing you from Agadir, or the R104 from Tafraoute. Several daily buses arrive from Sidi Ifni (1½ hours), Agadir (2 hours), and Tafraoute (2 hours). The bus station is a 15-minute walk along Avenue Hassan II from the medina entrance at Bab Jdid. The Compagnie de Transports au Maroc office is located inside the medina at the end of Avenue du 20 Août. There are also grands taxis from Agadir.

TIMING & PRECAUTIONS

With shops, restaurants, and a historic souk, Tiznit makes for a pleasant and relaxed day trip from Agadir.

EXPLORING

From the Méchouar, take the Rue Bain Maure. Follow it as it winds through neighborhood markets, and you'll emerge on a main medina street at a slim minaret (visible from the Méchouar). Cross the street and turn right along the arcade; then follow the cemetery walls around to the **Grande Mosquée** *(Great Mosque)* —unusual in Morocco for its sub-Saharan–style minaret, with sticks poking out from all sides that

9

make it look like someone forgot to take out the scaffolding after it was completed.

Facing the *pisé* (sun-dried mud) wall of the prison housed in the old Kasbah, continue to the left until you reach the **Lalla Zeina spring** on your left, which honors the saint after whom Tiznit is named. Legend has it that this shepherd girl brought her flocks to this spot and smelled the then-undiscovered spring below; her sheep dug (if you can imagine sheep digging) until they found the water, and the town was born. To catch a glimpse of her tomb on afternoons when devotees visit, follow the prison wall and turn left on the first narrow neighborhood street; the tomb is behind a green-painted door on your left.

Return to the main square and cross it to head into a **small square** lined with orange trees, where locals buy from the mint, date, and dried-thyme vendors whose carts are parked between the rows of clothing and housewares. The square gives way to a silver souk and a larger concentration of tourists (and hasslers).

WHERE TO STAY

$$ **Hotel Idou Tiznit.** It may cater primarily to the business market, but this is the best hotel in town, and, for women travelers, the one place that won't feel too intimidating, particularly at night. The marble lobby has a winding double staircase and an enormous, five-tier brass chandelier handcrafted in Fez. Rooms are standard for a luxury hotel, but the hand-laid tile work, marble, and carved plaster in the public areas make for a unique blend of fine Moroccan craftsmanship and modern technology. **Pro:** Full range of services. **Con:** Little local color. ⊠*Ave. Hassan II* ☎*028/60–03–33* ⊕*www.idoutiznit.com* ↘*87 rooms, 6 suites* ♿*In-hotel: 3 restaurants, bars, pool, hammam, no elevator* ▭*MC, V* ⦁⦁|*MAP.*

SHOPPING

Tiznit has earned a reputation as *the* place to buy silver jewelry in Morocco, and the local market has responded accordingly. Merchants cater increasingly to Western tastes and wallets. Many shops around the main square are owned by profiteers who ask inflated prices; to find unusual pieces for reasonable amounts, scour the backstreets for older men haggling with local women.

The low-pressure **Bijouterie** (⊠*6, Souk Joutia* ☎*028/86–40–93*) sells Saharan and Berber silver jewelry and tasteful, handwoven cream-color blankets made by local women.

Bijouterie Al Afran (⊠*32, Kissariat Louban, Pl. de Méchouar*) has a reputation for good prices on silver.

AGLOU PLAGE

17 km (10 mi) west of Tiznit, 115 km (72 mi) south of Agadir.

Aglou Plage is a world away from nearby Tiznit, both in climate and ambience, although connected by 17 km (10 mi) of good tarmac. It's the start of a good 75-km (47-mi) stretch of untouched beach that runs down to Sidi Ifni, where the stretches of beautiful sandy beach are surrounded by tall cliffs and wind-bitten scrub. On most weekends between May and October the lifeguard-protected beach is packed with vacationing Moroccans. About a kilometer up the beach are a series of troglodyte dwellings built into the cliff as shelter for fishermen (and, according to locals, the occasional hermit Frenchman) that you can reach on foot. A seat in a shared taxi from Tiznit should cost about 5 DH.

GETTING HERE & AROUND

Aglou Plage is a popular beach resort west of Tiznit. Take the main roads N1 or R104 to Tiznit and follow the signs.

TIMING & PRECAUTIONS

Aglou Plage has a dangerous undertow. In summer, lifeguards will allow swimming only if conditions are safe.

WHERE TO STAY

$$ ★ **Le Chant du Chameau.** It's got absolutely nothing to do with crooning dromedaries, but The Song of the Camel would get the most stubborn of the bunch cooing with approval. It's been done up in traditional rustic style, with deep-rose walls. Each room is designed differently, but united by a simple elegance. The guesthouse also offers guided tours around the area and to Souss Massa National Park. **Pro:** On the beach. **Con:** Isolated location. ⊠*Aglou Plage, Tiznit* ☎*067/90–49–91* ⊕*www.chantduchameau.com* ⋈*4 rooms* ⌂*In-hotel: beachfront* ⊟*No credit cards* ⁑*MAP.*

$ **Hotel Aglou Beach.** It may not look like much from the outside, but this rather bland building manages to conjure up a warm, familial feel thanks to its airy, spotlessly clean rooms and friendly service. Perched on the beach, many rooms have sea views (ask for Room 212 or 214). The restaurant serves up good seafood. **Pro:** Beachfront location. **Con:** Unimpressive exterior. ⊠*Aglou Plage, Tiznit* ☎*028/61–30–34* ⊕*www.agloubeach.com* ⋈*21 rooms* ⌂*In-hotel: restaurant, beach-front, no elevator* ⊟*No credit cards.*

SIDI IFNI

60 km (37 mi) south of Tiznit, 158 km (98 mi) south of Agadir.

Built in the 1930s, Sidi Ifni remains an architectural quirk of white-and-blue, Moorish-style, Art Deco buildings. It welcomes visitors seeking low-hassle, ocean-side beauty and a moderate climate. Many of Sidi Ifni's residents recall their Spanish rule with nostalgia and retain Spanish citizenship. Who can blame them, when the town feels so passed by in terms of care and attention. Western travelers are drawn to its rust-red, boulder-framed beaches and fresh fish.

9

CLOSE UP

Western Sahara

In 1975 nearly 400,000 Moroccans walked south to the former Spanish Sahara in the Green March, taking possession of what are now officially known as Morocco's Southern Provinces (though locally and internationally known as the western Sahara). Since 1975 the civil war between the Polisario (Saharan separatists) and the Moroccan military has been sporadic, and elections to determine the province's political future have been postponed numerous times. There is currently a truce, and the U.N. has a large presence in the big cities. The main attraction for the traveler, aside from the journey to the middle of nowhere, is a chance to set foot in the Sahara, as the cities are new and charmless, food and wine scarce, and the military presence pervasive.

THE TOWNS

Guelmim is known as the Gateway to the Sahara, and the ensuing drive south to Tan-Tan—on which the landscape turns ever more arid and desertlike—illustrates why. It's an easy trip (107 km [66 mi] south of Tiznit), shooting through empty stretches of flat hamada broken only by the occasional village or café and one gas station. You're likely to catch your first glimpse of large camel herds here.

As you approach **Tan-Tan** (125 km [78 mi] south of Guelmim), you may think you're seeing a giant mirage. Fear not, for your eyes do not deceive you: there really are two enormous kissing camels forming an archway over the road into town. Carved out of stone in the 1970s, these affectionate creatures are one of Tan-Tan's chief claims to fame and the subjects of many a western-Sahara postcard. Tan-Tan's main significance (beyond

the kissing camels) is that it was the official starting point for the Green March of 1975. The southern end of Boulevard Mohammed V is Tan-Tan's main square, Place de la Marche Verte (Green March Square). This is the main transportation hub for taxis and cars headed back to Guelmim and on to Laayoune. The town makes a logical stop on a trip farther south, and is a passable choice for an overnight stay.

At 150 km (93 mi) south of Tan-Tan, the modest fishing village of **Akhfenir** has the first gas station, cafés, and stores on the coastal route after Tan-Tan. Footpaths down to a gorgeous beach make Akhfenir a good place for an en-route swimming stop. At 85 km (53 mi) south of Akhfenir, and the largest of the few coastal towns on this route, **Tarfaya** offers panoramic ocean views, excellent seafood, and a nice place to explore before the road turns inland.

Laayoune, the former capital of the Spanish Sahara, has thrived under Moroccan rule. A calm and easy place to navigate, Laayoune (115 km [71 mi] south of Tarfaya) makes the best base for trips around the western Sahara. It's quite impressive to look around at surrounding dunes and landscape and contemplate the very existence of a town this size in the middle of the Sahara Desert.

Smara's central site has long been an important Saharan caravan stop, but most of the fun, it must be said, is in getting here. Once you *are* in Smara, however, the remains of the Palace Ma el Ainin make a great stopping point. The property is maintained by a kind guardian and his family, who will be happy to show you around and may even invite you for tea.

GETTING HERE & AROUND

Sidi Ifni can be reached either by an N12 from Guelmim or the more circuitous R104 from Tiznir. There are buses and grands taxis from both towns.

TIMING & PRECAUTIONS

Every June, Sidi Ifni holds a festival to celebrate it's reincorporation into the Kingdom of Morocco, having been relinquished by Spain in 1969.

EXPLORING

The most exemplary **Moorish Art Deco** buildings are clustered around

> **MASTER CLASS**
>
> If you like the look of the *tadelakt* (a hard, polished surface) in Le Chant du Chameau, it's because Ikhlaf, one half of the French-Moroccan couple who run the place, also runs courses on the craft, for €470. That may sound expensive, but it includes lodging, and just imagine being able to go home and decorate your own bathroom in the same style you've drooled over throughout Morocco.

Place Hassan II (locally called Plaza de España), near the coastal hillside, but small architectural gems are sprinkled about; along with an attractive sequence of residential doors, they make a walk around Ifni rewarding.

Place Hassan II is a circle with a well-kept garden in its center, adorned with colorful flowers and enclosed by a fence painted in Easter-egg hues. A former **church** now houses the courthouse.

Next door to the church is the now-deserted **Spanish consulate**, built in a stunning semicircular design.

Across the circle and down Avenue Hassan II, next to the Hôtel de Ville (town hall), is the streamlined Art Deco **Spanish cinema**, which may reopen as a cultural center.

Facing the Hôtel Belle Vue, take small Rue Ibn Toumert on your left toward a stocky **lighthouse**, now integrated into a family compound but still lighted every evening. The wall alongside the lighthouse is a perfect place to watch the sun set over the ocean.

From the lighthouse you can also see vestiges of the **Spanish port** farther down the coast. The Spaniards, who ruled Sidi Ifni from 1934 to 1969, hauled their daily catch up the cliff with a gondola system: boats moored at an offshore station and unloaded fish into a cable car that was lowered by an old diesel engine on the hillside. The rigging that supported the overhead cable mid-trip still rises from the water, but local authorities declared this system too expensive and closed it. They built a new, wholly unromantic port, now accessible from the beach farther south.

Follow the action to the town's **central market** any evening between 6 and 8, where you can then purchase calamari, shrimp, and sardines by the kilo from retailers. For a little extra, boys at the market will clean your purchase for you and you can take it back to your hotel, where the kitchen will prepare it.

WHERE TO STAY

Accommodations in Ifni are limited. Repeat visitors reserve their rooms weeks in advance, and in summer you should follow suit. Note that except for café-restaurants, all of Ifni's restaurants outside hotels are open only in summer.

¢ **Hôtel Belle Vue.** What the Belle Vue lacks in charm it makes up for with plenty of peace and quiet. The newest rooms are plain but comfortable and have gorgeous ocean views from the bedrooms and bathrooms. The patio bar overlooking the ocean is a great spot for the end of the day. **Pro:** Fantastic ocean views. **Con:** Not all rooms have hot showers. ⊠*Pl. Hassan II* ☎*028/87–50–72* ⬐*40 rooms* ⌂*In-hotel: 2 restaurants, bar, no elevator* ═*No credit cards.*

¢ **Hotel Suerte Loca.** This family-run hotel, whose name means "blind luck," is a favorite with surfers, budget travelers, and vacationing families. The cheerful mood, amplified with plenty of reggae, is often enhanced by the frequent presence of local guys mingling over the pool table, playing a game of chess, or starting an impromptu jam session. The rooms are clean and comfortable, and many have private balconies. The staff can help organize four-wheel-drive excursions into nearby villages on market days as well as beach trips for small groups, and is extremely helpful with general regional information. Even if you don't stay here, order dinner from the restaurant ahead of time and stop in for baked fish or paella. **Pros:** Lively and convivial atmosphere, family-friendly vibe. **Con:** Limited menu. ⊠*Rue Moulay Youssef* ☎*028/87–53–50* ⬐*16 rooms, 3 studios* ⌂*In-room: no TV. In-hotel: restaurant, bicycles, no elevator* ═*No credit cards.*

OUTDOOR ACTIVITIES

Keen walkers will find plenty of exciting day trips in the area around Sidi Ifni. For beachcombers, the highlight of these has to be Legzira, about 10 km (6 mi) to the north, where giant limestone arches hollowed out by the fierce sea have formed over the beach. Alternatively there's Sidi-Ouarzeg, 18 km (11 mi) to the south, a pristine stretch of deserted beach. ■TIP➔ **The beaches south of Ifni require a sturdy vehicle to navigate the pistes.** If strolling the beach isn't enough, it's possible to go out with local fisherman in their small craft for 400 DH per person from Ifni, but be prepared to get up early in the morning. The hotel Suerte Loca also rents surfing equipment for 120 DH per person, and bikes for 80 DH.

CLOSE UP

For the Birds: Souss Massa National Park & Estuary

Midway between Agadir and Tiznit, at the confluence of the Rivers Souss and Massa, is the world's last remaining colony of the endangered bald ibis. Stretching 64 km (40 mi) down the coast, the park provides refuge for a total of 257 bird species, 46 mammal species, 40 reptile species, and numerous butterflies. The most gorgeous vantage point, where you might spot cranes, great gray shrikes, cuckoos, and tufted ducks, is near the town of Sidi Rbat. Here you're surrounded by contrasting landscapes—mountains on one side, mimosa-lined sand dunes on another, and verdant fields flanking the river on a third. A place of natural beauty and true calm, Souss Massa is well worth the detour.

Recognizing the park's potential for ecotourism, the government has built an entrance to the grounds, and at press time foundations were being laid for an environmental museum on an overlooking hill that you can visit before touring the preserve.

Tours: For guided tours of Souss flora, fauna, and geology, contact Saïd Ahmoume at Taroudant's Environmental and Cultural Centre. Some of the best guided tours of the park are organized through the U.K.-based tour operator Naturally Morocco.

Getting Here: The entrance is 51 km (32 mi) south of Agadir. The park is almost halfway between Agadir and Tiznit, and can be reached from the main road between them. A place in a shared taxi to Sidi Rbat from Agadir should not exceed 20 DH. To get here from the main road, follow the signs to Sidi Rbat from the turning at Had Belfa (if you miss it, take the turn for Massa, farther south, and just follow the paved road to the right until it reaches Sidi Rbat). After 10 km (6 mi) of unspectacular scenery, you'll arrive at Massa village, and when the road forks, turn right (north). After about 5 km (3 mi) more, the road becomes a piste; keep going until you reach the park gates. You can park your car under the trees.

Tips: Pack your bag with binoculars and plenty of water for the two-hour walk to the beach from the entrance. Bird-watching is best between November and March, and in March and April the nature trail is carpeted with wildflowers.

MIRLEFT

25 km (15 mi) north of Sidi Ifni, 133 km (83 mi) south of Agadir.

Mirleft is going places. That may not be immediately obvious, but that's because the elite French residences springing up, particularly in the beachfront district of Les Amicales, are distinctly low-key and want to stay that way, to prevent a stampede. This upward mobility has given rise to some lovely hotels and a burgeoning adventure-sports industry, with an inevitable influx of quad bikes. The feel is different from the hippie vibe of coastal villages around Essaouira—this is more blue-blooded than purple haze.

GETTING HERE & AROUND

Route R104 takes you directly to Tiznit. The village is served by the number 26 bus, which runs every two hours between Ifni and Tiznit. There are also grands taxis operating along the same route. The village is easily explored on foot.

EXPLORING

The massive **red-sandstone arches** over the beach at Al Jazira, north of Ifni, are worth a quick visit or an afternoon jaunt; just watch your odometer, as the turn isn't signposted. Take the Tiznit road north 10 km (6 mi), and turn left onto the piste that dead-ends in a flat spot where, in high season, you might join European camper vans. Walk down to the beach below and head south to reach the arches.

> ### LOCAL FESTIVALS
>
> At Mirleft's annual Almuggar Issig, held the last Thursday in July, area girls seeking suitors assemble to sing and dance, with older, married women drumming in accompaniment around them. It's an interesting alternative to Imilchil's touristy marriage festival in September. In addition, Mirleft-area women celebrate the June festival of Ashura with a nighttime song to ward off pests that might spoil their flour supplies.

WHERE TO STAY

$ **Hotel Restaurant Atlas.** Small and simple, this is a great budget choice in the center of town. Enthusiastic owner Benedicte makes a special effort to interest guests in the color and customs of the region, and can organize all manner of excursions, from donkey rides to visits to women's cooperatives. The restaurant is a focal point for comings and goings, but upstairs rooms are peaceful and the shared bathroom facilities spotless. **Pros:** Helpful and friendly staff, easy on the wallet. **Con:** Rooms lack private bathrooms. ⊠ *Mirleft* ☎ *028/71–93–09* ⊕ *www.atlas-mirleft.com* ➥ *17 rooms without bath* ⟁ *In-hotel: restaurant* ▤ *No credit cards* ⏐⃝*CP.*

$$$$ **Les 3 Chameaux.** In a French fort, this guesthouse sits on a steep
Fodor's Choice hill behind town. A military-style spic-and-spanness hangs reassur-
★ ingly about the rambling old complex, but with a distinctly modern twist: the living room and library are a sumptuous collision of cream and colonialism. The Berber rooms located in the old stables are a bit like prisons, so you'll be better off in one of the suites, preferably one of the three with ocean views. The food, the setting, and the service are sumptuous. **Pros:** Great food, commanding views. **Con:** Rooms in stable are claustrophobic. ⊠ *On Sidi Ifni side of town* ✚ *follow signs that take you past market to hill behind town* ☎ *028/71–91–87* ⊕ *www.3chameaux.com* ➥ *9 rooms, 9 suites* ⟁ *In-hotel: restaurant, bar, pool* ▤ *V* ⏐⃝*MAP.*

OUTDOOR ACTIVITIES

The only place to go in Mirleft for adventure sports is **Aftas Trip** (⊠ *On road to Sidi Ifni* ☎ *066/02–65–37* ⊕ *www.aftastrip.com*), which is run by the friendly and competent Ahmed Bourma. A comprehensive range of activities includes surfing, fishing, snorkeling, trekking, donkey rides, quad bikes, and four-wheel-drive hire .

BEACHES

Tan-Tan Plage, 28 km (17 mi) southwest of Tan-Tan, combines a sand beach with a modern fishing port specializing in sardines for export. The town has several cafés, banks, and mosques, but no real sights or accommodations. The beach, being close to the port, can be littered with debris; for quality beaches, you'll do better to continue farther south.

Moroccan Adventures: A Primer

WORD OF MOUTH

"The shopping in Morocco was out of this world, the quality of crafts and the prices were amazing. Just be prepared to bargain a lot."

—Trish

"We also went to a hammam which is a Moroccan spa—it starts with a steam bath, followed by a body scrub with black sea salt, clay-and-olive-oil soap—it was very enjoyable until we had buckets of warm water dumped unexpectedly over our heads. All this 'cleansing' was followed by a wonderful one-hour massage—the Moroccans really know how to pamper themselves!"

—smgapp

HAMMAM 101

Updated
by Maryam
Montague

A hammam is a wonderful place to retreat from the hubbub of the souk and the ardors of shopping or to refresh yourself after hours of walking or trekking. If you go to the public variety, you'll have a rare opportunity to meet locals and participate in an important ritual.

Walking into a public hammam for the first time can be daunting or disenchanting if you're imagining a fairy-tale bathing chamber. It isn't an exotic spa—like those now offered in many of the upscale riads and hotels—but rather a basic, unadorned public bath, with no signs for the uninitiated. That said, if you know what to expect, there is nothing like it to make you feel you are truly in Morocco.

WHAT ARE THEY?

The hammam is not filled with steam like a Turkish bath, nor is it dry like a sauna. Like the tagines used to cook the national dish, it's a mixture of baking and steaming. Pipes of water running beneath the marble tiled floors are heated by wood fires underneath the hammam, the same fires used for the neighborhood's bread baking ovens. Water arrives in the hammam through taps and creates a light and constant hot steam before being removed by drains at the center of each room. Although many are old, all public hammams are very clean, as they are checked constantly.

HAMMAM HISTORY

The Islamic hammam came directly from the Roman and Greek baths. At first they were cold baths, and only men were permitted to use them. It wasn't until the prophet Mohammed learned that hot water (the word "hammam" means "spreader of warmth") could promote fertility that the heated hammam was inaugurated and its use permitted to women. It soon became central to Muslim life, with several in each city, town, and village annexed to the mosque, to make hygiene available to everyone in accordance with the laws of Islam. (A tour of the Hassan II Mosque in Casablanca includes a look at its magnificent hammams (☎022/48–28–86). The hammam's popularity also increased because the heat was thought to cure many types of diseases. The price of entry was, and still is, kept so low that even the poorest can afford it. Unlike the Romans' large open baths designed for socializing, hammams were mostly small, enclosed, and dimly lighted to inspire piety and reflection. Later, to show off their wealth and devoutness, the rich built larger ones. In time the hammams drew people to socialize, especially women, whose weekly visits became so important to them—the only time they were allowed to leave the confines of their house—that it became seen as a right.

These days Morocco's health and spa business is flourishing, and Marrakesh has one of the hottest spa scenes in Africa. As a result, privately run hammams that fall between the basic public hammam and the chic, expensive hotel or riad variety are also appearing.

HOW TO HAMMAM

HOW TO CHOOSE

If you make friends easily, are looking for an authentic experience, or are on a low budget, go to the public hammam. If you're shy, you may want to try one of the private hammams. If you want to share the hammam with a companion of the opposite sex, go to a hotel or riad hammam, since the public and private ones are segregated. While many hotels and riads have a hammam, check first, as they are not all open to nonguests. They are often not as hot as public ones, since they don't have a constant stream of bathers to warrant keeping it very hot, and they tend to heat it for the lowest common denominator, rather than for those who prefer higher temperatures. Also, if you're planning to go to an unlisted public hammam, check first with the concierge or ask a local. There are a few men's hammams for instance that have a reputation for easy pickups. If you're in a rural area, be prepared for the hammam to be extremely basic.

EQUIPMENT & SERVICE

Bring: Take your usual toiletries: soap, shampoo, lotion, comb and/or hairbrush, razor, two towels (one for drying, one to wear as a turban when you leave, as hair dryers are not permitted), and a spare pair of underwear. You may also want to bring a pair of flip-flops, as the hammam's tiled floors are slippery and hot. Don't bring any valuables with you, as you'll be leaving your belongings in an open cubbyhole. The hammam ladies watch diligently over these, so bring a few extra dirhams for a tip.

Purchase: If you're going to the public hammam, purchase the following at a grocer's shop: a glove called a *kees*, (10 DH), made of a coarse fabric that scrubs the skin well; 2 DH worth of *saboon bildi*, an organic dark-brown olive-oil soap-cum-paste that gets deep into the pores; a small plastic jug for pouring water over yourself (5 DH); and to condition your skin or hair and make it feel like silk, a handful of lava clay called *rhasoul* (2 DH). If you plan to hire a *tayeba* (or *ghalassa*, as they are also called), she will have the jug, kees, saboon bildi, and possibly the rhasoul on hand.

Tayebas: A tayeba does all the work for you: finds you a spot, fills the buckets, rubs the olive soap over you, rinses you, scrubs your body, rinses again, and washes and combs your hair. Some may do massage, but massage isn't customary in the public hammam. On arrival in the entrance room, you'll see several women: simply say "tayeba," and one of them will lead you into the hammam. You pay her afterward. If you're going alone for the first time, this is the best way to learn. If you're going with a friend, you can watch the other bathers and assist each other. Note that tayebas scrub vigorously, so if your skin is sensitive, tell her to go easy or you may end up red (a hand signal or grimace should do the trick). You will likely be amazed by the amount of skin sloughed off. Indeed, Moroccans who take hammams regularly often view themselves as "cleaner" than most foreigners.

HAMMAM RITUAL

Strip down to your underwear and give your bag of belongings to the attendant who will store it in one of the open cubbyholes. Take two buckets per person from the entry room and enter the hammam.

Most hammams consist of three rooms leading into one another through arches or doorways. They are usually dimly lighted from tiny windows in a small domed roof. The floors are of white marble tiles, hot and slippery, so tread carefully between the bathers. The first room is warm, the next hot, and the last is the hottest. ■TIP➡ **If at any point you feel too hot, go to the warm room for a few minutes—it will feel cool by comparison.**

Choose a spot to sit in the hot room and place your toiletries there. Then go to the taps and fill your buckets, one with hot water, the other with cold for mixing. Go back and rinse your sitting area, and sit on a mat. You can either stay here to let your pores open, or go to the hottest room for 15 minutes or so.

Now apply the olive soap all over yourself. Sit for a while before rinsing it off, then begin scrubbing your body all over with the kees mitt. At this point, one of the other women bathers may offer to scrub your back. It's polite to allow her to scrub yours and offer to scrub hers in return. Now rinse off with jugs of water mixed from the hot and cold buckets. You may refill your buckets at any time.

If you're using rhasoul, mix it into a thick paste with water and apply it all over your hair. Rinse out, leaning between your legs and combing from the roots until your hair feels silky clean. Now shampoo your hair and rinse again.

The last step is to lather your body with regular soap, followed by a final all-over rinse, including rinsing your sitting area clean before leaving. Wrapped in your towel, you can relax back in the changing room before dressing and going outside. If you hired a tayeba, pay her now, and tip the attendant who looks after the belongings. Moroccan women never leave the hammam with exposed wet hair, and you may want to wrap yours with a towel or scarf as well.

HAMMAM ETIQUETTE

The vibe in the hammam is generally relaxed, with a constant hum from the voices and splashing of water in each room. You might be stared at in a public hammam, but you can break the ice by smiling and

---

TIPS

Try to avoid going on crowded Thursday evenings, Friday, or Saturday afternoons.

Hair dryers are not permitted, so use an extra towel as a turban.

Take small bills, as there often isn't change.

The tayeba may greet your payment with a blank stare, or imply it isn't enough. If you've offered the going rate, just smile.

The men's hammam is a faster affair than the women's, with emphasis on stretching limbs and cracking bones rather than on beautifying treatments. Men can also hire tayebas.

saying *salaam waleykum* when you arrive. You could also offer some of your body lotion here, as it is seen as a luxury. Some women take a bottle of water or oranges into the hammam for cleansing the skin and for refreshment, so don't be surprised to see orange peel on the tiles.

Private hammams follow the ritual, but are more organized. In these you can rent towels and purchase specialized products. You may also hire a tayeba, though expect to pay a bit more than at the public hammam. A hotel hammam will be organized around you and will always have an attendant and a tayeba. In hotels and upscale private hammams you won't need to take anything with you, as towels and all products are included in the fee.

COSTS

Entry to a public hammam is between 5 DH and 10 DH. This includes the use of a cubbyhole for your belongings, two black rubber buckets (for rinsing soap and shampoo off: note that except for the upscale ones, there are no showers in public hammams), and all the hot water you desire. A tip of 3 DH–5 DH for the woman who looks after your belongings is expected. There's no fixed price in public hammams for the services of a tayeba; typically she receives anything from 20 DH to 50 DH, depending on how thorough she is, and on whether the hammam is small, new or old, in a town or a city.

Entry to private hammams generally costs 30 DH–60 DH, which includes the same items. A tayeba here will cost 40 DH–60 DH. Hotel or riad hammams usually cost between 150 DH and 500 DH per person (in some cases, per couple). This includes bath products, towels, and an attendant who will wash and scrub you. You may of course choose to bathe yourself.

BRINGING IT BACK

Shopping in Morocco, particularly in Marrakesh and Fez, is an experience you'll never forget. The narrow alleys contain some of the most colorful bazaars anywhere in the world, filled to bursting point with every item under the sun.

10

BEST BUYS

RUGS

Moroccan rugs vary tremendously in quality and design. There are basically two types: rural (Berber) and urban (*citadin*), but each has endless varieties. Generally, smaller bazaars in the souk carry the rural rugs, and larger bazaars and city stores carry a selection of both rural and urban. Urban rugs, generally short pile, arrived in Morocco via the East in the 18th century. These have higher knot counts (more "finely" woven) than the rural rugs, which technically makes them of higher quality. The rugs typically have seven colors and varied patterns including bands of different colors with geometric and floral designs. Urban carpets are made by women in cooperatives, Rabat and Salé being the main centers, but also in Meknès, Fez, and Marrakesh. Moroccans generally prefer to buy these rather than the rural rugs, but in terms of design and Western taste, they have less appeal as they represent commercial Moroccan interpretations of a Middle Eastern tradition rather than Berber tribal art.

Rural carpets, some of which are known as *kilims* (tapestry weave or flat weave) are identified first by region and then by tribe. Flat-weave rugs are mostly woven in the Middle Atlas (Azrou and Oulmes) and on the plains around Marrakesh (Chichaoua) by female weavers using traditional techniques of hand-tufting, hand-weaving, and hand-knotting. They're dark red and made of high-quality wool with the occasional detail in cotton or silk, and have bands of intricate geometric designs. A rug takes from several weeks to several months to complete. Special ones are brought out for weddings and other celebrations. No two rugs are ever alike, because each weaver blends tribal and individual patterns. The finished rugs are believed to ward off evil spirits.

> ### RUG-BUYING TIPS
>
> Check the rug for color. If it has been artificially aged, it'll be lighter on the back than the front.
>
> Check the weave's knot count. While the quality of urban carpets is measured by its high knot count—about 100 per square inch—rural carpets usually have a knot count less than 50 per square inch.
>
> Natural dyes are bright, rich, and somewhat uneven. Bright colors, like red, pink, or orange, are generally artificial. Ask to wipe a small area with a damp cloth to see if the color comes off (if it does, it's artificial).

Middle Atlas rugs are widely available in the town of Khemisset, between Meknès and Rabat, where the highly detailed red-striped *zemmour* rugs sell at near wholesale prices. Roadside bargains can also be had at weekly local markets. In the mountains north of Fez the women of the Beni Ouarain tribe weave rugs with patterns of fine stripes in black and white; they also weave the thick beige pile rugs with cross-hatching that have now become popular with the design set.

The flat-weave rugs of the High Atlas Mountains (Aït Ouaourguite, near Ouarzazate) have a natural background with beige and brown stripes. The wool-pile rugs from this region have alternating soft plush pile with intricate woven motifs—diamonds, zigzags, and tattoo-like motifs in warm tones like mustard-yellow and tomato-red, and are most plentiful in Taznakht and the Tifnout Valley. The white, sequined rugs-cum-blankets-cum-shawls you may see displayed on rural roadsides are made in the Middle and High Atlas, and are used both practically and ceremonially, their sequins prized for their reflection of light. Natural dyes are still used for most Berber rugs: orange from henna, blue from indigo, yellow from an indigenous shrub, and red from the madder plant.

Be wary when a vendor tells you a rug is very old; even they can only guess at its age, since rugs don't come with date or identification labels. Rural rugs may be up to 50 years old, but rarely older, because of heavy use. The price range for rural rugs is 900 DH–15,000 DH, depending on quality, age, and size. Flat-weave rugs are generally cheaper than pile rugs, and cotton is much less expensive than wool. Vintage rugs are typically long and narrow, to fit rooms that were traditionally built this way. Newer rugs and carpets can be bought in conventional sizes. That said, judging a rug or carpet for its value is more a matter of its particular charm than anything else. For pricing, a general rule is 200 DH–750 DH per square foot—again depending on quality, age, and condition. An urban rug of 5 feet by 10 feet will cost anything from 800 DH to 12,000 DH, depending on whether it was handmade or not and its quality. For both rural and urban rugs it's worth taking the time to check comparable prices at the Ensemble Artisanal, the state-run cooperatives found in all main cities. Generally speaking, the prices you'll find in Morocco are one-half to one-third those found in the United States.

> ### COLORS OF THE CARPET
>
> As a rule, carpets from the High Atlas region have mostly orange and red in them. In the Middle Atlas they tend to be red, and in the Anti-Atlas yellow and orange. The reason? Take a look at the soil of each region: it's used in handmade dyeing.

POTTERY & CERAMICS

They may be cumbersome carry-ons, but, apart from carpets, of all the handicrafts available in Morocco, ceramics may be the souvenirs that most become part of your daily life back home. Decorative styles, shapes, and colors vary from city to city, but due to increasing demand, each city has begun to imitate the styles of the others.

FROM FEZ Morocco's most stunning ceramics are the distinctive blue-and-white Fassi (from Fez) pieces. Many of the pieces you'll find actually have the word "Fas" (the Arabic pronunciation of "Fez") written in Arabic calligraphy incorporated into geometric designs. Ask a bazaar merchant in Fez's Souk el Henna to point these out. Fassi ceramics also come in a beautiful polychrome of teal, yellow, royal blue, and burgundy. These colors are a playful alternative to the often somber blue-and-white Fassi style, but they also have a folksier, less-sophisticated feel.

Another design unique to Fez is the simple *mataysha* (tomato flower) design. You'll recognize these by the repetition of a small four-petal flower design. Fez is also at the forefront of experimental glazes—keep your eyes out for solid-color urns of iridescent chartreuse or airy lemon yellow that would look at home next to a modernist Philippe Starck lamp or an Eames chair.

FROM SAFI Safi has had a flourishing pottery industry since the 12th century. Located near the phosphate mines known as Jorf el Asfar (*asfar,* like *safran,* means yellow), because of the local yellow clay, the pottery of Safi has a distinctive mustard color. The potters' elaborate designs and colors rival those of Fez, but are in black with curving lines of leaves and flowers, with less emphasis on geometric patterns. The pottery

10

is predominantly overglazed with a greenish blue, though brown, green, and dark reds are also used.

FROM SALÉ In Salé potters work on the clay banks of the River Bou Regreg estuary to produce glazed and unglazed wares in classic and contemporary styles, from huge garden urns to delicate dinner sets.

> **TIP**
>
> Though ceramic pieces overlaid with silver filigree are popular, be aware that they may either be chipped or cracked, or have other flaws that have been concealed by the overlay. Many can't hold liquids or are difficult to clean.

POTTERY KNOW-HOW The main things to keep an eye out for when shopping and bargaining are related to the kiln markings left after the ceramics have been fired. Pottery fired en masse is put in the kiln on its side and so the edges of bowls are often painted after they have been fired. The paint tends to flake off after a while, giving the bowls a more rustic or antiqued look. These should go for a lower price.

Another technique for firing en masse is to stack the bowls one on top the other. This allows for the glazing of the entire piece but results in three small marks on both the inside and outside of bowls from the stands where they were placed. Small touch-ups tend to disrupt the fluidity of the designs, but such blemishes can be used as a bargaining angle to bring down the price.

You can spot an individually fired piece by its lack of any interior faults. Only three small marks can be seen on the underside of the serving dish or bowl and the designed face should be immaculate. These pieces are the most expensive, upwards of 800 DH for a large, intricately glazed serving bowl with lid.

SILVER JEWELRY

The most popular silver jewelry in Morocco is crafted by Berbers and Arabs in the southern High Atlas and in the Anti-Atlas Mountains. Taroudant and Tiznit are particularly good places to shop. Desert nomads—Touaregs and Saharaouia—craft silver items for tribal celebrations. Smaller items include fibulas (ornamental clasps to fasten clothing), Touareg "crosses," delicate filigree bracelets, and hands of Fatima (or *khamsa,* meaning five, for the five fingers), which are said to offer protection from the evil eye. There's also a good variety of Moroccan Judaica that includes silver *yads,* Torah crowns, and menorahs.

Older pieces are usually collected by silver merchants from rural women who need cash, so used jewelry selections tend to reflect regional traditions. Silver items are priced by the gram (11 DH per gram; ask the silver merchant to weigh the piece) and according to intricacy of design. As with any other purchases, decide what the piece is worth to you before bargaining; an "old" piece might be anywhere from 5 to 50 years old. Merchants know that Westerners have a weak spot for antiques (so there's a tendency to exaggerate the age of a piece to get a better price), but many recently manufactured pieces are of just as high quality. For a small hand of Fatima or Touareg cross, prices typically start at 75 DH; for an ornate pair of earrings with gemstones from 200 DH to 500 DH; and for a silver bracelet without gemstones from 300 DH. You should pay about 50 DH for wide tin bracelets with large glass stones.

SLIPPERS

Leather and suede *babouches* are the ultimate house slipper. They're made all over Morocco, but you can see master craftsmen at work in the tanneries of Fez and Marrakesh. Myriad styles and colors of the classic women's slipper abound. Imagination is the key word here: slippers can be curly toed, embroidered, velvet, leather, suede, or woven hemp. Try leather slippers on to make sure they're made of the softer not harder leather, and if you want them to last, check that the soles are well made and the stitching secure. Note that slippers are crafted identically: wearing them will give them the shape of your feet. The less-expensive indoor slippers with sequins and soft soles are usually in baskets in front of the store, and you should be able to get them for 50 DH. As with everything else, the more expensive ones are inside, so you'll have to enter the lion's den to check them out. These vary from 80 DH to 150 DH a pair, depending on design, sole type, and quality of material. Ask the vendor specifically if the slippers are leather, as some are imitation. If you prefer to purchase without the aggravation of insistent vendors, try a boutique store (although prices will be marked up). The variety with a tonguelike high back, yellow, orange, or red in color, is much stronger, as they're made and worn in mountain areas like Tafraoute, which is a great place to get them.

LEATHER PRODUCTS

For centuries, Moroccan leather, known as *maroquinerie,* has been sought after worldwide. Fez and Marrakesh have large working tanneries, and as a result sell an enormous amount of inexpensive leather items in the bazaars. The best of these are bags, belts, luggage, jackets, and vests. Also look for embroidered calfskin ottomans. Many leather goods found in the souks are cheaply made, so examine pieces carefully. Check that the stitching is firm, the clasps well fixed, and the seams even. Check the insides of pieces to make sure that they are not surface dyed, and smell the leather to make sure it does not have an unpleasant odor.

ARGAN OIL

In Morocco, argan oil is the stuff of legends, much valued by the Berbers, who for centuries have seen it as an all-purpose salve, a healthy dip for their homemade bread, protection for skin and nails, scar and acne treatment, hair conditioning, moisturizer, and even a general cure for aches and pains. The oil comes from the *Argania Spinosa,* a thorny tree that has been growing wild in Morocco for some 25 million years. Today the argan forests are slowly receding due to over-exploitation, and are only found in a triangular belt along Morocco's Atlantic coast from Essaouira down to Tafraoute in the Anti-Atlas Mountains and eastward as far as Taroudant. Designated a UNESCO world biosphere reserve, the argan forests contain about 20 million trees, covering 829,000 square km (320,000 square mi), and provide a livelihood for

3 million rural Berbers. The argan nut (drupe) begins green, when it resembles a large olive, turns yellow then brown when ripe, and its kernels yield delicious deep gold-color oil, smooth and light in texture but rich in content, with a strong nutty and toasty flavor and aroma. The entire work of harvesting and extracting the oil is carried out by hand by local Berber women. The work is arduous and long, and it takes about 35 kilograms of sun-dried nuts to produce one liter of oil. In Europe, and to a lesser degree in the United States, argan oil has now become almost as legendary as in Morocco, used by top chefs, by beauty salons, and by naturopathic doctors for a variety of ailments.

Pure argan oil for culinary use is not an easy item to find. It is sold in grocery stores in Essaouira's souk (and in the Marrakesh spice market) for about 75 DH a half liter, but you need to go with someone reliable and knowledgeable who can vouch for the oil's purity, as vegetable oil is often added. Argan oil mixed with other essential oils for beauty treatments is easier to find. *(See Chapter 8 for places to buy argan.)*

THUYA WOOD

Essaouira is the source of all thuya-wood crafts, as the rare coniferous tree grows uniquely in the sandy countryside surrounding this popular seaside town. Only the gnarled burls that grow out of the tree's trunk are used to carve the vast variety of objects, from tiny boxes, picture frames, trays, games, and even furniture. The distinctive shine is created by repeated hand-polishing with vegetable oil and lemon. If you're not stopping in Essaouira, you can buy thuya articles in souks and stores all over Morocco. As wood is often not carefully dried before it's used, examine articles for hairline cracks and warping before purchasing.

OTHER GREAT SOUVENIRS

■ You can buy exquisitely embroidered caftans and table linens in Fez, Marrakesh, and Rabat. Check the stitching and seams for quality.

■ Lanterns are one of Morocco's most magical icons: from the smallest and plainest candleholder to the largest and most ornate ceiling lamps, they're typically made from brass or tin, and often have stained- or pressed-glass panels. Lanterns with complex piercings cast beautiful shadows when lighted but provide very little light.

■ Mirrors come in all sizes, colors, and motifs, often featuring geometric patterns or other details. Some are plain wood, brass, or tin; others have intricate patterns of bone and metal, or bone and wood.

■ Don't forget the local culinary accents at the spice seller's stand, such as cumin, ginger, cinnamon, *ras el hanout* (a blend of up to 20 spices used in lamb dishes, couscous, and for medicinal purposes), and saffron. Merchants also sell bulk lavender, assortments of incense, and fragrant oils such as jasmine, orange, and rose. Note that vendors hike up the price for foreigners. Saffron is much more expensive, but you'll get a better price at a simple hole-in-the-wall grocery than in the stalls. Don't be lured into buying the less-expensive saffron powder, as it includes no saffron at all.

CLOSE UP

The Art of Bargaining

Making a deal is a way of life in Morocco—an art form. It's considered serious business, and a satisfactory purchase is contingent on a mutually satisfying bargain.

THE GAME PLAN

Rest assured that you aren't a failure if you come home with a few over-priced items. Don't leave Morocco without buying things you want because the bargaining process is too daunting. Think of it as a game, and things will fall into place.

ROUND 1

Moroccan bazaar vendors are great hustlers, and will find a way to pounce upon you as soon as you blink in their direction. Your best defense is the proper mind-set: the first time you go into the souk, resolve firmly to browse rather than buy. Wander the stalls, get a sense of what's available, and do some comparison shopping. Don't make eye contact with or speak to vendors, and don't enter stores. Except for carpets, samples of almost everything sold in the bazaars are displayed outside. This will give you a good feel for what's on offer.

ROUND 2

Next time you venture out, set your mind to buying. This isn't simply a question of buying as cheaply as you can, but buying something you love at a price you feel good about. Once you've found your quarry and asked the price (make sure the vendor understands in which currency), start by halving the lowest price you are given for that item. (For carpets, a quarter of the starting price is reason-able.) If you didn't manage to find a price, don't worry. Keep a poker face and be persistent until you arrive at the price that suits both you and the vendor. Remember, the vendor will never look satisfied. If he won't come down far enough, try walking away, but you'll have to convince *yourself* you can't live with that price if you want to convince him in turn. You could try saying you saw the same item cheaper elsewhere, but it may not help you.

PHRASES FOR YOUR ARSENAL

Salaam waleykum. Peace be with you.
Sh'hal hedi bil dirhams? How much is this?
Rali bezzef. It costs too much.
Brit heda. I want this.
Ma'britsh . . . I don't want . . .
Iya. Yes.
La. No.
Biletti. Wait.
Arteni heda. Give me this.
Aufek. Please.
Chokran. Thank you.
M'andish floos. I have no money (often helpful)
Ma'es salema. Good-bye (or May you go in peace)

MORE TIPS

■ If you really don't want to buy anything, don't be persuaded to enter a store.

■ There are no hard-and-fast prices. It's typically cheaper to buy early in the morning before the crowds arrive or at the end of the day, right before the stalls close.

■ Even if a price is marked on an item, you're still expected to bargain, though the margin will be less than if it's unmarked.

–Pamela Windo

10

SHIPPING IT HOME

While many of the most common items purchased in Morocco can be carried on as hand luggage, large items like rugs, lamps, and large pottery pieces may need to be shipped back home. There are DHL and Federal Express offices in major cities, and main post offices also pack and ship medium-size boxes. (Packing requires an extra tip.) A 4-kilogram rug with a stated value of 2,000 DH costs about 420 DH to ship standard delivery to the United States, for example. Check out the Moroccan postal service's Web site (in French) at ⊕*www.bam. net.ma.*

■ The better crafts and antiques bazaars have been arranging shipments reliably for some years. An experienced guide or the concierge at a good hotel should know which to recommend. Note that there will be paperwork to be filled out, and custom duties to pay at the port of entry. The United States now has a free-trade agreement with Morocco that allows for handicrafts to be shipped without duties. Make sure to check customs and import tax regulations for your country before bringing your purchases home.

UNDERSTANDING MOROCCO

Books & Movies

French & Moroccan
Arabic Vocabulary

BOOKS & MOVIES

Books

Paul Bowles. Readings on Morocco in English begin and end with the works of the late Tangier-based American expatriate Paul Bowles and the many Moroccan writers whose work he has translated. Bowles's most famous novel, *The Sheltering Sky,* purports to take place in Algeria, but this tale of a doomed triangle of young Americans adrift in North Africa is quintessentially Moroccan in both tone and content. *The Spider's House* is a superb historical novel and portrait of Fez at the end of the French Protectorate. *Let It Come Down* paints a vivid portrait of life in Tangier's expatriate community, which Bowles inhabited for more than half a century. The most comprehensive collection of Bowles's short stories is *Collected Stories of Paul Bowles 1939–76.* *Days: Tangier Journal, 1987–1989* is the most recent addition to the Bowles bibliography, a series of musings and accounts of daily events that Bowles effortlessly (or so it seems) elevates to the level of artistic essays. All of Bowles's nonfiction is notable, but *Their Heads Are Green and Their Hands Are Blue* is the most revealing and informative on Morocco. Bowles also translated works from the Arabic and Berber canons into English.

Writings by Jane Auer Bowles, Paul's wife, are no less interesting than her husband's. A Tangier resident from the 1940s until her 1973 death in a Spanish insane asylum, Auer Bowles's *Everything Is Nice: Collected Stories* is a flawless portrait of expatriate life in Morocco. Millicent Dillon's biography of Jane Auer Bowles, *A Little Original Sin,* has key insights into both Mr. and Mrs. Bowles and their adopted country.

Fiction. Winner of France's Prix Goncourt, Moroccan author Tahar Ben Jelloun's novel *The Sand Child* tells the story of a girl brought up as a boy by her father. Also by Ben Jelloun are *Sacred Night* and *With Downcast Eyes.*

Travel Literature. Highlights include *The Voices of Marrakesh,* by Elias Canetti; *Tangier: City of the Dream,* by Ian Finlayson; and *A Year in Marrakesh,* by Peter Mayne. Among turn-of-the-20th-century accounts, French novelist Pierre Loti's *Voyage au Maroc* is a classic, as is Polish count Jean Potocki's *Voyage to Morocco.* Charles de Foucauld, a French nobleman, army officer, and missionary, chronicled his time as a Trappist monk in Morocco in his book *Voyage au Maroc.* For more historical and ethnographical accounts, find Edith Wharton's 1920 *In Morocco*; Antoine de Saint-Exupéry's *Wind, Sand and Stars* and *Southern Mail*; and Walter Harris's 1921 *Morocco That Was.* The most recent is *Zohra's Ladder & Other Moroccan Tales,* by Pamela Windo. In this collection of stories that took place during the author's seven years living in Morocco, Windo depicts both the stunning landscapes of the country and the genuine connections she made with the people. The book makes a good companion to a guidebook when traveling to Morocco.

Women Writers. The question of the Moroccan woman's experience has given rise to some excellent social critiques. *Scheherazade Goes West* is a prominent work by the Moroccan feminist Fatima Mernissi, who spoke only Arabic until the age of 20 but went on to earn a master's degree at the Sorbonne and a Ph.D. from Brandeis University. Mernissi has also written *The Forgotten Queens of Islam,* biographical studies of female leaders in the Muslim world, and *Dreams of Trespass,* tales of a harem girlhood. *Opening the Gates: A Century of Arab Feminist Writing,* edited by Margot Badran and Miriam Cooke, comprises three essays, one by Fatima Mernissi.

Food. Paula Wolfert's *Couscous and Other Good Food from Morocco* is excellent for its photographs and background on the Moroccan social context and fabulous recipes.

Current Events. Written by a former correspondent to the *New York Times*, Marvine Howe's 2005 *Morocco: The Islamist Awakening and Other Challenges* describes Morocco's development during the late King Hassan's reign, as well as the present King Mohammed VI's attempts to move the country away from autocracy to democracy.

Movies

A great many films that do not take place in Morocco were nonetheless shot there, most notably Orson Welles's *Othello,* David Lean's *Lawrence of Arabia,* David Cronenberg's *Naked Lunch,* Bernardo Bertolucci's *The Sheltering Sky,* and Martin Scorsese's *The Last Temptation of Christ* and *Kundun.* Scenes from *Gladiator* were shot in the desert just outside Ouarzazate. In Gillies MacKinnon's 1999 film *Hideous Kinky,* Morocco was featured in its own right: it's set in Marrakesh.

Alejandro González Iñárritu's 2006 *Babel,* with Brad Pitt and Cate Blanchett, was filmed partly in the High Atlas mountains (but if you watch before you go, don't worry—nothing like what happens to Cate Blanchett would happen in real life).

FRENCH & MOROCCAN ARABIC VOCABULARY

Most Moroccans are multilingual. The country's official languages are modern standard Arabic and French; most Moroccans speak Moroccan Arabic dialect, with many city dwellers also speaking French. Since the time of the French Protectorate, French has been taught to schoolchildren (not all children) starting in the first grade, resulting in several French-language newspapers, magazines, and TV shows. Spanish enters the mix in northern Morocco, and several Berber tongues are spoken in the south as well as the north. In the medinas and souks of big cities, you may find merchants who can bargain in just about any language, including English, German, Japanese, and Swedish.

A rudimentary knowledge of French and, especially, Arabic will get you far in Morocco. If you're more comfortable with French, by all means use it in the major cities; in smaller cities, villages, and the mountains, it's best to attempt some Moroccan Arabic. Arabic is always a good choice, as Moroccans will go out of their way to accommodate the foreigner who attempts to learn their national language. Some letters in Arabic do not have English equivalents. When you see "gh" at the start of a word in this vocabulary, pronounce it like a french "r," lightly gargled at the back of the throat. If unsure stick to a "g" sound.

FRENCH

ENGLISH	FRENCH	PRONUNCIATION

GREETINGS & BASICS

ENGLISH	FRENCH	PRONUNCIATION
Hello/Good morning/ Good afternoon	Bonjour	bohn-**zhoor**
Good evening	Bonsoir	bohn-**swahr**
Goodbye	Au revoir	oh ruh-**vwahr**
Mr./Sir	Monsieur	muh-**syuh**
Mrs./Madam	Madame	mah-**dahm**
Miss	Mademoiselle	mahd-mwah-**zel**
Pleased to meet you	Enchanté	ahn-shan-**tay**
How are you?	Comment ça va?	**koh**-mohn sa **va**?
Very well	Très bien	tray bee-ehn
And you?	Et vous?	ay **voo**?
yes/no	oui/non	wee/nohn
please	S'il vous plait	seal voo **play**
Thank you	Merci	mare-**see**
You're welcome	Je vous en prie	zhuh **voo** zahn **pree**

I'm sorry	Pardon	pahr-**dohn**
Excuse me	Je m'excuse	zhuh mex-**cues**

USEFUL PHRASES

Do you speak English?	Parlez-vous anglais?	par-lay **voo ahn**-glay
I don't speak . . .	Je ne parle pas . . .	zhuh nuh parl pah
French	français	frahn-**say**
I don't understand	Je ne comprends pas	zhuh nuh kohm-**prahn** pah
I understand	Je comprends	zhuh kohm-**prahn**
I don't know	Je ne sais pas	zhuh nuh say **pah**
I'm American/ British	Je suis américain/ anglais	a-may-ree-**kehn**/ ahn-**glay**
What's your name?	Comment vous ap pelez-vous?	ko-mahn voo za-pell-ay-**voo**
Where is . . .	Où est . . .	oo ay
the train station?	la gare?	la gar
the airport?	l'aeroport?	lehr-oh-**por**
the bus station?	la gare routière?	la **gahr** root-y-**air**
the rest room?	la toilette?	la twah-**let**

MOROCCAN ARABIC

ENGLISH	ARABIC TRANSLITERATION	PRONUNCIATION

GREETINGS & BASICS

Hello/Peace upon you	salaam ou alaikum	sa-**lahm** oo allah-ee-**koom**
(Reply:)		
Hello/And peace upon you	wa alaikum salaam	wa allay-koom sa-**lahm**
Goodbye	bislamma	bess-**lah**-ma
Mr./Sir	si	see
Mrs./Madam/Miss	lalla	lah-la
How are you? Fine, thank you	labass, alhamdul'Illah	la-**bahs**, al-**hahm**-doo-lee-**lah**
("No harm?") ("No harm, praise be to God")	labass	la-**bahs**

Pleased to meet you.	mitsharafin	mitsh-arra-**fayn**
Yes/No	namm/la	nahm/lah
Please	afek	**ah**-feck
Thank you	baraka Allahu fik	**ba**-ra-kah **la**-hoo **feek**
You're welcome	Allah yubarak fik	ahl-lah yoo-**bah**-rak feek
God willing	insh'Allah	in-**shah**-ahl-lah
Excuse me/I'm sorry (from a man)	smahali	**sma**-hah-li
Excuse me/I'm sorry (from a woman)	smahailia	sma-high-**lee**-ah

DAYS

Today	el yum	el yom
Yesterday	imbarah	im-ber-ah
Tomorrow	ghadaa	gha-dah
Sunday	el had	el had
Monday	tneen	t'neen
Tuesday	thlat	tlet
Wednesday	larbaa	lar-bah
Thursday	el khamis	el kha-mees
Friday	el jemaa	el j'mah
Saturday	sebt	es-sebt

NUMBERS

1	wahad	**wa**-hed
2	jouj	jewj
3	thlata	**tlet**-ta
4	rbaa	ar-**bah**
5	khamsa	**khem**-sah
6	sta	stah
7	sbaa	se-**bah**
8	taminia	ta-**min**-ee-ya
9	tseud	tsood
10	aachra	**ah**-she-ra
11	hadash	ha-**dahsh**

12	tanash	ta-**nahsh**
20	aacherine	ah-**chreen**
50	khamsine	khum-**seen**
100	milla	**mee**-yah
200	millatein	mee-ya **tayn**

USEFUL PHRASES

Do you speak English?	ouesh tat tkelem belinglisia	**wesh** tet te-**kel**-lem **blin**-gliz-**ee**-yah?
I don't understand.	ma fahemtsh	ma-**f'emtch**
I don't know.	ma naarf	ma-**nahr**-ef
I'm lost.	ana tilift	ahna t'-lift
I am American (for man).	ana amriqui	ahna am-ree-kee
I am American (for woman).	ana amriqiya	ahna am-**ree**-kee-yah
I am British.	ana inglisi	anna in-ge-**lee**-zee
What is this?	shnou hada	**shnoo** ha-da
Where is?	Fein?	fayn?
the train station	mahatat el tren	ma-ha-**tat** eh-tren
the city bus station	mahatat tobis	**ma-ha**-tat **toh**-beese
the intracity bus station	mahatat al cairan	**ma**-ha-tat al-kah-ee-rahn
the airport	el l'aéroport	el lehr-oh-por
the hotel	el l'hôtel	el l'oh-**teel**
the café	l'khaoua	al-kah-**hou**-wah
the restaurant	el restaurant	el rest-oh-**rahn**
the telephone	tilifoon	**til-lee**-foon
the hospital	el l'hôpital	el l'oh-bee-tahl
the post office	l'bosta	**al**-bost-**a**
the rest room	w.c.	**vay**-say
the pharmacy	pharmacien	far-**ma-cienn**
the bank	l'banca	**al** bann-**ka**
the embassy	sifara	**see**-far-**ra**
I would like a room.	bghit bit	**bgheet**-beet

I would like to buy	bghit nechri	bgheet-nesh-**ree**
cigarettes	garro	**gahr**-oh
a city map	kharretta del medina	kha-**ray**-ta del m'**dee**-nah
a road map	kharretta del bled	kha-**ray**-ta del blad
How much is it?	bi sha hal hada	**bshal hah**-da?
It's expensive.	ghaliya	**gha**-lee-ya
A little	shwiya	**shwee**-ya
A lot	bizzaf	bzzef
Enough	baraka	**ba**-rah-ka
I am ill. (a man)	ana marid	ah-na ma-**reed**
I am ill. (a woman)	ana marida	**ah**-na ma-**reed**-ah
I need a doctor.	bghit doctor	bgheet dok-**tohr**
I have a problem.	aandi mouchkila	**ahn**-dee moosh-**kee**-la
left	lessar	**lis**-sar
right	leemen	**lee**-men
Help!	awni!	**aow**-nee
Fire!	laafiya!	**lah**-fee-ya
Caution!/Look out!	aindek!	**aann**-deck

DINING

I would like	bghit	bgheet
water	l'ma	l'mah
bread	l'khobz	l'khobz
vegetables	khoudra	**khu**-dra
meat	l'hamm	l'hahm
fruits	l'fawakeh	el fah-**weh**-kee
cakes	l'haloua	el **hahl**-oo-wa
tea	atay	**ah**-tay
coffee	kahoua	**kah**-wa
a fork	forchette	for-**shet**
a spoon	maalka	**mahl**-ka
a knife	mousse	moose
a plate	tabsil	tahb-**seel**

Travel Smart Morocco

GETTING HERE & AROUND

▌BY AIR

Morocco is serviced by major airlines to and from North America and Europe. For long distances within Morocco, consider flying. If, for instance, you want to concentrate on the southern oasis valleys, land in Casablanca, fly to Ouarzazate, and rent a car there.

Domestic carriers may require reconfirmation to hold your seat. Remember to place this call ahead of time, or ask your hotel to do so for you. A call to the airline will also suffice to reconfirm your outbound seat.

On domestic flights, Royal Air Maroc offers a 50% discount for one member of a married couple traveling together, as well as additional discounts for children in family groups of three or more (not counting infants). The airline also gives 50% discounts to people between the ages of 12 and 22 and students 31 or younger. All the country's domestic airlines offer a standard 33% discount for children between 2 and 12.

Airline Security Issues Transportation Security Administration (⊕www.tsa.gov) has answers for almost every question that might come up.

AIRPORTS

Most people enter Morocco by flying into Casablanca's Mohammed V Airport (CMN). The airports at Agadir (AGA), Al Hoceima (AHU), Dakhla (VIL), Essaouira (ESU), Fez (FEZ), Ifrane (GMFI), Laayoune (EUN), Marrakesh (RAK), Ouarzazate (OZZ), Oujda (OUD), Nador (NDR), Rabat (RBA), Tangier (TNG), and Tétouan (TTU) have only domestic flights or limited international service. You can often arrange connecting flights to these cities from Casablanca. Another popular way to is to enter Morocco through Rabat or Marrakesh via several daily Air

France flights from Paris and other European cities

The airports themselves aren't remarkable. Casablanca's airport has a few restaurants and overpriced shops, as well as a bank and a pharmacy. Most of the other airports are very small, and you usually don't need to show up more than an hour and a half before your flight.

Airport Information Casablanca Mohammed V Airport (☎022/53–90–40 or 022/53–90–41). **Moroccan Airport Authority** (☎081/00–02–24 ⊕www.onda.ma).

GROUND TRANSPORTATION

Office National des Chemins de Fer, the national rail company, has a station directly under Casablanca's Mohammed V Airport. Trains come and go between 6:30 AM and 11 PM and make travel to and from the airport very easy and hassle-free. The ride to the city takes 30 minutes. Taxis are always available outside arrivals at the Casablanca airport; fares to the city are 250 DH. There's also a shuttle bus to Casablanca.

Contacts Office National des Chemins de Fer (⊕www.oncf.ma).

FLIGHTS

Currently, only Royal Air Maroc, in partnership with Delta and Air France, offers nonstop flights from New York City and Montréal to Casablanca every evening; these flights are convenient and dependable, and connect with domestic flights to other Moroccan destinations. Many other airlines offer connecting services in Europe, and it's worth shopping around for deals if you don't mind stopping along the way. Generally speaking, however, you'll get a better fare if you use the same carrier for the whole trip.

Royal Air Maroc and other major airlines offer daily direct or one-stop flights to Agadir, Casablanca, Fez, Marrakesh,

Rabat, and Tangier from nearly all Western European countries. In addition, discount airlines Atlas Blue and Easy Jet fly to Marrakesh from many European cities, including London and Paris.

Airline Contacts Air France (☎800/237–2747 in the U.S. ⊕www.airfrance.com). **Atlas Blue** (☎082/00–90–90 ⊕www.atlas-blue.com). **Delta** (☎800/221–1212 for U.S. reservations, 800/241–4141 for international reservations ⊕www.delta.com). **Easy Jet** (⊕www.easyjet.com). **Royal Air Maroc** (☎800/344–6726 New York and Montréal, 207/439–4361 London ⊕www.royalairmaroc.com).

▌ BY BOAT

If you're traveling from Spain, you'll need to take a ferry across the Strait of Gibraltar. The most popular crossing is from Algeciras, Spain, to Tangier. Algeciras to Ceuta (Spain inside mainland Morocco) is a popular and shorter route. High-speed ferries make the trip in about 30–40 minutes.

Unfortunately, disembarking in Tangier can be a traumatic way to arrive in Morocco. You're likely to be greeted by unpleasant characters who won't cease harassing you until you've parted company with some money, or at best suffered some verbal abuse. Don't admit to the brigands that you're visiting Morocco for the first time.

Information Comarit Ferry (☎09/93–12–20 ⊕www.comarit.com). **Southern Ferries Ltd** (☎207/491–4968). **Trasmediterránia** (☎09/94–11–01).

▌ BY BUS

For cities not served by train (mainly those in the south), buses are a good option. They're relatively frequent, and seats are usually available.

Compagnie de Transports Marocains (C.T.M.), the national bus company, runs trips to all destinations in the country and guarantees your seat and luggage service. No-smoking rules are enforced (the exception is the driver who sometimes smokes out his side window). These buses stop occasionally for bathroom and smoke breaks, but be sure to stay near the bus, as they have been known to leave quickly, stranding people without their luggage in unfamiliar places.

Another major bus company, Supratours, is connected to Morocco's national rail service. It offers comfortable service to major cities. Supratours has ticket counters at each train station and allows travelers to extend their trip past places where the train service ends. Departure times are designed to coordinate with the arrival of trains.

There are also plenty of smaller bus companies, called "souk buses." They're the only way to get to really rural areas not served by larger companies. They are neither comfortable nor clean. You're much better off shelling out a few extra dirhams for the punctual and pleasant C.T.M. or Supratours buses unless you're going to out-of-the-way places only served by small companies.

In each city the bus station—known as the *gare routière*—is generally near the edge of town. Some larger cities have separate C.T.M. stations. Ignore the posted departure times on the walls—they're never updated. Ask at the ticket booth when the next bus leaves to your chosen destination. There's nothing wrong with checking out a bus before you buy your ticket, as some are dilapidated and uncomfortable. The *greeson* will sell you a ticket, take you to the bus, and put your luggage underneath (you should tip a few dirhams for this).

Buy tickets at the bus station prior to departure; payment is by cash only. Tickets are only sold for the seats available, so once you have a ticket you have a seat. Other than tickets, there are no reservations. Often, tickets only go on sale an hour before departure. Inquire at the bus station for departure times; there are no printed schedules and the displayed schedules are not accurate. Children up to age four travel free. Car seats and bassinets are not usually available for children.

If possible, buy your ticket at least a day ahead of time to guarantee yourself a seat. The best method is to personally go to the station the day before. Remember you have to pay in cash. C.T.M. ticket offices are usually near the main bus stations. Any taxi driver *can* take you.

FARES

Fares are very cheap (currently around 20 DH for a one-hour journey to 250 DH for daylong trips). Luggage is usually charged by weight. Expect to pay no more than 10 DH per piece. Additionally, most C.T.M. stations have inexpensive luggage storage facilities.

Bus Information Compagnie de Transports Marocains (☎022/ 43–82–82 ⊕www. ctm.co.ma). Supratours (☎022/ 43–55–25 ⊕www.supratours.ma).

▌BY CAR

A car is not necessary if your trip is confined to major cities, but it's the best and sometimes the only way to explore Morocco's mountainous areas, small coastal towns, and rural areas, such as the Middle or High Atlas.

Driving in Morocco is relatively inexpensive and a fantastic way to see the country. Roads are generally in good shape and mile markers and road signs are easy to read (they're always written in Arabic and French). Remember that small mountain villages are still only reached by *piste* (gravel path), and that these rough roads can damage a smaller car. Watch for children selling herbs, fruit, oil, and honey on the side of the road—they will literally dart into traffic if they see a foreigner in a car, trying to make a sell.

Hiring a car and a driver is a great, if expensive, way to really get into the crevices of the country. Drivers also serve as protectors from potential faux guides and tourist scams. Be warned, however, that they themselves will often be looking for commissions and might steer you toward particular carpet sellers and tourist shops. Be sure to negotiate an acceptable price before you take off. Drivers must be licensed and official, so be sure to ask for credentials to avoid any unpleasantness down the road.

BOOKING YOUR TRIP

The cars most commonly available in Morocco are small European sedans, such as Renaults, Peugeots, and Fiats. Expect to pay at least 350 DH a day for these. Many companies also rent four-wheel-drive vehicles, a boon for touring the Atlas Mountains and oasis valleys; expect to pay around 2,500 DH a day for a new land cruiser. A 20% VAT (value-added tax) is levied on rental rates. Companies will often let you rent for the day or by the kilometer.

Note that you can negotiate the rental of a taxi with driver just about anywhere in Morocco for no more than the cost of a rental car from a major agency. Normally you negotiate an inclusive price for a given itinerary. The advantage is that you don't have to navigate; the disadvantage is that the driver may have his own ideas about where you should go. For less haggling, local tour operators can furnish vehicles with drivers at a fairly high daily package rate.

The best place to rent a car is Casablanca's airport, as the rental market is very competitive here—most of the cars are new, and you can often negotiate a discount. Local companies will give you a much better price for the same car than the international agencies (even after the latter have offered "discounts"). We list the agencies with offices at Casablanca's airport; most have other branches in Casablanca itself, as well as in Rabat and

Marrakesh. To get the best deal, book through a travel agent, who will shop around.

Rental Agencies Europ Car (☎022/53–91–61 airport). **First Car International** (☎022/22–30–00–07 city center). **Janoub Tours** (☎022/31–91–48 airport). **Jet Car** (☎022/53–83–67 airport). **Loca-Car** (☎022/53–86–92 airport). **National Car** (☎022/53–97–16 airport). **Nava Tour** (☎022/53–99–40 airport). **Prince Car** (☎022/53–94–92 airport). **Renaissance Car** (☎022/53–95–34 airport). **Siaha Car** (☎022/53–80–85 airport). **Sixt Car** (☎022/53–80–99 airport). **Thrifty Car** (☎022/53–20–01 airport). **Tourist Cars** (☎022/53–97–59 airport). **Union Car** (☎022/53–87–55 airport).

GASOLINE

Gas is readily available, if relatively expensive. The gas that most cars use is known as *super*, the lower-octane variety as *essence*. Unleaded fuel (*sans plomb*) is widely available but not currently necessary for local cars; it costs around 9.5 DH a liter. Diesel fuel (*diesel*) is significantly cheaper. All gas stations provide full service; tipping is optional. Some stations take credit cards.

PARKING

When parking in the city, make sure that you're in a parking zone or the authorities will put a boot on one of your wheels. In parking lots, give the *gardien* a small tip upon leaving. Some cities have introduced the European system of prepaid tickets from a machine, valid for a certain duration.

ROAD CONDITIONS

Road conditions are generally very good. A network of toll highways (*autoroutes*) runs from Casablanca to Larache (near Tangier) and east from Rabat to Meknès and Fez, and from Casablanca to Settat (south toward Marrakesh). These autoroutes are much safer than the lesser roads. There are periodic toll booths with tolls ranging from 5 DH to 20 DH.

On rural roads expect the occasional flock of sheep or goats to cross the road at inopportune times. In the south you'll see road signs warning of periodic camel crossings as well. In the mountains, side-pointing arrows designate curves in the road. However, be aware that some dangerous curves come unannounced. Also, in the countryside you're much more likely to encounter potholes, narrow roads, and speeding taxi drivers.

Night driving outside city centers requires extra caution. Beware of inadequate or unfamiliar lighting at night, particularly on trucks—it's not uncommon for trucks to have red lights in the front or white lights in the rear. Ubiquitous ancient mopeds rarely have working lights or reflectors.

ROADSIDE EMERGENCIES

In case of an accident on the road, dial 177 outside cities and 19 in urban areas. In case of fire, dial 15. Don't depend on the police or fire department to order an ambulance. Make that call yourself, if at all possible.

RULES OF THE ROAD

Traffic moves on the right side of the road. There are two main rules in Morocco; the first is "priority to the right," an old French rule meaning that in traffic circles you must yield to traffic entering from the right. The second is "every man for himself."

You must carry your car registration and insurance certificate at all times (these documents are always supplied with rental cars). Morocco's speed limits, enforced by radar, are 100 kph (63 mph) on autoroutes and 40 or 60 kph (25 or 37 mph) in towns. The penalty for speeding is a 400 DH fine or confiscation of your driver's license.

Wearing seat belts is mandatory for both drivers and passengers. Failure to do so will result in a hefty fine. Talking on cell phones while driving is illegal.

■ BY TAXI

Moroccan taxis take two forms: *petits taxis,* small taxis that travel within city limits, and *grands taxis,* large taxis that travel between cities. Drivers usually wait until the taxi is full before departing.

Petits taxis are color-coded according to city—in Casablanca and Fez they're red, in Rabat they're blue, in Marrakesh they're beige, and so on. These can be hailed anywhere but can take a maximum of three passengers. The fare is metered and not expensive: usually 5 DH to 30 DH for a short- or medium-length trip. Taxis often pick up additional passengers en route, so if you can't find an empty cab, try hailing a taxi with one or two passengers.

Grands taxis travel fixed routes between cities and in the country. One person can sit in front with the driver, and four sit, very cramped, in the back. Don't expect air-conditioning or even fully functioning windows. Fares for these shared rides are inexpensive, sometimes as little as 5 DH per person for a short trip. You can also charter a grand taxi for trips between cities, but you need to negotiate a price in advance.

■ BY TRAIN

If you're sticking mainly to the four Imperial Cities—Fez, Meknès, Rabat, and Marrakesh—you're best off taking the train and using petits taxis in the cities. Morocco's punctual rail system, Office National des Chemins de Fer, mostly serves the north. From Casablanca and Rabat the network runs east via Meknès and Fez to Oujda, north to Tangier, and south to Marrakesh. Bus connections link trains with Tétouan, Nador, and Agadir, and you can buy through tickets covering both segments before you leave.

Trains are divided into first class (*première classe*) and second class (*deuxième classe*). First class is a very good buy compared to its counterpart in Europe, but second class is comfortable, too. Long-distance trains seat six people to a compartment in first class, eight to a compartment in second class.

Fares are relatively inexpensive compared to those in Europe. A first-class ticket from Casablanca to Fez costs 155 DH. You can buy train tickets at any station up to six days in advance. Purchasing your ticket on the train is pricier and only in cash. Kids travel at half price on Moroccan trains.

Smoking is prohibited by law on public transport, but in practice people smoke in the corridors or in the areas between coaches.

Information Office National des Chemins de Fer (⊕ www.oncf.ma).

ESSENTIALS

▌ACCOMMODATIONS

Accommodations in Morocco range from opulent to downright spare, with everything in between. You'll have a range of options in most areas. Hotels can be on a par with those of Europe and the U.S., but the farther you venture off the beaten path, the farther you might feel from a five-star welcome. Particularly in some of the smaller towns and villages, hotels lack the amenities to call themselves top-tier. Look a bit closer, though—what they lack in luxury these hotels often make up in charm, character, and, most of all, location.

▌**TIP→** Assume that hotels operate on the European Plan (EP, no meals) unless we specify that they use the Breakfast Plan (BP, with full breakfast), Continental Plan (CP, Continental breakfast), Full American Plan (FAP, all meals), Modified American Plan (MAP, breakfast and dinner), or are all-inclusive (AI, all meals and most activities).

APARTMENT & HOUSE RENTALS

Book a room in or rent an entire well-furnished, traditional house (*riad*) in the medinas of the most visited cities, such as Fez, Marrakesh, and Essaouira, as well as in smaller seaside towns such as Asilah and Oualidia. This is a unique opportunity to experience traditional Moroccan architecture and live like royalty of old.

Moroccan Villas offers a selection of properties for families and groups. Marrakech Medina offers riads not only in Marrakesh, but in other destinations around the country. Splendia is a comprehensive booking engine to find exceptional riads in the city or countryside.

House Rentals Marrakech Medina (☎044/44–24–48 ⊕www.marrakech-medina. com). **Moroccan Villas** (⊕www.moroccovillas. com). **Riad Selection** (⊕www.riadselection. com/uk). **Splendia** (⊕www.splendia.com/ morocco.php).

HOSTELS

Hostels offer bare-bones lodging at low, low prices. In Morocco, hostels go under the French name *auberge de jeunesse* and are normally located near the medina walls in the old parts of town. A room is very inexpensive and averages around 30 DH to 60 DH.

Information Hostelling International—USA (☎301/495–1240 ⊕www.hiusa.org).

HOTELS

Hotels are classified by the Moroccan government with one to five stars, plus an added category for five-star luxury hotels. In hotels with three or more stars all rooms have private bathrooms, and there is an on-site bar. Air-conditioning is common in three-star hotels in Fez and Marrakesh and in all five-star hotels. Standards do vary, though; it's possible to find a nice two-star hotel or, occasionally, a four-star hotel without hot water. In the same vein, hotels that are beneath the star system altogether—"unclassified"—can also be satisfactory.

Prices for each government category are fixed within each region of the country, and are generally very reasonable (except in five-star luxury hotels, of course). Note that the large business hotels of this category in Casablanca and Rabat will systematically discount their published rates by applying "corporate rates" on the mention of the name of a company.

The hotels we list are the cream of the crop in each of our price categories (which do *not* parallel the Moroccan government's star system).

If your destination's high season is December through April and you're trying to book, say, in late April, you might save considerably by changing your dates by a week or two. Note, though, that many properties charge peak-season rates for your entire stay even if

LOCAL DO'S & TABOOS

CUSTOMS OF THE COUNTRY

Everyone is polite in Morocco, even to sworn enemies. If you have a problem and you lose your temper, you give up hope of solving it. A combination of courtesy and persistence is the best approach. Open transactions with the proper greetings (⇨ *Language & the French and Moroccan Arabic Vocabulary, at the end of this book*) before getting down to business, and remember that people come first; the actions to be accomplished are secondary. Status is another key concept. Morocco is a very hierarchical society; people are dealt with according to their position in the hierarchy, not the order in which they happen to arrive. In markets this phenomenon is modified: someone selling vegetables will deal with several customers at once, so don't wait meekly to be served in turn. Finally, Moroccans do not always say what they mean: what they say can be governed by the desire to please or, in the case of less-charitable characters, the perception of what will work to their advantage. You don't need to take all these guidelines into account for simple transactions like buying train tickets, but they'll help in more-complicated situations.

GREETINGS

Within and between the sexes, the two-cheek air kiss is customary when greeting and leave-taking and is likely the closest thing to a public display of affection you will observe between a Moroccan man and woman. While this is a moderate Islamic society, it's best to adhere to modesty in public. In rural, more-conservative areas, you will only see such greetings among people of the same sex.

SIGHTSEEING

With the exception of the Hassan II Mosque in Casablanca and the Tin Mal Mosque in the High Atlas, non-Muslims may not enter mosques.

Except at the beach, tank tops and shorts are not acceptable for either sex anywhere in Morocco, even in the hottest weather. Both women and men should cover up their arms and legs if they want better service and a friendly rapport with Moroccans; in the countryside locals consider T-shirts and shorts to be the same as underwear, and wearing such will increase the potential for harassment, especially for women. Apart from this, casual clothing is quite acceptable.

OUT ON THE TOWN

If you're invited to someone's home, do not enter until invited to do so. In more-traditional homes you'll have to leave your shoes at the door. Greet the assembled company in turn, starting with the person on your right. For all food served in a communal dish and meant to be eaten by hand, be sure to use only your right hand. Warning: Moroccan hospitality can be extremely generous, and you may need to pace your eating. It's not unusual to have two main meat dishes. It's customary to socialize before the meal rather than afterward, so food is not served upon guests' arrival, and it's acceptable to leave immediately after tea at the end of the meal.

DOING BUSINESS

Business appointments aren't usually scheduled more than a week in advance, and should be reconfirmed by phone the day before. Schedules are often changed at the last moment if something of higher priority comes up, so the prudent business traveler should always have a contingency plan in case meetings don't materialize. Punctuality is not a virtue: whatever time you're given is approximate, so don't expect to keep a series of tightly scheduled appointments. Never start a meeting by coming immediately to the point of business; always start with general conversation. Sensitive questions are approached politely and indirectly. Debt recovery in particular must be approached in a tactful way. Business cards are always appreciated.

It's generally fine to address business contacts by their first name. Moroccans use the respectful "Sidi" to precede last names. Note that with male business associates and acquaintances, inquiring about female spouses is not appropriate. Instead, one is asked about his "house" and the health of family members.

Moroccans tend to dress more formally than Americans in business dealings. Business attire is usually coat and tie for men and business skirt or slacks for women. A small gift or token is appreciated, but never expected.

LANGUAGE

Try to learn a little of the local language. Even just mastering a few basic words and terms is bound to make chatting with the locals more rewarding.

The main spoken language in Morocco is Moroccan Arabic, which has fewer vowels than other dialects and includes a number of Spanish and French words. There are also three Amazigh (Berber) languages—Tarifit, in the northern Rif; Tamazight, in the Middle Atlas and eastern High Atlas; and Tashelhit, in the western High Atlas, Souss Valley, and Anti-Atlas. French is widely spoken. There is no difference between the French spoken here and that used in France, except perhaps the presence of fewer colloquialisms, so any standard French phrase book will serve you well. There's usually no problem communicating in English at hotels in trafficked areas. The official written languages are Arabic and French, and most signs are written in both, so you don't need to know Arabic script to find your way around. Numerals within Arabic script are the same Arabic numerals we use in English (unlike those used in Middle Eastern countries).

It's difficult to learn Moroccan Arabic on location, because unless you look like a Moroccan you will nearly always be addressed in French. Generally, a good French phrasebook will be of much more use than an Arabic one. Still, it's useful to know some key words for proper greetings and for situations where no one speaks French.

A phrase book and language-tape set can help get you started. Consider a portable electronic translator for on-site assistance.

Fodor's French for Travelers (available at bookstores everywhere) is excellent.

Language Programs. Courses in Moroccan Arabic are taught at the American Language Center in Rabat, Casablanca, Fez, and Marrakesh. The center in Fez, in collaboration with some American universities, also offers an excellent program in classical and Moroccan Arabic through its ALIF (Arabic Language in Fez—*alif* is the first letter of the Arabic alphabet) program. The Centre Culturel Français offers French courses in all major cities.

The Center for Cross-Cultural Learning in the Rabat medina has excellent courses in Classical Arabic, Moroccan Arabic, and the Amazigh (Berber) languages. They offer intense learning sessions of two weeks as well as courses lasting two to three months. They also offer private lessons and occasional cultural tours with language learning.

Larger cities have many small companies offering classes in French and Moroccan Arabic, but quality and prices vary. Local public universities have been known to offer courses at greatly reduced prices (the same tuition charged Moroccan students) to foreigners staying in Morocco for a longer stint.

Centre Culturel Français (✉ *123, bd. Zerktouni, Casablanca* ☎ *022/23–79–14* ⊕ *www.ambafrance-ma.org/institut/marrakech/index.cfm*). **Center for Cross Cultural Leaning** (✉ *Ave. Lahlou, Derb Elijirani, 11, Zankat Elhassani, Rabat* ☎ *037/20–23–65 or 037/20–23–66* ⊕ *www.cccl-ma.com*).

your travel dates straddle peak and non-peak seasons. High-end chains catering to businesspeople tend to be busy only on weekdays, and often drop rates dramatically on weekends to fill up rooms. Ask when rates go down. At the height of summer when temperatures soar and tourists flock elsewhere, rooms are often discounted 20% to 30%.

Hotel reservations in Morocco nearly always require a faxed request and confirmation. Specify your room preferences on your fax. If you're looking for an en-suite bathroom, request a room *avec salle de bain*; for a two-person room, request *une chambre double*; for two beds, request *deux lits*; one large bed, *un grand lit*; and for a medina or garden view, request *coté medina/jardin*. Remember to ask whether breakfast is included in the rate.

■ COMMUNICATIONS

INTERNET

Internet use has exploded in Morocco, and you'll find cybercafés everywhere, even in the smaller towns. On average they charge 10 DH to 20 DH an hour. Wireless connections are also available in many areas within larger cities, which can be a treat if you have your laptop with you.

Take the same security precautions you would anywhere with your laptop, and always use a surge protector.

Contacts **Cybercafés** (⊕ www.cybercafes. com) is an excellent resource listing more than 4,200 Internet cafés worldwide.

PHONES

The country code for Morocco is 212. The area codes are as follows: Casablanca, 022; Settat and El Jadida, 023; Marrakesh, 044; Fez and Meknès, 035; Oujda, 056; Rabat, 037; Laayoune, 048; Tangier, 039; mobile phones, 061-071. When dialing a Moroccan number from overseas, drop the initial 0 from the area code. To call locally, within the area code, just dial the number.

For international calls *from* Morocco, dial 00 followed by the country code. Country codes: United States and Canada, 1; United Kindgom, 44; Australia, 61; New Zealand, 64. There are nine digits in local numbers, starting with "0." Note that when calling from out-of-country into Morocco you always drop the "0," and the number becomes an eight-digit code. After the zero there is a two-number area code. Numbers that start with 06 or 07 are mobile phones.

CALLING WITHIN MOROCCO

Morocco has an efficient phone system; you can call anywhere without difficulty. GSM cellular phones with international roaming capability work well in the cities and along major communication routes. (GSM is the mobile system used in Morocco and most of Europe.)

Morocco currently has two major cellular-phone companies, Maroc Telecom and Meditel. Both of these companies offer prepaid calling cards and phone sales. The frequent promotions and double phone card offers are a nice option for Moroccans and travelers alike.

Public phones are located on the street, and you must purchase a *telecarte*, or phone card, to use them. They come in denominations from 10 DH to 100 DH. You insert the card and then place your local or international call.

Téléboutiques are everywhere in Morocco. These little shops have individual coin-operated phones. You feed the machine with dirhams and make local calls. You can also make international calls by calling directory assistance or calling directly.

Access directory assistance by dialing **160** from anywhere in the country. Many operators speak English, and they all speak French. Phone numbers are given in French as a series of three two-digit numbers.

CALLING OUTSIDE MOROCCO
To call the United States directly from Morocco, call 001, then the area code and phone number. Calls from Morocco are expensive, but rates are cut by 20% if you call after midnight. The cheapest option in direct international dialing is to call from a public phone, using a telecarte. These rates are 4 DH a minute (about 42¢) during the day, and 3.16 DH (about 35¢) a minute after midnight.

Both AT&T and MCI have local access numbers for making international calls. These are especially useful if you already have calling cards with these companies.

Contacts **AT&T Direct Access** (☎002/11–00–11 in Morocco). **MCI** (☎002/11–00–12 in Morocco).

CALLING CARDS
Phone cards for use in public phones can be purchased at any téléboutique, *librarie*, photocopy shop, tobacco shop, or small convenience store. Maroc Telecom and Meditel phone cards, to be used with mobile phones, can also be purchased in these places in denominations of 20, 50, 100, 200, and 600 DH.

MOBILE PHONES
If you have a multiband phone (some countries use different frequencies than what's used in the United States) and your service provider uses the world-standard GSM network (as do T-Mobile, Cingular, and Verizon), you can probably use your phone abroad. Roaming fees can be steep, however: 99¢ a minute is considered reasonable. And overseas you normally pay the toll charges for incoming calls. It's almost always cheaper to send a text message than to make a call, since text messages have a very low set fee (often less than 5¢).

If you just want to make local calls, consider buying a new SIM card (note that your provider may have to unlock your phone for you to use a different SIM card) and a prepaid service plan in the destination. You'll then have a local number and can make local calls at local rates. If your trip is extensive, you could also simply buy a new cell phone in your destination, as the initial cost will be offset over time.

■**TIP→If you travel internationally frequently, save one of your old mobile phones or buy a cheap one on the Internet; ask your cell phone company to unlock it for you, and take it with you as a travel phone, buying a new SIM card with pay-as-you-go service in each destination.**

The mobile phone industry has taken off in the country—virtually everyone you meet, even High Atlas farmers, has a cell phone in his or her pocket. Moroccan cell phones are usually mono-band, which means they can work with dual and tri-band phones but not vice versa. For this reason it's a good idea to try to rent a phone or simply buy a cheap cell phone at your local Maroc Telecom or Meditel store. These can be bought for as little as 199 DH (about $27). If you're spending more than a few weeks in the country or traveling in remote spots, these are indispensable. You'll find cell-phone towers even in the most rural areas.

Contacts **Cellular Abroad** (☎800/287–5072 within the U.S., 310/862–7100 outside the U.S. ⊕www.cellularabroad.com) rents and sells GMS phones and sells SIM cards that work in many countries. **Mobal** (☎888/888–9162 ⊕www.mobalrental.com) rents mobiles and sells GSM phones (starting at $49) that will operate in 140 countries. Per-call rates vary throughout the world. **Planet Fone** (☎888/988–4777 ⊕www.planetfone.com) rents cell phones, but the per-minute rates are expensive.

■ CUSTOMS & DUTIES

Customs duties are very high in Morocco, and many items are subject to various taxes that can total 80%. You'll have no problem bringing in personal effects, a reasonable number of alcoholic drinks, cigarettes, food, or a laptop computer; there are no hard-and-fast rules for these things, though a friendly attitude always helps. Large electronic items will be taxed. (It's possible to import large electronics— such as laptop computers—temporarily without tax, but this will be marked in your passport, and the next time you leave the country you must take the equipment with you.) It's always easier to take things in person than to have them sent to you and cleared through customs at the post office, where even the smallest items will be taxed. Foreigners leaving the country are allowed to change up to 15,000 DH back into their native currency; this will be noted in the passport.

Information Government of Morocco Customs (⊕www.douane.gov.ma). **U.S. Customs and Border Protection** (⊕www.cbp.gov).

▌ EATING OUT

Moroccan cuisine is delectable. Dining establishments range from outdoor food stalls to elegant restaurants, the latter disproportionately expensive, with prices approaching those in Europe. Simpler, much cheaper restaurants abound. Between cities, roadside restaurants commonly offer delicious tagines or grilled meat with bread and salad; on the coast, fried fish is an excellent buy, and you can often choose your meal from the daily catch. Marrakesh and Fez are the places for wonderful Moroccan feasts in fairytale surroundings, and Casablanca has a lively and diverse dining scene. The restaurants we list are the cream of the crop in each price range and cuisine type.

MEALS & MEALTIMES

Moroccan hotels normally serve a continental breakfast (*petit déjeuner continental*): coffee or tea, fruit juice, croissants or crepes, bread, butter, and jam. You can buy an equivalent meal at any of numerous cafés at a much lower price. (Many urban Moroccans have the same breakfast, with the addition of olive oil and Moroccan pancakes. In rural areas, people have soup or a kind of porridge.) The more-expensive hotels have elaborate buffets. Hotel breakfasts are usually served from about 7 AM to 10 or 10:30. Lunch, typically the most leisurely meal of the day, is served between noon and 2:30. Hotels and restaurants begin dinner service at 7:30, though crowds are on the thin side until 8:30 or 9. In a Moroccan home you probably won't sit down to eat until 9 or 10 PM. Restaurants stay open later in the more cosmopolitan city centers.

Lunch (*déjeuner*) in Morocco tends to be a large meal, as in France. A typical lunch menu consists of salad, a main course with meat and vegetables, and fruit. In restaurants this is generally available à la carte. On Friday the traditional lunch meal is a heaping bowl of couscous topped with meats and vegetables.

At home, people tend to have afternoon tea, then a light supper, often with soup. Dinner (*diner*) in French and international restaurants is generally à la carte; you may select as light or heavy a meal as you like. Many of the fancier Moroccan restaurants serve fixed-price feasts, with at least three courses and sometimes upwards of five. If you're a vegetarian, or have other dietary concerns, state this when you make a reservation; many restaurants will prepare special dishes with advance notice.

Lunch and dinner are served communal style, on one big platter. Moroccans use their right hands to sop up the juices in these dishes with bread. Bread is used as an all-purpose utensil to pull up little pieces of vegetables and meat. In restaurants bread will always be offered in a basket. Utensils will be offered to foreigners. All restaurants, no matter how basic, have sinks for washing hands before and after your meal.

Unless otherwise noted, the restaurants listed in this guide are open daily for lunch and dinner.

Sunday is the most common day for restaurant closings.

During Ramadan, everything changes. All cafés and nearly all restaurants are closed during the day; the *ftir*, or "break fast," is served precisely at sunset, and most people take their main meal of the night, the *soukhour*, at about 2 AM. The main hotels, however, continue to serve meals to non-Muslim guests as usual.

PAYING
For price charts deciphering the price categories of restaurants and hotels (–$$$$), see "Planning" at the beginning of each chapter. Only the pricier restaurants take credit cards; MasterCard and Visa are the most widely accepted. Outside the largest cities you'll rarely be able to use your credit card.

RESERVATIONS & DRESS
Reservations are always a good idea: we mention them only when they're essential or not accepted. Book as far ahead as you can, and reconfirm as soon as you arrive. Jacket and tie are never required.

WINES, BEER & SPIRITS
Although alcohol is forbidden in the Islam religion, it is produced in the country. The more-expensive restaurants are licensed to serve alcohol. Morocco produces some red wines in the vicinity of Meknès, and the national beer is Flag Special. Heineken is produced under license in Casablanca. Apart from restaurants, drinks are available at the bars of hotels classified by the government with three stars or more. Supermarkets like Marjane, Label Vie, and Acima sell alcohol to foreigners with proper identification (except during Ramadan, when liquor shelves are restocked with tasteful displays of chocolates and dates). Little shops in small towns also sell beer and spirits.

▌ELECTRICITY

To use electric-powered equipment purchased in the United States or Canada, bring a converter and adapter. The electrical current in Morocco is 220 volts, 50 cycles alternating current (AC); wall outlets take the two-pin plug found in continental Europe. Power surges do occur.

Blackouts might occur in some remote areas, but these are nothing compared to neighboring African countries. Most small villages and midsize towns are connected to the national grid. The World Bank and other international NGOs have financed the electrification of rural Morocco. In midsize towns the electricity might go up and down, so bringing a small surge protector is advised. Problems are dealt with promptly by the local utilities board.

Consider making a small investment in a universal adapter, which has several types of plugs in one lightweight, compact unit. Most laptops and mobile phone chargers are dual voltage (i.e., they operate equally well on 110 and 220 volts), so require only an adapter. These days the same is true of small appliances such as hair dryers. Always check labels and manufacturer instructions to be sure. Don't use 110-volt outlets marked FOR SHAVERS ONLY for high-wattage appliances such as hair-dryers.

Contacts Steve Kropla's Help for World Traveler's (⊕ www.kropla.com) has information on electrical and telephone plugs around the world. **Walkabout Travel Gear** (⊕www.walkabouttravelgear.com) has a good coverage of electricity under "adapters."

■ EMERGENCIES

Local authorities are generally cooperative in emergency situations once they arrive on the scene. As with Moroccan businesses, services can be a bit slower than Western standards.

Although pharmacies maintain normal hours, a system is in place that ensures that one is always open. You'll find a schedule of late-closing pharmacies posted on the pharmacy door or the adjacent wall. Pharmacies are easy to spot, just look for the neon-green crescent moon symbol. Moroccan pharmacists are on par with European and American standards. Note that you don't need a prescription to purchase antibiotics.

■ HEALTH

The most common type of illness visitors suffer is traveler's diarrhea, usually caused by contaminated food or simply a change of diet. Moroccan tap water is usually safe, but many visitors have felt queasy after drinking the local water. To be on the safe side, drink only bottled, boiled, or purified water and soft drinks. Don't drink from public fountains, and resist the temptation to add ice to room-temperature beverages. Use bottled water to brush your teeth. Make sure food has been thoroughly cooked and is served to you fresh and hot; avoid raw vegetables and fruits unless you have washed or peeled them yourself. If you have problems, mild cases of traveler's diarrhea may respond to Imodium (known generically as loperamide) or Pepto-Bismol. Be sure to drink plenty of fluids; if you can't keep fluids down, seek medical help immediately.

Morocco is called "the cold country with the hot sun," and these two extremes can cause problems for travelers—especially in high mountain and desert regions. Winters bring biting cold that makes frostbite a real concern. Many smaller hotels don't have adequate heating. Do as the locals do and layer your clothing to keep warm. In summer, heatstroke and dehydration are big risks to travelers and Moroccans alike. Be sure to drink plenty of water and rest in the shade any chance you get. If you do get dehydrated, pharmacies sell rehydration salts called Biosel. ■TIP➡Sunscreen is widely available in pharmacies and specialty cosmetic stores, but is outrageously expensive. Pack your own.

Note that scorpions, snakes, and biting insects live in the desert regions. These rarely pose a problem, but it wouldn't hurt to shake out your shoes in the morning. Dog bites pose the risk of rabies, so it's worth getting vaccinated. If a dog approaches you, pick up a handful of rocks and throw them nearby—Moroccans do this so often that a dog usually runs away the moment you swing your arm.

Medical care is available but varies in quality. The larger cities have excellent private clinics. The rest of the county depends on government-run smaller clinics and *dispensaires*. The cost of medical care is low—an office consultation and exam will cost 250 DH. Seeing a specialist can cost up to 500 DH. While medical facilities can be quite adequate in urban areas, English-speaking medical help is rare.

OVER-THE-COUNTER REMEDIES

Nearly all medicines, including antibiotics and painkillers, are available over the counter at Moroccan pharmacies. Aspirin is sold as Aspro; ibuprofen is sold as Analgyl, Algantyl, or Tabalon. Acetaminophen, the generic equivalent of Tylenol, is sold as Doliprane and is widely available.

HOURS OF OPERATION

Moroccan banks are open Monday to Thursday 8:30 to noon and 2 to 4. On Friday, the day of prayer, they close slightly earlier in the morning and open a little later in the afternoon. Post offices are open Monday to Thursday 8:30 to noon and 2:30 to 6:30, Friday from 8:30 to 11:30 and 3 to 6:30. Government offices have similar schedules.

Museums are generally open 9 to noon and 2:30 to 6. Standard pharmacy hours are 8:30–12:30 and 3–9:30. Your hotel can help you locate which pharmacies are open around the clock. Shops are open every day except Sunday from about 9 to 1 and from 3 or 4 to 7.

Remember that during Ramadan the above schedules change, often with the midday closing omitted. On Friday many businesses close down for the day or for the noon prayer.

HOLIDAYS

The two most important religious holidays in Morocco are Aïd el Fitr, which marks the end of the monthlong Ramadan fast, and Aïd el Adha or Aïd el Kebir, the sheep-sacrifice feast commemorating the prophet Ibrahim's absolution from the obligation to sacrifice his son. Both are two-day festivals during which all offices, banks, and museums are closed. The other religious holiday is the one-day Aïd el Mouloud, commemorating the birthday of the prophet Mohammed. The dates change each year, so check ahead.

The monthlong Ramadan (beginning August 21 in 2009 and August 11 in 2010) is not a holiday per se, but it does change the pace of life. Because the Muslim calendar is lunar, the dates for Ramadan and other religious holidays shift each year.

The most important political holiday is Aïd el Arch, or Throne Day (July 30), which commemorates the coronation of King Mohammed VI. Morocco's other holidays are as follows: January 1, New Year's Day; January 11, anniversary of the proclamation of Moroccan independence; May 1, Labor Day; May 23, National Day; August 14, Oued ed Dahab, otherwise known as Allegiance Day; August 20, anniversary of the revolution of the king and the people (against the French); August 21, Youth Day; November 6, commemoration of the Green March, Morocco's claim on the Western Sahara in 1975; November 18, Independence Day.

MAIL

In Morocco the post office is called *l-bossta* in Arabic; the French word *timbre* is used for stamps. Post offices are available everywhere and are visible by their yellow signs. Outgoing airmail is completely reliable. Note that if you mail letters at the main sorting office of any city (usually situated on Avenue Mohammed V), they will arrive several days sooner than if you mail them from elsewhere, sometimes in as little as three days to Europe. Airmail letters to North America take between 5 and 14 days; to Europe between 3 and 10 days; and to Australia about two weeks.

For a 20-gram airmail letter or postcard, rates are 10 DH to the United States or Canada, 8 DH to the United Kingdom, and 14 DH to Australia or New Zealand.

You can have letters sent to *poste restante*—just note that about 2% of incoming mail gets lost, and letters with cash in them always get lost. Receiving packages by mail is not recommended, since you often have to pay customs duties almost equal to the value of the goods.

SHIPPING PACKAGES

Within Morocco, the Express Mail Service (EMS, or Poste Rapide) offers overnight delivery from main post offices to major cities. There is also same-day service between Rabat and Casablanca. The international EMS takes three to five days from Morocco to Europe. DHL is quicker but more than double the price. United Parcel Service operates in Casablanca.

When sending packages to Morocco by courier, bear in mind that only two courier services are represented outside Casablanca: the post office's Express Mail Service and DHL. If you use another service you may find that your recipient is only informed of the arrival of a package via postcard from Casablanca—and is then expected to show up in Casa to collect it. Note that if anything other than documents is sent to Morocco via courier, the package will be delayed, and the recipient will have to pay a customs broker and customs duty. The minimum time for a courier package to arrive is three days from the United Kingdom, five days from North America.

Sending packages *out* of the country is easy enough. Go to the Colis Postaux (parcel post office; one in each town), where you can also buy boxes. You'll need to fill in some forms and show the package to customs officials before wrapping it. Airmail parcels reach North America in about two weeks, Europe in about 10 days. For surface mail, count on from three to six months to North America, from one to three months to Europe. Airmail is more reliable. DHL offers a special rate for handicraft items shipped overseas, and some carpet stores can arrange shipping, though some scams have been reported whereby a substandard carpet is shipped to your home, so proceed with caution.

Express Services DHL (✉40, ave. de FranceRabat ☎037/77–99–34 ✉52, bd. Abdelmoumen, Casablanca ☎022/97–20–20 ⊕www.dhl.com). **FedEx** (✉313, bd. Mohammed V, Casablanca ☎022/54–21–33 ⊕www.fedex.com/ma). **United Parcel Service** (✉210, bd. Mohammed Zerktouni, Casablanca ☎022/48–36–36 ⊕www.ups.com).

▌MONEY

Costs in Morocco are low compared to those in both North America and Europe. Fruit and vegetables, public transportation, and labor are very cheap. (Cars, gasoline, and electronic goods, on the other hand, are relatively pricey.) Sample costs are in U.S. dollars:

Meal in cheap restaurant, $3 to $6; meal in expensive restaurant, $25 to $50; liter of bottled water, 65¢ ; cup of coffee, 70¢; museum admission, $1.50; liter of gasoline, $1.20; short taxi ride, $1 to $2. Prices throughout this guide are given for adults; reduced fees are usually available for children but not students or senior citizens.

Because the dirham's value experiences some flux, some of the more upscale hotels, tour operators, and activity specialists geared towards tourists publish their prices in euros, pounds, and sometimes even dollars, but accept dirhams (these places also usually take credit cards, which solves the problem).

▌TIP➔ **Banks never have every foreign currency on hand, and it may take as long as a week to order. If you're planning to exchange funds before leaving home, don't wait till the last minute.**

ATMS & BANKS

Your own bank will probably charge a fee for using ATMs abroad; the foreign bank you use may also charge a fee. Nevertheless, you'll usually get a better rate of exchange at an ATM than you will at a currency-exchange office or even when changing money in a bank. Extracting funds as you need them is a safer option than carrying around a large amount of cash.

▌TIP➔ **PIN numbers with more than four digits are not recognized at ATMs in many countries. If yours has five or more, remember to change it before you leave.**

Reliable ATMs are attached to banks in major cities, and there's one in the arrivals all at Casablanca's airport. BMCE and Wafabank belong to the Cirrus and Plus networks. The machines also give cash advances on Visa and MasterCard. ATM withdrawals impose a slight premium on the exchange rate compared to cash or traveler's checks.

CREDIT CARDS

Throughout this guide, the following abbreviations are used: **AE**, American Express; **D**, Discover; **DC**, Diners Club; **MC**, MasterCard; and **V**, Visa.

It's a good idea to inform your credit-card company before you travel, especially if you're going abroad and don't travel internationally very often. Otherwise, the credit-card company might put a hold on your card owing to unusual activity—not a good thing halfway through your trip. Record all your credit-card numbers—as well as the phone numbers to call if your cards are lost or stolen—in a safe place, so you're prepared should something go wrong. Both MasterCard and Visa have general numbers you can call (collect if you're abroad) if your card is lost, but you're better off calling the number of your issuing bank, since MasterCard and Visa usually just transfer you to your bank; your bank's number is usually printed on your card.

If you plan to use your credit card for cash advances, you'll need to apply for a PIN at least two weeks before your trip. Although it's usually cheaper (and safer) to use a credit card abroad for large purchases (so you can cancel payments or be reimbursed if there's a problem), note that some credit-card companies *and* the banks that issue them add substantial percentages to all foreign transactions, whether they're in a foreign currency or not. Check on these fees before leaving home, so there won't be any surprises when you get the bill.

Credit cards are accepted at the pricier hotels, restaurants, and souvenir shops. In all but the top hotels, however, the ven-dor occasionally has problems obtaining authorization or forms, so it's prudent to have an alternative form of payment available at all times. The most widely accepted cards are MasterCard and Visa; American Express is rarely taken.

CURRENCY & EXCHANGE

The national currency is the dirham (DH), which is divided into 100 centimes. There are bills for 20, 50, 100, and 200 DH, and coins for 1, 5, and 10 DH and 5, 10, and 20 centimes. You might hear some people refer to centimes as francs; others count money in *rials,* which are equivalent to 5 centimes each. A *million* is a million centimes, or 10,000 DH.

At press time, one U.S. dollar was equivalent to about 8.1 DH. The exchange rate is the same at all banks, including those at the airport. Moroccan law prohibits the export of dirhams, and the few places that sell dirhams outside the country are likely to have less-favorable rates. You can change dirhams back into U.S. dollars or Euros at the airport upon departure, as long as you've kept the exchange receipts from your time of entry.

■ TIP➔ **Even if a currency-exchange booth has a sign promising no commission, rest assured that there's some kind of huge, hidden fee. (Oh . . . that's right. The sign didn't say no *fee.*). And as for rates, you're almost always better off getting foreign currency at an ATM or exchanging money at a bank.**

Currency Conversion Google (⊕www. google.com). **Oanda.com** (⊕www.oanda.com). **XE.com** (⊕www.xe.com).

▌PACKING

Unless you come to Morocco in the hottest dog days of August or the biting cold snap in December, you will most likely need to pack for a range of temperatures. It's especially important not to underestimate how incredibly cold it gets in the mountains, where indoor heating is scarce. If you expect to hike and camp, pack all your gear, including a zero-degree sleeping bag.

Crucial items to bring to Morocco include: sunscreen, walking shoes, and for women a large shawl or scarf (that can be wrapped around your head or arms for respect or your shoulders for warmth), a French and/or Moroccan Arabic phrase book (in the countryside many people will not speak French).

Don't expect to find soap, washcloths, or towels in budget hotels. And do not expect toilet paper in most bathrooms; it's smart to pack your own. Tampons are rarely found in Morocco, so it is best to pack those, too.

Casual clothes are fine in Morocco; there's no need to bring formal apparel. Everywhere but the beach, however, you'll need to wear trousers or long skirts rather than shorts.

▌ PASSPORTS

Australian, British, Canadian, European Union, New Zealand, and U.S. citizens with a valid passport can enter Morocco and stay up to 90 days without a visa.

▌ RESTROOMS

All train stations and autoroute service stations have toilets. It's customary to tip the attendant 1 or 2 DH. Gas stations have toilets, and all cafés are obliged to have them, but these are of varying quality (usually they are Turkish-style squatters). ▌TIP➔ **Bring your own toilet paper in all cases—it's easy to find in stores, but only hotels can be counted on to provide it in bathrooms.**

Your best bet is to make a little "bathroom kit" to take with you: a small roll of toilet paper or Kleenex, a mini bar of soap, and a cotton bandanna for drying hands. Squat-style bathrooms are usually just a hole in the floor with a water tap

nearby. Under the tap is a small plastic bucket for flushing and cleaning.

It is acceptable to duck into a café bathroom without buying anything. And if you are ever in need, Moroccans are happy to locate a bathroom for you; they may even walk you to the front door to make sure you've found it.

Find a Loo The Bathroom Diaries (⊕www. thebathroomdiaries.com) is flush with unsanitized info on restrooms the world over—each one located, reviewed, and rated.

▌ SAFETY

Morocco is a safe destination. Violent crime is relatively rare. People who pester you to hire them as guides in places like Fez are a nuisance but not a threat to your safety. Pickpocketing can be a problem; carry your backpacks and purses in front of you in markets and other crowded areas. Cell phones, cameras, and other portable electronics are big sellers on the black market and should be kept out of sight whenever possible. Keep an eye on your belongings at the more-crowded beaches, as it is not unheard of for a roving gang of youths to make off with your stuff while you are swimming.

Female travelers—and especially single female travelers—sometimes worry about the treatment they'll receive on the streets of Morocco. There really isn't anything to worry about; you'll most likely be leered at, spoken to, and maybe even sometimes followed for about a block. Women walking alone are targeted by vendors hoping to make a sale. This attention, however, while irritating, isn't threatening. Don't take it personally; Moroccan women endure it, as well. The best way to handle it is to walk purposefully, avoid eye contact, and completely ignore men pestering you. If they don't let up, a firm reprimand with the Arabic "*hashuma*" (shame), or the French "*laissez-moi tranquille*" (leave me alone) should do the trick. In the event this still doesn't work, duck into a restaurant or museum, or look for a police officer.

As for what to wear, the basic rule is to dress modestly. Both men and women should leave the tank tops and shorts at home. Avoid bright colors and items that are low-cut, skin-tight, or even slightly see-through. In cities like Casablanca, Marrakesh, Essaouira, and Rabat, half of the local women you'll see wear traditional djellabas, and the other half wear jeans with high-necked, long-sleeved tunics. Even the most-modern women don't expose their legs or arms. As you get to more-traditional areas such as Fez and Meknès, almost all of the women wear traditional clothes.

The most likely scam in Morocco involves an unofficial guide whose questionable technique is harassment or even verbal abuse. Ignore them and walk quickly away. If they persist, report them to the police. Morocco created tourist police for exactly this problem in cities like Marrakesh and Fez.

Contacts U.S. Consulate (⊕casablanca. usconsulate.gov). **U.S. Department of State** (⊕www.travel.state.gov). **U.S. Transportation Security Administration** (TSA; ⊕www.tsa.gov)

▌TAXES

City, local, government, and tourism taxes range between 10 DH and 40 DH at all lodgings. There are no airport taxes above those originally levied on the ticket price. The VAT (called TVA in Morocco) is generally 20%. It is not refundable.

▌TIME

Morocco observes Greenwich Mean Time year-round (five hours ahead of Eastern Standard Time), so most of the year it's on the same clock as the United Kingdom: five hours ahead of New York and one hour behind continental Europe. During Daylight Saving Time, Morocco is one hour behind the United Kingdom,

four hours ahead of New York, and two hours behind continental Europe.

Time Zones Timeanddate.com (⊕www.time anddate.com/worldclock) can help you figure out the correct time anywhere.

▌TIPPING

Tipping is done in Morocco but not as commonly as in the United States. There are no hard-and-fast rules concerning how much and when you do it. Waiters in proper restaurants are always tipped up to 10% of the bill. In taxis, round up to the nearest 5 DH (for example, if the meter says 12 DH, pay 15 DH). At informal cafés the tip is normally 1 DH or 2 DH per person in the dining party. Porters, hotel or otherwise, will appreciate 5 DH or 10 DH. It's customary to give small tips of 1 DH or 2 DH to people such as parking and restroom attendants. When in doubt, you can't go wrong by tipping.

▌VISITOR INFORMATION

The Moroccan government's site has information in English, Arabic, French, and Spanish. The Moroccan National Tourist Office maintains a site in English, French, and German. Other helpful Web sites include Visit Morocco, with practical information for travelers and Weather Morocco, which has has current conditions and forecasts for 24 cities.

Contacts Government of Morocco (⊕www. maroc.ma). **Moroccan National Tourist Office** (☎212/557–2520 in New York ⊕www. tourism-in-morocco.com). **Weather Morocco** (⊕www.moroccoweather.com).

INDEX

ABOUT OUR WRITERS

Rachel Blech is a music broadcaster for RTÉ (Ireland's national radio and television network). Her love of world music first took her to Morocco in 2006 to make a documentary from the Gnawa Music Festival in Essaouira. Since then she has spent much time traveling in the desert, Drâa, and Souss Valley regions reporting for Irish radio, writing articles, and developing desert tourism projects. She has made programs for BBC Radio and RTÉ and has written for *Songlines* magazine, *Travelspeak, easyJet Inflight* magazine, and other publications. Rachel lives part of the year in Morocco, organizes tours occasionally, and one day hopes to write a novel set in the Sahara.

Maryam Montague gave up any plans she may have had for a white-picket fence in suburbia and moved to an olive grove in Marrakesh in 2006. For this guide, she was tasked with updating the Marrakesh and Adventures chapters. In addition to writing for a number of magazines, she pens a lifestyle blog called My Marrakesh (www.mymarrakesh.com). At this writing Maryam is also working on her first illustrated book—part memoir, part Moroccan design treatise—that's slated to be published by Artisan Books.

Tangier & the Mediterranean updater **Simona Schneider** is a teacher, freelance writer, and artist who has lived in Tangier since 2005. She originally went to Morocco to help found the Cinémathèque de Tanger, a nonprofit cinema in downtown Tangier. She has written travel articles for *Condé Nast Traveler* and the *Sun-Sentinel* and writes the monthly destination guide to Tangier for *easyJet Inflight* magazine. Her writing, translations, and photographs have been published in numerous publications in the United States and in Europe.

Although photographer and writer **Victoria Tang** currently calls Paris home, she has lived and traveled internationally since childhood. She's the author of two guidebooks translated into Dutch, Spanish, and Estonian and has written for numerous publications. Her visits to Morocco through the years have left an indelible impression that fuels a love affair with the country, its culture, history, and cuisine. With a passion for authenticity, extensive multicultural experience, and knowledge of French, German, and basic Arabic, Victoria updated the Fez & Meknes and Travel Smart chapters.

Washington State–based **Sarah Wyatt** is a travel, culture, and recreation writer whose work has appeared in the Associated Press, *Outdoors, Mensa Bulletin, Lighthouse Digest, Recommend, Women's International Perspective, Travel Muse,* and *Club Planet.* She enjoys wildlife photography, the outdoors, and the performing arts. Wyatt worked on the Northern Atlantic and Middle Atlas chapters.

Jillian C. York is a Boston-based writer who formerly taught English in Morocco and brings her love of that country to the Essaouira and High Atlas chapters. Jillian is the author of *Culture Smart! Morocco: A Guide to Customs and Culture* (Random House, 2006), and writes regularly for several publications, including *Global Voices Online* and *The Huffington Post.*